EVALUATION IN PRACTICE

A METHODOLOGICAL APPROACH

Richard D. Bingham

Cleveland State University

Claire L. Felbinger

Cleveland State University

Longman

New York & London

EVALUATION IN PRACTICE: A METHODOLOGICAL APPROACH

Longman Inc., 95 Church Street, White Plains, N.Y. 10601

Associated companies:
Longman Group Ltd., London
Longman Cheshire Pty., Melbourne
Longman Paul Pty., Auckland
Copp Clark Pitman, Toronto
Pitman Publishing Inc., New York

Senior editor: David J. Estrin
Production editor: Dee Josephson
Text design: Jill Francis Wood
Cover design: Jill Francis Wood
Production supervisor: Judi Stern

DEDICATED TO

Mary Ann and Ted Felbinger

Library of Congress Cataloging-in-Publication Data

Bingham, Richard D.
   Evaluation in practice.

   Bibliography: p.
   Includes index.
      1. Evaluation research (Social action programs) —
United States.   2. Social sciences — Research —
Methodology.   I. Felbinger, Claire L.   II. Title.
H62.5.U5B56   1989   361.6'1'072   88-612

ISBN 0-8013-0216-1 (pbk.)

94 93 92 91 90 89 9 8 7 6 5 4 3 2 1

Contents

Preface

This book is the product of the authors' frustrations. In teaching program and policy evaluation courses in various graduate public administration programs, we have found that students have serious difficulty in criticizing evaluations done by others. Many students have problems distinguishing one type of design from another. If the design used by a researcher is not a clone of one of the designs found in the textbook, many students are unable to classify, or categorize, it.

In addition, students often believe that merely because an article was published on a scholarly or professional journal, it is perfect. They fail to see how an author did or did not control for various methodological problems.

These, then, were our frustrations. We conceive of an evaluation course as a methods course in which students learn the techniques of program and policy evaluation and the methodological problems encountered when conducting evaluation research. Part of the learning process involves the ability to assess the evaluations of others—not solely to find fault with the work of others but to develop a keen understanding of the difficulties of conducting evaluations. Peter Rossi and Katharine Lyall make this point clearly:

> It is easy enough to be a critic: All pieces of empirical research are more or less flawed. There are simply too many points at which mistakes can be made or unforeseen events intrude to permit perfection in either design or execution. We believe that critics have a responsibility to make two kinds of judgments about the criticisms they offer: First it is necessary to make distinctions, if possible, between those mistakes that constitute serious flaws and those that are less serious defects. Admittedly, this is a matter of judgment, yet we do believe that some sort of weighting ought to be suggested by responsible critics as a guide to those who have not digested the enormous volume of memoranda, working papers, analyses, and final reports produced by the experiment. Second, it is only fair to distinguish between defects that arise from incorrect planning and other errors of judgment and those that arise out of events or processes that could not have been anticipated in advance. This is essentially a distinction between "bad judgment" and "bad luck," the former being a legitimate criticism and the latter calling for sympathetic commiseration.[1]

We would like to take Rossi and Lyall's comments one step further. According to the dictionary, a critic is, "One who expresses a reasoned opinion on any matter as a work of art or a course of conduct, involving a judgment of its value, truth, or righteousness, an appreciation of its beauty or technique, or an interpretation."[2]

Thus, to be a critic requires positive judgments as well as negative. We consider it important to point to cases in which researchers have developed interesting approaches to overcome problems of difficult evaluation design. Chapter 6 of this book is illustrative. Tim Newcomb devised a unique comparison group in his evaluation of an energy conservation program in Seattle. As "critics," we are delighted when we run across this kind of creative thinking.

It should be clear by now that the purpose of *Evaluation in Practice* is to illustrate the techniques of different research designs and the major design problems (termed *problems of internal validity*) encountered in real-world evaluation research. It is not our intent that *Evaluation in Practice* be used as a free-standing text but as a supplement to other textual materials. Each chapter presents a brief introduction to an evaluation design or problem, but these introductions are merely overviews and should not be substituted for more complete discussions found in traditional evaluation texts.

Another caveat: The book does not cover all forms of evaluation: monitoring, assessment, process evaluations, and the like (with the exception of brief discussions in Chapter 1). We are concerned with impact evaluations. This does not suggest that these functions are not important, only that the purpose of this book is much more modest.

Evaluation in Practice was written for students in graduate professional degree programs and for general graduate courses in the social sciences. Although we both teach in graduate public administration programs, this book is not that narrowly construed. The articles in the book are taken from a variety of disciplines illustrating the commonality of evaluation. The book provides examples of both policy and program evaluations from a multitude of disciplines. What is important is the methodology and not the substantive fields represented by the articles. The book has equal applicability in public policy courses, public administration, sociology, political science, criminal justice, education, social welfare, and the health professions, to name a few.

The book makes no assumptions about the readers' background beyond an undergraduate degree. A number of the articles use statistical techniques, but it is not necessary that the student be well versed in statistics. Unless we specify otherwise, the students can assume that the statistics are appropriately applied. It is the design methodology that is important in *Evaluation in Practice*—not statistics.

ORGANIZATION OF THIS BOOK

The book is composed of six parts: introduction, experimental designs, quasi-experimental designs, reflexive designs, cost benefit and cost effectiveness designs, and internal validity problems. Part I consists of one introductory chapter, "The Process of Evaluation." The chapter introduces process evaluations (Are program monies being disbursed in a timely fashion?), output evaluations (How many clients successfully completed the program?), outcome evaluations (Has the administration's job training program reduced long-term unemployment?), and meta-evaluations (On the basis of accumulated evaluations, what do we know about the impact of job training programs?). The chapter is based on the premise that evaluation is a continuous process in which different types of evaluation of a particular program are appropriate at different times and for different audiences.

Each of the following parts is composed of chapters divided into three sections. The first section consists of a short introduction describing a particular evaluation technique or threat to validity. The second section is an evaluation illustrating the techniques or problem. (Not every chapter contains an article because some articles are outstanding examples of more than one of the concepts covered in the book. For example, Chapter 2 contains the article "Improving Cognitive Ability in Chronically Deprived Children," which illustrates a thoughtful variation of the pretest-posttest control group design. The same article is the focus of Chapter 16, "Maturation," because the design presented there vividly shows how the effects of the program can be distinguished from the maturation effect.)

Articles often illustrate several concepts at once, as in the case of selection bias (Chapter 9). "The Effects of Early Education on Children's Competence in Elementary School" is an example of an evaluation that did not satisfactorily control for selection bias. However, it is by no means the only article dealing in one way or another with this threat to validity. Many others do also. Thus, a number of articles illustrate one concept whereas other articles illustrate several concepts. Following the article, we provide an "Explanation and Critique," which appraises the article, pointing out its strengths or weaknesses in terms of the topic under discussion.

Part II consists of four chapters discussing and illustrating four experimental evaluation designs. The feature common to each is the random assignment of subjects into experimental and control groups. The chapters cover the following designs: pretest-posttest control group design, Solomon Four-Group Design, posttest-only control group design, and the factorial design.

Part III covers quasi-experimental evaluation designs and is composed of five chapters. They are the pretest-posttest comparison (not control) group design, interrupted time-series comparison group design, regression-discontinuity design, posttest (only) comparison group design, and the use of statistical controls.

Part IV also concerns quasi-experimental designs but is differentiated from Part III in that in Part IV groups are compared only with themselves. The two types of evaluation design illustrated in this section are the one-group pretest-posttest design and the simple time-series design.

Part V covers two variations, or expansions, on other designs and are included for their uniqueness. These are cost benefit and cost effectiveness designs.

Part VI changes the focus somewhat in that it does not cover evaluations *per se* but problems that might invalidate the findings of an evaluation—threats to internal validity. These threats are history, maturation, testing, instrumentation, regression artifact, selection bias, and experimental mortality.

The final part, Part VII, attempts to integrate the material presented in the first

21 chapters. Chapter 22 attempts to put it all together by discussing several designs and threats to validity. Then the final chapter presents the students with an uncomplicated evaluation to appraise independently.

The table that follows lists all the illustrative articles in this volume and tells which concepts they illustrate. A "P" in the table indicates that the article is a "primary" example of a concept and an "S" indicates that it is a secondary illustration. Take, for example, the article in Chapter 10—"Evaluation of Residential Energy Conservation Programs in Minnesota." The article was included in this book because it illustrates the use of statistical controls. One of the events that it controls for is a substantial increase in energy costs during the period of the evaluation—a validity problem of history, thus the "S" under history.

We provide a bonus at the end of appropriate chapters. A number of dimensions (e.g., history) are discussed, controlled for, or may be a problem in a number of the evaluations in this book. In each "Explanation and Critique" we discuss in detail only one or two of these articles—typically those that are primary examples. We do not discuss the secondary examples. As an added learning tool, we have added a few questions for further study to the "Explanation and Critique" at the end of those chapters that have one or more secondary illustrations. This provides students with the opportunity to show that they have fully grasped the concept. For example, in Chapter 15 we discuss the impact of changing welfare eligibility on the New Jersey/Pennsylvania income maintenance experiment. At the end of Chapter 15, we also provide questions on all the other articles in which history was implicitly or explicitly a problem. Thus, students are afforded the opportunity to answer the questions: What effect of history would have had an impact on nonparticipants in the Minnesota Energy Conservation Program described in Chapter 10? Would this increase or decrease the estimated impact of the program?

We would like to thank a number of people for their assistance in this effort. First, thanks to Bobbie Horsman and Drew Dolan of the Division of Public Administration at Northern Illinois University for their assistance in the preparation of the manuscript. Second, we thank the Center for Governmental Studies and Division of Public Administration at Northern Illinois University and the Urban Research Center at the University of Wisconsin-Milwaukee for institutional support. We value the comments of Paul Culhane, Valerie Simms, and our other reviewers who functioned as critics of the first order, providing sound feedback for our venture. Finally, we appreciate the assistance of the people at Longman—Dee Josephson, Managing Editor; David Estrin, Senior Editor; his assistant, Victoria Mifsud—and Shirley Covington, our copyeditor. Of course, we retain the ultimate responsibility.

We have high hopes for this book. We are confident that if students thoroughly understand the readings and discussion presented here, they will be capable of rationally reviewing most of the program or policy evaluations or evaluation designs that they are likely to encounter during their professional careers.

Richard D. Bingham
Claire L. Felbinger

REFERENCES

1. Peter H. Rossi and Katharine C. Lyall, "An Overview Evaluation of the NIT Experiment," in *Evaluation Studies Review Annual, vol. 3,* ed. Thomas D. Cook, Marilyn L. Del Rosario, Karen M. Hennigan, Melvin M. Mark, and William M. K. Trochim (Beverly Hills, CA.: Sage, 1978), pp. 412-413.

2. *Webster's New International Dictionary* (2nd ed., Springfield, MA.: Merriam, 1950), p. 627.

THE CROSS-REFERENCE MATRIX

	Pretest-Posttest Control Group	Soloman Four Group	Posttest Only Control Group	Factorial Design	Pretest-Posttest Comparison Group	Interrupted Time Series Comparison Group	Regression-Discontinuity Design	Posttest Only Comparison Group	Use of Statistical Controls	One-Group Pretest-Posttest	Simple Time Series Design	Cost Benefit Design	Cost Effectiveness Design	History	Maturation	Testing	Instrumentation	Regression Artifact	Selection Bias	Experimental Mortality
	Experimental Designs					Quasi-Experimental Designs				Reflexive Designs		Cost Benefit & Cost Effectiveness Designs		Threats to Validity						
Chapter 2 "Improving Cognitive Ability in Chronically Deprived Children," by McKay et al.	P													S	P			S		S
Chapter 3 "Learning Factors as Determiners of Pretest Sensitizers," by Lana and King		P														S				
Chapter 4 "Community Posthospital Follow up Services," by Solberg			P								S	S								S
Chapter 5 "Overview of the Seattle-Denver Income Maintenance Experiment Final Report," by Skidmore			P													S			S	P
Chapter 6 "Conservation Program Evaluation: The Control of Self-Selection Bias," by Newcomb					P						S	S							S	
Chapter 7 "Impacts of SSI: A Re-Analysis of Federal Welfare Policy," by Albritton and Witayapanyanon						P														

	Experimental Designs						Quasi-Experimental Designs			Reflexive Designs		Cost Benefit & Cost Effectiveness Designs		Threats to Validity						
	Pretest-Posttest Control Group	Soloman Four Group	Posttest Only Control Group	Factorial Design	Pretest-Posttest Comparison Group	Interrupted Time Series Comparison Group	Regression-Discontinuity Design	Posttest Only Comparison Group	Use of Statistical Controls	One-Group Pretest-Posttest	Simple Time Series Design	Cost Benefit Design	Cost Effectiveness Design	History	Maturation	Testing	Instrumentation	Regression Artifact	Selection Bias	Experimental Mortality
Chapter 8 "Regression-Discontinuity Analysis: An Alternative to the Ex Post Facto Experiment," by Thistlethwaite and Campbell							P													
Chapter 9 "The Effects of Early Education on Children's Competence in Elementary School," by Bronson, Pierson, and Tivnan								P					S						P	S
Chapter 10 "Evaluation of Residential Energy Conservation Programs in Minnesota, by Hirst and Goeltz									P					S	S			S	S	
Chapter 11 "Nutrition Behavior Change: Outcomes of an Educational Approach, by Edwards, Acock, and Johnston										P									S	S
Chapter 12 "Impact Analysis of the Raised Legal Drinking Age in Illinois," by Maxwell											P									
Chapter 13 "The Costs and Benefits of Title XX and Title XIX Family Planning Services in Texas," by Malitz												P								

	Experimental Designs						Quasi-Experimental Designs			Reflexive Designs		Cost Benefit & Cost Effectiveness Designs		Threats to Validity						
	Pretest-Posttest Control Group	Soloman Four Group	Posttest Only Control Group	Factorial Design	Pretest-Posttest Comparison Group	Interrupted Time Series Comparison Group	Regression-Discontinuity Design	Posttest Only Comparison Group	Use of Statistical Controls	One-Group Pretest-Posttest	Simple Time Series Design	Cost Benefit Design	Cost Effectiveness Design	History	Maturation	Testing	Instrumentation	Regression Artifact	Selection Bias	Experimental Mortality
Chapter 14 "Performance Evaluation for Systems of Assigned Service Providers," by Houlden and Balkin													P						S	
Chapter 15 "An Overview of Labor Supply Results," by Rees														P		S				
Chapter 16 See Chapter 2																				
Chapter 17 "The Hawthorne Experiments: First Statistical Interpretation," by Franke and Kaul									S					S		P				S
Chapter 18 "Improving Effectiveness: Responsive Public Services," by Fukuhara																	P			
Chapter 19 "Regulatory Strategies for Workplace Injury Reduction," by Moran																		P		
Chapter 20 See Chapter 9																				
Chapter 21 See Chapter 5																				
Chapter 22 "Attitude Change and Mental Hospital Experience," by Hicks and Spaner	S	S			S									S		S			S	

PART ONE

Introduction

The Process of Evaluation

CLAIRE L. FELBINGER

The evaluation of agency programs or legislative policy is the use of scientific methods to estimate the successful implementation and resultant outcomes of programs or policies for decision-making purposes. Implicit in this definition are the many levels on which a program or policy can be evaluated and the many potential audiences that may be interested in utilizing the evaluation. There is not just one approach or method common to all evaluations. We hope that during the course of reading this book students of evaluation will become acquainted with the multiplicity of approaches to evaluation and develop the ability to choose appropriate designs to maximize internal validity and meet consumers' evaluation needs.

Good evaluations use scientific methods. These methods involve the systematic process of gathering *empirical* data to test *hypotheses* indicated by a program's or policy's *intent*. *Empirical data* are observable, measurable units of information. In evaluation, one does not just "feel" that a program is operating effectively; the data demonstrate that this is or is not the case. *Hypotheses* are assertions about program impacts. In other words, hypotheses state changes that should occur to program recipients as a direct result of the program. For example, children in a nutrition program should be healthier after the program than they were before. These hypotheses should be linked with the policy's or program's intent. Typically, *intent* refers to policymakers' hopes regarding the program's outcomes. Unfortunately, identifying intent is not always a simple process. Bureaucratic agencies attempt to translate legislative intent into procedures and regulations. When the intent is unclear or contradictory, the translation can be manipulated into a program that does not resemble anything the legislators had in mind. Even with clear intent, poor program design can obscure original intent. In the best of all worlds, evaluators look for broad-based goals and for clearly stated measurable objectives by which these goals can be reached. Nevertheless, it is the job of the evaluator to try to break through these often unclear guidelines and provide usable findings in a timely manner in the hopes of informing the decision-making process.

TYPES OF EVALUATION

There are several general types of evaluation corresponding to what some evaluators consider to be successive hierarchical levels of abstraction. One type of evaluation is not "better" than another; each is appropriate to a different set of research questions. Evaluation is a science and an art. The artful part of the work is the successful matching of the level of the evaluation and the appropriate scientific design within the resource and time constraints of the consumer of the evaluation.

Process Evaluations

The first sentence of this chapter mentions measuring the *implementation* of programs. *Implementation* is the process by which a program or policy is operated. *Process evaluations* focus on the means by which a program or policy is delivered to clients. Karen Sue Trisko and V. C. League identify five levels, or approaches, to evaluation, two of which are process or, as they also refer to them, formative evaluations.[1] Although Trisko and League refer to these as levels, the term *approach* seems to be more appropriate in the evaluation context. The *first* process level is monitoring daily tasks. In this level of evaluation, fundamental questions of program operation are the focus of inquiry. Indeed, questions such as "Are contractual obligations being met?" or "Are staff adequately trained for their jobs?" are pursued at this level. Basically, these evaluations look to uncover management problems or to assure that none are occurring.

These evaluations often involve an inspection of the fundamental goals and objectives of the program. Indeed, evaluations cannot occur in the absence of direction concerning what the program is supposed to do. It is shocking how many programs operate in the absence of written goals and objectives! Sometimes policymakers cannot satisfy all relevant political players unless they are *not* specific about goals and objectives. Even when such directives exist, evaluators often find that the actual operation does not seem to fit the intent of the written guidelines. This may be because the goals are outdated, at which point staff needs to reevaluate the goals and objectives in light of the current environment. Sometimes programs develop a life of their own, and evaluators can point out ways in which the program can get back on track.

Even if the purpose of the evaluation is not to assess process, evaluators find it necessary to gather an inventory of goals and objectives to determine the predicted impact of the program. They must then reconcile the written material with what they observe before a full-blown evaluation can occur. The process by which they do this is called evaluability assessment. *Evaluability assessments* are process evaluations that are performed so that the evaluator and the evaluation client can come to agreement on which aspects of the program will be part of the final product and what resources are necessary to produce the desired document. The benefits of process evaluations should not be underestimated.

The *second* level of process evaluation concerns assessing program activities and client satisfaction with services. Among the questions considered at this level are, "What is done to whom and what activities are actually taking place?" or "How could it be done more efficiently?" or "Are the clients satisfied with the service or image of the service?"

Both the first and second aspects of process evaluations involve subjective measures at times and also require staff and client involvement to complete. Donald Campbell and Julian Stanley and others refer to process evaluations as "pre-experiments."[2] The value of process evaluations should not be understated, though. It makes little sense to attempt to assess the impact of a program if it is run incorrectly or if the consumer actually being served is unknown. The results of these evaluations can be as basic as pointing out to an agency that they do not have evaluable goals or objectives or informing them that their accounting procedures are shoddy. If one ever wonders why it seems so difficult to evaluate the activities of federal bureaucrats, one need only look to the enabling legislation of many of our major national programs. Putting together congressional majorities in controversial legislation often leads to murky legislative intent.

Process evaluations frequently focus on the way a program is implemented. Program managers may be interested professionally in organizing and running a fine-tuned bureau and in periodically assessing the efficiency of operations. During the course of these evaluations, better ways of doing business may be discovered in addition to finding blatant inefficiencies. For instance, staff may suggest alternate ways of organizing the service production, or they may point out innovative techniques or tools discovered in their own professional development. Those who fund the activities are also concerned about efficiency (minimizing waste) — although sometimes to the detriment of effectiveness (obtaining the desired effect). During times of fiscal austerity, evaluations of this type can be beneficial. Unfortunately, evaluations are often the first activities to be cut during budget slashing.

Impact Evaluations

The next two approaches are referred to as *impact evaluations*. Impact evaluations focus on the end results of programs. The first impact evaluation, enumerating outcomes, looks at whether the program's or policy's objectives have been met. Questions may be "What is the result of the activities conducted by the program?" or "What happened to the target population because of those activities [was it the expected outcome?]?" or "Should different activities be substituted?" In other words, are the objectives of the program being met?

When people think of program evaluation, impact evaluations are what they usually have in mind. Impact evaluations are *easy* to conceptualize because they revolve around directly assessing outputs. How many output units were delivered? How many free lunches were served, applications processed, client hours logged, workers trained? Because these evaluations are easily conceptualized, designing them tends to be straightforward. In addition, because "impacts" are easily understood, these types of evaluation are more easily justified and fundable than process evaluations.

The second type of impact evaluation involves measuring effectiveness, which concerns either "Was the program cost effective?" or "What would have happened to the target population in the absence of the program?" In contrast to the previous approach, one looks at whether and to what extent the goals of the program or policy are being met. Impact evaluations tend to be more objective because it is not necessary to rely solely on clients or staff to gather data (although their assistance is often helpful). The data can be extracted from records (if process evaluations are favorable) or from observing or testing or measuring effects.

The evaluation methods covered in this book are generally of the impact variety. We say "generally" because both of us believe that scientific methodology and rigor can be used, though in varying degrees, in any type of evaluation. However, impact evaluations lend themselves quite easily to empirical investigation. The methods described here assume this empirical dimension.

Policy Evaluations

The final kind of evaluation described by Trisko and League considers the long-term consequences of a program or policy—assessing the impact on the problem. The kinds of question asked include, "What changes are evident in the problem?" or "Has the problem [e.g., poverty, illiteracy] been reduced as a result of the program or policy?" These evaluations are difficult to assess empirically. For instance, there are multiple programs dealing with poverty and malnutrition. Presumably there is a national policy concerning eradication of poverty and hunger. How does one assess the consequence of programs that are delivered simultaneously and sometimes at cross-purposes to a target population? How does one measure "poverty"? This type of evaluation truly can be called *policy evaluation*. David Nachmias and Claire Felbinger describe this type of evaluation as one that occurs when a political body considers changing or continuing a major social or political program—when prevailing policy is challenged in the agenda-setting forum.[3] In this situation, the role of the evaluator is rather vague. So many variables can have an impact on the long-term process concerning such broad social issues that it is difficult to assess impact. Many decisions regarding the relative "worth" of various policies are best debated in a political arena.

This does not mean that policies as such cannot be empirically evaluated. The example in Chapter 7 evaluates quite adequately the short- and longer-term impacts of a change in a social policy. Rather, evaluating policies such as the impact of "Great Society" programs relies less on empirical evidence than on ideological leanings.

Metaevaluations

There is an approach, or level of evaluation, that attempts to make sense out of accumulated evaluation findings. *Metaevaluations* are syntheses of evaluation research findings. They look for commonalities among results, measures, and trends in the literature. They reuse the extant research findings.

Metaevaluations are quite similar to literature reviews. In science, one is interested in the cumulative nature of research. Literature reviews attempt to make sense out of the research that precedes the current effort. Literature reviews are considered qualitative exercises: Equally equipped researchers can disagree on the interpretation of research results. Persons involved in metaevaluations try to quantify the review, presumably making a more objective statement. Harris Cooper argues that metaanalytic procedures can be systematic and scientific.[4] A number of quantitative methods for metaanalysis have been developed, most notably by Gene

Glass[5] and Richard Light.[6] Often, evaluations focus on whether the average, or mean, measure of the evaluation criterion variable for the group that participated in the program is any different from a similar group that did not participate. Glass and his associates found conceptually similar criterion variables across studies and developed what they call the "effect size" between means of the experimental and control groups, standardizing on the basis of standard deviation. They try to estimate the size of the total effect of these programs by aggregating across studies. Light, on the other hand, uses the original data (as opposed to group means), pools the findings in different sites, and reanalyzes the data. He includes only those measures that are identical across studies. This technique reduces the number of studies he can aggregate. However, the findings are not subject to measurement differences. Readers interested in these techniques should consult the references. The idea of systematically aggregating evaluation results has received considerable research attention.

UTILIZATION OF EVALUATION FINDINGS

Regardless of what type of evaluation is performed, it is not useful unless it is completed in time for decision makers to use the findings as input for their decision-making process. It makes little sense to perform an elegantly designed evaluation the results of which come in a day after the decision on the program's fate is cast. This is one difference between evaluation research and academic research. Academic researchers will usually risk a timely report for the elegance of a properly constructed, controlled design. Evaluation researchers hope to construct the "best" design, but they err on the side of expedience when a decision deadline is near. That does not mean that evaluation research is necessarily slipshod. Rather, evaluation research is not worth much if it is not utilized. Evaluators must recognize the trade-offs made in the interest of providing material in a timely manner.

How can one determine whether the results of an evaluation are utilized? In the 1970s, evaluation researchers spent a great deal of time trying to trace whether specific evaluations were utilized by decisionmakers. The first problem they encountered was that they could not agree on the definition of utilization. When restrictive definitions were proposed, the record of utilization was bleak. Less restrictive definitions led to more pleasing results. Evaluators, however, were frustrated with the degree to which they felt their efforts were being used to affect policy.

David Nachmias and Claire Felbinger recast the utilization question and put utilization into a broader perspective.[7] For them, utilization need not be a discreet action. Policymakers do not operate in an information vacuum; they bring to the decision-making process the variety of their life experiences. Indeed, when the results of an evaluation suggest some action that, to them, is counterintuitive or politically inexpedient, utilization is not immediately assured. However, as the volume of evidence grows, the information gleaned at an earlier time may be brought to bear in the context of a future decision. This type of utilization is virtually impossible to document.

Nachmias and Felbinger suggest that the process by which information is utilized can be conceptualized by viewing the decision process as part of a cycle of
life events that shape decision makers' perspectives. The diagram they use to explain this process is in Figure 1-1.

Figure 1-1 is instructive in this context because it displays the various points
at which decisions (hence, utilization) are made and the various levels and clients
for evaluation information of a single program. The feedback loop at point 1 stands
for ongoing, short-term evaluation of the implementation of a program—process
evaluations. This ongoing process is intended to inform program managers of the
success of basic program operations. The constant feedback allows them to fine-
tune the existing program. Generally then, evaluations at this point are short term
in nature, process oriented, and aimed at the needs of program managers (the
consumers and utilizers of the evaluation). Clearly, costly experimental designs are
inappropriate for evaluations at this level.

Evaluations at Point 2 are of the impact variety. They usually allow for a
longer-term evaluation. The designs described in this book are certainly appropri-

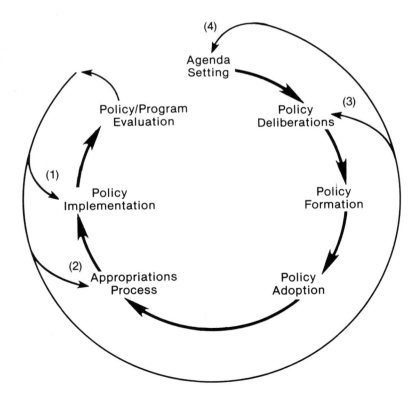

Figure 1-1

Evaluation Utilization Subcycles in the Legislative-Budgetary Cycle

Source: David Nachmias and Claire L. Felbinger, "Utilization in the Policy Cycle: Directions
for Research," *Policy Studies Review* 2 (November, 1982): 305.

ate for this level. The clients for evaluations at this level are decision makers who are interested in program oversight. In the Nachmias and Felbinger example, these consumers are members of Congress engaged in yearly appropriation hearings. However, these consumers can be any interested publics making decisions on the utility of programs. These decision makers are not constrained by the information presented in the specific impact evaluations; they are free to use the portions they think are relevant and politically feasible.

Point 3 evaluations are concerned with the outcomes of programs: policy evaluations. When programs are highly controversial or when new programs are competing for scarce dollars, policy evaluations affect whether the general policy should continue. When prevailing policies are being questioned, fundamental questions such as "Should the government really be involved in this?" or "Does this really matter?" come to the fore. The articles on the income maintenance experiments in Chapters 5 and 15 of this book are of this sort. Instituting the policy would constitute a major shift in national welfare policy. Evaluations performed at this level are typically of a long-term variety and command the most costly evaluations. Again, decision makers at this level may utilize the information from the evaluation. They cannot help, however, allowing their feelings to be shaped by ideological concerns and information from other sources.

The feedback loop at Point 4 is illustrative of how evaluations of the past affect decision making in the present and can be considered a personal metaevaluation exercise. Nachmias and Felbinger suggest that utilization research cast at this level would require longitudinal case studies. The loop is descriptive: The research suggested seems unmanageable. Nachmias and Felbinger hoped to end attempts to evaluate the utilization of specific results and to measure the behavior of decision makers. However, evaluators were still concerned about the value decision makers place on research results. Michael Patton and his colleagues suggest that evaluators should concern themselves with something they can control: the conduct of the evaluation. They suggest that evaluators should be concerned with designing utilization-focused evaluations.[8] William Tash and Gerald Stahler followed a step-by-step method to enhance the utilization of their research results:

1. Identify specific user audiences and tailor recommendations to these groups.
2. Formulate recommendations in cooperation with the user audiences.
3. Direct specific recommendations toward a broader policy and program model.
4. Assess the impact of recommendations over time.
5. Present recommendations in an empathetic way.[9]

Tash and Stahler caution against gearing evaluations toward one general "imaginary" user audience. They argue that this type of casting tends to develop recommendations that are not specific enough to provide managerial or policy-making direction. The recommendations often do not take into account the mid- and lower-level bureaucrats' needs—especially when the recommendations call for them to alter actions. Therefore, once the users are specified, it may be necessary to produce multiple versions of the same evaluation report to address the concerns of the different groups.

Tash and Stahler also suggest that evaluations, and especially the recommendation formulation process, be viewed as a joint venture that would make the role of staff more participatory. As such, the process would enhance utilization because those who participate have a stake in the process. In addition, staff involvement can lead to constructive and doable changes; otherwise, recommendations may not make sense in the given context for reasons unknown to the evaluator. Regular meetings regarding interim results are also suggested.

Tash and Stahler suggest that by casting the recommendations more broadly, the utilization of the research findings can be more generalizable to other contexts. Although this seems to contradict Step 2, they suggest that the broad implications can be the focus of an additional section of the report.

When possible, both strategically and financially, plans should be made to conduct a follow-up assessment sometime down the road to determine the extent to which the recommendations have been followed. Unfortunately, unless the users are committed to this reassessment, evaluators seldom know the extent to which their proposals have been followed. However, reassessment may be more likely if the evaluating unit is part of the evaluated organization.

In Step 5 Tash and Stahler are referring to the "style" of the recommendation presentations. Style demonstrates the respect the evaluator has for the evaluated and their environment. Respect detracts from the belief that all evaluators are interlopers who are quick to find fault with staff. Tash and Stahler suggest that rather than merely providing a laundry list of recommendations, an evaluator may present the recommendations in the form of case studies that hypothetically explain the intent of the recommendations. Regardless of the presentation, though, it makes sense that utilization would be enhanced by the common-sense method of presenting the results as you would like to receive them. This does not mean that the evaluator is co-opted by the organization, but neither is he or she aloof toward it.

INTERNAL VERSUS EXTERNAL VALIDITY

Another difference between academic and evaluation research is the different emphasis each puts on the value of internal versus external validity. A design is internally valid to the extent that the impact is attributable to the treatment and no other factors. External validity refers to the generalizability of the research findings to other sites and situations. Evaluators and laboratory scientists prefer to maximize the former, policy researchers the latter (although both would say they wished to maximize both simultaneously). Why the difference? Program managers, program funding agents, and interested publics are most interested in finding out whether their particular program works—whether the impacts can be traced to their program. In so doing, they tend to control for so many factors that the study becomes "generalizable" only to itself. In other words, the program has the observed impacts only under the conditions of the specific situation. In this way, evaluators are like scientists who seek to isolate the cause of a disease by ruling out all other factors with laboratory controls. On the other hand, policy researchers seek to build theory that is based on the generalizability of their findings. They wish to apply the results more broadly. For example, they may wish to explain expenditures in American cities: What general patterns seem to emerge? Their predictions are to American cities in general, not necessarily to the city in which you live. One approach is not more valid than another—only more appropriate to different situations. By maximizing specificity, however, generalizability is diminished.

The trade-offs between internal versus external validity need not result in the lack of appreciation of the findings of either practitioners or academics. When evaluators do what Tash and Stahler referred to in Step 3, they are increasing the external validity of their models by addressing the concerns of wider audiences. Careful academic research, likewise, can be used by evaluators to provide a grounding in theory for the relationships they hypothesize and a critique of the prevailing methodology. In other words, both types of research are complementary. Academics need the experience of the real-world evaluators and vice versa.

Because evaluations often occur after a program is in place and because they are often conducted under severe time constraints, evaluators are sometimes tentative about the quality of their findings. When they are overly cautious about accepting a treatment's impact when that impact truly exists, the researcher commits what is called a Type I error. When that occurs, a policy or program can be terminated when it in fact is beneficial. If an evaluator mistakenly concludes that an impact exists, he or she commits a Type II error. It seems that because the "best" design and "best" measures of variables are unavailable, evaluation findings tend to be attenuated and Type I errors arise. Students are cautioned not to be so critical of their findings that they cancel a program that appears to be effective when the evaluation findings are "not statistically significant."

ETHICS AND EVALUATIONS

Unlike most academic research in the social sciences, evaluation research has an ethical quality that in a very real sense touches people's lives and may cost jobs. These ethical considerations and trade-offs are all a part of the art and duty of evaluation at any level. A number of ethical considerations are involved in program evaluation. First, the evaluator should be aware of the purposes for which an evaluation is commissioned. Evaluations for covert purposes should be avoided. Those commissioned to white wash or to make a program look good are examples of unethical evaluations because the client dictates the results. Results should emerge from carefully constructed research; they should not be dictated from above. Evaluations commissioned to kill programs are also unethical for the same reason. Another covert purpose to be avoided is when it is clear that the consumer of the evaluation wants to target the replacement of present employees. Although some evaluations may show that the program is good or bad or that someone should be replaced, one should not design evaluations with a preconceived notion of what the results will be.

Unscrupulous evaluators who are in their profession just for the money and who will tailor results are often referred to as "Beltway Bandits." This phrase refers to the unscrupulous consulting firms that sprang up on the Washington, DC Beltway, a highway that encircles the District of Columbia, during the heyday of federal funding of social program evaluations. Not all these firms were unethical. There is evidence, however, to suggest that almost anyone at the time could get away with calling him- or herself an evaluator regardless of training. Over time, the reputations of these "bandits" became known, and they no longer were granted contracts.

Another ethical concern is confidentiality. The evaluator often has access to information of a confidential nature over the course of a study. Some of this information could be damaging to individuals who supply the information or to their superiors or subordinates. Also, some of the information (such as an individual's income) need not be divulged, although access to that information is necessary to arrive at aggregate statistics. An evaluator has to be conscious of confidentiality concerns whether or not confidentiality was assured.

As mentioned earlier, the results of an evaluation can have a real, personal impact on employees, clients, and agencies. Care should be taken to perform evaluations professionally and empathetically. These are the ethical considerations encountered in the business of evaluation.

STEPS IN EVALUATION

The chapters to follow define and outline how to conduct an evaluation. In general, though, the process of evaluation involves a number of similar steps, as follows:

1. Identify the goals and objectives of the program or policy in a manner that can be evaluated.
2. Construct an impact model of what you expect of the impact of the program or policy. This is the evaluability assessment.
3. Develop a research design that includes all the steps involved in the methodology and that is driven by an appreciation of the literature that suggests these expectations.
4. Measure the phenomena of interest (and deal with any measurement problems at this point).
5. Collect the data and analyze and interpret the results.

The following chapters provide the tools for effective evaluations.

REFERENCES

1. This classification is adapted from Karen Sue Trisko and V. C. League, *Developing Successful Programs* (Oakland, CA: Awareness House, 1978), chap. 7.
2. Donald T. Campbell and Julian C. Stanley, *Experimental and Quasi-Experimental Designs for Research* (Chicago: Rand McNally, 1963), pp. 6-12.
3. David Nachmias and Claire L. Felbinger, "Utilization in the Policy Cycles: Directions for Research," *Policy Studies Review* 2 (November 1982): 300-308.

4. Harris M. Cooper, "Scientific Guidelines for Conducting Integrative Research," *Review of Educational Research* 52, no. 2 (Summer 1982): pp. 291–302.

5. Gene V. Glass, "Primary, Secondary, and Meta-Analysis," *Educational Researcher,* 5 (1976): 3–8. Also, Gene V. Glass, "Integrating Findings: The Meta-Analysis of Research," in *Review of Research in Education,* ed. L. S. Schulman (Itasca, IL: Peacock, 1978), 5: 351–379.

6. Richard J. Light, "Capitalizing on Variation: How Conflicting Research Findings Can Be Helpful for Policy," *Educational Researcher* 8 (October 1979): 3–11. Also Richard J. Light and Paul V. Smith, "Accumulating Evidence: Procedures for Resolving Contradictions Among Different Research Studies," *Harvard Educational Review* 41 (November 1971): 429–471.

7. David Nachmias and Claire L. Felbinger, "Utilization in the Policy Cycle: Directions for Research," 300–308.

8. Michael Q. Patton, *Utilization-Focused Evaluation* (Beverly Hills, CA: Sage, 1978).

9. William R. Tash and Gerald J. Stahler, "Enhancing the Utilization of Evaluation Findings," *Community Mental Health Journal* 18, no. 3 (Fall 1982): 180–189.

PART TWO
Experimental Designs

There are experimental designs and then there are experimental designs. There is a distinction between experimental designs and the quasiexperimental designs that are discussed in Part III. The concern here is with the most powerful and "truly scientific" evaluation design—the controlled, randomized experiment. There are essentially three "true" experimental designs in the literature: (1) the pretest-posttest control group design, (2) the Solomon Four-Group Design, and (3) the posttest-only control group design.[1] There is actually a fourth variation—the factorial design—which is also examined in this section.[2]

As Peter Rossi and Howard Freeman note, randomized experiments (those in which participants in the experiment are selected for participation strictly by chance) are the "flagships" in the field of program evaluation because they allow program personnel to reach conclusions about program impact (or lack of impact) with a high degree of certainty. These evaluations have much in common with experiments in the physical and biological sciences particularly as they enable the research results to establish causal effects. The findings of randomized experiments are treated with considerable respect by policy makers, program staff, and knowledgeable publics.[3]

The key is randomization. True experimental designs always assign subjects to treatment randomly. As long as the number of subjects is sufficiently large, random assignment more or less guarantees that the characteristics of the subjects in the experimental and control groups are statistically equivalent.[4]

As David Nachmias points out, the classical evaluation design consists of four essential features: comparison, manipulation, control, and generalizability.[5] To assess the impact of a policy, some form of comparison must be made. Either a comparison is made of an experimental group with a control group or the experimental group is compared with itself before and after treatment. In a true experimental design, the experimental group is compared to a control group.

The second feature of an evaluation design is manipulation. The idea is that if a program or policy is actually effective, the individuals (or cities, or organizations) should change over the time of participation. If we are able to hold all other factors in the world constant during the evaluation, then the change in policy (manipulation) should cause a change in the target exposed to it (individuals, cities, or organizations).

The third feature of the experimental design—control—requires that other factors be ruled out as explanations of the observed relationship between a policy and its target. These other factors are the well-known sources of internal invalidity: history, maturation, testing, instrumentation, statistical regression, selection, experimental mortality, and selection-maturation interaction.[6] These "threats" to design validity are covered in detail in Part VI; it is not necessary for the student to understand these concepts at this point. As Nachmias points out, these sources of internal invalidity are controlled through randomization.[7]

The final essential feature of the classical design is generalizability, or the extent to which research findings can be generalized to larger populations and in different settings. Unfortunately, the mere use of the controlled, randomized experimental design will not in itself control for sources of external invalidity or the lack of generalizability.[8]

The four chapters contained in this section examine and critique four studies that illustrate the use of the pretest-posttest control group design, the Solomon Four-Group Design, the posttest-only control group design, and the factorial design.

REFERENCES

1. Donald T. Campbell and Julian C. Stanley, *Experimental and Quasi-Experimental Designs for Research* (Boston: Houghton Mifflin, 1963).

2. Ibid., pp. 27-31. See also David Nachmias, *Public Policy Evaluation: Approaches and Methods* (New York: St. Martin's Press, 1979), pp. 32-35.

3. Peter H. Rossi and Howard E. Freeman, *Evaluation: A Systematic Approach*, 3rd ed. (Beverly Hills, CA: Sage, 1985), p. 263.

4. Laura Irwin Langbein, *Discovering Whether Programs Work: A Guide to Statistical Methods for Program Evaluation* (Glenview, IL: Scott, Foresman, 1980), p. 67.

5. Nachmias, *Public Policy Evaluation*, pp. 23-29.

6. Campbell and Stanley, *Experimental and Quasi-Experimental Designs*, p. 5.

7. Nachmias, *Public Policy Evaluation*, pp. 27-28.

8. Campbell and Stanley, *Experimental and Quasi-Experimental Designs*, p. 8.

2

Pretest-Posttest Control Group Design

The pretest-posttest control group experiment, the classical experimental design, consists of two comparable groups: an experimental group and a control group. Although a number of authors use the terms *control group* and *comparison group* interchangeably, in a strict sense they are not. True control groups are formed by the process of randomization. Comparison groups are groups that are matched to be comparable in important respects to the experimental group. In this book, the distinction between control groups and comparison groups is strictly maintained.

When this design is used, individuals are randomly assigned to one of the two groups. Random assignment of members of a target population to different groups implies that whether an individual (city, organization) is selected for participation is decided purely by chance. Peter Rossi and Howard Freeman elaborate:

> Because the resulting experimental and control groups differ from one another only by chance, whatever processes may be competing with a treatment to produce outcomes are present in the experimental and control groups to the same extent except for chance fluctuations. For example, given randomization, persons who would be more likely to seek out the treatment if it were offered to them on a free-choice basis are equally likely to be in the experimental as in the control group. Hence, both groups have the same proportion of persons favorably predisposed to the intervention.[1]

But how is randomization accomplished? Randomization is analogous to flipping a coin, with all of those flipping heads being assigned to one group and all of those flipping tails being assigned to another. The most common ways of affecting random assignment are the following:

1. Actually flipping a coin for each subject (allowing all heads to represent one group and tails the other).
2. Throwing all the names into a hat or some other container, thoroughly mixing them, and drawing them out one at a time, allowing odd draws to represent one group and even draws the other.
3. Using a table of random numbers or random numbers generated by a computer program.

It is important to distinguish between random assignment and random sampling. At first glance, they may appear to be identical, and in some instances they may *be* identical. There are, however, major differences between the two techniques. Random sampling ensures representativeness between a sample and the population from which it is drawn. *Random selection* (sampling) is thus an important factor in the external validity of a study—that is, the extent to which a study's results can be generalized beyond the sample drawn. Let us take the case of the study presented in this chapter. McKay, Sinisterra, McKay, Gomez, and Lloreda evaluated a program of treatment combining nutrition, health care, and education on the cognitive ability of chronically undernourished children in Cali, Colombia. The children were not a random sample of undernourished children from around the world. Thus, the question is (assuming that the study itself is reliable): To what degree can the impact of this program conducted in Colombia be generalized to the probable impact of similar programs on other children throughout the world?

Random assignment, as opposed to random selection, is related to the evaluation's internal validity—that is, the extent to which the program's impact is attributed to the treatment and no other factors.

Obviously, the best course would be to select subjects randomly and then to assign them randomly to groups once they were selected.[2] This discussion has digressed a bit from the discussion of the pretest-posttest control group design, but the digression is important.

Returning to the design: Subjects are randomly assigned to an experimental group and a control group. To evaluate the effectiveness of the program, measurements are taken twice for each group. A preprogram measure is taken for each group before the introduction of the program to the experimental group. A postprogram measure is then taken after the experimental group has been exposed to (or has completed) the program. Preprogram scores are then subtracted from postprogram scores. If the gain made by the experimental group is significantly larger than the gain made by the control group, then the researchers can conclude that the program is effective. The pretest-posttest control group design is illustrated in Table 2-1. Group E is the experimental group, or the group receiving the program. Group C is the control group. The "O" indicates a test point and the "X" represents the program.

The critical question is: When should such a design be used? Although it is extremely powerful, this design is also costly and difficult to implement. It is not possible, for example, to withhold treatment purposely from some groups and to assign them randomly to control groups (in matters of life and death, for example). And in many cases, program participants are volunteers; there is no comparable control group (those persons who had the desire and motivation to participate in the program but who did not volunteer). Then there is the matter of cost. Experimental evaluation designs are generally more costly than other designs because of the greater amount of time required to plan and conduct the experiment and the

TABLE 2-1   The Pretest-Posttest Control Group Design

	Before		After
Group E	O_{e_1}	X	O_{e_2}
Group C	O_{c_1}		O_{c_2}

higher level of analytical skills required for planning and undertaking the evaluation and analyzing the results.

This design is frequently used in health or employment programs. A popular Urban Institute publication, *Practical Program Evaluation for State and Local Governments,* documents conditions under which such experimental designs are likely to be appropriate for state and local governments.[3] The more significant conditions include the following:

1. *There is likely to be a high degree of ambiguity as to whether outcomes were caused by the program if some other evaluation design is used.* The design is appropriate when the findings obtained through the use of a less powerful design may be criticized for not causing the results. Take a hypothetical example of a medical experiment involving a cold remedy. If no control group was used, would not the experiment be criticized by: "How do we know that the subject wouldn't have recovered from the cold in the same amount of time without the pill?"

2. *Some citizens can be given different services from others without significant danger or harm.* The experimental design may be used if public officials and the evaluators agree that the withdrawal or nonprovision of a service or program is not likely to have harmful effects. An example might be discontinuing evening hours at a local branch library, which is not likely to harm many individuals.

3. *Some citizens can be given different services from others without violating moral and ethical standards.* Some programs, although not involving physical danger, may call for not providing services to some groups. For example, an experiment to assess the effectiveness of a counseling program for parolees might be designed in such a way that certain parolees do not receive counseling (and thus might be more likely to commit a crime and be returned to prison). This could be seen by some as unethical or immoral.

4. *There is substantial doubt about the effectiveness of a program.* If a program is not believed to be working or effective, controlled, randomized experimentation is probably the only way to settle the issue once and for all.

5. *There are insufficient resources to provide the program to all clients.* Even when a program is expected to be helpful, the resources necessary to provide it to all eligible clients may not be available. In the article in this chapter, McKay et al. did not have sufficient financial resources to provide the program to all chronically undernourished children in Cali, Colombia. They thus were able to evaluate the program by comparing children receiving the program with those who had not— even though it would have been desirable to provide the program to all children.

6. *The risk in funding the program without a controlled experiment is likely to be substantially greater than the cost of the experiment; the new program involves large costs and a large degree of uncertainty.* The income maintenance experiments described in Chapters 5 and 15 were designed to test a new form of welfare payment. These evaluations are among the most expensive ever funded by the federal government. Yet the millions of dollars spent on the experiment are insignificant when compared to the costs of a nationwide program that did not provide the desired results.

7. *A decision to implement the program can be postponed until the experiment is completed.* Most experiments take a long time—a year or more. If there is considerable pressure (usually political) to fully implement a program, experimentation may be difficult to apply.

What all this means is that there are probably many occasions when an experimental design is not appropriate. On the other hand, there are times when such a design is clearly needed. The following article, "Improving Cognitive Ability in Chronically Deprived Children," is an example of the pretest-posttest control group design.

Improving Cognitive Ability
in Chronically Deprived Children

HARRISON McKAY
LEONARDO SINISTERRA
ARLENE McKAY
HERNANDO GOMEZ
PASCUALA LLOREDA

In recent years, social and economic planning in developing countries has included closer attention than before to the nutrition, health, and education of children of preschool age in low-income families. One basis for this, in addition to mortality and morbidity studies indicating high vulnerability at that age (1), is information suggesting that obstacles to normal development in the first years of life, found in environments of such poverty that physical growth is retarded through malnutrition, are likely also to retard intellectual development permanently if early remedial action is not taken (2). The loss of intellectual capability, broadly defined, is viewed as especially serious because the technological character of contemporary civilization makes individual productivity and personal fulfillment increasingly contingent upon such capability. In tropical and subtropical zones of the world between 220 and 250 million children below 6 years of age live in conditions of environmental deprivation extreme enough to produce some degree of malnutrition (3); failure to act could result in irretrievable loss of future human capacity on a massive scale.

Although this argument finds widespread agreement among scientists and planners, there is uncertainty about the effectiveness of specific remedial actions. Doubts have been growing for the past decade about whether providing food, education, or health care directly to young children in poverty environments can counteract the myriad social, eco-

---

Source: *Science* Vol. 200, April 21, 1987, pp. 270-278. Copyright © 1978 by the AAAS. (April 1987): 270-278.

nomic, and biological limitations to their intellectual growth. Up to 1970, when the study reported here was formulated, no definitive evidence was available to show that food and health care provided to malnourished or "at risk" infants and young children could produce lasting increases in intellectual functioning. This was so in spite of the ample experience of medical specialists throughout the tropical world that malnourished children typically responded to nutritional recuperation by being more active physically, more able to assimilate environmental events, happier, and more verbal, all of which would be hypothesized to create a more favorable outlook for their capacity to learn. (4).

In conferences and publications emphasis was increasingly placed upon the inextricable relation of malnutrition to other environmental factors inhibiting full mental development of preschool age children in poverty environments (5). It was becoming clear that, at least after the period of rapid brain growth in the first 2 years of life, when protein-calorie malnutrition could have its maximum deleterious physiological effects (6), nutritional rehabilitation and health care programs should be accompanied by some form of environmental modification for children at risk. The largest amount of available information about the potential effects of environmental modification among children from poor families pertained to the United States, where poverty was not of such severity as to make malnutrition a health issue of marked proportions. Here a large literature showed that the low intellectual performance found among disadvantaged children was environmentally based and probably was largely fixed during the preschool years (7). This information gave impetus to the belief that direct treatments, carefully designed and properly delivered to children during early critical periods, could produce large and lasting increases in intellectual ability. As a consequence, during the 1960s a wide variety of

individual, research-based preschool programs as well as a national program were developed in the United States for children from low-income families (8). Several showed positive results but in the aggregate they were not as great or as lasting as had been hoped, and there followed a widespread questioning of the effectiveness of early childhood education as a means of permanently improving intellectual ability among disadvantaged children on a large scale. (9).

From pilot work leading up to the study reported here, we concluded that there was an essential issue that had not received adequate attention and the clarification of which might have tempered the pessimism: the relation of gains in intellectual ability to the intensity and duration of meliorative treatment received during different periods in the preschool years. In addition to the qualitative question of what kinds of preschool intervention, if any, are effective, attention should have been given to the question of what amount of treatment yields what amount of gain. We hypothesized that the increments in intellectual ability produced in preschool programs for disadvantaged children were subsequently lost at least in part because the programs were too brief. Although there was a consensus that longer and more intensive preschool experience could produce larger and more lasting increases, in only one study was there to be found a direct attempt to test this, and in that one sampling problems caused difficulties in interpretation. (10).

As a consequence, the study reported here was designed to examine the quantitative question, with chronically undernourished children, by systematically increasing the duration of multidisciplinary treatments to levels not previously reported and evaluating results with measures directly comparable across all levels (11). This was done not only to test the hypothesis that greater amounts of treatment could produce greater and more enduring intellectual gains but also to develop for the first time an appraisal of what results could be expected at different points along a continuum of action. This second objective, in addition to its intrinsic scientific interest, was projected to have another benefit: that of being useful in the practical application of early childhood services. Also unique in the study design was the simultaneous combination of health, nutrition, and educational components in the treatment program. With the exception of our own pilot work (12), prior studies of preschool nutritional recuperation programs had not included educational activities. Likewise, preschool education studies had not included nutritional recuperation activities, because malnutrition of the degree found in the developing countries was not characteristic of disadvantaged groups studied in the United States (13), where most of the modern early-education research had been done.

EXPERIMENTAL DESIGN AND SUBJECTS

The study was carried out in Cali, Colombia, a city of nearly a million people with many problems characteristic of rapidly expanding cities in developing countries, including large numbers of families living in marginal economic conditions. Table 1 summarizes the experimental design employed. The total time available for the experiment was 3½ years, from February 1971 to August 1974. This was divided into four treatment periods of 9 months each plus interperiod recesses. Our decision to begin the study with children as close as possible to 3 years of age was based upon the 2 years of pilot studies in which treatment and measurement systems were developed for children starting at that age (14). The projected 180 to 200 days of possible attendance at treatment made each pro-

TABLE I   Basic Selection and Treatment Variables of the Groups of Children in the Study

Group	N In 1971	In 1975	Characteristics
TI(a)	57	49	Low SES, subnormal weight and height. One treatment period, between November 1973 and August 1974 (75 to 84 months of age)[a]
TI(b)	56	47	Low SES, subnormal weight and height. One treatment period, between November 1973 and August 1974 (75 to 84 months of age), with prior nutritional supplementation and health care
T2	64	51	Low SES, subnormal weight and height. Two treatment periods, between November 1972 and August 1974 (63 to 84 months of age)
T3	62	50	Low SES, subnormal weight and height. Three treatment periods, between December 1971 and August 1974 (52 to 84 months of age)
T4	62	51	Low SES, subnormal weight and height. Four treatment periods, between February 1971 and August 1974 (42 to 84 months of age)
HS	38	30	High SES. Untreated, but measured at the same points as groups TI–T4
T0	116	72	Low SES, normal weight and height. Untreated.

[a] SES is family socioeconomic status.

jected period similar in length to a school year in Colombia, and the end of the fourth period was scheduled to coincide with the beginning of the year in which the children were of eligible age to enter first grade.

With the object of having 60 children initially available for each treatment group (in case many should be lost to the study during the 3½ year period), approximately 7500 families living in two of the city's lowest-income areas were visited to locate and identify all children with birth dates between 1 June and 30 November 1967, birth dates that would satisfy primary school entry requirements in 1974. In a second visit to the 733 families with such children, invitations were extended to have the children medically examined. The families of 518 accepted, and each child received a clinical examination, anthropometric measurement, and screening for serious neurological dysfunctions. During a third visit to these families, interviews and observations were conducted to determine living conditions, economic resources, and age, education, and occupations of family members. At this stage the number of potential subjects was reduced by 69 (to 449), because of errors in birth date, serious neurological or sensory dysfunctions, refusal to participate further, or removal from the area.

Because the subject loss due to emigration during the 4 months of preliminary data gathering was substantial, 333 children were selected to assure the participation of 300 at the beginning of treatment; 301 were still available at that time, 53 percent of them male. Children selected for the experiment from among the 449 candidates were those having, first, the lowest height and weight for age; second, the highest number of clinical signs of malnutrition (15); and third, the lowest per capita family income. The second and third criteria were employed only in those regions of the frequency distributions where differences among the children in height and weight for age were judged by the medical

staff to lack biological significance. Figure 1 shows these frequency distributions and includes scales corresponding to percentiles in a normal population (16).

The 116 children not selected were left untreated and were not measured again until 4 years later, at which point the 72 still living in the area and willing once again to collaborate were reincorporated into the longitudinal study and measured on physical growth and cognitive development at the same time as the selected children, beginning at 7 years of age. At 3 years of age these children did not show abnormally low weight for age or weight for height.

In order to have available a set of local reference standards for "normal" physical and psychological development, and not depend solely upon foreign standards, a group of children (group HS) from families with high socioeconomic status, living in the same city and having the same range of birth dates as the experimental group, was included in the study. Our assumption was that, in regard to available economic resources, housing, food, health care, and educational opportunities, these children had the highest probability of full intellectual and physical development of any group in the society. In relation to the research program they remained untreated, receiving only medical and psychological assessment at the same intervals as the treated children, but the majority were attending the best private preschools during the study. Eventually 63 children were recruited for group HS, but only the 38 noted in Table 1 were available at the first psychological testing session in 1971.

Nearly all the 333 children selected for treatment lived in homes distributed throughout an area of approximately 2 square kilometers. This area was subdivided into 20 sectors in such a way that between 13 and 19 children were included in each sector. The sectors were ranked in order of a standardized combination of average height and weight for

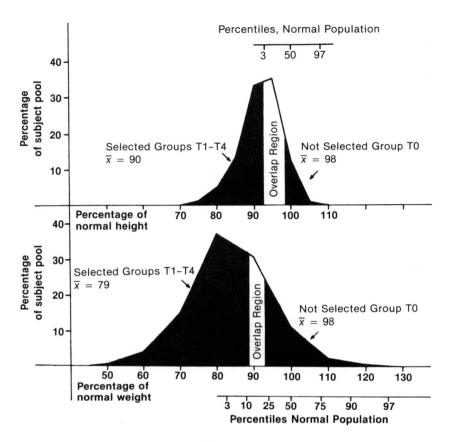

Figure 1

Frequency distributions of height and weight (as percent of normal for age) of the subject pool of 449 children available in 1970, from among whom 333 were selected for treatment groups. A combination of height and weight was the first criterion; the second and third criteria, applied to children in the overlap regions, were clinical signs of malnutrition and family income. Two classification systems of childhood malnutrition yield the following description of the selected children: 90 percent nutritionally "stunted" at 3 years of age and 35 percent with evidence of "wasting"; 26 percent with "second degree" malnutrition, 54 percent with "first degree," and 16 percent "low normal" (16).

age and per capita family income of the children. Each of the first five sectors in the ranking was assigned randomly to one of five groups. This procedure was followed for the next three sets of five sectors, yielding four sectors for each group, one from each of four strata. At this point the groups remained unnamed; only as each new treatment period was to begin was a group assigned to it and

families in the sectors chosen so informed. The children were assigned by sectors instead of individually in order to minimize social interaction between families in different treatment groups and to make daily transportation more efficient (17). Because this "lottery" system was geographically based, all selected children who were living in a sector immediately prior to its assignment were included in the assignment and remained in the same treatment group regardless of further moves. In view of this process, it must be noted that the 1971 N's reported for the treatment groups in Table 1 are retrospective figures, based upon a count of children then living in sectors assigned later to treatment groups. Table 1 also shows the subject loss, by group, between 1971 and 1975. The loss of 53 children—18 percent—from the treatment groups over 4 years was considerably less than expected. Two of these children died and 51 emigrated from Cali with their families; on selection variables they did not differ to a statistically significant degree from the 248 remaining.

A longitudinal study was begun, then, with groups representing extreme points on continua of many factors related to intellectual development, and with an experimental plan to measure the degree to which children at the lower extreme could be moved closer to those of the upper extreme as a result of combined treatments of varying durations. Table 2 compares selected (T1-T4), not selected (T0), and reference (HS) groups on some of the related factors, including those used for selecting children for participation in treatment.

TREATMENTS

The total number of treatment days per period varied as follows: period 1, 180 days; period 2, 185; period 3, 190; period 4, 172. A fire early in period 4 reduced the time available owing to the necessity of terminating the study before the opening of primary school. The original objective was to have each succeeding period at least as long as the preceding one in order to avoid reduction in intensity of treatment. The programs occupied 6 hours a day 5 days a week, and attendance was above 95 percent for all groups; hence there were approximately 1040, 1060, 1080, and 990 hours of treatment per child per period

from period 1 to period 4, respectively. The total number of hours of treatment per group, then, were as follows: T4, 4170 hours; T3, 3130 hours; T2, 2070 hours; T1 (a and b), 990 hours.

In as many respects as possible, treatments were made equivalent between groups within each period. New people, selected and trained as child-care workers to accommodate the periodic increases in numbers of children, were combined with existing personnel and distributed in such a way that experience, skill, and familiarity with children already treated were equalized for all groups, as was the adult-child ratio. Similarly, as new program sites were added, children rotated among them so that all groups occupied all sites equal lengths of time. Except for special care given to the health and nutritional adaptation of each newly entering group during the initial weeks, the same systems in these treatments were applied to all children within periods.

An average treatment day consisted of 6 hours of integrated health, nutritional, and educational activities, in which approximately 4 hours were devoted to education and 2 hours to health, nutrition, and hygiene. In practice, the nutrition and health care provided opportunities to reinforce many aspects of the educational curriculum, and time in the education program was used to reinforce recommended hygienic and food consumption practices.

The nutritional supplementation program was designed to provide a minimum of 75 percent of recommended daily protein and calorie allowances, by means of low-cost foods available commercially, supplemented with vitamins and minerals, and offered ad libitum three times a day. In the vitamin and mineral supplementation, special attention was given to vitamin A, thiamin, riboflavin, niacin, and iron, of which at least 100 percent of recommended dietary allowance was provided (18).

The health care program included daily observation of all children attending the treatment center, with immediate pediatric attention to those with symptoms reported by the parents or noted by the health and education personnel. Children suspected of an infectious condition were not brought into contact with their classmates until the danger of contagion had passed. Severe health problems occurring during weekends or holidays were attended on an emergency basis in the local university hospital.

The educational treatment was designed to develop cognitive processes and language, social abilities, and psychomotor skills, by means of an integrated curriculum model. It was a combination of elements developed in pilot studies and adapted from other programs known to have demonstrated positive effects upon cognitive development (19). Adapting to developmental changes in the children, its form progressed from a structured day divided among six to eight different directed activities, to one with more time

available for individual projects. This latter form, while including activities planned to introduce new concepts, stimulate verbal expression, and develop motor skills, stressed increasing experimentation and decision taking by the children. As with the nutrition and health treatments during the first weeks of each new period, the newly entering children received special care in order to facilitate their adaptation and to teach the basic skills necessary for them to participate in the program. Each new period was conceptually more complex than the preceding one, the last ones incorporating more formal reading, writing, and number work.

MEASURES OF COGNITIVE DEVELOPMENT

There were five measurement points in the course of the study: (i) at the beginning of the first treatment period; (ii) at the end of the first treatment period; (iii) after the end of the second period, carrying over into the beginning

TABLE 2

Selection variables and family characteristics of study groups in 1970 (means). All differences between group HS and groups T1–T4 are statistically significant (P < .01) except age of parents. There are no statistically significant differences among groups T1–T4. There are statistically significant differences between group T0 and combined groups T1–T4 in height and weight (as percent of normal), per capita income and food expenditure, number of family members and children, and rooms per child; and between group T0 and group HS on all variables except age of parents and weight.

Variable	Group		
	T1–T4	T0	HS
Height as percent of normal for age	90	98	101
Weight as percent of normal for age	79	98	102
Per capita family income as percent of group HS	5	7	100
Per capita food expenditure in family as percent of group HS	15	22	100
Number of family members	7.4	6.4	4.7
Number in family under 15 years of age	4.8	3.8	2.4
Number of play/sleep rooms per child	.3	.5	1.6
Age of father	37	37	37
Age of mother	31	32	31
Years of schooling, father	3.6	3.7	14.5
Years of schooling, mother	3.5	3.3	10.0

of the third; (iv) after the end of the third period, extending into the fourth; and (v) following the fourth treatment period. For the purpose of measuring the impact of treatment upon separate components of cognitive development, several short tests were employed at each measurement point, rather than a single intelligence test. The tests varied from point to point, as those only applicable at younger ages were replaced by others that could be continued into primary school years. At all points the plan was to have tests that theoretically measured adequacy of language usage, immediate memory, manual dexterity and motor control, information and vocabulary, quantitative concepts, spatial relations, and logical thinking, with a balance between verbal and nonverbal production. Table 3 is a list of tests applied at each measurement point. More were applied than are listed; only those employed at two or more measurement points and having items that fulfilled the criteria for the analysis described below are included.

Testing was done by laypersons trained and supervised by professional psychologists. Each new test underwent a 4 to 8 month developmental sequence which included an initial practice phase to familiarize the examiners with the format of the test and possible difficulties in application. Thereafter, a series of pilot studies were conducted to permit the modification of items in order to attain acceptable levels of difficulty, reliability, and ease of application. Before each measurement point, all tests were applied to children not in the study until adequate inter-tester reliability and standardization of application were obtained. After definitive application at each measurement point, all tests were repeated on a 10 percent sample to evaluate test-retest reliability. To protect against examiner biases, the children were assigned to examiners randomly and no information was provided regarding treatment group or nutritional or socioeconomic level. (The identification of

TABLE 3

Tests of cognitive ability applied at different measurement points (see text) between 43 and 87 months of age. Only tests that were applied at two adjacent points and that provided items for the analysis in Table 4 are included. The unreferenced tests were constructed locally.

Test	Measurement points
Understanding complex commands	1, 2
Figure tracing	1, 2, 3
Picture vocabulary	1, 2, 3
Intersensory perception (33)	1, 2, 3
Colors, numbers, letters	1, 2, 3
Use of prepositions	1, 2, 3
Block construction	1, 2, 3
Cognitive maturity (34)	1, 2, 3, 4
Sentence completion (35)	1, 2, 3, 4
Memory for sentences (34)	1, 2, 3, 4, 5
Knox cubes (36)	1, 2, 3, 4, 5
Geometric drawings (37)	3, 4
Arithmetic (38, 39)	3, 4, 5
Mazes (40)	3, 4, 5
Information (41)	3, 4, 5
Vocabulary (39)	3, 4, 5
Block design (42)	4, 5
Digit memory (43)	4, 5
Analogies and similarities (44)	4, 5
Matrices (45)	4, 5
Visual classification	4, 5

group HS children was, however, unavoidable even in the earliest years, not only because of their dress and speech but also because of the differences in their interpersonal behavior.) Finally, in order to prevent children from being trained specifically to perform well on test items, the two functions of intervention and evaluation were separated as far as possible. We intentionally avoided, in the education programs, the use of materials or objects from the psychological tests. Also, the intervention personnel had no knowledge of test content or format, and neither they nor the testing personnel were provided with information about group performance at any of the measurement points.

DATA ANALYSIS

The data matrix of cognitive measures generated during the 44-month interval between
the first and last measurement points entailed
evaluation across several occasions by means
of a multivariate vector of observations. A
major problem in the evaluation procedure,
as seen in Table 3, is that the tests of cognitive
development were not the same at every
measurement point. Thus the response vector was not the same along the time dimension. Initially, a principal component
approach was used, with factor scores representing the latent variables (20). Although this
was eventually discarded because there was
no guarantee of factor invariance across occasions, the results were very similar to those
yielded by the analyses finally adopted for this
article. An important consequence of these
analyses was the finding that nearly all of the
variation could be explained by the first component (21), and under the assumption of
unidimensionality cognitive test items were
pooled and calibrated according to the psychometric model proposed by Rasch (22) and
implemented computationally by Wright (23).
The technique employed to obtain the ability
estimates in Table 4 guarantees that the same
latent trait is being reflected in these estimates
(24). Consequently, the growth curves in Fig.
2 are interpreted as representing "general
cognitive ability" (25).

Table 5 shows correlations between pairs
of measurement points of the ability estimates
of all children included in the two points. The
correspondence is substantial, and the matrix
exhibits the "simplex" pattern expected in
psychometric data of this sort (26). As the
correlations are not homogeneous, a test for
diagonality in the transformed error covariance matrix was carried out, and the resulting
chi-square value led to rejection of a mixed
model assumption. In view of this, Bock's

TABLE 4

*Scaled scores on general cognitive ability, means and estimated standard errors, of the four treatment
groups and group HS at five testing points.*

Group	N	Average age at testing (months)				
		43	49	63	77	87
Mean score						
HS	28	− .11	.39	2.28	4.27	4.89
T4	50	− 1.82[a]	.21	1.80	3.35	3.66
T3	47	− 1.72	− 1.06	1.64	3.06	3.35
T2	49	− 1.94	− 1.22	.30[b]	2.61	3.15
T1	90	− 1.83	− 1.11	.33	2.07	2.73
Estimated standard error						
HS	28	.192	.196	.166	.191	.198
T4	50	.225	.148	.138	.164	.152
T3	47	.161	.136	.103	.123	.120
T2	49	.131	.132	.115	.133	.125
T1	90	.110	.097	.098	.124	.108
Standard deviation						
All groups		1.161	1.153	1.169	1.263	1.164

[a] Calculated from 42 percent sample tested prior to beginning of treatment.

[b] Calculated from 50 percent sample tested prior to beginning of treatment.

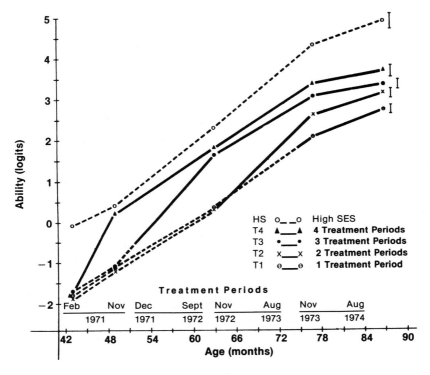

Figure 2

Growth of general cognitive ability of the children from age 43 months to 87 months, the age at the beginning of primary school. Ability scores are scaled sums of test items correct among items common to proximate testing points. The solid lines represent periods of participation in a treatment sequence, and brackets to the right of the curves indicate ± 1 standard error of the corresponding group means at the fifth measurement point. At the fourth measurement point there are no overlapping standard errors; at earlier measurement points there is overlap only among obviously adjacent groups (see Table 4). Group T0 was tested at the fifth measurement point but is not represented in this figure, or in Table 2, because its observed low level of performance could have been attributed to the fact that this was the first testing experience of the group T0 children since the neurological screening 4 years earlier.

multivariate procedure (27), which does not require constant correlations, was employed to analyze the differences among groups across measurement points. The results showed a significant groups-by-occasions effect, permitting rejection of the hypothesis of parallel profiles among groups. A single degree-of-freedom decomposition of this effect showed that there were significant differences in every possible Helmert contrast. Stepdown tests indicated that all components

were required in describing profile differences.

The data in Table 4, plotted in Fig. 2 with the addition of dates and duration of treatment periods, are based upon the same children at all measurement points. These are children having complete medical, socioeconomic, and psychological test records. The discrepancies between the 1975 N's in Table 1 and the N's in Table 4 are due to the fact that 14 children who were still participating in

TABLE 5 Correlation of Ability Scores Across Measurement Points

Measurement points	1	2	3	4	5
1	—	.78	.68	.54	.48
2		—	.80	.66	.59
3			—	.71	.69
4				—	.76
5					—

the study in 1975 were excluded from the analysis because at least one piece of information was missing, a move made to facilitate correlational analyses. Between 2 percent (T4) and 7 percent (HS) were excluded for this reason.

For all analyses, groups T1(a) and T1(b) were combined into group T1 because the prior nutritional supplementation and health care provided group T1(b) had not been found to produce any difference between the two groups. Finally, analysis by sex is not included because a statistically significant difference was found at only one of the five measurement points.

RELATION OF GAINS TO TREATMENT

The most important data in Table 4 and Fig. 2 are those pertaining to cognitive ability scores at the fifth testing point. The upward progression of mean scores from T1 to T4 and the nonoverlapping standard errors, except between T2 and T3, generally confirm that the sooner the treatment was begun the higher the level of general cognitive ability reached by age 87 months. Another interpretation of the data could be that the age at which treatment began was a determining factor independent of amount of time in treatment.

It can be argued that the level of cognitive development which the children reached at 7 years of age depended upon the magni-

tude of gains achieved during the first treatment period in which they participated, perhaps within the first 6 months, although the confounding of age and treatment duration in the experimental design prohibits conclusive testing of the hypothesis. The data supporting this are in the declining magnitude of gain, during the first period of treatment attended, at progressively higher ages of entry into the program. Using group T1 as an untreated baseline until it first entered treatment, and calculating the difference in gains (28) between it and groups T4, T3, and T2 during their respective first periods of treatment, we obtain the following values: group T4, 1.31; group T3, 1.26; and group T2, .57. When calculated as gains per month between testing periods, the data are the following: T4, .22; T3, .09; and T2, .04. This suggests an exponential relationship. Although, because of unequal intervals between testing points and the overlapping of testing durations with treatment periods, this latter relationship must be viewed with caution, it is clear that the older the children were upon entry into the treatment programs the less was their gain in cognitive development in the first 9 months of participation relative to an untreated baseline.

The lack of a randomly assigned, untreated control group prevents similar quantification of the response of group T1 to its one treatment period. If group HS is taken as the baseline, the observed gain of T1 is very small. The proportion of the gap between group HS and group T1 that was closed during the fourth treatment period was 2 percent, whereas in the initial treatment period of each of the other groups the percentages were group T4, 89; group T3, 55; and group T2, 16. That the progressively declining responsiveness at later ages extends to group T1 can be seen additionally in the percentages of gap closed between group T4 and the other groups during the first treatment period of each of the latter: group T3, 87; group T2, 51; and group T1, 27.

DURABILITY OF GAINS

Analysis of items common to testing points five and beyond has yet to be done, but the data contained in Fig. 3, Stanford-Binet intelligence quotients at 8 years of age, show that the relative positions of the groups at age 7 appear to have been maintained to the end of the first year of primary school. Although the treated groups all differ from each other in the expected direction, generally the differences are not statistically significant unless one group has had two treatment periods more than another. A surprising result of the Stanford-Binet testing was that group T0 children, the seemingly more favored among the low-income community (see Table 2), showed such low intelligence quotients; the highest score in group T0 (IQ = 100) was below the mean of group HS, and the lowest group HS score (IQ = 84) was above the mean of group T0. This further confirms that the obstacles to normal intellectual growth found in conditions of poverty in which live large segments of the population are very strong. It is possible that this result is due partly to differential testing histories, despite the fact that group T0 had participated in the full testing program at the preceding fifth measurement point, and that this was the first Stanford-Binet testing for the entire group of subject children.

The difference between groups T0 and T1 is in the direction of superiority of group T1 ($t = 1.507$, $P < .10$). What the IQ of group T1 would have been without its one treatment period is not possible to determine except indirectly through regression analyses with other variables, but we would expect it to have been lower than T0's, because T0 was significantly above T1 on socioeconomic and anthropometric correlates of IQ (Table 2). Also, T1 was approximately .30 standard deviation below T0 at 38 months of age on a cognitive development factor of a preliminary neurological screening test applied in 1970,

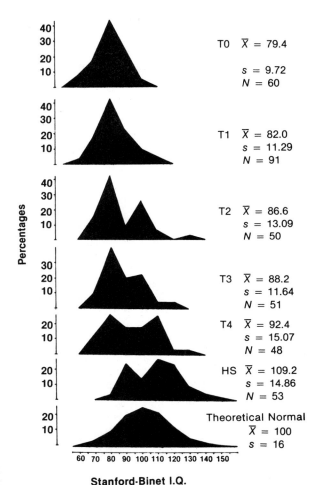

Figure 3

Mean scores on the Stanford-Binet Intelligence Test at 8 years of age. Groups T0–T4 had had 1 year of primary school. Group HS children had attended preschool and primary schools for up to five consecutive years prior to this testing point. Mental age minus chronological age is as follows:

Group T0 — 18 months
Group T1 — 15 months
Group T2 — 11 months
Group T3 —   9 months
Group T4 —   5 months
Group HS + 10 months

prior to selection. Given these data and the fact that at 96 months of age there is a difference favoring group T1 that approaches statistical significance, we conclude not only that group T1 children increased in cognitive ability as a result of their one treatment period (although very little compared to the other groups) but also that they retained the increase through the first year of primary school.

An interesting and potentially important characteristic of the curves in Fig. 3 is the apparent increasing bimodality of the distribution of the groups with increasing length of treatment, in addition to higher means and upward movement of both extremes. The relatively small sample sizes and the fact that these results were found only once make it hazardous to look upon them as definitive. However, the progression across groups is quite uniform and suggests that the issue of individual differential response to equivalent treatment should be studied more carefully.

SOCIAL SIGNIFICANCE OF GAINS

Group HS was included in the study for the purpose of establishing a baseline indicating what could be expected of children when conditions for growth and development were optimal. In this way the effectiveness of the treatment could be evaluated from a frame of reference of the social ideal. It can be seen in Table 4 that group HS increased in cognitive ability at a rate greater than the baseline group T1 during the 34 months before T1 entered treatment. This is equivalent to, and confirms, the previously reported relative decline in intelligence among disadvantaged children (29, p. 258). Between the ages of 4 and 6 years, group HS children passed through a period of accelerated development that greatly increased the distance between them and all the treatment groups. The result, at age 77 months, was that group T4 arrived at

a point approximately 58 percent of the distance between group HS and the untreated baseline group T1, group T3 arrived at 45 percent, and group T2 at 24 percent. Between 77 and 87 months, however, these differences appear to have diminished, even taking into account that group T1 entered treatment during this period. In order for these percentages to have been maintained, the baseline would have had to remain essentially unchanged. With respect to overall gains from 43 months to 87 months, the data show that reduction of the 1.5 standard deviation gap found at 43 months of age between group HS and the treated children required a duration and intensity of treatment at least equal to that of group T2; the group HS overall growth of 5.00 units of ability is less than that of all groups except T1.

As noted, group HS was not representative of the general population, but was a sample of children intentionally chosen from a subgroup above average in the society in characteristics favorable to general cognitive development. For the population under study, normative data do not exist; the "theoretical normal" distribution shown in Fig. 3 represents the U.S. standardization group of 1937 (30). As a consequence, the degree to which the treatments were effective in closing the gap between the disadvantaged children and what could be described as an acceptable level cannot be judged. It is conceivable that group HS children were developing at a rate superior to that of this hypothetical normal. If that was the case, the gains of the treated children could be viewed even more positively.

Recent studies of preschool programs have raised the question whether differences between standard intellectual performance and that encountered in disadvantaged children represent real deficits or whether they reflect cultural or ethnic uniquenesses. This is a particularly relevant issue where disadvantaged groups are ethnically and linguistically distinct from the dominant culture (*29*, pp. 262-272; *31*). The historical evolution of differences in intellectual ability found between groups throughout the world is doubtless multidimensional, with circumstances unique to each society or region, in which have entered religious, biological, and other factors in different epochs, and thus the simple dichotomy of culture uniqueness versus deprivation is only a first approximation to a sorely needed, thorough analysis of antecedents and correlates of the variations. Within the limits of the dichotomy, however, the evidence with regard to the children in our study suggests that the large differences in cognitive ability found between the reference group and the treated groups in 1971 should be considered as reflecting deficits rather than divergent ethnic identities. Spanish was the language spoken in all the homes, with the addition of a second language in some group HS families. All the children were born in the same city sharing the same communication media and popular culture and for the most part the same religion. Additionally, on tests designed to maximize the performance of the children from low-income families by the use of objects, words, and events typical in their neighborhoods (for example, a horse-drawn cart in the picture vocabulary test), the difference between them and group HS was still approximately 1.50 standard deviations at 43 months of age. Thus it is possible to conclude that the treated children's increases in cognitive ability are relevant to them in their immediate community as well as to the ideal represented by the high-status reference group. This will be more precisely assessed in future analyses of the relation of cognitive gains to achievement in primary school.

CONCLUSIONS

The results leave little doubt that environmental deprivation of a degree severe enough to produce chronic undernutrition manifested primarily by stunting strongly retards general cognitive development, and that the retardation is less amenable to modification with increasing age. The study shows that combined nutritional, health, and educational treatments between 3½ and 7 years of age can prevent large losses of potential cognitive ability, with significantly greater effect the earlier the treatments begin. As little as 9 months of treatment prior to primary school entry appears to produce significant increases in ability, although small compared to the gains of children receiving treatment lasting two, three, and four times as long. Continued study will be necessary to ascertain the long-range durability of the treatment effects, but the present data show that they persist at 8 years of age.

The increases in general cognitive ability produced by the multiform preschool interventions are socially significant in that they reduce the large intelligence gap between children from severely deprived environments and those from favored environments, although the extent to which any given amount of intervention might be beneficial to wider societal development is uncertain (*32*). Extrapolated to the large number of children throughout the world who spend their first years in poverty and hunger, however, even the smallest increment resulting from one 9-month treatment period could constitute an important improvement in the pool of human capabilities available to a given society.

REFERENCES AND NOTES

1. D. B. Jelliffe, *Infant Nutrition in the Tropics and Subtropics* (World Health Organization, Geneva, 1968); C. D. Williams, in *Preschool Child Malnutrition* (National Academy of Sciences, Washington, D.C., 1966), pp. 3-8; N. S. Scrimshaw, in *ibid.*, pp. 63-73.

2. N. S. Scrimshaw and J. E. Gordon, Eds., *Malnutrition, Learning and Behavior* (MIT Press, Boston, 1968), especially the articles

by J. Cravioto and E. R. DeLicardie, F. Monckeberg, and M. B. Stoch and P. M. Smythe; J. Carvioto, in *Preschool Child Malnutrition* (National Academy of Sciences, Washington, D.C., 1966), pp. 74-84; M. Winick and P. Rosso, *Pediatr. Res.* **3**, 181 (1969); L. M. Brockman and H. N. Ricciuti, *Dev. Psychol.* **4**, 312 (1971). As significant as the human studies was the animal research of R. Barnes, J. Cowley, and S. Franková, all of whom summarize their work in *Malnutrition, Learning and Behavior.*

3. A. Berg, *The Nutrition Factor* (Brookings Institution, Washington, D.C., 1973), p. 5.

4. In addition to the authors' own experience, that of pediatricians and nutrition specialists in Latin America, Africa, and Asia is highly uniform in this respect. In fact, a generally accepted rule in medical care of malnourished children is that improvement in psychological response is the first sign of recovery.

5. D. Kallen, Ed., *Nutrition, Development and Social Behavior.* DHEW Publication No. (NIH) 73-242 (National Institutes of Health, Washington, D.C., 1973); S. L. Manocha, *Malnutrition and Retarded Human Development* (Thomas, Springfield, Ill., 1972), pp. 132-165.

6. J. Dobbing, in *Malnutrition, Learning and Behavior*, N. S. Scrimshaw and J. E. Gordon, Eds. (MIT Press, Boston, 1968), p. 181.

7. B. S. Bloom, *Stability and Change in Human Characteristics* (Wiley, New York, 1964); J. McV. Hunt, *Intelligence and Experience* (Ronald, New York, 1961); M. Deutsch *et al.*, *The Disadvantaged Child* (Basic Books, New York, 1967). As with nutrition studies, there was also a large amount of animal research on early experience, such as that of J. Denenberg and G. Karas [*Science* **130**, 629 (1959)] showing the vulnerability of the young organism and that early environmental effects could last into adulthood.

8. M. Pines, *Revolution in Learning* (Harper & Row, New York, 1966); R. O. Hess and R. M. Bear, Eds., *Early Education* (Aldine, Chicago, 1968).

9. The 1969-1970 debate over the effectiveness of early education can be found in M. S. Smith and J. S. Bissel, *Harv. Educ. Rev.* **40,** 51 (1970); V. G. Cicirelli, J. W. Evans, J. S. Schiller, *ibid.* p. 105; D. T. Campbell and A. Erlebacher, in *Disadvantaged Child*, J. Hellmuth, Ed. (Brunner/Mazel, New York, 1970), vol. 3; *Environment, Heredity and Intelligence* (Harvard Educational Review, Cambridge, Mass., 1969); F. D. Horowitz and L. Y. Paden, in *Review of Child Development Research*, vol. 3, *Child Development and Social Policy*, B. M. Caldwell and H. N. Ricciuti, Eds. (Univ. of Chicago Press, Chicago, 1973), pp. 331-402; T. Kellaghan, *The Evaluation of a Preschool Programme for Disadvantaged Children* (Educational Research Centre, St. Patrick's College, Dublin, 1975), pp. 21-33; U. Bronfenbrenner, *Is Early Intervention Effective?*, DHEW Publication No. (OHD) 74-25 (Office of Human Development, Department of Health, Education, and Welfare, Washington, D.C., 1974).

10. S. Gray and R. Klaus, in *Intelligence: Some Recurring Issues*, L. E. Tyler, Ed. (Van Nostrand Reinhold, New York, 1969), pp. 187-206.

11. This study sprang from prior work attempting to clarify the relationship of moderate malnutrition to mental retardation, in which it became evident that malnutrition of first and second degree might be only one of many correlated environmental factors found in poverty contributing to deficit in cognitive performance. We selected children for treatment with undernutrition as the first criterion not to imply that this was the major critical factor in cognitive development, but to be assured that we were dealing with children found typically in the extreme of poverty in the developing world, permitting generalization of our results to a population that is reasonably well defined in pediatric practice universally. Figure 1 allows scientists anywhere to directly compare their population with ours on criteria that, in our experience, more reliably reflect the sum total of chronic environment deprivation than any other measure available.

12. H. McKay, A. McKay, L. Sinisterra, in *Nutrition, Development and Social Behavior*, D. Kallen, Ed., DHEW Publ. No. (NIH) 73-242

(National Institutes of Health, Washington, D.C., 1973); S. Franková, in *Malnutrition, Learning and Behavior*, N. S. Scrimshaw and J. E. Gordon, Eds. (MIT Press, Cambridge, Mass., 1968). Franková, in addition to showing in her studies with rats that malnutrition caused behavioral abnormalities, also was the first to suggest that the effects of malnutrition could be modified through stimulation.

13. *First Health and Nutrition Examination Survey, United States, 1971-72*, DHEW Publication No. (HRA) 75-1223 (Health Resources Administration, Department of Health, Education, and Welfare, Rockville, Md., 1975).

14. H. McKay, A. McKay, L. Sinisterra, *Stimulation of Cognitive and Social Competence in Preschool Age Children Affected by the Multiple Deprivations of Depressed Urban Environments* (Human Ecology Research Foundation, Cali, Colombia, 1970).

15. D. B. Jelliffe, *The Assessment of the Nutritional Status of the Community* (World Health Organization, Geneva, 1966), pp. 10-96.

16. In programs that assess community nutritional conditions around the world, standards widely used for normal growth of preschool age children have been those from the Harvard School of Public Health found in *Textbook of Pediatrics*, W. E. Nelson, V. C. Vaughan, R. J. McKay, Eds. (Saunders, Philadelphia, ed. 9, 1969), pp. 15-57. That these were appropriate for use with the children studied here is confirmed by data showing that the "normal" comparison children (group HS) were slightly above the median values of the standards at 3 years of age. Height for age, weight for age, and weight for height of all the study children were compared with this set of standards. The results, in turn, were the basis for the Fig. 1 data, including the "stunting" (indication of chronic, or past, undernutrition) and "wasting" (indication of acute, or present, malnutrition) classifications of J. C. Waterlow and R. Rutishauser [in *Early Malnutrition and Mental Development*, J. Cravioto, L. Hambreaus, B. Vahlquist, Eds. (Almqvist & Wiksell, Uppsala, Sweden, 1974), pp. 13-26]. The classification "stunted" included the children found in the range from 75 to 95 percent of height for age. The "wasting" classification included children falling between 75 and 90 percent of weight for height. The cutoff points of 95 percent height for age and 90 percent weight for height were, respectively, 1.8 and 1.2 standard deviations (S.D.) below the means of group HS, while the selected children's means were 3 S.D. and 1 S.D. below group HS. The degree of malnutrition, in accordance with F. Gomez, R. Ramos-Galvan, S. Frenk, J. M. Cravioto, J. M. Chavez, and J. Vasquez [*J. Trop. Pediatr.* **2,** 77 (1956)] was calculated with weight for age less than 75 percent as "second degree" and 75 to 85 percent as "first degree." We are calling low normal a weight for age between 85 and 90 percent. The 75, 85, and 90 percent cutoff points were 2.6, 1.7, and 1.3 S.D. below the mean of group HS, respectively, while the selected children's mean was 2.3 S.D. below that of group HS children. Examination of combinations of both height and weight to assess nutritional status follows the recommendations of the World Health Organization expert committee on nutrition, found in *FAO/ WHO Technical Report Series No. 477* (World Health Organization, Geneva, 1972), pp. 36-48 (Spanish language edition). In summary, from the point of view of both the mean values and the severity of deficit in the lower extreme of the distributions, it appears that the group of selected children, at 3 years of age, can be characterized as having had a history of chronic undernutrition rather than suffering from acute malnutrition at the time of initial examination.

17. The data analyses in this article use individuals as the randomization unit rather than sectors. To justify this, in view of the fact that random assignment of children was actually done by sectors, a nested analysis of variance was performed on psychological data at the last data point, at age 7, to examine the difference between mean-square for variation (MS) between sectors within treatment and MS between subjects within treatments within sectors. The resulting insignificant F-statistic ($F = 1.432$, d.f. 15,216) permits such analyses.

18. Food and Nutrition Board, National Research Council, *Recommended Dietary Allowances,* (National Academy of Sciences, Washington, D.C., 1968).

19. D. B. Weikart acted as a principal consultant on several aspects of the education program; D. B. Weikart, L. Rogers, C. Adcock, D. Mc-Clelland [*The Cognitively Oriented Curriculum* (ERIC/National Association for the Education of Young Children, Washington, 1971)] provided some of the conceptual framework. The content of the educational curriculum included elements described in the works of C. S. Lavatelli, *Piaget's Theory Applied to an Early Childhood Curriculum* (Center for Media Development, Boston, 1970); S. Smilansky, *The Effects of Sociodramatic Play on Disadvantaged Preschool Children* (Wiley, New York, 1968); C. Bereiter and S. Englemann, *Teaching Disadvantaged Children in the Preschool* (Prentice-Hall, Englewood Cliffs, N.J., 1969); R. G. Stauffer, *The Language-Experience Approach to the Teaching of Reading* (Harper & Row, New York, 1970); R. Van Allen and C. Allen, *Language Experiences in Early Childhood* (Encyclopaedia Britannica Press, Chicago, 1969); S. Ashton-Warner, *Teacher* (Bantam, New York, 1963); R. C. Orem, *Montessori for the Disadvantaged Children in the Preschool* (Capricorn, New York, 1968); and M. Montessori, *The Discovery of the Child* (Ballantine, New York, 1967).

20. M. McKay, L. Sinisterra, A. McKay, H. Gomez, P. Lloreda, J. Korgi, A. Dow, in *Proceedings of the Tenth International Congress of Nutrition* (International Congress of Nutrition, Kyoto, 1975), chap. 7.

21. Although the "Scree" test of R. B. Cattell [*Multivar. Behav. Res.* **2**, 245 (1966)] conducted on the factor analyses at each measurement point clearly indicated a single factor model, there does exist the possibility of a change in factorial content that might have affected the differences between group HS children and the others at later measurement periods. New analysis procedures based upon a linear structural relationship such as suggested by K. G. Jöreskog and D. Sörbom [in *Research Report 76-1* (Univ. of Uppsala, Uppsala, Sweden, 1976)] could provide better definition of between-occasion factor composition, but the number of variables and occasions in this study still surpass the limits of software available.

22. G. Rasch, *Probabilistic Models for Some Intelligence and Attainment Tests* (Danmarks Paedagogiske Institut, Copenhagen, 1960); in *Proceedings of the Fourth Berkeley Symposium on Mathematical Statistics* (Univ. of California Press, Berkeley, 1961), vol. 4, pp. 321-33; *Br. J. Math. Stat. Psychol.* **19**, 49 (1966).

23. B. Wright and N. Panchapakesan, *Educ. Psychol. Meas.* **29**, 23 (1969); B. Wright and R. Mead, *CALFIT: Sample-Free Item Calibration with a Rasch Measurement Model* (Res. Memo. No. 18, Department of Education, Univ. of Chicago, 1975). In using this method, analyses included four blocks of two adjacent measurement points (1 and 2, 2 and 3, 3 and 4, 4 and 5). All test items applied to all children that were common to the two proximate measurement points were included for analysis. Those items that did not fit the theoretical (Rasch) model were not included for further analysis at either measurement point, and what remained were exactly the same items at both points. Between measurement points 1 and 2 there were 126 common items included for analysis; between 2 and 3, 105 items; between 3 and 4, 82 items; and between 4 and 5, 79 items. In no case were there any perfect scores or zero scores.

24. Let M_W = total items after calibration at measurement occasion W; $C_{W, L + 1}$ = items common to both occasion W and occasion W + 1; $C_{W, L - 1}$ items common to both occasion W and occasion W − 1. Since $C_{W, L + 1}$ and $C_{W, L - 1}$ are subsets of M_W they estimate the same ability. However, a change in origin is necessary to equate the estimates because the computational program centers the scale in an arbitrary origin. Let $X_{W, L - 1}$ and $X_{W, L + 1}$ be the abilities estimated by using tests of length $C_{W, L - 1}$ and $C_{W, L + 1}$, respectively. Then:

$$X_{W, L - 1} = \beta 0 + \beta X_{W, L + 1} \qquad (1)$$

Since the abilities estimated are assumed to be item-free, then the slope in the regression will be equal to 1, and $\beta 0$ is the factor by which one ability is shifted to equate with the other. $X_{W, L + 1}$ and $X_{W + 1, L + 1}$ are abilities estimated with one test at two different occasions (note that $C_{W, L + 1} = C_{W + 1, L - 1}$); then by Eq. 1 it is seen that $X_{W, L - 1}$ and $X_{W + 1, L - 1}$ are measuring the same latent trait. Because the scales have different origins, $X_{W + 1, L - 1}$ is shifted by an amount $\beta 0$ to make them comparable.

25. It must be acknowledged here that with this method the interpretability of the data depends upon the comparability of units (ability scores) throughout the range of scores resulting from the Rasch analysis. Although difficult to prove, the argument for equal intervals in the data is strengthened by the fact that the increase in group means prior to treatment is essentially linear. Further discussion of this point may be found in H. Gomez, paper presented at the annual meeting of the American Educational Research Association, New York, 1977.

26. T. W. Anderson, in *Mathematical Methods in the Social Sciences*, K. J. Arrow, S. Karlin, P. Suppes, Eds. (Stanford Univ. Press, Stanford, Calif., 1960).

27. R. D. Bock, *Multivariate Statistical Methods in Behavioral Research* (McGraw-Hill, New York, 1975); in *Problems in Measuring Change*, C. W. Harris, Ed. (Univ. of Wisconsin Press, Madison, 1963), pp. 85-103.

28. Gain during treatment period is defined here as the mean value of a group at a measurement occasion minus the mean value of that group on the previous occasion. Thus the group T1 gains that form the baseline for this analysis are the following: treatment period 1 = .72; period 2 = 1.44; period 3 = 1.74.

29. C. Deutsch, in *Review of Child Development Research*, vol. 3, *Child Development and Social Policy*, B. M. Caldwell and H. N. Ricciuti, Eds. (Univ. of Chicago Press, Chicago, 1973).

30. L. M. Terman and M. A. Merrill, *Stanford-Binet Intelligence Scale, Form L-M* (Houghton, Mifflin, Boston, 1960), adapted for local use.

31. F. Horowitz and L. Paden, in *Review of Child Development Research*, B. M. Caldwell and H. N. Ricciuti, Eds. (Univ. of Chicago Press, Chicago, 1973), vol. 3, pp. 331-335; S. S. Baratz and J. C. Baratz, *Harv. Edu. Rev.* **40,** 29 (1970); C. B. Cazden, *Merrill-Palmer Q.* **12,** 185 (1966); *Curriculum in Early Childhood Education* (Bernard van Leer Foundation, The Hague, 1974).

32. Colombia has now begun to apply this concept of multiform, integrated attention to its preschool age children in a nationwide government program in both rural and urban areas. This is, among developing countries, a rarely encountered confluence of science and political decision, and the law creating this social action must be viewed as a very progressive one for Latin America. Careful documentation of the results of the program could give additional evidence of the social validity of the scientific findings presented in this article, and could demonstrate the potential value of such programs in the other regions of the world.

33. Adapted from a procedure described by H. G. Birch and A. Lefford, in *Brain Damage in Children: The Biological and Social Aspects*, H. G. Birch, Ed. (Williams & Wilkins, Baltimore, 1964). Only the visual-haptic modality was measured.

34. The measure was constructed locally using some of the items and format found in C. Bereiter and S. Englemann, *Teaching Disadvantaged Children in the Preschool* (Prentice-Hall, Englewood Cliffs, N.J., 1969), pp. 74-75.

35. This is a locally modified version of an experimental scale designed by the Growth and Development Unit of the Instituto de Nutrición de Centro América y Panamá, Guatemala.

36. G. Arthur, *A Point Scale of Performance* (Psychological Corp., New York, 1930). Verbal instructions were developed for the scale and the blocks were enlarged.

37. D. Wechsler, *WPPSI: Wechsler Preschool and Primary Scale of Intelligence* (Psychological Corp., New York, 1963).

38. At measurement points 3 and 4, this test is a combination of an adapted version of the

arithmetic subscale of the WPPSI and items developed locally. At measurement point 5, the arithmetic test included locally constructed items and an adaptation of the subscale of the WISC-R (39).

39. D. Wechsler, *WISC-R: Wechsler Intelligence Scale for Children-Revised* (Psychological Corp., New York, 1974).

40. At measurement points 3 and 4 the mazes test was taken from the WPPSI and at point 5 from the WISC-R.

41. Taken from (39). The information items in some instances were rewritten because the content was unfamiliar and the order had to be changed when pilot work demonstrated item difficulty levels at variance with the original scale.

42. At measurement point 4 the test came from the WPPSI, at point 5 from the WISC-R.

43. At measurement point 4 this was from *WISC: Wechsler Intelligence Scale for Children* (Psychological Corp., New York, 1949); at point 5 the format used was that of the WISC-R.

44. At measurement point 4 this test was an adaptation from the similarities subscale of the WPPSI. At point 5 it was adapted from the WISC-R. Modifications had to be made similar to those described in (38).

45. B. Inhelder and J. Piaget, *The Early Growth of Logic in the Child* (Norton, New York, 1964), pp. 151-165. The development of a standardized format for application and scoring was done locally.

46. This research was supported by grants 700-0634 and 720-0418 of the Ford Foundation and grant 5R01HD07716-02 of the National Institute for Child Health and Human Development. Additional analyses were done under contract No. C-74-0115 of the National Institute of Education. Early financial support was also received from the Medical School of the Universidad del Valle in Cali and the former Council for Intersocietal Studies of Northwestern University, whose members, Lee Sechrest, Donald Campbell, and B. J. Chandler, have provided continual encouragement. Additional financial support from Colombian resources was provided by the Ministerio de Salud, the Ministerio de Educación, and the following private industries: Miles Laboratories de Colombia, Carvajal & Cía., Cementos del Valle, Cartón de Colombia, Colgate-Palmolive de Colombia, La Garantía, and Molinos Pampa Rita.

Explanation and Critique

Students are typically critical of the McKay et al. article. First, they argue that the design is not experimental because the children participating in the program were not randomly selected and because there was no randomly assigned control group. In fact, children participating in the program were randomly selected, and although there was no completely untreated randomly selected control group, T1 served this purpose until the time it was subject to treatment.

First, let us examine the random selection of children. The researchers initially identified virtually all the children (333) in a target area (2 square kilometers) below normal in terms of (1) height and weight for age, (2) highest in number of signs of malnutrition, and (3) lowest in per capita family income. The remaining 116 children of the original 449 candidates identified did not show abnormally low weight for age or weight for height. Thus, the *population* for the study became all the 333 deprived children in the target area whose parents volunteered them for the program.

This population was then randomly assigned to groups T1 to T4 through a perfectly valid geographically random assignment process. The researchers describe the process and the reasoning behind geographic random selection:

> Nearly all the 333 children selected for treatment lived in homes distributed throughout an area of approximately 2 square kilometers. This area was subdivided into 20 sectors in such a way that between 13 and 19 children were included in each sector. The sectors were ranked in order of a standardized combination of average height and weight for age and per capita family income of the children. Each of the first five sectors in the ranking was assigned randomly to one of five groups. This procedure was followed for the next three sets of five sectors, yielding four sectors for each group, one from each of the four strata. At this point the groups remained unnamed; only as each new treatment period was to begin was a group assigned to it and families in the sectors chosen so informed. The children were assigned by sectors instead of individually in order to minimize social interaction between families in different treatment groups and to make daily transportation more efficient. Because this "lottery" system was geographically based, all selected children who were living in a sector immediately prior to its assignment were included in the assignment and remained in the same treatment group regardless of further moves.

Is this an experimental design? Yes, so long as the population consists of *below normal children*. Were children assigned to the groups T1–T4 randomly? Yes, through random assignment of geographic areas.

Could the researchers have identified a below-normal control group of children who remained untreated? Clearly, they could have expanded the geographic area.

But the real question is: Should the researcher assign malnourished children to a control group and then deny them treatment? In this case there was undoubtedly little alternative. The researchers were operating on limited funds and could obviously not feed all the undernourished children in Cali. The experiment thus took a group of equally undernourished children and, on the basis of randomization, decided who would be fed and who would not be fed. Given limited resources, was it ethical to conduct this experiment in the way in which it was conducted? There is always room for disagreement among honorable women and men.

REFERENCES

1. Peter H. Rossi and Howard E. Freeman, *Evaluation: A Systematic Approach*, 3rd ed. (Beverly Hills, CA: Sage, 1985), p. 235.

2. R. Barker Bausell, *A Practical Guide to Conducting Empirical Research* (New York: Harper & Row, 1986), pp. 87–91.

3. Harry P. Hatry, Richard E. Winnie, and Donald M. Fisk, *Practical Program Evaluation for State and Local Governments*, 2nd ed. (Washington, DC: Urban Institute, 1981), pp. 107–115.

3

The Solomon Four-Group Design

The Solomon Four-Group Design takes its name from its originator, Richard L. Solomon. In 1949 Solomon pointed out that a two-group, pretest-posttest design confounds or confuses training effects with the interaction between pretesting and training.[1] That is, pretesting may sensitize the subjects to the treatment.[2] The Solomon Four-Group Design depicted in Table 3-1 provides a method that shows whether groups are sensitized by the pretest. David Nachmias describes the design as follows:

> The Solomon Four-Group design . . . contains the same features as the classic [the pretest-posttest control group design], plus an additional set of comparison and experimental groups that are not measured prior to introduction of the program. Therefore, the reactive effect of measurement can be directly assessed by comparing the two experimental groups and the two comparison groups. The comparisons will indicate whether X (the policy) had an independent effect on the groups that were not sensitized by the preprogram measurement procedures.[3]

Note: Nachmias uses the terms *control group* and *comparison group* interchangably.

When is such a complicated design appropriate? Fortunately, only rarely. Because the design documents only the interactive effects of testing, or pretest sensitization, it is not recommended for most evaluations.[4] The design is ultimately appropriate only in cases in which a pretest is used and in which the independent effects of this pretest are thought to be substantial (perhaps more significant than the program itself).

The following article "Learning Factors as Determiners of Pretest Sensitization" is an example of the Solomon Four-Group Design.

TABLE 3-1   The Solomon Four-Group Design

	Before		After
Group E_1	O_{e_1}	X	O_{e_2}
Group C_1	O_{c_1}		O_{e_2}
Group E_2		X	O_{e_3}
Group C_2			O_{c_4}

Learning Factors as Determiners
of Pretest Sensitization

ROBERT E. LANA
DAVID J. KING

Several years ago Solomon (1949) suggested that the frequently used pretest-treatment-posttest research design was not adequately controlled in practice by most investigators. The possibility of an interaction between the pretest and the treatment affecting the posttest results was logically conceivable. This possibility would distort an interpretation of the effect of the treatment if the proper control groups were not utilized. Using a spelling examination as pretest and training in spelling as the treatment, he found that the pretest had a depressive effect on the results of the training as manifested by the posttest results. This was explained in terms of the preservation of the errors made on the pretest by the school children who acted as Ss in the experiment. Solomon indicated that a pretest-treatment effect of this sort may very well operate in the field of attitude change research where the pretest-treatment-posttest research design is frequently utilized.

Recently, Lana (1959a, 1959b) has shown that a pretest sensitization does not occur where certain attitudinal variables are involved. In one experiment an attitude of relatively little importance to the Ss was used as the dependent variable (vivisection) and in another experiment an attitude of somewhat greater concern (ethnic prejudice) was utilized. In both experiments no interaction effect between pretest and treatment or simple pretest sensitization (analysis of variance) was found. The examination of two probably divergent points along a continuum of importance of various attitudes held by an individual thus failed to indicate the existence of a pretest sensitization of any kind. The purpose of the present study is to examine the contention that pretest sensitization occurs when the pretest acts as a learning device, as in the case of Solomon's results with spelling training in school children, and that consequently, this is the more probable situation than the attitudinal case where one will find the need for careful consideration of the use of various control groups within the pretest-treatment-posttest research design.

In order to examine the effects of learning in a comparable situation to those of the experiments on attitude change (Lana, 1959a, 1959b) certain conditions had to be fulfilled which were different from the conditions used by Solomon. Adult Ss were employed in this study while Solomon used school children. Also, the treatment in the present investigation is identical to the treatment used in the second study mentioned above (Lana, 1959b), allowing for a greater degree of comparability among the three studies. The principal hypothesis of this study is that the administration of a pretest, which entails some learning process, will act to sensitize the individual so as to produce a differential posttest response from individuals not exposed to the pretest. The learning procedure used is the recall of meaningful connected material.

PROCEDURE

Seventy male students in four introductory psychology sections at the American University served as Ss in the experiment. Males

Source: *Journal of Applied Psychology* 44, no. 3 (1960): 189–191.

were used since they predominated in number over the females in the classes, and it has been pointed out by King and Cofer (1958) that consistent differences in the recall of meaningful connected material exist between the sexes. These groups were randomly assigned to four treatment conditions summarized in Table 1. All groups were read a story which consisted of a 388 word summary of the mental health film on ethnic prejudice, "The High Wall." Two of these groups were asked to recall the summary immediately after the reading by writing it as near to the original as possible on a sheet of paper provided by E. This first recall was conceptualized as the pretest. One of these two groups viewed the film 12 days after recalling the summary. A 12-day time interval between pretest and posttest was maintained for all groups in order to insure comparability in this respect with the two relevant studies alluded to previously. After treatment, Group I was asked to immediately recall the story as near to the original as possible by writing it on a sheet of paper. Group III was simply asked to recall the story 12 days later. Group II viewed the film without having been first asked to recall the story which was read to them 12 days previously. Group IV was asked to recall the story 12 days after it was read to them without having had an initial recall or having seen the film. The second recall for all groups is conceptualized as the posttest.

The two groups not receiving an initial recall condition were judged to be comparable with respect to recall ability to the two

TABLE 2   Means, Standard Deviations, and Ns for Posttests of All Groups on Accuracy of Recall

	M	SD	N
Group I (recall and film)	18.3	4.4	17
Group II (film)	11.6	5.3	20
Group III (recall)	20.1	3.6	17
Group IV (neither recall nor film)	10.0	5.8	16

groups receiving the initial recall since previous observations have shown introductory level students at American University to be similar in their abilities to recall meaningful connected material. (See Lana, 1959a for a discussion of the general problem of comparability of sample groups utilized in the pretest-treatment-posttest research design.) Scoring for the accuracy of recall was accomplished by dividing the story into 97 "idea units" and counting the number of units present in each protocol.

RESULTS

The difference between the two pretest mean scores was examined with a t test for independent means and found to be insignificant at the .05 level. The variances were tested by the F ratio and were homogeneous. The Ss receiving the pretest were judged to have similar abilities in recalling meaningful connected material. A Bartlett's test was then performed on the four posttest means and the resulting chi square was not significant. A factorial analysis of variance was then applied to the posttest means for the four groups. A summary of these results appears in Table 3.

The F ratio for the treatment effect was not significant at the .05 level. The interaction effect between pretest and treatment was not

TABLE I   Experimental Design

Group I	Group II	Group III	Group IV
Reading	Reading	Reading	Reading
Recall		Recall	
12 days	12 days	12 days	12 days
Film	Film		
Recall	Recall	Recall	Recall

TABLE 3 Summary of Analysis of Variance on Posttest Means for Accuracy of Recall

Source	SS	df	MS	F	p
Treatment	.01	1	.01	< 1	> .05
Pretest	70.56	1	70.56	4.80	< .05
T × P	2.89	1	2.89	< 1	> .05
Error		67	14.69		

NOTE

Error term was computed by the Walker and Lev approximation method for unequal N's.

significant, but the pretest effect was significant. As can be seen from Table 3, almost all of the variability was contained in the effect of the pretest on the posttest means. Thus one of the two possible types of sensitization has been demonstrated in the pretest-treatment-posttest design under conditions where the pretest acts as a learning device.

DISCUSSION

Apparently the pretest has acted differentially from the treatment in influencing the posttest scores. If one examines the various conditions to which each of the groups was exposed, a possible interpretation of the results becomes clear. It has previously been demonstrated (Clark, 1940; King & Cofer, 1957) that an immediate recall of meaningful connected material greatly increases the efficiency of a second recall some time later. Groups I and III were both pretested (recall immediately after presentation of the summary) so that one would expect their posttest scores to reflect this fact in showing a greater efficiency of recall during the posttest than Group II with one recall only two weeks after the reading. Since the treatment effect was not significant the implications are that the film, which presented all the material found in the summary in plot sequence, was not as effective in influencing recall of the original material, presented before the pretest, as was the act of recall occur-

ring twice. A pretest sensitization operating above the effect of the treatment condition is assumed to have been demonstrated by these results. This study, examined with the two previously cited studies (Lana, 1959a, 1959b), indicates that a pretest, which is in effect a learning task, may be the more usual situation in which a pretest sensitization occurs in the pretest-treatment-posttest experimental design. Solomon's study certainly supports the contention that the pretest as a learning task will sensitize the individual to a later posttest exposure. No attitude pretest sensitization by either a pretest-treatment interaction effect or a simple pretest effect has as yet been demonstrated. It should be pointed out that Solomon obtained a pretest-treatment interaction as a sensitizer, while the present study indicates a simple pretest sensitization to be operating rather than an interaction effect. Both, however, are important in the methodology associated with the design in question.

CONCLUSIONS

It is concluded:

1. In the use of a learning device, such as recall of a story, as pretest in the pretest-treatment-posttest research design, a pretest sensitization is evident. This sensitization differentially affects the reception of a memory aid, in the form of a film, in terms of recall of the original story in a posttest compared with groups having heard the story but who were not pretested in the form of this initial recall.

2. Some degree of learning by the S may have to occur during exposure to the pretest in order for a pretest sensitization to be evident since two previous studies (Lana, 1959a, 1959b) have failed to show pretest sensitization using attitude change as the pretest-posttest measure where little or no learning was involved.

REFERENCES

Clark, K. B. Some factors influencing the remembering of prose materials. *Arch. Psychol., N Y,* 1940, 35, No. 253.

King, D. J., & Cofer, C. N. *Some exploratory observations on the recall of stories varying in the adjective-verb quotient. USN, ONR Tech. Rep. No. 9,* 1957, Contract Nonr 595 (04), University of Maryland.

King, D. J., & Cofer, C. N. *Retroactive interference in meaningful material as a function of the degree of contextual constraint in the original and interpolated learning. USN, ONR Tech. Rep. No. 21,* 1958, Contract Nonr 595 (04), University of Maryland.

Lana, R. E. Pretest-treatment interaction effects in attitudinal studies. *Psychol. Bull.,* 1959, 56, 293-300.

Lana, R. E. A further investigation of the pretest-treatment interaction effect. *J. appl. Psychol.,* 1959, 43, 421-422.

Solomon, R. An extension of control group design. *Psychol. Bull.,* 1949, 46, 137-150.

Explanation and Critique

Robert Lana and David King apply the classical Solomon design to college students' recall of a summary of the plot of a mental health film on ethnic prejudice—"The High Wall." Lana and King were interested in knowing if a pretest—defined in terms of a written recall of a summary of the film—had any impact on students' ultimate recall of the film's plot. Students were randomly assigned to one of the four groups depicted in Table 3-2. Groups II and III, as described by Lana and King, are out of sequence so as to conform directly to the representation of the Solomon Four-Group Design depicted in the introduction to this chapter.

All students were read a story that consisted of a 388-word summary of the film, "The High Wall." Groups I and III were then asked to recall the summary immediately after the reading by writing it as near to the original as possible on a sheet of paper provided by the experimenter (this was the pretest). Twelve days later Groups I and II viewed the film (this was the treatment). Immediately after Groups I and II viewed the film, all four groups were asked to recall the story as near to the original as possible by writing it on a sheet of paper. Thus, Group IV was exposed to only one recall 12 days after the original reading.

What were the results? As Table 2 in the Lana and King article showed, the two groups subject to the pretest dramatically outscored the other two groups regardless of the film. The authors conclude:

> A pretest sensitization operating above the effect of the treatment condition is assumed to have been demonstrated by these results. This study . . . indicates

TABLE 3-2 Lana and King Application of the Solomon Four-Group Design

	Before		After
Group I	Recall	Film	Recall
Group III	Recall		Recall
Group II		Film	Recall
Group IV			Recall

that a pretest, which is in effect a learning task, may be the more usual situation in which a pretest sensitization occurs in the pretest-treatment-posttest experimental design.

This particular study exemplifies the significance of the Solomon design, but caution is advised. Most research finds little difference in experimental results due to the effects of pretesting. There are, however, unusual situations such as the one illustrated by the Lana and King article (e.g., learning) in which the pretest may have an important influence on the outcome of the evaluation. Under such situations, the Solomon Four-Group design can be an important evaluation tool.

REFERENCES

1. Richard L. Solomon, "An Extension of Control Group Design," *Psychological Bulletin* 46 (March 1949): 137-150.

2. Most research has shown that the actual impact of the pretest on the posttest is small to nonexistent. See Robert E. Lana, "Pretest Sensitization," in *Artifacts in Behavioral Research*, ed. Robert Rosenthal and Ralph L. Roshow (New York: Academic Press, 1969), pp. 119-141.

3. David Nachmias, *Public Policy Evaluation: Approaches and Methods* (New York: St. Martin's Press, 1979), p. 30.

4. R. Barker Bausell, *A Practical Guide to Conducting Empirical Research* (New York: Harper & Row, 1986), p. 102.

4

Posttest-Only Control Group Design

The posttest-only control group design (or the postprogram-only control group design, as it is sometimes called) is a variation on the pretest-posttest design and the Solomon design. The major difference is that it omits the pretested groups altogether. The posttest-only control group design is illustrated in Table 4-1.

Under this design, individuals are randomly assigned to Group E (experimental group) or Group C (control group). The first group is subjected to the treatment and progress is measured (observed) during or after the program.

Nachmias aptly describes the advantages of the posttest-only design by saying that it:

> controls for all intrinsic sources of invalidity. With the omission of the pretest, testing and instrument decay become irrelevant sources of invalidity. It can also be assumed that the remaining intrinsic factors are controlled, since both groups are exposed to the same external events and undergo the same maturational processes. In addition, the extrinsic factor of selection is controlled by the random assignment of individuals, which removes an initial bias in either group.[1]

What all this means is that with random assignment a pretest may be necessary, which provides some distinct advantages. For one thing, it is sometimes difficult to convene subjects for a pretest before a study. For another, repeated measurement can sometimes be expensive in terms of time and resources. In addition, some evaluations are quite transparent, and the researcher may wish to disguise the purpose of the experiment or even hide the fact that the study is in progress. Finally, it is possible (as demonstrated in Chapter 3) that the pretest may cause the subjects to react differently to the treatment—the pretest sensitization problem. To the extent that this problem exists, it is obviously eliminated if there is no pretest.

Why then have a pretest at all? If the posttest-only control group design is so good, why ever use the pretest-posttest control group design? Barker Bausell states that there is at least a moderate relationship between two administrations of the same test. Thus, a pretest can be used to increase the probability of obtaining statistically significant results if a true difference between an experimental and control group actually exists.

Another advantage of using a pretest is to reduce the size of the sample. The pretest itself is used statistically as a controlling variable in either a repeated measures analysis of variance or covariance. When subjects are in limited supply, a pretest is typically recommended.[2]

There is another good reason for having a pretest. It provides a good check

TABLE 4–1   The Posttest-Only Control Group Design

	Before		After
Group E		X	O_e
Group C			O_c

on the randomization process. Without a pretest one presumes but does not know that randomization causes the experimental and control group to start out at the same point, but one can never be sure. The pretest thus allows us to test for differences in the two groups that could be accounted for by what Lawrence Mohr terms "unhappy" randomization.[3]

Finally, there is always a concern about client preference. Clients frequently feel more comfortable with a pretest. Evaluators can point out the redundancy of a pretest, but if the client is not happy, a pretest may be appropriate. For these reasons, the pretest-posttest design is much more popular than the posttest-only design (even when the posttest-only is perfectly appropriate).

The following article "Community Posthospital Follow-Up Services" is an example of the posttest-only control group design.

Community Posthospital Follow-Up Services

ANN SOLBERG

In community mental health centers the psychiatric unit is only one phase in the continuum of mental health care. The role of the psychiatric unit is to stabilize acutely ill clients and refer them to other mental health services for continued care. These programs are referred to as posthospital or aftercare programs when they are included in the discharge plan of a client who has been hospitalized.

There is a general consensus among mental health professionals that attending posthospital programs is necessary to the client's continued progress and avoidance of rehospitalization. However, many discharged patients referred to such programs do not complete the referrals. Bass (1972) pointed out that the operational principles for maintaining the continuity of treatment were specified as requirements for federally funded centers. Therefore, it is the responsibility of each mental health center to promote continuity of care within its own system. Wolkon and associates (1978) concur that it is the responsibility of the community mental center to help discharged patients take advantage of needed services.

Studies in which the problem of rehospitalization has been examined from the view-

Source: Ann Solberg. "Community Posthospital Follow-Up Services," Vol. 7, No. 1 (February 1983), pp. 96–109. Copyright © 1983 by EVALUATION REVIEW. Reprinted by permission of Sage Publications, Inc.

point of aftercare program attendance have yielded inconsistent results. While most studies have shown that rehospitalization rates are lower for individuals who receive aftercare services compared to those who do not (Free and Dodd, 1961; Beard et al., 1963; Hornstra and McPartland, 1963; Mendel and Rappaport, 1963; Greenblatt et al., 1963; Purvis and Miskimins, 1970; Anthony and Buell, 1973; Smith et al., 1974; Winston et al., 1977), other studies show no differences between aftercare and no-aftercare groups (Brown et al., 1966; Michaux et al., 1969; Mayer et al., 1973; Franklin et al., 1975). Kirk (1976) attributes these diverse findings to differences in methodology, outcome measures, length of follow-up, type and size of patient samples, and treatment settings. Winston and associates (1977) identified the lack of systematic comparison of study groups as another possible source of conflicting results. Studies in which individuals who have attended aftercare programs were compared to those who have not may have been confounded by subject variables stemming from the process of self-selection.

The purpose of this article is to present the results of a 3-month demonstration project that ended in July 1980. The purpose of the project was to evaluate the effectiveness of community follow-up services in reducing both rehospitalization and the overall cost of mental health care of individuals hospitalized at the Fresno County Department of Health (FCDH) Acute Psychiatric Unit (APU). Clients discharged from the APU were randomly assigned to either the experimental group or the control group. The control group received only those aftercare services for which they completed referrals or services that they sought on their own. The experimental group received additional posthospital follow-up services from a team of four psychiatric social workers for a period of up to 30 days following their discharge from the APU. The follow-up team worked with clients, their families, and other treatment staff with the goals of improving clients' personal and community adjustments and increasing their involvement with the aftercare programs (outpatient, partial day, or residential) to which they were referred by APU staff. The follow-up services were treated as an additional aftercare service. They were intended to supplement rather than substitute for aftercare services specified in a client's discharge plan.

The effectiveness of the project was evaluated by comparing the two study groups on selected outcome measures. The evaluation period lasted for the 60 days following each client's discharge from the APU. The decision to extend the evaluation period was based, in part, on a statistical consideration. The total number of clients rehospitalized from both study groups was larger in the 60-day period. The larger sample improved the discriminating power of the test used to compare the survival rates of the study groups. In addition, it was believed that any beneficial effects produced by the follow-up services should extend beyond the service period. In this study no attempt was made to associate client characteristics with differences in predisposition to hospitalization or in relative success in the follow-up project.

Two hypotheses concerning the effectiveness of the follow-up services were tested.

- The follow-up services will prevent or at least delay the rehospitalization of clients.
- The follow-up services will reduce the cost of mental health services.

METHOD

Subjects

The population studied was defined to include all persons who were hospitalized at the Fresno County Department of Health (FCDH) Acute Psychiatric Unit (APU), with the exception of individuals meeting one or more of the following disqualifying criteria:

1. residence outside of Fresno County,
2. supervision by the law enforcement system,
3. referral to alcohol or drug abuse programs,
4. referral to FCDH Advocare program,
5. referral to subacute locked facilities,
6. transfer to a psychiatric unit in another hospital.

These criteria helped ensure that the subjects (1) would be accessible to the follow-up workers, (2) were not in need of specialized treatment programs, (3) did not have another mental health worker supervising their treatment plan, and (4) would return to the APU in the event of future need for hospital services.

The sample consisted of 143 persons discharged from the APU during a three-month period ending in July 1980. The subjects were randomly assigned to two groups—experimental and control—upon their discharge from their first hospital episode during the study period. (The first hospital episode was not necessarily the first hospital admission in the client's psychiatric history.) There were 71 subjects in the experimental group and 72 subjects in the control group. The experimental group received the posthospital follow-up services for 30 days, and the control group did not.

The characteristics of the experimental group were as follows: females (45 percent); males (55 percent); age (X = 29.4; SD = 10.8); psychoses (51 percent); neuroses (49 percent); global impairment rating (X = 3.6; SD = 1.2). Similarly, the characteristics of the control group were as follows: females (43 percent); males (57 percent); age (X = 32.8; SD = 12.1); psychoses (51 percent); neuroses (49 percent); global impairment rating (X = 3.6; SD = 1.3).

Measures and Analysis

Information for testing the hypotheses was based on a 60-day evaluation period following each client's discharge from his or her first hospital episode during the study period. Hospital data were limited to hospitalizations taking place at the APU. Following clients closely for 60 days to record possible admissions to other hospitals was neither practical nor necessary. The likelihood that rehospitalization would take place at the APU was increased considerably by including in the sample only those persons who completed their hospital episode at the APU, rather than being transferred to another facility. The exceptions (hospitalizations at other facilities) were treated as a random variable, assumed to affect both study groups equally.

Survival Time. Survival time was defined as the length of time between a client's discharge from the first hospital episode and the onset of their first rehospitalization at the APU during the 60-day evaluation period. The 60-day fixed evaluation period resulted in incomplete information (censored observations) on the actual length of survival for many of the clients. All that is known about these clients is that they did not return to the hospital for at least 60 days after their first hospital episode. The test developed by Gehan (1965), which compares two groups with respect to the length of survival when one or both samples contains censored observations, was used in this study.

Cost Analysis. There were three sources of mental health care costs included in the cost analysis: (1) the cost of rehospitalization, including treatment and intake evaluations at outpatient clinics; (2) the cost of aftercare program participation; and (3) the cost of the follow-up services, which were applicable to the experimental group only. Overhead expenses were included in all cost categories.

PROCEDURE

Clients were assigned to groups at the time of discharge from their first hospital episode during the study period. Clients were not considered for reassignment upon their discharge from subsequent hospitalizations. A clerk at the APU notified the research assistant as soon as the decision to discharge a client had been reached. The research assistant determined, based on the aftercare referrals made for the client by APU staff, if the client being discharged met the target group criteria. A client who met the target group criteria was randomly assigned to the experimental group or the control group by the research assistant using a group assignment sheet. The assignment sheet was prepared by the project evaluator prior to the study using the one-digit columns of a table of random numbers. The numbers were assigned to subjects according to their order of appearance, beginning at the top of the column and progressing downward. Even numbers designated assignment to the experimental group and odd numbers designated assignment to the control group. The last subject was assigned 30 days prior to the last day of the study period to allow for a full 30 days of follow-up. Precautions were taken to ensure that the assignment of clients to groups was not biased by special interests. The APU staff were not informed about the target-group criteria. The project social workers and evaluator were not involved with subject assignment beyond defining the target group and preparing the initial assignment list based on the table of random numbers.

The research assistant contacted one of the social workers when a client was assigned to the experimental group. The social workers then decided among themselves who would accept the case, considering immediate availability and size of caseloads. After reaching a decision, a social worker met the client at the APU. Within 24 hours, the social worker made the first home visit. Follow-up services were provided for a period of 30 days after a client's initial discharge from the APU during the study period. Clients were given only one follow-up period, regardless of subsequent hospitalizations. At the end of the 30-day period, the social worker discharged the client from the follow-up project and made referrals to aftercare programs according to the client's need for continued care.

The project evaluator collected the data for the outcome measures and made periodic visits to the project site. Information regarding hospitalizations was obtained from records at the APU. A 24-hour report showed the date and time of admission and discharge. Aftercare program participation was obtained from the FCDH management information system (MIS). The type and frequency of follow-up contacts were recorded by the project social workers. Cost information was obtained from the MIS and the accounting office.

RESULTS

Description of Follow-up Services

Of the group of 71 clients who received follow-up services, 58 (82 percent) were seen by a social worker at the APU prior to their discharge. Forty-six clients (65 percent) received a home visit within 24 hours of their discharge. The clients, as a group, received a total of 546 client contacts (face-to-face and telephone contacts) during the 30-day follow-up period. The median number of contacts was five per client. Collateral contacts—a second category of follow-up contacts—included face-to-face and telephone contacts with mental health staff and family members. There were 551 collateral contacts in the 30-day period, with a median of four contacts per client. Figure 1 shows the percentage of total client contacts (546) and total collateral

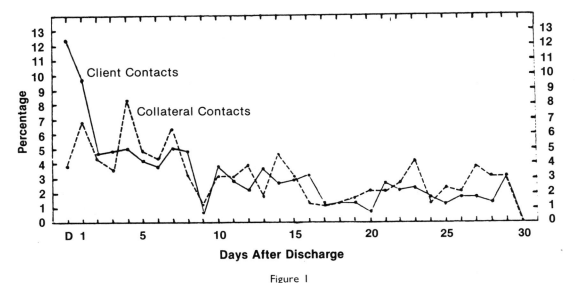

Figure I

Percentage of Client and Collateral Follow-Up Contacts Received by Experimental Group Subjects Each Day of the 30-Day Follow-Up Period

contacts (551) that were provided each day of the 30-day follow-up period. Not shown on this figure are 19 client and 42 collateral contacts that took place after the 30-day follow-up period ended. It was not in the best interest of 26 (37 percent) clients to discharge them on precisely the 30th day.

There were 54 clients (76 percent) who were identified as "service completers," because they cooperated with the social workers throughout the 30-day period. The other 17 clients (24 percent) were designated as drop-outs because they refused services during the first few contacts or were resistive to the extent that the social workers stopped initiating contact with them before the follow-up period ended.

Hospital Contacts

During the 60-day evaluation period, 8 experimental subjects (11.3 percent) and 20 control subjects (27.8 percent) were rehospi-

talized at least once. Two experimental subjects and four control subjects were rehospitalized twice. Clients in the experimental group were in the hospital a total of 83.9 days, compared to 206.6 days accumulated by the control group. The total hospital days for the control group was estimated for 71 clients by multiplying the group average, based on 72 clients, by 71.

The survival-time distributions for the study groups are presented in Figure 2. Comparing the groups on survival time, the results of Gehan's test support the hypothesis that the follow-up services are effective in preventing or at least delaying the recurrence of hospitalization (V = 2.77; p < .05). The median survival time for the experimental group was 22.8 days, compared to 17.4 days for the control group. Also, none of the experimental subjects was rehospitalized within 14 days of discharge from the APU, compared to nine control subjects (12.7 percent) who were rehospitalized during the same period. The

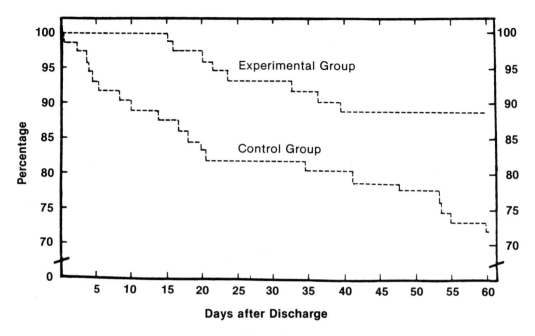

Figure 2
Survival Rates for Study Groups

two-week period after discharge has been identified as a period of high risk for rehospitalization.

Cost of Mental Health Care

Table 1 shows the cost of mental health care for the study groups during the 60-day evaluation period. The total cost for the experimental group ($60,165) was $10,298 less than the total cost for the control group ($70,463). The t-test for these outcomes showed no significant differences between the two groups regarding total program costs ($t = 1.21 < 1.96$; $p > .05$). The total hospital cost (Acute Psychiatric Unit) was $13,407 for the experimental group and $49,703 for the control group. A significant difference was found between the two groups, indicating a reduction in the cost of hospitalization for the experimental group ($t = 8.50 \geq 1.96$, $p \leq .05$). The cost of aftercare services was ob-

servably higher for the experimental group ($25,093) compared to the control group ($20,760), but the t-test showed that the costs were not statistically different from one another ($t = 1.18 < 1.96$, $p > .05$). The cost figures for aftercare services were based on 439 aftercare contacts for 40 experimental subjects and 355 aftercare contacts for 37 control subjects.

DISCUSSION

In this study, the event of readmission was used as a complex index of the individual's overall adjustment and acceptance by the family and community. Solomon and Doll (1979) have indicated that there are many factors that contribute to a decision to rehospitalize a person, other than the individual's psychiatric status. These include family and community acceptance of the individual,

TABLE I   A Comparison of Study Groups on the Cost of Mental Health Care During a 60-Day Period after Subjects' Discharge from Acute Psychiatric Unit

Cost Components	Experimental Group		Control Group		t
	Total	SD	Total	SD	
Acute Psychiatric Unit	$13,407	$15,882	$49,703	$32,583	8.50[a]
Aftercare Services	$25,093	$24,072	$20,760	$19,733	1.18
Follow-up Services	$21,665	$15,219	—	—	
Total	$60,165	$40,650	$70,463	$52,313	1.32

NOTES

The cost of follow-up services includes the salaries of 3.5 full-time equivalent psychiatric social workers, a part-time psychiatric social worker supervisor, a full-time research assistant, supplies, travel expenses, and all overhead expenses.

[a] $p < .05$

characteristics and perceptions of admitting personnel, factors in the mental health delivery system (e.g., hospital policies, census, and availability of community alternatives), and the individual's perception of the hospital as being a solution to his or her problems. The follow-up team dealt with all factors that had the potential for increasing a client's community tenure. Rehospitalization was considered only when no other solution could be found.

The results showed that community follow-up services, as provided in this demonstration project, provide an effective means of reducing the rehospitalization of individuals who have been hospitalized in a short-term acute psychiatric facility at the Fresno County Department of Health. The results of the survival-time analysis showed that the follow-up services were effective, at least in delaying further hospitalizations. Many clients who received follow-up services and were not hospitalized during the 60-day evaluation period may have been hospitalized afterward. While it is doubtful that clients with a history of relapse will be prevented from ever returning to the hospital, persons whose psychiatric condition is not chronic are more likely to have future hospitalizations prevented altogether. Because not all rehospitalizations can be prevented, the follow-up period should be renewed each time a person is hospitalized. The

limit of one follow-up period in this study was a requirement of the design used for the evaluation.

The cost analysis showed that the savings in hospital costs were substantial ($36,296). The follow-up staff stated that they could have served an additional ten cases (total 81) without reducing the effectiveness of their follow-up efforts, and therefore, the potential for savings may be somewhat underestimated. In addition, the cost analysis showed that there were no significant increases in aftercare program costs nor in total mental health care costs as a result of adding the follow-up component to the service delivery system. In other words, the savings in hospital care paid for the additional cost of providing follow-up services.

Factors in the follow-up model that are believed to be effective in reducing hospitalization include (1) an assertive approach to follow-up, (2) contact with the client and staff prior to the client's discharge, (3) more frequent contact in the beginning of the follow-up period, (4) services provided to the client in his or her natural environment, and (5) the role of follow-up workers as case managers. The follow-up workers were strongly encouraged to contact clients more often at the beginning of the follow-up period. Consequently, most clients (82 percent) received an initial visit by a follow-up worker on the psychiatric unit, and a greater percentage of contacts took place early in the follow-up period. Previous readmission data for the psychiatric unit in this study have consistently shown that a greater percentage of clients return within the first two weeks after discharge than during any other time period up to 90 days after discharge. Therefore, follow-up services were especially emphasized during the early days of the follow-up period identified as a high risk period. The effectiveness of this strategy was demonstrated by the result that none of the experimental subjects returned to the hospital within two weeks after their discharge from the psychiatric unit, whereas nine control subjects were rehospitalized during the same period.

Because this study was carefully conducted, following principles of controlled research, it is believed that these results can be replicated using different samples from the same population. The decision to continue the project was based on this rationale. However, there will be two changes in the follow-up procedure. First, the follow-up period will be renewed each time a client is discharged from the hospital. A second change will allow the follow-up period to vary between 30 and 40 days. The social workers judged that for about one-third of the clients, a strict adherence to a 30-day period may result in abrupt discharges, which are potentially detrimental to their progress.

It is believed that posthospital community follow-up services have a likelihood for similar success in other locations. Characteristics that are unique to clients in other settings may need to be considered in developing an effective follow-up strategy.

SUMMARY

The purpose of this project was to evaluate the effectiveness of community follow-up services in the context of a true experimental design. One hundred forty-three clients ready for discharge from the Fresno County Department of Health Acute Psychiatric Unit were randomly assigned to either an experimental group or a control group. There were 71 subjects in the experimental group and 72 subjects in the control group. The individuals in the experimental group received community follow-up services from one of four psychiatric social workers for a period of 30 days after their discharge from the acute psychiatric unit. The control group received no follow-up services from the project staff.

The evaluation period lasted for 60 days following each client's discharge from the hospital. The results showed that posthospital community follow-up, as provided in this demonstration project, is effective in increasing the survival time of clients and in reducing the cost of mental health care. The survival time—length of time outside of the hospital—was significantly greater for the experimental group compared to the control group ($p \leq .05$). The median survival time for the experimental group was 22.8 days and for the control group, 17.4 days. The percentage of experimental subjects who were rehospitalized (28 percent), and the number of hospital days for the experimental group (84) was less than one-half the number of hospital days for the control group (207). The savings in hospital costs ($35,896) more than paid for the cost of the follow-up services ($21,665), and the total cost for the experimental group ($60,165) was $10,298 less than the total cost for the control group. It was concluded, based on the results of the cost analysis, that hospital expenditures were substantially reduced, and this savings paid for the cost of the follow-up program.

Note: One of the four social workers left the project during the fifth week. This social worker was not replaced, because the project was found to be overstaffed relative to the number of clients being included as experimental subjects.

REFERENCES

Anthony, W. A. and G. J. Buell (1973) "Psychiatric aftercare clinic effectiveness as a function of patient demographic characteristics." J. of Consulting and Clinical Psychology 41, 1: 116-119.

Bass, R. (1972) A Method for Measuring Continuity of Care in a Community Mental Health Center. Report 4, Series on Mental Health Statistics. Washington, DC: National Institute of Mental Health.

Beard, J. N., R. B. Pitt, S. H. Fisher, and V. Goertzel (1963) "Evaluating the effectiveness of a psychiatric rehabilitation program." Amer. J. of Orthopsychiatry 33: 701-712.

Brown, G., et al. (1966) Schizophrenia and Social Care. London: Oxford Univ. Press.

Franklin, J., L. D. Kittredge, and J. H. Thrasher (1975) "A survey of factors related to mental hospital readmissions." Hospital and Community Psychiatry 26, 11: 749-751.

Free, S. and D. Dodd (1961) "Aftercare for discharged mental patients." Presented at the Five-State Conference on Mental Health, Richmond, Virginia.

Gehan, E. A. (1965) "A generalized Wilcoxon test for comparing arbitrarily singly censored samples." Biometrika 52: 203-223.

Greenblatt, M., R. F. Moore, R. S. Albert, and M. H. Soloman (1963) The Prevention of Hospitalization. New York: Grune & Stratton.

Hornstra, R. and T. McPartland (1963) "Aspects of psychiatric aftercare." Int. J. of Social Psychiatry 9: 135-142.

Kirk, S. A. (1976) "Effectiveness of community services for discharged mental hospital patients." Amer. J. of Orthopsychiatry 46, 4: 646-659.

Mayer, J., M. Motz, and A. Rosenblatt (1973) "The readmission patterns of patients referred to aftercare clinics." J. of Bronx State Hospital 1, 4.

Mendel, W. M. and S. Rappaport (1963) "Outpatient treatment for chronic schizophrenic patients." Archives of General Psychiatry 8: 190-196.

Michaux, W., et al. (1969) The First Year Out: Mental Patients After Hospitalization. Baltimore: Johns Hopkins Press.

Purvis, S. A. and R. W. Miskimins (1970) "Effects of community follow-up on post-hospital adjustment of psychiatric patients." Community Mental Health J. 6, 5: 374-382.

Smith, W., J. Kaplan, and D. Siker (1974) "Community mental health and the seriously disturbed patient." Archives of General Psychiatry 30: 693-696.

Solomon, P. and W. Doll (1979) "The varieties of readmission: the case against the use of recidivism rates as a measure of program effectiveness." Amer J. of Orthopsychiatry 49, 2: 230-239.

Winston, A., H. Pardes, D. S. Papernik, and L. Breslin (1977) "Aftercare of psychiatric patients and its relation to rehospitalization." Hospital and Community Psychiatry 28, 92: 118-121.

Wolkon G., C. Peterson, and A. Rogawski (1978) "A program for continuing care: implementation and outcome." Hospital and Community Psychiatry 29, 4: 254-256.

Explanation and Critique

One of the most interesting facets of program or policy evaluation is that real-world projects do not always exactly fit the model. In fact, they seldom do. The article by Ann Solberg is a perfect example. As we have seen, Solberg's research reported on a project to evaluate the effectiveness of community follow-up services in reducing both rehospitalization and the overall cost of mental health care of individuals hospitalized at the Fresno County Department of Health Acute Psychiatric Unit (APU). Solberg details the following in her article:

> Clients discharged from the APU were randomly assigned to either the experimental group or the control group. The control group received only those after-

care services for which they completed referrals or services that they sought on their own. The experimental group received additional posthospital follow-up services from a team of four psychiatric social workers for a period of up to 30 days following their discharge from the APU. The follow-up team worked with the clients, their families, and other treatment staff with the goals of improving clients' personal and community adjustments and increasing their involvement with aftercare programs (outpatient, partial day, or residential) to which they were referred by APU staff. The follow-up services were treated as an additional aftercare service. They were intended to supplement rather than substitute for aftercare services specified in a client's discharge plan.

When one thinks of the posttest-only control group design, eliminating the pretest comes to mind. For example, one might envision an experimental reading program in which students are randomly assigned to experimental and control groups and are given reading tests before and after the program. In the posttest-only design the pretest is simply eliminated—knowing that randomization has, in effect, made the two groups equal and thus the pretest unnecessary.

In Solberg's evaluation, however, a pretest was not possible. What could be pretested? Nothing. Thus, in evaluations such as this, the pretest-posttest design and the Solomon Four-Group Design are not used because they cannot be used. The posttest-only design is the only real experimental alternative.

In examining Solberg's research, consider her application of the posttest-only control group design. The randomized assignment was obviously the key to the validity of the design, but this was not the only strength of the paper. For one thing, Solberg provided data on the characteristics of the experimental group and the control group (gender, age, psychosis, neurosis, global impairment rating). Given that randomized assignment of the patients was used, presentation of such comparisons was not really necessary. In the introduction to Part II, "Experimental Designs," it was stated that as long as the number of subjects is sufficiently large, random assignment guarantees that the characteristics of the subjects in the experimental and control groups are statistically equivalent. With only 71 subjects in the experimental group and 72 in the control group, Solberg apparently wanted to assure the reader that the groups were, in fact, statistically equivalent. A nice touch.

This discussion has emphasized the fact that the key to experimental designs is random assignment. Random assignment, again, means that the treatment or program to which the subject is assigned bears no relation to any characteristic of the subject. It is important, however, as we pointed out in Chapter 2, that random assignment be distinguished from random selection.

To illustrate, look again at the Solberg article. Solberg first selected the subjects of her study from the Fresno APU. To achieve true external validity, she should have selected subjects at random from the population of persons discharged from psychiatric hospitals. For Solberg to do this, however, the costs would have been prohibitive. Instead, she randomly assigned all subjects discharged from the Fresno County Department of Health Acute Psychiatric Unit who met the inclusion criteria to experimental and control groups. This procedure reduced the generality of findings, but it also reduced costs and random errors. Random selection is not a requisite for a true experimental design.[4] Solberg abandoned random selection entirely (but not random assignment), but still had a valid experimental design. However, she lost generalizability. This is an example of one of the trade-offs discussed in Chapter 1. To her credit, Solberg was very careful about this. She reported the following:

> The results showed that community follow-up services, as provided in this demonstration project, provide an effective means of reducing the rehospitalization of individuals who have been hospitalized in the short-term acute psychiatric facility *at the Fresno County Department of Health* [emphasis ours].

Solberg was certainly correct in not generalizing beyond this unit.

Overall, although we may have questions about some segments of Solberg's article (e.g., How were hospitalization costs determined?), the research reported provides a fine example of a variation on the posttest-only control group design.

REFERENCES

1. David Nachmias, *Public Policy Evaluation: Approaches and Methods* (New York: St. Martin's Press, 1979), p. 32.
2. R. Barker Bausell, *A Practical Guide to Conducting Empirical Research* (New York: Harper & Row, 1986), p. 93.
3. Lawrence B. Mohr, *Impact Analysis for Program Evaluation* (Chicago, IL: Dorsey, 1988), p. 46.
4. Laura Irwin Langbein, *Discovering Whether Programs Work: A Guide to Statistical Methods for Program Evaluation* (Glenview, IL: Scott, Foresman, 1980), pp. 67-68.

5

The Factorial Design

The last of the experimental designs considered is the factorial design. A *factorial design* is used to evaluate a program that has more than one treatment or component. It is also usually the case that each level of each component can be administered with various levels of other components. In a factorial design, each possible combination of program variables is compared—including no program. Thus, a factorial evaluation involving three program components is similar to three separate experiments, each investigating a different component.

One of the major advantages of the factorial design is that it allows the researchers to identify any interaction effect between variables. Again, we rely on David Nachmias, who states:

> In factorial experiments the effect of one of the program variables at a single level of another of the variables is referred to as the simple effect. The overall effect of a program variable averaged across all the levels of the remaining program variables is referred to as its main effect. Interaction describes the manner in which the simple effects of a variable may differ from level to level of other variables.[1]

Table 5-1 illustrates a program with two components, A and B (this is termed a 2^2 design).[2] Let us illustrate with an overly simplistic situation. In an evaluation of the operation of a special program to teach calculus to fifth graders, component A is a daily schedule of 30 minutes of teaching with a_1 indicating participation in the program and a_2 indicating nonparticipation. Component B is a daily schedule of 30 minutes of computerized instruction with b_1 indicating participation and b_2 nonparticipation. The possible conditions include the following:

a_1b_1 teaching and computer
a_1b_2 teaching only
a_2b_1 computer only
a_2b_2 neither teaching nor computer

Also suppose that a_1b_2 improved the students' knowledge of calculus by one unit, that a_2b_1 also improved the students' knowledge of calculus by one unit, but that a_1b_1 improved the students' knowledge of calculus by three units. This is an example of an interaction effect. The combination of receiving both components of the program produces greater results than the sum of each of the individual components.

The following article, "Overview of the Seattle-Denver Income Maintenance Experiment Final Report," exemplifies the use of the factorial design.

TABLE 5–1 The 2² Factorial Design

		Treatment A	
		a_1 (yes)	a_2 (no)
	b_1 (yes)	a_1b_1	a_2b_1
Treatment B			
	b_2 (no)	a_1b_2	a_2b_2

Overview of the Seattle-Denver Income Maintenance Experiment Final Report

FELICITY SKIDMORE

The Seattle-Denver Income Maintenance Experiment (SIME/DIME) was the last in a series of four large-scale income maintenance experiments undertaken in the late 1960s and early 1970s to measure the disincentive effects of cash transfers on the market work of those eligible for them.

The purpose of this summary is to provide an overview of the rationale behind the income maintenance experiments in general and SIME/DIME in particular; a brief description of SIME/DIME experimental design; and a synopsis of the SIME/DIME research results.

THE POLICY CONTEXT

In the mid 1960s, a consensus emerged among policy analysts that there were potential problems with the existing set of transfer programs available to those in need. Programs were believed to be fragmented and characterized by variations in benefit levels

and administrative access among different types of families. In particular, the working poor in two-parent families were largely excluded. In 1966, the Aid to Families with Dependent Children-Unemployed Father (AFDC-UF) program covered less than 100,000 families, although one-third of all the poor were in two-parent families where the husband worked full-time all year round. The existing set of transfer programs was also asserted to be antifamily. For example, one possible way a poor father could help his family would be to leave his wife and children—thus enabling them to apply for AFDC.

A variety of policy reform proposals were being developed during this period, such as the Heineman Commission's 1969 proposal for a federal negative income tax with universal eligibility. Since a major objective of such proposals was to extend coverage to the working poor, it was considered important to determine if the benefits of increased coverage would be offset by reductions in work. The major reason for the income mainte-

Source: "Overview of the Seattle-Denver Income Maintenance Experiment Final Report," Felicity Skidmore, U.S. Department of Health and Human Services, May 1983.

nance experiments was to measure how strong the work disincentive of such a program might be.

Other policy concerns of the period also shaped the design of SIME/DIME. First, the 1960s and early 1970s saw a rapid increase in rates of divorce and separation, and hence, the proportion of female-headed families. This development focused attention on whether a negative income tax with universal eligibility would increase marital stability. Second, "Great Society" programs were not conceived primarily as income support, but rather as a way to increase the ability of the poor to be economically self-sufficient. This led to the question of whether a job counseling and education or training subsidy program administered simultaneously with a negative income tax could offset the reductions in work that might result from the negative income tax alone.

Four income maintenance experiments were undertaken, starting with the New Jersey Experiment in 1967, including the Rural (1968) and Gary (1971) Experiments, and ending with SIME/DIME, the subject of this overview. SIME/DIME was the largest of the four experiments—indeed larger than the other three combined—and lasted for the longest period of time. For this reason, its results can be viewed with the most confidence.

The next section of the overview discusses the potential of social experimentation as a policy research tool. The third section describes the design and administration of SIME/DIME, and the rest of the overview presents the major research findings that resulted from the analysis of SIME/DIME data.

SOCIAL EXPERIMENTATION

A social experiment is a field test of one or more social programs—or, to use the phraseology of the natural sciences, a test of one or more "treatments." A social experiment is a field test in the sense that families or individuals are actually enrolled in a pilot social program offering some type of special benefit or service. It is "experimental" in the sense that families or individuals are enrolled in each of the tested programs on the basis of a random assignment process, for example, the flip of a coin. To draw conclusions about the effects of the treatments, it is necessary to collect information about the people who are enrolled in each experimental program and about those who receive no special treatment (called the control group), and then to compare them on the basis of the collected information. If the composition of each of the groups is determined by a random process and the groups are composed of similar families or individuals, any differences in measured behavior between the groups can be attributed to the effects of the programs being tested.

It is the random assignment procedure that gives social experimentation its advantage as a policy research tool. Most nonexperimental data sources are simply observations of behavior or situations resulting from a myriad of unspecified and indeterminate influences. With such nonexperimental data, one can observe factors that appear to change simultaneously or sequentially. However, at best, only tentative conclusions can be drawn about causality. Since experimentation can deliberately inject a new element into an environment, keeping everything else the same, subsequent changes can be attributed to the influence of the new element within known statistical confidence intervals.

This cause-effect characteristic does not, of course, guarantee that social experiments will produce definitive findings; the treatment may turn out to have no effect or to have an effect that is not precisely measurable. And even if there are definitive findings, there is no guarantee that these findings will be those that were expected by the designers of the experiment or will be useful for policy purposes. The scientific success of the experiment depends on several important factors:

- how precisely the propositions to be tested can be formulated;
- how well the experiment is designed to test those propositions;
- how large the experimental and control groups are and how long is the period over which they experience the treatment;
- how much difference the treatment makes to the environment faced by the experimental group compared to the otherwise identical environment faced by the control group—in other words, how strong the treatment is;
- the extent to which unforeseen or uncontrollable situations and events distort the observed experimental-control comparison.

It is worth expanding briefly on each of these factors.

The Propositions to Be Tested. In order to test whether something is the cause of something else, it is important not only to define the treatment and the hypothesized effect clearly and unambiguously, but also to be able to spell out the logic of the mechanism connecting the treatment to the hypothesized effect. If the issue of policy interest cannot be given prior shape in this manner, the unique analytic strength of the experimental approach is not worth its expense.

The primary focus of SIME/DIME—the effect of income maintenance on work effort or labor supply—was a good subject for experimentation from this point of view. Economists had developed a rigorous and widely accepted theory of how changes in effective wage rates and unearned incomes caused changes in individual labor supply, i.e., the number of hours people worked. The direction of the expected experimental effect was clear and so was the expected cause-effect

mechanism. An increase in unearned income or a decrease in the effective wage rate were hypothesized to lead to decreases in labor supply. By the late 1960s, analyses of nonexperimental survey data had yielded numerical estimates of the magnitude of such decreases. However, the wide range of available estimates suggested that social experimentation was an appropriate research strategy to improve the accuracy of the numerical estimates.

The Design of the Experiment. Given a well-defined treatment, an expected effect, and an expected cause-effect mechanism, the next step is to design an experiment that will clarify the cause-effect relationship. Developing such a design is complex. The basic aim, however, is straightforward: to introduce deliberate and systematic variations in the strength of the treatment and in the characteristics of those people exposed to it, so that the resulting pattern of behavioral responses permits identification of how the effects vary both as the treatment changes *and* as the characteristics of those exposed to the treatment change. If the number of treatment variations is numerous in comparison to the number of enrolled families or individuals, the experiment may fail to detect the impact of each of the tested variations with adequate precision. In this case the experiment will have failed in its basic purpose.

For this reason, experiments cannot be designed to test everything. While large-scale social experiments can and do collect a great deal of information on many issues, the most precise data collected will relate to the central issues motivating the experimental design. In the case of SIME/DIME, the experiment was in fact designed to test the effect of two different kinds of social programs on participant work effort. As has been noted, the two policies were a variety of cash transfer or negative income tax programs and several combinations of job counseling and education or training subsidy programs. Many other topics were examined in SIME/DIME—in particular, the relationship between cash transfers and marital stability—but it should be kept in mind that the statistical advantages of the experimentally generated data are somewhat greater for the labor supply analysis.

Size of Sample and Strength of Treatment.

Other things equal, the larger the sample size, the greater the ability of an experiment to detect treatment effects and the greater the statistical confidence that can be placed in the findings. Having a larger sample size than all the other income maintenance experiments combined, SIME/DIME produced the results to which one could attach the greatest degree of confidence.

The "strength" of the cash transfer treatment was greater in SIME/DIME than in the other experiments, both in terms of the generosity of the benefit levels and in terms of the length of the treatment period. The more generous the benefit levels, the greater the expected effects on behavior. Given this expectation, the more generous the benefit level, the smaller is the treatment group size required to detect the effect of the treatment at any given level of statistical confidence. In addition, to the extent that it takes time for families to learn what the treatment means and to make adjustments in behavior, longer treatment periods will also increase the likelihood of detectable response.

With respect to treatment generosity, however, a caveat is in order. Although a stronger treatment is more likely to advance scientific understanding of labor supply behavior, it will not yield better estimates of the probable labor supply response to a national cash transfer program if the benfits proposed in that program differ substantially from those in the experiment. Care must be exercised, therefore, in drawing policy implications from the experimental results.

The Treatment-Control Comparison.

We have been discussing random assignment of treatments to subjects in an experimental study. One "treatment" that is frequently tested is no treatment at all, in other words the "control" treatment. Families or individuals enrolled in the control group are not eligible for any special benefit or service, but provide the same information to the experimenters as that provided by the enrollees in the experimental treatments. The control families, of course, do not exist in a vacuum. They are eligible for and participate in ongoing programs similar to the experimental treatments. It is possible to imagine a situation in which, midway through an experiment, a regular government program is implemented that is exactly like the experimental treatment. In such a case, all the difference in behavior between the experimental and control groups might disappear. This is not to say that the treatment has lost its effect—merely that the difference in environments experienced by experimental and control families has disappeared. In the case of SIME/DIME, for example, the members of the control group were potentially eligible for the AFDC and AFDC-UF programs and Food Stamps as well as for a variety of job training programs. Any observed effects of the experiment, therefore, must be interpreted as the differential effects of the experimental treatment compared to existing government programs. Thus, any observed experimental-control differences in outcomes must be interpreted as estimates of the effect of replacing the early 1970s status quo with the experimental programs.

In addition to such external influences, certain occurrences within the experimental environment may pose problems for the interpretation of the results. Two that are inevitable in any experiment are sample attrition and mismeasurement of behavior. Attrition occurs when members of the experimental and control groups drop out of the sample and stop providing information to the experimenters.

Mismeasurement occurs when information used to measure the effect of the treatments turns out to be inaccurate. Since most of the information used to evaluate SIME/DIME was supplied in personal interviews, the predominant form of mismeasurement here consisted of misreporting of income or hours worked and earnings information.

If we could guarantee that the incidence of attrition and misreporting are random and thus identical for the experimental as well as the control group, the observed experimental responses would provide undistorted estimates of treatment effects. But the incentives to drop out of the experiment and to report income incorrectly may differ for the two groups. With respect to the misreporting bias, experimentals might be expected to underreport in comparison with controls, because the less income they report the larger will be their benefit. Of course, controls receiving AFDC face a similar incentive vis-à-vis the welfare office, but less so with respect to the SIME/DIME interviewers. Controls' incentive to underreport earnings to the welfare office, however, may be relatively lower than experimentals', since AFDC benefit levels were lower than SIME/DIME benefit levels. If controls report to the interviewers a higher fraction of their earnings than do experimentals, then the effect of misreporting bias is to overestimate the actual work reduction effect. Of course, if experimentals report a higher fraction of their earnings than controls, the actual work reduction effect is underestimated. With respect to attrition, people in the control group and in low-benefit treatment might be expected to drop out with greater frequency than those on the high-benefit plans—because they have less to lose by leaving the experiment. But those on the high-benefit plans can be expected to have a larger behavioral response to the experiment. Therefore, attrition may cause the observed experimental-control difference to overestimate the actual effect, unless the difference in attrition rates

can be explained by measurable family characteristics and these characteristics are controlled for in the analysis.

Additional difficulties in interpreting results may arise in an experiment like SIME/DIME, where different types of treatments were tested in combination. While SIME/DIME was designed so that the independent effects of the two different types of treatment (cash transfers and job counseling/training subsidies) could be separately measured, the separation of effects introduces additional statistical complexity, and thus, potential controversy into the analysis of the experimental data.

Finally, there are inherent limitations in social experiments regardless of design quality. Because experiments have finite durations, they may not completely represent the conditions of a fully implemented, permanent national program. Participants may alter their behavior in response not only to the program options being tested, but to the experiment itself, a phenomenon known as the "Hawthorne effect". Furthermore, participants, knowing the experimental conditions are only temporary, may not respond in the same way they would to a permanent program. For example, given the opportunity to participate in an income maintenance experiment, individuals may use it to increase their schooling, also a temporary activity.

THE DESIGN AND IMPLEMENTATION OF SIME/DIME

SIME/DIME was launched in Seattle, Washington, in 1970 and extended in 1972 to a second site in Denver, Colorado. The prime contractors for SIME/DIME were the States of Washington and Colorado, which subcontracted with SRI International for the design, operation, and research evaluation of the experiment. SRI International, in turn, subcontracted with Mathematica Policy Research

(MPR) for the administration of the cash transfer or negative income tax (NIT) treatment and all the field data collection from both experimental and control groups. For the administration of the job counseling/training subsidy treatment, SRI subcontracted with the Seattle Central Community College and the Community College of Denver.

The experiment involved almost 5,000 families. In order to test whether, and if so to what extent, behavioral responses varied by duration of treatment, the families in the experimental groups were also randomly assigned to a three-year or five-year treatment duration. The four basic treatment combinations were (a) NIT only, (b) counseling/training only, (c) NIT and counseling/training, (d) no treatment. The NIT and counseling treatments are described briefly below.

Cash Transfer (NIT) Treatments. The cash transfer treatment tested in SIME/DIME, as in the previous income maintenance experiments, consisted of a series of negative income tax plans. A negative income tax is simply a cash transfer program in which there is (a) a maximum benefit (called the guarantee) for which a family is eligible if it has no other income and (b) a rate (called the benefit reduction or tax rate) at which the maximum benefit is reduced as other income rises. The combination of a guarantee and a tax rate defines an income level (called the breakeven level) at which the benefit falls to zero. Families whose incomes rise above this breakeven

level no longer receive benefits, although they retain program eligiblity and regain benefit entitlement should their income fall below the breakeven level at some future date.

In all the experiments, more than one version of the negative income tax treatment was tested. This was to provide information on how behavioral responses might differ as program structure varied—making the results useful for predicting response to a wide range of cash transfer plans. Table 1 shows the plans tested: three guarantee levels and four tax rates, combined in such a way as to produce 11 negative income tax plans in all. The three guarantee levels for a family of four in 1971 dollars were $3,800, $4,800, and $5,600.[1] The dollar guarantee levels varied with family size (as does the poverty line) with larger families qualifying for higher guarantee levels under a given NIT plan. In the three earlier income maintenance experiments, only constant tax rates were tested (that is, tax rates that remained the same for every level of family income below the breakeven). SIME/DIME tested two constant tax rates: 50 percent and 70 percent. In addition to constant tax rates, however, SIME/DIME also tested two declining tax rate schedules. These rates were 80 percent and 70 percent, respectively, for the first $1,000 of nonexperimental income and then declined by 5 percentage points for each additional $1,000 of nonexperimental income.[2]

A major point to keep in mind about the cash transfer plans tested is that they consti-

TABLE I   Negative Income Tax Plans Tested in SIME/DIME

Initial guarantee[a]	Tax rate			
	50 percent	70 percent	70 percent (declining)	80 percent (declining)
$3,800	X	X	X	X
$4,800	X	X	X	X
$5,600	X	X		X

[a] 1971 dollars.

tuted a rather generous benefit range compared with transfer programs now in place or contemplated in most policy proposals. The SIME/DIME treatments averaged out to a negative income tax plan with a maximum benefit for those with no other income of about 115 percent of the poverty line and an effective marginal tax rate of about 50 percent. (The effective marginal tax rate was this low because families assigned to the declining tax plans typically face rather low marginal rates). With respect to breakeven level (that is, the income level below which experimental families receive positive benefits), 88 percent of the two-parent families had breakeven levels above 150 percent of the poverty line, and 58 percent were above twice the poverty line. For female-headed families the proportions were 83 percent and 43 percent respectively.[3]

The relative generosity of the average benefit received by experimental families as compared with the average received by the control group can be seen in Table 2, which shows the average amount of experimental and other transfers received over the course of the experiment, expressed in 1971 dollars.[4] It should be noted that, over the life of the experiment, there was a rising income trend among the sample families independent of the experiment, leading to a decline for

TABLE 2 Average Transfers Received by SIME/DIME Families

	Experimental groups		Control groups	
	Sample size[a]	Average transfer	Sample size	Average transfer
Husbands:				
Year:				
1	1,393 (440)	$1,361	1,071	$263
2	1,294 (415)	1,296	990	220
3	1,183 (392)	1,276	851	210
4	(374)	1,233	804	195
5	(340)	990	562	165
Wives:				
Year:				
1	1,408 (445)	1,455	1,089	295
2	1,343 (427)	1,524	1,026	327
3	1,253 (416)	1,564	895	383
4	(406)	1,618	849	397
5	(372)	1,323	600	348
Single female heads:				
Year:				
1	1,102 (304)	2,105	699	1,171
2	1,066 (294)	2,185	649	1,089
3	997 (286)	2,032	562	1,014
4	(278)	1,908	525	932
5	(260)	1,776	381	748

[a] The sample sizes for the 5-year sample are in parentheses.

NOTE

For experimental families the transfer total includes SIME/DIME payments plus AFDC, AFDC-UF, and bonus value of food stamps as reported in interviews. For control families the transfer total includes AFDC, AFDC-UF, and the Food Stamp bonus value as reported in interviews. The husband and wife sample size differ because of family splits.

Source: *Final Report*, Volume 1, Part III, Chapter 4, Tables 3.1 and 3.2.

both groups in the percentage of families with incomes low enough to receive transfer benefits of any kind.

Counseling/Training Subsidy Treatments

There were three variants of the counseling/ training subsidy treatments: counseling only, counseling combined with a 50 percent subsidy for approved education[5] or training courses, and counseling combined with a 100 percent subsidy for approved education or training. Within a family enrolled in the counseling/training subsidy programs, every family member aged 16 and older was eligible for the experimental counseling and training subsidies. The counseling component of the treatment can be characterized as voluntary, informational, and nondirective. Included in the training of the SIME/DIME counselors, all of whom had extensive previous counseling experience, was a special three-day workshop in nondirective counseling at the start of the experiment. Within this nondirective framework, the counseling had three main features: self-assessment, labor market assessment, and job search assistance.

Self-assessment consisted not only of getting sample members to evaluate their own employment records and work skills, if any, but also of encouraging them to explore their long-range hopes and unfulfilled expectations without regard to the feasibility of these goals. Feasibility was discussed at a later stage. Labor market assessment consisted of providing counselors with detailed reports on occupations of interest to clients including specific tasks involved, credentials and experience required, usual hiring channels, and career potential of the occupation. Although job openings were indicated in cases where that information happened to be available, such information was not usually provided to counselors. The job search assistance component did not involve direct job placement or referrals but, rather, general help in preparing resumes and in practicing job interview skills.

The culmination of the counseling process was the formulation of a "plan of action". Although the counselor did at this stage examine with the participants the obstacles in the way of successfully completing the proposed plan, the participant selected the goal and the counselor helped the participant assess the assets and liabilities of the participant's choice.

The training subsidy component of the treatment was also flexible and geared to providing maximum freedom of choice with respect to the type of education or training subsidized. Two subsidy plans were tested. In one, individuals who chose to receive job-related training were reimbursed for 50 percent of the direct costs of training (tuition, fees, materials, transportation, and child care expenses); in the other, clients were reimbursed for 100 percent of training costs. In both subsidy plans, the amount of training subsidized was limited to the cost of the least expensive local institution providing the desired training. Within that constraint, individuals were free to use the subsidy at the institution of their choice. The requirement that training be "job related" was liberally interpreted so that individuals could receive subsidized training that was required for ambitious career goals (like professional and managerial positions). There was no fixed limit on the amount of training that would be subsidized, either with respect to cost or duration, except that subsidies were limited to the three- or five-year period of experimental eligibility.

Administration of the Treatments.

The cash transfer treatment, as has been noted, was defined by a guarantee and a tax rate. The amount of payment actually received by a family was calculated according to information regarding nonexperimental income, assets, and expenses contained in a monthly Income Report Form submitted by the family to the SIME/DIME payments office. This information was used to calculate the benefit to be paid by check to the family in the subsequent month.

Such a reporting and payment system differed from what was then common state welfare policy, where benefits were calculated for a future period based on projected income and the expected expenses for that future period.[6] Another important difference between the payment calculations used in the income maintenance experiments and those still prevailing under state welfare policy is that, in the former, the underlying basis for experimental benefits was the income received over the previous year. This ensured that families with the same annual income received the same total benefit over the course of a year. For those families whose income remained below their breakeven level throughout the year (most of the sample), this constraint made no difference to the amounts received each month. For those whose incomes fluctuated around their breakeven levels—so that in some months they were above it and in some months below it—receipt of benefits in any month depended not only on whether the family income was below the breakeven level for the most recent month, but also on the family's nonexperimental income over the previous twelve-month period. A third important difference in SIME/DIME was the monthly Income Report Form. The conventional welfare system had no regular reporting form for clients.

Families were enrolled into the experiment in a face-to-face interview at which they were told about the guarantee level and tax rate of the negative income tax plan to which they had been assigned, how the benefit payments were calculated, and how long the experiment would last for them. The filing and record-keeping responsibilities of the sample families, the specifics about what counted as income and what were deductible expenses, the details of the payment calculation formula, and the conditions under which the experiment could withhold benefit checks were

all spelled out in considerable detail in a set of rules and regulations given each family. Penalties for misrepresentation were also specified, and appropriate audit and appeal procedures were set up. Although, as in any program, some cases of misreporting did occur, the incidence of deliberate fraud seems to have been low and repayments were usually achieved through appropriate deductions from future payment streams.

Throughout their period of experimental eligibility, families in the treatment group who were also eligible for AFDC or AFDC-UF were allowed to choose which program they wished to receive benefits from in any given month. They were not, however, allowed to receive checks from both SIME/DIME and AFDC simultaneously. A major part of the auditing functions thus involved making sure that families were not benefiting from both SIME/DIME and AFDC in the same payment period.

The administration of the counseling/training subsidy treatment involved informing families of their eligibility for the counseling/training subsidy program at the time of the enrollment interview mentioned above. A counselor then contacted them and arranged individual or group sessions for those individuals who desired counseling.

Data Collection. The primary data for analysis of behavioral responses to the experiment came from a series of face-to-face interviews administered three times a year, for the duration of the treatment period and at least one year beyond. These took about forty minutes each, were administered in the families' homes by specially trained interviewers, and were identical for both experimental and control group families.

Detailed questions on every aspect of labor force participation, earnings, and job change for the period since the previous interview were included in each questionnaire. The database thus contained a continuous work history on each family member (age 16 and over) from two years prior to enrollment until at least one year after treatment ended. In addition to the regular labor force core questions, each questionnaire included modules covering other aspects of behavior. In all, 53 questionnaire modules were developed, covering additional economic information such as consumption and wealth as well as family functioning, education, and social and psychological attitudes.

In addition to the rich body of information from these periodic interviews, Social Security and Internal Revenue Service records were collected so that validation studies of the interview-reported earnings information could be conducted.

The Sample. The composition of the SIME/DIME sample was defined partly with reference to the likely population to be included in any national negative income tax program and partly to assure that important questions about the magnitude of the overall work effort response and about possible differential responses by different population groups could be satisfactorily answered.

The sample was restricted to families with heads between 18 and 58 years of age at enrollment in order to focus on those at least potentially in the prime-aged labor force. For this reason, families with disabled heads were excluded. In addition, eligibility was limited to families with total earnings of less than $9,000 a year if one head was employed, or earnings of $11,000 a year if both husband and wife were employed. These earnings cutoffs were a compromise between the need to include those who, although above their breakeven income level at enrollment, could be expected to fall below it during the period of the experiment, and the wish to exclude people whose incomes were so high that potential eligibility for cash transfers appeared highly unlikely. These earnings cutoffs do

raise the potential problem of sample selection bias in the results.

To be able to detect differences by family type, both one-parent families with a dependent child present and couples were included in the sample. For convenience, the latter type of family is frequently referred to as two-parent, although there was no requirement that such families contain a dependent child. Nor was there a requirement that the two family heads be legally married, although for convenience they are often referred to as husbands and wives. Three ethnic groups were included in the SIME/DIME sample—blacks, whites, and (in Denver only) Chicanos. All enrolled families were residents of selected low-income Census tracts in Seattle and Denver.

The experimental sample was designed using a sophisticated mathematical procedure to yield the maximum amount of useful information within a fixed budget. To achieve this purpose, enrolled families were divided into a large number of different types of "strata." For example, families were divided into seven different income levels, depending on their average incomes over a number of years prior to the start of the experiment. They were further subdivided according to race and the number of family heads present (one or two). In addition to including a large number of family types or strata, the experiment tested a variety of treatment combinations: twelve NIT treatments (the eleven NIT plans tested plus the control treatment) combined with four counseling/training subsidy treatments (three experimental plans plus the control treatment), in combination with two different periods of experimental eligibility (three and five years). In the interests of economy, the experiment did not test every possible combination of these treatments, but a large number were tested.

After determination of the treatment combinations to be tested and family types to be enrolled, the essence of the sample design problem is to determine the number of families of each family type to be assigned to each treatment combination. For a particular family type and treatment combination, this number is known as the "cell size". Obviously, the average experimental cost of families in a given cell will depend both on the characteristics of the family and the generosity of the treatment combination. Low-income families, for example, will receive higher NIT benefits under a given plan than high-income families. Families assigned to high-guarantee NIT plans or to 100 percent training subsidy plans will cost more to enroll than families in the control group or in low-guarantee and less generous training subsidy plans. It should also be mentioned that not every treatment combination tested was of equal interest or importance. For example, certain guarantee/tax-rate combinations were considered more feasible than others (basically, those in the middle range were considered the more policy-relevant), and consequently the designers put greater emphasis on obtaining precise behavioral response estimates for these combinations.

Taking account of the cost differences of the various cells and their varying degrees of policy relevance as well as their relative contributions to statistically precise measurement of the response pattern, the mathematical procedure alluded to earlier was used to determine the cell sizes in SIME/DIME. A family of a given type which had been selected for the sample was then randomly assigned to a particular treatment combination on the basis of the cell sizes computed by this mathematical model. Since assignment to particular treatment combinations was completely random for all families of a given family type, the hoped-for result was that measured differences in the behavior of people subject to different treatment combinations measured the effect of the treatment differences.

In all, 4,800 families were enrolled in SIME/DIME including control families. The way the initial sample was distributed by family structure and race and by assignment to site, treatment, and treatment duration can be seen in Table 3. Note that the "pure" control group (that is, the group eligible for neither the cash transfer nor the counseling/training subsidy treatments) accounts for less than one quarter of the sample because the same comparison group can be used for all the treatment variants. The groups eligible for the cash transfer treatment only and the counseling/training subsidy treatment only were slightly smaller than the control group. The group eligible for both a cash transfer and a counseling/training subsidy treatment is about twice as large as either group receiving a single type of treatment.

Families were located through an inten-

TABLE 3 The Distribution of the SIME/DIME Sample at Enrollment

Site:	
Seattle	2,042
Denver	2,758
Family structure:	
2-parent families	2,769
1-parent families	2,031
Ethnic group:	
White	2,071
Black	1,862
Chicano	867
Treatment/control status:	
Negative income tax (NIT) only	946
Counseling/training subsidy only	1,012
NIT plus training/counseling	1,801
Control group	1,041
Treatment Duration:	
3 years	2,638
5 years	1,121
Control Group	1,041

Source: Murarka, B. A. and R. G. Spiegelman, "Sample Selection in the Seattle and Denver Income Maintenance Experiments," SRI International Technical Memorandum 1, July 1978, p. 53, as quoted in the *Final Report*, Volume 1, Part 1.

sive survey effort, which first identified the areas in Seattle and Denver that would be most fruitful in terms of the expected yield of eligible families and then canvassed those areas on an individual dwelling-unit basis.

During the period of the experiment, in spite of strenuous efforts to keep track of sample families and persuade them to continue in the experiment, some families dropped out. Over the first thirty months of the experiment, 20 percent of the originally enrolled husbands, 15 percent of originally enrolled wives, and 15 percent of single heads of families dropped out. The husband-wife differences are due to differential drop-out rates in the cases of couples that split up.

SIME/DIME RESULTS

Introduction

The major SIME/DIME results are presented under three headings. First, the effects of the experiment on work effort or labor supply are presented. The primary focus is the effect of eligibility for a negative income tax plan, but the analysis sample used to obtain these findings includes all families enrolled in the experiment, including those families enrolled only in the counseling/training subsidy treatments. Second, the effects on hours worked and earnings of the counseling/training subsidy treatments are discussed specifically. Third, the effects of the experiment treatments on "marital stability" are described. Recall that marital stability is not used in the literal sense here since couples were not required to be legally married. For the marital stability research, the analysis sample included those who were eligible for the negative income tax and counseling/training subsidy treatments alone plus those who were eligible for both, as well as those eligible for neither—the control group. Many other types of behavioral response to the experimental treatments have

also been analyzed and are discussed in the *Final Report*. . . .

In all cases, unless otherwise noted, the results presented in this overview are experimental-control differences, adjusted by statistical methods to control for the variation in sample characteristics across treatment combinations.

Cash Transfer Effects on Labor Supply

The labor supply results for husbands, wives, female family heads, and youth will be summarized in turn. For each group, the overall response to the SIME/DIME negative income tax plans taken together is described first. A discussion of differences in response among the different NIT plans follows.

As mentioned above, the samples used for the labor supply analysis include families that were eligible for the counseling/training subsidy treatment. There is no statistically significant evidence that the counseling/training subsidy treatment altered the effect of the negative income tax treatment on labor supply behavior. Consequently, the labor supply analysis can statistically separate the effect of the two treatments, and the results described in this section can be interpreted as the effect of just the negative income tax plans on work effort.

The NIT treatment was administered for two different lengths of time (three and five years) to get some information both on how long the family members took to adjust their behavior to the change and on whether a long-term program might have a different effect from a short-term one. Obviously the experiment could not go on indefinitely. The hope was, however, that any differences between the responses of the three- and five-year sample would help predict long-term program effects. In addition, interview information was collected for at least one post-experimental year in order to measure any effects of the cessation of benefits.

Husbands. The results for husbands show that the combination of negative income tax plans tested in SIME/DIME—which, as already mentioned, represents on average a relatively generous cash transfer program with a guarantee of 115 percent of the poverty line and a tax rate of 50 percent—has a significant negative effect on hours worked per year. Table 4A shows the findings by experimental year and duration of treatment. The best measure of the overall labor supply effect for the combined three- and five-year samples is probably the disincentive effect as measured in the second year—after all the experimentals have had time to adjust to the treatment but before the three-year families start preparing for the treatment to end. This percentage reduction in hours of labor supplied for the three- and five-year families combined, as measured in the second experimental year, is about 9 percent. For the three-year sample, the maximum labor supply response is a 7.3 percent decline, occurring in both the second and third years. For the five-year sample, the maximum response is a 13.6 percent decline, occurring in the fourth year of the five-year treatment period. These maximum percentage responses represent in absolute terms a decline of about 133 and 234 hours of work per year, respectively.

The larger response for husbands enrolled in the five-year group suggests that the response to a long-term national program of comparable generosity might be higher than the response measured for the three-year sample, or even for the combined three- and five-year sample. It should be noted, however, that no general statement about the effect of treatment duration on response can be made, since this effect depends critically on the generosity (i.e., the guarantee/tax rate combination) of the NIT.

By the end of the first post-treatment year, labor supply for NIT-eligible husbands had again returned essentially to the same level as that for controls, indicating strongly

TABLE 4 Labor Supply Response of Husbands

A. *Overall NIT response* (percentage difference in annual hours worked)

	Year				
	1	2	3	4	5
3-year sample	−1.6	−7.3	−7.3	−0.5	−0.2
5-year sample	−5.9	−12.2	−13.2	−13.6	−12.3
Total sample	−3.1	−9.0	−9.3		

B. *Second year response by NIT plan* (percentage difference in annual hours worked)

Guarantee	Tax rate			
	50 percent	70 percent	70 percent (declining)	80 percent (declining)
$3,800	−6.7	−5.6	−10.0	−8.9
$4,000	−8.8	−1.5	−14.5	−9.9
$5,600	−11.8	−10.4		−8.7

Source: Derived according to the formula in the *Final Report.* Volume I, Part III, Chapter 5, footnote 3 and data in Tables 3.4 and 3.9.

both that the observed response was indeed a result of the treatment and that husbands can adjust their labor supply fairly rapidly to changed incentives. Average work reductions were observed to be larger among black and Chicano men than among white men. However, these results were not statistically significant. Similarly, work reductions were observed to be larger in Denver (which had a tight labor market during the experiment) than in Seattle (which had high unemployment during most of the experiment). Again, these results failed to be statistically significant.

When the results for all 11 negative income tax plans are estimated separately, as shown in Table 4B, we begin to see how the pattern of response changes with changes in the negative income tax plan. As the guarantee becomes more generous, the labor supply response becomes generally more negative. Response does not, however, change in any clear pattern as the tax rate changes. This result may at first appear surprising. However, recall that plans with higher tax rates—and greater associated work disincentives for NIT recipients—also have lower breakeven levels. Consequently, higher tax plans will have fewer recipients, and a smaller fraction of the population will be affected by their work disincentives.

When the plans are grouped according to relative overall generosity as measured by the breakeven level (not shown), the magnitude of the labor supply reductions for husbands increases as the generosity of the plan increases. Findings by plan again indicate greater responses for the five-year sample than the three-year sample. In addition, although the response is uniformly greater for the five-year sample than the three-year sample, the difference between the two is less for the lower than for the higher generosity plans.

What form did the decrease in annual hours worked take? Was it mainly that people worked with the same regularity but for fewer hours each week, or was it that they spent more time not working at all—that is, unemployed or out of the labor force? Experimental husbands did work significantly fewer weeks than control husbands: annual weeks worked were 2.8 weeks less during the second year. Most of this reduction came about through a significant increase in unemployment.[7] Weeks unemployed for experimental husbands were on average 2.2 more than for controls. One interpretation of this result might be that the cash transfer program enabled husbands to take more time to find a better job. However, other findings from the experiment show that husbands in the experimental group did not find measurably better jobs than their control counterparts, at least as judged by the wage rate. Disregarding the distinction between unemployment and out of the labor force, a safer conclusion is that NIT eligibility induced men who were out of work to spend more time between jobs than men in the control sample. For a few men, the time spent out of employment was increased quite considerably. For example, during the second experimental year the proportion of men in the NIT-eligible group who worked at least one week during the year dropped by 7 percent in comparison to that observed in the control group. For those experimentals who did work, there was a significant reduction in the proportion who worked full time, but no significant impact on the proportion working overtime or only part time.

A question remains as to whether the missing observations of those who dropped out during the experiment and/or possible misreporting bias cause the estimates presented above to be distorted in any measurable way. This is, by its very nature, a difficult question to answer. Examination of other earnings records (particularly from Social Security, but also, on a more fragmentary basis, from the Washington and Colorado Departments of Employment Security) on both experimental and control families suggests that for husbands any attrition and misreporting bias is probably small.

Wives. The labor supply response of wives to the SIME/DIME negative income tax treatment was significantly negative and larger in percentage terms than the response for husbands, at least when that response is measured with SIME/DIME interview data. As shown in Table 5A, the average work reduction for the three- and five-year samples taken together, as measured in the second experimental year, is about 20 percent. For the three-year sample the maximum effect was a decrease in annual hours of 16.5 percent in hours worked, occurring in the second year. For the five-year sample, the maximum effect was a decrease in annual hours of approximately 27.1 percent, occurring in the fourth year. In absolute terms these decreases—just over 100 hours a year and just over 200 hours per year, respectively—are smaller than for husbands. The larger percentage decreases should be interpreted in the context

of the smaller average hourly commitment of these women to market work than the average hourly commitment of their husbands. Wives readjusted at the end of the experiment as quickly as husbands, with the wives in the three-year sample even showing a tendency to work more than comparable control families during the second post-experiment year.

When response is estimated separately for the eleven plans tested (see Table 5B), the response for wives, as for husbands, generally increased in magnitude as the guarantee became more generous and, again as for husbands, showed a somewhat inconsistent pattern with respect to the tax rate. When plans are arrayed by generosity of the breakeven level, wives show the expected pattern of generally increasing response magnitude as generosity increases. The five-year responses are uniformly although not significantly larger than the three-year responses for wives. The treatment duration differences that do exist are again smaller for less generous NIT plans than for plans with higher breakeven levels.

TABLE 5 Labor Supply Response of Wives

A. *Overall NIT response* (percentage difference in annual hours worked)

	Year				
	1	2	3	4	5
3-year sample	−4.0	−16.5	−15.2	−2.0	+13.4
5-year sample	−15.1	−26.5	−21.6	−27.1	−24.0
Total sample	−8.1	−20.1	−17.4		

B. *Second year response by NIT plan* (percentage difference in annual hours worked)

Guarantee	Tax rate			
	50 percent	70 percent	70 percent (declining)	80 percent (declining)
$3,800	−24.7	−13.2	−1.6	−19.7
$4,800	−29.3	−23.2	−20.7	−18.7
$5,600	−28.1	−40.1		−12.6

Source: Derived according to the formula in the *Final Report*, Volume I, Part III, Chapter 5, footnote 3 and data in Tables 3.5 and 3.9.

There are some interesting differences between the behavior of wives and husbands with respect to the form the decrease in work actually took. Weeks worked per year were about 3.8 less for experimental wives than for control wives in the second experimental year. Virtually all of this difference took the form of an increase in weeks out of the labor force (rather than weeks unemployed as was the case with husbands).[8] The probability of working at least one week during the year was also significantly less for experimental wives during the second experimental year. With respect to changes in the amount worked by those who did work, there was a significant reduction in the probability of both full-time and part-time work.

Analysts have investigated the importance of possible misreporting and attrition biases on the experimental results for wives. Employment and earnings checks with the same records used to validate the results for husbands suggest that both the attrition bias and the misreporting bias for wives may be substantial—with both working in the direction of exaggerating observed experimental-control differences. Once again, incomplete data make it impossible to come up with precise estimates of the magnitude of the biases, though examination of the Social Security and unemployment insurance records suggests that as much as half of the measured response may be attributable to differential attrition bias and that a large fraction of the remaining response may represent misreporting bias. The reader should therefore be cautioned that the observed labor supply response for wives might overstate the work reduction that actually occurred.

Female Family Heads. As with the previous two groups, female family heads responded to the SIME/DIME negative income tax treatment by reducing work effort significantly. The overall response of the three-year and five-year samples taken together, as measured in the second treatment year, was 14 percent. Their maximum response was larger in absolute and percentage terms than that of either husbands or wives. For the three-year sample (see Table 6A) the maximum reduction was about 22 percent, occurring in the final treatment year; for the five-year sample the maximum response was about 32 percent, also occurring in the final treatment year. These correspond to absolute reductions of about 220 and 405 hours per year, respectively. These maximum responses, it should be noted, are about double the average response.

Unlike husbands and wives, female heads do not seem to have responded differently to the three- and five-year treatments, since the responses for the two samples measured over the same period of time are not significantly different. However, their adaptation both to the experiment and to its end appears to have been slower, suggesting that female heads adjust more slowly to changes in financial incentives than do husbands or wives. This suggests that the response observable in any brief-duration experiment, such as three or five years duration, will understate the work reduction of female family heads relative to a permanent program.

When the responses are calculated separately for the eleven plans tested (see Table 6B) no obvious pattern of variation between the labor supply response and either guarantee or tax rate is found.

How did the average reduction in annual hours worked manifest itself in patterns of employment for female family heads? First, as with the other two groups, there was a significant reduction in weeks worked. For female heads this reduction was higher than for husbands but lower than for wives. As with wives, but not husbands, this was accounted for by dropping out of the labor force rather than by being unemployed. The probability of working at all during the year also decreased significantly for female heads—again, the

TABLE 6   Labor Supply Response of Female Heads

A. *Overall NIT response* (percentage difference in annual hours worked)

	Year				
	1	2	3	4	5
3-year sample	−5.5	−14.1	−21.6	−8.9	−7.7
5-year sample	−7.9	−15.0	−21.2	−28.3	−31.8
Total sample	−6.3	−14.3	−21.4		

B. *Second year response by NIT plan* (percentage difference in annual hours worked)

Guarantee	Tax rate			
	50 percent	70 percent	70 percent (declining)	80 percent (declining)
$3,800	−7.0	−19.4	−2.5	−16.0
$4,800	−21.7	−11.7	−20.9	−10.5
$5,600	−6.9	−23.7	—	−25.1

Source: Derived according to the formula in the *Final Report*, Volume I, Part III, Chapter 5, footnote 3 and data in Tables 3.6 and 3.9.

magnitude of the labor force participation decline is between those for husbands and for wives. With respect to changes in full-time, part-time, or overtime work by those who worked, female heads reacted more like the husbands than the wives. The only significant change for those that worked was a decrease in full-time work.

With respect to the question of possible misreporting and attrition bias in the observed responses, comparison with other data records suggests that there was no misreporting bias. There is, however, evidence of moderate attrition bias that goes in the other direction from that observed for wives. When interpreting the results for female heads, therefore, it should be kept in mind that the observed responses might underestimate slightly the actual reduction.

Youth. Based on their own interview-reported hours and earnings, both male and female youth (at least age 16 but under age 21) appeared to respond to the negative income tax plans tested in SIME/DIME by reducing their labor supply significantly. For the three- and five-year samples for males taken together, the observed reduction was substantial; reported hours worked per week decreased on average by about 24 percent and the proportion of the year during which they reported working decreased by about 17 percent. Although the proportional reductions in work effort are large for both young men and women, the absolute reductions are quite small, since average work effort among teenagers is low.

When the labor supply response of youth is estimated for the three- and five-year samples separately, the differences between the two are not generally significant. However, the fact that the observed effects for the five-year sample are larger (and, in the case of young men, sometimes much larger) than for the three-year sample suggests that the work effect of a permanent program might be larger than the observed response in this limited-duration experiment. Differentiating response by plan yields the same lack of tax rate effect as appeared for the other groups; and for youth there is no systematic guarantee effect either.

Labor supply response does vary in an important respect according to whether the youth remained dependents or set up separate households. For males who continued to live at home and for males who left their original family to form new, two-parent families (both eligible for continued payments), the observed work disincentive is substantial. By the second half of the third experimental year, hours worked by the new husbands had declined by about 33 percent (mainly accounted for by increased unemployment), and the hours worked by those continuing to live at home had declined by about 43 percent (about equally accounted for by increased unemployment and increased time out of the labor force). But for young men who left their parental family to live as single individuals, there is no significant work disincentive effect. For females there is a significant work disincentive (about a 42 percent decrease in hours worked) only for those who continue to live with their parental family. For none of the youth groups was the decrease in hours worked accompanied by an increase in time spent in school. The observed work reductions tend to be largest for those who are not in school, but labor supply declines are not restricted to youths in that group.

Generalizing to the National Population. As emphasized earlier in this overview, the observed labor supply responses presented so far are effects that are specific to the population enrolled in SIME/DIME and relate only to NIT programs actually tested in that experiment. In order to predict from the observed SIME/DIME responses the effects of national programs of differing generosity, the SIME/DIME analysts developed a more general form of the work disincentive response.

The most noteworthy pattern they found

is that, although the decrease in hours worked by participants gets larger the higher the tax rate (holding the guarantee constant), the work disincentive for the U.S. population as a whole gets smaller. This is because a higher tax rate implies a lower breakeven income level and a smaller number of participants. The positive labor supply response among those losing eligibility is big enough to offset the larger negative response among the program participants.

Counseling/Training Subsidy Effects

A unique feature of SIME/DIME among the four NIT experiments was the testing of a labor market counseling and training subsidy program in addition to a negative income tax transfer program. The rationale for including these programs was to determine whether increased labor market information and increased education and training could offset the decline in work effort that was predicted to occur due to the negative income tax program. As described at the beginning of this overview, the SIME/DIME counseling treatment was informational and nondirective in nature, and types of training deemed appropriate for subsidization were very flexibly defined. The expectation was that the counseling would lead, at least eventually, to better labor market match of skills to jobs and thus higher wage rates, earnings and, possibly, job status. The training subsidy was expected to lead to the same general outcomes, possibly after a brief period of decreased labor market activity in the short run as the extra training was acquired.

Participation.   There was substantial participation in the counseling and subsidized training programs, particularly among single women. Many of those who participated in the counseling program demonstrated interest in obtaining additional training, including even some who were not eligible for a training subsidy. There was marked diversity in the goals of those who planned to seek training. A majority chose relatively modest occupational and training objectives, but a substantial minority chose quite ambitious objectives that presumably held lower prospects for successful attainment.

Table 7 shows the proportions of the SIME/DIME sample that participated in the counseling and training subsidy programs. Participation rates for counseling rose consistently as the amount of subsidy offered increased. Husbands and wives participated at similar rates (nearly 40 percent for the counseling-only group, just over 50 percent for the 50 percent subsidy group and about 60 percent for the 100 percent subsidy group). Female heads participated in counseling at uniformly higher rates (54 percent for the counseling-only group, 64 percent for the 50 percent subsidy group, and 72 percent for the 100 percent subsidy group). A similar pattern emerges for participation in the training subsidy programs, though the percentages

are lower. Just over 20 percent of husbands and wives chose to participate in the 50 percent subsidy option and 36 percent chose to participate in the 100 percent subsidy option. For female heads the figures are 35 percent and 47 percent, respectively.

For those who participated in counseling, the average number of sessions also increased as the amount of subsidy offered increased—from the 4.8-to-5.8 range for the counseling-only group to the 6.5-to-7.7 range for the 100 percent subsidy group. The average amount of the subsidy for those who chose to participate ranged from a low of $363 for husbands on the 50 percent subsidy plan to a high of $954 for wives on the 100 percent subsidy plan. The average number of academic quarters subsidized ranged between 3.6 and 4.1.

With respect to the amount of schooling received, counseling-only did not make a difference. The subsidies did tend, however, to increase the amount of schooling received—mildly for husbands, more strongly for wives,

TABLE 7   Rates of Participation in the Counseling Training Subsidy Treatments

	Counseling only			Counseling and 50 percent subsidy			Counseling and 100 percent subsidy		
	H	W	FH[a]	H	W	FH	H	W	FH
Number of eligibles	510	510	374	671	670	481	391	392	313
Percent attending at least 1 counseling session	39.8	38.2	54.0	51.4	52.8	64.4	60.6	56.6	71.9
Of those participating: Average number of sessions	4.8	4.9	5.8	6.6	6.4	7.3	6.5	7.4	7.7
Percent receiving some subsidy				21.0	21.3	34.9	36.3	36.5	46.6
Of those receiving subsidy: Average amount				$363	$401	$650	$666	$954	$857
Average number of academic quarters subsidized				4.0	3.6	4.1	3.8	3.9	4.1

[a] Demographic groups are husbands (H), wives (W), and female heads (FH).

Source: *Final Report,* Volume I, Part IV, Chapter 3, Table 4.1.

and most strongly for female heads. For the latter two groups the effects on schooling were generally stronger the more generous the subsidy.

Impact on Labor Market Performance.

The counseling/training subsidy treatment did not have the expected positive effects for most groups. The effects on average annual earnings and hours of work are shown in Table 8. Earnings declined during the experimental period and, quite unexpectedly, the negative results tended to continue into the post-program period as well, though these post-program reductions were not statistically significant. Not all results for all groups are statistically significant, but the negative pattern shows clearly throughout the estimates— in earnings, hours worked, and wage rates.

Table 8 shows the results for the three- and five-year samples for years 1, 4, and 6, to indicate both in-program and post-program effects. For husbands, the three-year counseling-only program had virtually no impact on earnings. In contrast, the five-year counseling program had a predominantly negative impact on earnings, even in the sixth year when experimentals were no longer eligible for counseling. In addition, eligibility for counseling resulted, for those husbands who were working, in consistently lower wage rates than those of their control counterparts. The training subsidy programs led to substantial and significant first year decreases in earnings and hours. The 50 percent subsidy, for example, led to a $248 decrease in annual earnings for the three-year sample and a $398 decrease for the five-year sample. The 100 percent subsidy, administered to only the three-year sample, led to a $317 decrease. In year 4 the decrease in earnings was smaller and not significant; in year 6 it had practically disappeared.

Wives show a similar pattern of response to the counseling-only program with even larger negative effects. Both the three-year

and five-year counseling programs resulted in lower earnings and hours of work for wives in every year, and these effects are generally significant for the five-year program. For example, in the first post-program year, wives eligible for the five-year counseling treatment earned $430 less than did comparable controls, a 19 percent reduction. Wives eligible for the training subsidy programs also had lower earnings and worked fewer hours than did controls. These effects tend to be significant in the early years but are also large and negative in the later years.

For single female heads, the counseling-only program probably did have positive results on earnings. Although not statistically significant, the effect on earnings is substantial: in the fifth year, female heads eligible for the counseling-only program earned between $275 and $300 more per year than did controls, approximately a 10 percent increase. Furthermore, the counseling-only program did have some significant post-program impacts on the wage rates and hours of work of female heads.

For the combined counseling/training subsidy program, in contrast, the effects were negative for female heads, as for the other groups. As for husbands and wives, female heads eligible for subsidies generally had lower earnings and worked fewer hours than did comparable controls even in the post-program period.

It would be instructive to be able to separate out the effects of the counseling from the effects of the training subsidies, to test the possibility that the counseling was the driving negative influence. While no definitive conclusion on this point can be drawn, because counseling was a prerequisite to the subsidy program, it is possible to infer the separate impact of subsidies when added to an existing counseling program. Here the results for female heads suggest strongly and those for husbands suggest weakly that the addition of a training subsidy program causes even larger

TABLE 8 Effect of Counseling and Training Subsidies on Annual Earnings and Hours of Work

| | Experimental year | | | | | |
| | 1 | | 4 | | 6 | |
	Earnings	Hours	Earnings	Hours	Earnings	Hours
Husbands						
Counseling only:						
3-year sample	+$6	−3.0	−$5	+24.1		
5-year sample	−31	−2.8	−185	−80.6	−$239	−115.6
Counseling and 50 percent subsidy:						
3-year sample	−248[b]	−71.7[b]	−101	+22.4		
5-year sample	−398[b]	−105.6[a]	−161	−73.7	−33	−18.7
Counseling and 100 percent subsidy:						
3-yr sample	−317[b]	−88.8[a]	−245	−37.9		
Wives						
Counseling only:						
3-year sample	+21	−8.6	−215	−61.8		
5-year sample	−187[c]	−77.1[c]	−534	−197.9[a]	−430[c]	−125.8
Counseling and 50 percent subsidy:						
3-year sample	+6	−14.9	−199	−63.9		
5-year sample	−255[a]	−107.8[a]	−124	−43.1	−301	−52.1
Counseling and 100 percent subsidy:						
3-year sample	−37	−10.0	−222[c]	−96.1[c]		
Female Heads						
Counseling only:						
3-year sample	+148	+36.1	+144	+13.2		
5-yr sample	+123	+31.8	+184	+81.1	+426	+183.4[c]
Counseling and 50 percent subsidy:						
3-year sample	−32	−4.6	−207	−98.1		
5-year sample	−114	−81.3	−89	−77.9	−37	−112.8
Counseling and 100 percent subsidy:						
3-year sample	−11	−20.7	−45	−35.7		

[a] Significant at the 1 percent level.

[b] Significant at the 5 percent level.

[c] Significant at the 10 percent level.

Source: *Final Report*, Volume 1, Part IV, Chapter 5, Table 4.5–4.7.

earnings and hours reductions than counseling by itself. For wives, the negative impact of counseling plus subsidies is approximately equal to the impact of counseling by itself.

Possible Reasons for the Effects.   How did programs intended to improve the employment and earnings experiences of eligibles actually lead to lower earnings? If the results had indicated no effects, one might be able to explain the results by hypothesizing that very little actually happened in the counseling and training programs. The finding of negative effects, however, cannot be so dismissed. Something did occur in counseling and in training that actually reduced the earnings prospects of participants.

Analysis of data gathered on the objectives of participants suggests that a substantial fraction of the subsidized training was oriented to achieving ambitious career goals. For an important fraction of participants, the goals were evidently overambitious, and the training did not translate into higher earnings even though it may have provided immediate satisfaction to the participants. Evidently, the SIME/DIME counseling/training subsidy program induced short-run reductions in earnings without supporting the type of training or education that would enable participants to secure better paying jobs, at least during the one to three year follow-up period. This "training ineffectiveness argument" would explain a zero treatment response, but it doesn't really offer an explanation of the observed negative response. Perhaps the counseling and training experiences of those with ambitious upward mobility goals actually made it more difficult to pursue a career consisting of a series of relatively low-paying jobs. In any case, a different type of counseling might have resulted in training and education decisions that were less ambitious, but this is entirely conjectural.

Effects on Marital Stability

Although, as mentioned earlier, the experiment was not explicitly designed to test effects on marital stability, much attention was paid to the issue in terms of both data collection and analysis.[9] To the extent that the effects of the experiment on marital dissolution were expected to depend on the guarantee and the tax rate, and to the extent that they were ex-

pected to differ according to income, ethnicity, and family type, the experimental design was well suited to the task of determining such effects. But to the extent that response might depend on other factors—such as presence or absence of children, degree of stigma attached to the program, or to some unanticipated combined effect of the cash benefit and counseling/training subsidy treatments—the design was not optimal for testing those hypotheses. This nonoptimality implies only that the response is measured with less statistical efficiency than with an optimal design, not that the design affects the validity of the response analysis.

Expected Effects. Previous research on the possible determinants of marital stability had not reached as well-defined a consensus on the expected effects of cash transfers on marital dissolution and the chain of causation through which these effects might occur, as was the case with respect to labor supply. There was some theoretical basis in the literature for believing both that cash transfers would reduce marital dissolution and that they would increase it.

The "conventional wisdom" at the time the experiment began, however, was relatively unambiguous. The widely held view then was that the welfare system might be contributing to marital dissolution. AFDC was restricted largely to one-parent families. The AFDC-UF program for which two-parent families with children were eligible was not available in every state and, even where available, was so highly restrictive in its eligibility requirements that few two-parent families actually participated. The empirical evidence on whether AFDC increased marital dissolution was mixed, but the policy presumption was that, if it did, a negative income tax for which both one-parent and two-parent families were eligible would be a stabilizing influence. A negative income tax with universal eligibility would be available to all families as soon as their incomes fell below a certain level, regardless of who was part of the family. Therefore, the argument went, the incentive to leave one's family in order to make them eligible for cash transfers would no longer exist.

The Analysis. As already noted, two-parent families with children did not have to be legally married, or even claim to be, in order to be eligible for SIME/DIME benefits. All they needed was to be living together on a continuing basis. Unmarried couples without children were ineligible for SIME/DIME. The SIME/DIME rules also permitted persons who had left their original partner to retain SIME/DIME eligibility and continue receiving negative income tax payments if their current incomes were below the breakeven level given their new family size. Thus, if an original two-parent family split up, the experiment permitted both halves of the original family to continue receiving (separate) NIT payments. If a member of the original couple formed a new continuing relationship, the new person was counted after a short waiting period as an eligible family member in computing SIME/DIME benefits.

During the first three years of SIME/DIME, roughly one in five of the couples married at enrollment were observed to break up. Table 9 shows the proportion of original marriages that dissolved during the first three payment years, broken down by duration of treatment and ethnic group.

The methodology used in the statistical analysis of the SIME/DIME data is complex and need not be spelled out in this overview. A number of points are worth keeping in mind as the analytical results are discussed below. First, the estimation methodology properly places substantial emphasis not only on the number of events but also on their timing.[10] Second, the analysts place more emphasis on their findings for the smaller number of families in the five-year treatment group than for the larger number of families in the three-year treatment group, arguing that the longer treatment more closely approximates a permanent program. In addition, as the raw data in Table 9 suggest, the statistical analysis demonstrates that the different ethnic groups react differently to the treatments, and hence need to be analyzed separately, thus reducing further the size of the samples used in the analysis.

Third, the treatment group on which the statistical results are based includes those who received both the negative income tax treatment and the counseling/training subsidy treatment, as well as those on the negative income tax treatment only. The statistical procedure used in the marital dissolution analysis to adjust for the counseling/training subsidy treatment is basically the same as that used in the labor supply analysis. Although the interaction between the NIT and counseling/training subsidy treatments is statistically significant for whites (but not for blacks or Chicanos),

TABLE 9 Proportions of Originial Marriages Observed to End During the First 3 Years of SIME/DIME[a]

	Blacks	Whites	Chicanos
Control group	0.205 (435)	0.145 (608)	0.185 (200)
NIT treatment group	.278 (504)	.203 (691)	.222 (338)
3-year sample	.270 (333)	.198 (479)	.223 (238)
5-year sample	.292 (171)	.212 (212)	.220 (100)

[a] The number of original couples is shown in parentheses.

Source: *Final Report*, Volume I, Part V, Chapter 5, Table 5.3.

the analysts conclude that the unsystematic nature of the interaction is most plausibly explained by sampling variability. An additional finding that leads the authors to discount the importance of the interaction between the two types of treatments is that when they used their statistical methodology to reestimate rates of marital dissolution in the New Jersey income maintenance experiment, they found the NIT effects to be similar in New Jersey (where there was no counseling or training subsidy) and SIME/DIME.

The Overall Effect.   Table 10 shows the estimated effect of the negative income tax treatment for the three-year treatment and five-year treatment families, by ethnic group. The rate of marital dissolutions among Chicanos is unaffected by the NIT. As can be seen, the overall effect on marital dissolution rates is positive and substantial for black and white families in both the three-year and five-year NIT treatment groups.

To confirm the observed effects for blacks and whites, the analysis differentiated the dissolution rates during the experiment from those occurring in the period after the treatments ended. For this analysis, three time periods were used—enrollment to three years later, three years after enrollment to five years after, and five years after enrollment to seven years after (i.e., the post-experimental years for the five-year treatment group). The impact of the NIT on marital dissolution was al-

lowed to vary for each period. With this specification, the marital dissolution effects for both the three-year and five-year treatments are again positive and significant for blacks and whites but not for Chicanos. In the post-treatment period, the experimental-control difference disappears altogether for both the three-year and five-year treatment groups. Thus, the observed response in dissolution is clearly attributable to the experiment.

A separate analysis of the experimental effect on remarriage concludes that the NIT treatments did not affect remarriage rates for single white or black women, but did reduce the rate by over 60 percent for single Chicano women. Furthermore, after an analysis of how sample attrition may have biased estimates of the change in dissolution rates, the analysts concluded that the unadjusted estimates for whites and blacks, which range in Table 10 from 40 percent to 50 percent, should be reduced about 10 percentage points for blacks and about 5 percentage points for whites.

Explanation of Effects.   What is the reason for the experimental effect on black and white marriages and single Chicano women, given that this effect is the differential effect of the SIME/DIME NIT treatments compared to the effect of the public assistance (AFDC) option present in the control environment? The analysts begin explaining the increase in marital dissolution rates by noting a surprising general

TABLE 10   Estimated Percentage Change in Marital Dissolution Rates Caused by the NIT Treatments: All Marriages[a]

	Blacks	Whites	Chicanos
3-year treatment sample	+47[b]	+41[b]	+19
5-year treatment sample	+43[b]	+43[b]	+2
Number of marriages	1,203	1,714	698

[a] Includes relationships entered into after the start of the experiment; 3-year treatment effect is estimated over a 3-year period and 5-year effect over 5 years.

[b] Significant at 1 percent level.

Source: *Final Report,* Volume 1, Part V, Chapter 5, Table 5.5.

pattern of the experimental effects when estimated separately by NIT plan. There was no perfectly consistent pattern, but what pattern there was suggested the paradox that lower marital dissolution rates are associated with higher guarantees.

Grouping by guarantee confirms that the experimental effect tends to decrease as the generosity of the guarantee increases. In fact, for white couples the effect is statistically significant only for the low $3,800 guarantee (an 82 percent increase in the rate of marital dissolution), and for blacks the effect is statistically significant only for the $3,800 guarantee (a 60 percent increase) and the medium $4,800 guarantee (a 91 percent increase). For neither blacks nor whites is the effect significant for the high $5,600 guarantee. This pattern of effects is especially striking in view of the fact that the $3,800 guarantee most closely approximates the generosity of the AFDC and AFDC-UF programs available to the control group.

Recognition of two aspects of the situation may account for this pattern of findings. First, according to the existing literature, an increase in cash transfers can be expected to have two opposing effects on the marital dissolution rate. Increases in family income tend to stabilize marriages, giving rise to an *income* effect; but a cash transfer program that provides financial alternatives to marriage for low-income women also tends to destabilize marriage, causing an *independence* effect. Depending on the strength of the two effects, which are opposite in direction, a negative income tax reform may increase marital dissolution, decrease it, or leave it unchanged. Second, since the basic income support offered to low-guarantee experimentals is similar to that already available to controls with children, it is also clear that the relevant difference between the two environments must be nonpecuniary.

Three nonpecuniary differences between the NIT and existing welfare programs may be relevant. Knowledge of the availability of benefits in the event of marital dissolution is likely to be greater for experimentals under the SIME/DIME rules than for controls who would have to go to the local welfare office to apply for AFDC and Food Stamps. The time and nuisance cost of becoming eligible for benefits in the event of a dissolution is lower for the experimentals. Experimental families already had eligibility for SIME/DIME; the only change due to a dissolution would be noting a change in family composition and available family resources on the regular monthly income report form. The necessary procedure for applying for AFDC and Food Stamp benefits is more difficult and more time consuming. Finally, the social and psychological costs (or stigma) of applying for AFDC and using Food Stamps are likely to be higher. The SIME/DIME payments process was largely private. The use of Food Stamps or AFDC exposes applicants to public acknowledgment of dependence or to interaction with possibly condescending welfare workers. One way to sum up these nonpecuniary differences between the programs is to say that a dollar from welfare is less attractive than a dollar from SIME/DIME.

CONCLUSIONS SUGGESTED BY THE SIME/DIME RESULTS

Marital Stability

How can the SIME/DIME results be used as a guide to the possible effects on family structure of new public policy initiatives? The analysts themselves "caution the reader against uncritically extrapolating from these or any other summary measures of the effects of SIME/DIME on marital dissolution."[11] They stress as reasons for this statement the following facts: the SIME/DIME sample is nationally unrepresentative, the relationship of the impact of a limited duration experiment to that of a permanent national program is ambiguous, nonpecuniary differences in programs (caused by different administrative procedures and/or work requirements, for example) seem to have important effects on the family structure impact, the social context of SIME/DIME and of a national program are likely to differ in important respects, the remarriage effects of a national program would probably differ because of the possible incentive to marry into the experiment, and the differences among ethnic groups in the treatment effects suggest strongly that the behavioral effects of SIME/DIME on family structure are not yet fully understood. Yet after discussing all these reasons, the analysts conclude: "We have discussed a number of factors that complicate any attempt to extrapolate from SIME/DIME to any other NIT program. None of these factors alter our qualitative conclusions. Given the magnitude of these findings, it is unlikely that any national NIT program would be neutral with respect to marital stability. Although the effects of a national NIT program are unlikely to be as dramatic as the experimental effects, the potential for such effects must not be ignored."[12]

Labor Supply. The work responses to be expected from transfer programs of varying generosity are much more precisely known as a result of SIME/DIME than they were before. It is now possible, as a consequence of the SIME/DIME labor supply analysis, to predict with some confidence how much more or less people will work as a result of new policy initiatives and what the cost implications of new programs will be. The response to tax rate variations turns out to be smaller than was formerly thought, permitting the imposition of higher—and more cost saving—marginal tax rates. The responses to guarantee variations turn out to be systematic and predictable. The responses to *breakeven* variations turn out to be very important because (a) the income level at which benefits cease is

the critical determinant of the size of the beneficiary population, and (b) the size of the beneficiary population is the most important determinant of program costs and aggregate work reductions.

Counseling/Training. With respect to the counseling/training subsidy results, two major points deserve emphasis. Participation in both the counseling and training-education programs was strongly related to the amount of the subsidy. Both the 50 percent and 100 percent subsidy plans induced statistically significant increases in formal schooling (although not work-related training). These increases provide a plausible explanation of the negative results—namely that hours worked and earnings both during and (to a lesser extent) after program participation tended to be reduced. While in formal schooling it is reasonable to expect employment to be reduced, and the employment records of participants to become less regular. The formal schooling was not, however, typically job-related. Therefore, the potentially deleterious effect of the reduced work history was not compensated for by any job-related skills acquired during the subsidy period.

APPENDIX

Enormous effort was devoted to the development of counterattrition measures for SIME/DIME. . . . It was the responsibility of the sample maintenance department to counteract this attrition by developing successful ways for clients to report address information and effective methods of updating this address information, plus locating families who moved without reporting new addresses.

Monitoring Address Information

NIT Treatment Sample. The families in the NIT treatment group had a greater incentive to report current address information on a regular basis both because it was required if they were to receive payment and because it was easy to do, being reported on the regular income report form (IRF). Any address change information reported on an IRF was given to the sample maintenance department to be entered into the address card file (which will be discussed later in this section).

Control Sample. The control group had less of an incentive to report address changes. First, they received no benefits. Second, most of them did not fill in an IRF form regularly every month. Third, when lost they were more difficult to track down because the experiment only contacted them for the periodic interviews about every 4 months, by which time the trail was often cold. To keep track of control families between interviews and to give them a small financial incentive to continue, the experiment paid them $8 each month for filling out and sending in a postcard giving any address or family composition changes. A secondary reason for implementing this procedure was that one of the goals of the experiment was to collect comparable data on family stability from both experimentals and controls. The family composition change data from NIT treatment families were reported on the monthly IRF; this postcard was the control analog. If a family indicated a composition change on their card, they received a family change letter form on which to provide the details of the change.

The control assistant at each site managed the control sample and the postcard and $8 check mailings. Family change letters when received were turned over to sample maintenance for processing. Address changes were also turned over to sample maintenance for updating the address card file.

Processing of the monthly control checks was routine. The only input needed was an address card for the family in question. The monthly schedule allowed families plenty of time to submit their address cards, with the normal cut-off date for payment being about the 23d of the month and the payment (along with the next month's card) going out on the last working day of the month. There was no provision for late payments. If a family failed to file four postcards in succession, they were dropped from the system. Over 90 percent of the active control sample usually submitted their card in time to be paid. The disbursements to control group families are summarized in Table V-2.

Control IRFs. In Denver, 50 percent of the control group was required to submit monthly income and expense reports (IRFs), rather than simply submitting postcards. For this they were paid $15 each month. The IRFs were, of course, the same reports filed by the families in the experimental group. The purpose was to be able to measure any differences in the respondents' reporting of income and expenses on the periodic interview that might be due to a learning effect from the regularly repeated task of completing an IRF. The reporting habits of the IRF control sample were good. Over the course of the experiment, about 88 percent of them submitted IRFs each month.

TABLE V-2 Disbursement of Control Group Payments to Enrolled Families

Fiscal year	Seattle	Denver[a]
1971	$15,304	
1972	94,870	$38,598
1973	83,776	136,493
1974	101,464	123,608
1975	152,090	152,661
1976	95,240	166,850
1977	77,779	101,351
1978	16,288	95,688
1979		81,984
Total	622,507	847,233

[a] Includes payments for both postcards and control IRFs.

TABLE V–3 Sample Dynamics and Attrition in Seattle

[Families of two or more persons]

Periodic interview	(1) Active families from previous interview $(10_p - 16_p)$	(2) Cumulative attrition: Prior interviews (14_p)	(3) Net changes due 10 family splits, marriage, etc.	(4) Cumulative family units in experiment $(3 + 4_p)$	(5) Dropped from experiment	(6) Former drops now restored	(7) Moved out of area[a]	(8) Interview sample $(1 + 4 + 6 - 5 - 7)$
1	2,038	0	28	2,066	51	0	47	1,968
2	1,964	55	14	2,080	43	3	30	1,905
3	1,897	103	28	2,108	29	2	41	1,857
4	1,820	107	18	2,126	17	10	13	1,818
5	1,799	193	9	2,135	6	0	4	1,798
6	1,720	277	11	2,146	16	31	22	1,724
7	1,689	297	−42	2,102	9	2	16	1,624
8	1,590	338	−18	2,084	17	4	12	1,557
9	1,537	371	−2	2,082	35	51	6	1,605
10	1,602	359	17	2,099	40	81	20	1,668
11	1,661	325	26	2,075	42	5	13	1,637
12	1,336	NA	20	NA	17	29	7	1,361
13	895	NA	16	NA	15	20	10	906
14	580	NA	7	NA	5	4	7	579
15	562	NA	4	NA	9	5	2	561
16	545	NA	16	NA	14	5	7	545
17	400	NA	0	NA	20	5	4	381
Total			152		385	256	261	23,494

[a] Still in experiment; interviewed annually as part of Moved Out of Area Project.

[b] Families were administered periodic interviews for their entire period of enrollment this 1 year.

NOTE

See text for explanation of column headings and derivation.

Searching Activities

Mobility rates were relatively high for both the Seattle and Denver families. Even with the address reporting procedures detailed above, families often moved without reporting their new address. Interviewers made an initial effort to locate these families by contacting neighbors and checking with office personnel for updated address information. Questionnaires belonging to those respondents who could not be located by the interviewers were then turned over to a full-time searcher in the sample maintenance department at each site.

The qualifications for this position included knowledge of the Seattle or Denver area, plus an imaginative and tenacious approach to searching. The following is a list of various sources used in attempting to locate "moved-not-found" families.

- *Payments files and previously completed questionnaires:* Typically, the searcher first collected any information available from these data sources that could be useful. This included former addresses, telephone numbers, union affiliations, birthdates, social security numbers, school histories of

TABLE V–3 Sample Dynamics and Attrition in Seattle (Continued)

[Families of two or more persons]

(9)	(10)	(11)	(12)	(13)	(14)	(15)	(16)
Interviews not completed	Completed interviews (8 − 9)	Completion rate (10 ÷ 8) (percent)	Marginal attrition (5 + 9 − 6)	Attrition rate (12 ÷ (4 − 12)) (percent)	Cumulative attrition (2 + 12)	Attrition rate (14 ÷ 3) (percent)	Completing interview series[b]
4	1,964	99.8	55	2.7	55	2.7	0
8	1,897	99.6	48	2.4	103	5.0	0
37	1,820	98.0	64	3.2	167	8.1	0
19	1,799	99.0	26	1.3	193	9.2	0
78	1,720	95.7	84	4.3	277	13.1	0
35	1,689	98.0	20	1.1	297	14.3	0
34	1,590	97.9	41	2.3	338	16.1	0
20	1,537	98.7	33	1.9	371	17.8	0
3	1,602	99.8	− 12	− 0.7	359	17.3	0
7	1,661	99.6	− 34	− 2.1	325	15.5	0
12	1,625	99.3	49	NA	NA	NA	289
6	1,355	99.6	− 6	NA	NA	NA	460
1	905	99.9	− 4	NA	NA	NA	326
11	568	98.1	2	NA	NA	NA	5
16	545	97.1	20	NA	NA	NA	0
5	540	99.1	14	NA	NA	NA	140
6	375	98.4	21	NA	NA	NA	375
302	23,192	98.7			431		

children, and utilization of public services. Contact with any public or private agency had to be done with extreme care in order to avoid violating the confidentiality pledge with the families.

- *Personal contacts with neighbors, land-lords, mailmen, and people at local hang-outs:* These contacts often proved successful.
- *The searcher's file:* This file consisted of a listing of the friends and relatives of the families, compiled by the searcher from other sources. As this file built up, it developed into an invaluable source of information.
- *Telephone information operators and tele-phone directories:* Often new listings for respondents could be found.
- *Other family members in SIME/DIME:* Oc-

casionally, missing families had other relatives in SIME/DIME who could be contacted for information.

- *Letters to old addresses:* Sometimes there were reasons to believe that letters to old addresses might be productive. Occasionally, for example, an interviewer checked the wrong address or another family's name appeared in the mailbox causing the interviewer to think the original family had moved when they were, in fact, still living there.
- *Reverse street directory:* The library provided a directory that listed telephone subscribers by their street address; however, this was less useful than initially thought because it did not provide very current information.
- *AFDC warrant register:* MPR had access to

TABLE V–4 Sample Dynamics and Attrition in Denver

[Families of two or more persons]

Periodic interview	(1) Active families from previous interview $(10_p - 16_p)$	(2) Cumulative attrition: Prior interviews (14_p)	(3) Net changes due to family splits, marriage, etc.	(4) Cumulative family units in experiment $(3 + 4_p)$	(5) Dropped from experiment	(6) Former drops now restored	(7) Moved out of area[a]	(8) Interview sample $(1+4+6-5-7)$
1	2,699	0	20	2,719	18	0	26	2,675
2	2,660	33	11	2,730	29	4	45	2,601
3	2,588	71	25	2,755	28	4	28	2,561
4	2,541	115	26	2,781	44	19	33	2,499
5	2,483	166	3	2,784	28	16	20	2,454
6	2,425	207	30	2 314	31	33	16	2,441
7	2,412	234	11	2,825	24	29	17	2,411
8	2,398	267	29	2,854	25	13	8	2,407
9	2,394	306	30	2,884	26	12	10	2,400
10	2,375	359	13	2,897	24	14	27	2,351
11	2,327	NA	29	NA	30	20	35	2,311
12	2,182	NA	34	NA	30	23	20	2,189
13	1,431	NA	18	NA	15	22	− 15	1,471
14	1,076	NA	20	NA	9	10	−7	1,104
15	1,033	NA	17	NA	22	12	9	1,031
16	998	NA	7	NA	10	15	4	1,006
17	976	NA	15	NA	6	11	6	990
18	479	NA	6	NA	27	17	5	470
Total			344		426	264	285	35,372

[a] Still in experiment; interviewed annually as part of Moved Out of Area Project.

[b] Families were administered periodic interviews for their entire period of enrollment plus 1 year.

the Aid to Families with Dependent Children monthly warrant register. It listed public assistance recipients by name, birthdate, social security number, and case-load number. If a family was currently receiving assistance, the searcher could contact the caseworker for updated address information.

- *Housing authorities:* MPR had agreements with local housing authorities that enabled the searcher to call the appropriate housing project to obtain information. This source was used more productively in Seattle than in Denver.
- *Post Office address correction cards:* For a

fee, the Customer Service Department of the U.S. Post Office would verify or correct an address. Address correction cards were sent in bulk, distributed to the appropriate carriers, filled in, and returned in bulk to the searcher.

- *Counselors administering the counseling/ training component of the treatment:* These individuals had direct contact with a subset of the families and often knew something about their habits.
- *Motor Vehicle Department:* In Denver, the Motor Vehicle Department provided, for a slight fee for each request, current driver's license address information.

TABLE V–4   Sample Dynamics and Attrition in Denver (Continued)

[Families of two or more persons]

(9)	(10)	(11)	(12)	(13)	(14)	(15)	(16)
Interviews not completed	Completed interviews $(8-9)$	Completion rate $(10 \div 8)$ (percent)	Marginal attrition $(5+9-6)$	Attrition rate $(12+(-12))$ (percent)	Cumulative attrition $(2+12)$	Attrition rate $(14 \div 3)$ (percent)	Completing interview series[b]
15	2,660	99.6	33	1.2	33	1.2	0
13	2,588	99.5	38	1.4	71	2.6	0
20	2,541	99.2	44	1.6	115	4.2	0
16	2,483	99.4	51	1.9	166	6.0	0
29	2,425	98.8	41	1.6	207	7.4	0
29	2,212	98.8	27	1.0	234	8.3	0
13	2,398	99.5	8	0.3	242	8.6	0
13	2,394	99.5	25	1.0	267	9.4	0
25	2,375	99.0	39	1.5	306	10.6	0
24	2,327	99.0	34	1.3	340	11.7	0
23	2,288	99.0	33	NA	NA	NA	106
33	2,156	98.5	40	NA	NA	NA	725
23	1,448	98.4	16	NA	NA	NA	372
11	1,087	98.5	16	NA	NA	NA	54
17	1,003	97.3	38	NA	NA	NA	5
28	979	97.0	25	NA	NA	NA	0
30	957	96.7	28	NA	NA	NA	478
33	470	100.0	10	NA	NA	NA	470
384	34,988	98.9					

If the searcher had continued to look for a lost family for two months and found no productive lead, the family was dropped administratively from the experiment. Of course, as provided in the rules of operation, a family could rejoin the experiment at any time, provided they completed the interviews and met other payments-reporting requirements for the period they were unavailable. In both Seattle and Denver, many lost families were, in fact, found.

Processing Address Information

Address information from all previously described sources was processed in a variety of ways in Seattle and Denver. A computer disk file of names and addresses of all active families was maintained by the department. As address changes were received, they were noted on departmental forms. Near the end of each month, these forms were used to update the address file. Once information was updated, two address computer card decks were created. One deck included all active NIT families and was used by the payments department to produce checks and mailing labels. Another deck was created including all control families. This deck was used for the same purpose in processing the control group monthly address postcards and control IRF payments. Additional listings of the control-experimental sample were also produced in alphabetical and family number order. These were used throughout the month as aids to IRF and postcard processing.

Sample Dynamics

There are a number of different approaches to measuring the attrition that occurred during the experiment. From the point of view of measuring attrition as it might affect research inferences, the appropriate procedure is to calculate separate attrition rates for husbands, wives, and single female heads of household for each experimental group (NIT treatment and control) and for each city and racial group. About 20 percent of husbands and 15 percent of wives and single female heads of household attrited during the first two and one-half years of the experiment. Further, as expected, the attrition rate was greater among controls than among NIT treatment families.

An alternative approach to attrition measurement, and one that is more useful in planning for survey administration, is to examine how the sample of enrolled families changed over time. Due to the numerous family composition changes, attrition, and efforts to counter attrition, the sample of families receiving the periodic interviews changed markedly over the course of the experiment. A summary of the changes that occurred over time is presented in Tables V-3 and V-4.

Each line of the tables depicts the sample changes that occurred during each periodic interview period. The numbers in parentheses below some column headings refer to the columns used to calculate that entry. The numbers with the subscript "p" signify that the number has come from the previous periodic number in the appropriate column. Thus, the numbers in column 1 (active families from previous interviews) are derived by subtracting the number for the previous periodic interview given in column 16 (families completing interview series) from the number for the previous periodic interview given in column 10 (completed interviews). The basic data for the tables come from project records. Column 3

(net changes due to family splits, etc.) represents the net changes in the size of the sample due to family composition changes. For example, a married couple splitting into two famly units (that is, each having at least one dependent) would increase the number of families in the experiment by one. However, if one head of a married couple left without taking any dependents, that would not be reflected as a change in this table, which excludes individuals living alone.

Column 7 (moved out of area) refers to the net number of families who moved out of the greater Seattle or greater Denver area during that interview period. These families were not included in the periodic interview sample, but were interviewed once each year in a special moved-out-of-area interview effort.

The interview completion rates are presented in column 11. Due to the efforts to counter attrition and convert interview refusals, the completion rates are high—almost 99 percent in each city. The results of the counterattrition efforts can probably be most clearly seen in column 15, which shows the cumulative attrition rate over time. More than four years after the first families were enrolled, only 15.5 percent had attrited in Seattle and only 11.7 percent in Denver.

The figures on cumulative attrition are presented in these tables only up to the point where families were dropped from the sample because they had completed their interview series. Each experimental family was interviewed for one full year after the completion of their treatment. The tables are discontinued at that point because attrition data were confounded by families leaving the experiment because they had completed the interview series.

NOTES

1. These correspond to 95 percent, 120 percent, and 140 percent of the official poverty line for

a family of four ($4,000 in 1971 dollars). The relationship of these levels to the poverty line was preserved throughout the experimental period by adjusting the dollar guarantee levels regularly according to increases in the Consumer Price Index, as is the poverty line itself.

2. The last two variants were introduced because a declining tax rate schedule provides less of a work disincentive than a constant tax rate plan with the same guarantee and breakeven level and therefore needs a smaller cash transfer budget.

3. Under the 1981 AFDC amendments, there is a limit on total non-AFDC income at 150 percent of the state needs standard. On the basis of the poverty lines and state needs standards of 1980, the breakeven level at 150 percent of the needs standard is below the poverty line in all but 15 states.

4. All citations are to the *Final Report of the Seattle-Denver Income Maintenance Experiment* (denoted *Final Report*), Washington, D.C.: U.S. Government Printing Office, 1983.

5. It is important to note that the subsidy was available for a wide range of training or education, including liberal arts courses. However, for simplicity, the remainder of the paper re-

fers to this treatment as the counseling/training subsidy treatment.

6. Projected income and expected expenses were typically based on the most recently verified monthly data, which were assumed to hold true in future months.

7. Unemployed means out of work but looking for a job. Out of the labor force means not working and not looking for a job.

8. The difference, again, is whether they are looking for a job or not.

9. The reader is reminded that, for simplicity, the term "marital stability" is used in this overview, but legal marriage was not a condition of eligibility for SIME/DIME couples.

10. Essentially, earlier marital dissolutions counted more heavily in the analysis than later dissolutions. For example, suppose two groups of families had the same proportion of dissolutions over the course of the experiment, but in one group all the dissolutions were observed near the beginning of the experiment, whereas in the other the dissolutions occurred toward the end. The estimation methodology correctly attributes to the first group a higher rate of marital dissolution.

11. *Final Report*, Volume 1, Part V, Chapter 11.

12. *Ibid.*

Explanation and Critique

The preceding article by Skidmore provides an excellent example of the factorial design. The income maintenance experiment had two major components: (1) cash transfer (NIT) treatments and (2) a counseling/training component. The four basic treatment combinations were (1) NIT only, (2) counseling/training only, (3) NIT and counseling/training, and (4) no treatment. The basic design is depicted in Table 5-2.

Actually, the procedure was much more complicated because more than one version of both NIT and counseling/training were tested. With NIT, the three guarantee levels and four tax rates combined in such a way as to produce 11 negative income tax plans (one control group receiving no treatment made 12 groups in all). For counseling/training, there were three treatment variants plus a control group receiving no counseling/training, making a total of four. Table 5-3 illustrates the complete factorial design for the experiment. Notice that NIT_{12} and C/T_4 are control groups that did not receive the respective treatments.

Table 5-3 thus shows 48 possible combinations of the 12 NIT plans and four

TABLE 5–2 Basic Design of Income Maintenance Experiment

	Counseling/Participation Training/Participation	
	Counseling/Training	No Counseling/ Training
NIT	NIT and C/T	NIT but No C/T
No NIT	No NIT but C/T	No NIT No C/T

counseling/training plans. These 48 plans obviously include the group NIT_{12}/CT_4 that received no treatment of any kind beyond the traditional welfare support systems already in place (e.g., AFDC). In addition, in order to test whether (and if so, to what extent) behavioral responses varied by duration of treatment, the families were also randomly assigned to a 3-year or 5-year treatment duration. Thus, instead of 48 possible treatment/control groups, there were 95 if all possible combinations were considered given the two treatment durations.

Such a massive experiment would obviously have cost a small fortune so, in the interests of economy, the experiment did not test every possible combination of the treatments. Nor was every combination tested of equal interest or importance. As the researchers point out:

> Certain guarantee/tax-rate combinations were considered more feasible than others (basically, those in the middle range were considered the more policy-rele-

TABLE 5–3 Factorial Design for the Seattle-Denver Income Maintenance Experiment

Negative Income Tax Plans	Counseling/Training			
	CT_1	CT_2	CT_3	CT_4
NIT_1	NIT_1/CT_1	NIT_1/CT_2	NIT_1/CT_3	NIT_1/CT_4
NIT_2	NIT_2/CT_1	NIT_2/CT_2	NIT_2/CT_3	NIT_2/CT_4
NIT_3	NIT_3/CT_1	NIT_3/CT_2	NIT_3/CT_3	NIT_3/CT_4
NIT_4	NIT_4/CT_1	NIT_4/CT_2	NIT_4/CT_3	NIT_4/CT_4
NIT_5	NIT_5/CT_1	NIT_5/CT_2	NIT_5/CT_3	NIT_5/CT_4
NIT_6	NIT_6/CT_1	NIT_6/CT_2	NIT_6/CT_3	NIT_6/CT_4
NIT_7	NIT_7/CT_1	NIT_7/CT_2	NIT_7/CT_3	NIT_7/CT_4
NIT_8	NIT_8/CT_1	NIT_8/CT_2	NIT_8/CT_3	NIT_8/CT_4
NIT_9	NIT_9/CT_1	NIT_9/CT_2	NIT_9/CT_3	NIT_9/CT_4
NIT_{10}	NIT_{10}/CT_1	NIT_{10}/CT_2	NIT_{10}/CT_3	NIT_{10}/CT_4
NIT_{11}	NIT_{11}/CT_1	NIT_{11}/CT_2	NIT_{11}/CT_3	NIT_{11}/CT_4
NIT_{12}	NIT_{12}/CT_1	NIT_{12}/CT_2	NIT_{12}/CT_3	NIT_{12}/CT_4

vant), and consequently the designers put greater emphasis on obtaining precise behavioral response estimates for these combinations.

Once the various cells in the factorial table that were of interest had been identified (including, obviously, NIT_{12}/CT_4), a family of a given type that had been selected for the sample was randomly assigned to a particular treatment combination on the basis of cell sizes computed by a mathematical model. We might add as an aside that eliminating cells for practical, political, or policy reasons does not invalidate the experiment so long as the control group is maintained.

Now to the findings. What did the factorial design contribute to the experiment? First, notice the reasons why a labor market counseling and training subsidy program was included in the experiment. The rationale for including these programs was to determine whether increased labor market information and increased education and training could offset the decline in work effort that was predicted to occur due to the negative income tax program.

What actually happened was that the counseling/training subsidy treatment did not have the intended effects for most groups. For husbands, the counseling-only program had no impact on savings, whereas the training/subsidy programs led to substantial and significant decreases in earnings and hours worked in the short run and had little measurable impact in the long run.

The counseling-only program resulted in a significant lowering of earnings and hours for wives. Wives eligible for the training subsidies also had lower earnings and hours than did those in the control group—even in the long testing.

It was only for single female heads of household that counseling-only had the intended impacts. But, once training was introduced, these results were the same for the single heads as for other groups.

Because counseling/training was a voluntary program, one might conclude that had the effects been positive, then self-selection might have been the real reason for the results. Would not one expect that people volunteering for job counseling/training would want a job? The negative impact is entirely believable and must be attributed to the counseling/training program. Skidmore concluded:

> Evidently, the SIME/DIME counseling/training subsidy program included short-run reductions in earnings without supporting the type of training or education that would enable participants to secure better paying jobs, at least during the one- to three-year follow-up period. This "training ineffectiveness argument" would explain a zero treatment response, but it doesn't really offer an explanation of the observed negative response. Perhaps the counseling and training experiences of those with ambitious upward mobility goals actually made it more difficult to pursue a career consisting of a series of relatively low-paying jobs. In any case a different type of counseling might have resulted in training and education decisions that were less ambitious, but this is entirely conjectural.

Although the results did not work out as the experimenters had hoped, the article still provides an excellent example of the factorial design.

Actually, this was not the first large-scale income maintenance experiment. The "original" of these large-scale experiments was conducted in New Jersey and Pennsylvania.[3] Peter Rossi and Katharine Lyall are quite critical of this evaluation.[4] For them, the major weaknesses in the study included the fact that the target population was limited to work-eligible male-headed families, the "haphazard" selection of sites, the fact that no attention was paid to ethnicity or race in the initial design of the sample, and the fact that the definition of eligibles resulted in a truncated sample. The eligible population consisted of intact families whose total income was less than 150 percent of the poverty level. This led to a sample in which families tended to be larger than the poverty population in general, had fewer wives in the labor force, had lower levels of homeownership, and so on.

Although it is not clear why Seattle and Denver were selected for the last of these experiments, the evaluation design was much tighter than the New Jersey-Pennsylvania projects. Attention was paid to ethnicity, unmarried women were included in the sample, the sample was larger than those in the other experiments, and the evaluation covered an extended time. This evaluation thus clearly benefited from the earlier income maintenance experience. Because it was so carefully conceived and was so thorough in its execution, the results can be viewed with confidence.

REFERENCES

1. David Nachmias, *Public Policy Evaluation: Approaches and Methods* (New York: St. Martin's Press, 1979), p. 33.
2. *Ibid.,* pp. 33-34.
3. See Albert Rees, "An Overview of the Labor-Supply Results," *Journal of Human Resources* 9 (Spring 1974): 158-180.
4. Peter H. Rossi and Katharine C. Lyall, "An Overview Evaluation of the NIT Experiment," in *Evaluation Studies Review Annual,* vol. 3, ed. Thomas D. Cook, Marilyn L. DelRosario, Karen M. Hennigan, Melvin M. Mark, William M. K. Trochin (Beverly Hills, CA.: Sage, 1978), pp. 412-428.

PART THREE

Quasi-Experimental Designs

It is the absence of random assignment that distinguishes quasi-experiments from true experiments. Quasi-experiments employ comparison groups just as do experiments. In the quasi-experimental design, the researcher strives to create a comparison group that is as close as possible to the experimental group in all relevant respects. And, just as there is a variety of experimental designs, there are basic designs that fall into the quasi-experimental category. These include the pretest-posttest comparison group design, the interrupted time-series comparison group design, the regression-discontinuity design, and the posttest-only comparison group design. We also include the use of statistical controls in quasi-experimentation even though some refer to their use as "nonexperimental".

Laura Langbein identifies a number of ways in which quasi-experiments are distinct from randomized experiments in practice. First, quasi-experiments tend to be retrospective—that is, to occur after a program is in practice. When the decision to evaluate comes after the program has been implemented, the option of conducting a true experiment is usually foreclosed.

Second, the internal validity of most quasi-experiments is usually more questionable than that of experiments. The researcher must identify and measure all the relevant characteristics of the experimental group and attempt to construct a similar comparison group. Successfully executing this task is frequently problematic.[1]

Although quasi-experiments are not true experiments, they are far from useless. Peter Rossi and Howard Freeman are actually quite positive about them. They state:

The term "quasi-experiment" does not imply that the procedures described are necessarily inferior to the randomized controlled experiment in terms of reaching plausible estimates of net effects. It is true that, without randomization, equivalence . . . cannot be established with as much certainty. The possibility always remains that the outcome of a program is really due to a variable or process that has not been considered explicitly in the design or analysis. However, quasi-experiments, properly constructed, can provide information on impact that is free of most, if not all, of the confounding processes [threats to validity]. . . . Indeed, the findings from a properly executed quasi-experimental design can be more valid than those from a poorly executed randomized experiment.[2]

REFERENCES

1. Laura Irwin Langbein, *Discovering Whether Programs Work: A Guide to Statistical Methods for Program Evaluation* (Glenview, IL: Scott, Foresman, 1980), pp. 87–89.
2. Peter H. Rossi and Howard E. Freeman, *Evaluation: A Systematic Approach*, 3rd ed. (Beverly Hills, CA: Sage, 1985), p. 267.

6

Pretest-Posttest
Comparison Group Design

The pretest-posttest comparison group design, sometimes referred to as the non-equivalent group design, is similar in every respect to the pretest-posttest control group design except that the individuals (cities, organizations) in the program being evaluated and in the comparison group are not assigned randomly—the comparison group is nonequivalent. The researcher attempts to identify a group for comparisons comparable in essential respects to those in the program. The validity of the quasi-experiment depends in large part on how closely the constructed control group resembles the intervention group in all essential respects. Table 6-1 illustrates the design.

There are obviously a multitude of uses for this design and, in fact, it is one of the designs most frequently found in the literature. If randomization is not possible, researchers attempt to find a group similar to the experimental group to use as a "pseudo-control." In many cases this is extremely difficult. In fact, it is so difficult that one research scholar, Barker Bausell, recommends against its use, as follows:

> Although this is probably a minority opinion, I recommend against the use of nonequivalent control groups, especially for beginning researchers. In many ways, quasi-experimental research (as these models are sometimes called) is more difficult to perform well than research involving the random assignment of subjects. Such research is also seldom conclusive, since it is subject to so many alternative explanations.[1]

One way in which evaluators seek to establish a comparison group as similar as possible to the experimental group is through the matched-pair design. This approach assigns subjects to experimental and "control" conditions on the basis of some common characteristic the evaluator wishes to measure. For example, in education research, students in an experimental group might be matched with other students on the basis of grade and reading level to form a comparison group.

TABLE 6-1 The Pretest-Posttest Comparison Group Design

	Before		After
Group E	O_{E_1}	X	O_{E_2}
Group C	O_{C_1}	X	O_{C_2}

However, only these two factors are controlled. Other factors that could affect the outcome (home, environment, intelligence) are not controlled.[2]

When is this design most often used? It is used in retrospective analysis when it is too late to assign a control group. It is also frequently used in evaluating programs in which the participants are volunteers and thus a true control group cannot be found.

Finding an adequate comparison group for a volunteer program is precisely the problem that was facing Tim Newcomb in the article to follow: "Conservation Program Evaluations: The Control of Self-Selection Bias."

Conservation Program Evaluations

The Control of Self-Selection Bias

TIM M. NEWCOMB

Public and private electric utilities across the United States have developed a variety of conservation programs for their residential customers during the past five years. This effort has been spurred in part by the federal Residential Conservation Service, which began in 1979 and requires the larger utilities to offer a home energy audit service to their customers. From the point of view of the utilities, these programs are beneficial to the extent that they reduce the residential load in a cost effective way.

Precise analyses of the cost-effectiveness of these programs are difficult to make because relatively little is known about the amount of electricity conserved by the programs. Several recent reviews have noted the lack of accurate research on residential electricity conservation and have called for better evaluation strategies to measure conservation (Berry, 1981; Pease, 1982). In the early stages of conservation program planning, estimates of potential electricity savings came from engineering studies. Recent evaluation studies by Seattle City Light (Weiss and New-

comb, 1982; Newcomb, 1982) and by Oak Ridge National Laboratory (Hirst et al., 1983a) found that conservation estimates developed prior to program implementation were considerably larger than the observed amount of conservation.

Inaccuracies in engineering estimates may be due, in part, to the tremendous variation in electricity consumption patterns among residential customers. Olsen and Cluett (1979) and Hirst et al. (1983a) report that some of this variation can be explained by differences in home size, income level, and number of occupants. More than half of the variation among households remains after these factors are accounted for. Engineering studies, which are conducted in a few homes, cannot take into account the complex relationships among unique home dwellers, unique homes, and varying combinations of energy conservation measures. For these reasons, accurate estimation of the conservation achieved by a residential program must be based upon actual field measurements of electricity use by the participating population.

Source: Tim Newcomb, "Conservation Program Evaluations: The Control of Self Selection Bias," Vol. 8, No. 3 (June 1984), pp. 425-440. Copyright © 1984 by EVALUATION REVIEW. Reprinted by permission of Sage Publications, Inc.

The purpose of this article is to describe a quasi-experimental design for estimating average household electricity conservation that controls for the major threats to internal validity and does not require complex statistical methods for analysis. The design uses a non-equivalent control group as described by Campbell and Stanley (1966) consisting of residential customers who participated in the same conservation program at a later date. This research strategy is useful in situations where a program operates over a period of several years and maintains constant and restrictive guidelines for accepting participants. Under these conditions, early participants will resemble later ones with respect to important preprogram characteristics.

This approach to estimating electricity conservation has been applied to three residential conservation program evaluations at Seattle City Light. The evaluation of electricity savings for the Low Income Electric Program (LIEP) will be presented here as an example of the approach.

Seattle City Light serves approximately 270,000 residential customers and plans to weatherize 20,000 homes by 1989 through the LIEP. This is expected to yield between 60 and 70 million kilowatt-hours of conserved electricity each year. The predicted cost of the weatherization over 8 years is 25 million in 1980 dollars. The LIEP offers a free home energy audit and free home weatherization to applicants whose total annual household income is less than 90 percent of the median income for the Seattle-Everett Standard Metropolitan Statistical Area. All applicants must accept ceiling and underfloor insulation as needed, as well as duct insulation, hot-water tank insulation, and repairs that are judged necessary by the utility auditors. Wall insulation, pipe insulation, and weatherstripping and caulking are optional. The participants included in this analysis all had electric heat as their primary source of space heat. The average 1981 LIEP participant received approxi-

mately $1400 in weatherization materials and labor at no cost.

The average cost to Seattle City Light for a weatherization job was approximately $2500 in 1981, including administration, home energy audits, and inspection of weatherization. An accurate assessment of the electricity savings is essential to evaluate and justify such large expenditures.

REASONS FOR SELECTING LIEP PARTICIPANTS AS A CONTROL GROUP

A simple pre-post experimental design could not provide accurate program conservation estimates for several important reasons. Weather fluctuations from one year to the next have a strong impact upon electricity use in homes that use electric space heat, and could easily mask or magnify the effects of home weatherization. Seattle City Light increased its residential rates approximately 65 percent in August of 1980, causing its customers to decrease their consumption of electricity. This effect coincided with the LIEP weatherization and, while the rate hike cannot be separated cleanly from the effects of the program, it probably produced reductions in electricity use beyond the results of weatherization. There were no time series data available of sufficient quality to allow the estimation of weather and rate hike effects using multiple regression.

All of these reasons demonstrate the need for the inclusion of a control group in this study that is as similar as possible to the LIEP participants. No group of residential customers fitting this description had been selected for analysis prior to the program, and current household income data were not available for any group except participants. Further, since the program is voluntary, participants almost certainly differ from the average low-income customer in attitudes and education. Recent studies by Olsen and Cluett (1979) and by Berry (1981) report that participants in voluntary residential conservation programs tend to have more education and use more electricity than the average customer. Without knowing beforehand exactly what the attributes of the program participants were, the best choice for a control group was the group of people who would later sign up for the program. This choice was confirmed through a comparison of survey data and electricity consumption figures for the LIEP weatherized homes and the control group to be presented in a later section.

A description of the experimental and the control groups, and the general approach to calculating electricity conservation estimates from the program are outlined as follows:

- The program participants, or "experimental group," received home conservation measures *in 1981*. The electricity use for this group prior to the program (September 1980 to May 1981) will be referred to as E_1. The electricity use for this group after the program weatherized the homes (September 1981 to May 1982) is referred to as E_2.

- The "control group" of homeowners received home conservation measures *in 1982*. The electricity consumption during the period from September 1980 to May 1981 will be called C_1. The electricity in use from September 1981 to May 1982 for this group is C_2. In this case, C_2 represents electricity use for the control group *before* the homes were weatherized.

- The computation of the estimates of conservation due to the program involves computing the pre-to-post change in consumption for the experimental group. $E_2 - E_1$, and the corresponding change for the control group, $C_2 - C_1$. The latter difference is subtracted from the former to find the estimate of conserved electricity, which is $(E_2 - E_1) - (C_2 - C_1)$.

ESTIMATING THE IMPACT OF WEATHERIZATION ON ELECTRICITY USE

Comparison of the Preprogram Attributes of the Weatherized Homes and the Control Homes

Three sources of information about the experimental and control groups of homes were available. Data collected at the time of the home energy audit describe the age and size of the home, the number of occupants, and the type of space heating. A mail survey of a random sample of each of the groups gathered information on the conservation actions taken in addition to the LIEP, and on the reasons for the homeowner's participation. Finally, the utility's customer metering system provided electricity consumption figures for each customer in periods of two months. Each of these sources can be used to test the assumption that the two groups were similar before the weatherization occurred.

Table 1 compares the groups with respect to average heated floor area, percentage of homes having each type of electric space heat, and average number of nighttime occupants. The reports by Hirst et al. (1983a) and by Olsen and Cluett (1979) showed that home size and number of occupants were positively correlated with level of consumption. The fact that there is little difference between the experimental and control groups for these two measures is strong support for the argument that the groups are similar. The close similarity in types of space heating is also significant because different types of space heating respond differently to fluctuations in temperature.

The survey responses to the mailed questionnaire are shown in Table 2. The response rates to these surveys were 81 percent and 76 percent for the experimental group and the control group, respectively, indicating that the responses are representative of the

TABLE I LIEP Participants, 1981 and 1982: Selected Demographic and Dwelling Characteristics

	1981 Participants Experimental Group (N = 326)	1982 Participants Control Group (N = 227)	t-Tests of Differences Between Groups Two-Tailed
Floor area of home			
Mean sq. feet	1258	1323	t = −1.26
Std. error	35	38	p>.10
Number of occupants			
Mean number	2.6	2.5	t = 0.71
Std. error	0.1	0.1	p>.10
Type of electric heat			
% Furnaces	20.4	21.6	t = −0.34
% Baseboard	70.6	73.6	p>.50
% Other	3.5	3.0	t = −0.77
			p>.10
			t = 0.33
			p>.50

respective survey populations sampled. There is little difference with regard to the respondents' stated reasons for participating in LIEP, except for a small increase in those who mentioned saving on electricity bills in 1982. The percentage of respondents who took each of the four conservation actions in addition to the LIEP is also very similar, which shows that any measured effects of the program weatherization are not affected by differences in extraprogram weatherization. The two groups appear to resemble each other with respect to their motivation and their reliance on the program for changes in home weatherization.

The single most critical test of the similarity of the two groups must be their respective levels of electricity use during the same time period before the experimental group received weatherization. Any differences in either the amount of electricity used or in the response curves of electricity use to weather would require adjustments before the impact of the program could be measured. Table 3 presents the average electricity consumption figures and the standard errors for these aver-ages, for five two-month billing periods prior to LIEP participation. The differences between the groups are not significant at the 5 percent level for any of the five two-month periods. Since electricity use is the criterion variable in this analysis, the similarity offers strong support for the choice of later participants as the control group.

The evidence for similarity was judged strong enough to support the estimation of electricity conservation using the calculations described earlier. A further discussion of the advantages and disadvantages of this design follows the estimation of the annual program conservation.

Calculation of the Electricity Conservation Estimates

The description of the quasi-experimental design that has been developed up to this point is oversimplified. This is so because homes were weatherized under LIEP continuously during 1981 and 1982, rather than in a short period. Figure 1 shows that as homes were

TABLE 2 LIEP Participants, 1981 and 1982: Survey Responses—Reasons for Participating in LIEP and Conservation Actions Taken Outside LIEP

	1981 Participants Experimental Group (N = 197) %	1982 Participants Control Group (N = 110) %	t-Tests of Differences Between Groups Two-Tailed
Reasons for participating			
Program is free	70	70	t = 0
Save on bills	89	97	t = 2.85 p < .01
Believe in conservation	75	77	t = −0.40 p > .50
Increase value of home	55	58	t = −0.51 p > .50
Increase comfort of home	80	77	t = 0.61 p > .50
Help solve energy crisis	61	57	t = .68 p > .10
Conservation actions taken outside LIEP within 12 months of weatherization			
Installed thermal windows	10	12	t = −0.54 p > .50
Installed storm windows	16	21	t = −1.06 p > .10
Installed energy-efficient water heater	9	7	t = 0.63 p > .50
Installed solar water heater	1	1	t = 0

weatherized in 1981, they were dropped from the preprogram consumption averages, and added to the postprogram averages. As homes in the control group were weatherized in 1982, they were dropped from the control group consumption averages.

All of the preprogram bimonthy billing records for the experimental group were grouped by two-month periods and an average was computed for each period, although the number of cases in each preprogram period changed (decreased) as homes received weatherization and were removed from the preprogram group. In a similar fashion, all of the electricity billing data for postprogram periods for the experimental group were grouped by period and averaged. The number in each billing period changed (increased) over times as more homes were weatherized.

The control group remained stable throughout the preprogram period. However, as these homes entered the program in early 1982, they were dropped from the control group, and the number of cases available for control purposes declined during successive billing periods in 1982 through May of 1982, which was the last period used in the analysis.

The varying numbers of homes in the two groups is a problem that will occur in a design of this type unless the treatment is applied to the entire group of participants in a brief period. The evaluation of programs op-

TABLE 3 LIEP Participants, 1981 and 1982: Electricity Consumption Before and after Weatherization of the Experimental Group

Bimonthly Billing Period	1981 Participants Experimental Group	1982 Participants Control Group	t = Tests of Differences Between Groups One-Tailed
Preperiod			
September 1980			
Mean Kwh/2 months	1893	1902	t = −0.08
Std. Error	98	55	p > .05
N	68	201	
November 1980			
Mean Kwh/2 months	3686	3829	t = −0.70
Std. Error	160	128	p > .05
N	113	208	
January 1981			
Mean Kwh/2 months	5195	5434	t = −1.13
Std. Error	155	144	p > .05
N	185	210	
March 1981			
Mean Kwh/2 months	4389	4567	t = −1.11
Std. Error	105	121	p > .05
N	293	209	
May 1981			
Mean Kwh/2 months	3010	3114	t = −.91
Std. Error	76	86	p > .05
N	293	209	
Postperiod			
September 1981			
Mean Kwh/2 months	1780	1871	t = −.85
Std. Error	91	57	p > .05
N	68	209	
November 1981			
Mean Kwh/2 months	3232	3960	t = −3.95
Std. Error	137	123	p < .05
N	113	209	
January 1982			
Mean Kwh/2 months	5031	6169	t = −5.03
Std. Error	156	164	p > .01
N	185	208	
March 1982			
Mean Kwh/2 months	4116	5027	t = −4.92
Std. Error	98	157	p > .01
N	293	160	
May 1982			
Mean Kwh/2 months	2631	3519	t = −4.15
Std. Error	70	202	p > .01
N	293	39	

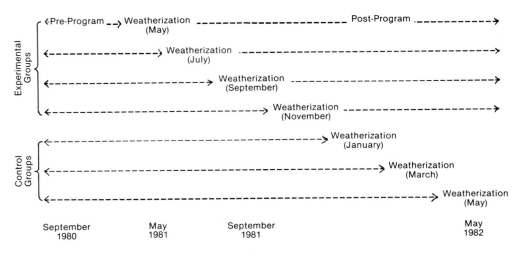

Figure 1

erating in a natural setting is more likely to face the continuous mode of program operation described here. An accurate system for tracking and assigning participants to one or the other of the two groups as the treatment occurs is helpful for a design of this kind.

Figure 2 is a graph of each two-month electricity consumption average for the experimental group and the control group using the method described above. While the two groups are similar during the period up to September 1980, they diverge after that time. The small difference during the September 1980 period is due to the relatively minor impact of weatherization during summer months when consumption for space heating is very low. The number of heating degree days during the period from November 1980 to April 1981 was only 87 percent of the number of heating degree days from November 1981 to April 1982. The colder winter of 1981-1982 had an obvious impact upon the consumption of the control group homes in Figure 2. This increased consumption was not shared by the experimental group; however, a simple pre-post design would have reduced the estimate

of electricity conservation over this period for the experimental group because the colder winter raised the consumption of electricity by comparison with the previous year.

Table 3 displays the mean values for the experimental and control groups, before and after the experimental group received weatherization. The t-test values for each of the ten differences between mean values are listed in the third column with the probability that such a value would occur by chance. One-tailed t-tests were used for both the before and after periods, because the hypothesis to be tested is that the experimental group does not have a lower bimonthly electricity level at each period than the control group. While all of the preperiod differences between means are significantly different from zero, four of the five postperiod differences are highly significant.

The actual computations of electricity conservation are presented in Table 4. The first column contains the pre-to-post changes by billing period for the experimental group, referred to earlier as E_2-E_1. The corresponding differences for the control group are given in column 2, and referred to as C_2-C_1. The

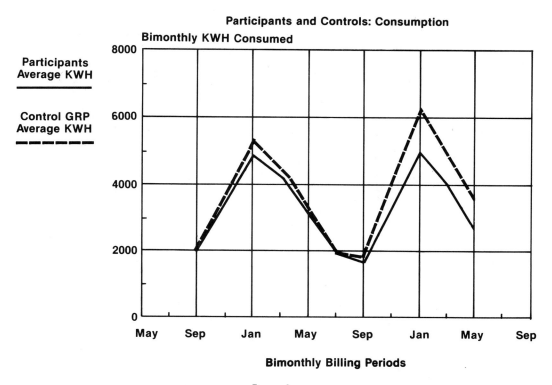

Figure 2
LIEP Electricity Consumption (KWH) 1980–1982.

net change $(E_2-E_1) - (C_2-C_1)$ is computed in column three. The total net change for the ten-month period under study is -3083 Kwh. To compute an estimated annual amount of electricity conservation, the ratio of electricity use by the control group for one full year (July 1980 to May 1981) to that group's use for ten months (September 1980 to May 1981), equal to 1.11, was multiplied by -3083 Kwh/10 months. The result is -3422 Kwh/year of electricity conservation. The value of the conserved electricity to the average LIEP participant is $485 (1981 dollars) over the 30-year lifetime of the weatherization measures (Weiss, 1983; this is also the net present value to the customer since the weatherization was free).

DISCUSSION

From the point of view of quasi-experimental design theory, the design described here has some significant strengths. The assumption that the control and experimental groups are alike can be examined carefully. The somewhat unique group of customers that participated in the LIEP can be compared to another very similar group without performing a multiple-regression analysis of the relationship between income levels, electricity consumption, and weatherization levels.

Most of the threats to internal validity described by Campbell and Stanley (1966) can be discounted in this study. The problem of selection in the LIEP study is a recurrent one

TABLE 4   LIEP Participants, 1981 and 1983: Computation of Electricity Conservation from Bimonthly Changes in Consumption of the Experimental and Control Groups

Bimonthly Comparison Periods	Changes for the 1981 Participants Experimental Group E_2-E_1	Changes for the 1982 Participants Control Group C_2-C_1	Net Change Due to LIEP Program Weatherization $(E_2-E_1) - (C_2-C_1)$
September 1981 minus September 1980	−113 Kwh/2 mo.	−31 Kwh/2 mo.	−82 Kwh/2 mo.
November 1981 minus November 1980	−454	131	−585
January 1982 minus January 1981	−164	735	−899
March 1982 minus March 1981	−273	460	−733
May 1982 minus May 1981	−379	405	−784

NOTE

Net change over ten-month period: −3083 Kwh.

in residential energy conservation research (Hirst et al., 1983b). Since voluntary participants may be unlike a random sample of customers, this difference must either be controlled through the proper design, or counteracted through statistical techniques. The nonequivalent control group design used here effectively dispenses with this threat through its comparison of two groups of customers who have volunteered for the same program during adjacent time periods.

The problem of mortality in the experimental group has its counterpart here in those LIEP participants who had to be excluded from analysis either because they moved into homes shortly before the weatherization, or moved out shortly after the weatherization. For these cases there were not enough two-

month billing periods under one owner to permit pre-post comparison. Approximately 10 percent of the controls and 13 percent of the experimentals were discarded for this reason. An examination of the impact of change of ownership on consumption shows that in 50 percent of the cases the level of electricity consumption changed by more than 25 percent with the ownership change. Given this large impact, a comparison of preprogram and postprogram levels regardless of ownership is not possible. These large changes underscore the high level of variability in electricity use among the single-family customers of Seattle City Light.

Table 5 presents preprogram consumption data for the experimental group and for a sample of homes excluded due to ownership

**TABLE 5   The LIEP Experimental Group and Excluded LIEP Cases
Average Preprogram Electricity Use for Four Billing Periods**

Bimonthly Billing Period	1981 Participants Experimental Group	1981 Participants Excluded	t-Tests of Differences Between Groups Two-Tailed
September 1980			
Mean Kwh/2 months	1893	1840	t = 0.29
Std. Error	98	155	p > .50
N	68	20	
November 1980			
Mean Kwh/2 months	3686	3837	t = −0.41
Std. Error	160	336	p > .50
N	113	24	
January 1981			
Mean Kwh/2 months	5195	4870	t = −0.90
Std. Error	155	328	p > .10
N	185	28	
March 1981			
Mean Kwh/2 months	4389	3928	t = 1.55
Std. Error	105	278	p > .10
N	293	25	

changes. The comparison suggests that the excluded cases may have used slightly less electricity than the cases that were included in the analysis. The result of this exclusion may have been to overestimate the average conservation due to the program.

The use of future program participants has limitations for program evaluation that stem from the method's dependence upon constant program guidelines for participation. As the requirements for entry into a program change, the possibility of finding a similar group of future participants disappears.

The design employed in this analysis can only be used when a program operates continuously under relatively unchanging guidelines for a sufficient period to permit the accumulation of large groups for statistical analysis. Even under these conditions, such a design will be difficult to defend if the dependent variables are qualitative, or less well defined than bimonthly electricity consumption. In such cases, it must be defended on theoretical grounds rather than by comparing preprogram characteristics of the experimental and control groups.

REFERENCES

Berry, L. (1981) Review of Evaluations of Utility Home Energy Audit Programs, ORNL/CON-58. Tennessee: Oak Ridge National Laboratory.

Campbell, D. T. and J. C. Stanley (1966) Experimental and Quasi-Experimental Designs for Research. Chicago: Rand McNally.

Hirst, E., E. Broneman, R. Goeltz, J. Trimble, and D. Lerman (1983a) Evaluation of the BPA Residential Weatherization Pilot Program, ORNL/CON-124. Tennessee: Oak Ridge National Laboratory.

Hirst, E., J. Trimble, R. Goeltz, and S. Cardell (1983b) Methods to Deal with Self-Selection in Estimating Conservation Program Energy Savings: Use of Synthetic Data to Test Alternative Approaches, ORNL/CON-120. Tennessee: Oak Ridge National Laboratory.

Newcomb, T. M. (1982) Electricity Conservation Estimates for the Low Income Electric Program. Washington: Seattle City Light Department.

Olsen, M. and C. Cluett (1979) Evaluation of the Seattle City Light Neighborhood Energy Conservation Program. Seattle, WA: Battelle Human Affairs Research Center.

Pease, S. (1982) An Appraisal of Evaluations of Utility-Sponsored Programs for Residential Energy

Conservation, N-1925-DOE. Washington, DC: U.S. Department of Energy.

Weiss, C. (1983) Low Income Electric Program Cost-Effectiveness Analysis. Washington: Seattle City Light.

Weiss, C. and T. M. Newcomb (1982) Home Energy Loan Program Energy Savings Analysis. Washington: Seattle City Light.

Explanation and Critique

Developing an evaluation is an exercise of the dramatic imagination. The art of evaluation involves using the science of evaluation to create a design and gather information that is appropriate for a specific situation and a particular policy-making context. The quasi-experiment with constructed controls provides the researcher with the opportunity to exercise artistic creativity. Tim Newcomb rose to this challenge. "Conservation Program Evaluations: The Control of Self-Selection Bias" is absolutely elegant.

Seattle City Light operates a Low Income Electric Program (LIEP) that offers a free energy audit and free home weatherization to applicants whose total annual household income is less than 90 percent of the median income for the Seattle-Everett Standard Metropolitan Statistical Area. The average 1981 LIEP participant received approximately $1,400 in weatherization materials at no cost. The average cost to Seattle Light for each job was $2,500 including administration and energy audits. The company planned to weatherize 20,000 homes by 1989 through LIEP at a cost of $25 million in 1980 dollars. Given such cost, it was imperative to develop an approach to accurately estimating electricity conservation that could be attributed to the program. How could this be done?

Because the program was voluntary, Newcomb could not use an experimental design and randomly assign low-income utility customers into program and control groups. Furthermore, a comparison of low-income participants with nonparticipants would be inappropriate because simply by volunteering for the program a select group of low-income utility customers showed their concern with utility costs. They thus might be assumed to conserve more in response to the 1980 rate increase than nonvolunteers. The simple pretest-posttest design could not be used because of year-to-year fluctuations in the weather. Nor were time-series data available to allow the estimation of weather and rate hike effects using multiple regression.

Thus, Newcomb was faced with the need to find a comparison group for the study as similar as possible to LIEP participants. Obviously, no true control group was available. He describes his predicament:

> No group of residential customers fitting this description had been selected for analysis prior to the program, and current household income data were not available for any group except participants. Further, since the program is voluntary,

participants almost certainly differ from the average low-income customer in attitudes and education.

Newcomb found his comparison group and overcame the self-selection problem by using as "controls" the group of people who would later sign up for the program. The characteristics of the control group in terms of housing, income, preweatherization electricity use, and so on were proven to be comparable. Most important, the self-selection problem was overcome through Newcomb's unique design. The pretest-posttest control group design used in this study effectively dispensed with the selection threat to validity through its comparison of two groups of customers who volunteered for the same program during adjacent time periods.

Substantively, what did this evaluation show? Newcomb compared the energy consumption of both groups for the before-and-after periods by using the one-tailed t-test. The t-test was used to determine whether the average energy consumption of weatherized residents was different from the average consumption by those not weatherized. Thus Newcomb used a "difference of means" test with the t-statistic to determine whether there was a statistically significant difference between the means. In general, the t-test is an inferential statistic used to determine whether the null hypothesis (that there is no difference) is true. If one is able to reject the null hypothesis, the test or alternate hypothesis (that there is a difference) is accepted. The one-tailed t-test was appropriate in this case because Newcomb's hypothesis was that the experimental group would have *lower* bimonthly electricity consumption rates than the control group. When a direction (lower) is implied in a hypothesis (rather than just "different"), a one-tailed test is dictated.

Newcomb found that there was no significant difference between the energy consumption of the two groups in all the pretest periods. After the homes of the experimental group had been weatherized, however, there was a significant difference in energy consumption between the two groups for four of the five periods. It was only in the warmest months that the difference between the two groups was not significant.

By using this carefully selected comparison group, Newcomb was able to show that the program resulted in a savings of 3,422 kilowatt hours per year for the average participant. The value of the conserved electricity (1981 dollars) amounted to $485 per participant over the 30-year lifetime of the weatherization measures. Given variations in the temperature from winter to winter, Newcomb never could have made these calculations without having a credible comparison group. More simply, because winters are different, the energy consumption of the families participating in the program will vary from year to year so it is not possible to simply compare this year's energy use with last year's.

REFERENCES

1. R. Barker Bausell, *A Practical Guide to Conducting Empirical Research* (New York: Harper & Row, 1986), p. 138.
2. Ronald D. Sylvia, Kenneth J. Meier, and Elizabeth M. Gunn, *Program Planning and Evaluation for the Public Manager* (Monterey, CA.: Brooks/Cole, 1985), p. 99.

7

Interrupted Time-Series
Comparison Group Design

The interrupted time-series comparison group design is a very strong quasi-experimental design. This design examines whether and how an interruption (treatment, program, or whatever) affects a social process and whether the observed effect is different from the process observed in an untreated group or among different types of treatments. The design assumes that data are collected at multiple points before the treatment and at multiple points after the treatment and that the same data are collected for units not treated. The design is schematically shown in Table 7-1, in which "O" is the observation, "t_1" and "t_2" are treatment groups 1 and 2 respectively; "c" is the untreated comparison group; "$t - 1$" and "$t - 2$" are observation times at two points before the treatment, whereas "$t + 1$" and "$t + 2$" are observation times following the treatment; and "X_1" and "X_2" denote two different treatments.

For a design to be an interrupted time-series with comparison group, the comparison group can be an untreated group similar with respect to the treated group on as many variables as possible, or the comparison can be made to similar units receiving a different form of the treatment, or both. (The experimental example in Chapter 15 is one in which comparisons are made between eight different forms of the treatment and a separate *control* group. Chapter 5 distinguishes between 11 treatments and a *control* group.)

This is a strong design because the nature of the time-series design eliminates the bias that results when one makes only one observation of a phenomenon. In other words, when data are collected at only one point, the researcher must determine whether the observation is reflective of the normal trend in the data. Without this assurance, the researcher cannot be sure that the collected data are not reflective of an abnormal high or low fluctuation. The model is strengthened further by the number of observations over time. Models with data collected at four points before and after the treatment are superior to models with two points but inferior to those with 10 observation points before and after the treatment. This is reasonable because the more points of data, the better one can specify the trend—the more certain the researcher is that the observations are reflective of the social process. Consequently, researchers try to assemble as many data points before and after the treatment as possible or as resources will allow.

The type of intervention dictates the type of impact the researcher expects. In other words, the hypothesized impact is driven by theory—that is, knowledge of the form the impact will take. Laura Langbein provides a graphic presentation of

TABLE 7-1   Interrupted Time Series Comparison Group Design

Before			After	
$O_{t1_{t-2}}$	$O_{t1_{t-2}}$	X_1	$O_{t1_{t+1}}$	$O_{t1_{t+2}}$
$O_{t1_{t-2}}$	$O_{t2_{t-1}}$	X_2	$O_{t2_{t+1}}$	$O_{t2_{t+2}}$
$O_{c_{t-2}}$	$O_{c_{t-1}}$		$O_{c_{t+1}}$	$O_{c_{t+2}}$

the different forms the impacts can take in Figure 7-1 from her book, *Discovering Whether Programs Work*.[1] The following is a paraphrased description from her original work.

The patterns shown in Figure 7-1(a) and 7-1(b) indicate that the program has had an immediate and abrupt impact. The treated group in Figure 7-1(a) rises immediately after the treatment, but the untreated group remains basically unchanged. In Figure 7-1(b), both groups continue an upward trend. However, the rapid change in slope for the treated group immediately after the treatment displays the program impact above and beyond that which one would expect through history or maturation. Moreover, the effect is permanent; the treated group's scores remain high in the period following the treatment. Langbein warns that investigators should not expect patterns like these when program impact is hypothesized to be gradual or incremental. Figures 7-1(c) and 7-1(d) suggest a delayed result. When this is the case, researchers should attempt to rule out any changes that occurred subsequent to the treatment that could explain the delayed change. Figure 7-1(e) could indicate a gradual intervention that was effective. Figure 7-1(f) shows a program that only increased the instability of the outcome measure. Thus, the researcher must have in mind the kind of impact he or she is expecting in order to interpret the results of the time-series analysis.

When using time-series analysis, the researcher can plot the outcome measures discretely (as is demonstrated in Figure 7-1) or smooth the curve by using a moving average to plot points. For example, the plotted point at $t - 3$ would be the average of the outcome measures at $t - 2$, $t - 3$, and $t - 4$; the point at $t - 2$ would be the average of $t - 1$, $t - 2$, and $t - 3$. And so on. Physically this removes some abrupt or drastic changes ("noise") caused by spurious events. It captures the trend in the data. The fact that time-series analysis takes account of trends in the data and "noise" make it superior to simple before-and-after designs.[2]

One can assess the impact of an interruption or treatment on a preexisting trend in a number of different ways. Perhaps the easiest is a simple, visual assessment of the data arrayed by year. According to Lawrence Mohr, this technique is most effective in "well-behaved" series—those without a great deal of noise and with visually consistent slopes.[3] Simply, one tries to get an impression of the trend before the treatment and compares that with the posttreatment trend (sometimes referred to as the *transfer function*). Dramatic changes either in the slope or the intercept during the posttest time is indicative of the treatment's effects. It always is a good idea for evaluators to visually assess the relationships in their data to get a feeling for the form of the transfer function.

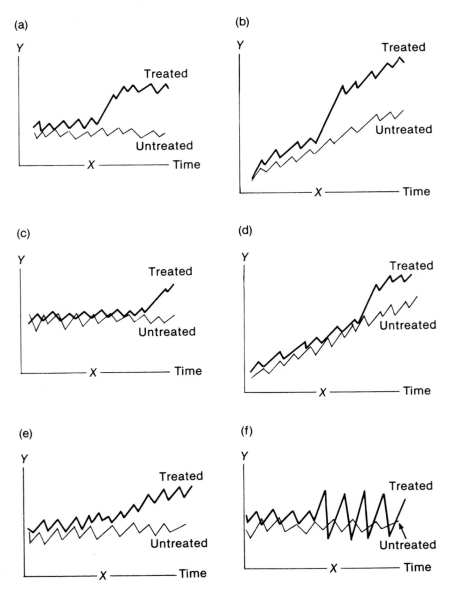

Figure 7–1
Possible Results from ITSCG Design

When there is a great deal of noise, it becomes difficult to assess trends. Unfortunately, social processes seldom exhibit purely linear trends. This problem is confounded by the fact that not all noise is "white noise"—that is, nonrandom disturbances or correlated error terms result in what is called autocorrelation. Autocorrelation violates a fundamental assumption of ordinary least squares regression, that assumption being independent, random errors—among other things. Although violation of this assumption does not bias the regression coefficient (b) over infinite trials, the variance estimates are understated. This not only makes it easier to get a statistically significant result but reduces the confidence that the particular b in a specific equation is accurate. Fortunately, there are ways to control for autocorrelation statistically. For example, the ARIMA procedure accomplishes that.

The recent availability of computer programs that easily compute time-series statistics has increased the number of time-series evaluations. Systematic collection of data on a myriad of topical areas has also assisted in the growth of use. Many of the assumptions and mathematics involved are complex—surely beyond the boundaries of this book. However, it is our intent to afford students the opportunity to be exposed to such analysis so that they can attempt to interpret time-series results. In the following article, Robert Albritton and Tamasak Witayapanyanon use ARIMA (Auto Regressive Integrated Moving Average) modeling to estimate the impact of Medicare and Supplemental Social Security income on health care costs and numbers of recipients. ARIMA models estimate moving averages for different model specifications. Oversimplistically, the procedure combines interpreting different forms of impacts while relying on a moving average technique. It also handles noise from the measures' being correlated over time. In other words, it controls when the value at t + 2 is dependent on the level of t + 1. As a result, only white noise remains, and the transfer function can be accurately estimated.[4] Notice how Albritton and Witayapanyanon question accepted modeling techniques and how they devise a comparison group.

Impacts of SSI:

A Reanalysis of Federal Welfare Policy

ROBERT B. ALBRITTON
TAMASAK WITAYAPANYANON

One of the most significant developments in policy analysis is the growing interest in and attention to time-series data in analyzing outcomes or impacts of public policy decisions. Indeed, use of research designs employing time-series data is no longer novel in policy and other social science research. Increasingly, studies employ serial data in the form of interrupted time-series (Campbell and Stanley, 1966; Cook and Campbell, 1979), in which a series of observations over time is regressed on one or a set of binomially coded or otherwise specified variables to estimate changes in level or direction of that series associated with a specific policy intervention. Properly conceptualized and applied, this design is effective for estimating policy and other impacts in a variety of permutations and, in

Source: Original article written for this book. Printed with permission of the authors.

the case of policy analysis, for answering a basic question: Does a change in policy produce a corresponding change in policy results?

Its increased use notwithstanding, there are problems peculiar to time-series analysis that are by now familiar to most researchers. Among the most important of these is the potential statistical dependence of observations. In many time-series, such dependence can constitute a significant source of difficulty in testing hypotheses that particular policies have or have not been effective. Box, Jenkins, Tiao, and others have addressed this issue by modeling time-series as autoregressive integrated moving averages processes (ARIMA), which provides statistical corrections to control for nonstationarity and the presence of autoregressive or moving averages components biasing the analysis (Box and Jenkins, 1976; Box and Tiao, 1975). These statistical corrections substantially increase the utility of serial data by controlling for plausible rival hypotheses as explanations of research results.

The availability of computer packages offering easy solutions to these statistical problems tends to draw attention away from many other factors that work to pose plausible alternative interpretations of observed effects. Perhaps one reason for neglect of these issues, at least with regard to policy analysis (in which such methods are most commonly employed), is that studies typically concentrate on unique time-series or on effects associated with a unique policy shift. Given this emphasis, the analyst using interrupted time-series techniques tends to be preoccupied with problems of measuring changes in a specifically selected series. Problems of other plausible threats to the conclusions are seldom addressed as a part of the policy analytic process.

One problem characteristic of policy applications of interrupted time-series designs is attenuation of the posttest series. When the analysis is based on yearly data, such problems are unavoidable unless researchers are prepared to wait indefinitely before impacts of policy innovations are determined. Still, if researchers undertake the analysis, conclusions as to more fundamental changes in the data, particularly sustained impacts of a policy initiative, lie beyond reach of the data. Perhaps even more important, there is always nagging doubt as to whether the analysis correctly models intervention effects in conjunction with the intervention, in which case observed impacts might be spurious or erroneously measured as occurring at all.

A case in point is the article by Albritton (1979) showing that executive and legislative decision making leading to the Supplemental Security Income program (SSI) represented a significant shift in policy toward the poor. This analysis lends support to suggestions such as Kenneth Bowler's that SSI represented "radical" change in welfare policy leading to "substantially expand(ed) costs and recipients of federal cash welfare benefits" (Bowler, 1974, p. 167). An important implication is the establishment of linkages between conceptual shifts in policy and subsequent outputs. If outputs do not vary as a result of so-called conceptual or technical changes or if there is sizable disparity between intended and actual consequences, can a case be made that significant policy change has taken place? Reliance on professed policy intentions, as President Reagan's disavowal of negotiations with hostage takers should illustrate, leaves a society vulnerable to deception by what Murray Edelman calls the "symbolic uses of politics" (1967). According to this logic, hypothesized qualitative shifts in policy structures should be linked to corresponding quantitative changes in indicators of outputs or outcomes.

In this discussion, we replicate the Albritton analysis by extending the time period an additional 10 years (1976 to 1986). Extension of the data permits not only a reanalysis of the findings but the ability to model the posttest series sufficiently to test for long-term effects. We exploit this advantage in the present work by modeling the transfer function as outlined by Cook and Campbell (1979, pp. 261-293). The results provide important new evidence on impacts of SSI and implications as to the course of welfare policy in the United States beyond the original Albritton analysis.

MEASURING IMPACTS OF SSI: APPLICATIONS OF THE ARIMA MODEL

Hypotheses tested here suggest that implementation of the Supplemental Security Income program in 1974 resulted in expanded coverage and increased participation of aged, blind, and disabled persons as well as in significant advances in benefits arising from the national minimum income guarantee for persons qualifying under SSI (Burke and Burke, 1974, p. 194). When the ARIMA model is applied to time-series representing outputs of this innovation in welfare policy (numbers of recipients and average monthly payments per recipient) for each SSI category, estimates of change in each series associated with SSI implementation should show "significant" changes in these indicators associated with antecedent legislative and executive decision making (Albritton, 1979, pp. 562-563). For purposes of this analysis, time-series data on numbers of recipients and average monthly payments per recipient (in constant 1967 dollars) are examined for selected SSI categories.

Albritton's analysis indicated significant increases in numbers of recipients and average monthly grants in all categories of SSI except numbers of blind recipients (Albritton, 1979). Blindness is a clearly identifiable disability and blind persons are often successful in obtaining and holding employment, so there was and is now no large pool of eligible blind persons not already on welfare rolls. This group is excluded from the present anal-

ysis in order to focus on the elderly and disabled poor, those identified as benefiting most from the SSI policy initiative.

In most respects, treatment of the data approximate the 1979 study. The yearly average monthly payments per recipient are just that, yearly averages, not the average December payments more readily available in standard data sources. In addition, the payments data include state-administered supplementation. Average monthly expenditures per year for transfer payments in each category are divided by average monthly number of recipients in each category to obtain the average monthly payment.

The most important difference is the inclusion of an additional 10 years in the posttest data series. Representing the period 1937 to 1986, this treatment offers 37 pretest and 13 posttest observations in contrast with 37 pretest and 3 posttest observations of the 1979 study of impacts on the elderly; the series reflecting policy toward the disabled, which is based on the period 1952 to 1986, provides 22 pretest and 13 posttest observations compared with 22 pretest and 3 posttest observations in the previous study.

The extended time-series allows several important additions to the analysis. First, it provides information on long-term effects so that policy conclusions are not limited to generalizations based on temporary fluctuations. Second, it accommodates the posttest series as part of the modeling process so that the analyst is not limited to the assumptions of the 1979 study that the posttest series structure conforms to the pretest model. Finally, it furthers modeling the intervention process and simultaneous estimation of all parameters—that is, ARMA identification and estimation are performed simultaneously with the estimate of the intervention parameter.

A procedure for testing hypotheses modeling the intervention is suggested by Cook and Campbell (1979, pp. 261-293). The alternatives for modeling the intervention when actual effects are unknown suggest choices among models specifying (1) continuous effects in the form of abrupt, permanent change; (2) continuous effects in the form of gradual, permanent change; or (3) discontinuous effects in the form of abrupt, temporary change (Cook and Campbell, 1979, pp. 208–209). Because of the attenuated posttest series, the 1979 analysis assumed an abrupt, permanent change by necessity. Yet, if the extended series indicates an abrupt, temporary change, for example, conclusions as to the impact of SSI require considerable modification.

Importance of the more extended analy-

sis is evident in Figures 1 and 2. All series show sharp shifts associated contemporaneously with or immediately after SSI implementation. This shift is, essentially, what is measured in the 1979 study. The extended posttest series, however, poses a variety of interpretations. Caseloads among the elderly seem to drop sharply after an initial rise following the intervention. Both grants series imply temporary, abrupt increases followed by a return close to a normal trend. Only the number of disabled recipients seems to approximate the abrupt, permanent change assumed in the earlier study.

Following Cook and Campbell, hypoth-

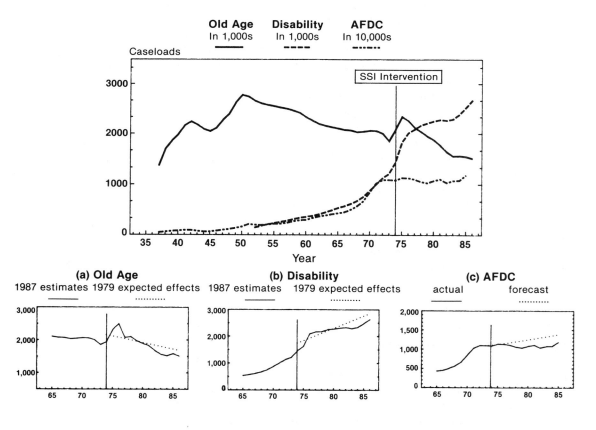

Figure 1
Average Monthly Caseloads, 1937–1986

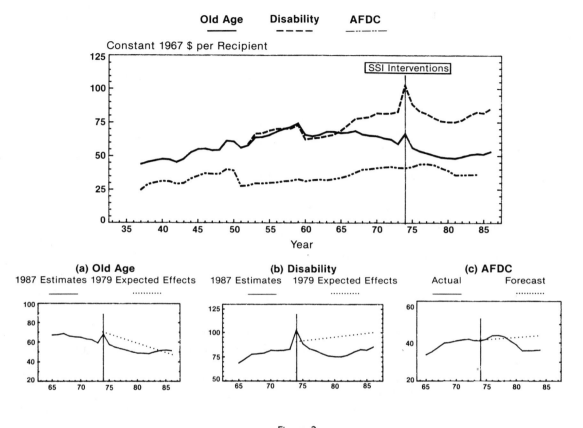

Figure 2
Average Monthly Payments, 1937–1986

eses of the impact of SSI on recipient levels and average monthly payments per recipient will be tested by modeling the intervention in two steps.

Step One

Modeling the transfer function or intervention as an abrupt, temporary impact is the first step, and it is accomplished by expressing the intervention as a pulse function coded 1 in the intervention year and 0 for all other years. In addition, a rate of change function, the lagged endogenous variable, is included in the equation as a test of the continuity of

intervention effects (δ). If the coefficient (δ) is large, this is taken as evidence of a permanent effect. If, by contrast, the coefficient is small, the analyst takes this as evidence that the effect is temporary and abrupt. The equation is expressed as follows:

$$y_t = \delta\, y_{t+-1} + \omega I$$

If δ turns out to be small or nonsignificant, an abrupt, temporary model is assumed and the intervention function is expressed as a pulse function.

Step Two

If δ turns out to be significant or large, the second step is to posit a permanent effect. This is accomplished by specifying the transfer function coded 1 for the intervention and subsequent years and 0 during the pretest period. In this case, the effect is interpreted as abrupt and permanent when the ω is significant. If the delta is also significant, it indicates an asymtotic increase in level beyond the step function. If the intervention function is significant but the δ is absent, the intervention effect is inferred to be abrupt and constant—a step-level change in the time series (Box and Tiao, p. 72).

Figure 3 presents eight recognizable specifications of the intervention function. Models a, b, c, d, e, and h represent abrupt effects of either a temporary or permanent type. The other models suggest nonabrupt intervention effects. These models include those identified in the succeeding analysis.

Table 1 presents the specified intervention functions based on ARIMA identifications and parameter estimations for the four series of output indicators analyzed in this study in comparison with Albritton's 1979 findings. One important outcome of the intervention modeling process is that the posttest series conform to widely differing specifications. In other words, they are not all consistent with Albritton's conclusion of step-level impacts of the SSI policy innovation. This finding alone requires some reinterpretation of the original analysis.

Another interesting outcome is that the two series representing numbers of elderly recipients and payments to the elderly are close to identifications of the 1979 study in the ARIMA estimates. The series associated with the disabled, by contrast, turn out to be considerably simpler models in the extended series. The more complex moving average components of the earlier study give way to simple $(1, 1, 0)$ and $(0, 1, 0)$ models with the

addition of 10 time points to the posttest series. The indication is that the shorter series used in the 1979 analysis were probably misidentified, not a surprising finding in view of the extremely limited number of time points in the previous study.

SUBSTANTIVE FINDINGS: EFFECTS OF THE SUPPLEMENTAL SECURITY INCOME PROGRAM

Estimation of changes in the time-series associated with enactment and implementation of SSI under new identifications and intervention function specifications produces results at some variance with the earlier analysis. When the longer time period is analyzed, estimates of the number of additions to the elderly caseload rise from somewhat over 163,000 to over 220,000 (Table 1). In addition, the delta function indicates that despite a visual decline in the indicator (Figure 1), the gap between current levels and what would have resulted from previous trends is not only continuous but probably widening. The reanalysis indicates an intervention specification close to that of model f in Figure 3. The larger omega (ω) and strong delta (δ) imply that the earlier study substantially underestimated SSI impacts in bringing elderly persons who were not receiving assistance under federal welfare programs onto assistance rolls.

The differences in evaluating the time-series for numbers of disabled are important as well. Although the step-change, or change in level associated with SSI, declines from 349,000 to 164,000 persons, the delta (δ) function indicates a strong upward trend in increasing caseloads subsequent to the program's onset. The difference in level is a significant one. However, the 1979 analysis was not sensitive to the profound change in slope during the posttest period. Accordingly, the entire change was measured as a step function. A better fit of the model implies an inter-

Policy effective at t = 0

(a) An Abrupt Discontinuous Effect

Pulse Function (P_t) where

$I = 1$ for $t = 0$

$I = 0$ otherwise

$I = P_t$

$\delta = 0$

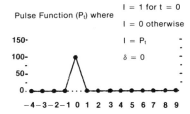

(b) An Abrupt Temporary Effect

$I = P_t$

$0 < \delta < +1$

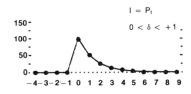

(c) An Abrupt Discontinuous Impact with a Residual Effect

$I = P_t + s_t$

$\delta = 0$

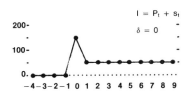

(d) An Abrupt Temporary Impact with a Residual Effect

$0 < \delta < +1$ for P_t

$I = P_t + s_t$

$\delta = 0$ for s_t

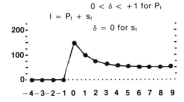

(e) An Abrupt Permanent Effect

Step Function (s_t) where

$I = 1$ for $t >= 0$

$I = 0$ for $t < 0$

$I = s_t$

$\delta = 0$

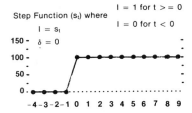

(f) A Gradual Permanent Effect

$I = s_t$

$0 < \delta < +1$

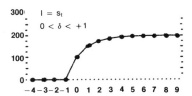

(g) A Constant Cumulative (Slope) Effect

Rump Function (R_t) where

$I = 0$ for $t < 0$

$I = 1.2.3.....n + 1$

for $t = 0.1.2.....n$

$I = R_t$

$\delta = 0$

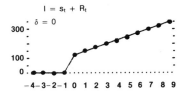

(h) An Abrupt Continuous and Cumulative Effect

$I = s_t + R_t$

$\delta = 0$

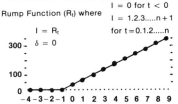

Adapted from Box and Tiao (1975: 75); Cook and Campbell (1979: 208–9).

Figure 3

A General Class of Intervention Analytic Models for Evaluation of Policy Impact on Posttreatment Outcomes of Time-Series

TABLE I Impacts of the Supplemental Security Income Program on Numbers of Recipients and Average Monthly Payments (Comparisons with 1979 Study in Parentheses)

Indicator	ARIMA Identification (p, d, q)	Autoregressive[b] Component ϕ	Moving Averages[b] Component θ	Intervention Specification	Intervention Coefficient ω	Rate of Change Coefficient δ	R^2
Old Age Assistance:							
Number of Aged Recipients	1, 1, 1	.41	−.69	Step & Delta	221.49[a]	.62[a]	.97
(1979 Study)	(1, 1, 1)	(.51)	(−.65)	(Step)	(163.5[a])	—	(.95)
Average Monthly Payments to Aged	0, 1, 1	—	−.32	Pulse & Delta	10.01[a]	.11	.92
Recipients (1979 Study)	(0, 1, 1)	—	(−.69)	(Step)	(15.2[a])	—	(.95)
Aid to the Permanently and Totally Disabled:							
Number of Disabled Recipients	1, 1, 0	.56	—	Step & Delta	164.27[a]	.77[a]	.99
(1979 Study)	(1, 1, 2)	(.88)	(−.46) (−.54)	(Step)	(349.3[a])	—	(.98)
Average Montly Payments to Disabled	0, 1, 0	—	—	Pulse & Delta	20.62[a]	.35[a]	.90
Recipients (1979 Study)	(0, 1, 1)	—	(−.56)	(Step)	(8.4[a])	—	(.91)

[a] $p < .05$

[b] Coefficients of ϕ and θ are significantly different from zero and within the invertibility-stationarity criteria. The analysis results in a white noise process in the residuals for all indicators.

vention function specification also similar to model *f* in Figure 3, a significant shift upward in the level of disabled persons receiving assistance under the federal program and a significant rate of increase in subsequent years bringing persons onto the rolls, reflective of greater use of welfare and entitlement programs to meet needs of the disabled poor.

Major differences from the previous analysis identified in this study are in the average monthly amounts paid out in transfer payments for both the elderly and the disabled. The longer time period indicates a decline in the original estimated increase from $15 a month to only $10 for elderly SSI recipients. In addition, specification of the transfer function implies an abrupt, unsustained increase as in model *a* of Figure 3, because the delta (δ) function is not significantly different from zero. The estimate of average monthly payments to the disabled indicates an increase over the previous finding from $8.40 per month to more than $20 per month. Unfortunately, the specification of an abrupt, temporary phenomenon also obtains for this series as a pulse function plus a modest level of delta (model *b* of Figure 3), indicating a relatively rapid decline in increasing payments associated with the intervention.

In summary, reanalysis indicates confirmation of the general thrust of previous findings that SSI resulted in substantively significant increases in numbers of persons receiving benefits in both old age and disability categories. Measurement of impacts on average monthly payments, however, indicates that significant increases paid out in transfer payments were short-lived.

There are confounding effects that might account for the attentuation in benefits increases. Enactment in 1978 and subsequent implementation of cost-of-living allowances for Social Security recipients may represent a discounting of reliance on SSI for assistance. Such a policy shift could easily account for the

observation of temporary increases in SSI payments, yet this possibility extends beyond the scope of this analysis.

TEST OF AN ALTERNATIVE HYPOTHESIS: A COMPARISON GROUP

Results of such quasi-experimental analysis are always open to rival explanations. Were significant increases in the series of indicators actually due to experimental intervention or to other factors influencing not only the observed series but other variables as well? Failure to consider and eliminate systematically alternative explanations of observed impacts undermines confidence that changes in a time-series are linked to an experimental treatment in a direct causal sense.

As in the previous study, the most plausible rival explanations would have a similar impact on other welfare programs. Were there economic or social conditions coinciding with the advent of SSI that stimulated significant changes in number of persons seeking and obtaining welfare assistance independently of SSI effects? Was there a general liberalizing of public sentiment regarding welfare recipients so that all categories of welfare expanded dramatically in response to needs of the poor?

Failure of the Congress in 1972 to provide federally guaranteed cash assistance to families offers one means of testing such rival hypotheses by examining the course of policy toward welfare recipients not covered by SSI. With younger, able-bodied heads of households, economic fluctuations should have even more dramatic effects on the Aid to Families with Dependent Children (AFDC) program. Likewise, any general outpouring of support for the plight of welfare recipients apart from categories covered under SSI should be reflected in similar abrupt discontinuities in time-series of AFDC indicators similar to those observed for SSI recipients in Table 1.

Applications of the ARIMA model and estimation of intervention effects on indicators of welfare policy for the Aid to Families with Dependent Children program tests the rival hypothesis that observed changes in welfare policy associated with the advent of SSI may be explained by coincident phenomena having a bearing on all welfare programs. Table 2 shows that there are no corresponding increases in AFDC indicators that would support the rival hypothesis of more ubiquitous effects. As in the previous analysis, the series show *declines* rather than increases. Unlike the earlier study, such declines are not statistically significant. Still, the estimation strongly implies that whatever caused rises in SSI indicators is not a factor in the AFDC welfare policy area. The evidence reinforces the view that changes observed in SSI programs are a result of policy changes associated with that program alone and that the 1972 decision to exclude families from federal welfare reform resulted in lasting differences in treatment of this category of welfare recipients from treatment of the so-called "deserving poor," those dependents now covered by Supplemental Security Income.

CONCLUSIONS

Results of this study generally support earlier findings that executive and legislative decisions resulting in enactment and implementation of the Supplemental Security Income program produced substantial changes in numbers of persons having access to federal assistance and in average monthly transfer payments for aged and disabled persons. Addition of 10 time points to all series, however, shows that payments effects are temporary rather than constant as the previous study assumed. The difference in the payments series from that of the numbers of recipients may well be a function of subsequent changes in related programs that have the effect of reducing reliance on SSI payments. In this case, the original findings would be accurate as a description of short-term effects. The ability to examine longer-term consequences, however, indicates the extent to which changes in important factors such as model identification affect the analysis.

From a methodological perspective, even more important implications derive from the ability to model the intervention effect. In the case of SSI, the question of whether effects are temporary or permanent is a crucial substantive issue. The fact that this dimension is not possible to measure in a short posttest series requires reanalysis of the data after an appropriate interval. Not only does it answer questions concerning validity of the previous analysis; it also opens new issues for consideration and study. Among the most obvious of these is the impact of cost-of-living allowances in Social Security on the burden of SSI payments.

Finally, the analysis indicates several points at which qualitative analysis of policy effects fails to present an accurate picture of what is occurring in the policy arena. An intuitive analysis of Figure 1, for example, would indicate significant declines from initial levels of elderly recipients below those before enactment of SSI. The methodology of interrupted time-series suggested here indicates that despite overall declines, the level of program coverage is significantly and constantly higher than federal income support for the elderly would have been without SSI. Many, if not most, policies promise significant quantitative changes that can be evaluated by this means, and effective evaluation of public policy provides information and knowledge necessary for individuals as well as societies to choose among alternative future paths.

TABLE 2 Association of Aid to Families with Dependent Children Program with Implementation of the Supplemental Security Income Program (Comparisons with 1979 Study in Parentheses)

Indicator	ARIMA Identification (p, d, q)	Autoregressive[b] Component ϕ	Moving Averages[b] Component θ	Intervention Specification	Intervention Coefficient ω	R^2
Aid to Families with Dependent Children:						
Number of Recipients	1, 1, 0	.61	—	Step	−330.25	.99
(1979 Study)	(1, 1, 1)	(.72)	(− .67)	(Step)	(−408.91[a])	(.39)
Average Monthly Payments	0, 1, 0	—	—	Step	−0.39	.80
(1979 Study)	(0, 1, 0)	—	—	(Step)	(−0.18)	(.84)

[a] $p < .05$

[b] Coefficients of ϕ and θ are significantly different from zero and within the invertibility-stationarity criteria. The analysis results in a white noise process in the residuals for all indicators.

REFERENCES

Albritton, Robert B., "Measuring Public Policy: Impacts of the Supplemental Security Income Program," *American Journal of Political Science* 23, no. 3 (1979): 560-578.

Bowler, M. Kenneth. *The Nixon Guaranteed Income Proposal: Substance and Process in Policy Change* (Cambridge, MA: Ballinger, 1974).

Box, G. E. P., and Gwilym M. Jenkins. *Time Series Analysis: Forecasting and Control* (San Francisco: Holden-Day, 1976).

Box, G. E. P., and G. C. Tiao. "Intervention Analysis with Applications to Economic and Environmental Problems," *Journal of the American Statistical Association* 70 (March 1975): 70-79.

Burke, Vincent J., and Vee Burke. *Nixon's Good Deed: Welfare Reform* (New York: Columbia University Press, 1974).

Campbell, Donald T., and Julian C. Stanley. *Experimental and Quasi-Experimental Designs for Research* (Boston: Houghton-Mifflin, 1963).

Cook, Thomas D., and Donald T. Campbell. *Quasi-Experimentation: Design and Analysis for Field Settings* (Geneva, IL: Houghton-Mifflin, 1979).

Edelman, Murray C. *The Symbolic Uses of Politics* (Urbana: University of Illinois, 1967).

Explanation and Critique

Albritton and Witayapanyanon have provided a clearly written description of what would otherwise be a complicated analysis. They performed a reanalysis of the work Albritton published in 1979. In 1979, Albritton had data on 37 pretest points and three posttest points that he used to estimate the impact of the institution of the Supplemental Security Income (SSI) program, which provides a national income floor for aged, blind, and disabled Americans. Basically, he found that the SSI had an immediate, nonincremental effect in important aspects of welfare policy. Refer to the 1979 article for the conceptual framework for the analysis.

The reanalysis is justified on a number of accounts. First, apparently Albritton had a nagging doubt as to the form of the impact the post program had in the initial study because he relied on only three post-program points. The initial study suggested a long-term impact at a level much higher than the preprogram estimates would predict. This does not mean that the initial analysis was flawed. It is often important to measure programmatic impact shortly after the institution of a new program to provide data to decision makers to enable them to make future funding decisions. However, as Albritton and Witayapanyanon point out, it is often reasonable to reanalyze (or reestimate) the impacts in view of the passage of time. As discussed in our introduction, it is always preferable to have more data points than fewer when using a time-series design. Also, the new data allow the evaluators to test for the long-term effects of the policy.

Notice that Albritton and Witayapanyanon used a measure of yearly average monthly payments in constant 1967 dollars. The time aspect controls for variations and seasonality associated with income conditions in December—when data like these are typically collected. The 1967 dollar controls for inflation, allowing the researchers to compare dollars received across years.

The impact of the different analyses is displayed in the article's illustrations. Figures 1 and 2 plot the actual pre- and post-program data points. Figures 1 and

2 show the actual preprogram points and the post-program estimates using 3 post-program points (the 1979 estimates) and the 10 post-program points (the 1987 analysis). The area between the post-program line estimates shows the difference in projections based on 3 and 10 points. Clearly, the long-term trend anticipated in 1987 is not as dramatic as the 1979 estimates suggested. Nonetheless, the impact of SSI is still measurable.

Reexamine Figures 1 and 2 of the article. Visually assess the preprogram trends, and plot the expected post-program trends that you would have expected had there been no interruption. Compare your findings (expectations regarding the values on the Y axis) with the values given in the tables. To the extent that your visual assessment controls for noise and matches the table values, you have visually performed an ARIMA analysis.

The explanation of the coefficients in the tables is clearly described by Albritton and Witayapanyanon, relying on the interpretation of Cook and Campbell. The substantive explanations are apparent in the tables and figures. Although the thrust of the 1979 findings was confirmed, the analysis shows that the burst in increased benefits paid was short-lived.

In the initial portion of the analysis, the aged and disabled programs are compared, using as a comparison group another form of treatment. In their search for other plausible explanations for the findings, Albritton and Witayapanyanon use a comparison group of welfare recipients (those receiving AFDC) to test rival hypotheses that there could possibly be other economic or social conditions that affect the number of persons receiving assistance. They wanted to know if changes in program indicators for aged and disabled poor were a result of policy change or were antecedent effects.

Using the same ARIMA model, they found the results in Table 2 and Figures 1 and 2. Because there were no corresponding increases in AFDC indicators over this period, they ruled out the rival hypothesis that spurious factors were present in all welfare programs.

This article is important in that it demonstrates the value of reanalysis of time-series findings and the impact of estimating on the basis of fewer than optimal post-program data points. Although the estimate of the short-term impacts was valid in the 1979 study, the study reprinted here demonstrates the impact in the long term which may or, as in this case, may not be identical. Again, it is important to have a theoretical understanding of the form of impact that is expected in order to choose the best modeling technique. Although the availability of computerized time-series analysis packages has increased, Albritton and Witayapanyanon demonstrate that an evaluator should be cognizant of the form before using the default statistics from the computer package.

REFERENCES

1. Laura Irwin Langbein, *Discovering Whether Programs Work: A Guide to Statistical Methods for Program Evaluation*, (Glenview, IL: Scott, Foresman, 1980), p. 91.

2. "Noise" refers to departures from the underlying trend—that of fluctuations above or below the trend line. Errors which are completely random (e.g., as opposed to systematic errors in measurement or due to historical effects), are referred to as "white noise".

3. Lawrence B. Mohr, *Impact Assessment for Program Evaluation* (Chicago: Dorsey Press, 1988), pp. 155-156.

4. In ordinary least squares regression noise is reduced by the addition of control variables. In ARIMA the past values of the series variable and of the error terms function as independent or control variables. For a full description of this technique, see Gene V. Glass, V. L. Wilson, and J. M. Gottman, *Design and Analysis of Time-Series Experiments* (Boulder, CO: Associated University Press, 1975).

8

Regression-Discontinuity Design

The regression-discontinuity design is a quasi-experimental design with limited applicability.[1] However, in those cases for which the design is appropriate, it is a very strong method used to determine program performance. Two criteria must be met for the use of the regression-discontinuity design:

1. The distinction between treated and untreated groups must be clear and based on a quantifiable eligibility criterion.
2. Both the eligibility criterion and the performance or impact measure must be interval level variables.[2]

These criteria are often met in programs that use measures such as family income or a combination of income/family size to determine program eligibility. Examples of these include income maintenance, rent subsidy, nutritional and maternal health programs, or even in some cases more aggregate programs such as the Urban Development Action Grants. The U.S. Department of Housing and Urban Development's Urban Development Action Grants' (UDAG) eligibility criteria consisted of a summated scale of indexes of urban distress. This scale approximates an interval scale and determined a city's ranking for eligibility. For a regression-discontinuity analysis, one would array the units of analysis (cities) by their UDAG scores on the X axis and cut the distribution at the point where cities were funded (impact), and then plot a development score of some kind on the Y axis. See the following example for further explanation. Donald Campbell and Julian Stanley caution that these eligibility cutting points need to be clearly and cleanly applied for maximum effectiveness of the design.[3] Campbell refers to the unclear cut points as "fuzzy cut points."[4]

In the regression-discontinuity design the performance of eligible program participants is compared to that of untreated ineligibles. The example in Figure 8-1 from Laura Langbein depicts a regression-discontinuity design assessing the impact of an interest credit program of the Farmer's Home Administration on the market value of homes by income level.[5] Figure 8-1 shows that the income eligibility cut-off for the interest credit program is $10,000. Because income is an interval variable and it is assumed that the eligibility criterion is consistently upheld, the program's impact is measured as the difference in home market value at the cut-off point. For the program to be judged successful, estimated home values for those earning $9,999 should be statistically significantly higher than for those with incomes of $10,001.

Market Value of Home

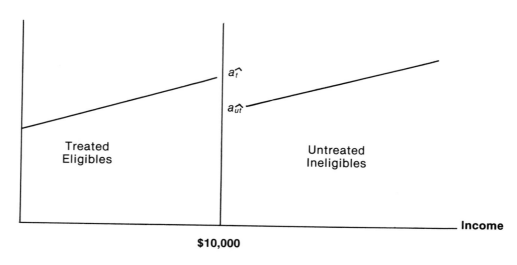

Figure 8–1

Regression-Discontinuity Design: The Impact of Subsidized Interest Credit on Home Values

To perform the analysis, two regression lines must be estimated—one for the treated eligibles and the other for the untreated ineligibles. For each, the market values of the home (Y) is regressed on income (X). Although it is intuitively pleasing in this example that both lines are upward sloping (i.e., that market value increases with income), the measure of program impact is at the intercepts (a) of the regression lines. If the difference between a_t ("a" for treated eligibles) and a_{ut} ("a" for untreated ineligibles) is statistically significant, then the program is successful. If not, the program is ineffective (the "a"s were the same) or dysfunctional (a_{ut} was statistically significantly different from a_t and higher than a_t).

Langbein describes the rationale of the design as follows:

> It assumes that subjects just above and just below the eligibility cut point are equivalent on all potentially spurious and confounding variables and differ only in respect to the treatment. According to this logic, if the treated just-eligibles have homes whose value exceeds those of the untreated just-ineligibles, then the treatment should be considered effective. The linear nature of the regression makes it possible to extrapolate these results to the rest of the treated and untreated groups.[6]

Thus, the design controls for possible threats to internal validity by assuming that people with incomes of $9,999 are similar in many respects to those who earn $10,001.

Several cautions are advanced to those considering using this design. First, if the eligibility cut-off for the program in question is the same as that for other programs, multiple treatment effects should be considered so as not to make the results ambiguous. Second, the effects of self-selection (Chapter 20) or volunteerism among eligibles should be estimated. Langbein suggests that a nested experiment within the design can eliminate this threat to internal validity.[7] Third, when people with the same eligibility are on both sides of the cut point line, a fuzzy cut point has been used. If the number of such misclassifications is small, the people in the fuzzy gap can be eliminated. However, one should use this technique cautiously. The further apart on the eligibility criterion the units are, the less one is confident that the treated and untreateds are comparable. A variation of a fuzzy cut point occurs when ineligibles "fudge" their scores on the eligibility criterion. This nonrandom measurement error is a threat to the validity of the design. These effects should be minimized (by careful screening) and at least estimated. Fourth, because regression is a linear statistic, a visual examination of the bivariate distributions ensures that nonlinear trends are not being masked. An associated caution is that one should remember that the program's effect is being measured at only a relatively small band of eligibility/ineligibility; consequently, a visual inspection of overall trends seems reasonable for one's claiming programmatic impact.

The following article, "Regression-Discontinuity Analysis: An Alternative to the Ex Post Facto Experiment," provides an overview of the replication of Thistlethwaite's earlier work using what the authors argue to be a more appropriate design.

Regression-Discontinuity Analysis:

An Alternative to the Ex Post Facto Experiment[1]

DONALD L. THISTLETHWAITE
DONALD T. CAMPBELL

While the term "ex post facto experiment" could refer to any analysis of records which provides a quasi-experimental test of a causal hypothesis, as described by Chapin (1938) and Greenwood (1945), it has come to indicate more specifically the mode of analysis in which two groups—an experimental and a control group—are selected through *matching* to yield a quasi-experimental comparison. In such studies the groups are presumed, as a result of matching, to have been equivalent prior to the exposure of the experimental group to some potentially change inducing event (the "experimental treatment"). If the groups differ on subsequent measures and if there are no plausible rival hypotheses which might account for the differences, it is inferred that the experimental treatment has caused the observed differences.

This paper has three purposes: first, it

Source: "Regression-Discontinuity Analysis: An Alternative to the Ex Post Facto Experiment," Donald L. Thistlethwaite and Donald T. Campbell. JOURNAL OF EDUCATIONAL PSYCHOLOGY, Vol. 51, No. 6, December 1960. "In the Public Domain."

presents an alternative mode of analysis, called regression-discontinuity analysis, which we believe can be more confidently interpreted than the ex post facto design; second, it compares the results obtained when both modes of analysis are applied to the same data; and, third, it qualifies interpretations of the ex post facto study recently reported in this journal (Thistlethwaite, 1959).

Two groups of near-winners in a national scholarship competition were matched on several background variables in the 1959 Thistlethwaite study in order to study the motivational effect of public recognition. The results suggested that such recognition tends to increase the favorableness of attitudes toward intellectualism, the number of students planning to seek the MD or PhD degree, the number planning to become college teachers or scientific researchers, and the number who succeed in obtaining scholarships from other scholarship granting agencies. The regression-discontinuity analysis to be presented here confirms the effects upon success in winning scholarships from other donors but negates the inference of effects upon attitudes and is equivocal regarding career plans.

METHOD

Subjects and Data[2]

Two groups of near-winners—5,126 students who received Certificates of Merit and 2,848 students who merely received letters of commendation—answered a questionnaire approximately 6 months after the announcement of awards in the second National Merit Scholarship program. The C of M group received greater public recognition: their names were published in a booklet distributed to colleges, universities, and other scholarship granting agencies and they received approximately two and one-half times more newspaper coverage than commended students. The

decision to award some students the Certificate of Merit, which meant greater public recognition, was made chiefly on the basis of "qualifying scores" on the CEEB Scholarship Qualifying Test (SQT). A second aptitude test, the Scholastic Aptitude Test, was used to confirm the high ability of all finalists, i.e., all students scoring above the SQT qualifying score for the state in which the student attended high school.[3] Two hundred and forty-one students who voluntarily withdrew from the program before the second test or whose scores were not confirmed received neither award while 7,255 students who satisfactorily completed the second test received Certificates of Merit. The latter were subsequently screened by a selection committee and 827 of these students were awarded Merit Scholarships. Since the interest is in estimating the effects of honorary awards, questionnaire responses from Merit Scholars are not included in these analyses. As Table 1 shows, response rate did not vary systematically by test score interval, and there is no reason to believe that differential response bias can account for the effects to be described.

Regression-Discontinuity Analysis

In situations such as the foregoing, where exposure to an experimental treatment (in this case, increased public recognition) is determined by the subject's standing on a single, measured variable, and where the expected effects of the treatment are of much the same nature as would be produced by increasing magnitudes of that variable, examination of the details of the regression may be used to assess experimental effects. The experimental treatment should provide an additional elevation to the regression of dependent variables on the exposure determiner, providing a step-like discontinuity at the cutting score.

The argument—and the limitations on generality of the result—can be made more specific by considering a "true" experiment

TABLE I Participants in 1957 Merit Program Classified by Aptitude Score Interval

Group	Scholarship qualifying test score interval[a] (1)	Number of Merit Scholars excluded (2)	Number in designated sample[b] (3)	Number of respondents (4)	Percentage of designated sample responding (5)	Percentage of C of M winners in each interval awarded Merit Scholarships (6)
Commended students	Below 1		419	322	76.8	
	1		318	256	80.5	
	2		368	281	76.4	
	3		320	258	80.6	
	4		407	338	83.1	
	5		324	259	79.9	
	6		333	267	80.2	
	7		280	213	76.1	
	8		301	248	82.4	
	9		256	201	78.5	
	10		262	205	78.2	
Totals			3,588	2,848	79.4	
Certificate of Merit winners	11	17	476	380	79.8	3.4
	12	22	466	370	79.4	4.5
	13	16	399	319	79.9	3.9
	14	17	371	298	80.3	4.4
	15	19	361	300	83.1	5.0
	16	34	358	289	80.7	8.7
	17	13	319	247	77.4	3.9
	18	18	345	256	74.2	5.0
	19	17	254	211	83.1	6.3
	20	23	301	237	78.7	7.1
	Above 20	631	2,778	2,219	79.9	18.5
Totals		827	6,428	5,126	79.7	11.4

[a]Intervals show the student's SQT score relative to the qualifying score in the student's state (e.g., subjects whose scores equaled the qualifying score are classified in Interval 11, those whose scores were one unit less than the qualifying score are classified in Interval 10, etc.).

[b]The designated sample for commended students consisted of a 47% random sample of all commended students.

131

for which the regression-discontinuity analysis may be regarded as a substitute. It would be both indefensible and infeasible to conduct an experiment in which a random group of students along the whole range of abilities would be given the C of M award while a randomly equivalent group received merely the letter of commendation. However, a group of commended students who narrowly missed receiving the higher award might be given the opportunity of receiving extra recognition. Thus students in Interval 10 in Figure 1 might be randomly assigned to the different treatments of C of M award and no C of M award. The two half-circle points at 10 for Line AA' in Figure 1 illustrate a possible outcome for such a true experiment, the solid half-circle representing the award group, and the hollow half-circle the no award group. Alternatively, a similar true experiment might be carried out among students just above the cutting point (Score 11 in Figure 1). For reasons discussed below, the regression-discontinuity analysis attempts to simulate the latter of these two experiments, by extrapolating from the below-cutting-point line to an "untreated" Point 11 value (an inferred substitute for the no award "control group"). Thus the major evidence of effect must be a distinct discontinuity or difference in intercept at the cutting point. Outcomes such as those shown in Line AA' would, of course, be strictly demonstrated only for aptitude intervals adjacent to the cutting point, and inferences as to effects of the C of M award upon persons of other ability levels would be made in hazard of unexplored interactions of award and ability level. Inferences as to what the regression line would have looked like without the C of M award become more and more suspect the further the no award experience of Points 1 to 10 has to be extrapolated. The extrapolation is best for Point 11 and becomes increasingly implausible for Points 12 through 20.

To better illustrate the argument several hypothetical outcomes are shown in Figure 1.

Line AA' indicates a hypothetical regression of the percentage exhibiting Attribute A as a function of score on the decision variable. The steplike discontinuity which begins at the point where the experimental treatment begins to operate would be convincing evidence that the certificate has had an effect upon Attribute A. Similarly, outcomes such as those shown by Lines BB' and CC' would indicate genuine treatment effects. Line DD' is a pure case of no effect. Lines EE' and FF' are troublesome: there seems to be a definite change in the regression lines, but the steplike discontinuity at the cutting point is lacking. Consequently the points could merely represent continuous, curvilinear regressions. It seems best not to interpret such ambiguous outcomes as evidence of effects.

In applying this mode of analysis to the present data, the qualifying score in each state was used as a fixed point of reference, and students were classified according to the number of score intervals their SQT score fell above or below the qualifying score in *their* state. For example, in Figure 2 all students whose scores equaled the qualifying score in their state have been classified in Interval 11, while all those whose scores were one less than the relevant qualifying score have been classified in Interval 10. Data were analyzed only for subjects whose scores placed them within 10 score intervals of the relevant cutting point. Because of nonresponse to particular questionnaire items the Ns for percentages and means in Figures 2 to 4 differ slightly from those shown in Column 4 of Table 1.

RESULTS

Graphic Presentation of Results

Figures 2, 3, and 4 present the results for five variables, with least squares linear regression lines fitted to the points. In Figure 2, both regression lines for scholarships received seem

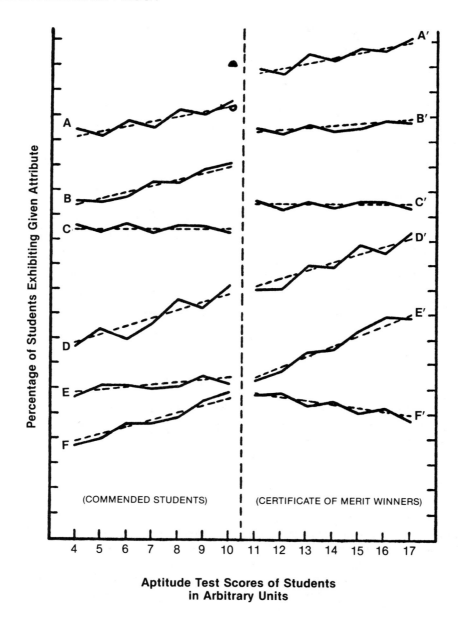

(COMMENDED STUDENTS)   (CERTIFICATE OF MERIT WINNERS)

**Aptitude Test Scores of Students
in Arbitrary Units**

Figure 1
Hypothetical Outcomes of a Regression-Discontinuity Analysis

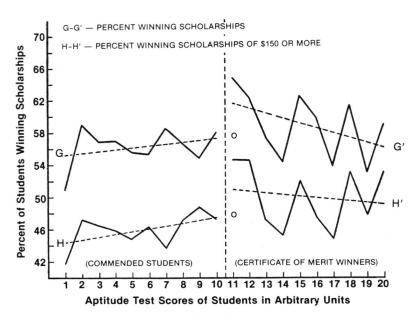

Figure 2
Regression of Success in Winning Scholarships on Exposure Determiner

to show a marked discontinuity at the cutting point. The persuasive appearance of *effect* is, however, weakened by the jaggedness of the regression lines at other points, particularly to the right of the cutting score. In addition, the slopes of the right-hand lines indicate that the effects are specific to students near the cutting score. The downward trend with high scores is presumably a result of eliminating from consideration those receiving Merit Scholarships. Where those of high aptitude test scores are passed over for National Merit Scholarships, it is usually for undistinguished high school grades, which likewise affect the scholarship awards by other agencies as plotted in Figure 2. Table 1 shows that, in general, larger proportions of C of M winners in the highest score intervals were selected for Merit Scholarships.

The two plots in Figure 3 show less discontinuity at the cutting point: there is little or no indication of effect. In II' the difference

between observed values at 10 and 11 is small, and while in the hypothesized direction, is exceeded by five other ascending gaps. In JJ' the observed 10-11 jump is actually in the wrong direction. On the other hand, it is confirming of the hypothesis of effect that *all* of the observed Points 11 through 20 lie above the extrapolated line of best fit for Points 1 to 10, in both II' and JJ'. But this could well be explained by the rival hypothesis of an uninterrupted curvilinear regression from Points 1 to 20. The picture is ambiguous enough to leave us skeptical as to the effects upon the student's study and career plans. The analysis neither confirms nor denies the ex post facto findings.

In Figure 4 no such ambiguity remains. It is inconceivable in view of this evidence that the Certificate of Merit award has increased favorableness of attitudes toward intellectualism, a finding clearly contradicting the ex post facto analysis.

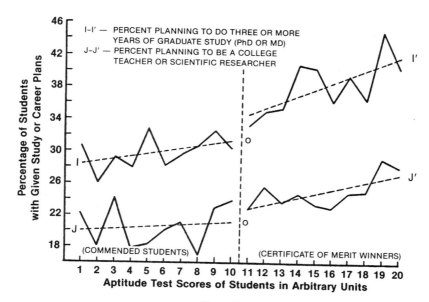

Figure 3

Regression of Study and Career Plans on Exposure Determiner

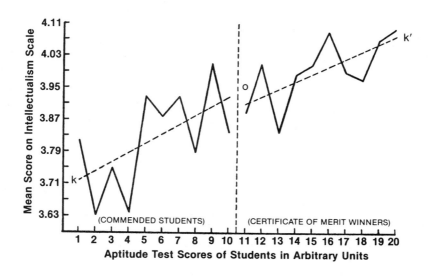

Figure 4

Regression of Attitudes Toward Intellectualism on Exposure Determiner

The Problem of Tests of Significance

In discussing tests of significance in this case, it is probably as important to indicate which tests of significance are ruled out as to indicate those which seem appropriate. Again, reference to the pure cases of Figure 1 will be helpful. A simple t test between Points 10 and 11 is excluded, because it would show significance in an instance like DD' if the overall slope were great enough. That is, such a test ignores the general regression obtained independently of the experimental treatment. Such a test between adjacent points is likewise ruled out on the consideration that even if significant in itself, it is uninterpretable if a part of a very jagged line in which jumps of equal significance occur at numerous other places where *not* expected. Similarly, a t test of the difference between the means of all points on each side of the cutting point would give significance to cases such as DD' or EE', which would be judged irrelevant. Furthermore, covariance tests applied to the regression lines (e.g., Walker & Lev, 1953, pp. 390-395) are judged inappropriate, because of the differential sample bias for the score intervals arising from the exclusion of Merit Scholars. Even in the ideal case, if the hypothesis of common slope is rejected (as it would be for lines such as EE' and FF') we presumably could not proceed further with a simple linear version of the covariance model.

Mood (1950, pp. 297-298) provides a t test appropriate for testing the significance of the deviation of the first experimental value beyond the cutting point (i.e., the observed Point 11) from a value predicted from a linear fit of the control values (i.e., the encircled point in Figures 2, 3, and 4, extrapolated from Point 1 through 10). As applied here, each plotted point has been treated as a single observation. On this basis, both of the plots in Figure 2 show a significant effect at Point 11. For GG', $p < .025$; for HH', $p < .01$ (one-tailed tests). Thus the Certificate of Merit

seems to have significantly increased chances of obtaining scholarships from other sources. For none of the other figures does this test approach significance.

The test in this form fails to make use of the potentially greater stability made available by considering the trend of all of the Values 11 through 20. Potentially the logic of the Mood test could be extended to provide an error term for the difference between two extrapolated points at 10.5, one extrapolated from Points 1 through 10, the other from Points 11 through 20. In many applications of the regression-discontinuity analysis, this would be the most appropriate and most powerful test. In our present instance, we have judged it inappropriate because of the differential sampling bias felt to exist in the range of Points 11-20, as explained above.

DISCUSSION

A critic may easily question the results of an ex post facto experiment by supposing that one or more relevant matching variables has been inadequately controlled or entirely overlooked. In contrast the regression-discontinuity analysis does not rely upon matching to equate experimental and control groups, hence it avoids the difficulties of (a) differential regression-toward-the-mean effects, and (b) incomplete matching due to failure to identify and include all relevant antecedent characteristics in the matching process.

Edwards (1954, pp. 279-282) has shown how pseudo effects may be produced in ex post facto designs through differential regression effects. Suppose, for example, we were to match, with respect to aptitude test scores, a group exposed to recognition and a group not exposed to recognition. Since exposure to recognition tends to be positively correlated with aptitude test score we expect that the matched experimental subjects will have low aptitude scores relative to other exposed subjects, while the matched control subjects will have high aptitude scores relative to other unexposed subjects. To the extent that there are errors of measurement on the aptitude variable, however, our experimental group is apt to contain subjects whose aptitude scores are too low through error, while our control group is apt to contain subjects whose aptitude scores are too high through error. Simply on the basis of regression effects, then, we can predict that the matched experimental group will excel the matched control group on a subsequent administration of the aptitude test and on any other variable positively correlated with aptitude. Following Thorndike (1942, pp. 100-101), who discussed a similar problem, one might attempt to match individuals on the basis of predicted true score on the background trait—i.e., score predicted by the regression equation between original test and a retest at the time of the experimental comparison. However, the predicted true score for each individual must be determined from the regression equation for his own population, and for groups when the special treatment is not applied. Unfortunately such matching is usually impossible in situations where we wish to use the ex post facto design, since we typically cannot obtain pretest and posttest measures on control variables for "experimental" groups from which the special treatment has been withheld. Indeed if we had the power to withhold the treatment from some subjects we would usually be able to test our causal hypotheses by an experiment with true randomization. In short, the suggested procedure for controlling regression effects in ex post facto studies presupposes knowledge which we typically cannot obtain.

In the present analysis exposed and unexposed groups are subdivided according to their closeness to receiving a treatment other than the one they have received. Background traits correlated with the probability of exposure to recognition (e.g., rank in high school

graduating class, scholastic aptitude, etc.) presumably vary systematically with the score intervals which represent the student's nearness to the cutting point. All of these traits contribute to the observed slopes of the regression lines plotted in Figures 2 to 4. Since there is no reason to believe that the composite effect of all relevant background traits fluctuates markedly at the cutting point, regression discontinuities emerging at the 10-11 gap must be attributable to the special experimental treatment—the only factor which assumes an abrupt change in value in this region. Thus the new analysis seems to provide a persuasive test of the presence or absence of experimental effects.[4]

The value of the regression-discontinuity analysis illustrated here is that it provides a more stringent test of causal hypotheses than is provided by the ex post facto design. Admittedly the class of situations to which it is applicable is limited. This class consists of those situations in which the regression of dependent variables on a single determiner of exposure to an experimental treatment can be plotted. Whenever the determiners of exposure are multiple or unknown this mode of analysis is not feasible.

Of the five variables described in Figures 2 to 4 the regression-discontinuity analysis indicated significant effects only for those shown in Figure 2. The ex post facto experiment, on the other hand, indicated significant effects for all variables except HH' (success in winning a freshman scholarship of $150 or more). For six other variables, not reported here, neither analyis indicated a significant effect.[5] Considering the regression-discontinuity analysis to be the more definitive, it appears that the ex post facto experiment underestimated effects for one variable and wrongly indicated effects for three variables.

We conclude that increased public recognition tends to increase the student's chances of winning scholarships. There is no clear-cut evidence in the present analysis that such recognition affects the student's career plans, although an effect upon plans to seek graduate or professional degrees is not ruled out. In this regard, Thistlethwaite (1961) has reported that when near-winners in a subsequent National Merit program were asked, "How did winning a C of M help you?" approximately two out of every five reported that it "increased my desire for advanced training (MA, PhD, MD, etc.)." In short, while other evidence indicates that the hypothesis of effect upon study plans may be correct, the present analysis does not provide confirmation.

SUMMARY

The present report presents and illustrates a method of testing causal hypotheses, called regression-discontinuity analysis, in situations where the investigator is unable to randomly assign subjects to experimental and control groups. It compares the results obtained by the new mode of analysis with those obtained when an ex post facto design was applied to the same data. The new analysis suggested that public recognition for achievement on college aptitude tests tends to increase the likelihood that the recipient will receive a scholarship but did not support the inference that recognition affects the student's attitudes and career plans.

NOTES

1. This study is a part of the research program of the National Merit Scholarship Corporation. This research was supported by the National Science Foundation, the Old Dominion Foundation, and by Ford Foundation grants to the National Merit Scholarship Corporation. The participation of the second author was made possible through the Northwestern University Carnegie Corporation Project in Psychology-Education. The mode of analysis illustrated in

Figure 1 of this paper was first suggested by the second author. . . .

2. Details of the sample of students, the experimental treatment, and dependent variables are described in . . . Thistlethwaite, 1959, and only the essential features of the data collection will be discussed here.

3. Recognition awards in the 1957 Merit program were distributed so that the number of students recognized in each state was proportional to the number of public high school graduates in each state. Since there were marked state differences in student performance on this test, qualifying scores varied from state to state. All SQT scores represented a composite in which verbal scores were weighted twice as heavily as mathematical scores.

4. Background traits uncorrelated with the probability of exposure to recognition will, of course, not vary systematically with score intervals, but these traits are irrelevant. Even if partialed out they would not affect the correlation between the dependent variable and degree of exposure to recognition.

5. No significant differences were found with respect to the percentages enrolling in college immediately, well satisfied with their choice of college, believing their college offers the best training in their field of study, going to college more than 250 miles from home, applying for two or more scholarships, or receiving encouragement from their high school teachers and guidance counselors to go to college.

REFERENCES

Chapin, F. S. Design for social experiments, *Amer. sociol. Rev.,* 1938, 3, 786–800.

Edwards, A. L. Experiments: Their planning and execution. In G. Lindzey (Ed.), *Handbook of social psychology.* Vol. 1. Cambridge, Mass.: Addison-Wesley, 1954.

Greenwood, E. *Experimental sociology: A study in method.* New York: King's Crown, 1945.

Mood, A. M. *Introduction to the theory of statistics.* New York: McGraw-Hill, 1950.

Thistlethwaite, D. L. Effects of social recognition upon the educational motivation of talented youth. *J. educ. Psychol.*, 1959, 50, 111-116.

Thistlethwaite, D. L. The recognition of excellence. *Coll. Univer.* (Spring, 1961), 36, 282-295.

Thorndike, R. L. Regression fallacies in the matched group experiment. *Psychometrika*, 1942, 7, 85-102.

Walker, Helen M., & Lev. J. *Statistical inference.* New York: Holt, 1953.

Explanation and Critique

Donald Thistlethwaite and Donald Campbell used what was in 1960 the relatively new technique of regression-discontinuity analysis to reassess the results Thistlethwaite found using an ex post facto analysis (posttest-only comparison group design; see Chapter 9). In the earlier analysis, Thistlethwaite found that students receiving Certificates of Merit in the National Merit Scholarship competition had more favorable attitudes toward intellectualism, and they more often planned to seek a masters or PhD degree and to become college teachers or scientific researchers. These students also succeeded in obtaining more scholarships than a matched group of other reasonably intelligent students. The programmatic impact of the recognition was hypothesized to cause these attributes.

The two groups included in the Thistlethwaite and Campbell analysis were runners-up for the National Merit Scholarship. The "treated" group was composed of the students who received Certificates of Merit (C of M) from the Scholarship Commission but not the Merit Scholarship itself. The treatment was the increased public recognition afforded these students as opposed to the personal letter of commendation awarded to the second runners-up (commended students). This increased recognition was hypothesized to make these students more positive to the proacademic attitudes listed in the preceding paragraph. The "untreated" students received personal letters of commendation from the Scholarship Commission but not the public exposure given to the C of M students.

For this study, the eligibility criterion is the scholarship qualifying test score interval of "11." These scores are arrayed along the X axis in Figures 2, 3, and 4. For each of the attitudinal and behavioral scales (arrayed on the Y axis), the effect of the treatment is determined by examining the difference in the regression intercepts between that which would have been predicted given no treatment (the open circle at score "11") and that estimated by the treated scores. Notice that Thistlethwaite and Campbell plot both the actual responses and the estimated regression lines. This allows them visually to assess the extent to which the line reflects fluctuations in the actual data and supplies more information to inform their conclusions.

The propositions examined are those found significant in the ex post facto analysis. The ex post facto results were refuted in three of the five equations. In Figure 2 it was demonstrated that the behavioral aspects, winning scholarships, showed the expected discontinuities. However, the downward sloping line among the treated was unexpected. Thistlethwaite and Campbell conclude that the omission of Merit Scholars from the treated group and the fact that scholarship awarders consider criteria (e.g., grade point average) similar to those considered by the

Scholarship Commission affected the slope of the line. They consider all other explanations and information before accepting the statistical significance of the discontinuity at the "11" point.

Figure 3 demonstrates less continuity at the cutting point, whereas Figure 4 clearly refutes the earlier findings with the counterintuitive result of the intercept of the higher scores that are actually *lower* than predicted by the lower scores. But how much difference in the intercepts does there need to be before the impact can be established? One would typically answer that the difference should be statistically significant. Thistlethwaite and Campbell discuss the considerations involved in choosing an appropriate set of statistics. Notice that the test is always one-tailed because the hypothesis suggests that public exposure leads to higher scores on proacademic items. The only statistically significant differences were found for lines GG' and HH'. Basically, these tests determine whether the confidence intervals around the intercepts overlap. If they do, there is no difference between the points. Langbein points out that an exact formula for such a test can be found in Hubert Blalock's statistics text.[8]

One other interesting aspect of this article is that Thistlethwaite and Campbell suggest how a nested experiment could be performed within this regression-discontinuity analysis. The experiment could involve randomly assigning students who scored just below the cutting point ("10") to C of M or commended status. The results of such an experiment, if in fact there were an impact, are shown in Figure 1, lines AA'. Had there been an impact of increased public recognition, those students assigned to the C of M group would hold attitudes similar to level "11" C of M winners (see the closed half circle), whereas those in the commended group would be more like their level "10" peers (open half circle). Obviously, Thistlethwaite and Campbell were unable to perform this experiment after the fact; however, they could do this in future years. One must be careful, though, that such experimentation does not run counter to any fairness principle when determining award or program eligibility. It would be unfair to withhold a service or an award from a student who would otherwise be eligible.

The regression-discontinuity design is powerful when it is appropriate, and it avoids some of the difficulties encountered when using a design that relies on matching subjects' characteristics. The Thistlethwaite and Campbell article demonstrates how investigators can use a sophisticated method in the absence of the ability to assign subjects randomly into groups and estimate programmatic impact or, as in this case, lack thereof.

REFERENCES

1. Lawrence Mohr notes that most of the use of regression-discontinuity designs lately has been in the area of compensatory education, and he cites the work of William M. Trochim, *Research Design for Program Evaluation: The Regression-Discontinuity Approach* (Beverly Hills, CA: Sage, 1984). This reference is from *Impact Analysis for Program Evaluation* (Chicago: Dorsey, 1988), p. 98.

2. Laura Irvin Langbein, *Discovering Whether Programs Work: A Guide to Statistical Methods for Program Evaluation* (Glenview, IL: Scott, Foresman, 1980), p. 95.

3. Donald T. Campbell and Julian C. Stanley, *Experimental and Quasi-Experimental Designs for Research* (Boston: Houghton Mifflin, 1963), p. 62.

4. Donald T. Campbell, "Foreword", in Trochim, *Research Designs for Program Evaluation*, pp. 29-37.

5. Langbein, *Discovering Whether Programs Work*, p. 95. The example and explanation in this chapter are largely drawn from Langbein's explanation on pages 95-96 of her book.

6. *Ibid.*

7. *Ibid.*, p. 97. For an example of a nested design, Langbein cites Robert F. Boruch, "Coupling Randomized Experiments and Approximations to Experiments in Social Program Evaluation," *Sociological Methods and Research* 4 (1975): 31-53.

8. Hubert M. Blalock, Jr., *Social Statistics,* 2d ed. (New York: McGraw-Hill, 1972), p. 404.

9

Posttest-Only Comparison
Group Design

The posttest-only comparison group design is similar to the posttest-only control group design. The only difference between the two designs is that one design uses a randomly assigned control group for comparison and the other uses a nonrandomly assigned comparison group. The design is shown in Table 9-1. In this design neither group is pretested, and both groups are posttested after the experimental group receives the treatment.

This form of evaluation is used primarily when an evaluation is proposed after the fact and is one of the most commonly used designs. For instance, if a city is experiencing fiscal constraints, the council may ask staff or a consultant to prepare evaluations of existing programs and provide the results before budget deliberations the following month. Within these time constraints (and certainly budget constraints) full-fledged experimental designs are out of the question. However, the decision makers will need to make budgetary decisions on the basis of something more than hearsay. Consequently, the posttest-only comparison group design is appropriate.

One of the weaknesses of the design is that the data are collected at only one point. The lack of time-series data do not allow the researcher to tell if the observation is really "true" or if it is a result of random fluctuations. In addition, the evaluator needs to be sure of the form the outcome should take and collect the data to reflect it. In other words, if the treatment is supposed to have an immediate effect, then the data should be collected as soon after the treatment as possible. However, if the impact is incremental, a longer time between treatment and measurement is necessary. The consequences of poor timing are critical; the problems of committing Type I and Type II errors should be apparent. In the example of a city that is facing fiscal problems, the future of programs is at stake. The classic example is the results of the early evaluations of the Head Start programs, which showed little short-term impact. On the basis of those data, it was proposed that the program be terminated. However, subsequent tracking of Head Start graduates demonstrated a substantial long-term impact. Fortunately for the follow-on children, the directives of the early results were not followed.

Choosing a comparison group is also a major consideration. Because the posttest-only comparison group design is ex post facto, random assignment is impossible. However, if a good comparison group can be identified, valid comparison across the groups is possible. Members of the comparison group should be similar to the treated group on as many relevant variables as possible save the treatment.

TABLE 9–1 The Posttest-Only Comparison Group Design

	Before	After
Group E	X	O
Group C		O

To enhance internal validity, the measurement of the characteristics of the treated and comparison groups should be taken at the same time.

In the following article, Martha Bronson, Donald Pierson, and Terrence Tivnan use the posttest-only comparison group design to estimate the long-term impact of the Brookline Early Education Program (BEEP) on children's in-classroom behavior.

The Effects of Early Education on Children's Competence in Elementary School

MARTHA B. BRONSON
DONALD E. PIERSON
TERRENCE TIVNAN

Over the past twenty years there have been a large number of early education programs designed to provide services to preschool children and their families. These programs have provided major challenges for evaluators because of the diversity of program goals, settings, and types of families for whom these programs are intended. Partly as a result of this diversity it has been difficult to come to any conclusions about the overall efficacy of such early interventions. It has only been relatively recently that any consistent evidence of long-term effects has emerged. The Consortium for Longitudinal Studies (Lazar and Dar- lington, 1982) has documented that early education programs for children from low-income families have important and lasting effects. The effects—evident several years after conclusion of the intervention—include fewer assignments to special education services and fewer retentions in grade. At the present time, however, neither the Consortium data nor other available studies (e.g., Gray and Wandersman, 1980; Schweinhardt and Weikart, 1980) have determined adequately whether the effects of early education can be identified in elementary school classroom behaviors and, if so, whether such effects extend to chil-

Source: Martha B. Bronson, Donald E. Pierson, and Terrence Tivnan, "The Effects of Early Education on Children's Competence in Elementary School," Vol. 8, No. 5 (October 1984), pp. 615–629. Copyright © 1984 by EVALUATION REVIEW. Reprinted by permission of Sage Publications, Inc.

dren other than those from low-income backgrounds.

In developing measures to evaluate early education programs, many psychologists and educators have criticized the traditional reliance on intelligence tests (Zigler and Butterfield, 1968; McClelland, 1973; Seitz et al., 1975; Zigler et al., 1973). Others have stressed the importance of focusing on social or functional competence, including cognitive, social, and motivational components (Anderson and Messick, 1974; Zigler and Tricket, 1978; Gotts, 1979; Zigler and Seitz, 1980; Scarr, 1981). Despite these persuasive appeals to measure how children function within the classroom domain, the prekindergarten and elementary education evaluation literature has shown little response. The difficulties encountered in developing and implementing innovative methods for assessing effectiveness have limited most evaluations to more traditional measures.

In only very few instances have early education program evaluations been carried out on heterogeneous groups of participants. Fewer still have focused on children's behaviors in classrooms. Pierson et al. (1983) found significant behavioral advantages during fall and spring of the kindergarten year for a heterogeneous group of early education participants. The outcome measures were designed to assess the child's functional competence in social and learning situations in the classroom setting. These measures corresponded closely to the goals of the intervention and to the notions of competence held by the school system in which the children were enrolled. The study reported in this article extends the earlier work by following up on children when they were enrolled in second grade, using the same classroom observation instrument. Children who had been enrolled in an early education program were observed in their second grade classrooms. The observations focused on assessing their functional or educational competence.

Thus this study provides an approach to evaluation of early education programs that addresses several of the limitations of the available literature. First, the participants come from a wide range of family backgrounds, not just low-income families. Second, this study represents an opportunity for follow-up evaluation of a program that ended at the children's entry into kindergarten. Finally, the evaluation involves the use of classroom observations, focusing on behaviors considered important by the project as well as the local school system.

METHOD

Program Description

The Brookline Early Education Project (BEEP) involved a combination of services: parent education, periodic monitoring of the children's health and development, and early childhood programs. The parent education services were administered at three levels to assess the cost effectiveness of different service packages. Families were assigned at random to one of three cost levels: Level A included home visits and meetings at least once per month as well as unlimited contacts with staff and some child care in the project Center; Level B offered home visits and meetings about once every six weeks as well as the Center options; Level C was restricted primarily to services available at the Center. BEEP staff were available to families at the Center but no home visits, meetings or child care services were scheduled. In working with parents, teachers followed curriculum goals that were oriented toward supporting the parents in the role of primary educators of their child.

The monitoring of health and development was intended to prevent or alleviate conditions that might interfere with learning during the first five years of life. A team of psychologists, pediatricians, and a nurse conducted the examinations of hearing, vision, neurologic status, and language, perceptual, and motor skills. Follow-up conferences and advocacy work were pursued by teachers and social workers as needed. These diagnostic services were available equally to all participants in the project.

The early childhood programs involved a weekly play group at age two years and a daily prekindergarten program at ages three and four years. These were held in the Center or at elementary schools and were focused on individually tailored educational goals (Hauser-Cram and Pierson, 1981). As with the exams, the children's educational programs were available to all families regardless of the parent education cost-level assignment.

The project's primary goal was to reduce or eliminate school problems. For this reason, the evaluation focuses on whether the program decreased the proportion of children who fell below certain minimal competencies defined as necessary for effective functioning in second grade.

Subjects

The experimental subjects were 169 second grade children who participated from birth to kindergarten in BEEP. Enrollment was open to all residents of Brookline and to ethnic minority families from the adjacent city of Boston. Participants were recruited through the schools, health, and social service agencies, and neighborhood networks. Recruitment strategies were designed to locate and inform families who were expecting to have babies in the coming months and who ordinarily would not seek or hear about such a program. All participants in BEEP had the option of attending the public schools of Brookline either as town residents or through METCO, a state-funded desegregation program.

At second grade, 104 of the participants were enrolled in the Brookline public schools;

another 65 children had moved to other schools, but were within commuting distance of Brookline and available to the study.

A comparison group of 169 children was selected from the same classrooms as the BEEP children. Each comparison child was matched with a BEEP participant by selecting a child at random from within the same classroom and sex group as the participant group child. The children were spread out over 82 classrooms in over 50 different elementary schools. Table 1 shows that demographic characteristics of the two groups are quite similar and that the children involved in this study represent a heterogeneous collection of families. For example, the education levels of the families range from those with less than a high school education to those with college and postcollege degrees. Over 10 percent of the families spoke first languages other than English.

Measure

The outcome measures in this study are taken from a classroom observation instrument. The instrument was developed in response to the well-documented evidence that a dearth of adequate measures had hindered previous efforts to evaluate Head Start and other early education programs (Smith and Bissell, 1970; Walker et al., 1973; Butler, 1974; Raizen and Bobrow, 1974). Trained observers recorded the frequency of specific classroom behaviors. The instrument thus avoided the traditional reliance of educational evaluations on tests individually administered outside the classroom milieu. The instrument also focused on specific behaviors that reflected the project's position on what constitutes competent functioning in young school-age children.

The observation instrument, entitled the Executive Skill Profile (Bronson, 1975, 1978, 1981), provided a way of recording a child's performance in planning and organizing work, interacting with others, and carrying

TABLE 1 **Distribution of Background Characteristics for BEEP and Comparison Group**

Characteristics		Percentage Number of Children	
		BEEP (N = 169)	Comparison (N = 169)
Mother's education	College graduate	59	54
	High school graduate	33	37
	Not high school graduate	8	9
Father's education	College graduate	63	65
	High school graduate	29	29
	Not high school graduate	8	6
Number of parents in home	Two	83	81
	One	17	19
First language	English	87	82
	Spanish	9	4
	Chinese	4	2
	Russian	0	4
	Hebrew	0	2
	Other	0	6
Birth order	First	44	50
	Second	38	27
	Third	11	12
	Fourth or later	7	11
Gender	Female	48	48
	Male	52	52

out social interactions and learning tasks. The concept of "executive skill" is applied to both social and learning activities in the sense of using effective strategies for choosing and reaching goals.

The trained observers followed and recorded the behavior of each child for six 10-minute periods in the spring of the second grade year. The modified time-sampling procedure required that three of the observations begin at the start of a social interaction and three at the start of academic work. The observers were instructed to make certain that at least one of the academic tasks be a language arts (reading/writing) task and at least one be a math activity. Each 10-minute observation was scheduled for a different day, spread out over no less than three and no more than six

weeks. Sometimes children's absences from school or scheduling difficulties extended or compressed the observation period.

Behaviors were recorded on a sheet that allowed both the frequency and duration of specific behaviors to be collected. The duration of behaviors was measured either with a small timing device that clicked at 15-second intervals into an earphone worn by the observer (Leifer and Leifer, 1971) or with a stop watch (some observers found this easier). During a two-week training period observers studied a manual (Bronson, 1983) and were trained in classrooms to record each behavior variable to a criterion of 90 percent interobserver agreement with the observation supervisor. Observers were not informed about the specific purposes of the study and safeguards were employed to avoid divulging children's membership in the participant versus comparison group.

The observations covered eleven variables divided into three categories of behavior: mastery skills, social skills, and use of time. The mastery skills category included three variables designed to measure a child's success in planning and carrying out school learning tasks: resistance to distraction, use of appropriate task attack strategies, and successful completion of tasks.

The social skills category included four variables pertaining to interpersonal relations: cooperative interaction with peers, successfully influencing others, use of effective cooperative strategies and use of language rather than physical force to persuade and gain the attention of others.

The use of time category consisted of four variables related to a child's degree of involvement in activities within the classroom: proportion of time spent in social activities, proportion of time in mastery tasks (not necessarily mutually exclusive with social time), proportion of time spent without any focused activity (mutually exclusive with both preceding variables) and rate of social acts. Each observation variable yielded a rate or percent score based on a full set of six 10-minute observations.

Taken as a whole, the observation procedures used in this study provide several important advantages for this evaluation. Information is collected on a wide range of important behaviors. Observation is directed at the behavior of individual children rather than on groups or classrooms or teacher behavior. The focus is on in-classroom behavior, rather than individualized, out-of-classroom assessment. In addition, the Executive Skill Profile has been successfully used in other settings (Bronson, 1975, 1978, 1981; Pierson et al., 1983), and it attempts to measure behaviors that are consistent with the goals of the local school system that is the setting for the evaluation. Thus it addresses some of the important limitations of more traditional evaluation instruments used in elementary schools.

A major goal of the Brookline Early Education Project was to prevent school problems—or, conversely, to increase the proportion of children attaining minimal competencies. Thus it was considered important to analyze the data by looking at the proportions of children who were having difficulty in school as well as by looking at average performance. Criteria for determining adequate performance versus "concerns" or "problems" were derived from clinical impressions of effective behavior and from analyses of data on non-BEEP children. The pivotal point for determining whether a given score should be regarded as "adequate" or "concern" always fell at least one standard deviation below the group mean score for that category. Concerns were considered to indicate a "problem" if scores for two or more variables in a given area (i.e., mastery skills, social skills, or use of time) fell below the criteria for "concern." The results of the comparison of mean scores and the comparisons of percentages of children showing problems will be presented separately.

RESULTS

Table 2 shows the differences between the category means of the BEEP participants and the randomly selected comparison group. The BEEP participants show significant advantages over the comparison group in both mastery and social skills, with the strongest effects in the mastery skills area. There is no difference between the two groups in the use of time area.

Another way of viewing the data is by focusing on the proportions who have prob-

TABLE 2   Differences Between the Means of BEEP and Comparison Children in Second Grade Spring Classroom Observations

	BEEP (N = 169)		Comparison (N = 169)		
	Mean	SD	Mean	SD	Significance[a]
Mastery Skills Area					
Percentage tasks completed successfully	84	18	76	23	< .001
Rate task attack strategies	2.13	.86	1.82	.83	< .001
Percentage time attending, not distracted	94	6	91	12	< .001
Social Skills Area					
Percentage time in cooperative interaction	79	20	77	23	ns
Rate cooperative strategies	.50	.41	.41	.36	< .01
Percentage success in influencing others	97	4	96	5	< .05
Percentage use of language to influence	97	5	95	6	ns
Use of Time Area					
Percentage time in mastery tasks	54	13	53	13	ns
Percentage time in social activities	51	12	51	12	ns
Rate of social acts	5.34	1.29	5.34	1.32	ns
Percentage time involved	98	2	98	3	ns

[a] Significance is based on t tests for matched pairs.

lems. Table 3 shows the percentage of children with "concerns" (low scores in categories) or "problems" (two or more low scores in an area) in the BEEP and comparison groups. Again the BEEP group shows a significant advantage over the comparison group in both mastery and social skills with the strongest effect in the mastery skills area. The BEEP group has fewer overall problems and many fewer children with problems in more than one area.

The reduction in severity of difficulties for BEEP participants can also be seen in the numbers of children with low scores across several of the eleven categories. Figure 1 presents the frequency distributions, showing more children with multiple concerns in the comparison group than in BEEP.

Figure 2 shows the numbers of children in the BEEP and random comparison groups who met the criteria for competence in the observations (by having no problems in any of the three areas assessed) with distinctions for mother's education and program cost level. BEEP children with highly educated mothers (college graduates) show advantages over their counterparts. For these subgroups, even the minimal cost-level program resulted in significant (p < .01) advantages. However, for children whose mothers were not so highly educated (less than college graduates) a more substantial investment and outreach, represented by cost-level A, was required to attain significant (p < .01) advantages over the comparison group.

Focusing on the cost levels within BEEP, we find that no significant overall differences across the three groups emerge. The only trend is for the Level A participants to be ahead of Levels B and C among the less educated families. These results are consistent with other analyses of the within-program differences.

CONCLUSIONS AND DISCUSSION

Children who participated in the Brookline Early Education Project showed several advantages in second-grade classroom behavior

**TABLE 3 Percentage Number of Children with Concerns[a] or Problems[b]
for BEEP Participants and Randomly Selected Comparison Group
in Second Grade Classroom Observations**

	Percentage Number of Children Below Competence Criteria		
	BEEP (N = 169)	Comparison (N = 169)	Significance[c]
Mastery Skills Concerns			
Tasks not completed successfully	14	27	< .01
Inadequate rate of task attack strategies	18	32	.001
Time distracted	18	29	< .05
Social Skills Concerns			
Inadequate time in cooperative interaction	6	8	ns
Inadequate rate of cooperative strategies	18	21	ns
Unsuccessful in influencing others	2	7	< .05
Ineffective use of language to influence	3	7	ns
Use of Time Concerns			
Inadequate time in mastery tasks	11	11	ns
Inadequate time in social activities	17	18	ns
Inadequate rate of social acts	2	2	ns
Time not involved	1	2	ns
Problem in Mastery Skills	12	25	< .01
Problem in Social Skills	2	8	< .05
Problem in Use of Time	2	1	ns
Overall Difficulty: Problems in One or More Areas	14	29	< .01

[a] A "concern" is a score below the established criterion in any single category.

[b] "Problems" are two or more scores below the criteria in an area.

[c] McNemar's matched-pairs test.

indices over comparison children. Advantages for the BEEP participants were apparent both in mean differences in the behavior categories and in the relative numbers of children performing below competence criteria. The BEEP advantage was most pronounced in the mastery, or academic learning area. BEEP children with highly educated mothers showed significant advantages over comparison children regardless of program level, but children whose mothers were less highly educated showed significant advantages only with the relatively intensive level A program.

Observations of BEEP and comparison children in kindergarten (Pierson et al., 1983) with the same observation instrument showed significant advantages for the program group, with the greatest differences appearing in the social and use of time areas. In the second grade observations the BEEP advantage is greatest in the mastery area. This shift in the pattern of BEEP advantages over comparison children is interesting. In the fall of kindergarten year classroom behavior differences favoring BEEP children were strongest in the social and use of time areas. In the spring of kindergarten year there was a shift in the pattern of BEEP advantages, with use of time behaviors being less important, mastery behaviors becoming more important, and social behaviors continuing to be strong discriminators between the two groups. By second

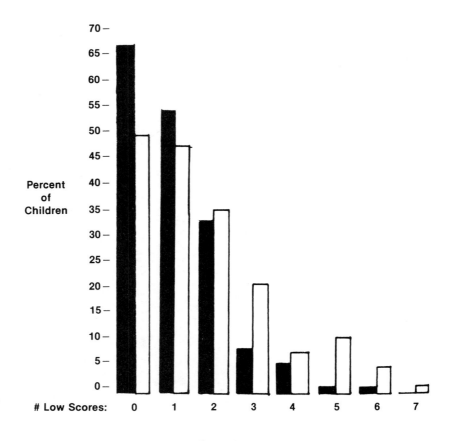

Figure 1

Frequency Distribution of the Number of Low Scores Obtained by BEEP (solid bars) and Comparison (clear bars) Children on Eleven Observation Variables

grade, mastery behaviors are the strongest discriminators. The social behavior categories show a consistent but less strong BEEP advantage, and the use of time categories reveal no differences between the BEEP and comparison groups.

This shift in the pattern of the relative advantages of BEEP over comparison children seems to be related to the changing patterns of classroom demands at these three time periods. In the fall of kindergarten year, academic demands are few and the emphasis in classroom is on school adjustment and learn-

ing school routines. The behaviors in the social and use of time areas are those most likely to pick up differences in school-related competence under these circumstances. In the spring of kindergarten year some academic demands are being introduced—numbers, letters, printing, and so on—and most children have adapted to school routines. This shift in emphasis in the classroom away from routines and toward academic demands is reflected in the changing pattern of advantages of BEEP children, away from use of time categories and toward differences in mastery cat-

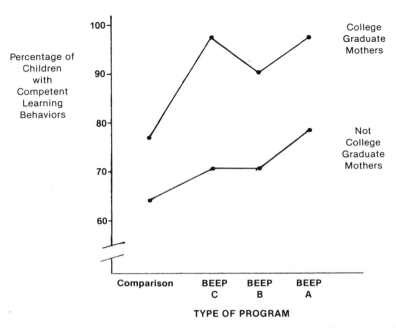

Percentage of Children with Competent Learning Behaviors

100 —
90 —
80 —
70 —
60 —

College Graduate Mothers

Not College Graduate Mothers

Comparison | BEEP C | BEEP B | BEEP A

TYPE OF PROGRAM

NOTE: Percentage of children with no difficulties in mastery skills, social skills, or use of time behaviors, analyzed by level of mother's education and type of program, is shown.

Figure 2
Overall Competencies Observed

egories. By the second grade, the primary demands in the classroom are academic. There is less time for social interaction and less room for differences in use of time categories since children's involvement in various activities is much more controlled. The pattern of BEEP advantages reflects these shifts in classroom demands and constraints.

An additional finding that deserves some attention was the lack of strong main-effect differences across the three program service levels. For the highly educated families the least intensive level of service was as effective as the most intensive level. For the less highly educated, there were no differences between the moderate and lowest levels of service, and only the most intensive level showed a significant advantage over the comparison

group. Of the three major service components that were part of BEEP—parent education, diagnostic monitoring of children's status, early childhood programs for children— only the parent education services were offered differentially; diagnostic and education programs for children were equally available to all. So it should not be surprising that in this study, focusing on outcomes for children some years after the provision of services, few differences among the service levels should be observed. Nevertheless, the search for interaction effects, or differential impact on different types of families, is important in evaluating and planning early education programs. The evidence here, although limited, suggests that service levels need to be more intensive when parents are less educated. More educated parents appear to benefit from even minimal services. This finding indicates the potential usefulness of early education for all children, not only the less educated or economically needy groups. The benefits may well vary across different types of families, and the types of services that will be helpful may also vary considerably. This issue deserves more attention from evaluators.

From the evaluation perspective, the results suggest the value of classroom observations as an evaluation technique and the importance of tailoring outcome measure to intervention goals. It is noteworthy, in this regard, that there were few differences between BEEP and comparison groups on a traditional measure of IQ or ability obtained at entry into kindergarten (see Pierson et al., 1983). So without the use of observations in the classrooms the impact of the early intervention would be very difficult to detect, and criticisms similar to those cited earlier concerning reliance on traditional tests (e.g., Zigler and Seitz, 1980; Scarr, 1981) would be relevant.

The reduction in classroom behavior problems also has significant practical implications for elementary schools. Even if behavior problems are not so severe as to require expensive special services, behavior problems in the classroom require teacher attention and reduce the amount of productive teacher time and energy available to all children. Fewer behavior problems in a classroom result in a more positive classroom atmosphere and more "learning time" for all children.

In summary, the results of this study suggest the importance of a carefully planned program like the Brookline Early Education Project for all school systems. Education and support services to parents of young children coupled with early education programs for the children should be recognized as an essential part of a high quality elementary school curriculum. Early detection and prevention of learning difficulties is more effec-

tive, and less expensive in the long run, than remediation.

REFERENCES

Anderson, S. and S. Messick (1974) "Social competence in young children." Developmental Psychology 10: 282-293.

Bronson, M. B. (1975) "Executive competence in preschool children." Presented to the annual meeting of the American Educational Research Association, Washington, D.C., April. ERIC (Document Reproduction Service ED 107 378.

Bronson, M. B. (1978)"The development and pilot testing of an observational measure of school-related social and mastery skills for preschool and kindergarten children." Doctoral dissertation, Harvard Graduate School of Education.

Bronson, M. B. (1981) "Naturalistic observation as a method of assessing problems at entry to school." Presented to the annual meeting of the Society for Research in Child Development, Boston, April.

Butler, J. A. (1974) Toward a new cognitive effects battery for Project Head Start. Santa Monica, CA: Rand Corp.

Gotts, E. E. (1979) "Early childhood assessment." In D. A. Sabatino and T. L. Miller (Eds.) Describing learner characteristics of handicapped children and youth. New York: Grune & Stratton.

Gray, S. W. and L. P. Wandersman (1980) "The methodology of home-based intervention studies: Problems and promising strategies." Child Development 51: 993-1009.

Hauser-Cram, P. and D. E. Pierson (1981) The BEEP Prekindergarten Curriculum: A Working Paper. Brookline, MA: Brookline Early Education Project.

Lazar, I. and R. Darlington (1982) "Lasting effects of early education: A report from the Consortium for Longitudinal Studies." Monographs of the Society for Research in Child Development 47 (2-3, Whole No. 195).

Leifer, A. D. and L. J. Leifer (1971) "An auditory prompting device for behavior observation." J. of Experimental Child Psychology 2: 376-378.

McClelland, D. C. (1973) "Testing for competence rather than for 'intelligence'." Amer. Psychologist 28: 1-14.

Pierson, D. E., M. B. Bronson, E. Dromey, J. P. Swartz, T. Tivnan, and D. K. Walker (1983) "The impact of early education as measured by classroom observations and teacher ratings of children in kindergarten." Evaluation Rev. 7: 191-216.

Raizen, S. and S. B. Bobrow (1974) Design for a National Evaluation of Social Competence in Head Start Children. Santa Monica, CA: Rand Corp.

Scarr, S. (1981) "Testing for children: Assessment and the many determinants of intellectual competence." Amer. Psychologist 36: 10 1159-1166.

Schweinhart, L. and D. P. Weikart (1980) Young Children Grow Up. Ypsilanti: Monographs of the High/Scope Educational Research Foundation Seven.

Seitz, V., W. D. Abelson, E. Levine, and E. F. Zigler (1975) "Effects of place of testing on the Peabody Picture Vocabulary Test scores of disadvantaged Head Start and non-Head Start children." Child Development 45: 481-486.

Smith, M. S. and J. S. Bissell (1970) "Report analysis: the impact of Head Start." Harvard Educ. Rev. 40: 51-104.

Walker, D. K., M. J. Bane, and A. S. Bryk (1973) The Quality of the Head Start Planned Variation Data (2 vols.) Cambridge, MA: Huron Institute.

Yurchak, N. J. H. (1975) Infant Toddler Curriculum of the Brookline Early Education Project. Brookline, MA: Brookline Early Education Project.

Zigler, E. F. and E. C. Butterfield (1968) "Motivational aspects of changes in IQ test performance of culturally deprived nursery school children." Child Development 39: 1-14.

Zigler, E. F. and V. Seitz (1980) "Early childhood intervention programs: A reanalysis." School Psychology Rev. 9(4): 354-368.

Zigler, E. F. and P. K. Trickett (1978) "I.Q., social competence, and evaluation of early childhood intervention programs." Amer. Psychologist 33: 789-798.

Zigler, E. F., W. D. Abelson, and V. Seitz (1973) "Motivational factors in the performance of economically disadvantaged children on the Peabody Picture Vocabulary Test." Child Development 44: 294-303.

Explanation and Critique

This evaluation is a reexamination of children observed at two points in time while in kindergarten and who are now in second grade. Martha Bronson, Donald Pierson, and Terrence Tivnan provided a posttest comparison of children who received early education programming with similar children who did not. One goal was to determine whether the programming had a long-term impact on children's competence as defined by the consumers of the evaluation—the school district. Competence was assessed on the basis of the children's mastery of task skills, social skills, and use of time. A second goal of the evaluation was to assess the cost effectiveness (Chapter 15) of three levels of early education programming. The idea was that if all three levels were equally effective, then the least expensive alternative should be pursued in the future.

Parents of children who could potentially participate in the BEEP program were recruited at the time the children were born. The recruitment included births in Brookline, Massachusetts, an affluent suburb of Boston, and low-income minority family births in Boston. Participation was not mandatory; families volunteered for the program. The problems of self-selection in this evaluation are discussed in detail in Chapter 20 and will not be covered here.

The researchers concluded that BEEP had a positive impact on children's in-classroom kindergarten behavior and sought to see if that impact was carried over into the second grade and whether the form of the impact changed over the two-year period. The subjects were the 169 second graders who had participated in BEEP from birth to kindergarten. The researchers observed children who had left the school district as well as those still in the district.

The children in the comparison group were chosen randomly from the class-rooms of the BEEP students, matching them by sex. This method was used to control for variations in classroom exposure, teacher style, or any other variable in the learning environment. The characteristics of the BEEP and comparison students are shown in Table 1 of the article. The comparison group members are similar to the BEEP students. One possibly relevant variable that is missing from Table 1 is how many of the children were not from Brookline. This missing information is discussed in Chapter 20.

The evaluators used trained classroom observers to gather data on the BEEP and non-BEEP students. Notice that they did not divulge the specific purposes of the study or the experimental/control status of the students. This was done to maximize the observers' objectivity. The time-sampling technique and the validity of the instrument are reasonable and well documented.

Tables 2 and 3 of the article summarize the comparisons of the BEEP and non-BEEP students. Notice that the tests of significance used were for matched pairs, not the typical t-test of differences of group means. This is appropriate because the research question revolves on the differences in otherwise similar matched students. The findings indicate that BEEP students scored significantly higher than the comparison group on all measures of mastery skills and on some measures of social skills. In addition, BEEP students had a lower incidence of problems or concerns in these two areas. The BEEP and non-BEEP students did not differ in their use of time.

Figure 2 of the article provides the cost effectiveness results. Bronson, Pierson, and Tivnan controlled for the home educational environment by examining separately the percentage of children with educational competence who had college educated mothers and those whose mothers were not college-educated. Presumably they used the education of the mother because mothers traditionally spend more time with children than working fathers do. The article is not explicit in this regard. The findings indicated that children of college-educated mothers scored higher on competence ratings than those whose mothers were not college educated. It appears from Figure 2 that, even when given the most expensive early education program, children of mothers who were not college educated only barely excelled in competence over nontreated (comparison) students whose mothers were college educated. Level A training affords children the best chance at increased competence, according to Figure 2, whereas the program type does not seem to make much difference among children of college-educated mothers. The policy implications indicate that to decrease the competence gap between those whose parents are more educated and others, the early education program at Level A should be targeted to children whose parents do not have a college education.

A few concerns are not addressed in the article. First, the home environment of the children seems to have been captured by the education variable. However, it would have been useful also to control for Brookline versus Boston residence, and it is not clear that the authors did so. In fact, there is no indication in the article just how many Boston students are in the BEEP group. Perhaps the implication is that Boston students (the low-income minority) need early education to keep up with their suburban counterparts, thereby increasing the educational level of the area more effectively. Again, the whole issue of self-selection will be covered in later chapters.

Second, it is not clear from the article why the impact of BEEP lasted through the second grade. From Figure 1 it is clear that BEEP children score higher than the comparison group on the competence scores, but how is that directly attributable to BEEP? Could any historical events leading to or causing participation in the program account for the results? The authors could have statistically controlled for a variety of the variables listed in Table 1 to disentangle the competence results. Perhaps space limitations did not allow the authors to characterize the form of the effect of BEEP. In other words, was the effect to be incremental, long-term, short-term, episodic? However, it is of some intrinsic value to follow and at least describe what happened to children who received school district resources.

This article documents a carefully designed posttest-only comparison group design in terms of the collection of outcome data and selection of the comparison group. Some of the shortcomings lie in threats to the internal validity of the evaluation. When searching for other plausible explanations of the outcomes of programs, evaluators should take pains to be candid about both the strengths and weaknesses of their approach. Sometimes this type of evaluation is the best one can do within the limitations of resources and data. Carefully constructed evaluations of this type can provide valuable information for policymakers.

10

Use of Statistical Controls

The final quasi-experimental design that we discuss is the use of regression analysis to control for extraneous variance. In true experiments, one need not worry about this variance because random assignment of subjects to experimental and control groups randomly distributes characteristics across the two (or more) groups. In quasi-experimentation the comparison group is matched with the treated group on as many characteristics as possible in order to control for differences. There does not need to be a one-to-one correspondence between individuals in the experimental and control groups, but there should be a general correspondence on aggregate traits. The use of *statistics* to remove the effects of potentially spurious and confounding variables is the subject of this chapter. Statistical control eliminates the necessity of grouping subjects (randomly or otherwise).

Some scholars refer to the use of statistical controls as "nonexperimentation" instead of quasi-experimentation.[1] We do not wish to enter into the debate as to whether the use of statistical control is experimental. The appropriate use of such statistics is an accepted practice and is often the only method available to control for spurious effects.

A variety of statistics can be used to remove spurious effects. The choice of what statistic is appropriate depends on the level of measurement of the independent and dependent variables and the presence or absence of a causal linkage. However, many of these statistics use the assumptions and interpretations of multiple-regression analysis as a basis for analysis. For example, path analysis and aspects of time-series analysis rely on the linear model and assumptions of linear regression. Therefore, it seems appropriate to include regression analysis in the present treatment.

Students should not be overwhelmed when interpreting regression statistics. The main stipulation in regression analysis is that all variables be measured at the interval level. Dummy variables approximate this interval requirement. The general formula for regression is:

$$Y = a + b_1 x_1 + b_2 x_2 + \ldots b_n x_n + e$$

where

Y = the dependent variable or phenomenon to explain.

a = the intercept or point at which the regression line crosses the Y axis.

b_{1-n} = the regression coefficients. A unique 1 is attached to each independent variable indicating its effect on the dependent variable.

x_{1-n} = the independent variables.

e = random measurement error.

In regression, the effects of each independent variable are simultaneously, statistically controlled. In other words, when one interprets a regression coefficient, one does so knowing that the effects of all the other variables have been partialed out. The unstandardized regression coefficients (b) can be interpreted in a straightforward manner:

A one-unit increase in the independent variable (X) results in a dependent variable unit (b) (increase/decrease) in the dependent variable.

For example, let us say that the dependent variable is measured as the average number of workplace injuries in mines for a calendar quarter (see this example in Chapter 19) and that one of the independent variables is a time counter measured by quarterly increments. The following partial equation:

$$\text{Injuries} = a + 0.0258 \text{ (time counter)} + \ldots + e$$

is interpreted in this way:

The passage of one additional quarter was associated with an average increase of 0.0258 injuries.[2]

or

The increase of one quarter results in a 0.0258 average increase in workplace injuries (controlling for all the other variables in the equation).

Thus, one can verbalize the impact of each independent variable. One must be careful not to confuse the regression coefficient (b) with the standardized coefficient (beta), which allows one to determine which independent variable contributed most to the equation. Beta cannot be interpreted verbally as can b and cannot be compared across equations as can b. In evaluation, this is the most important coefficient because it can be used by decision makers to make alterations in funding and programmatic priorities so that the estimated impact can be expected.

One final statistic of importance in regression analysis is the R^2. Squaring the multiple-correlation coefficient yields the percentage of variance in the dependent variable that is explained by knowledge of the combined effects of the independent variables. The higher the R^2, the better the job the variables do of explaining the dependent variable. One should be skeptical of interpretation of results with very low R^2. In Chapter 17 we argue that the testing effect was not a relevant explanation of the Hawthorne studies because other independent variables explained 97 percent of the variance, leaving only 3 percent left over for the testing, or original, explanation.

In the following article, "Evaluation of Residential Energy Conservation Programs in Minnesota," two stages of regression analysis are used to demonstrate the impact of energy audit and loan programs on conservation of natural gas.

Evaluation of Residential Energy Conservation Programs in Minnesota

ERIC HIRST
RICHARD GOELTZ

The federal Residential Conservation Service (RCS) was mandated by the 1978 National Energy Conservation Policy Act (U.S. Congress, 1978; U.S. Department of Energy, 1982). The major goal of the RCS is to improve energy efficiency of existing homes. Its main feature is an on-site home energy audit. Information collected during the audit is used to develop recommendations to the household to reduce home energy use.

During the past few years, several evaluations of utility home energy audit programs have been completed (Centaur Associates, 1983; Hirst, 1984). The typical evaluation uses one year of fuel consumption data before the audit plus one year of comparable data after the audit. At best, this allows one to estimate the energy saving effect of the program during the first year after program participation. Questions naturally arise about the long-term durability of program-related energy savings. How quickly do households respond to the suggestions in their energy audit and install recommended measures? Would they have installed some or all of these measures anyway, in response to the economic forces of rising fuel prices? How quickly? These questions, related to the dynamics of program energy savings, cannot be

answered on theoretical grounds; they are best addressed with empirical data.

This article discusses the methods used and results obtained in an evaluation of home energy audit and loan programs in Minnesota (see Hirst et al., 1983 and Hirst and Goeltz, 1984a and 1984b). The evaluation included samples of households that participated in these programs between April 1981 and June 1982; fuel consumption data, for both these participants and for samples of nonparticipants, were obtained for nearly four years— from Fall 1980 through Spring 1984. This allowed comparison of preprogram consumption (1980/1981) with two full years of postprogram consumption (1982/1983 and 1983/1984).

Northern States Power (NSP) is the largest utility in Minnesota, serving about 750,000 Minnesota households with electricity; this represents about half the households in Minnesota. NSP's service area includes the Minneapolis–St. Paul Twin Cities, St. Cloud, and many communities in the southern half of the state.

Between April 1981 and December 1982, NSP mailed the Minnesota Energy Conservation Service (MECS)[1] offers to almost 350,000 of its Minnesota customers. Al-

Source: Eric Hirst and Richard Goeltz, "Evaluation of Residential Energy Conservation Programs in Minnesota," Vol. 9, No. 3 (June 1985), pp 329-347. Copyright © 1985 by EVALUATION REVIEW. Reprinted by permission of Russell Sage Publications, Inc.

most 12,000 audits were conducted during this period. The average cost of providing these audits totaled $145, of which $10 was recovered through the audit fee charged by NSP to audit households.

NSP conducts a related program in portions of its service area, the Public Utility Conservation Investment Program (PUCIP). The St. Paul PUCIP loan program offered low-interest loans to St. Paul area households for installation of retrofit measures recommended by a MECS audit. About 450 PUCIP loans were made between Fall 1981 and September 1982, averaging almost $3000 per home. PUCIP loans were offered at 7 percent and 9.75 percent interest rates. About 25 percent of the audited households eligible for PUCIP loans actually applied for and obtained loans (see Griffin, 1982 and City of St. Paul, 1983 for additional information on PUCIP).

It is important to note (see Appendix A of Hirst et al., 1983) that the MECS and PUCIP programs operate in different geographic settings. Our evaluation of the PUCIP program focused primarily on the city of St. Paul, an urban area. Evaluation of the MECS program focused primarily on the surrounding communities, a suburban area. Unfortunately, this complicates interpretation of evaluation results; the PUCIP and MECS results are difficult to compare due to the combination of differences between the programs and differences in structure and household characteristics between the urban and suburban areas.

Results presented here are likely to be of interest for two reasons. First, analysis of program energy savings are based on utility natural gas billing data rather than on household self-reports of conservation action taken. Thus, the estimates of energy savings should be reliable. Second, the analysis includes at least two years of postparticipation data, allowing examination of the temporal effects of home energy audits on natural gas consumption.

EVALUATION DATA

The major purpose of this evaluation was to estimate the energy savings that could be attributed to the NSP MECS and PUCIP programs. We therefore decided at the outset (March 1982) to limit attention to NSP customers that use natural gas as their primary heating fuel and that purchase gas from NSP. This restriction made it possible to collect all fuel bill information from only one source (NSP) and eliminated the substantial data quality problems inherent in fuel oil data (Energy Information Administration, 1983). This does not severely limit generalizability of evaluation results because about 85 percent of NSP's residential customers heat with natural gas.

The evaluation was also restricted to households that owned their own home and that lived in single-family homes. NSP's experience (as well as that in many other RCS programs) showed that most program participants were homeowners living in single-family units; exclusion of tenant-occupied homes and of multifamily units simplified later analyses.

We had initially intended to limit attention to participants that received a MECS audit in mid-1981. This would have simplified analysis of energy savings because participation in the NSP programs would have occurred entirely between heating seasons. However, this would have greatly reduced the sample sizes of MECS and PUCIP participants. As a consequence, this evaluation includes households that received audits between April 1981 and June 1982 (Figures 1 and 2).

To analyze the issues selected for evaluation, several types of data were collected (see Appendix B of Hirst et al., 1983):

- Monthly natural gas consumption records for program participants and nonparticipants from October 1980 through May 1984 (four full heating seasons)

Household
Surveys
— —
Mail Phone

MECS Energy Audits

Monthly Natural Gas Bills

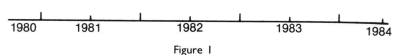

| 1980 | 1981 | 1982 | 1983 | 1984 |

Figure 1

Timing and Major Activities in Evaluating MECS and PUCIP

- Daily temperature data for each weather station (three), to match with gas consumption records to adjust for changes in weather
- Energy audit reports for MECS and PUCIP participants

- Household demographics, structure characteristics, and information on recent and planned conservation actions (July 1982 mail screener survey)
- Detailed information on recent conservation actions (what, when, who did it, at

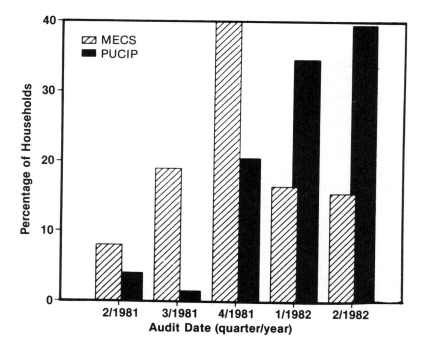

Figure 2

Distribution of Audit Dates for Participant Households in Evaluation

what cost) and on energy-related attitudes (November 1982 telephone survey)

The data set used in this evaluation of the NSP programs included 581 households with "complete" data: 245 MECS audit, 107 MECS nonaudit, 68 PUCIP audit plus loan, 56 PUCIP audit only, and 105 PUCIP nonaudit. Complete data include four years of natural gas billing data, mail survey responses, and telephone survey responses. We conducted several tests to determine the existence of bias among these 581 households relative to larger data sets (e.g., those households for which we had natural gas data but no telephone survey; those households for which we had only three years of natural gas data). Results suggest that the 581 households in this analysis are representative of the populations sampled (Hirst et al., 1983; Hirst and Goeltz, 1984a and 1984b).

MODELS OF HOUSEHOLD ENERGY USE

The most important purpose of the evaluation was to develop credible estimates of the natural gas savings that could be attributed to the NSP MECS and PUCIP programs. In designing this evaluation, we relied primarily on actual natural gas consumption records, in the belief that these data would provide the most reliable measure of actual program performance. Chapters 2 and 5 of the 1983 evaluation report examine program performance in terms of the retrofit measures households report they installed, the influence of the energy audit on their decisions to install these measures, and their attitudes and opinions about the NSP energy audit and loan programs.

Because accurate analysis of energy consumption and of changes in consumption is difficult, we developed and implemented a variety of approaches to estimate the energy saving effects of these programs (Johnson, 1983; Hirst et al., 1983).

We begin with a brief discussion of the factors that affect household energy use and how these factors might be included in models of household energy consumption, from which estimates of program energy saving are derived. These models are implemented later in this article. The first stage of our approach models annual consumption for each household and year, normalizing for differences in weather and billing cycles. The second stage uses the normalized annual consumption (NAC) estimates from the first stage, accounting for individual differences among households in a cross-sectional model. Other approaches are discussed in Chapter 3 and Appendix C of Hirst et al. (1983).

Princeton Scorekeeping Model[2]

Household energy use is the sum of energy use for the various end-uses (e.g., space heating, water heating, air conditioning). Because space heating accounts for about 75 percent of total natural gas use for the households in this evaluation and is strongly temperature-dependent, we write a model of energy use as:

$$E_{it} = a_i + b_iHDD_{it}, \qquad [1]$$

where the unit of analysis is one year of natural gas billing data called a household-year.[3] E is gas use for household i during monthly billing period t. HDD is the number of heating degree days to reference temperature Tref, for the same time period as the utility bill for the weather station closest to that household.[4] Daily HDD is defined as maximum (0, Tref— average daily temperature); daily HDD values are summed to obtain billing period totals.

The reference temperature (Tref) is the temperature that yields the highest explanatory power (R^2) in the above model; we restricted Tref to integers in the range 40-75°F. Physically, Tref is the outdoor temperature below which the heating system must operate to maintain the desired indoor air temperature. The coefficient a_i reflects household use of natural gas for nonspace heating purposes[5] and b_i reflects use of gas for space heating (more accurately nonweather- and weather-sensitive consumption, respectively).

The parameters (a, b, Tref) are estimated for each household for each of the four years in the present analysis (Fels et al., 1983). The parameters are used to define NAC, the primary output of the scorekeeping model:

$$NAC_{ij} = 365 \cdot a_{ij} + b_{ij} \cdot \overline{HDD} \, (Tref_{ij}),$$
$$j = 1, 2, 3, 4 \qquad [2]$$

where NAC is normalized (weather-adjusted) annual natural gas consumption for household i and year j, and $\overline{HDD}$ is the long-run normal HDD at Tref. The NAC formula corrects household gas use for year to year changes in winter severity and for temporal misalignment across households in fuel bills.

Cross-Sectional Model

We assume that this "first-stage" NAC estimation process removes the effects of changing weather (and more generally of all short-run time dependence) from household gas use. Then, variations in NAC are assumed to be a function solely of cross-sectional (i.e., individual household) factors and of program participation. Thus, the "second-stage" analysis treats NAC as the dependent variable:

$$NAC_{ij} = C_o + \sum_K C_k Z_{ik} \qquad [3]$$

where Z_{ik} is a vector of k demographic and dwelling unit characteristics (e.g., income, number of household members, floor area of home, participation in MECS or PUCIP).[6] The c_k coefficients show how weather-ad-

justed annual natural gas use depends on these cross-sectional variables and program participation status.

Before we estimated the models discussed in this section, we spent considerable time examining the data for anomalous outliers and for missing data elements. Some observations were missing individual data elements (e.g., income, floor area) from the screener and telephone surveys. To avoid loss of these observations from the regression models, we assigned the sample means for the missing values to these households. In addition, we added dummy variables to reflect "missingness." For example, if a household did not report income in the screener survey, we assigned the mean value of income to that household. The dummy variable for missing income was set equal to one for that household (and for all other households missing income). The coefficients of these dummy variables were consistently insignificant, suggesting that there was no bias due to missingness. As a consequence, these dummy variables were not included in the final equations.

We limited the present analysis to only those households with clean data (i.e., NAC model $R^2 > 0.75$) that used gas as the primary heating fuel (i.e., Heating > 50 MBtu/ year and Heating/NAC > 0.4) for each of the four years of analysis. These restrictions eliminated 21 percent of the households, which used gas as only a supplemental heating fuel, did not use gas for any heating, or had poor NAC model performance in any of the four years.[7]

We also identified and attempted to correct anomalous individual monthly bills. For example, if two large residuals (difference between actual gas use and the NAC model prediction) of opposite sign are identified, and if they are temporally adjacent to each other, they are combined to make one bimonthly bill. The assumption is that the gas meter was read incorrectly one month and correctly the following month, which explains two outliers of opposite sign. The NAC model is then re-estimated with the combined bill instead of the two original bills; if the new model is better than the original, its NAC estimates are retained for further analysis. If a single large outlier is identified, the bill is dropped and the NAC model reestimated. Again, the new model is retained for further analysis if its performance is better than that of the original.

ESTIMATED ENERGY SAVINGS

Scorekeeping Results

We began analysis of natural gas consumption with development of the simple NAC models discussed above (equations 1 and 2). These models yield estimates for each household of reference temperature, non-weather-sensitive (baseload) consumption, weather-sensitive (primarily space heating) consumption, and total normalized consumption for each of the three years (see Table 1). The predictive power of these simple models is very high, with an average R^2 of 0.97. The heating slope and baseload coefficients are almost always highly significant, at the 1 percent level or better.

Both MECS- and PUCIP-audited households consumed more natural gas preprogram (year 1, 1980/1981) than did the non-audit households. The PUCIP households (most of whom live within the city of St. Paul) consumed more energy than did the MECS households (who live in suburban and outstate areas).

All five groups cut their gas use during each of the succeeding three years. The reductions in gas use are greater for audit households. Although nonparticipants in both groups cut annual gas use by an average of 13 MBtu between years 1 and 4, MECS audit and PUCIP audit only households cut gas use by 17 MBtu and PUCIP audit plus loan households cut gas use by 36 MBtu. It is likely that some of these gas savings, especially for nonparticipants, were due to increases in natural gas prices during this time.[8]

All five groups showed declines in both baseload and space heating gas during this four-year period. The participant groups, especially the PUCIP loan households, cut space heating gas use by more than they cut baseload gas use. On the other hand, the nonparticipants' reductions in baseload and heating use were roughly equivalent. Thus, the greater total savings experienced by participants was due primarily to their larger space heating gas use reductions. This is to be expected because the audits emphasized space heating measures.

Average reference temperatures increased by 2° or 3°F for all five groups. We found this puzzling because we had expected that the space heating retrofit measures installed by these households (especially program participants) would have lowered the reference temperature of their homes.

In addition to examination of the mean values of NAC (Table 1), we also computed and examined the medians and adjusted means (using the LSMEANS option in the SAS Institute, 1981 GLM procedure). Because the estimates of net and total energy savings are similar to those discussed above, we do not present the medians and adjusted means. However, this similarity of results lends confidence to our use of the unadjusted means.

Cross-Sectional Results

We next used results of the NAC analysis as the dependent variable to estimate the cross-section model discussed previously (equation 3). That is, for each household, values of Normalized Annual Consumption for the four years are the dependent variables. This en-

TABLE I Summary (Means) of Normalized Annual Consumption Models for Each Household

	MECS		PUCIP		
	Audit	Nonaudit	Audit Plus Loan	Audit Only	Nonaudit
Gas use (MBtu/year)					
Total NAC[a]					
year 1	162	146	172	168	159
year 2	152	140	162	162	155
year 3	150	138	142	155	150
year 4	146	133	137	150	146
Baseload[b]					
year 1	42	40	45	42	41
year 2	38	39	39	41	40
year 3	36	37	32	35	36
year 4	36	35	34	37	34
Heating[c]					
year 1	120	106	127	125	118
year 2	114	101	124	121	115
year 3	114	101	110	120	115
year 4	110	98	103	114	112
Total saving (MBtu/year)					
year 1–2	10.4	5.9	10.2	5.5	3.8
year 1–3	12.2	7.9	30.1	12.6	8.2
year 1–4	16.8	12.9	35.7	17.2	12.7
Model R^2	0.97	0.97	0.97	0.97	0.97
No. of days/ household-year	335	335	335	335	335
No. of households	250	107	69	58	105

[a] Normalized annual consumption (NAC) is the sum of the baseload and heating components. The heating component is computed on the basis of the long-run value heating degree days for each household at its Tref (average of 8000 at 65°F base).

[b] Nonweather-sensitive gas use.

[c] Weather-sensitive gas use.

sures that the observations for each household are for the same time periods and for the same weather.

The explanatory variables (Table 2) include factors related to household demographics, structure characteristics, and program participation. Household income and number of household members are the demographic factors included. House age, number of stories in house, heated floor area, and a binary (dummy) variable indicating use of gas as the primary water heating fuel are the structure characteristics included. The price of natural gas is included to capture the temporal effects of price increases on gas use. Finally, we include two sets of binary variables related to program participation—one to capture preprogram differences in gas consumption across groups and the second to capture postprogram reductions in gas use. Separate variables are used for each participant group—MECS audit, PUCIP audit plus loan,

TABLE 2   Regression Results for Model of Normalized Annual Consumption of Natural Gas (MBtu/year)[a]

Explanatory Variable	Model Coefficient	Significance Level
Intercept	21.6	0.214
House age (years)	0.471	0.000
Number of floors in house	12.2	0.000
Floor area (ft²)	0.0144	0.000
Number of household members	8.62	0.000
Household income (thousands of dollars)	0.770	0.000
Price of natural gas ($/MBtu)	−7.21	0.002
Binary variables		
Gas is water heating fuel	19.6	0.001
Program participant		
MECS	14.0	0.001
PUCIP audit plus loan	11.5	0.067
PUCIP audit only	12.4	0.053
Postprogram		
MECS		
year 2	−7.2	0.000
year 3	−3.7	0.008
year 4	−4.0	0.005
PUCIP audit + loan		
year 2	−17.6	0.000
year 3	−22.9	0.000
year 4	−24.2	0.000
PUCIP audit only		
year 2	−1.1	0.811
year 3	−4.2	0.058
year 4	−4.1	0.067

[a] Based on 2324 observations (581 households × four years), telephone survey respondents; $R^2 = 0.29$.

and PUCIP audit only. Separate postprogram variables are used to reflect savings in years 2, 3, and 4.

We used the SAS (1983) procedure TS-CSREG (time-series/cross section regression) to estimate this model. This procedure accounts for the correlation among the four NAC terms for each household (i.e., it explicitly recognizes that the observations are not independent of each other for each household).

Unfortunately, the NSP evaluation data set does not fully meet the criteria for time-series/cross section analysis. With only four years of annual data, there may be insufficient

data to adequately identify the dynamics of natural gas use. Also, most of the variables listed above vary across households but not over time (a consequence of the fact that household demographic and economic data were collected only once, during the 1982 mail and telephone surveys). Thus we are forced to assume that these factors are constant from year 1 through year 4. Natural gas price, on the other hand, varies only over time; because all these households purchase gas from the same utility, at any given time they all pay the same price. Despite these data limitations, it is preferable to explicitly recognize the dependence among the four

NAC values for each household, which is why we used TSCSREG instead of the simpler ordinary least squares method.

This model explains almost 30 percent of the variation across households and years in NAC. Only the intercept and PUCIP audit only energy saving in year 2 are not statistically significant at reasonable levels.

Model results show that normalized annual natural gas use increases with house age and size, and with number of household members and household income. If natural gas is used as the primary water heating fuel, gas use is increased by an average of 20 MBtu/year relative to homes that do not use gas for water heating. Natural gas use declines with increasing gas prices, by about 7 MBtu per $/MBtu increase in price.

The model shows that program participants consumed about 12MBtu/year (almost 10 percent) more preaudit than did nonparticipants. However, participants cut their energy use by more than nonparticipants in years 2, 3, and 4. The year 3 and year 4 coefficients are more meaningful than the year 2 coefficients because so many of the audits were conducted during the second year.[9] The coefficients show savings for MECS households (3.7 MBtu in year 3 and 4.0 MBtu in year 4), for PUCIP audit plus loan households (22.9 MBtu in year 3 and 24.2 MBtu in year 4), and for PUCIP audit only households (4.2 MBtu in year 2 and 4.1 MBtu in year 4). These estimates for MECS and PUCIP audit plus loan households are statistically significant at the 1 percent level; the estimated savings for PUCIP audit only households are significant at about the 6 percent level. These estimates imply that the MECS audit and PUCIP audit only households cut consumption—relative to nonparticipants—by 2 percent-3 percent and the PUCIP audit plus loan households by 14 percent. These are the net energy savings that can be directly attributed to the NSP programs.

A similar evaluation of the Michigan RCS program (Kushler et al., 1984) also collected and analyzed two years of postaudit energy consumption records for gas-heated homes. Their results also showed a slight increase in net annual energy saving from the first to the second postaudit year, from 7.9 MBtu to 8.4 MBtu.

Effects of Winter Severity and Electricity Use

As noted earlier, winters 2 and 4 were 15 percent-20 percent colder than were winters 1 and 3. We were initially concerned that changes in the seasonal efficiency of gas furnaces from year to year would partially obscure the energy-saving effects of retrofit measures installed because of the NSP home energy audits. The seasonal efficiency of a typical residential gas furnace decreases with increased furnace on-off cycling. In colder winters, the furnace will cycle less frequently, yielding a higher seasonal efficiency than in milder winters.

Conversations with engineers at the Honeywell Corporate Technology Center, National Bureau of Standards, Brookhaven National Laboratory, and Minnesota Energy Division suggested that the net effect of differences in winter severity on gas furnace efficiency would be very small. The available literature confirmed this; Patani et al., (1983) showed that a 100 percent increase in furnace load (equivalent to a 100 percent increase in the difference between outdoor and reference temperatures) yields only a 4 percent-6 percent increase in furnace seasonal efficiency.

To test the effect of the colder winters in years 2 and 4, we added a binary variable to the TSCSREG model discussed earlier (Table 2); this variable is zero for years 1 and 3 and one for years 2 and 4. The coefficient had the expected negative sign, but it was statistically insignificant. We conclude that the NAC model adequately corrects for differences in winter severity from year to year; the effect of differences in gas furnace performance on NAC is very small.

We were also concerned that the exclusion of household electricity use from our analysis would complicate interpretation of the energy-saving estimates. If, for example, households reduced consumption of electricity during the time period studied (by turning off lights and replacing old, inefficient appliances with more energy-efficient units), then the space heating system would have to operate for longer periods to offset the lost internal gains from electric appliances. The NAC model estimates would then show less saving than actually occurred.

Examination of NSP's data on residential electricity use during this four-year period showed no change: average weather-adjusted electricity use for NSP's nonelectric space heating residential customers averaged 6500 kWh (equivalent to 22 MBtu) in 1980/ 1981 and 1983/1984. Therefore our analysis

of natural gas use should be, on average, un-affected by household electricity consumption.

CONCLUSIONS

Several approaches were used to develop estimates of total and net energy savings. The range in estimated savings, given the diversity of analytical approaches and data subsets, is small. Total savings for the two nonparticipant groups were similar, 8 MBtu in year 3 and 13 MBtu in year 4 (see Figures 3 and 4). Total savings for the MECS audit and PUCIP audit only groups were also quite similar, 12 MBtu in year 3 and 17 MBtu in year 4. Finally, the PUCIP audit + loan households had the largest total savings, 30 MBtu in year 3 and 35 MBtu in year 4. The total savings increase from the first to the second postaudit years for participants because of both their participation

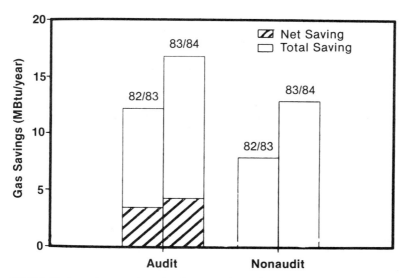

NOTE: Net savings refers to that portion of the total saving that can be directly attributed to the NSP program.

Figure 3

Total and Net Natural Gas Savings per Household One and Two Years after Participation in the NSP MECS Home Energy Audit Program

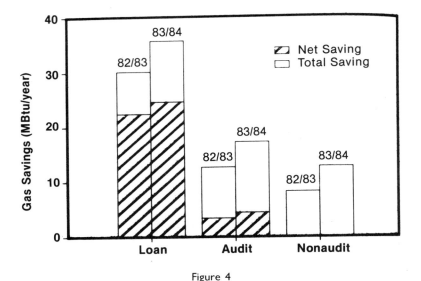

Figure 4

Total and Net Natural Gas Savings per Household One and Two Years after Participation in NSP PUCIP Home Energy Audit Plus Loan Program

in NSP's residential conservation programs and increases in natural gas prices. The savings experienced by nonparticipants are due primarily, we think, to rising gas prices, although other factors such as increasing awareness of energy issues, growing knowledge of household energy conservation options, and changes in income may also have affected household energy use trends.

Net savings for the two audit only groups were similar to each other and roughly constant from years 3 and 4 at about 4 MBtu/year; the net savings increased from year 3 to year 4 for both groups but the increases were small and statistically insignificant. The PUCIP audit plus loan households showed a net savings of 23–24 MBtu/year for both years 3 and 4; here again, the slight increase in savings from year 3 to year 4 was programmatically uninteresting and statistically insignificant.

These results suggest that the net energy savings attributed to the NSP audit and loan programs remain roughly constant between

the first and second years after participation. The net saving for households that received an audit averaged 4 MBtu/year (2 percent–3 percent of preprogram gas use). The net saving of households that received both an audit and low-interest retrofit loan was about six times higher, 24 MBtu/year (14 percent of preprogram gas use).

Results presented here show near constancy of *net* program energy savings between the first and second postparticipation years and substantial increase in *total* energy savings during this time. This suggests that the relative influence of the NSP programs declines over time. That is, after a few years, the effects of rising natural gas prices on household energy use are likely to be much larger than the effects of the energy audit. The much larger effect of the PUCIP loan is likely to be felt for many more years, regardless of increases in natural gas prices.

Our evaluation also included analysis of the economic effects of the MECS and PUCIP programs on participants, nonparticipating

NSP natural gas ratepayers, and society in general (see Chapter 4 of Hirst et al., 1983). Results showed that both NSP programs were very cost-effective to participants. Both programs were economically unattractive to nonparticipating ratepayers because of the assumption that the marginal price of natural gas would remain, on average, $1/MBtu *below* the average price of gas throughout the forecast period. If, on the other hand, the marginal price was $3/MBtu *higher* than the average price, the MECS program would be attractive to nonparticipants; similarly, if the marginal price was $8/MBtu above the average price, then the PUCIP program would be attractive to nonparticipants. Finally, the MECS program is economically neutral and the PUCIP program is not cost-effective from the social (i.e., state of Minnesota) perspective. The PUCIP program would be cost-effective to the state if the marginal price of gas was $3/MBtu above the average price.

NOTES

1. The Minnesota Energy Conservation Service is their version of the federal Residential Conservation Service.

2. The approach used here was developed by Fels et al. (1983) at Princeton University.

3. For this project, each household-year includes 11 monthly bills. The billing data cover natural gas use from October 1980 through May 1984, a total of 44 months. Dividing these bills equally among four years yielded 11 bills per household-year.

4. Daily temperature data were provided by NSP for three weather stations: Minneapolis/St. Paul (89 percent of the households), St. Cloud (6 percent), and LaCrosse, WI (5 percent). The Minneapolis/St. Paul station experiences a long-run average of 8000 HDD (65°F base). The first heating season (1980/1981) was 11 percent warmer, the second season was 6 percent colder, the third season was 9 percent warmer, and the fourth season was 7 percent colder than the long-run average.

5. Use of electricity (for nonspace heating uses such as lighting and operation of appliances) is not included in the present analysis.

6. Because information on the Z_{ik} were obtained at only one time (from the 1982 mail and telephone surveys), we assume that these variables are independent of year j.

7. As noted in the preceding section, these 581 households are a representative sample of the full data set. That is, no important biases were observed in comparisons of the 581 households used in this analysis with the larger sample from which these households used in this analysis with the larger sample from which these households were drawn. In addition, we estimated the time-series/cross section model previously discussed (see Table 2) with the full data set and obtained results very close to those obtained with the 581 households.

8. The real price (in 1982 dollars) of natural gas to NSP's residential customers increased from $3.21/MBtu in Fall 1980 to $3.84 during the 1980/1981 heating season, $4.56 during the 1981/1982 season, $5.30 during the 1982/1983 season, and $5.34 during the 1983/1984 season—a 66 percent increase between Fall 1980 and the 1983/1984 winter. All the increases occurred between Fall 1980 and Spring 1983; prices declined slightly since then.

9. Almost 85 percent of the MECS households and more than 95 percent of the PUCIP households received their audits *during* year 2.

REFERENCES

Centaur Associates, Inc. (1983) 1983 RCS Highlights: Cost-Benefit Evaluation of the Residential Conservation Service. Prepared for the U.S. Department of Energy, Washington, DC.

City of St. Paul (1983) Saint Paul Energy Resource Center, Program Evaluation Report. Department of Planning and Economic Development.

Energy Information Administration (1983) Residential Energy Consumption Survey. Consumption and Expenditures—April 1980 through March

1981. Washington, DC: U.S. Department of Energy, DOE/EIA-0321/2.

Fels, M. F. et al. (1983) Scorekeeping for Electricity Savings in Houses, Methodology Development (Phase I). Princeton, NJ: Princeton University Center for Energy and Environmental Studies.

Griffin, T. (1982) Energy Resource Center 1981-82 Annual Report. St. Paul, MN.

Hirst, E. (1984) "Household energy conservation: a review of the federal residential conservation service." Public Administration Rev. 44, 5: 421-430.

Hirst, E. and R. Goeltz (1984a) Energy Savings One and Two Years After Participation in Minnesota Home Energy Audit and Retrofit Loan Programs, report ORNL/CON-168. Oak Ridge, TN: Oak Ridge National Laboratory.

Hirst, E. and R. Goeltz (1984b) "Testing for nonresponse bias: evaluation of utility energy conservation programs." Evaluation Rev. 8, 2: 269-278.

Hirst, E., M. Thornsto, and D. Sundin (1983) Evaluation of Home Energy Audit and Retrofit Loan Programs in Minnesota: The Northern States Power Experience, report ORNL/CON-136. Oak Ridge, TN: Oak Ridge National Laboratory.

Johnson, K. E. (1983) "Qualitative response models and the estimation of energy-savings from utility conservation programs." Energy 8, 10: 775-780.

Kushler, M. G., P. M. Witte, and G. C. Crandall (1984) RCS in Michigan: Where Do We Go from Here? ACEEE 1984 Summer Study on Energy Efficiency in Buildings. American Council for an Energy-Efficient Economy.

Patani, A., U. Bonne, and G. J. Gustafson (1983) "Analysis of hybrid residential heating systems on the basis of cost and life cycle cost efficiencies." Presented at the 1983 International Gas Research Conference, London.

SAS Institute, Inc. (1983) SUGI Supplemental Library User's Guide. Cary, NC: Author.

SAS Institute, Inc. (1981) SAS for Linear Models: A Guide for the ANOVA and GLM Procedures. (R. J. Freund and R. C. Littel, authors.) Cary, NC: Author.

U.S. Congress (1978) National Energy Conservation Policy Act. Public Law 95-619,

U.S. Department of Energy (1982) "Residential conservation service program, final rule." Federal Register 47.

Explanation and Critique

Eric Hirst and Richard Goeltz maintain that one of the problems with earlier energy conservation evaluations was that energy use tended to be compiled for only one year after the conservation treatment. In this article, they try to estimate the longer-term effect of such activities following energy consumers' participation in the Minnesota Energy Conservation Service (MECS) and the Public Utility Conservation Investment Program (PUCIP), both operated by Northern States Power (NSP) utility.

Hirst and Goeltz used regression analysis to estimate the weather-adjusted annual natural gas consumption for each household, which acted as the dependent variable for the subsequent analysis. By the time they reached the second stage of the analysis, they had made a number of concessions that should be noted. First, the MECS and the PUCIP programs are operative in different types of areas—the former in suburban areas and the latter in St. Paul, which Hirst and Goeltz acknowledge could complicate the interpretation of the results. Fortunately, however, they used dummy variables in the second stage to account for these differences. It would have been reasonable for them to suggest what they expected the urban/suburban differences could be and the subsequent impact on the results. Apparently, urban consumers had higher normalized annual consumption rates, as shown in Table 1 of the article.

Hirst and Goeltz also restricted their analysis to consumers of NSP services living in owner-occupied, single-family homes. The first of these restrictions seems reasonable on two counts. First, 85 percent of southern Minnesota energy consumers use NSP, and second, gathering data from one source increases the reliability of the data. However, the second restriction did pose some problems (although Hirst and Goeltz implied that this "simplifies" later analyses). In terms of external validity, then, Hirst and Goeltz could only generalize conservation policy impacts to owner-occupied, single-family homes. Now, consider the differences between the urban and suburban housing stock. Urban areas tend to have an older housing stock with many more multifamily dwellings. Older urban homes are sometimes larger and usually less efficiently constructed than their suburban counterparts. The overall impact of PUCIP in urban areas (for which it was designed) was not adequately tapped, given these restrictions.

To their credit, Hirst and Goeltz used several types and sources of data. Had they relied solely, for instance, on survey data, they would have been measuring *perceptions* rather than energy-use *behavior*. To maintain their large N in the regression, cases with missing data were assigned the sample mean value. "For example, if a household did not report income in the screener survey, we assigned the mean value of income to that household." When using regression, researchers will often do this to avoid problems with "listwise deletion." When listwise deletion is operative (and it usually is), a case is deleted from the analysis if it has a missing value on any *one* of the independent variables. Because Hirst and Goeltz used quite a few independent variables, this could pose a problem. One should use caution when assigning sample means to missing values. First, if there are many cases with missing values, the assignment of the mean restricts the variance in the independent variable. Second, if the mean is not reflective of the sample (because it is either skewed or the remaining cases are not typical), then the results are misleading. Although Hirst and Goeltz did not show the extent to which this was a problem in their study, they did report that analyses using the "missingness" dummy variable demonstrated no apparent bias caused by the mean assignment.

Although Hirst and Goeltz did not use an ordinary least squares method, for purposes here the interpretation of the coefficients are essentially the same as outlined in the introduction to Chapter 10. Table 2 of the article displays the regression results. The "model coefficient" is the b value. Entered simultaneously into the equation are variables known to affect energy usage—housing age, number of floors, square footage, household income, and use of gas for water heating. In effect, the impact of all these variables was controlled in order to estimate programmatic impact. In addition, Hirst and Goeltz controlled for the impact of rising gas prices (Chapter 15), which typically reduces energy use. Their results were consistent with expectations on these variables.

The next step was to determine the extent to which program participation explained usage above and beyond (controlling for) these initial variables. An examination of the coefficients for the dummy variables showed that program participants initially consumed more MBtu/year than nonparticipants (see the positive bs). This was demonstrated in Table 1 of the article. The MBtu/year decreases reported come directly from the postprogram bs in Table 2. Notice how they can convert these bs into meaningful MBtu/year interpretations. When interpreting a b for a dummy variable, the presence of the attribute (e.g., the score of "1" on the year 3 PUCIP) decreases (minus sign) MBtu/year by 22.9. In every case, participation in the programs decreased MBtu/year even when controlling for the other variables.

One may be tempted to conclude that the "best" program for reducing energy consumption is the PUCIP audit + loan (with reductions of 24.2 MBtu/year 4 as compared to MECS of 4.0 MBtu/year 4). This, however, is misleading not only because of the urban/suburban differences cited previously but also because of an apparent interaction between self-selection bias (Chapter 20) and regression artifact (Chapter 19). People who *choose* to participate in audits or act on audit advice (e.g., apply for a loan) do so overwhelmingly because they perceive their gas bills to be too high. They self-select participation on the basis of their extreme scores (usage). The effects of self-selection suggest that they would *do* something as a result of the audit, and the regression effect predicts some easing back to the mean usage. Given these effects, one would expect PUCIP + loan (with the most initial extreme values) to show the greatest improvement. Apparently, each program works relatively well for participants considering their heating usage similarities in year 4 in Table 1.

Two final points merit mention. With all the included variables, Hirst and Goeltz were able to explain only 29 percent of the variance. Consequently, many of the safeguards included in the first stage did not "purify" the analysis—71 percent of the variance remains unexplained. Finally, they mention that nearly all the included variables were statistically significant. With such a large N, goodness-of-fit criteria (such as R and R^2) are more important than statistical significance.

Hirst and Goeltz demonstrate that long-term effects of energy conservation programs that are beneficial to consumers (i.e., cost about $10.00) are felt regardless of increases in natural gas prices. It would be quite another analysis to determine whether it is beneficial to program funders (Part V).

REFERENCES

1. For example, Laura Langbein, *Discovering Whether Programs Work: A Guide to Statistical Methods for Program Evaluation* (Glenview, IL: Scott, Foresman, 1980), chaps. 8 and 9.

2. Moran, Garrett E., "Regulatory Strategies for Workplace Injury Reduction: A Program Evaluation," *Evaluation Review* 9, no. 1 (February 1985): 29.

PART FOUR
Reflexive Designs

The classifications, experimental designs and quasi-experimental designs, the subjects of the previous two parts, are relatively straightforward. That is, they are easy to define. Not so with the subjects of this part, which is concerned with evaluations that use the target group of the program as its own control. Such designs are termed reflexive controls by Peter Rossi and Howard Freeman.[1] Donald Campbell and Julian Stanley considered them to be preexperimental designs.[2] The two types of reflexive designs covered by this part are simple before-and-after studies that are formally known as the *one-group pretest-posttest design* and the *simple time-series design*.

For full-coverage programs (i.e., for programs for which most of the population is eligible), it may be impossible to define randomized or constructed-control groups or, in fact, to locate nonparticipants. Many programs, for example, are directed at all targets within a specific geographic area. In these cases, the researcher may have no choice but to use reflexive controls.

The essential justification of the use of reflexive controls is that in the circumstances of the experiment it is reasonable to believe that targets remain identical in relevant ways before and after the program. Without the program, pretest and posttest scores would have remained the same. Try to determine whether the use of a reflexive design in Chapter 11 is reasonable.

REFERENCES

1. Peter H. Rossi and Howard E. Freeman, *Evaluation: A Systematic Approach*, 3rd. ed. (Beverly Hills, CA.: Sage, 1985), p. 297.
2. Donald T. Campbell and Julian C. Stanley, "Experimental and Quasi-Experimental Designs for Research on Teaching," in *Handbook of Research on Teaching*, ed. N. L. Gage (Chicago: Rand McNally, 1963), pp. 171–247.

One-Group Pretest-Posttest Design

Probably the most commonly used form of reflexive design is the one-group pretest-posttest design, sometimes called a comparison of before-and-after data. It is not a powerful design and is subject to most of the traditional validity problems. It is typically used when nothing better can be done. The one-group pretest-posttest design is shown in Table 11-1.

The target group is measured before the implementation of the program (O_1) and again after the program is completed (O_2). The difference scores are then examined and any improvement ($O_2 - O_1$) is usually attributed to the impact of the program. The major drawback of this design is that changes in the target may be produced by other events and not the program. The longer the time lapse between the preprogram and postprogram measurements, the more likely it is that other variables besides the program affected the postprogram measurement. Harry Hatry, Richard Winnie, and Donald Fisk give the conditions under which this design might be applied as follows:

> This design often is the only type that is practical when time and personnel are limited. It is most appropriate (1) when the period covered by the evaluation is short (thus making it less likely that nonprogram related factors will affect the evaluation criteria); (2) when the link between the program intervention and the outcomes being measured is close and direct so no other major events are likely to have had a significant influence on the values measured with the evaluation criteria; or (3) when the conditions measured have been fairly stable over time (and are not, for example, likely to be distorted by seasonal changes), and there is reason to believe such stability will continue.[1]

Rossi and Freeman give a hypothetical example, as follows:

> In evaluating the outcome of a nutritional education program testing participants' knowledge of nutrition before and after participation in a three-week set of lectures, the use of reflexive controls is likely to provide a good measure of the

TABLE 11-1 The One-Group Pretest-Posttest Design

	Before		After
Group E	O_1	X	O_2

impact of the course because knowledge of nutrition is unlikely to change sponta-
neously over such a short period of time.[2]

The following article, "Nutrition Behavior Change: Outcomes of an Educational
Approach" reads much like the Rossi and Freeman example.

Nutrition Behavior Change:

Outcomes of an Educational Approach

PATRICIA K. EDWARDS
ALAN C. ACOCK
ROBERT L. JOHNSTON

A major responsibility of evaluators is to test the basic theoretical premises underlying the delivery of human service programs (Flay and Best, 1982; Neigher and Schulberg, 1982). With respect to health education programs, numerous studies have examined the assumption that an expansion in pertinent knowledge and positive changes in beliefs is associated with improvements in health-related behavior. Findings from an array of programs—for example, weight reduction (Becker et al., 1977), alcohol use (Goodstadt, 1978), smoking (Thompson, 1978), and breast self-examination (Calnan and Moss, 1984)—suggest that the viability of health education in promoting positive health behavior is highly problematic. Moreover, the nature of causal linkages between knowledge, belief, and behavior changes remains in question. Although the consistency model predicts that valid knowledge change is the first stage in a pathway proceeding to changes in beliefs and attitudes—which then culminate in behavior change (Swanson, 1972; Stanfield, 1976; Zeitlan and Formacion, 1981)—some researchers propose alternative causal mod-

els. Changes in attitudes may be, in fact, a necessary prior step to the acquisition of health-related knowledge (Mushkin, 1979; Rosander and Sims, 1981), and health-related beliefs can be modified subsequent to changes in behavior to maintain consistency among the affective and behavioral domains (Almond, 1971; McKinlay, 1972).

This body of research is highly relevant to the evaluation of nutrition education programs. However, although a considerable amount of investigation has focused on the magnitude of cognitive, belief, and behavioral outcomes, extant studies suffer from a number of constraints that limit our understanding of the basic premises and potential of nutrition education programs. Firstly, most of the research has examined programs designed for and targeted to specific subpopulations such as low-income mothers (Ramsey and Cloyd, 1979; Rosander and Sims, 1981), primary school children (St. Pierre and Cook, 1981), hospital staff (Looker et al., 1982), and pregnant teenagers (Perkin, 1983). Little is known about the efficacy of programs aimed at a broadly based constituency. Secondly, to our

---

Source: Patricia K. Edwards, Alan C. Acock and Robert L. Johnson, "Nutrition Behavior Change: Outcomes of an Educational Approach," Vol. 9, No. 4 (August 1985), pp. 441-459. Copyright © 1985 by EVALUATION REVIEW. Reprinted by permission of Sage Publications, Inc.

knowledge, there are no studies involving nutrition education programs that report the extent to which positive cognitive, belief, and behavioral changes are sustained over time. Most health education programs are of a relatively short duration, but their objectives—particularly those that are behavior oriented—are not timebound (Hochbaum, 1982; Flay and Best, 1982). Despite long-range expectations, evaluations of the effectiveness of nutrition education programs, and most other health change programs as well, are generally confined to a pretest-posttest design.

A third problem endemic to many nutrition education evaluations deals with the reliability of outcome measures. In some studies the reliability of scales is estimated from tests piloted with samples that are not equivalent to the target audience of the program (i.e., Looker et al., 1982). We cannot assume that because a test is reliable for one population it will be equally reliable for others (Talmage and Rasher, 1981). Other studies, which use internal consistency as a measure of the reliability of their scales, present pretest results only, ignoring the possibility that the scales may have a different level of internal consistency for the posttest stage (i.e., St. Pierre and Cook, 1981; Rosander and Sims, 1981). The difficulty in constructing reliable outcome scales, even when they are administered to fairly homogeneous groups, is demonstrated by the wide variation of reliability coefficients. For example, Sullivan and Schwartz (1981) report a coefficient as low as .00.

Finally most nutrition education program evaluations measure the intended effects of the program in isolation, making assumptions regarding causal linkages between outcome domains, while failing to demonstrate the actual relationships between cognitive, belief, and behavioral changes. Thus, it is impossible to determine if there is, indeed, an empirical association among the knowledge, belief, or behavioral changes that do occur.

This study addresses four issues in the evaluation of nutrition education programs: (1) Can reliable and valid measures of nutrition knowledge, beliefs, and behavior be developed that will enable longitudinal assessment of programs targeted to the general public? (2) Can a program directed to a broad audience be effective in terms of changing nutrition knowledge, beliefs, and behavior? (3) Are positive changes sustained over time? (4) What is the relationship of changes in the cognitive, belief, and behavioral domains? At a time when federal funds for nutrition education programs have been drastically curtailed, these issues are of critical importance in terms of demonstrating the potential of educational interventions as a strategy for promoting positive dietary behavior.

THE AMERICAN RED CROSS NUTRITION COURSE EVALUATION

This article draws from the results of an evaluation of a nutrition course, "Better Eating for Better Health," developed jointly by the American Red Cross (ARC) and the United States Department of Agriculture (USDA). The primary goals of the course—presently being offered by many of the 3000 ARC chapters nationwide—concern the promotion of nutrition knowledge, positive beliefs, and improved dietary behavior of the general public. The curriculum consists of six two-hour modules that may be presented over a period ranging from two to six weeks. Participant workbooks and supplementary reading materials are provided to each attendee. Prior to conducting a course, ARC instructors are expected to have completed the Nursing and Health Services core curriculum, as well as the Nutrition Instructor Specialty Course. Evaluation was carried out in five separate stages concurrently with the development of the course and included both formative and summative elements. The selected findings reported here are derived from the final stage of the project, a national field test, conducted at 51 ARC chapter sites.[1]

Data Collection Procedures

Course participants were surveyed at three distinct points in time: prior to the beginning of the nutrition course, immediately after the last session of the course, and approximately 10 weeks following completion of the course. Group-administered questionnaires, provided by course instructors who had been trained to implement the surveys, were used to collect baseline (N = 1461) and posttest (N = 1031) data. All individuals attending the first and last sessions of the nutrition course participated in the first two surveys. Although we were unable to use random selection for our sampling procedures, because participation in ARC classes is voluntary, our baseline sample is differentiated along an array of sociodemographic variables.[2] The third participant survey was conducted by means of telephone interviews with a systematically selected subsample of baseline respondents. A total of 248 interviews were attempted to achieve a quota of 200 telephone survey respondents, accounting for a completion rate of 81 percent. Respondents to the telephone survey are representative of the initial sample along the range of background characteristics.[3]

In order to assess the possible effects of exogenous factors on changes in the nutrition course participant's knowledge, beliefs, and behavior, we solicited volunteers for a nonequivalent control group from individuals who were simultaneously attending other Red Cross courses during the field test. Again, random selection was not possible without severe disruption of ARC chapter activities. The control group completed both the baseline (N = 212) and posttest questionnaires (N = 133). An earlier analysis indicates that although there are some statistically significant sociodemographic differences between the experimental and control groups, these differences are not influential in interpreting the effects of the nutrition education intervention (Edwards et al., 1983a: 15-17, 100-107).

Measurement Techniques

Items for the outcome scales were constructed cooperatively by the course development and evaluation teams, composed of personnel from ARC and USDA, as well as outside consultants. Each item reflects a major knowledge, belief, or behavioral objective of the course.[4] The three outcomes scales were initially tested with a prototype sample of participants during the third stage of the evaluation, which constituted a "best chance" pilot assessment of course materials and teaching strategies at six ARC chapter sites. (The nutrition course was taught by experienced ARC instructors who were assisted and observed by members of the course development and evaluation teams). Subsequent to this stage of the evaluation, the course development team revised course objectives, materials, and teaching strategies to more adequately coincide with participant needs identified in the evaluation. In addition, the evaluation scales were examined, using factor analysis and alpha reliability to assess the accuracy and validity of each measure. Inadequate items were deleted, and new measures reflecting changes in the nutrition course objectives were added.

The evaluation team conducted a second pilot test of the revised instruments at ten ARC sites during the fourth stage of the evaluation, in a more naturalistic setting, without either observation or supervision. Again, changes were made in the instrumentation to improve the validity and reliability of the items, as well as to ensure that the items represented the fourth-stage modifications in the nutrition course.

The final nutrition knowledge scale consisted of 15 multiple-choice items pertaining to facts about nutrients, sodium, vitamins, food additives, weight loss, and the relationship of disease to nutrition. Responses were coded so that a score of one indicates a correct answer and zero an incorrect response. Nutrition beliefs, operationalized as a dimension of the affective domain (see Fishbein and Raven, 1962), were constructed using a five-category Likert-type scale. The items were coded so that a score of one represents the least positive belief, three denotes the respondent was undecided, and five indicates the most desirable response in terms of the course objectives. The scale included 8 items concerning beliefs that related to the content areas addressed in the knowledge items. The nutrition behavior scale measured the frequency of participant's conduct related to the knowledge and belief questions. The 12 items making up this scale were coded so that one represents the least positive behavior pattern and five the most desirable, according to

course objectives. Belief and behavior items were constructed in both positive and negative terms to avoid a response set.

RELIABILITY OF NUTRITION OUTCOME SCALES

Developing adequate scales to measure nutrition outcomes has been a thorny problem confounding the evaluations of nutrition education programs. Even when a single domain of outcomes is divided into subtests dealing with specific content areas of nutrition knowledge, beliefs, or behaviors, the internal consistency of each subscale is often unacceptable (i.e., Sullivan and Schwartz, 1981). Moreover, as St. Pierre and Cook (1981) illustrate, the reliability of scales may vary considerably among subsamples of a target population.

The Cronbach alpha coefficients for the field test surveys shown in Table 1 demonstrate the problematic nature of achieving reli-

TABLE 1   Reliability of Nutrition Knowledge, Belief, and Behavior Scales

| | | Alpha Reliability | | | | |
| | | Course Participants | | | Control Group | |
Scale	Number of Items	Baseline	Posttest	Telephone	Baseline	Posttest
Field Test Survey						
Participants and Controls						
Knowledge	15	.75	.79	—	.72	.62
Beliefs	8	.56	.65	—	.46	.49
Behavior	11	.79	.82	—	.82	.83
Number of respondents		1461	1031	—	212	133
Telephone Survey						
Participants						
Knowledge	7	.66	.70	.58	—	—
Beliefs	5	.53	.60	.69	—	—
Behavior	7	.78	.77	.71	—	—
Number of respondents		196–199	137–147	196–200	—	—

NOTE

Number of respondents varies due to missing data. The lower number of respondents included in the posttest results reflects the proportion of participants dropping the class before it was completed, approximately 25%.

able nutrition outcome measures. For course participants, the inter-item reliability is only slightly differentiated between the baseline and posttest points on the knowledge and behavior scales. Despite the fact that the scales were administered to a heterogeneous population and include a range of content areas, the reliability coefficients are within an acceptable range. Both scales were examined using principal component factor analysis. All 15 items of the knowledge scale have a positive loading on the first factor, accounting for 21.9 percent of the variance on the baseline and 25.6 percent on the posttest. There is a clear first factor on the 11-item behavior scale, explaining 36.0 percent and 39.1 percent of the variance on the baseline and posttest, respectively.

Measurement of nutrition beliefs on a single scale had been highly problematic from the start of the project. On our pretest analysis, it was evident that many of the belief objectives of the course were not integrated along a single dimension. Baseline and posttest reliabilities for the eight items that were finally selected are relatively low for course participants. The eight-item scale has a first principal factor explaining 25.8 percent of the baseline and 29.7 percent of the posttest variance.

Comparisons between the reliability coefficients for the participant and control group baseline scales show a great deal of consistency for the knowledge and behavior scales. The reliability coefficient for the control group belief scale, however, is considerably lower than that for the treatment group. This difference persists in the comparison of the posttest coefficient. Moreover, the knowledge reliabilities deteriorate for controls on the second test, to a less satisfactory range. The differences between the reliability of scales administered to both groups may, indeed, be a result of the fact that they constitute samples of two separate populations. The participant

group, by virtue of electing to take the course, perhaps had a more acute "nutrition awareness," resulting in the higher level of internal consistency of responses. These findings underscore the need to pretest scales with controls, as well as experimentals, when nonequivalent samples are expected.

In order to keep length of the telephone survey to a minimum, it was necessary to reduce the number of items in each scale for this follow-up survey. Table 1 presents a reexamination of the scales in their reduced form for telephone respondents only. The results show that decreasing the number of items and the pool of respondents has a deleterious effect on scale reliability. Of particular concern here is the deterioration in the interitem coefficients for the knowledge scale used in the telephone survey. Our findings suggest that caution must be taken when developing multiple choice knowledge items for telephone surveys. Although it may be necessary to utilize several different data collection techniques in longitudinal studies, it is evident that each technique must be thoroughly pretested to assure consistent results.

As mentioned previously, prior research has shown that scale reliability can vary among sociodemographic subsets of a sample. When these groups are important in assessing differential outcomes of the program under examination, their responses should be analyzed for scale reliability. Table 2 presents reliabilities for the baseline knowledge, belief, and behavior scales by gender, race, age, education, and income. The findings show that pattern of scale reliability found in the aggregated sample is generally maintained among subsets of respondents. However, none of the scales perform as well for nonwhites and the youngest group of participants. Furthermore, those participants with the lowest level of educational attainment have considerably lower knowledge and belief scale reliabilities than participants who have completed high school

TABLE 2 Reliability of Baseline Scales by Selected Subsamples of Participants

	Knowledge	Beliefs	Behavior	N
Gender				
Male	.78	.49	.81	177
Female	.74	.56	.78	1269
Race				
White	.72	.57	.80	1105
Nonwhite	.68	.43	.75	298
Age				
<24	.66	.47	.75	219
25–54	.74	.56	.78	855
54+	.76	.60	.78	320
Education				
<HS	.63	.42	.78	143
HS/some college	.69	.51	.77	919
Bachelors+	.69	.56	.82	380
Income				
<15,000	.67	.50	.77	353
$15,000–29,999	.71	.49	.80	427
$30,000+	.71	.58	.80	468

NOTES

Variation in the total number for each subsample is due to unreported data.

or college. Although these findings illustrate the need to test for scale reliability among relevant subsets of a sample, the overall consistency found here does not pose a serious problem in interpreting outcome results for this study.

EFFECTIVENESS OF NUTRITION EDUCATION ON A VARIEGATED CONSTITUENCY

The second issue posed in this study concerns the potential of a health education course targeted to a broadly based audience. Table 3 shows that the ARC nutrition course had substantial positive cognitive, belief, and behavioral effects on the overall sample of participants.[5] In contrast, no significant changes are found between the baseline and posttest scores for the control group, despite the fact that their baseline means are not statistically different from those of the treatment group. The key point is that the control group makes no statistically significant improvement and, therefore, the improvement in the treatment group is most reasonably attributed to the course itself.

Our analysis further indicates that positive knowledge, belief, and behavior changes are consistent among subgroups of course participants. There are no statistically significant differences in improvements on the basis of sex, race, and income in the three outcome measures. Although age is a factor that differentiates the degree of positive effects, of the four age groups examined (under 19, 19 to 24, 25 to 54, and 55 or over), all made significant improvements in nutrition knowledge and behavior, and only those participants under 19 years of age did not gain in terms of positive nutrition beliefs. Marital status and education also affect the level of change. Nonetheless, statistically significant and sub-

TABLE 3   Changes in Nutrition Knowledge, Beliefs, and Behavior: Immediate Effects

	Participants				Controls			
Scale	Means (N = 883)	S.D.	Change	Probability (2-tailed)	Means (N = 104)	S.D.	Change	Probability (2-tailed)
Knowledge								
Baseline	8.91	3.24	1.96	.000	8.09	3.36	.10	NS
Posttest	10.87	3.24			8.19	3.14		
Beliefs								
Baseline	27.49	4.17	3.29	.000	26.82	3.67	−.10	NS
Posttest	30.78	4.38			26.72	3.70		
Behavior								
Baseline	36.00	7.76	5.05	.000	36.08	8.01	.94	NS
Posttest	41.05	7.10			37.02	7.91		

NOTES

Possible ranges for each scale are: Nutrition knowledge, 0–15; Nutrition beliefs, 5–40; Nutrition behavior, 5–55. It should be noted that the absolute degree of change cannot be compared across the scales due to differences in the length and coding of the instruments. The probabilities are based on individual t-tests.

stantial improvements in nutrition knowledge, beliefs, and behavior are found within each category of these two variables. Our results show that although sociodemographic variables have selected influences on how much participants gain from the course, they do not differentiate to the extent that certain groups fail to improve their nutrition knowledge, belief, or behavior after taking the course.[6]

One reservation must be noted here, however. Participation in the ARC nutrition course is, by design, voluntary. There is no reason to expect that we could find the same dramatic positive results with a group of participants who had not been motivated to participate in the course. Our reservations may, however, be tempered by the fact that the reasons for participating in a health-related Red Cross class are extremely complex. Analysis of open-ended responses elicited from course participants indicates that though many of the respondents decided to attend the course to improve their own dietary behavior, others were motivated to do so because the course was job-related or provided an opportunity for social interaction.

ARE POSITIVE CHANGES SUSTAINED OVER TIME?

Our third concern in evaluating a nutrition education program relates to the longitudinal effects of the intervention. Table 4 presents the mean changes in nutrition knowledge, beliefs, and behavior for the modified instruments used in the telephone survey undertaken approximately ten weeks after the course was completed. Our analysis only includes participants who had been involved in the follow-up telephone survey. Because we wanted to acquire further information from individuals who had, for some reason, dropped the course, the attrition rate is reflected in the lower number of cases available for analyses involving posttest responses.

The first two rows in Table 4 provide the change when baseline and posttest scores are compared. These changes are substantial and significant for all three measures in a positive direction. Thus, the outcome results for this subsample of participants are consistent with the full complement of participants. We expected a significant drop-off in the scores be-

TABLE 4 Telephone Survey Comparison: Follow-Up Effects

	Knowledge				Beliefs				Behavior			
	N	Means	S.D.	Change	N	Means	S.D.	Change	N	Means	S.D.	Change
Baseline to posttest	147	5.11	1.80	.82[a]	136	16.62	3.05	2.53[a]	132	22.32	5.50	3.16[a]
		5.93	1.50			19.15	2.98			25.48	4.82	
Posttest to telephone	147	5.93	1.50	−.24[a]	137	19.12	2.99	−.41	132	25.56	4.79	1.07[a]
		5.69	1.39			18.71	3.18			26.63	4.39	
Baseline to telephone	200	5.21	1.75	.48[a]	197	16.67	3.06	1.95[a]	193	21.84	5.49	4.49[a]
		5.69	1.42			18.62	3.20			26.33	4.84	

NOTES

Possible ranges for each scale are: Nutrition knowledge, 0–7; Nutrition beliefs, 5–25; Nutrition behavior, 5–35. Because some of the original items were deleted in the telephone survey instruments, these scores are not comparable to the change scores in Table 2.

[a] $p \leq .05$ based on individual t-tests.

tween the posttest and the telephone survey. In the weeks that elapsed between the two measurements, a great deal of information and the motivation to change behavior could be lost. Indeed, there is a significant reduction in the score on the nutrition knowledge scale. We can conclude that although participants learn a great deal initially, a substantial proportion of this new knowledge is lost soon after completing the course. In contrast, although there is some loss in terms of positive beliefs, the deterioration is not statistically significant. What is, perhaps, most surprising is the significant improvement in the quality of behavior at the end of the ten week period. Finally, looking at the comparison of the baseline and telephone responses in the last two rows of Table 4, we can see that, despite the drop in knowledge subsequent to completion of the course, knowledge, belief, and behavior improvements persist.[7]

We might speculate that the initial improvement in nutrition knowledge provides a cognitive influence in the beliefs that participants have about good nutrition. Even after the students lose some of their specific knowledge, the improved beliefs are retained. Perhaps behavioral changes become self-reinforcing elements in the participant's lifestyle.

THE RELATIONSHIP OF COGNITIVE, BELIEF, AND BEHAVIORAL DOMAINS

Table 5 presents the correlations between changes in the outcome domains for two data sets. The first column of correlations shows the changes between the baseline and the posttest. The second column does the same for the changes between the posttest and subsequent telephone interview. These correlations refer to change scores rather than the actual scores on the scale themselves. For example, the correlation of .21 between knowledge and belief means that the more a person improves their knowledge between the base-

TABLE 5   Correlation of Changes in Nutrition Knowledge, Belief, and Behavior Scales

Change	Baseline to posttest (N = 883)	Posttest to telephone (N = 134)
Knowledge/belief	0.21[a]	−0.08
Knowledge/behavior	0.15[a]	−0.10
Belief/behavior	0.26[a]	−0.05

[a] $p \leq .05$.

line and the posttest, the more they also improved their beliefs.

The changes between the baseline and the posttest are positively correlated across all three domains. These correlations are modest, but all are statistically significant. The more a person improves his or her knowledge, the more beliefs ($r = .21$; $p \leq .05$) and behavior ($r = .15$; $p \leq .05$) also improve. Similarly, the more one's beliefs improve, the more one's behavior improves ($r = .26$; $p \leq .05$).

Analyzing the pattern of these correlations, we can see that changes in beliefs may have a greater influence on improvements in behavior ($r = .26$) than do changes in knowledge alone ($r = .15$). Although both of these correlations are statistically significant by themselves, the difference between them does not achieve statistical significance ($p = .11$, one-tail). Therefore, we hesitate to generalize these results beyond this particular data set. Nonetheless, these results do suggest that educational interventions should address changing beliefs, along with providing relevant knowledge. At the very least, these results emphasize that changing beliefs are an important covariate of changing behavior.

Examining the correlations that appear in the last column of Table 5 provides very different results. These correlations reflect the relationship between changes in knowledge, beliefs, and behavior that occur from the posttest to the subsequent telephone interviews. Earlier we demonstrated that behaviors continue to improve after the completion of the course, whereas knowledge deteriorates significantly and beliefs deteriorate somewhat, but not significantly. The fact that none of these correlations is statistically significant means that changes after the course in one domain are independent of changes in the two other domains. This is especially true for nutrition behavior. Nutrition behavior improves after the course, regardless of what happens to the participant's knowledge and beliefs following the course. Thus, a subject who forgets much of what is learned from the course is nearly as likely to continue improving nutrition behavior as a person who remembers all of the nutrition information and belief material.

These results indicate that change in knowledge and especially change in beliefs are important to produce the initial changes in behavior (baseline to posttest). Just as important, however, the maintenance and enhancement of improved nutrition behavior is largely independent of how much of the knowledge and belief information is retained subsequent to the course.

CONCLUSIONS

At the beginning of this article we raised four questions about the measurement of nutrition outcome variables; what can be accomplished on a large and heterogeneous population; the ability to sustain changes over time; and the interdependence of changes in cognitive, belief, and behavioral domains.

This study has the advantage of being a formative evaluation. This allowed two systematic pretests of the measurement scales prior to the actual implementation of the evaluation. There is an additional advantage in terms of having the opportunity to share the empirical results of the pretest with the program personnel and combine the empirical and expert opinions in developing the final scales. Unfortunately, much evaluation research will not have these advantages.

It was possible to develop a highly reliable scale to measure nutrition behavior. This high reliability is consistent using the group-administered long form of the questionnaire (11 items) for the case of both the baseline and the posttest in both the treatment group and in the control group. The long-form result is also consistent with the short form of the scale (7 items) used in the telephone interviews. This consistency is evident, even though fewer items were used and the method of measurement was changed from group-administered to telephone interview.

Beliefs are consistently problematic. The reliability for the control group is poor. Interestingly, for the experimental group there is improvement in the reliability between the baseline and the posttest and even more improvement moving from the posttest to the telephone survey. Perhaps there is a tendency to organize one's beliefs about nutrition as a result of the course. Thus, the respondent's nutrition beliefs not only improve but become more integrated due to the systematic exposure to nutrition information in the course.

Knowledge is reliable, but the reliability appears to drop off on the telephone follow-up. Perhaps this is because knowledge is the most likely of the three domains to deteriorate after the course is completed. Thus, nutrition knowledge not only deteriorates, but the integration of that knowledge in a coherent fashion also drops off.

A general conclusion regarding the reliability of the scales is that it is possible to develop reasonably reliable scales even though we are applying them to a heterogeneous population and using different methods to administer them. Impressively, the telephone interviews do nearly as well as the group administered questionnaire method even though the telephone interviews have fewer items in the scales.

The second major question concerns the ability to produce changes in a broad audience. Our results show that progress is substantial with a diverse population. However, as we have dealt with a volunteer population, we do not know if such impressive improvements in knowledge, belief, and behavior are possible with a less motivated, nonvoluntary population.

The third issue concerns the ability to sustain changes over time. What happens after the course was completed? As our results show, there is a significant deterioration in nutrition knowledge, a slight (nonsignificant) decrease in the quality of beliefs, and an actual improvement in nutrition behavior after the course is completed.

Although we had hoped behavior would be sustained after the course, we were surprised that it actually improved significantly. One possible explanation for this improvement can be gained by examining some of the classic studies conducted by social psychologists on the effect of fear on changes in attitudes and behavior. Leventhal (1980) reports great inconsistency in the results of the use of fear in change programs. He suggests that fear produces two possible effects. One of these is a realistic fear that can be controlled by directed changes in behavior. Thus, when people are scared and are told what specific behavior will mitigate this fear, they are likely to change their behavior dramatically.

The nutrition course did not intend to produce high levels of fear among the participants. Still, the substantial changes in knowledge and beliefs could be expected to make people fearful of practicing poor nutrition behavior. On the other hand, proper nutrition conduct could be expected to give a very positive feeling because it mitigates concerns developed because of the improved knowledge and beliefs.

This argument means that proper dietary behavior may become a self-reinforcing behavior. For example, proper diet makes people feel good because they do not need to be concerned about their health (at least as far as nutrition is a health issue). Even after the participant forgets some of the details they learned in the course, the good feeling associated with proper nutrition behavior retains its self-reinforcing property and continues to improve.

If this argument is valid, then the findings have far-reaching implications for change programs. The creation of moderate levels of fear based on improved knowledge and beliefs *combined* with clear guidelines on specific behavior to control such fear can make the behavior self-reinforcing. Once the behavior becomes self-reinforcing, it can continue to improve long after the completion of the intervention and in spite of a deterioration in the level of specific knowledge and beliefs.

The final major issue of this article is the relationship among the three domains (cognitive, belief, and behavioral) of nutrition. Some interventions focus on only one or two of these domains, however, we have demonstrated that all three are interrelated. In particular, positive beliefs appear to be even more important improvement than knowledge as a precursor of changes in behavior. Although change in knowledge and beliefs are influential on changes in behavior as a result of the course, postcourse changes (drop-off) in beliefs and knowledge are not associated with changes in behavior. This is further evidence that nutrition behavior can become self-reinforcing after the completion of the course.

NOTES

1. This article reports only selected findings from the field test, which included a more comprehensive analysis of the relationship between participant attributes, program delivery variables (e.g., instructor training and experience), exogenous factors, and a variety of program outcomes, such as attendance, extent of in-

volvement, level of difficulty of the course, and participant satisfaction with course content, materials, and teaching strategies. A description of the evaluation model and results of the analysis have been reported elsewhere (Edwards, 1984, Edwards et al., 1983a, Edwards et al., 1983b). Data from two additional field test surveys directed to course instructors and chapter administrators are not included in this analysis.

2. For example, gender: female (88 percent); age: < 25 years (16 percent); 25-34 (24 percent); 35-54 (39 percent); 55+ (21 percent); marital status: married (54 percent), single (25 percent), divorced/widowed (21 percent); ethnicity: white (77 percent), black (17 percent), Hispanic (4 percent), other (2 percent); household income: < $15,000 (28 percent); $15,000-34,999 (44 percent); $35,000+ (28 percent); employment status: full time (43 percent), part time (15 percent), not employed (42 percent); education < high school (10 percent), high school graduate (28 percent), some college (36 percent), college graduate (26 percent).

3. There are no statistically significant differences among the baseline sample and telephone respondents in terms of sex, age, educational attainment, income, race, marital status, mean household size, or participant's perception of their personal health status.

4. To illustrate, an objective of session 3 was to clarify knowledge of health problems related to excess sugar consumption and suggest strategies for reducing sugar in the diet. Examples of survey questions used to measure this objective within each outcome domain are shown below.

- *Knowledge:* The most common disease in the United States related to excessive sugar consumption is: (1) diabetes, (2) tooth decay, (3) obesity, (4) cirrhosis, (5) gastrointestinal disorders.
- *Beliefs:* Honey and molasses are better for you than table sugar (strongly disagree, disagree, undirected, agree, strongly agree).
- *Behavior:* (I) eat fruits canned in their own juice without sugar added rather than fruits canned in syrup (never, rarely, sometimes, usually, always).

The complete sets of scale items can be obtained from the authors.

5. Analysis of the effects of the course showed that sociodemographic factors explained only a small proportion of the variance on those outcome measures (Edwards et al., 1983a).

6. Multivariate analyses of the effect of process and participant perception variables (e.g., extent to which the course design was followed, team versus individual instruction and participant assessments of course content, activities, length, difficulty, and quality of instruction) on the three outcome domains are reported elsewhere (Edwards, 1984, Edwards et al., 1983a).

7. Because 25% of the telephone sample had dropped the course, these results may underestimate the longer range positive effects of the intervention for participants who attended most of the course.

REFERENCES

Almond, R. (1971) "The therapeutic community." Scientific Amer. 224: 34-42.

Becker, M. H., L. A. Maiman, J. P. Kirscht, E. P. Haefner, and R. H. Drachman (1977) "Dietary compliance: a field experiment." J. of Health and Social Behavior 18: 348-366.

Calnan, M. W. and S. Moss (1984) "The health belief model and compliance with education given at a class in breast self-examination." J. of Health and Social Behavior 25: 198-210.

Edwards, P. K. (1984) "The American Red Cross nutrition course: findings from the field test," pp. 575-586 in Agricultural Outlook 85. Washington, DC: U.S. Department of Agriculture.

Edwards, P. K., A. C. Acock, R. L. Johnston, and K. L. Demicco (1983a) American Red Cross Nutrition Course Field Test: Technical Report. Washington, DC: American Red Cross.

Edwards, P. K., R. Mullis, and B. Clarke (1983b) "A comprehensive model for evaluating innovative nutrition education programs." Paper presented at the Evaluation Research Society meetings, Baltimore, MD.

Fishbein, M. and B. H. Raven (1962) "The AB

scales: an operational definition of beliefs and attitudes." Human Relations 15: 35-44.

Flay, B. R. and J. A. Best (1982) "Overcoming design problems in evaluating health behavior programs." Evaluation and the Health Professions 5: 43-69.

Goodstadt, M. (1978) "Alcohol and drug education: models and outcomes." Health Education Monographs 6: 263-279.

Hochbaum, G. W. (1982) "Certain problems in evaluating health education." Amer. J. of Public Health 6: 14-20.

Leventhal, H. (1980) "Findings and theory in the study of fear communications." pp. 120-186 in L. Berkowitz (ed.) Advances in Experimental Social Psychology, Vol. 5. New York: Academic.

Looker, A., S. Walker, L. Hamilton, and B. Shannon (1982) "Evaluation of two nutrition education modules for hospital staff members." J. of the Amer. Dietetic Assn. 81: 158-163.

McKinlay, J. B. (1972) "Some approaches and problems in the study of the use of services: an overview." J. of Health and Social Behavior 14: 115-151.

Mushkin, S. J. (1979) "Educational outcomes and nutrition," pp. 269-302 in R. F. Klein et al., (eds.) Evaluating the Impact of Nutrition and Health Programs. New York: Plenum.

Neigher, W. D. and H. C. Schulberg (1982) "Evaluating the outcomes of human service programs: a reassessment." Evaluation Rev. 6: 731-752.

Perkin, J. (1983) "Evaluating a nutrition education program for pregnant teenagers: cognitive vs. behavioral outcomes." J. of School Health 53: 420-422.

Ramsey, C. E. and M. Cloyd (1979) "Multiple objectives and the success of educational programs." J. of Nutrition Education 11: 141-145.

Rosander, K. and L. S. Sims (1981) "Measuring effects of an affective-based nutrition education intervention." J. of Nutrition Education 13: 102-105.

St. Pierre, R. G. and T. D. Cook (1981) "An evaluation of the nutrition education and training program." Evaluation and Program Planning 4: 335-344.

Stanfield, J. P. (1976) "Nutrition education in the context of early childhood malnutrition in low resource communities." Proceedings of the Nutrition Society 35: 131-144.

Sullivan, A. D. and N. E. Schwartz (1981) "Assessment of attitudes and knowledge about diet and heart disease." J. of Nutrition Education 13: 106-108.

Swanson, J. E. (1972) "Second thoughts on knowledge and attitude effects upon behavior." J. of School Health 42: 362-363.

Talmage, H. and S. P. Rasher (1981) "Validity and reliability issues in measurement instrumentation." J. of Nutrition Education 13: 83-85.

Thompson, E. L. (1978) "Smoking education programs 1960-1976." Amer. J. of Public Health 68: 250-257.

Zeitlan, M. F. and C. S. Formacion (1981) Nutrition Education in Developing Countries: Study II, Nutrition Education. Cambridge, MA: Oelgeschlager, Gunn, & Hain.

Explanation and Critique

The first thing a student is likely to say on reading the Edwards, Acock, and Johnston article is, "This is not an example of the one-group pretest-posttest design; it had a comparison group. It is really a quasi-experimental design." *But is it?* Look at the article another way.

   Assume that you are taking a course in program evaluation at Cleveland State University and Professor Felbinger is your instructor. Down the hall from you is a class in astrophysics. Professor Felbinger decides to find out how much you learn about evaluation research during the course, so she gives you a comprehensive

200-question, multiple-choice test on evaluation research on the first day of class. The class performs miserably. She gives you the same test on the last day of class, and you all do quite well. She also gives the same test on the first and last days of class to the physics students. They perform miserably on both the pretest and the posttest. Has the use of a comparison group—the physics students—somehow magically transformed Professor Felbinger's evaluation from a reflexive design into a quasi-experimental design? Of course it has not. There is no reason in the world to expect that the population in general, including physics students, would show a statistically significant increase in their knowledge of program evaluation practices during the course of a semester.

Remember, when identifying a comparison group, to carefully match characteristics of the comparison group with those in the experimental group. If, for example, your experimental group consists of cities, make the matches on the basis of similar size, revenue base, services delivered, and so on. Select groups of people on normal demographic variables so that the groups are similar in all possible *relevant* respects except the treatment. In the Edwards, Acock, and Johnston article, there is no reason to expect that a comparison group of individuals attending other Red Cross courses (e.g., life saving) would either be similar in relevant respects to those interested in nutrition training or would show a statistically significant improvement in their knowledge of nutrition during the time that the nutrition course was being offered. One might call this the use of a pseudo-control group—at most, it controls for the effects of history (Chapter 15). It certainly is not a systematically chosen comparison group.

In reality, the Edwards, Acock, and Johnston article presents an example of the one-group pretest-posttest design. Volunteers for a "Better Eating for Better Health" course consisting of six two-hour modules (presented over a period ranging from two to six weeks) were tested at three points before the beginning of the course, immediately after the last session of the course, and approximately 10 weeks later. The results showed a statistically significant change in knowledge, beliefs, and behavior (Table 3 of the article). Pretty simple, is it not? There is no reason to expect that exogenous factors caused these changes. Nor is there any reason to cloud up a simple (and appropriate) design with a pretense of elegance.

The article can be criticized from the standpoint of the comparison group, but the evaluation has its strengths. In particular, the authors handled the problem of measuring the outcome of their nutritional education program very well. They were careful in the selection of their measurement items and took the time to compute reliability coefficients. They also examined reliabilities for knowledge, belief, and behavior scales by gender, race, age, education, and income.

Their analysis indicated significant changes in participants' knowledge, belief, and behavior as a result of the course. Furthermore, there were no significant improvements based on gender, race, or income. Age, marital status, and education, however, did affect the level of change.

Edwards, Acock, and Johnson were quite thorough in this evaluation in that they were also interested in how well the results held up over time. To test this, they used a telephone survey of participants 10 weeks after the course was completed— expecting a significant drop in the scores between the original program posttest and the telephone survey. They found a significant reduction in the score on the nutrition knowledge scale, a smaller reduction in terms of positive beliefs (the deterioration was not statistically significant), and a significant improvement in the quality of nutrition behavior at the end of the 10 weeks. Thus, despite a drop in knowledge, changes in belief and behavior brought about by the course persist. The authors conclude that:

> The creation of moderate levels of fear based on improved knowledge and beliefs *combined* [emphasis theirs] with clear guidelines on specific behavior to control such fear can make the behavior self-reinforcing. Once the behavior becomes self-reinforcing, it can continue to improve long after the completion of the intervention and in spite of a deterioration in the level of specific knowledge and beliefs.

Without the second posttest, such conclusions would never have been possible.

REFERENCES

1. Harry P. Hatry, Richard E. Winnie, and Donald M. Fisk, *Practical Program Evaluation for State and Local Governments,* 2nd ed. (Washington, DC: Urban Institute, 1981), p. 28.
2. Peter H. Rossi and Howard E. Freeman, *Evaluation: A Systematic Approach,* 3rd ed. (Beverly Hills, CA: Sage, 1985), pp. 297–298.

12

Simple Time-Series Design

The second type of reflexive design that we discuss is the time-series design.[1] Although this design is a significant improvement over the one-group pretest-posttest design, it is still in the reflexive category, although some, such as David Nachmias, consider the time-series design to be quasi-experimental.[2] This design is often referred to as a single interrupted time-series design as the implementation of the program acts to interrupt the prevailing time series. The impact of the interruption is interpreted as programmatic impact. The simple time-series design is shown in Table 12-1.

Time-series designs are useful when preprogram and postprogram measures are available on a number of occasions before and after the implementation of a program. The design thus compares actual postprogram data with projections drawn from the preprogram period.

The design is useful when adequate historical data are available (e.g., numerous data points) and when there appears to be an underlying trend in the data—that is, the data are fairly stable and not subject to wild fluctuations. Crime or accident statistics are good examples of data that are adaptable to the use of the time-series design. Finally, a simple time-series design is considered appropriate when no other rival explanations of the effect can be entertained. In the following article, Delmas Maxwell uses this design to estimate impact for a target population: male drivers 19 to 21 years old.

TABLE 12–1   The Simple Time-Series Design

	Before		After
Group E	$O_1 \ O_2 \ O_3$	X	$O_4 \ O_5 \ O_6$

Impact Analysis of the Raised Legal Drinking Age in Illinois

DELMAS M. MAXWELL

BACKGROUND

Drivers between the ages of 16-25 are consistently overrepresented in traffic accidents, including fatal accidents. Young male drivers comprise a substantial portion of single vehicle accidents and alcohol involved fatal accidents.

Fatal accident involvement has been shown to be related to driver alcohol consumption. It has been determined that the risk of accident involvement increases as a function of driver blood alcohol content (BAC). In addition, alcohol related traffic accidents have been shown to be highly correlated with driver involvement age and sex. Also, studies show that most alcohol related accidents occur during nighttime hours.[1,4]

Driver sex, driver age, and accident hour are characteristics with which alcohol involved accidents are identified. Previous work[4] has shown that lowering the minimum legal drinking age increases the number of accidents involving drivers less than 25 years of age. Fourteen States since 1976 have passed legislation raising the minimum legal drinking age. Raising the legal drinking age has been found to reduce nighttime alcohol-involved accidents with younger drivers.[10,11]

Eight States (Florida, Georgia, Iowa, Minnesota, Montana, New Jersey, Rhode Island, and Tennessee) raised their minimum legal drinking age from 18 to 19. Maine, Massachusetts, and New Hampshire have raised the age from 18 to 20. A recent study of the raised legal drinking age in Maine[8] found a reduction in traffic accidents for drivers in the affected age groups.

Nebraska raised its minimum age from 19 to 20. In Michigan, where the legal drinking age was raised from 18 to 21, a recent study[10] found a reduction of 31 percent in alcohol involvement for those drivers affected by the law change, the 18-20 year old drivers. Increases of 9 percent and 5 percent in alcohol involvement were found for drivers 21-24 years old and 25-45 years old, respectively.

Illinois raised its minimum legal drinking age in January 1980 from age 19 to 21 years. As a result, drivers age 19 and 20 who could previously purchase alcohol can no longer do so. This analysis attempts to determine what reduction, if any, in alcohol involvement can be attributed to the law change in Illinois.

LEGAL DRINKING AGE LAW — IMPACT ANALYSIS

Data for single vehicle [night] male driver involvements (SVNMD) occurring between 8 P.M. and 3 A.M. were obtained from the State of Illinois. SVNMD was used as a surrogate for alcohol related accidents. Surrogate measures for alcohol involvement are typically used since BAC reporting for driver accident involvement is often incomplete.

Figures 1-9 (see Appendix) are graphs of each SVNMD raw data series along with the 12-month moving average. Monthly involvements by age group for 1977-1980 were analyzed as an impact measure. A total of nine series, each consisting of 48 data points, were used. The nine age groups used are shown in Table 1.

Source: Delmas M. Maxwell, "Impact Analysis of the Raised Legal Drinking Age in Illinois." NHTSA Technical Report DOT HS-806-115 U.S. Department of Transportation, December 1981.

TABLE 1 SVNMD Series

LT16	Driver Age Less Than	16
EQ16	Driver Age Equals	16
EQ17	Driver Age Equals	17
EQ18	Driver Age Equals	18
EQ19[a]	Driver Age Equals	19
EQ20[a]	Driver Age Equals	20
EQ21	Driver Age Equals	21
EQ22	Driver Age Equals	22
GT22	Driver Age Greater Than	22

[a] Ages affected by law change.

A statistical evaluation model was developed for each series (age group) to quantify the relationship between the impact measure (SVNMD) for the affected ages and a possible explanatory variable, the intervention of the legal drinking age law. The method used is a least-squares analysis technique known as Box-Tiao Intervention Analysis.[2,3] This approach has been used extensively to determine traffic safety program impact (e.g., the 55 MPH National Maximum Speed Limit) using State and National data.[6,7,8]

If a statistically significant reduction was found in the impact measure for the affected ages, 19–20 years old, and not found for the other age groups, we could reasonably conclude that these drivers exhibited behavior unlike the others. Therefore, this reduction is attributable to the law change.

The first step in the analysis was to develop a univariate model for each series. The univariate models would relate future SVNMD based on its own past. This was done to examine the time series characteristics exhibited in the raw data, which would serve as a basis for constructing impact assessment models[9] relating changes in SVNMD to the intervention, i.e., law change.

Figures 1–9 were used to identify possible similarities in the behavior of SVNMD for the nine age groups.

Univariate models were estimated for each series and are summarized in Table 2. Eight of the series were characterized by nonstationary behavior, i.e., observations at time period show high correlation with observations 12, 24, 36, etc. months apart. Nonstationarity was accounted for by taking a seasonal (12-month) difference of the original series and estimating a moving average parameter of order 12. Box-Jenkins Time Series Analysis was used to arrive at univariate model estimates.[2]

All series except LT16 required a seasonal (12-month) difference and a seasonal moving average parameter. The EQ19, EQ20, EQ21, and GT22 univariate models also required a moving average parameter of order 1. All model parameters were significant and residual analysis indicated that the models were adequate.

TABLE 2 SVNMD Univariate Models

Series	Difference Required	θ_1	s.d. (θ_1)	δ^{12}	S.D. (θ^{12})
LT16	Regular				
EQ16	Seasonal	—	—	0.75	0.07
EQ17	Seasonal	—	—	0.73	0.07
EQ18	Seasonal	—	—	0.74	0.07
EQ19[a]	Seasonal	0.50	0.15	0.80	0.07
EQ20[a]	Seasonal	0.40	0.16	0.76	0.07
EQ21	Seasonal	0.49	0.15	0.73	0.07
EQ22	Seasonal	—	—	0.79	0.07
GT22	Seasonal	0.42	0.16	0.74	0.07

[a] Ages affected by law change.

The next step in the analysis was to create a variable to represent the (intervention) raising of the legal drinking age in Illinois. The dummy variable LAW was created where:

$$LAW_t = 0, \ t < \text{January 1980}$$
$$1, \ t > \text{January 1980}$$

to represent the absence/presence of the new legal drinking age law.

Next, a model was developed for each series which would relate SVNMD and the intervention, LAW. This impact assessment model would provide a measure of the change associated with the raised minimum legal drinking age in Illinois. The following model form was entertained:

$$Y_t = w_o \, LAW_{t-b} + N_t$$

where

Y_t = SVNMD age group at month t

w_o = impact of raised minimum legal drinking age, i.e., monthly average change in SVNMD

b = delay time before impact is "felt"

N_t = noise series, a function of normal, independently distributed error, $N(0, \sigma^2)$

Impact assessment models were estimated for each SVNMD age group. For driver age = 19 (EQ19) and driver age = 20 (EQ20) the following models were estimated:

$$(8.7)$$
EQ19 $Y_t = -17.7 \, LAW_t + N_t$

where

$$N_t = \frac{(1 - .69B^{12})}{(1 - B^{12})} a_t$$

TABLE 3   Impact Assessment Estimates

Series	Impact W_o	s.d. (w_o)	t-value
LT16	−11.5	15.1	0.76
EQ16	−4.6	6.6	−0.70
EQ17	−5.1	8.3	−0.61
EQ18	−5.7	9.7	−0.59
EQ19	−17.7	8.7	−2.03[a]
EQ20	−11.2	6.4	−1.75[a]
EQ21	11.3	7.6	1.49
EQ22	2.5	7.7	0.33
GT22	31.9	102.2	0.31

[a] Significant at $\alpha = 0.05$

$$(6.4)$$
EQ20 $Y_t = -11.2 \, LAW_t + N_t$

where

$$N_t = \frac{(1 - .77B^{12})}{(1 - B^{12})} a_t$$

Values appearing in parentheses represent the standard errors of the estimates.

The model parameters and their standard errors for each of the SVNMD age groups are given in the Appendix. The values for W_o, impact of the raised legal drinking age, are summarized in Table 3. Delay time for all series was 0.

Both impact estimates for the affected ages were statistically significant (using a one-sided t-test) at the $\alpha = 0.05$ level.[5] Impact assessment estimates for the other age groups were not statistically significant.

Analysis of the model residuals revealed no model inadequacies.

From these models, estimates can be made of the steady state reduction in single vehicle night male driver involvements for the affected ages attributable to Illinois legal drinking age law change. The steady state estimate of the reduction attributable to the law change

TABLE 4   Annual SVNMD

	1977	1978	Base 1979	Avg.	1980	All Yrs. Avg.
EQ19	2,145	2,243	1,965	2,118	1,897	2,063
EQ20	1,863	1,845	1,708	1,805	1,689	1,776
TOTAL	4,008	4,008	3,673	3,923	3,586	3,839

TABLE 5 1980 Reduction in SVNMD

	Number	Percentage
EQ19	212	10.0
EQ20	134	7.4
TOTAL	346	8.8

for drivers age 19 and age 20 is 17.7 and 11.2 per month, respectively. Those reductions can be compared to annual SVNMD for EQ19 and EQ20. Annual SVNMD are shown in Table 4.

Thus, the 1980 reduction in single vehicle night male driver involvements, using the model estimates and comparing these to base year (before the law change) averages yields Table 5.

CONCLUSION

From the above results, the raising of the legal drinking age law has been effective in the reduction of single vehicle night male driver involvements for drivers ages 19 and 20 in Illinois. Single vehicle night male driver involvements was used as a surrogate measure for alcohol involvement in accidents for these drivers.

The percent[age] reduction attributable to the law change in Illinois in single vehicle night male driver involvements for 1980 totals 8.8 percent.

REFERENCES

1. *Alcohol Safety Action Projects, Evaluation of Operations,* 1974, Vol. II, Chapter 1, DOT-HS 801 726.

2. Box, G. E. P. and Jenkins, G. M. *Time-Series Analysis Forecasting and Control.* Holden-Day, 1970.

3. Box, G. E. P. and Tiao, G. C. *Intervention Analysis with Application to Economic and Environmental Problems. Journal of the American Statistical Association, March 1975.*

4. Douglas, R. L., Filkins, L. D., Clark, F. A.
The Effect of Lower Legal Drinking Age on Crash Involvement, September 1974. DOT-HS 801 213.

5. Hogg, R. V., Craig, A. T. *Introduction to Mathematical Statistics,* 4th edition, Macmillan Publishing Co., Inc., 1978.

6. Johnson, P., Klein, T. M., Levy, P., Maxwell, D. *The Effectiveness of the 55 MPH National Maximum Speed Limit as a Life Saving Benefit.* DOT-HS 805 694. October 1980.

7. Klein, T. M. *The Effect of Raising the Minimum Legal Drinking Age on Traffic Accidents in the State of Maine.* DOT Technical Note (in print), December 1981.

8. Maxwell, D. *The Effect of the Speed Enforcement Program in Massachusetts.* DOT-HS 805 977. August 1981.

9. McCleary, R. and Hay R. A. *Applied Time-Series Analysis for the Social Sciences.* Sage Publications, 1980.

10. Wagenaar, A. C. *Effects of the Raised Legal Drinking Age on Motor Vehicle Accidents in Michigan,* HSRI Research Review, January-February 1981.

11. Williams, A. F., Zador, P. L., Harris, S. S., Karpf, R. S. *The Effect of Raising the Legal Minimum Drinking Age on Fatal Crash Involvement.* Insurance Institute for Highway Safety, June 1981.

APPENDIX A

Series: SVNMD, LT16

Impact Estimate, W_o	-11.5
s.d. (W_o) 15.1	
t-value	-0.76

Model $Y_t = -11.5 \, LAW_t + N_t$

where $N_t = \dfrac{a_t}{(1 - .85B)}$

Series: SVNMD, EQ16

Impact Estimate, W_o	-4.6
s.d. (W_o) 6.6	
t-value	-0.70

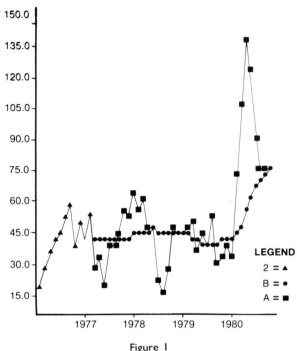

Figure 1
SVNMD-LT16

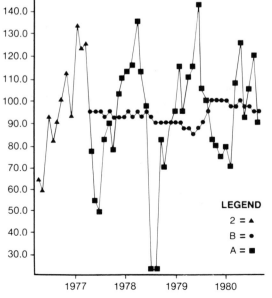

Figure 2
SVNMD-EQ16

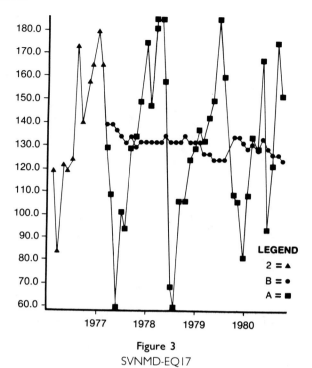

Figure 3
SVNMD-EQ17

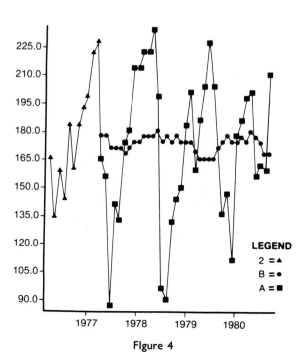

Figure 4
SVNMD-EQ18

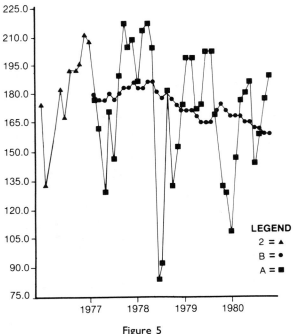

Figure 5
SVNMD-EQ19

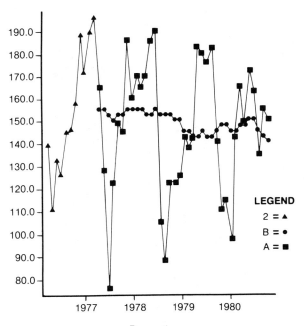

Figure 6
SVNMD-EQ20

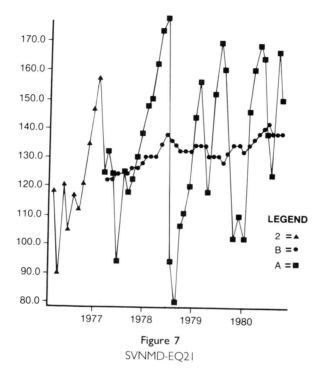

Figure 7
SVNMD-EQ21

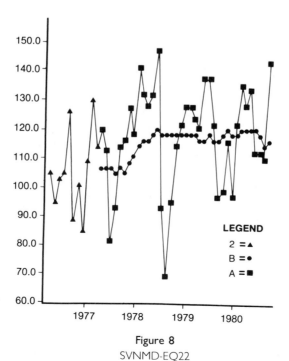

Figure 8
SVNMD-EQ22

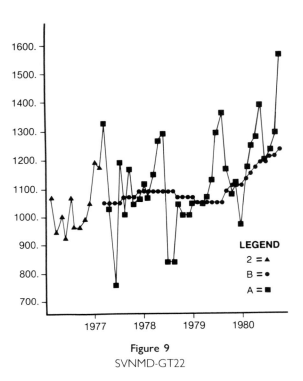

Figure 9
SVNMD-GT22

Model $Y_t = -4.6\ LAW_t + N_t$
where $N_t = \dfrac{(1\ -\ .81B^{12})}{(1\ -\ B^{12})}\ a_t$

Series: SVNMD, EQ17

    Impact Estimate, W_o -5.1

    s.d. (W_o) 8.3

    t-value -0.61

Model $Y_t = -5.1\ LAW_t + N_t$
where $N_t = \dfrac{(1\ -\ .46B^{12})}{(1\ -\ B^{12})}\ a_t$

Series: SVNMD, EQ18

    Impact Estimate, W_o -5.7

    s.d. (W_o) 9.7

    t-value -0.59

Model $Y_t = -5.7\ LAW_t + N_t$
where $N_t = \dfrac{(1\ -\ .65B^{12})}{(1\ -\ B^{12})}\ a_t$

Series: SVNMD, EQ19

    Impact Estimate, W_o -17.7

    s.d. (W_o) 8.7

    t-value -2.03

Model $Y_t = -17.7\ LAW_t + N_t$
where $N_t = \dfrac{(1\ -\ .69B^{12})}{(1\ -\ B^{12})}\ a_t$

Series: SVNMD, EQ20

    Impact Estimate, W_o -11.2

    s.d. (W_o) 6.4

    t-value -1.75

Model $Y_t = -11.2 \, \text{LAW}_t + N_t$

where $N_t = \dfrac{(1 - .77B^{12})}{(1 - B^{12})} \, a_t$

Series: SVNMD, EQ21

Impact Estimate, W_o 11.3

s.d. (W_o) 7.6

t-value 1.49

Model $Y_t = 11.3 \, \text{LAW}_t + N_t$

where $N_t = \dfrac{(1 + .47B)}{(1 - B^{12})} \, a_t$

Series: SVNMD, EQ22

Impact Estimate, W_o 2.5

s.d. (W_o) 7.7

t-value 0.32

Model $Y_t = 2.5 \, \text{LAW}_t + N_t$

where $N_t = (1 + .48B) \, a_t$

Series: SVNMD, GT22

Impact Estimate, W_o 31.9

s.d. (W_o) 102.2

t-value 0.31

Model $Y_t = 31.9 \, \text{LAW}_t + N_t$

where $N_t = \dfrac{(1 - .67B)(1 + .58B^{12})}{(1 - B)} \, a_t$

Explanation and Critique

Evaluation literature is awash in studies linking driver safety laws and the reduction of traffic fatalities. The 55 mile per hour speed limit, mandatory seat belt and child restraint laws, and drinking age legislation have been the foci of this research. Decision makers are interested in determining just what intrusive measures or constraints can be justified in terms of saving lives.

Delmas Maxwell joined this research tradition by estimating the impact of raising the drinking age in Illinois on accidents involving single vehicles driven by males between the hours of 8:00 P.M. and 3:00 A.M. In Figures 1 through 9 of his article, Maxwell plotted the actual number of accidents per month from 1976 through 1980 (plotted points marked by "2" and "A") plus the 12-month moving average of the accidents (plotted "B") for each age group. The average, beginning in 1977, was based on the previous 12 months' reports. Box-Jenkins Time-Series Analysis was used for the univariate model estimates, and Box-Tiao Intervention Analysis assessed overall impacts of the programs.

The dependent variable was a surrogate for alcohol-related traffic fatalities, the single vehicle night male driver (SVNMD) index. Although Maxwell contended that surrogates are frequently used in these studies, this particular measure is curious in that it will overestimate some impacts while grossly underestimating others. Consider the assumptions in the measure. The single vehicle aspect suggests that most fatalities in which a vehicle runs off the road or hits a fixed object will be alcohol-related. Included in this measure would be fatalities caused by the driver's falling asleep at the wheel (a reasonable possibility between 8:00 P.M. and 3:00 A.M.), suffering a heart attack or other seizure, or suicide. The single vehicle assumption obviously did not include alcohol-related multiple-car crashes (e.g., cars crossing the center line or failing to stop and thus hitting another vehicle). The second assumption concerned night driving, which underestimated fatalities occurring after "happy hours" or any other alcohol-related fatalities. Including only male drivers in the count obviously underestimated fatalities due to females' drinking. Also, all the other concerns were exacerbated by including only males.

Why, then, did Maxwell use such a seemingly flawed measure? Surrogates are not necessarily poor measures. Historically, the correlations between the characteristics of the measure and alcohol consumption and related behavior are high. That was the justification used by Maxwell. These data (SVNMD) were readily available and collected systematically. Thus, Maxwell opted for a reliable measure expressing a trend over time even though it can be argued that the measure is not valid. That is a concern when one wishes to use the single interrupted time-series design. One must rely on how data were gathered—usually by someone else who probably did not have the analyst's research question in mind while gathering the data. Researchers are infrequently afforded the luxury of constructing such measures for bureaus. Even if they could, they might not have the research question in mind at the time.[3]

Concern about the criterion aside, Maxwell hypothesized an impact of the law if there is a significant reduction in the number of SVNMD fatalities for 19 and 20 year olds with the introduction of the law in 1980. The estimates for the univariate models controlled for seasonal variations, and an examination of the residuals indicated that the models were adequately specified.

The impact analysis related changes in SVNMD to the introduction of the law. The analysis revealed a significant reduction in SVNMD for the target categories. The one-tailed test was appropriate because the impact was hypothesized to be negative. Although the t-value was relatively low, it did satisfy the $p \leq 0.05$ baseline. Therefore, Maxwell concluded that the imposition of the law reduced fatalities among the groups affected by the law. This is consistent with the visual results of the moving averages in the article's Figures 5 and 6, which are downward sloping at the end of the time period (after the intervention). Moreover, the fluctuations in the actual monthly rates appear to be smaller than those demonstrated in earlier time periods, indicating a smoother, less erratic trend. The impact coefficient (W_o) indicated that the presence of the law ($LAW_t = 1$) contributed to the monthly reduction in fatalities of 17.7 and 11.2 for drivers aged 19 and 20 respectively. Notice that the interpretation of W_o is similar to that of the regression coefficient (b) discussed in Chapter 10. The only interpretable W_os in Table 3 are those that are statistically significant—in this case for EQ19 and EQ20. The overall reduction of fatalities for the targeted group in 1980 was 346 (8.8 percent) (article Tables 4 and 5). Consequently, Maxwell concluded that raising the drinking age in Illinois had the expected, significant result for the targeted group.

As stated in the introduction to this chapter, use of the single interrupted time-series design is justifiable in cases where no rival hypotheses could be entertained to produce the observed impact. The classic study in this regard was Robert Albritton's study of the impact of a permanent federal program to eradicate measles in the school-aged population in 1966.[4] Finding that the program had a substantial impact that continued over time, Albritton sought rival explanations for the impact. Because the number of school children had not declined and the impact remained even when statistically controlling for the private use of measles vaccine, he concluded that the impact of the program was real. Even though the federal program required improved measles reporting procedures, thus increasing reported incidence, the impact remained. Albritton pointed out that this result attenuated his estimates of the impact. Therefore, in reality, the impact was even greater than that estimated. No rival hypothesis could have possibly explained the impact.

What about Maxwell's analysis? Could any rival hypotheses have been introduced to falsify the findings? Maxwell did not include any; however, some reasonable ones should have been investigated. The introduction of the law came during a time of heightened awareness about drunk driving. Did police tighten their enforcement of drunk driving laws coincidentally with the raising of the drinking age? If so, some possible fatalities would have been averted. One thing that did occur was that patrolling and enforcement were intensified in counties bordering Wisconsin (which had a lower drinking age than Illinois), including the setting up of roadblocks to inhibit interstate drinking and driving among 18 to 20 year olds. These factors provide rival hypotheses that were not addressed by Maxwell.

One way Maxwell could have possibly addressed the rival hypotheses would have been that if intensified patrolling was actually stopped and the impact (i.e., reduction of fatalities) continued, he could have eliminated this rival. Therefore, one must be cautious with this design although it can be a powerful tool in that it controls for random variances for which one cannot control in single time pretest-posttest designs.

REFERENCES

1. Hatry, Winnie, and Fisk call this "Comparison of Time Trend Projection of Preprogram Data with Actual Postprogram Data." See Harry P. Hatry, Richard E. Winnie, and Donald M. Fisk, *Practical Program Evaluation for State and Local Governments*, 2nd ed. (Washington, DC: Urban Institute, 1981), pp. 30-39.

2. David Nachmias, *Public Policy Evaluation: Approaches and Methods* (New York: St. Martin's Press, 1979), p. 57.

3. Tamasak Witayapanyanon, "Evaluation of the Illinois Drinking Age Law," unpublished manuscript, Northern Illinois University, 1985. In a reanalysis of Maxwell's article using a more valid measure of alcohol-related fatalities, Witayapanyanon found that the overall number of alcohol-related deaths *increased* with the increase in the drinking age although it decreased dramatically within the *target group*.

4. Robert B. Albritton, "Cost-Benefits of Measles Eradication: Effects of a Federal Intervention," *Policy Analysis* 4 (1978): 1-22.

PART FIVE

Cost-Benefit
and Cost-Effectiveness Designs

The preceding parts discussed the various methodologies for assessing the impact of a program or treatment. These experimental, quasi-experimental, and reflexive designs answer the fundamental question, "Do these programs work as intended?" These statistical or manipulable methods are referred to by Laura Langbein as methods of "evaluation research."[1] This part is related to the earlier ones; however, its applications address more practical, and certainly political, decision making. The questions answered by cost benefit and cost effectiveness are, "Is this program worth it?" and "How much do constituents receive as a result of the program?"

The designs described here and earlier can be (and are) used in tandem to evaluate the impact of programs. It makes little sense to estimate the cost benefits of a program that had no impact; the benefits did not exist. Likewise, it is important for decision makers to know which of competing programs work or have the greatest impact. If the costs to operate the *best* program are prohibitive, however, it would be politically and fiscally responsible to offer a program with slightly less estimated impact that a political unit could afford than offer no program at all.

Cost-benefit and cost-effectiveness measures are relative; it is sometimes difficult to interpret them outside of the evaluation site. However, one way to evaluate the measures is to compare them with some established standard. Service level standards, or goals, are often published by professional associations (e.g., the International City Management Association, the National Education Association, the American Library Association). For instance, the American Library Association publishes circulation and holdings goals by type of library and population characteristics of the catchment area.[2] Peter Rossi and Howard Freeman call such goals *generic controls*.[3]

Care should be taken in determining the difference between a well-established norm and professional aggrandizement. In the absence of established norms, researchers may wish to compare their results with those from similar studies to know if they are "in the ballpark." Finally, they can use others' results to predict outcomes in their own evaluations. The article in Chapter 13 uses generic controls.

The applications of cost-benefit and cost-effectiveness analysis are not confined to overtly political realms such as city councils and state legislatures. These tools are useful in such nonprofit realms as hospital and psychiatric settings. They can even be useful in the private sector where maximizing corporate profit while maintaining product and service integrity is important. The following two chapters provide examples of these two methods, which differ in assumptions, problems, and utility. As with other designs, the appropriateness of either method depends on the questions the evaluation client needs answered and the constraints of the available data.

REFERENCES

1. Laura Irwin Langbein, *Discovering Whether Programs Work: A Guide to Statistical Methods for Program Evaluation* (Glenview, IL: Scott, Foresman, 1980), p. 9.

2. Henry Hatry and his colleagues chronicle a number of measures and standards related to effectiveness in *How Effective Are Your Community Services* (Washington, DC: Urban Institute, 1977).

3. Peter H. Rossi and Howard E. Freeman, *Evaluation: A Systematic Approach* 3rd ed. (Beverly Hills: Sage, 1985), pp. 279-282.

13

Cost-Benefit Designs

Cost-benefit analysis is an intuitively easy process to conceptualize and appreciate. One gathers all the costs of providing a good or service and weighs those costs against the dollar value of all the subsequent benefits provided by the good or service. If the benefits outweigh the costs, the good or service should be continued; if the costs of providing the service exceed the benefits obtained, the service should be terminated. All decision makers can relate to break-even points. Private sector managers wish benefits (i.e., profit) to far exceed costs, whereas public sector managers hope at least to break even.

This is not to say that public sector managers never attempt to economize or provide efficient services. The nature of governmental involvement has been historically to provide "collective goods"—those for which exclusion is infeasible and joint consumption possible. The private market has no incentive to provide collective goods through normal market structures because they cannot make a profit by doing so. Therefore, government must get involved to provide these services.[1]

However simplistic this analysis seems conceptually, the actual adding up of costs and benefits is anything *but* simple. First, you must list all the costs and all the benefits associated with a program. Do you include only the costs to a *particular* agency when more than one agency supports the program? How do you apportion overhead costs? What about the costs of in-kind contributions? And as for benefits, do you consider short-term benefits or long-term benefits, or both? How do you divide programmatic benefits when a recipient participates in several related programs (e.g., general assistance, job training, child nutrition, and subsidized day care)? Once these costs and benefits are delineated, how do you attach a dollar amount to the numerator or denominator? What is the dollar value of one nonhungry child or the deterrent effect of keeping one child out of the juvenile justice system?

These are not easy questions. These are the very questions confronted by any researcher involved in cost benefit analysis. A fundamental assumption of this design is that the researcher is able to assign dollar values to both the numerator and denominator. Typically, costs are easier to assign than are benefits. When we described time-series analysis earlier, we gave some attention to the fact that some impacts of programs occur instantaneously, some over time, some extinguish quickly whereas others deteriorate over time. When determining benefits, the researcher must be aware of the expected impact and judge benefits accordingly. This is not often an easy task.

When you can make such assignments, cost-benefit analysis becomes a very strong tool to assist decision making—especially when you can make comparisons among competing programs or the ways service is delivered. However, some major ethical considerations come into play when interpreting cost benefit ratios. Should the interpretation and utilization of the ratios be taken literally? Should you abolish a program merely on the basis of the cost benefit result? If so, you can understand why researchers must be extremely careful in partialling out costs and benefits. Moreover, what role must government play in providing basic social services? If there were positive benefit-to-cost ratios in all social programs, would not the marketplace step in to provide such services? Would strict attention to cost-benefit ratios nail the lid on the coffin of the delivery of social services?

"The Costs and Benefits of Title XX and Title XIX Family Planning Services in Texas" is an excellent example of a careful, well-conceived, cost-benefit analysis. Notice that Malitz is in a precarious position with regard to estimating benefits. The benefits are actually negative costs (expenditures) not incurred as a result of the estimated impact of the program. He cannot *directly* measure the benefits because the benefits are the consequences of averted pregnancies!

Malitz's article refers to the Titles XIX and XX amendments to the Social Security Act. Title XIX refers primarily to Medicaid services (health care) for poor people covered by the Aid to Families with Dependent Children. Title XX provides health and social service assistance (subsidized day care, maternal health and family planning, home health care) for low-income individuals—even those above "the poverty line."

The Costs and Benefits of Title XX and Title XIX Family Planning Services in Texas

DAVID MALITZ

Publicly funded family planning services in Texas are administered by two state agencies: the Texas Department of Human Resources (TDHR) and the Texas Department of Health. In fiscal year (FY) 1981, TDHR spent about $22 million in Title XX and XIX funds to provide services to more than a quarter of a million patients, representing about 79 percent of all women receiving family planning services from organized providers in Texas (Alan Guttmacher Institute, 1982). In 1982, TDHR commissioned a study to evaluate the

---

Source: David Malitz, "The Costs and Benefits of Title XX and Title XIX Family Planning Services in Texas," EVALUATION REVIEW, Vol. 8, No. 4 (August 1984), pp. 519-530. Copyright © 1984 by EVALUATION REVIEW. Reprinted by permission of Sage Publication, Inc.

impact of this large program (Malitz et al., 1981). One component of this evaluation was a cost-benefit analysis, the results of which will be reported in this article.

The costs of the programs were relatively easy to ascertain and consisted of expenditures for the programs during FY 1981. The benefits, however, were considerably more difficult to measure. For this study, consideration was limited to direct, first-year cost savings to TDHR which arose through the prevention of unwanted births. These cost savings consisted of expenditures which would have been incurred within the first year following birth in TDHR's Aid to Families of Dependent Children (AFDC), Food Stamp, and Medicaid programs.

It is important to note some of the possible benefits that were not considered in the analysis. These include prevention of long-term welfare dependency and adverse social and health consequences due to births by adolescent mothers, as well as the health benefits which may result from health screening by family planning providers. In addition, although estimates were made of the number of abortions and miscarriages averted, no attempt was made to quantify these benefits in financial terms.

The methodology is patterned after Chamie and Henshaw's (1982) analysis of governmental expenditures for the national family planning program. It requires estimates of the number of births averted by the program, the proportion of such births which lead to the receipt of public assistance, and the cost of this assistance.

The number of births averted was estimated by examining patterns of contraceptive use among family planning patients (Forrest et al., 1981). Data were collected regarding the use of various contraceptive methods (including no method) by family planning patients before they entered the program (the premethod) and after their last visit to the program (the postmethod). Use-effectiveness

rates for each of these contraceptive methods was applied to the preprogram distribution to estimate the number of women who would become pregnant within a year if they continued using the contraceptive methods observed just prior to their first program visit. Similarly, estimates were made of the number of women who would become pregnant within a year using the postmethods of contraception. The difference between these two estimates represents the number of pregnancies averted by the program.

Using available data regarding the outcomes of unwanted pregnancies in the United States (Dryfoos, 1982), calculations were made of the number of births, abortions, and miscarriages which would have resulted from the pregnancies averted. Finally, public assistance costs were estimated for the births averted and compared with the costs of the program to derive the cost-benefit ratio.

METHODOLOGY

As noted above, the number of averted pregnancies was estimated from data on pre and postprogram use of contraceptive methods by family planning patients. To gather these data, a survey was conducted of a randomly selected sample of case records maintained by the 78 providers of Title XX family planning services in Texas. Technical problems made it impossible to draw a separate sample of patients from the Title XIX program in the time available. Although estimates of the costs and benefits of the Title XIX program will be made below, it should be understood that these are based upon contraceptive use data gathered from the Title XX program.

The sampling frame for the Title XX survey consisted of billing records for all 227,253 Title XX patients served in FY 1981 (September, 1980 through August, 1981). Patients were stratified by provider and by age: adolescents (19 years and younger) and adults

(20 years and over). Patient records within each age group were sampled from the 78 providers in proportion to the number of patients served by each provider.

Based upon this sampling plan and upon an expected rate of return, the sample size was determined and a sample drawn from the billing records. The final sample consisted of 1606 adolescents (about 2.5 percent of the Title XX adolescent population) and 1605 adults (about 1.0 percent of the adult population). Given an expected response rate of about 70 percent, a 95 percent confidence interval of about ±18 pregnancies per 1,000 women would be achieved.

Survey forms were printed which identified each patient sampled, and which solicited information from the providers to determine the date when the patient first visited the agency, the date of the last visit in FY 1981, and the method(s) of contraception used by the patient before her first visit and after her last visit in FY 1981. Agency staff were assured that patient confidentiality would be maintained, and the survey form was designed in such a manner that patient names could be detached so they could not be identified with patient information.

Survey forms were returned by 65 of the 78 providers. Among those returning forms, the completion rate was quite high. Overall, 1252 complete and usable survey forms for adolescents (78.0 percent) were returned and 1283 (79.9 percent) complete forms for adults were obtained.

RESULTS

Pregnancies, Births, Abortions and Miscarriages Averted

Table 1 presents the survey results for adolescents and adults. On the left-hand side of Table 1, the various contraceptive methods are listed along with the number of pregnancies

expected within a year's time among 1,000 sexually active women using each method (Forrest et al., 1981). It can be seen that the use-effectiveness rates range from a low of zero for sterilization to a high of from 490 to 640 pregnancies per 1,000 women using no method of contraception.

Following the use-effectiveness rates are data from the sample of case records for adolescent Title XX patients. Shown first is the percent distribution of preprogram contraceptive use, followed by the post-program distribution. Similar pre and postdistributions are shown for adult patients. When multiple methods, either at the pre or postlevel were indicated by agency staff, the patient's most effective method was chosen as the primary method for purposes of data analysis.

It can be seen from Table 1 that, among adolescents, the most common premethod was "none," indicated for 68.7 percent of the 1252 patients from whom data were available. This percentage is considerably higher than the 50.4 percent reported by Forrest et al. (1981) for a 1975 national sample of adolescents visiting family planning clinics. However, data collected by the Alan Guttmacher Institute (AGI) (AGI, 1981, AGI, 1982) show a fairly steep rise between 1972 and 1980 in the proportion of family planning patients using no method of birth control before entering clinics. When patients of all ages are combined, the percentage rose from 31 percent in 1976 to 55 percent in 1979. Among adolescents, data for 1980 show 70 percent using no premethod in a national sample. Thus, the percentage for Texas adolescents is slightly lower than the national average for 1980, the latest year for which data were available.

Examination of the distribution of post-program usage among adolescents in Table 1 reveals a dramatic shift from preprogram usage. Whereas 68.7 percent used no preprogram method, only 14.4 percent used no method after the program, a drop of more than 50 percentage points. Thus, by the time

TABLE I   Contraceptive Method Use Patterns and Expected Number of Pregnancies Averted Among Title XX Patients Served

| Contraceptive Method | Expected Number of Annual Pregnancies per 1,000 Women | Percentage Using Each Method Before First Visit and After Last Visit to Program | | | |
| | | Adolescents | | Adults | |
		Pre	Post	Pre	Post
Pill	25	21.4	74.7	42.9	62.9
IUD	71	0.8	1.8	3.7	6.7
Diaphragm	172	0.3	1.1	0.6	1.9
Foams, creams, jellies	184	1.9	0.8	2.3	2.4
Rhythm	250	0.2	0.0	0.2	0.2
Sterilization	0	0.0	0.1	1.7	6.9
Condom	123	5.9	6.5	4.8	7.9
Other	189	0.8	0.6	1.1	1.2
None	490 to 640	68.7	14.4	42.6	9.9
Total	—	100.0	100.0	100.0	100.0

| Expected Number of Annual Pregnancies per 1,000 Patients | Adolescents | | Adults | |
	Pre	Post	Pre	Post
Low estimate	357	103	237	90
High estimate	460	124	301	104
Midpoint estimate	408.5	113.5	269.0	97.0
Pregnancies averted	295		172	

Source: Forrest, Hermalin, and Henshaw (1981) for expected number of annual pregnancies per 1,000 women.

NOTES

Based upon surveys of contraceptive failures among married women using the methods listed. The estimates of pregnancy rates among users of no method are based upon surveys of unmarried, sexually active adolescents.

of the last agency visit in FY 1981, the majority of the adolescent patients (85.6 percent) were using one of the more effective contraceptive methods. The percentage using no method after the program (14.4 percent) is slightly higher than the 12 percent figure reported among adolescents in 1980 (Alan Guttmacher Institute, 1982). It is also higher than the 8.1 percent reported in 1975 (Forrest et al., 1981).

Among adolescents using an effective method after the program, the vast majority left the agency using the pill. This method was used by 74.7 percent of the sample, slightly more than the 69 percent reported by AGI for 1979. The condom was the next most common method, and was used by 6.5 percent of the Texas sample after leaving the program.

It should be noted that among the 14.4 percent of the adolescent patients who left the agency using no method, most (88.3 percent) also entered the agency using no method on their first visit (not shown in Table 1). To a somewhat lesser degree, this was true for adults, for whom 66.4 percent of those leaving with no method also entered with no method.

Patients who entered and exited with no method would appear to represent program failures because ideally all patients should leave the agency using an effective contraceptive method. However, inquiries made to clinic personnel indicated that many of these patients came to the agencies for pregnancy tests. Some of these patients were found to be pregnant and therefore could not be given contraceptives. Unfortunately, it was not possible, with the data at hand, to determine how many of those exiting with no method were pregnant and how many refused or were not given contraceptives for other reasons. However, AGI data (1982) indicate that among patients who had no contraceptive method at their last clinic visit, about half were pregnant, while the remainder were seeking pregnancy, came to the clinic for infertility services, did not receive a method for medical reasons, or, for nearly one-third, failed to receive a method for some other reason.

At the bottom of Table 1 is the expected number of pregnancies per 1,000 patients based upon the pre- and postmethod distributions. These estimates were derived by multiplying the number of pregnancies among 1,000 users of each method by the percent using each method, and summing the resulting products across methods. Given that a range is indicated for the pregnancy rate among users of no contraceptive method, low and high estimates were calculated in each column.

It can be seen that among adolescent users of the preprogram methods, between 357 and 460 pregnancies per 1,000 patients would be expected (the midpoint of this range is 408.5). Nearly all of these pregnancies would be attributable to patients using no method, who accounted for 337 to 440 of these pregnancies.

Among adolescent users of the postprogram methods, fewer pregnancies (103 to 124 per 1,000 patients with a midpoint of 113.5) would be expected. This is due primarily to the shift from no method to some effective method.

To simplify future calculations, the midpoints of each range were used as the best

estimate of the expected number of pregnancies. The difference between the pre- and postmidpoints represents the number of pregnancies averted. Thus, approximately 295 pregnancies per 1,000 adolescent patients were averted by the Title XX program. This is higher than the 240 pregnancies averted among U.S. adolescents in 1975 reported by Forrest et al. (1981). It also compares favorably with the 1979 figure of 282 pregnancies averted per 1,000 adolescents aged 15-19 reported by AGI (1981).

Turning to the adult data presented in the second part of Table 1, it can be seen that the percentage of patients using no preprogram method (42.6 percent) is lower than was found among adolescents, but is still substantial. Only 9.9 percent of the adults used no postprogram method, the remainder using the pill most frequently, followed by condoms, sterilizations, and the IUD. Forrest et al. do not present data for adults, but AGI (1982) data from 1980 show that among women aged 20 and over, 39 percent used no preprogram method and 12 percent used no postprogram method. Thus, the Texas figures show slightly more adult women using no preprogram method and slightly fewer using no postprogram method than the national figures for this age group.

In terms of pregnancies averted, the estimate in Table 1 of 172 pregnancies per 1,000 patients is higher than the estimates reported by AGI for 1970-1972, the latest years for which adult estimates were made. These national estimates are 141 pregnancies averted per 1,000 women aged 20-29 and 52 pregnancies averted among women 30 and over.

Table 2 uses the Title XX estimates of pregnancies averted to make additional estimates of the number of births, abortions, and miscarriages averted by the Title XX and XIX programs. At the top of the table is shown the number of pregnancies averted, computed by multiplying the program counts by the mid-

TABLE 2 Estimated Number of Pregnancies, Births, Abortions, and Miscarriages Averted by the Title XX and Title XIX Family Planning Programs

| Age Group | Number in Program | Pregs. Averted | Total Births, Abortions, and Miscarriages Averted | | | Births Averted per 1,000 Patients |
			Births	Aborts.	Miscar.	
Title XX Program						
Adolescents	63,176	18,637	6,784	9,542	2,311	107
Adults	164,077	28,221	15,614	8,592	4,015	95
Total	227,253	46,858	22,398	18,134	6,326	99
Title XIX Program						
Adolescents	11,653	3,438	1,251	1,760	426	107
Adults	32,823	5,646	3,122	1,716	802	95
Total	44,476	9,084	4,342	3,516	1,226	99

| U.S. Pregnancy Outcomes | Percentage Distribution of Unintended Pregnancies by Outcome | | |
Age Group	Births	Aborts.	Miscar.
Adolescents	36.4	51.2	12.4
Adults	55.3	30.4	14.2
Total	47.8	38.7	13.5

Source: Dryfoos (1982) for distribution of unintended pregnancies by outcome.

NOTES

Pregnancies averted are calculated by multiplying program counts by Title XX rates in Table 1. Rows may not sum to totals due to rounding.

point of the pregnancies-averted rates from Table 1. It can be seen that almost 19,000 adolescent pregnancies and more than 28,000 adult pregnancies were averted, for a total of nearly 47,000 pregnancies averted by the Title XX program in FY 1981.

At the bottom of Table 1 are listed the percent distribution of births, abortions, and miscarriages, for unintended pregnancies to women of low and marginal income (Dryfoos, 1982). This distribution is based on the assumption that pregnancies that occur to women who are visiting family planning clinics would be unintended. The figures are also appropriate because they were computed for women of low and marginal income in 1979, income levels similar to those among Title XX women in 1981.

These percentages were multiplied by the

number of pregnancies averted to estimate the number of births, abortions, and miscarriages averted by the program. At the top of Table 1 it can be seen that nearly 7,000 adolescent births and more than 15,000 adult births were averted by the program, for a total of about 22,000 births averted. About 18,000 abortions were averted, approximately half by adolescents and half by adults. About 6,000 miscarriages were also averted by the program.

The final column at the top of Table 2 expresses the births averted as a rate per 1,000 patients served. It can be seen that the program averted about one birth for every ten patients served.

The second section of Table 2 repeats the calculations for the Title XIX program based upon the Title XX pregnancies-averted rates. It can be seen that about 9,000 pregnancies were averted by the Title XIX program, and that these pregnancies would have resulted in about 4,300 births, 3,500 abortions, and 1,200 miscarriages.

Cost-Benefit Analysis of the Title XX Program

Direct first-year costs to TDHR are incurred by births to Title XX women in two ways. First, a certain percentage of Title XX women will become Title XIX eligible due to the birth of a child. For these women, TDHR will pay, through Medicaid, certain delivery and birth-related expenses. In addition, the department will pay AFDC and Medicaid benefits for each woman and her child for one year. Finally, because of the birth of a child, some women may be entitled to additional food stamp allotments. Births in this category will be termed "AFDC births."

TDHR can incur direct first-year expenses for non-AFDC births as well. Although at least some of these women will depend upon city and county funds to pay delivery and birth-related expenses, these costs will not be paid by TDHR and will therefore not be included in this analysis. However, some of the Title XX family planning patients will be food stamp recipients, and may therefore be entitled to an increased allotment due to an increase in family size.

Let a equal the costs associated with an AFDC birth, b equal the cost associated with a non-AFDC birth, p equal the proportion of Title XX women who would go onto AFDC due to a birth, and $1 - p$ equal the proportion who would not go onto AFDC.

Given these parameters, the total average cost per Title XX birth, t, will be:

$$t = (p \times a) + [(1 - p) \times b].$$

In other words, the two costs are weighted by the proportion of women incurring each cost, and summed to produce a total average cost

per Title XX birth. Looked at another way, this figure represents the average cost savings per Title XX birth averted. This figure can then be multiplied by the probability of averting a birth for each Title XX patient. The resulting figure will be the average cost savings per patient, which can be compared with the average cost of serving a patient to derive the cost-benefit ratio.

The following discussion will first outline the costs that can be incurred by TDHR due to births to Title XX women who become AFDC recipients. Following this, there will be a discussion of the increased food stamp costs to the remaining Title XX recipients. Estimates derived for these two groups will then be combined in the manner described above and will be used to estimate the overall cost savings brought about by averting births to Title XX women.

The first step involves computing the annual Title XIX cost in FY 1981 that would be expected for each case that went onto AFDC due to the birth of a child. This includes $1304, the average Title XIX payment per delivery; and $807, the average cost for inpatient hospital care for infants aged zero to one year of age (due primarily to premature births and birth defects); for a total Title XIX cost of $2,111 associated with the birth of a child.

The next figure needed is the cost of welfare maintenance for a mother and one child during FY 1981. Although some of the cases which go onto AFDC due to the birth of a child will have family sizes larger than this (and will therefore incur additional expenses), a conservative approach was taken by assuming all cases would consist of only two recipients.

Based upon a grant amount of $86 per month for twelve months, TDHR will pay $1032 to maintain a mother and one child on AFDC. In addition to this, it was calculated that the department will pay an estimated $1,006 in the first year for non-birth-related Medicaid benefits for the family. Thus, the cost for AFDC and Medicaid is $2,038 per year. Adding this to the birth-related expenses yields the total first-year Title XIX cost for an AFDC birth: $4,149.

The department will also incur added food stamp costs for the new AFDC cases that receive food stamps. The maximum allotment for increasing the family size from one to two recipients is $50 per month ($600 per year). About 87 percent of all AFDC cases receive food stamps, and the average allotment for these cases is about 91 percent of the maximum. Therefore, the average per-case yearly increase in food stamp allotments for a mother and one child who go onto AFDC is about $475 ($600 × .87 × .91).

To summarize, the costs to TDHR for cases that would go onto AFDC include $4149 for birth-related costs and welfare maintenance, plus $475 in increased food stamp allotments. This totals to $4,624 per AFDC birth.

The next parameter needed is the percentage of Title XX women who would go onto AFDC due to the birth of a child. A direct estimate was not available from TDHR. Therefore, an indirect method was used to derive this parameter.

National and local data were used to ascertain the number of family planning patients (both Title XIX and XX) who were mothers. Also estimated was the proportion of these family planning mothers who were already Title XIX recipients (i.e., the proportion who were on AFDC). It was reasoned that this proportion, the proportion of family planning mothers already on AFDC, represented the probability that a Title XX nonmother would go onto AFDC due to the birth of a child. This reasoning was based on the assumption that Title XX women will go onto AFDC in the same proportions as current family planning mothers who are enrolled in AFDC.

In this way it was estimated that 30.4 percent of all family planning mothers are on AFDC in Texas. Among adolescents, the proportion was 35.8 percent, whereas among adults, the proportion was 28.3 percent. These figures are somewhat lower than national estimates made by Chamie and Henshaw (1982) who estimated that among women of low and marginal income, 47.8 percent of adolescents and 31.0 percent of adults would go onto AFDC if they had a child. However, because Texas income requirements for AFDC eligibility are among the lowest in the country (McManus and Davidson, 1982), it makes sense that the Texas proportions would be lower than the national estimates.

These estimates of the percent of Title XX women who would go onto AFDC were multiplied by the total cost per AFDC birth, resulting in the first component of the average cost per birth to a Title XX family planning patient: $1,309 for adults and $1,655 for adolescents, with an average of $1,406 for all Title XX births (this average is weighted in accordance with the size of the adolescent and adult Title XX populations).

The second manner in which the department can incur costs is due to increased food stamp allotments for those Title XX women who give birth but do not go onto AFDC. It will be recalled that the maximum increase in the food stamp allotment for increasing the family size from one to two would be $600 per year. However, only about 27.4 percent of Title XX family planning patients receive food stamps, and the average allotment for a non-AFDC case is only about 50 percent of the maximum. Thus, the average yearly increase in the food stamp allotment for non-AFDC births is about $82 ($600 × .274 × .50).

The proportion of women not going onto AFDC would simply be 100 percent minus the proportion that would go onto AFDC. Thus, about 64.2 percent of adolescents, 71.7 percent of adults, the 69.6 percent of all Title XX women would not go onto AFDC due to the birth of a child. Applying these proportions to the $82 figure yields the second component of the cost of a Title XX birth: $43 for adolescents, $59 for adults, and about $57 for all patients combined.

The total cost per Title XX birth equals the sum of the two components (for AFDC and non-AFDC births): $1,708 for adolescents, $1,368 for adults, and $1,463 for births to all Title XX women combined. Table 3 uses these estimates to compute the overall costs and benefits attributable to the Title XX program. The above figures represent the average cost savings per birth averted. Multiplying these figures by the births-averted rates (in Table 2) yields the average cost savings per patient. Table 3 shows these costs savings to be $183 per adolescent, $130 per adult, and about $145 per patient of any age.

In FY 1981, 227,253 contraceptive and sterilization patients were served at a cost of $17,187,782; an average cost per patient of about $75. Dividing the average cost savings per patient by the average cost of delivering

services, cost-benefit ratios were computed to be 1:2.44 for adolescents, 1:1.73 for adults, and 1:1.93 for all Title XX patients. Thus, for every dollar spent on the Title XX family planning program, about $1.93 is saved. For every dollar spent on services to adolescents, about $2.44 is saved, and about $1.73 is saved from services to adults.

Total first-year savings to TDHR attributable to births averted by the Title XX program were computed by multiplying the total program cost by the ratio of benefits to costs. These total savings amounted to nearly $33 million, with $11.7 million attributable to adolescent services and about $21.5 million attributable to adult services. Subtracting the cost of delivering services from total savings yields a net savings of nearly $16 million to the Department. Roughly $6.9 million of these savings can be attributed to adolescent services, and approximately $9 million can be attributed to adult services.

The cost-benefit ratio of 1:2.44 for ado-

TABLE 3 Costs and Estimated Savings Associated with the Title XX Family Program for Adolescents and Adults

	Adolescents Only (19 and Under)	Adults Only (20 and Over)	All Patients
Savings			
Total estimated savings per birth averted	$1,708	$1,368	$1,463
Births averted per family planning patient	.107	.095	.099
Savings per family planning patient	$ 183	$ 130	$ 145
Costs			
Average Title XX expenditure per family planning patient (including sterilizations)	$ 75	$ 75	$ 75
Cost-Benefit Ratio	**1:2.44**	**1:1.73**	**1:1.93**
Total Cost and Savings in FY 81			
Number of patients	63,176	164,077	227,253
Total cost	$ 4,778,000	$12,410,000	$17,188,000
Total estimated savings	$11,658,000	$21,469,000	$33,173,000
Net estimated savings	$ 6,880,000	$ 9,059,000	$15,985,000

NOTE

Summing figures for adolescents and adults may not equal totals due to rounding.

lescents is somewhat lower than the national estimate of 1:2.92 computed by Chamie and Henshaw (1982). Although the methodologies were similar, there are two reasons why the estimates reported here are not directly comparable to Chamie and Henshaw's. First, the cost per patient served was higher in the Title XX program than the national average. The Texas Title XX program served patients at an average cost of about $75, compared to the 1979 national average of about $63. This will, of course, lower the ratio of benefits to costs.

The second reason the Title XX ratio is lower is that Chamie and Henshaw's cost-savings calculations include estimates of birth-related costs to all public sector entities. In contrast, only a portion of these birth-related costs, those billed directly to TDHR, were included here. Thus, costs incurred by city and county hospitals, for example, to help women of low and marginal income pay for deliveries and first-year care were included in Chamie and Henshaw's estimates, but not in those used for this study.

Cost-Benefit Analysis of the Title XIX Program

Having estimated the costs and cost savings associated with the Title XX program, similar estimates can be made for the Title XIX program. For Title XIX women receiving family planning services, TDHR incurs direct costs due to the birth of a child through birth-related expenses and welfare maintenance and increased food stamp allotments for the child (because the mother is already a Title XIX recipient, her costs represent no increased expense). The costs associated with birth-related expenses (delivery and first-year care) were outlined above and were seen to be approximately $2,111 per birth. AFDC grants for an additional child are $30 per month, or $360 per year, and Medicaid expenses for the new child recipient are about

$503 per year. Added to this is $475 in increased food stamp allotments, for a total of $3,449 per birth to a Title XIX recipient.

In Table 4, this cost per birth is multiplied by the births-averted rates to yield the cost savings per Title XIX family planning patient: approximately $369 per adolescent patient, $328 per adult, and $341 per patient of any age. In FY 1981, $4,959,614 Title XIX dollars were spent to deliver services to 44,476 patients through organized family planning providers (this includes patients who received sterilizations, other contraceptive methods, or drug refills, but does not include services delivered by private physicians). This averages to about $112 per patient.

When this average cost is compared with the average cost savings, a cost-benefit ratio of 1:3.04 results for all Title XIX patients, 1:3.29 for adolescents, and 1:2.93 for adults. Thus, for every Title XIX dollar spent on family planning, the department saves about $3. For adolescents, the savings are even greater. Total first-year savings in FY 1981 are calculated to be about $15.1 million. Net savings, after subtracting the cost of service, are about $10.1 million: $3.0 million attributable to adolescent services and $7.1 million to adult services.

It should be noted that the per-patient cost of delivering Title XIX services ($112) is substantially higher than either the average Title XX cost ($75) or the 1979 national average ($63). Nevertheless, the cost-benefit ratio was higher than that calculated for Title XX or for the nation as a whole. This is because TDHR pays delivery and birth-related expenses for all Title XIX recipients who give birth, but for only a portion of Title XX patients who give birth (those who go onto AFDC). Even in Chamie and Henshaw's national study (1982), it was estimated that, on the average, only 65 percent of the birth-related expenses for women of low and moderate income would be assumed by the public sector. Thus, it is the high expense to TDHR

TABLE 4 Costs and Estimated Savings Associated with the Title XIX Family Program for Adolescents and Adults

	Adolescents Only (19 and Under)	Adults Only (20 and Over)	All Patients
Savings			
Total estimated savings per birth averted	$3,449	$3,449	$3,449
Births averted per family planning patient	.107	.095	.099
Savings per family planning patient	$ 369	$ 328	$ 341
Costs			
Average Title XIX expenditure per family planning patient (including sterilizations)	$ 112	$ 112	$ 112
Cost-Benefit Ratio	**1:3.29**	**1:2.93**	**1:3.04**
Total cost and Savings in FY 81			
Number of patients	11,653	32,823	44,476
Total cost	$1,300,000	$ 3,660,000	$ 4,960,000
Total estimated savings	$4,277,000	$10,724,000	$15,078,000
Net estimated savings	$2,977,000	$ 7,064,000	$10,118,000

NOTE

Summing figures for adolescents and adults may not equal totals due to rounding.

for each Title XIX birth that makes the Title XIX family planning program so cost-effective.

DISCUSSION

Many potential benefits of the family planning program's services were not included in this analysis. These include certain human and long-range benefits that can be attributed to the prevention of about 56,000 unwanted pregnancies and 27,000 births. Also not included are the benefits, financial and otherwise, of preventing nearly 22,000 abortions and over 7,000 miscarriages.

Even certain financial cost savings were not included in this analysis. For example, many Title XX women who give birth but who are not eligible for AFDC and Medicaid depend upon the financial resources of city and county governments to pay for their births. By preventing births in this group of women, cost savings are realized by city and county governments that are not included in this analysis. Nevertheless, even when consideration is limited only to direct, first-year, financial cost savings experienced by a state welfare department, the demonstrable benefits of the program are substantial.

It is important to note that, as in many cost-benefit analyses, many estimates and assumptions were required to calculate the cost savings attributable to the program. Although every attempt was made to do this as accurately and, when necessary, as conservatively as possible, the conclusions of the study are only as valid as these estimates and assumptions. Nevertheless, the fact that the final cost-benefit ratios and the estimates of pregnancies and births averted are generally consistent with previous estimates lends credence to the results.

One key parameter was the estimate of

the number of pregnancies averted based upon the survey of contraceptive use among Title XX patients. Leridon (1977) states that this method of calculating pregnancies and births averted "often leads to an over-optimistic estimate, since one does not know whether the methods prescribed are effectively and correctly used" (p. 130). To some extent, this problem was overcome by employing use-effectiveness rates for the various contraceptive methods, for these rates reflect contraceptive effectiveness by taking into account factors that lead to less than maximal performance. Perhaps more problematic is the issue of discontinuation or switching of methods because the calculation of pregnancies averted assumes that women have used the premethods for one year in the absence of the program, and that they will also continue to use the postmethod for a period of one year following their last clinic visit.

Data from the National Survey of Family Growth (Vaughan et al., 1980) indicate that most women seeking to prevent an unwanted pregnancy continue using contraceptives over a period of a year, and that only between 3 percent and 9 percent will abandon use of a contraceptive method altogether. However, this abandonment could affect the estimate of the number of pregnancies averted, probably leading to an overestimate. Switching among methods could also affect the estimates, although the effect should be relatively minor as long as the switching occurs primarily among the more effective methods. The reason for this is that most of the pregnancies averted, according to the estimation procedure used in this study, are due to the switch from no method before coming to a clinic to some effective method at the last clinic visit. Any of the effective methods are so much more effective than no method, that switching among them will not have a great effect on the estimate of the number of pregnancies averted.

Despite these apparent problems with the method of estimation used in this study, Forrest et al. (1981) found that in one instance, at least, this method yielded an estimate of pregnancies and births averted which was quite comparable to one obtained using areal multivariate analysis. Although the two methods used completely different analytical methods and data bases, both yielded fairly similar estimates of the number of births averted in the United States in 1975 (75 to 98 births per 1,000 patients based upon the contraceptive-use methodology compared with approximately 101 births from the areal multivariate analysis methodology).

Nevertheless, further research is needed comparing the contraceptive-use methodology with other methods that estimate averted pregnancies. The contraceptive-use methodology is a simple and economical method to employ, and could be implemented in a variety of settings if found to be valid. Although not routinely reported in data systems that currently exist, it was found in the course of conducting this study that the pre and postmethod data were readily accessible in clinic records. Using these data, it would be possible to estimate the number of pregnancies, births, abortions, and miscarriages averted on any level of analysis from the level of the individual clinic or provider all the way up to the state or national level. It is therefore hoped that additional research will be undertaken to validate this simple method of assessing the impact of family planning services.

REFERENCES

Alan Guttmacher Institute (1982) Current Functioning and Future Priorities in Family Planning Services Delivery. New York: The Alan Guttmacher Institute.

Alan Guttmacher Institute (1981) Data and Analyses for 1980 Revisions of DHHS Five-Year Plan for Family Planning Services. New York: The Alan Guttmacher Institute.

Chamie, M. and S. K. Henshaw (1982) "The costs and benefits of government expenditures for family planning programs." Family Planning Perspectives 13: 117-126.

Dryfoos, J. G. (1982) "Contraceptive use, pregnancy intentions and pregnancy outcomes among U.S. women." Family Planning Perspectives 14:81-94.

Forrest, J. D., A. I. Hermalin, and S. K. Henshaw (1981) "The impact of family planning clinic programs on adolescent pregnancy." Family Planning Perspectives 13: 109-116.

Heridon, H. (1977) Human Fertility: The Basic Components. Chicago: Univ. of Chicago Press.

Malitz, D., R. L. Casper, and P. Romberg (1981) Impact Evaluation of the Texas Department of Human Resources Family Planning Program. Austin, TX: Texas Department of Human Resources.

McManus, M. A. and S. M. Davidson (1982) Medicaid and Children: A Policy Analysis. Evanston, IL: The American Academy of Pediatrics.

Vaughan, B., J. Trussel, J. Menken, and E. F. Jones (1980) Contraceptive Efficacy Among Married Women Aged 15-44 Years. Hyattsville, MD: National Center for Health Statistics.

Explanation and Critique

David Malitz's study attempts to estimate the benefits of a $22 million family planning program funded by the Texas Department of Human Resources (TDHR). In the beginning paragraphs, he sets up the parameters of the study outlining which aspects were and were not to be considered. He acknowledges that the cost estimates were easily obtained; the TDHR commissioned the study to see how *their* funds were spent. He limits the benefits to direct, first-year cost savings due to the prevention of unwanted pregnancies among Title XIX and Title XX family planning patients. He immediately makes his benefits estimate more conservative by eliminating long-term dependency costs and costs due to predicted abortions and miscarriages. In other words, he resisted the urge to pad the benefits, making the favorable relationship more difficult to obtain.

The benefits are the lack of expenditures that would have been incurred had the program not been in place, which complicates the matter. Family planning agencies cannot withhold services from eligible recipients, assigning them randomly into treated and untreated groups. Therefore, Malitz could not estimate averted pregnancies by counting the number of pregnancies in an untreated group, nor could he pull the figures out of thin air. Instead, he used national standards regarding contraceptive use among family planning patients and data regarding the outcomes of unwanted pregnancies in the United States as the basis from which he estimated averted pregnancies and their associated costs. There is face validity in using these measures as standards because the Texas women *were* family planning patients and the consequences of nontreatment (unwanted pregnancies) had been tabulated in another setting. In a sense, Malitz could use these standards as a comparison group in determining whether his findings were consistent with other research, in addition to using these prior results to project expenditures. In other words, he used generic controls.

Malitz reasonably assumed that in the absence of the family planning services, women would use the contraceptive methods they had been using when they entered the program. He used this preprogram information on Title XX recipients to estimate the number of averted pregnancies for both sets of recipients as a result of FY 1981 services. One could argue that in the absence of the program, women could have learned about or received other contraceptive advice resulting in averted pregnancies; however, the short time frame reduces the impact of this random effect. From the survey results and the baseline study that estimates the expected number of pregnancies per 1,000 women per method, Malitz estimated the number of adolescent and adult pregnancies averted (Table 1 of the article). "These estimates were derived by multiplying the number of pregnancies amount per 1,000 users of each method, and summing the resulting products across methods." Malitz used the midpoint estimates (again a relatively conservative measure) as the basis for extrapolating to the population served (Table 2 of the article). Again, notice that he compared his findings with the Forrest et al. (1981) and AGI (1981) studies to determine whether the Texas experience was at all similar to the other studies. To the extent that they are similar, he was confident in his estimation techniques. Again, this illustrates a use of generic controls. Because the costs to TDHR differed by whether one was a Title XX or Title XIX recipient, the estimates were calculated separately for each population.

All of this was accomplished before the actual cost-benefit analysis. The cost-benefit analysis takes into account the TDHR'S responsibility for AFDC births as opposed to the reduced expenditure for non-AFDC births—those Title XX women who would not become AFDC eligible due to a birth. The only TDHR increment for those remaining Title XX eligible women would be an increase in eligibility for food stamps. Therefore, three calculations are necessary to estimate benefits (non-additional costs to TDHR)—one for current AFDC recipients, one for Title XX eligibles who would become AFDC eligible with a birth, and one for those who would remain only Title XX eligible. Notice how carefully (and often conservatively) Malitz used existing information to calculate portions of the benefits. For example, consider the added food stamp costs for new AFDC cases that receive food stamps:

> The maximum allotment for increasing family size from one to two recipients is $50 per month ($600 per year). About 87 percent of all AFDC cases receive food stamps, and the average allotment for these cases is about 91 percent of the maximum. Therefore, the average per-case yearly increase in food stamp allotments for another child who goes on AFDC is about $475 ($600 × 0.87 × 0.91).

In this and other examples Malitz tried to incorporate existing knowledge from the Texas program and the standards to arrive at realistic benefits. One seeming anomaly is that the current cost of supporting the averted-birth AFDC family was not subtracted from the AFDC birth calculation (the portion THDR would pay anyway for maintenance without a birth). Although Malitz did not say so directly, it seems that this amount was taken care of by estimating maintenance at a two-person family amount (by Malitz's terms a conservative approach). This is because AFDC assumes *at least* a two-person family. A birth to an existing AFDC family assumes *at least* a three-person family. Moreover, Title XX eligibles who become

AFDC eligible are a 100 percent liability to TDHR—those expenditures are all *new* expenditures.

Malitz then took the average cost savings per Title XX birth averted, multiplied that by the birth-averted rates (his Table 2) to show the average cost savings per patient (his Table 3). From there a traditional cost-benefit analysis was straightforward. For example, TDHR cost to the adolescent family planning patient was $75 divided by the cost savings for that group (benefits) of $183, which yielded a cost-benefit ratio of 1:2.44. That ratio means that for every $1 (cost) provided by TDHR for family planning services to adolescents, the Department saved $2.44 (benefits) in costs that they would have had to provide for a Title XX adolescent birth. This procedure was duplicated for adults, all patients and groups of Title XIX eligibles (Malitz's Table 4).

At the bottom of his Tables 3 and 4, Malitz calculated the total cost savings (the "bottom line") of providing family planning services to the population of recipients. The net savings estimate was calculated by taking the total cost from the total estimated savings to arrive at the amount TDHR was ahead, given the current level of services.

The only question Malitz could not adequately address was the "What if?" question. What would Title XX eligible (or Title XIX, for that matter) women do in the absence of the family planning services if they were truly concerned about averting pregnancies? How many would pay a private doctor for contraceptive services? How many would require partners to supply condoms? Because of the sliding fee scale used to provide many Title XX services, one would expect that those women at the top of the scale (those with higher incomes) would be able to provide a few extra dollars for private assistance. In the absence of information on these questions, Malitz could not make an informed guess. He tried to overcome this weakness by consistently using conservative benefit estimates.

All in all, Malitz presented an analysis suggesting that the benefits of providing family planning services in Texas were greater than the costs incurred. Does this automatically mean that Texas will continue funding those services? That is a political question. Social conservatives may argue that government has no business being in the family planning business—or supporting indigent welfare mothers, for that matter. Cost benefit analysis is a tool to assist decision makers to make informed decisions based on sound empirical evidence regardless of whether one believes the ultimate decision to be sound.

Malitz's research is not the first article in the book that might benefit from cost-benefit analysis. Given the data presented by Ann Solberg in Chapter 4, it would be relatively simple to calculate the cost-benefit of posthospital follow-up of psychiatric patients.

REFERENCE

1. For an excellent treatment of alternate forms of service delivery mechanisms, see E. S. Savas, *Privatizing the Public Sector* (Chatham, NJ: Chatham House, 1982).

14

Cost-Effectiveness Designs

In the previous chapter, cost-benefit analysis was used to determine if program objectives were economically beneficial or justifiable. In cost-effectiveness analysis, the results of a project are assumed to be intrinsically worthwhile. Cost-effectiveness analysis "explores how such results might be efficiently achieved and which costs are attached to them for reaching different levels of the desired outcomes."[1] Like cost-benefit analysis, cost-effectiveness analysis assumes that all the costs (both direct and indirect) of a program can be calculated. The difference arises in the determination of the denominator. Rather than using only a dollar amount, a meaningful unit of effectiveness measure (or *unit of service*) is attached. For example, the evaluation would be, for example, in terms of the number of dollars spent per ton of garbage picked up per day or dollars spent per life saved.[2]

Cost-effectiveness designs are reasonably employed when it is difficult to attach a dollar amount to the denominator (e.g., the value of a life saved). The utility of this kind of design is traditionally associated with the exploration of a number of different alternatives to a specified, desired outcome. Like cost-benefit analysis, cost-effectiveness results are valuable tools for decision makers, particularly during budgetary deliberations. In addition, cost-effectiveness designs can act as a good measure of internal evaluation. It allows an evaluator to determine how well an organization is performing now as compared to before a change program was started. An example would be comparing the cost per ton of garbage collected in 1988 to the cost in 1985, controlling for inflation. Generic controls are often used to compare a program's cost effectiveness with national or professional standards (e.g., library book circulation standards, parkland acquisition standards). Finally, elected officials in one jurisdiction may wish to gauge their performance relative to other jurisdictions that are similar to them in order to see how well they are performing.

Whether it is a before-after, cross-community, or across-alternative process, cost effectiveness is based on comparisons. It is seldom useful if no comparisons are made. R.D. Peterson outlines three approaches to cost-effectiveness comparisons: constant-cost analysis, least-cost analysis, and objective-level analysis.[3] In a constant-cost analysis, the job of the researcher is to determine how much of an objective can be obtained within given cost constraints. Peterson's example is a program to reduce road accidents. He says:

> A legislature may vote to allocate only $2.5 million to accomplish the objective.
> A constant-cost analysis would focus on the total number of deaths that could be

prevented by spending $2.5 million for each alternative that could achieve that objective.

The least-cost analysis goal is to reach a prespecified goal for the least cost. Peterson goes on to say:

> For example, suppose that the stated objective was "to reduce deaths due to automobile accidents by 10 percent each year." Based on this criterion, the cost-effectiveness question involves finding the alternative that will achieve that end in the least expensive way. Each alternative way of achieving the stated objective would be analyzed in terms of the dollar amount of expenditures required to reach the specified goal.

The objective-level analysis compares varying performance levels under a single alternative: As Peterson says:

> In preventing highway deaths, the analyst might seek to determine costs according to 10 percent, 20 percent, 40 percent and 80 percent reductions in deaths for each specific program alternative. . . . The costs per unit of objective reached are then computed for each successive level.

The researcher involved in cost-effectiveness analysis usually identifies alternatives for reaching objectives and calculates cost-comparison ratios. In the following article, although the objectives are not clearly specified by the legal system, Pauline Houlden and Steven Balkin perform a version of the least-cost analysis to compare the costs of the services of ad hoc public defenders versus the services of those who are on staff part time.

Performance Evaluation for Systems of Assigned Service Providers

A Demonstration Assessing Systems of Indigent Defense

PAULINE HOULDEN
STEVEN BALKIN

Modern American society confronts any number of situations in which it wishes to provide services: health care, education, legal representation, and so on to individuals who cannot afford to purchase such services for themselves. Regardless of the service area, taxpayers, government managers, and consumers desire the best service for the least

---

Source: Pauline Houlden and Steven Balkin, "Performance Evaluation for Systems Assigned Service Providers: A Demonstration Assessing Systems of Indigent Defense," EVALUATION REVIEW, Vol. 9, No. 5 (October 1985), pp. 547–573. Copyright ©1985 by EVALUATION REVIEW. Reprinted by permission of Sage Publications, Inc.

cost. Often there is more than one way in which services can be provided, so a decision must be made between systems of service provision. For instance, choices might be made between reimbursement for fee for service, vouchers, direct public provision, or contracting with the private sector.

To evaluate the quality and cost of these systems it has seemed inappropriate to simply compare the performance of assigned providers with that of privately purchased providers. There are any number of dimensions along which assigned and privately retained providers will differ (e.g., years of experience, quality of education) and these may well be related to consumers' outcomes. In addition, there are any number of attributes along which the clients of assigned and retained providers will differ (e.g., education, lifestyle, prior medical, legal, or educational experiences) and these may also be related to system performance. Therefore, a comparison of assigned versus retained systems may yield spurious results. In addition, the contrast of assigned and retained providers sheds little light on how assigned service providers may differ among themselves. Yet this is an important policy choice issue.

Unfortunately, an analysis comparing systems of assigned service providers has its own limitations, because almost inevitably, different systems will be operating in different locales, or the same locale at two different times. Whatever differences are observed may therefore be due to differences in the locations or times, rather than system characteristics (Campbell and Stanley, 1972). Using a health care example, if Medicaid patients in one county are found to spend eight days in the hospital after a C-section, and public hospital patients in another city are found to spend five days, is this a true indication of greater cost savings associated with the patients of public hospital doctors? Or might the difference be due to countywide hospitalization practices? To answer this latter question

we need to know the length of hospitalization after a C-section for patients of privately retained doctors. Thus, although a comparison of assigned and retained service providers was previously argued to be insufficient for evaluating systems of assigned service providers, information about the relative functioning of assigned and retained service providers in a locale is, we believe, extremely valuable as a control. But it must be combined with information about the relative functioning of different systems of assigned service providers.

If patients of privately retained doctors in the first county are found to spend seven days in the hospital, whereas those in the second county spend four days, we have learned that there are differences in hospitalization between the counties. These must be taken into account in assessing the performance of Medicaid versus public hospital doctors. Examination of length of hospitalization for only assigned physicians led to the conclusion that Medicaid doctors were less quick to release patients than public hospital doctors. Yet once we are aware of the differences in county hospitalization practices, it appears that the patients of Medicaid doctors fare as well as the patients of privately retained doctors, whereas the patients of public hospital doctors spend a day longer in the hospital. It is the difference in the functioning of assigned versus retained service providers that must be determined in order to evaluate systems of assigned service providers.

A demonstration of the value of this technique for choosing between two systems of legal defense for the indigent is presented in this article. This approach is consistent with use of a performance ratio model (Grizzle, 1984) for comparing agencies across locations. For those confronted with the problem of evaluating a system of assigned providers, it is our contention that this can best be done by (1) collecting performance and cost data on whatever assigned systems are of interest, holding constant as many variables between the sites in which the systems operate as is reasonably possible, (2) collecting performance data for the privately retained service providers in the same locales, and (3) analysing statistically significant differences in the *differences* between the services provided by assigned and retained providers in the different locales.

INDIGENT DEFENSE

Several U.S. Supreme Court decisions of the 1960s have made it mandatory that defense attorneys be provided for any indigent criminal defendant who faces the possibility of incarceration (*Gideon* v. *Wainwright,* 1963; *Argersinger* v. *Hamlin,* 1972). In response to these decisions, jurisdictions have devised a variety of methods for providing such representation. Larger jurisdictions expanded or created public defender offices; smaller jurisdictions developed a variety of private bar systems. These range from loosely structured ad hoc assignment by a judge of any attorney who comes to mind, to a highly structured assignment process by a county official according to a list of private attorneys who have volunteered for such work and been judged competent in specified areas of criminal law (Houlden and Balkin, 1985).

In recent times of fiscal austerity, smaller jurisdictions have been distressed as the costs of assigned counsel yearly have surpassed budgeted amounts and shown no sign of slowing their rate of increase. Jurisdictions have, therefore, become interested in determining whether any particular method of private bar indigent defense is less expensive to operate. However, county governments are also acutely aware that they must provide competent representation. This is not only a moral consideration, it is based on the knowledge that incompetent counsel provides a basis for appeal and appeals will cost the county far more than may have been saved. Thus, in evaluating private bar indigent defense ser-

vices, both cost and quality of representation must be considered.

The typical research paradigm for studies investigating indigent defense systems has compared only one example of each of two or three forms of legal representation (Nagel, 1973; Wheeler and Wheeler, 1980; Cohen et al., 1983). As discussed above, such comparisons confound system and jurisdictional differences. If each system is operating in a different jurisdiction (or the same jurisdiction at two different times), it is unclear whether observed differences reflect counsel system or jurisdictional characteristics. Yet comparing only types of representation in the same jurisdiction has problems of its own. First, this comparison confounds type of counsel with type of clientele. Prior research has indicated that different types of defendants are represented by different types of attorneys (e.g., Sterling, 1983). Privately retained lawyers are more likely to represent clients whose demographic characteristics make them more likely to be acquitted or sentenced more leniently. Although covarying the characteristics of defendants could help to resolve this problem, a comparison of retained and assigned counsel is associated with another shortcoming. It is unclear how to interpret the results. If one takes the position that an assigned counsel system has to match the performance of its own retained counsel system to be considered adequate, then this comparison has meaning. However, it is reasonable to expect that retained counsel will usually outperform an assigned counsel system. An assigned counsel system would then be considered inadequate if it underperforms too much. But what is too much? Further, the decision to be made is between assigned counsel systems. Privately retained counsel will simply not be available to everyone. One is trying to evaluate systems of assigned counsel to choose that which best compares to the performance of retained counsel at the price the county can afford. It requires comparisons of assigned and retained counsel across jurisdictions to be able to evaluate different assigned counsel systems.

In a midwestern state we found two rural jurisdictions that were similar on twelve social-demographic measures, yet differed in their mode of providing defense services for indigent defendants. One utilized an ad hoc method of representation (jurisdiction AH) and one a part-time public defender (jurisdiction PD). With ad hoc assignment, when a defendant requests counsel but declares himself or herself unable to afford representation, the judge in the courtroom decides which attorney shall be asked to represent the defendant. The judge makes the decision on whatever basis he or she perceives to be appropriate. The attorney is notified of appointment by a court clerk and may accept or decline. Defendants are informed of the name of their counsel, and are told either to assume responsibility for contacting the lawyer or that the lawyer will contact them.

Although this system is simple to operate, questions have been raised about the quality of representation provided by such counsel. It has been alleged that attorneys receive assignments as compensation for supporting the judge during the appointment process, or that they are unlikely to be skilled or interested in criminal law. Certainly the incentive structure for the attorney—fee for service—would appear to encourage the development of a full defense, but this is limited by the possible higher fee per hour the attorney could earn for other work and jurisdictional restrictions on total reimbursement. In addition, counties are unable to predict in advance how much it will cost to provide representation for indigent defendants in any approaching twelve-month period. Thus, jurisdictions have explored alternatives to ad hoc appointment.

One of these alternatives is the appointment of a part-time public defender. In jurisdictions where the volume of crime is insufficient to justify the employment and payment of an attorney to defend the indigent on a full-time basis, the decision is sometimes made to contract with an attorney for less than 40 hours of defense services per week. A jurisdiction will hire an attorney for a year, for whatever number of hours was required by the preceding year's caseload adjusted by an estimation of likely increases or decreases in the local indigent defendant crime rate. This attorney is given the title of public defender and paid monthly, in lump-sum amounts for his or her services. The amount paid is constant, regardless of whether the actual number of defendants to be represented is greater or less than projected.

This system would seem to eliminate the impact of judicial political patronage, and might therefore improve the qualify of representation. As noted by the National Advisory Commission on Criminal Justice Standards and Goals (1973), the fact that one individual must repeatedly appear to represent criminal defendants may enhance defense skills. However, frequent appearance may also engender a fear of reprisals on later clients that restricts an attorney's willingness to actively defend. In addition, because the part-time public defender is paid a flat fee, the income of a marginal hour of work is zero. Extra time spent on cases means sacrificing either leisure or income from a private caseload (regardless of how high private fees are). An attorney receiving a flat fee is likely to allocate less time to his or her caseload than one receiving income on a fee-for-service basis.

Clearly, there are potential shortcomings in both systems. Yet in this, as in other situations where decisions must be made between alternative systems of providing services, one would like to determine whether one system is superior to the other. The value of the evaluation design demonstrated in this article is that it allows a more accurate assessment of the relative performance of assigned service providers than any previous methodology.

In approaching the evaluation of private bar indigent defense systems, we discovered that much prior research has restricted itself to investigating the quality of representation provided in isolation of cost. Yet quality cannot be separated from cost. If a jurisdiction is willing to spend an unlimited amount of money, surely any system of representation could provide excellent defense services. Jurisdictions, however, are limited in the amount of money they have to spend. To properly evaluate the quality of counsel provided, one needs to consider the resource cost per case.

Furthermore, a review of the literature indicates that when cost has been considered in evaluating defense systems, it has been estimated as a single aggregate cost per case. Specifically, cost per case has been defined as total system cost divided by number of cases. This approach fails to control for case mix. At the least level of differentiation, felonies utilize more resources than misdemeanors; trials utilize more resources than pleas and dismissals. Differences in case mix between jurisdictions need to be corrected for before comparing system costs.

To determine differentiated cost per case is relatively easy in an ad hoc system. One merely needs to determine the costs associated with the reviewed vouchers submitted by appointed counsel for particular case types. However, determining cost per case in a part-time public defender system, where one lump sum is paid, is more difficult. Data about hours spent on different types of cases are not readily available. We interviewed the part-time public defender in the jurisdiction we studied, asking about approximately how many hours he spent on various case types. This and knowledge of his salary allowed us to determine the per-case cost of different case types. As detailed below, our cost-per-case estimates relied only on relative time information contained in these interviews, not on absolute time information. Thus, the en-

demic problem of lawyer overestimation of time spent per case did not affect our cost-per-case estimates.

In sum, this article presents an evaluation of the quality of representation provided to indigent defendants in two jurisdictions. It is unique in four respects. First, it utilizes retained counsel in each jurisdiction as a control for jurisdictional differences. This is a new design that has application for any tiered system of providing services. In conducting our test of this design we did three further things that advance the evaluation of systems of indigent defense: (1) we recognized the need to consider the costs associated with providing representation, (2) we estimated how much cases cost for an array of case types, and (3) we developed a method for estimating cost per case among case types for a system where only a lump-sum payment is made.

Finally, we acknowledge that there was one problem that we simply cannot resolve. Evaluation is not possible unless there are agreed upon objectives and goals, yet such an agreement does not exist within the criminal justice system, nor within society (see Feeley, 1983). The objectives and goals of indigent defense depend upon whether one is the defendant, the prosecutor, the victim, a member of the county board, or a relatively uninvolved citizen. Defendants will think that a desirable indigent defense is acquittal or the least possible sentence. Victims will likely think otherwise. Prosecutors may think a positive indigent defense system involves speedy disposition. The county board will be concerned mainly with lowering costs. We were forced to recognize therefore that although we can provide an assessment of the relative performance of indigent defense systems, the attachment of "good" or "bad" labels to systems of indigent defense depends on one's position or role in society in general and the criminal justice system in particular. We can gather quality and cost data, but which method of defense seems best will depend upon the objectives and goals of the individual. The method of defense that "should" be adopted by a jurisdiction will depend upon the objectives and goals of that jurisdiction.

Again, in viewing the results presented below we want to emphasize not the substantive outcomes—though it is hoped they will be useful to those who have to choose a system of indigent defense—but the methodological approach used in the design and analysis.

METHOD

Sample

Our resources allowed a sample of 400 cases at each site. Two hundred cases at each site (jurisdictions AH and PD) were to be cases represented by assigned council, and 200 to be cases represented by retained counsel. Half were to be felony, and half to be misdemeanor cases. Because these were rural jurisdictions with small caseloads, we discovered that we were able to study all criminal cases filed in each jurisdiction for the two-year period, 1981–1982 and still obtain an N of less than 800 cases.

Data Collection Instruments

Information in the court files regarding the processing and outcome of the sampled cases was gathered with respect to the following: defendant bond status at the time of first appearance and time of case disposition, method of case disposition (e.g., dismissal, trial, plea), nature of the case disposition (e.g., innocent, guilty), sentence received, number of motions filed, number of attorney appearances in court, and number of days from first appearance to disposition and sentencing. In addition, we sought information about the defendant's prior convictions, race, sex, and age.

In the jurisdiction utilizing ad hoc assignment of counsel, information was taken from

the bills submitted by attorneys appointed to handle indigent cases and approved by the criminal court judge. Information was gathered about fee paid and the number of hours attorneys claimed to have worked on cases. Information about the costs of representing indigent defendants in the jurisdiction with a part-time public defender were calculated on the basis of information received from the public defender.

RESULTS

Overview

Considering both felony and misdemeanor cases, differences between the ad hoc assigned and part-time public defender system emerged with respect to bond status, the likelihood of incarceration, and speed of disposition. The ad hoc assigned counsel system is less likely than the part-time public defender system to have clients out of jail at the time of case disposition and more likely to have its clients receive sentences of incarceration. In addition, ad hoc assigned counsel appear less likely than the part-time public defender system to secure the release of initially incarcerated felons from jail prior to disposition and to process misdemeanor cases more slowly.

These results were obtained from analyses of covariance.[1] In what follows, we present first the results of a comparison in each jurisdiction between assigned and retained counsel, covarying defendant's initial bond status and whether other offenses were charged. This analysis (a 4 × 2 design) also tested for interactions between type of counsel and type of offense (felony/misdemeanor). Then we present the results of the comparison central to our proposed design, a test of significant interactions between assigned and retained counsel between the two sites. Again, this analysis of covariance tests for interactions with type of offense.[2]

TABLE I   Indicators of Performance for Defense Counsel in Jurisdiction AH

Variable	Assigned Counsel				Retained Counsel			
	Felony (N = 109)		Misdemeanor (N = 39)		Felony (N = 76)		Misdemeanor (N = 154)	
A. Percentages and Frequencies of Dichotomous Performance Measures								
Bond status at time of case disposition								
In jail (1)[a]	59.8	(64)	60.5	(23)	27.2	(21)	5.1	(7)
Out of jail (0)	40.2	(43)	39.5	(15)	72.8	(56)	94.9	(131)
Change in bond status from first appearance to disposition								
Change—was in jail, now out (0)	60.3	(38)	78.2	(18)	90.4	(19)	71.4	(5)
No change—was in jail, still in (1)	39.7	(25)	21.8	(5)	9.6	(2)	28.6	(2)
Case disposition								
• Dismissal								
Case dismissed (0)	9.3	(10)	25.7	(9)	9.1	(7)	21.9	(33)
Not dismissed (1)	90.7	(98)	74.3	(26)	90.9	(70)	78.1	(118)
• Trial								
Case tried (0)	7.4	(8)	11.4	(4)	11.7	(9)	25.1	(38)
Case not tried (1)	92.6	(100)	88.6	(31)	88.3	(68)	74.9	(113)
• Trail vs. plea								
Plea entered (0)	91.8	(89)	84.6	(22)	87.1	(61)	67.8	(80)
Case tried (1)	8.2	(8)	15.4	(4)	12.9	(9)	32.2	(38)
• Type of plea								
Original charge (0)	52.8	(47)	63.6	(14)	39.3	(24)	55.0	(44)
Lesser charge (1)	47.2	(42)	36.4	(8)	60.7	(37)	45.0	(36)
• Trial outcome								
Guilty (0)	87.5	(7)	75.0	(3)	88.9	(8)	78.9	(30)
Not guilty (1)	12.5	(1)	25.0	(1)	11.1	(1)	21.1	(8)
• Trial outcome								
Guilty of original charge (0)	85.7	(6)	66.6	(2)	37.5	(3)	70.0	(21)
Lesser charge (1)	14.3	(1)	33.4	(1)	62.5	(5)	30.0	(9)
• Motions filed								
Filed none (0)	15.7	(17)	47.4	(18)	24.7	(19)	20.0	(31)
Filed any (1)	84.3	(91)	52.6	(20)	75.3	(58)	80.0	(124)
• Overall disposition								
Guilty (0)	89.7	(96)	71.4	(25)	89.6	(69)	72.8	(110)
Not guilty (1)	10.3	(11)	28.6	(10)	10.4	(8)	27.2	(41)
Sentence								
• Incarceration								
Yes (0)	53.1	(51)	52.0	(13)	31.8	(22)	11.9	(13)
No (1)	46.9	(45)	48.0	(12)	68.1	(47)	88.1	(96)
Type								
Incarceration (3)	53.1	(51)	52.0	(13)	31.9	(22)	11.9	(13)
Probation (2)	38.5	(37)	8.0	(2)	53.6	(37)	19.3	(21)
Other (1)	8.4	(8)	40.0	(10)	14.5	(10)	68.8	(75)

TABLE I (Continued)

Variable	Assigned Counsel		Retained Counsel	
	Felony (N = 109)	Misdemeanor (N = 39)	Felony (N = 76)	Misdemeanor (N = 154)
B. Means of Interval Level Performance Measures				
Length of incarceration (range)	21.6 months (1–324)	1 (n/a)	6.1 months (1–48)	1.2 (1–3)
Number of motions filed (range)	1.9 motions (0–8)	.74 (0–5)	1.8 motions (0–6)	.22 (0–2)
Number of attorney appearances (range)	5.1 appear (1–25)	2.7 (1–11)	5.1 appear (1–15)	2.3 (1–8)
Days from first appearance to disposition (range)	84.8 days (1–355)	81.3 (1–174)	111.8 days (7–387)	91.7 (14–376)
Days from first appearance to sentencing (range)	93.4 days (1–355)	72.8 (1–162)	129.8 days (7–417)	86.8 (14–261)

[a] In this column, numbers in parentheses indicate how a variable was coded for the analyses of covariance.

Jurisdiction AH

We examined 184 felony and 192 misdemeanor court files.[3] Frequencies and means for the performance indicator variables (dichotomous and interval level) utilized in the analyses of covariance[4] are presented in Table 1. The data in Table 1 or a combination of the data about assigned counsel systems in Tables 1 and 3 represent the usual material on which an evaluation of tiered service providers would be based. The advantage of the methodology proposed in this article is that it allows a statistical integration of the results of both tables.

Significant differences between assigned and retained counsel in jurisdiction AH emerged for the following measures of performance: (1) bond status at time of case disposition [$F(1,688) = 34.70$, p $<.001$],[5] (2) likelihood of change in bond status from first arraignment to time of case disposition [$F(1,177) = 4.19$, p$<.042$], (3) likelihood a case would resolve by trial [$F(1,666) = 5.16$, p$<.023$], (4) likelihood that a case would be resolved by plea versus trial [$F(1,481) = 4.23$, p $< .040$], (5) if a case were resolved by trial, likelihood that the defendant would

be found guilty of original versus lesser charges [$F(1,52) = 4.85$, p $< .032$], (6) days from first arraignment to sentencing [$F(1,450) = 5.16$, p $< .024$], (7) likelihood of incarceration [$F(1,463) = 13.17$, p $< .001$], (8) sentence severity [$F(1,463) = 10.84$, p $< .001$], (9) number of motions filed [$F(1,673) = 7.72$, p $< .006$], and (10) likelihood of motions being filed [$F(1,675) = 13.31$, p $< .001$].

Examination of means adjusted for the covariates, presented in Table 2, reveals that clients of retained counsel are more likely than are clients of assigned counsel to be released before case disposition. Similarly, retained counsel are more likely than are assigned counsel to change the bond status of their clients, such that those who were incarcerated at the time of first arraignment will be released from jail before the time of case disposition. Adjusted means also indicate that clients of retained counsel are more likely to have their cases resolved by trial (rather than dismissed or settled by plea). More specifically, retained counsel appear more likely than assigned counsel to take a case to trial rather than arrange a plea. If a case is taken

TABLE 2   Cell Means Adjusted for Covariates for Statistically Significant Differences in Jurisdiction AH

Variable	Retained Counsel	Assigned Counsel
Bond status at time of case disposition	.98	.79
Change in bond status from first appearance to case disposition	.19	.29
Case disposition: case tried vs. not tried	.81	.90
Case disposition: plea entered vs. case tried	.23	.13
Trial disposition: guilty of original vs. lesser charge	.51	.15
Days from first appearance to sentencing	105.34	88.10
Incarceration: yes vs. no	.73	.56
Type sentence: incarceration, probation, other	1.88	2.15
Number of motions filed	1.07	1.21
Likelihood of filing motions	.49	.64

to trial, clients of assigned counsel are more likely to be found guilty of their original, rather than lesser charges. Cases represented by assigned counsel move more quickly, both from first arraignment to disposition and from first arraignment to sentencing. In addition, the adjusted means indicate that clients of assigned counsel are more likely to receive sentences of incarceration. This same finding emerges in the analysis of the variable comparing incarceration, probation, and alternative sentences. The adjusted means reveal that clients of assigned counsel are more likely than the clients of retained counsel to be incarcerated and less likely to receive probation or alternative sentences. Assigned counsel appear to file more motions than retained counsel. Assigned counsel also appear more likely than retained counsel to file motions.

This last main effect is, however, qualified by an interaction with the type of crime with which a defendant was charged (felony/misdemeanor; $F(1,675) = 4.78$, p < .029). Assigned counsel are more likely to file a motion only when misdemeanors are charged [$F(1,675) = 11.7$, p < .001; adjusted means = assigned counsel and a felony = 1.8; retained counsel and a felony = 1.7; assigned counsel and a misdemeanor = 1.5; retained counsel and a misdemeanor = 1.2].

TABLE 3   Indicators of Performance for Defense Counsel in Jurisdiction PD

Variable	Assigned Counsel		Retained Counsel	
	Felony (N = 98)	Misdemeanor (N = 103)	Felony (N = 90)	Misdemeanor (N = 114)
A. Percentages and Frequencies of Dichotomous Performance Measures				
Bond status at time of case disposition				
In jail (1)[a]	39.6 (36)	13.9 (11)	20.5 (18)	11.9 (8)
Out of jail (0)	60.4 (55)	86.1 (68)	79.5 (70)	88.1 (59)
Change in bond status from first appearance to disposition				
Change—was in jail, now out (0)	66.1 (22)	45.5 (5)	64.7 (11)	75.0 (6)
No change—was in jail, still in (1)	38.9 (14)	54.5 (6)	35.3 (6)	25.0 (2)

TABLE 3 (*Continued*)

Variable	Assigned Counsel				Retained Counsel			
	Felony (N = 98)		Misdemeanor (N = 103)		Felony (N = 90)		Misdemeanor (N = 114)	
Case disposition:								
• Dismissal								
Case dismissed (0)	41.2	(40)	40.6	(41)	33.3	(30)	41.2	(47)
Not dismissed (1)	58.8	(57)	59.4	(60)	66.7	(60)	58.8	(67)
• Trial								
Case tried (0)	6.2	(6)	6.9	(7)	4.4	(4)	7.0	(8)
Case not tried (1)	93.8	(91)	93.1	(94)	95.6	(86)	93.0	(106)
• Trial vs. plea								
Plea entered (0)	89.5	(51)	88.3	(53)	93.3	(56)	88.1	(59)
Case tried (1)	10.5	(6)	11.7	(7)	6.7	(4)	11.9	(8)
• Type of plea								
Original charge (0)	25.5	(13)	69.8	(37)	28.6	(16)	71.2	(42)
Lesser charge (1)	74.5	(38)	30.2	(16)	71.4	(40)	28.8	(17)
• Trial outcome								
Guilty (0)	50.0	(3)	85.7	(6)	75.0	(3)	75.0	(6)
Not guilty (1)	50.0	(3)	14.3	(1)	25.0	(1)	25.0	(2)
• Trial outcome								
Guilty of original charge (0)	66.7	(2)	100.0	(6)	33.3	(1)	83.3	(5)
Guilty of lesser charge (1)	33.3	(1)	0.0	(0)	66.7	(2)	16.7	(1)
• Motions filed								
Filed none (0)	60.8	(59)	91.3	(94)	72.2	(65)	94.7	(108)
Filed any (1)	39.1	(38)	8.7	(9)	27.8	(25)	5.3	(6)
• Overall disposition								
Guilty (0)	55.7	(54)	58.4	(59)	65.6	(59)	57.0	(65)
Not guilty (1)	44.3	(43)	41.6	(42)	34.4	(31)	43.0	(49)
Sentence								
• Incarceration								
Yes (0)	11.1	(6)	8.5	(5)	10.2	(6)	3.1	(2)
No (1)	88.9	(48)	91.5	(54)	89.8	(53)	96.9	(63)
• Type								
Incarceration (3)	11.1	(6)	8.5	(5)	10.2	(6)	3.1	(2)
Probation (2)	50.0	(27)	16.9	(10)	27.1	(16)	12.3	(8)
Other (1)	38.9	(21)	74.6	(44)	62.7	(37)	84.6	(55)

B. Means of Interval Level Performance Measures

Variable	Assigned Counsel		Retained Counsel	
Length of incarceration	2.8 months	1	16.3 months	1.5
(range)	(1–6)	(n/a)	(6–36)	(1–2)
Number of motions filed	.56 motions	.14	.42 motions	.06
(range)	(0–4)	(0–3)	(0–8)	(0–2)
Number of attorney appearances	1.8 appear	1.4	1.5 appear	1.3
(range)	(0–8)	(0–7)	(0–8)	(0–5)
Days from first appearance to disposition	76.0 days	47.9	71.8 days	69.9
(range)	(1–344)	(1–265)	(0–266)	(0–523)
Days from first appearance to sentencing	68.8 days	41.4	76.4 days	54.8
(range)	(1–278)	(1–149)	(0–284)	(0–256)

[a] In this column, numbers in parentheses indicate how the variable was coded for the analyses of covariance.

Jurisdiction PD

The court files of 187 felonies and 217 misdemeanors were examined.[6] Frequencies and means for the performance indicator variables (dichotomous and interval level) utilized in the analyses of covariance[7] are presented in Table 3.

In jurisdiction PD differences between assigned and retained counsel emerged on two measures of performance, bond status at time of case disposition [$F(1,688) = 4.54$, $p < .033$] and sentence severity [$F(1,463) = 4.06$, $p < .044$]. Adjusted cell means for these statistically significant effects are presented in Table 4. As in jurisdiction AH, it appears that clients of assigned counsel are more likely than the clients of retained counsel to be in jail at the time of case disposition. Again as in jurisdiction AH, these clients are more likely than the clients of retained counsel to receive sentences of incarceration and less likely to receive probation or alternative sentences.

The analyses also reveal a significant interaction between type of counsel (assigned/retained) and type of offense (felony/misdemeanor) for the variable days from first arraignment to disposition [$F(1,649) = 7.72$, $p < .006$]. Simple effects tests indicate that assigned and retained counsel do not differ in the days to disposition for felonies (adjusted means = 80.5 and 71.5 days, respectively) but that misdemeanors are moved to disposition more quickly by assigned than retained counsel [$F(1,649) = 8.83$, $p < .003$; adjusted means = 46.6 and 80.1 days, respectively).

Analysis of the Differences Between the Systems of Indigent Defense in Jurisdictions AH and PD

Statistically significant differences between assigned and retained counsel between the two jurisdictions are found for bond status at the time of case disposition [$F(1,688) = 7.42$, $p < .007$] and likelihood of incarceration [$F(1,463) = 5.69$, $p < .017$]. The first of these effects reflects a greater difference in the performance of assigned and retained counsel than the part-time public defender and retained counsel. Compared to the part-time public defender, the ad hoc assigned counsel system is more likely to have clients in jail at the time of case disposition. The second effect is a result of the occurrence of a statistically significant difference between assigned and retained counsel and the lack of such a difference between the part-time public defender and retained counsel. Thus, assigned counsel are more likely to obtain sentences of incarceration for their clients then are part-time public defenders.

In addition, the analyses indicate an interaction between type of counsel, site, and type of crime for likelihood of change in bond status between first arraignment and case disposition [$F(1,177) = 3.92$, $p < .049$], and the number of days between first arraignment and case disposition [$F(1,649) = 7.31$, $p < .007$]. The first of these three-way interactions occurs because of a marginally significant difference between assigned and retained counsel in jurisdiction AH in the handling of felony versus misdemeanor cases that does not occur in jurisdiction PD.[8] It ap-

TABLE 4   Cell Means Adjusted for Covariates for Statistically Significant Differences in Jurisdiction PD

Variable	Retained Counsel	Assigned Counsel
Bond status at time of case disposition	.94	.88
Type sentence: incarceration, probation, other	1.38	1.57

pears that in jurisdiction AH, assigned counsel may be less likely to secure the release of initially incarcerated felony clients before the date of case disposition than retained counsel. This difference does not occur for misdemeanant clients in jurisdiction AH and does not occur in jurisdiction PD.

The second three-way interaction is a reflection of the difference between the part-time public defender and retained counsel in speed of bringing cases to disposition. As discussed above, the part-time public defender is significantly quicker for bringing misdemeanors to disposition. Because the ad hoc assigned counsel system does not differ from retained counsel in speed of bringing cases to disposition, a three-way interaction is created. There is a difference in case disposition speed between assigned counsel systems with respect to misdemeanors. The part-time public defender is quicker.

In sum, the ad hoc assigned counsel system appears less likely to release clients from jail prior to disposition, and particularly unlikely to secure the release of felons if they are initially incarcerated and more likely to have its clients incarcerated. The part-time public defender, however, appears to process misdemeanor cases more quickly.

Cost Data Overview

In jurisdiction AH we obtained the fee requests for the felony and misdemeanor cases handled by assigned counsel analyzed in our assessment of quality of representation. From these requests data were obtained to estimate fee per case, time spent per case, and fee per hour. In addition, overhead costs for jurisdiction AH were calculated.[9] In jurisdiction PD the part-time public defender was paid an annual salary. Therefore, data do not exist on fees for individual cases. Data were obtained from the part-time defender about number of cases handled, distribution of case types, and the number of hours spent on average on different types of cases. From this we were able to construct an estimate of cost per case. There is negligible overhead to the jurisdiction associated with the use of a part-time public defender, and therefore, overhead costs were not estimated for this location. Following the presentation of cost estimates for each jurisdiction, a comparison is made of costs between the two jurisdictions.[10]

Jurisdiction AH

Fee/Case, Hours/Case, Fee/Hour. As can be seen in Table 5, for the sample of 98 felony fee requests by ad hoc assigned counsel (aggregating across trial and nontrial methods of disposition), the average fee per case was approximately $284. The average fee per hour was approximately $24. Although the sample of felony trial cases is admittedly very small (7), it appears that trials were more

TABLE 5 Fee per Case, Hours per Case, Fee per Hour, Overhead, and Cost per Case for Ad Hoc Assigned Indigent Defense Counsel System

Case type and mode of disposition	Fee/Case	Hours/Case	Fee/Hours	Overhead/ Case	Cost/Case
Felonies	$ 284.15	11.5	$24.71	$9.16	$ 293.31
Trial (7)	1080.67	38.9	27.73	9.16	1089.83
Nontrial (91)	229.22	9.3	24.59	9.16	238.38
Misdemeanor	112.03	4.4	25.29	9.16	121.19
Trial (4)	139.75	5.3	26.72	9.16	148.91
Nontrial (30)	108.33	4.3	25.08	9.16	117.49

expensive than nontrial dispositions. A trial cost over four times as much as nontrial (plea and dismissal) disposition. The higher cost of a trial is attributable to either the greater time spent or greater cost per hour, or both, as is evident from Table 5, given that trials required more hours of work from assigned counsel. But the fee per hour for a felony trial is only slightly great than the fee per hour for a felony nontrial. The much greater fee per case for a felony trial case is a result of the greater amount of attorney time spent on that type of case.

For the entire sample of 34 misdemeanor case fee requests, average fee per case was $112 and the average fee per hour was $25.59. Assigned counsel spent on average 4.4 hours on misdemeanor cases. Although there are extremely few misdemeanor trial cases (4), Table 5 does show that misdemeanor trial cases were almost three times more expensive than misdemeanor nontrial cases. This difference is less than the cost difference in trial versus nontrial modes of resolution for felony cases. However, as in felony cases, the fee per hour for cases resolved at trial is only slightly greater than the fee per hour for nontrial cases. The difference in cost per case is again due to the relative number of hours devoted to each type of case.

A comparison of felony cases in general to misdemeanor cases reveals that felony fee per case is approximately two-and-a-half times greater than misdemeanor cases. The difference appears primarily to be a result of the greater number of hours required for the disposition of felony cases.

Overhead Costs and Cost per Case. The overhead costs associated with this ad hoc assigned counsel system consist of costs associated with the assignment process and the payment process. The assignment process requires approximately five minutes of a judge's time to select an assigned attorney and ten minutes of a court clerk's time to telephone

the attorney and mail him or her the Notice of Appointment and Complaint. Using an annual salary of $60,000 for the judge and $20,000 for the court clerk, the assignment process adds a cost of $2.50 for judicial resources and $1.67 for court clerk resources expended. Thus, for the assignment process, we roughly estimate that each case costs the jurisdiction an additional $4.17.

The payment process requires approximately five minutes of a judge's time to review and approve the voucher submitted by the appointed attorney. In addition, the payment process requires five minutes of a court clerk's time to transmit the attorney's claim form to the treasurer's office, five minutes of a clerk's time in the treasurer's office to submit the claim for approval at the monthly county board meeting, and five minutes of a county clerk's time to enter the transaction into the county budget book and cut the check. Using the same values as above about judicial and clerical salaries, the value of the judge's time can be imputed to be approximately $2.50 and the value of each five minutes of clerk's time $.83. The per-case cost of the payment process is then roughly estimated to be $4.99.

The total overhead cost per case would be equal to the cost of the appointment process ($4.17) plus the cost of the payment process ($4.99), or approximately $9.16. Each case is attributed the same overhead cost. Returning to Table 5, one can see the estimated cost per case for each case type as a function of fee per case plus overhead per case.

Jurisdiction PD

The methodology used to calculate the costs associated with the part-time public defender system necessarily differed from that utilized in the jurisdiction employing ad hoc assignment of counsel. A part-time public defender is paid an annual salary for the entire caseload. He or she does not submit vouchers indicating hours worked and requested reimbursement for each case. However, data were obtained from the part-time public defender about salary, number of cases represented, distribution of cases, and number of hours spent on average on different types of cases. On the basis of this information we were able to estimate cost per case. To calculate this we used a weighted average formula using only "relative" time per case.[11] The cost of a case is considered to be determined by the number of attorney hours required for that type of case multiplied by the cost per attorney hour. For purposes of this analysis, it was assumed that the cost per attorney hour was the same for all types of cases. It needs to be emphasized that although data on absolute hours spent per case types were provided by the part-time defender, only relative hours are entered into the analysis.

In both jurisdictions, cases were gathered from each of two years. Because the public defender's salary and the number of cases represented varied in the two years, costs had to be calculated separately for each of the two years.[12] Table 6 reports the time data provided by the part-time defender with respect to the average number of hours required by each type of case. It will be noted that the

part-time defender also provided information about time spent on cases other than adult criminal cases: traffic, juvenile, ordinance violation, and family cases. Because the part-time defender's salary is expected to encompass work on these types of cases, information on the frequency and time required by these cases had to be obtained so that these cases could be partialed out in estimating the cost of the adult criminal case load.

The string of ratios describing the relative time required per type of case is as follows (in order of Table 6): 3.2: 3.2: 1.2: 1.62: .44: .2: 1.6. Using "misdemeanor nontrial" as the arbitrary base of one, this string of ratios can be interpreted in the following way: a felony case, on average, takes three-and-one-fifth as much time as a misdemeanor nontrial case; a felony trial case, on average, takes as much time as a felony nontrial case; or a misdemeanor trial takes 20 percent longer than a misdemeanor nontrial case.

Using the frequency distributions presented in Table 6, the ratios of relative time spent per case and a weighted average formula (cost per case) was calculated for each of the six case types for which cost data were calculated in jurisdiction AH. These cost-per-case estimates are presented in Table 7.

TABLE 6 Hours per Case and Distribution of Caseload Reported by Public Defender in Jurisdiction PD

Case Type	Hours/Case	1982 Frequency	1982 Relative Frequency (%)	1982 Frequency	Relative Frequency (%)
Felony trial	8.0	3	1.3	2	1.0
Felony nontrial	8.0	53	23.1	37	19.3
Misdemeanor trial	3.0	5	2.2	5	2.6
Misdemeanor nontrial	2.5	74	32.2	60	31.3
Traffic	1.5	58	25.3	40	20.8
Juvenile	1.1	27	11.8	35	18.2
Ordinance	.5	9	3.9	9	4.7
Family	4.0	0	0.0	4	2.1
Total		229	100	192	100

TABLE 7   Cost per Case in Jurisdiction PD

Case Type	1981 ($)	1982 ($)	Combined 1981 + 1982 ($)
Felonies	218.72	293.84	249.56
Felony trial	218.72	293.84	248.77
Felony nontrial	218.72	293.84	249.61
Misdemeanors	69.21	93.25	80.06
Misdemeanor trial	80.02	110.19	96.11
Misdemeanor nontrial	68.35	91.83	78.87

Comparisons of Jurisdiction AH and PD

The overall conclusion is that cost per case is greater in jurisdiction AH. Cost per hour is essentially the same for the two counties (see Table 8). Therefore, the higher cost per case in jurisdiction AH is attributable to the extra time that attorneys in that system report devoting to their cases.

By comparing the cost/case columns in Tables 5 and 7, it can be observed that a felony case cost more to defend for the ad hoc assigned counsel system ($293.31 versus $249.56). This constitutes a 16 percent difference in costs. This type of difference would occur even if one excluded the estimated overhead costs. However, if one disaggregates by disposition mode, a more complex pattern appears. Felony trials are more expensive in jurisdiction AH ($1089.83 versus $249.56), but felony nontrial cases are less expensive in jurisdiction AH ($238.38 versus $249.62).

By comparing the cost/case columns in Tables 5 and 7 it can also be observed that misdemeanors cost more to defend in jurisdiction AH ($121.19 versus $80.06). This constitutes a 41 percent difference in cost per case. When one dissaggregates by mode of disposition, the same pattern holds. Ad hoc counsel is more expensive per misdemeanor case, regardless of mode of disposition.

A comparison of Tables 5 and 6 allows an assessment of the time devoted to cases by attorneys in the two jurisdictions. It appears that assigned counsel spend more time on cases.[13] The greatest difference is for felony trial cases (38.9 hours versus 8 hours). By dividing cost per case data by time spent data, one obtains estimates of cost per hour. These estimates are presented in Table 8. The estimates reveal that the costs per hour are roughly similar for the two jurisdictions. They are a few cents more in jurisdiction AH for trial cases and a little lower in jurisdiction AH for nontrial cases. The only substantive difference (and that is still small) is for felony nontrial cases. Cost per hour was $1.83 less in jurisdiction AH. This similarity in cost per

TABLE 8   Cost per Hour for Jurisdictions AH and PD

Case Type	Cost per Hour	
	Jurisdiction AH ($)	Jurisdiction PD ($)
Felony trial	27.97	27.34
Felony nontrial	25.58	27.34
Misdemeanor trial	27.99	27.34
Misdemeanor nontrial	27.20	27.34

hour again implies that cost per case differences are due to differences in time spent per case.

CONCLUSION

The analysis of both felony and misdemeanor cases, covarying the two attributes of bond status after first appearance and whether other offenses were charged, revealed four statistically significant differences between the part-time public defender and ad hoc assignment of counsel. Ad hoc assigned counsel are more likely to have clients in jail at the time of case disposition and are less likely to get initially incarcerated felony defendants released prior to the date of case disposition. Ad hoc counsel are also more likely to have clients receive sentences of incarceration. The part-time public defender, however, appears to move misdemeanors more quickly from first appearance to disposition.

From a defense perspective, the first three measures clearly suggest the superiority of the part-time public defender system. It is more difficult, however, to interpret the value of speedier disposition of misdemeanors. No one wants overly hasty justice, but neither do we desire a system that takes longer than necessary for a determination of innocence or guilt. Examination of statistical tests and adjusted cell means reveals that although part-time public defenders are speedier in disposing of misdemeanors, on no indicator of quality of performance is their work revealed to be inferior. The speedier case disposition for misdemeanors seems to be a positive attribute. In all respects, then, the part-time public defender appears superior to ad hoc assigned counsel.

Further support for the part-time defender system emerges from our analysis of cost per case. Cost per case is lower in the part-time defender system. This is true for both felony and misdemeanor cases and for trial and nontrial cases. This result holds even if the ad hoc system overhead is not added in to calculations of that system's cost per case.

In sum, this study presents a demonstration of a technique for evaluating assigned counsel systems and more generally any tiered system involving professional services. It shows the value of comparing how assigned systems differ with reference to a benchmark (privately retained providers) in each site. The study also shows the desirability of estimating cost per case for a set of case types, not just an aggregate cost per case. In addition, it demonstrates that it is possible to estimate cost per case across case types, even for a system receiving lump sum payments.

For government managers who must choose between assigned counsel systems we hope this study has provided useful information about the relative advantages of part-time public defenders versus ad hoc assignment of counsel. More generally, we hope this provides a useful framework for continued comparisons of systems of providing professional services.

NOTES

1. Although such a statistical test is unquestionably appropriate for interval-level measures, a probit/logit formulation might be preferred for the dichotomous dependent variables. Using analysis of covariance for a model with a binary (0,1) dependent variable implies that the distribution of errors is likely to be heteroscedastic and the model is sensitive to specification error (Pindyck and Rubinfeld, 1976). We therefore conducted a probit analysis, as well as the analyses of covariance, for each binary dependent variable, making 88 comparisons between the two analyses. Differences emerged on only three measures.

In jurisdiction AH, the difference between assigned and retained counsel with respect to likelihood of change in bond status becomes nonsignificant. However, in the central comparison of assigned counsel systems, the probit analysis confirms that there is a difference on this measure. Thus, both statistical techniques detect the interaction, whereas only the analysis of covariance uncovers a statistically significant simple effect. In jurisdiction PD, the difference between the part-time public defender and retained counsel with respect to bond status at the time of case disposition also becomes nonsignificant. Yet again in the comparison of assigned counsel systems, the probit analysis detects the interaction. The alteration in these statistical outcomes would not affect the conclusions of the article.

With respect to the analysis comparing types of assigned counsel systems, a probit analysis would not have revealed the statistically significant difference in likelihood of incarceration. Instead, it would have detected a difference that was marginally significant in the ancova—and therefore not reported—likelihood of resolving a case at trial rather than through dismissal or plea. Thus a probit analysis would have suggested one different conclusion.

To keep the data presentation as simple and understandable as possible, we have chosen to present only the results of the analyses of covariance, rather than moving the reader back and forth between statistical procedures as a function of the level of measurement of specific dependent measures.

2. For those concerned about the effect of variables related to outcome that may not have been included in our statistical model, we would note that with respect to our central analysis, the effects of such variables are not likely to be crucial. Because we are comparing

differences in performance between assigned counsel systems any such possible effects are likely to cancel out.

There might nonetheless be differences between the clients represented by assigned and retained counsel that affect the quality of their outcomes yet were not included in our analyses of covariance. Research into differences between indigent defense systems has sometimes concluded that differences in outcome are eliminated when differences in clientele are controlled (e.g., Sterling, 1983). We were aware of this at the time the study was planned and were able to gather information on defendant sex, race, age, and prior record for felony defendants. We computed analyses of covariance for the felony data using these covariates, plus bond status and whether other offenses were charged. The results generally revealed that the additional covariates were nonsignificant. Thus the inclusion of covariates likely to affect the interpretation of our results did not increase the predictive ability of the model.

3. For the analyses, cases are classified by the type of counsel that disposed of them rather than by the type of counsel initially representing them. Twelve defendants changed from retained to assigned counsel and fourteen from assigned to retained representation.

4. The frequency distributions of the two variables used as covariates: initial bond status, and whether other offenses were charged at the time of this arrest in jurisdiction AH were as follows:

| | Frequency (%) | | | | | | | |
| | Assigned Counsel | | | | Retained Counsel | | | |
	Felony		Misdemeanor		Felony		Misdemeanor	
Initial bond status:								
Bond	25.0	(27)	36.8	(14)	67.5	(52)	82.6	(128)
Jail	59.3	(64)	60.5	(23)	27.3	(21)	4.5	(7)
ROR	14.8	(16)	2.6	(1)	5.2	(4)	1.9	(3)
No information	.9	(1)	0.0	(0)	0.0	(0)	10.4	(16)
Other offenses charged at time of arrest:								
Yes	13.1	(14)	36.8	(14)	23.4	(18)	23.4	(118)
No	86.9	(93)	63.2	(24)	76.6	(59)	76.6	(36)

5. For analyses of dependent variables concerned with bond status, the covariate related to bond status was omitted.

6. The data indicate that 11 defendants switched from retained counsel to the part-time public defender, and 23 changed from the public defender to retained counsel.

7. The frequency distributions of the two covariates—initial bond status, and whether other offenses were charged at the time of this arrest—for the clients of both assigned and retained counsel in jurisdiction PD were as follows:

	Frequency (%)							
	Assigned Counsel				Retained Counsel			
	Felony		Misdemeanor		Felony		Misdemeanor	
Initial bond status:								
Bond	14.4	(14)	39.8	(40)	41.1	(37)	47.4	(54)
Jail	37.1	(36)	10.7	(11)	20.0	(18)	7.0	(8)
ROR	42.3	(41)	26.2	(27)	36.7	(33)	4.4	(5)
No information	6.2	(6)	23.3	(24)	2.2	(2)	41.2	(47)
Other offenses charged at time of arrest:								
Yes	14.6	(14)	14.6	(15)	22.2	(20)	13.3	(15)
No	85.4	(82)	85.4	(88)	77.8	(70)	86.7	(98)

8. Because the effect was only marginally significant it was not reported in the main body of the text [$F(1,177) = 3.48$, $p < .063$].

9. We use the term "overhead" to mean nonfee costs attributable directly to running the assigned counsel system. We intend to include in this category only those cost items that would differ across the jurisdictions.

10. Only direct costs to the county of the assigned council systems were estimated. A broader perspective would include indirect costs to the county (e.g., jail cost attributable to a defendant not obtaining bond), and a consideration of cost to the defendant (e.g., loss of work time due to court appearances). Evaluating indigent defense services in a rigorous cost-benefit framework would involve including costs and benefits to society wherever they are incurred.

11. The weighted average formula used was

$$\text{Cost/Case} = \sum^{m} (\text{Hours/Case} \times \text{Cost/Hours} \times \text{Percentage Caseload})$$

where M is the number of case types.

12. This did not need to be done in jurisdiction AH, because the sampled vouchers that formed the basis of our cost estimates were gathered from cases in each of the two years.

13. Even though this comparison involves using the absolute time data provided by the part-time defender, the conclusions seem to be valid because the expected bias would be that the defender would overreport hours of work.

REFERENCES

Campbell, D. T. and J. C. Stanley (1972) Experimental and Quasi-Experimental Designs for Research. Chicago: Rand McNally.

Cohen, L., P. P. Semple, and R. E. Crew (1983) "Assigned counsel vs. public defender systems in Virginia: a comparison of relative benefits," pp. 127-150 in W. F. McDonald (ed.) The Defense Counsel. Beverly Hills, CA: Sage.

Feeley, M. M. (1983) Court Reform on Trial: Why Simple Solutions Fail. New York: Basic Books.

Grizzle, G. (1984) "Developing standards for interpreting agency performance: an exploration of three models." Public Admin. Rev. pp. 128–133.

Houlden, P. and S. Balkin "Quality and cost comparisons of private bar indigent defense systems: contract vs. ordered assigned counsel." J. of Criminal Law and Criminology, 26 (Spring 1985): 176–200.

Nagel, S. S. (1973) "Effects of alternative types of counsel on criminal procedure treatment." Indiana Law J. 48: 404–426.

National Advisory Commission on Criminal Justice Standards and Goals (1973) Courts. Washington, DC: Author.

National Study Commission on Defense Services (1976) Guidelines for Legal Defense Systems in the U.S.: Report of the National Study Commission on Defense Services. Chicago: National Legal Aid and Defender Association.

Pindyck, R. S. and D. L. Rubinfeld (1976) Econometric Models and Economic Forecasts. New York: McGraw-Hill.

Sterling, J. (1983) "Retained counsel vs. the public defender: the impact of type of counsel on charge bargaining," pp. 151–170 in W. F. McDonald (ed.) The Defense Counsel, Beverly Hills, CA: Sage.

Wheeler, G. R. and C. L. Wheeler (1980) "Reflections on legal representation of the economically disadvantaged: beyond assembly line justice." Crime and Delinquency 26: 319–332.

Explanation and Critique

Pauline Houlden and Steven Balkin sought to determine whether a system of indigent defense was delivered in a more cost-effective manner by part-time public defenders or by judicial ad hoc assignment of counsel. They made a cogent argument that it was difficult to make direct cost-effectiveness comparisons between two disparate legal systems, or even within the same system, over time unless the comparisons had a more firm grounding. Therefore, they proposed to compare the two indigent defense systems with privately purchased services available coincident with those systems.

Houlden and Balkin chose two rural jurisdictions in a midwestern state that were similar on 12 social and demographic measures but that differed on the model of indigent defense (as in any good comparison-group design). In one system, the presiding judge chose a defender for each defendant on whatever basis he or she deemed appropriate—an ad hoc (AH) system. Attorneys chosen in the ad hoc system were reimbursed at an hourly rate. The second jurisdiction appointed a part-time public defender (PD) who worked on a monthly lump-sum retainer that was paid regardless of the actual number of defendants handled. To control for fee and other judicial customs in the jurisdictions, Houlden and Balkin drew a control group for each locality consisting of privately retained attorneys for similar cases. All felony and misdemeanor cases filed over a two-year period in both jurisdictions were included in the analysis.

Houlden and Balkin acknowledged two weaknesses of their design. Cost-effectiveness analyses are preferably based on agreed-on desired outcomes, which assumes agreement on the goals and objectives of the program. What Houlden and Balkin encountered in this analysis was probably more typical of actual evaluations: Judgments regarding the success of the outcome depend on the evaluation consumer. In their example, what would have been a successful result? For the victim of the crime, prosecution and incarceration; for the defendant, acquittal. And the list can go on. Houlden and Balkin tried to maintain objectivity, hypothesizing the best and the worst consequences of either mode of assignment. It certainly would have been easier if those who had a stake in choosing the ultimate defense method had agreed on which measures of effectiveness were critical to their choice *before* the analysis. Then Houlden and Balkin could have made substantive interpretations and recommendations.

The second weakness was the cost measures—typically the easiest measure to assemble in cost-effectiveness designs. To their credit, Houlden and Balkin acknowledged that it would have been simplistic and misleading to add total costs of the system and divide by the number of cases—a general cost per case measure. Instead, they wanted the ratios to reflect (or control for) case mix. This was relatively easy for them to do in the ad hoc system where vouchers specified the services and time provided and reimbursement was made on the basis of those vouchers. To the extent that assigned and retained attorneys in the AH jurisdiction and retained attorneys in the PD jurisdiction accurately reported their time allocations, this was a reliable cost measure.

The estimates of cost per case in the public defender's office were less straightforward because the defender submitted no vouchers. The authors had to rely on interview information regarding the relative amount of time the attorney perceived to have been spent on a range of cases, aggregate the kinds of actual cases handled, and, on the basis of the attorney's salary, estimate a relative cost-per-case measure. This is perhaps the best the authors could have done short of requiring the public defender to keep a diary or following the defender around for two-years. The costs of either course could have been prohibitive.

A third weakness was that this design was a posttest-only comparison group design even though there was no treatment of it as such. Although the cost-effectiveness portion of the design was well executed, it lacked generalizability of the results to other systems in the state. The only conclusion that could be drawn was that County A's process appeared to be more cost effective than County B's. In other words, the design as reported here inherited all the weaknesses discussed in Chapter 9.

The performance (effectiveness) indicators are listed in Tables 1 and 3 of the article for AH and PD jurisdictions, respectively. Houlden and Balkin were not provided direction regarding which effectiveness measures were most important, so they listed 17 performance measures, allowing research consumers to pick and choose among the alternatives. Their first investigation was to determine by means of an analysis of covariance whether there were differences between assigned and retained counsel on the performance measures. To do this, they assigned dummy values to categorical variables (see values in Tables 1 and 3 in order to interpret the adjusted cell means in Tables 2 and 4). The summaries of statistically significant differences *within* jurisdictions are in Tables 2 and 4.

The second stage of the analysis was to examine differences *between* jurisdictions, using a two-way analysis of covariance. Houlden and Balkin found that "compared to the part-time public defender, the ad hoc assigned counsel system is more likely to have clients in jail at the time of case disposition" and that "assigned counsel are more likely to obtain sentences of incarceration for their clients than are part-time public defenders." The three-way interactions (between site and type of defense and type of crime) showed that in "jurisdiction AH, assigned counsel may be less likely to secure the release of initially incarcerated felony clients before the date of case disposition than retained counsel," and that the "part-time public defender is significantly quicker for bringing misdemeanors to disposition."

The differences in cost effectiveness between the AH and PD assigned counsel are reported in Tables 5 and 7 of the article. The authors chose cost per case as the ultimate cost-effectiveness measure. Overhead costs were relevant for the AH jurisdiction and were based on the time the court took to assign cases. The estimates for the PD jurisdiction were extrapolated from the relative frequency of cases, discounting other activities in which the public defender was engaged. Overall, AH costs were higher than PD costs per case by type of crime. Houlden and Balkin attributed this finding to padding of vouchers or at least the "extra time" those attorneys reported spending on cases.

The authors do not directly address the gross differences between time spent on felony trials across jurisdictions and the lack of difference between trial and nontrial felonies in the PD city relative to the gross differences in the AH jurisdiction. Remember, these two rural jurisdictions were similar on 12 demographic characteristics—a fairly comparable match. It may strike one as odd that such gross differences were apparent when attorneys typically must chronicle their time (as the AH attorneys presumably did in their own firms and for the vouchers' sake) for billing purposes. A number of AH attorneys reported such distinctions (based on reported means with no standard deviations), but the *one* PD attorney reported no distinction between time spent on trial and nontrial preparation. This finding is rather curious. Houlden and Balkin apparently trusted the interview data more than the unobtrusive voucher reports.

From the perspective of defense and cost effectiveness, Houlden and Balkin concluded that the public defender system was superior to that of the ad hoc system. The quality of assigned versus retained counsel was more variable in ad hoc versus public defender jurisdictions. (Other audiences interested in different measures of performance may have a different interpretation. The crux of this interpretation rests on how an audience interprets the measure of the relative time spent by the single public defender.) However, Holden and Balkin provided a useful general framework for conducting cost-effectiveness analysis.

Having now been introduced to cost-effectiveness analysis, you can test what you have learned by referring to earlier articles in this book. For example, is Ann Solberg's evaluation of community post-hospital follow-up services (Chapter 4) a good example of cost-effectiveness analysis? Concerning the Seattle energy conservation program (LIEP, Chapter 6), is it possible to calculate the cost effectiveness of the program using kilowatt hours reduced as the effectiveness measure? And, thinking about the Bronson, Pierson, and Tivnan article (Chapter 9), what can be said of the cost effectiveness of the different BEEP levels? (See Figure 2 in the article.)

REFERENCES

1. R. D. Peterson, "The Anatomy of Cost Effectiveness Analysis," *Evaluation Review* 10, no. 1 (February 1986): 31.

2. A slightly dated but still a relatively good survey of effectiveness measures for local government services can be found in Harry Hatry et al., *How Effective Are your Local Government Services?* (Washington, DC: Urban Institute, 1977).

3. R. D. Peterson, "The Anatomy of Cost Effectiveness Analysis," p. 32. The remaining examples are also from p. 32.

PART SIX

Internal Validity

As was discussed in Part II, one reason experimental designs are preferred over other designs is their ability to eliminate problems of internal validity. Internal validity is the degree to which a research design allows the investigator to rule out alternative explanations concerning the potential impact of the program on the target group. Or, to put it another way: Did the experimental treatment make a difference?

In presenting practical program evaluation designs for state and local governments, Harry Hatry, Richard Winnie, and Donald Fisk constantly alert their readers to look for external causes that might "really" explain why a program works or does not work. For example, in discussing the one-group pretest-posttest design, they warn:

> Look for other plausible explanations for the changes. If there are any, estimate their effect on the data or at least identify them when presenting findings.[1]

For the simple time-series design they caution:

> Look for plausible explanations for changes in the data other than the program itself. If there are any, estimate their effects on the data or at least identify them when presenting the findings.[2]

Concerning the pretest-posttest comparison group design, they say:

> Look for plausible explanations for changes in the values other than the program. If there are any, estimate their effect on the data or at least identify them when presenting the findings.[3]

And even for the pretest-posttest control group design, they advise:

> Look for plausible explanations for the differences in performance between the two groups due to factors other than the program.[4]

For many decision makers, issues surrounding the internal validity of an evaluation are more important than those of external validity (the ability to generalize the research results to other settings). This is because they wish to determine specifically the effects of the program *they* fund, *they* administer, or in which *they* participate. These goals are quite different from those of academic research, which tends to maximize the external validity of findings. This difference often makes for heated debate between academics and practitioners, which is regrettable. Such conflict need not occur at all if the researcher and consumer can reach agreement on design and execution of a project to meet the needs of both. With such understanding, the odds that the evaluation results will be used is enhanced.

Donald Campbell and Julian Stanley identify eight factors that, if not controlled, can product effects which might be confused with the effects of the experimental (or programmatic) treatment. These threats to internal validity are history, maturation, testing, instrumentation, statistical regression, selection, experimental mortality, and selection-maturation interaction.[5] The chapters to follow define these threats and present examples of situations in which these factors provide serious alternative explanations to the reported impacts of the program under study.

The table that follows shows the probable impact of the various potential sources of invalidity on the evaluation designs discussed in the previous chapters but in a very crude way. The table does not replace the discussions in the text; it is merely a guide and makes a variety of assumptions. It assumes, for example, that in the experimental designs, the experimental and control groups are alike in all significant respects. In other words, it assumes that randomized assignment indeed produced two equivalent groups—that there is no "unhappy" randomization.

The table also assumes that the quasi-experimental design comparison groups were selected to minimize the potential impact of sources of invalidity. As will be seen, such selection is often difficult in evaluation research. If the comparison group is not equivalent to the experimental group in all relevant respects, then many of the plus signs in the table should actually be question marks or minus signs.

REFERENCES

1. Harry P. Hatry, Richard E. Winnie, and Donald M. Fisk, *Practical Program Evaluation for State and Local Governments* 2nd ed. (Washington DC: Urban Institute, 1981), p. 27.
2. *Ibid.,* p. 31.
3. *Ibid.,* p. 35.
4. *Ibid.,* p. 40.

SOURCES OF INTERNAL INVALIDITY OF EVALUATION DESIGNS

	History	Maturation	Testing	Instrumentation	Regression Artifact	Selection Bias	Experimental Mortality	Interaction
Experimental Designs								
Pretest-Posttest Control Group Design	+	+	+	+	+	+	+	+
Solomon Four-Group Design	+	+	+	+	+	+	+	+
Posttest-Only Control Group Design	+	+	+	+	+	+	+	+
Factorial Design	+	+	+	+	+	+	+	+
Quasi-Experimental Designs								
Pretest-Posttest Comparison Group	+	+	+	+	?	+	+	−
Interrupted Time-Series Comparison Group	+	+	+	+	+	+	+	+
Regression-Discontinuity Design	+	+	+	+	+	?	+	+
Posttest-Only Comparison Group Design	+	+	+	+	?	?	?	~
Reflexive Designs								
One-Group Pretest-Posttest Design	−	−	?	?	−	?	?	
Simple Time-Series Design	−	+	+	?	+	+	+	

Threats to Internal Validity

NOTES

A minus sign indicates a weakness, a question mark (?) indicates a source of concern, and a plus (+) indicates that the factor is controlled. This table is only a broad guide and does not replace more comprehensive discussions in the chapters to follow. It assumes no unfortunate event such as "unhappy randomization."

Sources: Donald T. Campbell and Julian C. Stanley, *Experimental and Quasi-Experimental Designs for Research,* (Boston: Houghton Mifflin, 1963) pp. 8. 40; Lawrence B. Mohr. *Impact Analysis for Program Evaluation,* (Chicago: Dorsey Press, 1988), pp. 50-51.

5. Donald T. Campbell and Julian C. Stanley, *Experimental and Quasi-Experimental Designs for Research* (Boston: Houghton Mifflin, 1963), p. 5. Selection-maturation interaction is not covered in this text because it is such an obscure concept that real-world evaluations ignore it. Campbell and Stanley state than an interaction between such factors as selection with maturation, history, or testing is unlikely but mostly found in multiple-group, quasi-experimental designs (pp. 5, 48). The problem with the interaction on the basis of selecting the control and/or experimental groups with the other factors is that the interaction may be mistaken for the effect of the treatment.

15

History

Donald Campbell and Julian Stanley define history simply as "the specific events occurring between the first and second measurement in addition to the experimental variable."[1] Historical factors are events that occur during the time of the program that provide rival explanations for changes in the target or experimental group. Although most researchers use the Campbell and Stanley nomenclature as a standard, Peter Rossi and Howard Freeman choose different terms for the classical threats to validity. They distinguish between long-term historical trends, referred to as "secular drift," and short-term events, called "interfering events."[2] Regardless of the terminology, the events are the "history" of the program.

Time is always a problem in evaluating the effects of a policy or program. Obviously, the longer the time lapse between the beginning and end of the program, the more likely that historical events will intervene and provide a different explanation. For some treatments, however, a researcher would not predict an instantaneous change in the subject, or the researcher may be testing the long-term impact of the treatment on the subject. In these cases, researchers must be cognizant of intervening historical events besides the treatment itself that may also produce changes in the subject. Not only should researchers identify these effects; they should also estimate or control for these effects in their models. For example, many investigators use automobile fuel consumption as a hypothetical example of the potential impact of history. Any study of automobile usage in 1973 would have to contend with the tremendous price increase during that year caused by the Arab oil embargo. This incident is clearly associated with a decrease in miles driven.

Although experimental designs traditionally deal well with internal validity problems, the following article is unique in that even though the evaluation uses an experimental design, it has to contend with historical events beyond the control of the researchers. Consider the possible problems of the New Jersey Income Maintenance Experiment summarized in "An Overview of the Labor Supply Results." This overview presents the results of only one aspect evaluated in this well-funded evaluation project. Unlike previous articles, the portion of the study that explicitly addresses history is not presented because it is extremely complex and requires mathematical knowledge well beyond the skills of typical social science students. Read the article to get a feel for the project. The Explanation and Critique explains how researchers coped with historical interference.

An Overview of the Labor-Supply Results

ALBERT REES

The purpose of this article is to provide a summary of the findings of the Graduated Work Incentive Experiment on labor supply, and to do so in a way that makes them accessible to readers who are not concerned with the finer points of methodology and technique. . . . As a necessary preface to the summary of findings, we begin with a discussion of what we expected to find, and why.

WHAT WE EXPECTED TO FIND

The sponsors of the experiment and the researchers all expected, from the outset, that the payment of substantial amounts of unearned income to poor families would reduce the amount of labor they supplied, though not by very large amounts. These expectations were based in part on theory and in part on the results of nonexperimental empirical research. We begin by reviewing what will be called here the static theory of labor-leisure choice.

Static Theory

Figure 1 shows the labor-leisure choices of a hypothetical worker who is capable of earning $2.00 an hour. We assume that he is able to vary his weekly hours by such devices as voluntary overtime, part-time work, and multiple job holding; we also assume, for simplicity, that all hours worked are paid at the straight-time rate. In the initial situation, the worker is in equilibrium at point X on indifference curve I_0, where he works 40 hours a week and receives a weekly income of $80. He is then offered a negative income tax plan that guarantees him $60 a week if he has no earned income and "taxes" earned income at 50 percent by reducing the guaranteed payment as earned income rises. This plan has a "break-even" at point C at an earned income of $120; to the left of this point he receives no payments. The opportunity set facing the worker is now BCA rather than OA, and he chooses point Z on indifference curve I_1. His hours and earned income have decreased and his total income has increased.

The reduction in hours from X to Z can be divided into an income effect and a substitution effect by drawing line DE parallel to AO, which is tangent to I_1 at Y. The distance DO shows the amount of payments that would yield as much satisfaction as the original negative tax plan if the tax rate were zero. The horizontal distance from X to Y is the pure income effect on hours, since the wage rate, or the price of leisure, is the same at both points. The horizontal distance from Y to Z is the pure substitution effect of the tax rate, since the level of satisfaction is the same at both points. It should be noted that the income effect refers to the combined effect on welfare or satisfaction of the guarantee and the tax, and not that of the guarantee alone. A guarantee of $60 a week with no tax would enable the worker to reach an indifference curve lying above I_1.

As Figure 1 is drawn, both the income effect and the substitution effect of the negative income tax reduce hours of work. The negative substitution effect follows from the usual constraints of neoclassical utility theory

Source: "An Overview of the Labor-Supply Results," Albert Rees. THE JOURNAL OF HUMAN RESOURCES Vol. 9 (Spring 1974): 158–180.

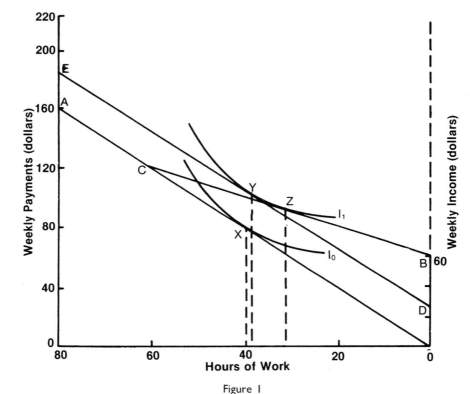

Figure I

Response to a Negative Income Tax

on the shapes of indifference curves. If the curves are convex from the Southwest and BC is flatter than OA, then Z must lie to the right of Y. There is no such necessary relation between X and Y. The expectation that Y will lie to the right of X rests on empirical evidence. This is the evidence that as real income has risen through time, hours of work have tended to fall and that, in cross-section, hours of work tend to be shorter in high-paid than in low-paid jobs. In other words, the empirical evidence all indicates that "leisure" (the term used, for convenience, to include all nonwork activity) is a normal good. That leisure is not an inferior good might be expected from the fact that most inferior goods have

preferred close substitutes, and there is no close substitute for leisure.

In the case of wage increases, not only is the income effect negative, but it is sufficiently large to outweigh the positive substitution effect of a wage increase, which of course makes leisure more expensive. In the case of a negative income tax, both the income effect and the substitution effect will tend to reduce the amount of work supplied. The experiment enables us to observe points X and Z as the behavior of the control and experimental subjects, respectively. (It should be noted that point Y is not observable.)

The preceding discussion has been cast in terms of the choice of hours of work by a single worker. If we think of the family as a single decision-making unit having a collective indifference map, the same analysis would apply to the family. Moreover, it would apply to decisions about labor-force participation as well as to decisions about hours. Thus, a negative income tax might be expected to induce some members of the household to withdraw from the workforce, particularly those whose wage rate was low and who had good nonmarket uses for their time. Teenagers might withdraw to devote their full time to schooling, or wives to devote full time to keeping house.

Our expectations about labor-force participation rest more heavily on substitution effects than do those about hours of work. As real wages have risen through time, male labor-force participation rates have fallen, suggesting, as in the case of hours, that negative income effects outweigh the positive substitution effects of real wage increases. For married women, however, the evidence is mixed. In cross-section, holding education constant, the participation rate of wives falls as husbands' incomes rise. However, the participation rate of wives has risen through time as real wages have risen. Either the income effects are smaller than the substitution effects in this context, or they are offset by other changes in the opportunity set confronting wives—such as the availability of work-saving home appliances and prepared foods.

In the presentation above, we have assumed only one specification of the negative income tax plan. In the actual experiment there are eight, with four different guarantee levels and three different tax rates. (The eight plans are defined in Table 1). The general expectation from the theory is that the plans with higher tax rates will have larger substitution effects and hence will produce greater reductions in labor supply, though, strictly speaking, this is true only as among plans that permit the family to achieve the same level of

TABLE I   Number of Experimental Families by Plan

Guarantee Level[b] (Percentage)	Tax Rate[a] (Percentage)		
	30	50	70
125	no plan	138	no plan
100	no plan	77	86
75	100	117	85
50	46	76	no plan

[a]The tax rate, sometimes called the "offset rate," is defined as the rate at which the transfer payment is reduced as the family's income increases. All plans are linear and have the algebraic form: $P = G - tY$ for $Y < G/t$, where P is the dollar amount of transfer payment; G is the dollar amount of guarantee for a given family size; t is the tax or offset rate; Y is the family income; and G/t defines the "break-even" level of income.

[b]Guarantee as a percentage of the following basic support levels, referred to here as the "poverty levels": 2 persons, $2,000; 3 persons, $2,750; 4 persons, $3,300; 5 persons, $3,700; 6 persons, $4,050; 7 persons, $4,350; 8+ persons, $4,600. These differ slightly from the official poverty levels as of 1968. They were increased annually by the change in the Consumer Price Index.

satisfaction. Similarly, one would expect from the empirical evidence on hours of work that, at the same tax rate, the plans with the most generous payments would cause the largest reduction in labor supply, whether generosity is measured in guarantee levels or in the average payments that would be made at the family's normal (preenrollment) income.

Dynamic Considerations

The theory sketched above is too simple in at least three respects. (1) It assumes that the wage rate confronting each worker is exogenously given and that he can do nothing to affect it. (2) It implicitly assumes that the negative income tax is a permanent change in the opportunity set facing the worker. (3) It assumes that the negative income tax plan is introduced into a world without existing welfare plans. Relaxation of these assumptions gives rise to what can loosely be called dynamic modifications of the standard theory. Each will be discussed in turn.

Endogenous Wage Change. The worker could change his market wage in at least three different ways. First, he might withdraw from the labor force or reduce his hours in order to undertake training that would raise his wage at some future time. A permanent negative income tax would make it easier to do this by providing some income during the period of training. A temporary experiment provides an even stronger incentive in the short run, since in this case the training would have to be completed before the end of the experiment. These considerations suggest that there might be a greater reduction in labor supply early in the experiment than the static theory suggests, but that toward the end of the experiment this might no longer be true. If labor supply is measured in earnings rather than in man-hours, the effect toward the end of the experiment could even be to have a larger labor supply from the experimental group than from the control group. However, few of us gave sufficient weight to this line of argument at the beginning of the experiment to expect this result.

A second set of arguments suggests that earnings might fall more than hours throughout the experiment. The jobs open to a person of given skill and experience usually differ in the extent to which they are pleasant or unpleasant. Some involve heavy physical labor, disagreeable working conditions, inconvenient working hours, or inaccessible places of work. Others are lighter, more pleasant, and more convenient. Under conditions of sustained full employment, the less desirable jobs can be filled only at higher wages; the wage differentials thus called forth are known as compensating differentials.

The payment of a negative income tax could lead workers to shift toward pleasant jobs, sacrificing compensating differentials

previously earned. Instead of substituting leisure for labor, they would substitute more agreeable work for disagreeable work. Such behavior would cause earnings to fall more than hours.

To the extent that average hours are reduced, there is another source of reduction in hourly earnings. By choosing not to work voluntary overtime, workers would reduce the hours paid at premium rates. In shifting from full-time to part-time jobs, workers might have to accept lower straight-time rates. It is not uncommon for part-time workers to receive less than full-time workers receive for similar work; for example, such differentials are often found in collective bargaining agreements for clerks in retail food stores.

Another possible influence of experimental payments on wages is through their effects on job search. One of the standard arguments in favor of unemployment insurance is that it permits the unemployed worker to search for a suitable job, rather than being forced by lack of income to accept one of the first job offers he receives, even if the wage offered is very low. More generally, any payments that are increased when a worker is not working will lower the cost of search and increase the expected wage of the job offer finally accepted. Negative income tax payments fall into this category, as supplements to unemployment insurance and even more strongly for those workers who are not eligible for unemployment insurance payments. Low-income workers are more likely than others not to receive unemployment insurance benefits. Some are in uncovered industries such as local government, domestic service, and agriculture. Some are new entrants to the labor force, or new residents in the state. Finally, some will have quit their last jobs or have been discharged for cause. Any difference between experimental and control families in the incidence and duration of unemployment should be considered as a change in labor supply, rather than as a result of deficient demand, because experimentals and controls were selected from the same population and face the same demand conditions.

Limited Duration of Experiment. We turn next to consideration of the effects on labor supply of the limited duration of the experiment. These, too, do not all work in the same direction. Consider first the male household head with a steady job involving hard work and long hours. If he knew that the negative tax payments were permanent, he might decide to take a job with lighter work and more normal hours. Yet, for a period of three years, such a shift might seem too risky. At the end of the experiment, he would need the higher earned income but might be unable to get his old job back. For the steadily employed male head, the probability is that an experiment of limited duration will have smaller effects on labor supply than would a permanent program.

For other members of the household, whose attachment to the labor force is less secure, the effects of limited duration may be quite the opposite. Wives, teenagers, and other adults in the household are likely to be in and out of the labor force as family circumstances change. To the extent that periods of withdrawal from the labor force are planned in advance, a temporary experiment encourages the concentration of such periods during the experimental years, when the costs of not working are lower than normal. This may be particularly true toward the end of the experiment.

Presence of Welfare. The final consideration is the presence of preexisting welfare plans. At the beginning of the experiment, New Jersey did not give welfare to households with a male head—that is, it did not have a program known as Aid to Families of Dependent Children with Unemployed Parents (AFDC-U). This, indeed, was one of the important reasons for choosing New Jersey as the experimental site. Moreover, at the outset, we did not plan to include a site in Pennsylvania, but it became necessary to do so in order to enroll enough non-Spanish-speaking whites. In January 1969 (three months after the Trenton enrollment but before enrollment in the other sites), New Jersey introduced a welfare program for intact families. Until they were cut back in July 1971, benefits under this plan were more generous than those of most welfare programs in the country.

The presence of welfare complicates the comparison between control and experimental families. In the ninth experimental quarter, 25 percent of control families and 13 percent of experimental families were on welfare (these figures are the highest percentages for any quarter). Among experimental families, the percentage varied by plan, decreasing with plan generosity; ninth quarter figures show 23 percent on the 50-50 and 75-70 plans choosing welfare, compared with only 7 percent on the 125-50 plan. (These abbreviations for the plans are defined in Table 1). It also varied by site, from 6 percent in Jersey City to 21 percent in Paterson-Passaic in the ninth quarter.

The general effect of welfare is to make the observed differences between experimental and control groups smaller than they would be in the absence of welfare. The underestimate occurs essentially because welfare may induce some withdrawal of work effort in the control group. On the other hand, the estimates derived from an experiment in the presence of welfare are perhaps more accurate estimates of the effect of a new national income maintenance program that is superimposed on existing programs.

A very careful analysis of the effects of welfare on the experiment is given in the full report.[1] This analysis suggests that the presence of welfare did not have a major effect on the estimated labor-supply differentials.

Taken as a group, these three arguments lead us to look for certain patterns in the experimental results. However, they do not modify substantially the overall expectations generated by the static theory because, for the household as a whole, they tend to be offsetting.

The Nonexperimental Literature

In the postwar period, there has been a substantial empirical literature on labor supply, and this literature was important in forming our initial expectations. The studies fall into three general groups—studies of hours of work, studies of labor-force participation, and studies concentrating on the effects of nonlabor income.

Hours of Work. The studies of hours of work have already been mentioned. It is these studies that lead us to expect some reduction in labor supply for the experimental group, because they suggest that the income effect as well as the substitution effect of a negative income tax will be to diminish the amount of work supplied.

It should be noted, however, that the studies of hours of work have not been confined to low-income workers. They suggest that at or near the mean wage, increases in wage rates are associated with decreases in hours worked, but this need not be true at wages well below the mean, when the desire for added consumer goods may be stronger and the desire for additional leisure weaker. Low-income workers may have a stronger desire to reach the average level of living of their communities than middle-income workers have to rise above it. Indeed, this is exactly what is shown by the usual textbook diagrams of the backward-bending supply curve of labor, which show a forward-rising curve at very low wages, becoming vertical and then bending back as some higher level of wages is reached. Unfortunately, there is no empirical

basis for the forward sloping portion of the curve. Moreover, even if substitution effects are stronger than income effects at low wages, the total effect of a negative income tax will still be to reduce hours, since the tax-induced reduction in net wage rates will not produce an income loss, as would a wage cut with no income transfer. The unique feature of a negative income tax plan is that income is increased at the same time as the net wage rate is reduced.

Labor-Force Participation. The portion of the labor-force participation literature that is relevant deals with the differences in strength of attachment to the labor force by age, sex, and marital status. The studies of such attachment show very high rates of participation by married men with wife present, only weakly affected by differences in education or the strength of demand. For teenagers, the elderly, and married women, average rates of participation are much lower, and such forces as differences in education or in the strength of demand induce much larger differences in participation rates.

Because of the previous studies of participation rates, we never expected any substantial fraction of the male heads of households to withdraw from the labor force when they received payments. It seemed much more likely that the response of male heads would be shorter hours or longer periods of search between jobs. For wives, teenagers, and the elderly, however, reductions in labor-force participation rates seemed a much more likely outcome.

We were aware, of course, of the popular view that large transfer payments can cause widespread idleness. There are experiences that support such a view, such as the experience with unemployment benefits for returning veterans after World War II—payments that were sometimes called "rocking chair money." However, many of the veterans involved were single rather than household heads, and they lacked recent civilian work experience. Popular current views on the effect of welfare on work behavior are similarly based largely on experience other than that of male household heads—in this case, mothers without husbands—and, even here, they tend to be based on anecdotal information rather than on systematic evidence. If there were people who expected our experimental treatment to cause large declines in the participation rates of male heads, they were not in our research group.

Nonlabor Income. The last kind of research that is relevant consists of studies that have emphasized the effects of nonlabor income on labor supply. Several of them were designed explicitly to simulate from nonexperimental data the effects of a negative income tax program. Nevertheless, they were not influential in forming our expectations—in part, of course, because most of them have appeared since we began the experiment. The most striking thing about them is the very wide range of values of their results, and this lack of agreement weakens confidence in any of the findings.

First of all, these studies face a problem that may be insurmountable. Much of the nonlabor income reported in income surveys consists of transfer payments such as unemployment compensation; workmen's compensation; old age, survivors, and disability insurance; and temporary disability insurance. All of these payments except survivors insurance are totally or partially work conditioned—that is, they cannot legally be received by those who work, or by those who work or earn more than a stated amount. Work behavior determines whether nonlabor income is received and in what amount. If any of these types of work-conditioned transfers are included in the measure of nonlabor income used to simulate a negative income tax, the size of the negative effects on work effort will be overestimated, perhaps very

greatly. There are, of course, types of nonlabor incomes that are not work conditioned—particularly dividends, interest, and certain types of pensions. However, the amount of dividend and interest income of the nonaged poor is negligible, and pensions tend to be received by those past prime working age. The nonlabor income of the working poor that is not work conditioned is hard to find in such existing data bases as the Census or the Survey of Economic Opportunity. Some investigators, searching for this needle in the haystack, seem to have seized in desperation at the handiest pitchfork instead. Even those who are clearly aware of the problem of work-conditioned transfers sometimes report amounts of nonlabor income (supposedly *not* work conditioned) that are so large as to call their definitions or procedures into question.

A second general difficulty with the simulation studies of negative income taxes is that they sometimes truncate their samples by current income, thus tending to include a disproportionate number of households that supply, perhaps temporarily, less than average amounts of labor—a selection which could bias the estimated coefficients toward large supply effects. Truncation on a measure such as hourly wages, which is uncorrelated or less highly correlated with the amount of labor currently supplied, would be far preferable. To be sure, the New Jersey-Pennsylvania sample is also truncated on family income, which may not have been the best variable to choose for this purpose. However, the problem is far less serious in a study that estimates labor-supply effects in a period subsequent to that used to select the sample and derives these estimates from a comparison of experimental and control groups where the experimental group receives an exogenous treatment.

It should also be pointed out that the nonexperimental studies estimate substitution effects from cross-sectional differences in average hourly earnings that may not be entirely independent of the effects of the amount of labor supplied. Those who work over 40 hours per week will receive premium pay for overtime; those who want to work only part time may have to accept lower hourly earnings. In an experiment, differential tax rates create a truly exogenous source of differences in net wages.

Despite these deficiencies, the studies that focus on the effects of nonlabor income reinforce the more general labor-supply studies in one important respect—they consistently find larger supply effects for women than for men; indeed, the estimated effects for men are sometimes very close to zero.

A Summary of Expectations

The researchers involved in the experiment never agreed on and set down in advance a summary of what they felt was the most likely outcome for labor supply. In retrospect, this is unfortunate. Any attempt to do so now is bound to reflect to some extent our present knowledge of the results and thus to understate the degree to which we have been surprised. Despite this caveat, it still seems useful to attempt a summary in retrospect.

We never expected able-bodied male heads of households to withdraw from the labor force in response to temporary payments too small to support large families. We did expect some of them to reduce their hours of work, or to spend more time searching for new jobs when they lost or quit a job. We expected some teenagers to return to school or to stay in school longer as a result of the payments. We expected some working wives to leave the labor force to spend all their time in household work.

On the whole, the reduction in labor supply we expected to find in the experimental group was of the order of 10–15 percent. We did not expect to find any differential effects by ethnic group. However, we did expect to find that higher tax rates would produce

greater reductions in labor supply, and so would higher guarantees.

HOW WE ANALYZE THE DATA

The results . . . are more complex and somewhat more ambiguous than we anticipated they would be, and they are not easy to summarize. In attempting to do so, we must explain why we regard some of the results as more salient than others. This, in turn, requires some brief discussion of our methods of analysis, which will deal with dependent variables, the control variables, the treatment variables, and the time period.

The Dependent Variables

There are at least four possible measures of the amount of labor supplied by the household: labor-force participation rates, employment rates, total hours of work, and total earnings. The total hours of work measure includes those not at work as supplying zero hours, and therefore the average level of this variable will be below the average weekly hours of those who are at work. With hours defined this way, the measures listed above are in order of increasing comprehensiveness. Employment includes changes in labor-force participation and in unemployment, which (as pointed out earlier) must be considered as a supply phenomenon in the context of differences between experimentals and controls. Hours includes variations in the two preceding variables and, in addition, variations in hours per week of those at work. Earnings reflects variations in all three preceding variables and, in addition, variation in earnings per hour worked.

It would therefore seem that earnings furnishes the best summary measure of the effects on labor supply. Unfortunately, however, there is a possible bias in the use of the earnings variable not present in the other measures. Experimental families filled out an income reporting form every four weeks; control families did not. The experimental families, therefore, may have learned more quickly than did the control families that what was to be furnished was gross rather than net earnings (that is, earnings before taxes and other deductions, *not* take-home pay). This differential learning process could have caused a spurious differential in earnings in favor of the experimental group, especially during the early part of the experiment.

The analysis of differences in hourly earnings between experimentals and controls supports the idea of this learning effect. For all three ethnic groups, reported average hourly earnings of male experimentals rise relative to those of controls early in the experimental period. For white and Spanish-speaking males, this differential is later reversed or disappears. For black males, it grows even larger toward the end of the experiment, a phenomenon that seems to result from an unusually small rise in hourly earnings in the black control group.

Because of the possible bias in the earnings measure, we shall emphasize the hours measure in summarizing the results. An exception is made in discussing the labor supply of the household as a *whole,* where the earnings measure, despite its defects, serves as an appropriate way of weighting the hours of different members of the household by the value of the labor they supply. It should also be recalled that family earnings are the basis on which payments were determined.

Control Variables

In measuring supply effects, a large set of control variables was typically entered on the right-hand side of the regression equations. In part these were necessary to control for differences between the experimental and control groups resulting from the fact that families were not assigned to these groups by simple random assignment, but by a more complex stratified design. In part, however, their inclusion was in response to the fact that even in a simple random design, it is important to control for systematic differences that may survive the randomization process.

The control variables are used in two different ways. First, they are entered into the labor-supply equations as variables in their own right. Second, they are often interacted with the variables representing experimental treatments to see whether the treatment has differential effects in different subgroups of the treated population. A control variable that is highly significant in the first of these contexts may not be significant in the second.

One of the most important control variables is the preenrollment value of the dependent variable. Thus, if the dependent variable is hours, hours at preenrollment are usually entered on the right-hand side. This procedure captures the effect of many taste variables that cannot be specified individually, but will also reduce the significance of the control variables that are separately specified. It is worth noting that this kind of control variable cannot be used in a nonexperimental study based on a single body of cross-sectional data.

Some of these control variables, although they could have been expected to be very significant, in fact were not. Thus, after control for ethnicity, there was little systematic difference among experimental sites. On the other hand, health status and ethnicity turned out to be very important variables even when many other control variables were present. For this reason, most of the papers that follow run separate regressions for the three ethnic groups (white, black, and Spanish-speaking) and control for health status.

It is also important to control for potential earned income, since average income levels are not the same in experimental and control groups as a result of the complexities of the design model, and since there may be differential responses at different income levels.

The income variable used for this purpose should be free of any influence from the experimental treatment. For this purpose we have used estimates of normal hourly earnings, either based entirely on observations from the control group or derived by methods that isolate and abstract from treatment effects. Full descriptions of these normal wage variables are given in the papers that follow.

The foregoing brief account is by no means a complete listing of control variables. Some variables were important in some of the analyses and not in others, . . .

Treatment Variables

In one sense, the experimental treatment in this experiment is very simple—it consists of giving families cash payments. These payments can be specified much more precisely than can the more amorphous treatments involved in experimental evaluation of counseling, training, or psychotherapy programs. In another sense, however, the treatment is complex. There were eight different payment plans, and within each plan there was variation in payments by family size. Table 1 shows the number of experimental families by payments plan.

In the design stages of the experiment, we all confidently expected significant overall effects of the treatment on labor supply, and attention was focused on measuring differential effects of the treatment plans. In retrospect, this emphasis may have been somewhat misplaced, since the overall treatment effect is not always unambiguous.

In general, two different methods of introducing treatment effects are used. The first is to include a dummy variable for any experimental treatment and two additional sets of variables that specify tax rates and guarantee levels. The second method uses the experimental dummy and a variable measuring average payments levels. The payments reflect the guarantee level, the tax rate, family size,

and earned income. To avoid introducing experimental response into the treatment variable, the preenrollment level of income is used in calculating payments. The payments calculation is useful in identifying families who are initially above the breakeven point of their plans, since, although they will be in the experimental group, they all will appear with zero payments.

In practice, two of our plans were dominated by New Jersey welfare during most of the period of the experiment, and attrition from these plans was very high. These were, of course, the two least generous plans—the 50 percent of poverty guarantee with a 50 percent tax rate (50-50 plan) and the 75 percent guarantee with a 70 percent tax rate (75-70 plan). In much of the analysis, these plans are omitted from the treatment group.

Before we discuss effects, it will be useful for the reader to have some idea of the size of the payments and their variation by plan. Table 2 gives, by experimental site, the average size of payments to continuous husband-wife families who received payments in a given four-week period for each of the three years of the experiment. The average payments per period can, of course, be converted to annual averages by multiplying by 13. Thus, the first-year annual average for all such families is $1,183. The average payments are slightly lower for all families than for continuous husband-wife families. We show the data for the latter here, since most of the labor-supply analysis is based on these families.

The data in Table 2 show a mildly rising trend through time, except in Trenton. This trend arises from two sources. First, guarantee levels were escalated annually during the course of the experiment according to the Consumer Price Index. The increase was based on July-to-July changes in the CPI and was implemented in all sites where payments were then being made in September 1969 (5.5 percent), October 1970 (5.9 percent),

TABLE 2 Average Payments per Four-Week Period, Continuous Husband-Wife Families by Site

	All Sites	Trenton	Patterson-Passaic	Jersey City	Scranton
First year	$91.03	$69.93	$79.43	$107.80	$91.46
Second year	93.25	71.91	80.67	109.86	94.72
Third year	96.84	58.67	84.92	120.35	98.26
Percentage change, first to third year	6.4%	−16.1%	6.9%	11.6%	5.2%
Percentage increase in guarantee amount due to CPI		11.7	16.6	16.6	10.5

and September or October 1971 (4.4 percent). Because of differences in the timing of the experimental period in different cities, Trenton received the first two cost-of-living adjustments, cumulating to 11.7 percent; Paterson-Passaic and Jersey City received all three, cumulating to 16.6 percent; and Scranton received the last two, cumulating to 10.5 percent. In Paterson-Passaic and Jersey City, the third increase in guarantees was in effect for less than a full year before the end of payments; in Scranton it was in effect less than two months, and in Jersey City about seven months. The average increase in guarantee levels for the final experimental year in the two sites that received all three increments thus lies between 11.7 and 16.6 percent, closer to the former figure in Paterson-Passaic, and slightly closer to the latter in Jersey City. When these increases are compared with the increases in average payments shown in Table 2, it can be seen that in every case the increase in payments is less than the increase in guarantees—and by substantial amounts in all sites but Jersey City.

The second factor tending to produce increasing average payments over time is rising unemployment rates. A weighted average unemployment rate for the four sites rose from 4.4 percent in 1969 to 7.1 percent in 1971, a factor that would also tend to produce rising payments as members of the experimental families who lost jobs experienced greater difficulty finding new ones.

In light of the increases in guarantees and the rise in unemployment, the smallness of the rise in average payments over the life of the experiment suggests that there was not an increasing withdrawal of labor supply or any growing falsification of income reports as experimental subjects learned to "beat the system." Either of these kinds of behavior would have produced more rapidly rising payments.

Table 3 gives, by ethnic group, the same kind of data as Table 2. The average payments rise most rapidly for Spanish-speaking families. Since these payments rise more than those for all ethnic groups in any one site, something more than the distribution of ethnic groups by site must be at work.

Table 4 shows the average payments to continuous husband-wife families by experimental plan for the second experimental year. These payments vary from $187 per four-week period in the most generous plan to $22 in the least generous. In addition, of course, there is substantial variation within plans because of differences in family size and earned income.

Changes in payments from the first to the third year also vary by plan, as shown in Table 5. In the three plans with a guarantee equal to or above the poverty line, payments increase

TABLE 3 Average Payments per Four-Week Period, Continuous Husband-Wife Families by Ethnic Group

	All	White	Black	Spanish-Speaking
First year	$91.03	$87.65	$ 97.65	$ 86.96
Second year	93.25	91.03	96.59	92.23
Third year	96.84	90.11	102.83	100.32
Percentage increase, first to third year	6.4%	2.8%	5.3%	15.4%

between 9 and 14 percent. The low guarantee plans vary more, but three of the five show decreases in payments. The decreases include both the plans with the lowest (30 percent) tax rate.

Experimental Time

We had expected, before the experiment began, that the best results from the experiment would be obtained during the middle part of the experimental period. At the outset, participants might still be learning how to report income and how their payments would vary with changes in income. Toward the end of the experiment, anticipation of the termination of payments might also affect labor supply, producing unknown kinds of "end game" effects. When results are presented separately by years, results for the middle year generally should be the most reliable. Often we use the central two years—that is, quarters 3 through

10; for some purposes we average observations over the entire period.

It also should be recalled that experimental time does not have the same meaning in each site in terms of calendar time, because each site entered and left the experiment at a different date. To control for trends in the economy, calendar time is sometimes entered into the analysis in addition to experimental time.

WHAT WE FOUND

The principal findings for three groups of participants—married men, married women, and the family as a whole—are presented [elsewhere], and only a brief summary will be offered in this section.

A succinct summary of the findings is presented in Tables 6 to 8, which show a regression-estimated mean difference in several measures of labor supply for a selected subset

TABLE 4 Average Payments in Dollars per Four-Week Period, Continuous Husband-Wife Families by Plan (Second Experiment Year)

Guarantee Level (Percentage)	Tax Rate (Percentage)		
	30	50	70
125	no plan	187.28	no plan
100	no plan	123.72	66.07
75	103.54	44.17	34.91
50	46.23	21.66	no plan

TABLE 5 Percentage Change in Average Payments per Period by Plan, First to Third Year, Continuous Husband-Wife Families

Guarantee Level (Percentage)	Tax Rate (Percentage)		
	30	50	70
125	no plan	8.9	no plan
100	no plan	9.1	13.9
75	−4.5	−10.3	15.1
50	−2.6	3.2	no plan

of the sample observations—namely, 693 husband-wife families who met criteria for continuous reporting. This subset of families is selected because they are a relatively homogeneous group representing the modal family type among the working poor, for whom the analysis is not complicated by the problems of changes in family composition and missing data. . . . Negative differentials, both absolute and percentage, indicate smaller labor supply on the part of the experimental families compared with control families. Within each table, results are reported separatey for each ethnic group. It should be

noted that these groups showed important differences in responses.

Male Heads

As brought out in Table 6 . . . , the differences in work behavior between experimentals and controls for male heads of continuous husband-wife families were, as we expected, very small. Contrary to our expectations, all do not show a clear and significant pattern; indeed, they show a discernible pattern only after a great deal of refined analysis. Experimentals show a slightly higher partici-

TABLE 6   Husband Totals: Regression Estimates of Differentials in Labor-Force Participation, Employment, Hours, and Earnings for Quarters 3–10[a]

	Labor-Force Participation Rate	Employment Rate	Hours Worked Per Week	Earnings Per Week
White				
Control group mean	94.3	87.8	34.8	100.4
Absolute differential	−.3	−2.3	−1.9	.1
Treatment group mean	94.0	85.5	32.9	100.5
Percentage differential	−.3	−2.6	−5.6	.1
Black				
Control group mean	95.6	85.6	31.9	93.4
Absolute differential	0	.8	.7	8.7
Treatment group mean	95.6	86.4	32.6	102.1
Percentage differential	0	.9	2.3	9.3
Spanish-speaking				
Control group mean	95.2	89.5	34.3	92.2
Absolute differential	1.6	−2.4	−.2	5.9
Treatment group mean	96.8	87.1	34.1	98.1
Percentage differential	1.6	−2.7	−.7	6.4

[a] The data for these tables consist of 693 husband-wife families who reported for at least 8 of the 13 quarters when interviews were obtained. The reported differentials in each measure of labor supply are the experimental treatment group mean minus the control group mean, as measured in a regression equation in which the following variables were controlled: age of husband, education of husband, number of adults, number of children, sites, preexperiment labor-supply variables of the husband. These means and the associated control-treatment differentials may therefore be interpreted as applicable to control and treatment groups with identical composition in terms of these variables. Percentage differentials are computed using the mean of the control as base.

Official government labor-force concepts, used in the experiment, define someone as in the labor force if he is employed or unemployed. Someone is unemployed if he is actively seeking employment, waiting recall from layoff, or waiting to report to a new wage or salary job.

This and the following two tables appear as Tables 1, 2, and 3 in U.S. Department of Health, Education, and Welfare, *Summary Report: The New Jersey Graduated Work Incentive Experiment*, a Social Experiment in Negative Taxation sponsored by the Office of Economic Opportunity (December 1973), pp. 22–27.

pation rate than controls, a lower employment rate, and a correspondingly higher unemployment rate. The unemployment rate difference carries over into hours worked per week. However, on the two measures of earnings, experimentals do better than controls—a result that may reflect greater misreporting of earnings by controls. As a generalization, these differences are all quantitatively small and not statistically significant.

By far the most surprising result of the analysis for male heads is the complete failure to find any significant effect for black male heads in any of the analyses, despite the fact that black husband-wife families received larger average payments than did similar families in the other two ethnic groups. Indeed, the estimated supply response for blacks is not only insignificant, but preponderantly positive. This kind of finding for blacks is not limited to male heads; it recurs in the analysis of other components of the household.

We certainly did not anticipate this outcome; moreover we have no plausible explanation for it after the fact. There is some indication in the earnings data that something peculiar happened to the black control group, but we don't know why. While there is always some possibility that the result arises from sampling variability, we should note that black continuous husband-wife families comprise more than a third of the total and are a larger group than the Spanish-speaking, for whom consistent and negative supply effects were found.

Married Women, Husband Present

One of the first things to note about the labor supply of wives is that the participation rates are very low—around 16 percent, which is less than half the 1971 rates of all married women in the U.S. population as a whole. . . . This rate is low in part because the average family size in the experiment is very large,

and we overrepresent families with small children. In part it is an unfortunate consequence of the decision to truncate the sample by family income, a decision that leads to an underrepresentation of working wives even among large families. In retrospect, it might have been preferable to truncate on the basis of husband's income or, better still, husband's wage rate. The same decision probably accounts in part for the rather sharp rise in participation rates of control wives over time, since at the outset we overrepresent families where the wife is temporarily out of the labor force.

The effect of the treatment is shown in Table 7 for the three ethnic groups separately. The measured work disincentives are seen to arise mainly from the behavior of white wives; the effects of the treatment on the labor-supply variables of black wives are close to zero and sometimes positive, and the effects on Spanish-speaking wives are negative in Table 7, sometimes positive, . . . but never statistically significant.

The results thus indicate that a temporary negative income tax program would cause a substantial percentage reduction in the proportion of working wives in large low-income families, at least among white wives. How such a result is evaluated in terms of social priorities will depend on one's views about the value of having mothers care for their own children. It should be remembered that these estimated effects are probably larger than those to be expected in an otherwise similar permanent income maintenance program. For the control families, no more than 19 percent of wives were in the labor force in any one quarter, but 41 percent were in the labor force in at least one of the 13 quarters (counting preenrollment). In other words, this is a group that enters and leaves the labor force frequently. The experimental treatment creates a strong incentive to concentrate periods out of the labor force during the life of the experiment. A permanent pro-

TABLE 7 Wife Totals: Regression Estimates of Differentials in Labor-Force Participation, Employment, Hours, and Earnings for Quarters 3–10[a]

	Labor-Force Participation Rate	Employment Rate	Hours Worked Per Week	Earnings Per Week
White				
Control group mean	20.1	17.1	4.5	9.3
Absolute differential	−6.7[b]	−5.9[b]	−1.4	−3.1
Treatment group mean	13.4	11.2	3.1	6.2
Percentage differential	−33.2	−34.7	−30.6	−33.2
Black				
Control group mean	21.1	16.8	5.0	10.6
Absolute differential	−.8	−.3	−.1	.8
Treatment group mean	20.3	16.5	4.9	11.4
Percentage differential	−3.6	−1.5	−2.2	−7.8
Spanish-speaking				
Control group mean	11.8	10.7	3.4	7.4
Absolute differential	−3.8	−5.2	−1.9	−4.1
Treatment group mean	8.0	5.5	1.5	3.3
Percentage differential	−31.8	−48.3	−55.4	−54.7

[a] The data for these tables consist of 693 husband-wife families who reported for at least 8 of the 13 quarters when interviews were obtained. The reported differentials in each measure of labor supply are the experimental group mean minus the control group mean, as measured in a regression equation in which the following variables were controlled: age of wife, number of adults, number and ages of children, sites, preexperiment family earnings (other than wife's), and preexperiment labor-supply variables of the wife. These means and the associated control-treatment differentials may therefore be interpreted as applicable to control and treatment groups with identical composition in terms of these variables. Percentage differentials are computed using the mean of the control as base. See ft. a of Table 6 for the definition of labor-force participation.

[b] Significant at the .95 level (two-tailed test).

gram, therefore, could be expected to have a somewhat smaller impact.

The Labor Supply of the Family

[Another] analysis applies to the family as a whole, including male heads, wives, and all other members of the household 16 years of age and over, and it covers the full three years of the experiment. A summary of the results is shown in Table 8. The sample is still restricted to continuous husband-wife families. The hours and earnings effects for whites are consistently negative and range from 8 to 16 percent. For blacks, the earnings effects of the experimental treatment are large and positive. The hours effects are small and differ in sign. For Spanish-speaking families, all estimates are negative.

The results for the family as a whole for whites are thus consistent with those from the separate analyses of male heads and wives in showing appreciable and significant negative effects on labor supply. For blacks, the results again show predominantly anomalous positive responses, though not consistently so for hours. For Spanish-speaking families, the effects are negative, though they are generally smaller and less significant than those for whites.

CONCLUSIONS

In general, the estimated effects of the experimental treatment on labor supply are in accord with our expectations. The major surprise is the absence of any negative effect on

TABLE 8 Family Totals: Regression Estimates of Differentials in Labor-Force Participation, Employment, Hours, and Earnings for Quarters 3–10[a]

	Number in Labor Force Per Family	Number Employed Per Family	Hours Worked Per Week	Earnings Per Week	Percentage of Adults in the Labor Force Per Family	Percentage of Adults Employed Per Family
White						
Control group mean	1.49	1.30	46.2	124.0	57.6	51.1
Absolute differential	−.15[b]	−.18[b]	−6.2[b]	−10.1	−5.3[b]	−6.1[b]
Treatment group mean	1.34	1.12	40.0	113.9	52.3	45.0
Percentage differential	−9.8	−13.9	−13.4	−8.1	−9.1	−12.0
Black						
Control group mean	1.38	1.17	41.7	114.0	54.3	46.9
Absolute differential	−.07	−.07	−2.2	4.1	−1.6	−1.6
Treatment group mean	1.31	1.10	39.5	118.1	52.7	45.3
Percentage differential	−5.4	−6.1	−5.2	3.6	−2.9	−3.3
Spanish-speaking						
Control group mean	1.15	1.04	39.0	102.4	48.9	44.7
Absolute differential	.08	−.02	−.4	5.0	2.4	−1.0
Treatment group mean	1.23	1.02	38.6	107.4	51.3	43.7
Percentage differential	6.7	−1.5	−.9	4.9	5.0	−2.2

[a] The data for these tables consist of 693 husband-wife families who reported for at least 8 of the 13 quarters when interviews were obtained. The reported differentials in each measure of labor supply are the experimental treatment group minus the control group mean, as measured in a regression equation in which the following variables were controlled: age of husband, education of husband, education of wife, number of adults, number and ages of children, sites, and preexperiment labor-supply variables for the husband and wife. These means and associated control-experimental differentials may therefore be interpreted as applicable to control and experimental groups with identical composition in terms of these variables. Percentage differentials are computed using the mean of the control as a base. See fn. a of Table 6 for the definition of labor-force participation.

[b] Significant at the .99 level (two-tailed test).

the labor supply of black households. For white and Spanish-speaking families, and for the group as a whole, the effects are negative, usually significant, but not very large. They consist of a reduction in hours of white male heads, an increase in the unemployment rate of Spanish-speaking male heads, and a large relative reduction in the labor-force participation rate of white wives.

If one calculates the cost of a negative income tax program on the assumption of no supply response, then these results strongly suggest that the estimated cost will be too low. However, the added cost produced by the supply response is a rather small portion of the total cost—not over 10 percent and probably closer to 5 percent. The estimates suggest that a substantial part of this will, in effect, represent added benefits for mothers whose withdrawal from paid employment is likely to be offset by increased "employment" at home. There is a further suggestion that tax rates higher than 50 percent may lead to a more pronounced supply response and, consequently, a larger increment to total cost. Whatever the percentage change in income, a higher tax rate requires that more of that change will be made up in benefits.

If the results we found by ethnic group were applied to the national low-income urban population using national ethnic weights, then the importance of our results for whites would rise and the importance of the results for the Spanish-speaking would fall. It is not at all clear that results for Puerto Ricans in New Jersey say anything at all about Mexican-Americans in the Southwest.

We place less weight on our results for blacks for a different reason. They are strange results that appear to arise from the unusual behavior of the black control group, whose labor supply and especially earnings fell relative to other control groups for reasons we do not understand. That the experimental treatment effects for blacks are often statistically significant is no assurance that they are not biased.

The patterns of labor-supply response that we have found are not as clear as we had expected. Yet in many ways they are clearer and more sensible than the results of much of the nonexperimental literature. Certainly they call into serious question the very large effects estimated in some of the nonexperimental studies. The burden of proof would now appear to be on those who assert that income maintenance programs for intact families will have very large effects on labor supply. Considering how little had been done in the experimental testing of economic policies when we began, we do not find our results disappointing.

REFERENCES

1. Irwin Garfinkel, "The Effects of Welfare on Experimental Response," in *Final Report of the Graduated Work Incentive Experiment in New Jersey and Pennsylvania*, Ch. C-II (Madison: Institute for Research on Poverty, University of Wisconsin, 1973).

Explanation and Critique

The New Jersey Income Maintenance Experiment was designed to test whether provision of a negative income tax could take the place of welfare with more beneficial results. Simply, the effort would guarantee a minimum dollar benefit for each family and would tax earned income at a lower than current rate up to a predetermined income bracket. Thus, it would encourage recipients to continue in the workforce by not penalizing (taxing) them for their efforts.

Although experimental designs are expensive in terms of time and resources, the results of a good experiment can have a potentially huge impact on future expenditures and is often worth the initial investment. That was the idea behind the New Jersey Income Maintenance Experiment. If the plan worked in the experimental setting, it could then be implemented in the rest of the country. This would be a major national policy shift that could potentially cost the government a lot of money (or save money, depending on the findings).

Many dimensions of behavior were examined in the experiment. The article by Albert Rees summarizes the findings regarding the impact of the experiment on the labor supply.[3] Although the evaluation was set up as an experiment, some of the rules regarding experiments were relaxed. For example, using the stratified random method, families were assigned to experimental and control groups. The control families continued operating within the existing tax and welfare system, and experimental families were assigned to one of the eight guarantee and tax systems shown in Table 1 of the article. Experimental families were free to move back to the existing system whenever they wished, however. This back-and-forth movement could have been because of the families' desire to gain more benefits, or because the families were more familiar with the existing system, or because they wanted to take advantage of Medicaid benefits that were not available for experimental families. Whatever the reason for the changes, self-selection in and out of the program and experimental mortality (see Chapters 20 and 21 of this book) were problems with which the investigators had to cope.[4]

Why were the subjects allowed to switch back and forth? Could not the investigators have forced them to continue in the experiment? No. Ethical considerations always take precedence over experimental concerns, which is disturbing to the "purist" investigator. Evaluators of social programs have to be aware of subjects' rights, however. This has allowed some researchers to suggest that one cannot ever use an experimental design when evaluating social programs. Evaluators have to choose the "best" design, given the objective and political situation, which often means that an evaluator must relax model assumptions. This prompts students to ask, "Why bother doing anything but the best design?" Decision makers need to base their decisions on the empirical evidence that evaluators present. For this reason, evaluators strive to provide the best available information.

New Jersey was chosen as the site for the experiment on the basis of characteristics of the welfare system that existed before the experiment. A number of events occurred after the start of the experiment that could potentially have had an impact on the results. These historical events could not be controlled by the investigators. However, they identified the events and took great pains either to cope with them or to estimate their effects.

The first historical factor was the institution of the AFDC-U program shortly after the experiment began, an event that could not be controlled by the evaluators because it was a *political* decision to begin the program. Irwin Garfinkel estimated the effect of the presence of this program on experimental subjects and the subsequent impact on the labor supply.[5] First he looked at the percentage of experimental and control families on welfare during the experiment. This number included switchers from the experimental group to preexperiment welfare or

AFDC-U status. He found that the percentage of experimental families on welfare increased over time but that their rate of participation was below that of the controls. He also found that those on welfare, expectedly, worked less than those not on welfare.

From 1969 to 1971, the benefits under the AFDC-U program were more substantial than those of many of the experimental plans. Therefore, it was reasonable to expect those families in groups whose benefits were dominated by these welfare benefits to switch out of their experimental group. This, in fact, is what Garfinkel found. The percentage of families in the more generous programs who switched to welfare was less than those with an economic incentive to do so. Here history caused experimental mortality.

In 1971 the New Jersey AFDC-U benefits for a family of four was cut from $347 a month to $216. At this point, welfare benefits dominated only two of the experimental plans. Garfinkel states that despite some logical nonmonetary draws of staying on welfare (Medicaid, food stamps, increased benefits for larger families), budgetary constraints explain much of the switching (participation) behavior.[6] The general impact of the presence of the program, then, was an underestimation of the differences between the experimental and control groups.

In terms of the impact of historical factors on the labor supply, Garfinkel carefully reasoned that the impact of the AFDC-U program would not have a major detrimental impact because a relatively small number of current recipients would be eligible for AFDC-U. His analysis was performed using intact families—the ones potentially eligible for AFDC-U. So his estimates were overestimations of effects. Because the impact he found was minimal, the impact generalized to the welfare population would be low.

Other nonspecified historical events were controlled by use of calendar time in the analysis as a variable. Rees states that both fluctuations in the economy (most relevant for his analysis) and the differential entry of sites were controlled by use of this variable.

This article also demonstrates other threats to internal validity that are acknowledged by Rees. The effects of testing are covered in Chapter 17 of this book. Instances of testing in the Rees study can be summarized, however. First, Rees points out that the limited duration of the experiment could have caused some potential experimental subjects to eschew the treatment for fear of not regaining their current job at the end of the experiment. Although Rees did not explicitly say so, there appeared to have been a trade-off between the job behavior of these people and those whose attachment to the labor force was less secure. Apparently, these effects evened out over the course of the experiment. There was no method of specifically measuring these effects.[7]

Another effect of testing is the learning by the experimental group that caused a spurious differential in reported earnings. Notice that when this impact was discovered, Rees and his colleagues relied more on hours worked than on earnings.[8]

Even though the use of an experimental design should have controlled for threats to internal validity, Rees and his colleagues included a large number of variables to control statistically when using regression analysis. This practice is an additional safeguard when unhypothesized effects occur. In this way, the study religiously followed the Hatry, Winnie, and Fisk directives listed in the introduction to this section; Rees and his colleagues looked for any conceivable alternate explanation for the observed effects. Unfortunately, so many of the uncontrollable problems encountered in this study (some of which were described in Chapter 5) rendered many of the results suspect. Peter Rossi and Katharine Lyall state that:

> Overlaying the experimental treatments with a competing AFDC-UP program made it more difficult to determine whether the "treatment" was the nominal guarantee and tax rates, the difference between these and the competing AFDC rates with "kinks" at points where there occurred strong incentives to switch from one program to another.[9]

Apparently Rossi and Lyall did not buy the results.

Evaluation is an art. As can be seen from the overview of the New Jersey experiment, the evaluators patched together the best design ethically possible, were aware of and estimated (where possible) the threats to the study's internal validity, and sought alternate explanations for their findings. It also shows that evaluators must be patient and aware of possible flaws in their design but strive to produce the most valid findings within these constraints.

The impact of history can also be questioned in several earlier articles. For example, what historical impacts were controlled for by the inclusion of a comparison group in Tim Newcomb's evaluation of Seattle's energy conservation program? And what effect of history would have had an impact on *non*participants in the Minnesota energy conservation program described in Chapter 10? Would this increase or decrease the estimated impact of the program? As a result, would a researcher be more apt to commit a Type I or Type II error?

REFERENCES

1. Donald T. Campbell and Julian C. Stanley, *Experimental and Quasi-Experimental Designs for Research* (Boston: Houghton Mifflin, 1963), p. 5.

2. Peter H. Rossi and Howard E. Freeman, *Evaluation: A Systematic Approach* 3rd ed. (Beverly Hills, CA: Sage, 1986), pp. 192–193.

3. Four volumes are available that describe the experiment and the results. The volumes are part of the Institute for Research on Poverty Monograph Series. The series was published in 1977 by Academic Press, New York.

4. Part Two of Volume III in the series edited by Harold W. Watts and Albert Rees is devoted to the validity and generalizability of the evidence from the experiment. Chapters 18 and 20 document how attrition affected the results.

5. Irwin Garfinkel, "The Effects of Welfare Programs on Experimental Responses," in *The New Jersey Income-Maintenance Experiment, Volume III: Expenditures, Health, and Social Behavior, and the Quality of the Evidence*, ed. Harold W. Watts and Albert Rees (New York: Academic Press, 1977), pp. 279–302.

6. *Ibid.*, p. 287.

7. See the article by Charles E. Metcalf, "Predicting the Effects of Permanent Programs

from a Limited Duration Experiment," in Watts and Rees, *The New Jersey Income-Maintenance Experiment,* pp. 375–398, for additional analyses of these short-term effects.

8. For more information regarding this impact, see also "Analysis of Wage-Rate Differentials" by Harold W. Watts and John Maner, pp. 341–352, and "Differences Among the Three Sources of Income Data" by Charles E. Metcalf, pp. 375–398, both in Watts and Rees, *The New Jersey Income-Maintenance Experiment.*

9. Peter H. Rossi and Katharine Lyall, "An Overview of the NIT Experiment," in Thomas D. Cook et al., *Evaluation Studies Review Annual* (Beverly Hills, CA: Sage, 1978), 3:48.

16

Maturation

Another potential cause of invalidity is maturation or changes produced in the subject simply as a function of the passage of time. Maturation is different from the effects of history in that history may cause changes in the measurement of *outcomes* attributed to the passage of time whereas maturation may cause changes in the *subjects* as a result of the passage of time.

Programs that are directed toward any age-determined population have to cope with the fact that, over time, maturational processes produce changes in individuals that may mask program effects. Suppose, for example, that a researcher wants to evaluate the effects of a new reading program in school and records students' achievement before and after the program. Between the preprogram and postprogram tests, however, the students grow older. How much of the difference in the test scores can be attributed to the program and how much simply to the fact that the students have grown older?

The problem of maturation does not pertain only to people. A large body of research conclusively shows the effects of maturation on both private corporations and public organizations.[1]

The article "Improving Cognitive Ability in Chronically Deprived Children" by Harrison McKay et al was used in Part 2, "Experimental Designs," as an example of the pretest-posttest control group design. Now review this article, but think about it in terms of the maturation effects as shown in Table 16-1.

Explanation and Critique

The McKay et al. article was selected as an example of the potential impact of maturation in program evaluation not because maturation interfered with the outcome but because the results so vividly portray the impact of maturation. The clearest impact of maturation is shown in Table 2 of the article. The table shows the growth of general cognitive ability of the children from age 43 months to 87 months, the age at the beginning of primary schools. Ability scores are scaled sums of the test items correct among the items common to proximate testing points. Table 4 shows the same information as Figure 2 but in slightly different form. The preprogram mean cognitive ability scores for the four groups are as follows (average age at testing 43 months).

	TI	T2	T3	T4
Ability Score (43 months)	−1.83	−1.94	−1.72	−1.82

During the next six months, treatment was given only to group T4. At the end of the six-month period, all four groups were tested again. The change in the mean test scores for each group is shown in Table 16-1.

For group T4, the treatment improved the children's mean cognitive ability dramatically from −1.82 to +0.21 for a gain of 2.03. The treatment has been successful! But the three untreated groups also improved their cognitive ability by an average of 0.69. Some of the improvement in group T4 must be explained by maturation and not the program. If one assumes that the children in the program would have shown the same growth in cognitive ability as the children not receiving treatment (0.69), then it is probably safe to conclude that the program accounted for about two-thirds of the children's change in cognitive ability (2.03 − 0.69/2.03) and maturation the other one-third (0.69/2.03).

These computations are not shown to downgrade the article or the substantial impact of the program. They merely show how the authors' design allows us to estimate both the program impacts and the influence of maturation on the children's performance.

Now, consider another question. McKay et al. state: "The total number of treatment days per period varied as follows: period 1, 180 days; period 2, 185; period 3, 190; period 4, 172. A fire early in period 4 reduced the time available owing to the necessity of terminating the study before the opening of primary school. The original objective was to have each succeeding period be at least as long as the preceding one in order to avoid reduction in intensity of treatment." Does this impact of history invalidate the fourth year results?

REFERENCES

1. See the following examples: Herbert Kaufman, *Time, Chance, and Organizations: Natural Selection in a Perilous Environment* (Chatham, NJ: Chatham House, 1985); Howard E. Aldrich, *Organizations and Environments* (Englewood Cliffs, NJ: Prentice-Hall,

TABLE 16-1   Maturation Effects in McKay Study

	TI (N = 90)	T2 (N = 49)	T3 (N = 47)	T4 (N = 50)
Ability Score (49 months)	−1.11	−1.22	−1.06	−0.21
Ability Score (43 months)	−1.83	−1.94	−1.72	−1.82
Change	+0.72	+0.72	+0.66	+2.03

1979); W. Richard Scott, *Organizations, Rational, Natural, and Open Systems* (Englewood Cliffs, NJ: Prentice-Hall, 1981); John R. Kimberly, Robert H. Miles, and Associates, *The Organizational Lifestyle* (San Francisco: Jossey-Bass, 1980); Paul C. Nystrom and William H. Starbuck (eds.), *Handbook of Organizational Design, Vol. 1, Adapting Organizations to Their Environments* and *Vol. 2, Remodeling Organizations and Their Environments* (New York: Oxford University Press, 1981).

17

Testing

The effects of testing are among the most interesting internal validity problems. Testing is simply the effect of taking a test (pretest) on the scores of a second testing (posttest). A difference between preprogram and postprogram scores might thus be attributed to the fact that individuals remember items or questions on the pretest and discuss them with others before the posttest. Or the pretest may simply sensitize the individual to a subject area—for example, knowledge of political events. The person may then see and absorb items in the newspaper or on television relating to the event that the individual would have ignored in the absence of the pretest.

Recall the discussion in Chapter 3 of the Solomon Four-Group Design. One of the goals of the design is to determine the extent to which a subject is sensitized by a pretest that affects the posttest performance. The Solomon Four-Group Design allows the investigator to directly assess the effects of testing in the experiment by allowing for enhanced internal validity of the design. However, remember also that the Solomon Design is an experimental design and that most evaluation researchers have neither the resources to conduct such an experiment nor do they often find themselves able to shelter respondents from competing stimuli that may affect performance. Fortunately, much research indicates an insignificant impact of the pretest on posttest performance. However, in cases where one suspects this to be true (as in the learning factors described in Chapter 3), the researcher must be conscious of the consequences of a pretest even if a Solomon Design cannot be executed.

The best-known example of the effect of testing is known as the "Hawthorne effect" (named after the plant where the experiment was conducted). The Hawthorne experiment was an attempt to determine the effects of varying light intensity on the performance of individuals assembling components of small electric motors.[1] When the researchers increased the intensity of the lighting, productivity increased. They reduced the illumination, and productivity still increased. The researchers concluded that the continuous observation of workgroup members by the experimenters led workers to believe that they had been singled out by management and that the firm was interested in their personal welfare. As a result, worker morale increased and so did productivity.

Another phenomenon similar to the Hawthorne effect is the placebo effect. Subjects may be as much affected by the knowledge that they are receiving treatment as by the treatment itself. Thus, medical research usually involves a placebo control. One group of patients is given neutral medication (i.e., a placebo, or sugar pill), and another group is given the material under study. In the following article, Richard Franke and James Kaul describe the importance of the Hawthorne studies and empirically test the extent to which the Hawthorne effect actually affected worker behavior in the Western Electric Plant.

The Hawthorne Experiments

First Statistical Interpretation

RICHARD HERBERT FRANKE
JAMES D. KAUL

The massive Hawthorne experiments of some 50 years ago serve as the paradigmatic foundation of the social science of work.[1] The insights gleaned from these experiments provide a basis for most current studies in human relations as well as for subareas such as participation, organizational development, leadership, motivation, and even organizational design. But aside from visual inspection and anecdotal comment,[2] the complex of data obtained during the eight years of the Hawthorne experiments has never been subjected to thoroughgoing scientific analysis. Indeed, as was pointed out in this journal by Carey (1967), the data necessary for statistical analysis are not available in the scientific literature. It is the purpose of this report to make the Hawthorne data accessible, to interpret systematically the most important of these, and to draw from the results thus obtained some conclusions regarding the use of social science in industry.

Since interpretation and criticism of the Hawthorne studies to date have been little more than opinion, most of this introduction will be a simple description of the Hawthorne experiments over 1924 to 1933, with brief note of the conclusions and impact of these studies.[3] Systematic review of the secondary literature is presented following the analytical section, so that these evaluations may be judged in light of the results of quantitative analysis.

The Hawthorne studies began in 1924 at the Hawthorne plant of the Western Electric Company in Chicago with an inquiry by the National Academy of Sciences and Western Electric into relationships between illumination levels and worker production rates. Inexplicably worker output and job satisfaction generally increased regardless of increase or decrease in illumination. Their curiosities piqued, Western Electric management and social scientists from the Harvard School of Business Administration initiated experiments to examine effects of social as well as physical factors upon work efficiency. A chronology of the experiments is presented in Figure 1. The exploratory illumination experiments (1924–27) were followed by the main Hawthorne experiment, in the first relay assembly test room (1927–33), and by four derivative experiments (1928–32). The first four experimental programs were reactive; that is, condi-

---

Source: "The Hawthorne Experiments: First Statistical Interpretation," Richard Herbert Franke and James D. Kaul. AMERICAN SOCIOLOGICAL REVIEW, Vol. 43, 1978. Reprinted by permission of American Sociological Association.

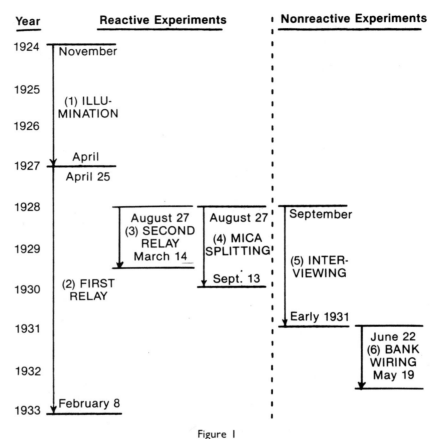

Figure 1

Chronology of the Hawthorne Experiments

tions were manipulated by the experimenters, who then noted changes in work satisfaction and performance. The final two experiments did not include advertent manipulation of independent variables. However, the presence of interviewers and observers was itself a change in the conditions of work.

A flowchart and description of events is presented in Figure 2.[4] From sole attention to environmental conditions of work in (1) the illumination experiments, the studies expanded in (2) the first relay experiment to scrutinize effects of work environment, physical requirements, management, and social relations upon output. All issues dealt with

subsequently were initiated, at least broadly, in the first relay experiment. The derivative studies were: (3) the second relay experiment, which tested and discounted effects of small group incentive payment; (4) the mica splitting experiment, which tested and discounted effects of rest pauses upon performance; (5) the interviewing program, which indicated that relations with management and with peers were important to worker satisfaction, and that informal group organization could be used by workers to regulate and reduce the pace of their work; (6) the bank wiring observation, which confirmed the latter conclusion regarding output restriction, and

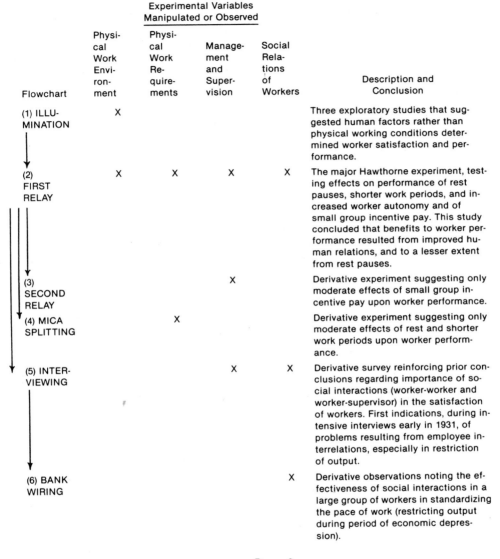

	Experimental Variables Manipulated or Observed				
Flowchart	Physical Work Environment	Physical Work Requirements	Management and Supervision	Social Relations of Workers	Description and Conclusion
(1) ILLU- MINATION	X				Three exploratory studies that suggested human factors rather than physical working conditions determined worker satisfaction and performance.
(2) FIRST RELAY	X	X	X	X	The major Hawthorne experiment, testing effects on performance of rest pauses, shorter work periods, and increased worker autonomy and of small group incentive pay. This study concluded that benefits to worker performance resulted from improved human relations, and to a lesser extent from rest pauses.
(3) SECOND RELAY			X		Derivative experiment suggesting only moderate effects of small group incentive pay upon worker performance.
(4) MICA SPLITTING		X			Derivative experiment suggesting only moderate effects of rest and shorter work periods upon worker performance.
(5) INTER- VIEWING			X	X	Derivative survey reinforcing prior conclusions regarding importance of social interactions (worker-worker and worker-supervisor) in the satisfaction of workers. First indications, during intensive interviews early in 1931, of problems resulting from employee interrelations, especially in restriction of output.
(6) BANK WIRING				X	Derivative observations noting the effectiveness of social interactions in a large group of workers in standardizing the pace of work (restricting output during period of economic depression).

Figure 2

Flow, Content, and Conclusions of the Hawthorne Studies

thus underlined the importance of social relations among workers. Counseling, supervisory training, and other nonexperimental programs also were undertaken by Western Electric to make use of the conclusions from the six experiments. In experiments (2), (3), (4), and (6), research attention focused on small group activities. Three separate groups of five female workers each were involved in the first relay, second relay, and mica splitting experiments, while 14 male workers participated in the bank wiring study. The (1) illumination and (5) interviewing studies, on the other hand, involved whole departments of workers.

The researchers concluded from both the primary and the derivative experiments that measured experimental variables had little effect, but that the unmeasured quality of human relations of workers to management and peer group was responsible for most output improvements observed in the first four experiments. This rather unspecific conclusion, providing a foundation for modern humanitarian and human relations approaches to work, led other researchers to focus upon worker satisfaction, as in the Ohio State supervision studies and their descendants (cf. Fleishman et al., 1955; Miner, 1965), to studies of authoritarianism (cf. Sales, 1966; Vroom, 1960), informal organization (Whyte, 1955), leadership (Bass, 1960; Stogdill, 1974), participative management (cf. Likert, 1967; Marrow, 1975; Pusić, 1973), and to the use of sensitivity training and related techniques in organizational development (cf. Beer, 1976; Bradford et al., 1964; Golembiewski and Blumberg, 1970). It should be stated here that the initial concern of the Hawthorne experiments was with output. Concentration upon worker satisfaction in subsequent studies is sometimes justified by assuming it to be an intervening factor in job performance. This is an assumption often made in practice if not in word (as by Kahn, 1975, and Price, 1968), in the face of contradicting evidence (cf. Locke, 1976; Vroom, 1964). Attempts to demonstrate empirically a linkage between human relations and work performance have not received primary attention since the time of the seminal Hawthorne experiments. To cast further doubt upon the human relations conclusion, we should again note that there have never been meaningful statistical analyses of the data from the Hawthorne experiments. The absence of statistical analysis may have resulted from the nature of the experiments: (a) there were no control groups

other than the experimental groups themselves prior to manipulation; (b) since these were field experiments over extended periods of time, it would have been difficult to eliminate all extraneous variables from the experiment.[5]

Fortunately, quasi-experimental approaches and time-series analytical procedures have been developed since the original researchers' interpretations of the Hawthorne experiments (Mayo, 1933; Roethlisberger and Dickson, 1939; Whitehead, 1938). These methods allow the use of periodic data, with testing for effects of measured variables and adjustment for changes over time in unmeasured historical factors. Rough schematic approaches have been suggested for analysis in education and psychology by Campbell and Stanley (1963) and Cook and Campbell (1976), while quantitative regression procedures have been developed in the field of econometrics (cf. the analytical procedures described below).

One investigation at Hawthorne, the first relay experiment, included a variety of dependent and independent variables that could be expressed quantitatively over 23 experimental periods,[6] allowing convenient use of time-series regression. Measures of quantity and quality of output could be obtained for the group of five workers and for each individual, and measures of independent variables also could be obtained. Rest pauses, hours of work per day, and days of work per week were intentionally manipulated, and a small group incentive system was introduced. A number of inadvertent categoric changes which occurred over the five years of the experiment also could be identified. Most interesting of these changes were the replacement by management of two of the workers after period 7, because of their unsatisfactory attitudes in response to requests for greater diligence and more output, and the onslaught of the great depression early in period 15. The analyses that follow will use the available evidence to test directly for the sources of differences in worker performance over time, to determine whether the substantial performance variances obtained in the experiment can be explained quantitatively.

METHOD

Data

The original documents from the Hawthorne experiments were reviewed and then borrowed during visits to the Hawthorne plant between November 1976 and May 1977. Copies of the documents are now on microfilm in the libraries of the University of Wisconsin, Milwaukee, and the Worcester Polytechnic Institute. The data of the first relay experiment are summarized in Appendix 1 (group) and Appen<dix 2 (individuals). Quantity of output is recorded as net hourly and net weekly rate per worker, while quality of output is recorded as repair time required per day. Hours worked per day and per week and the number of weeks per experimental period describe the basic work schedules, with time taken for scheduled and voluntary rest pauses reducing actual work time. Categoric changes in working conditions are expressed as dummy variables of zero to one for managerial discipline (the replacement by management of two of the five workers, with one of the replacements assuming the role of straw boss), and for the occurrence of the economic depression, the supply of defective raw materials for two periods, the temporary voluntary replacement of one worker, and for the change from a large group to a small group incentive system of pay after the first two experimental periods. A list of these variables and their dimensions is provided in the first results presented in Table 1. Data were available over the 23 periods for all variables, except for repair time (18 periods) and voluntary rest time (21 periods), each unmeasured in several early and late periods.

Analytical Procedures

The data of the first relay experiment are suitable for rigorous analysis using time-series econometric techniques. With these, even influences of inadvertent experimental changes can be examined specifically.[7] In addition, influence of other (generalized) historical factors as well as the passage of time can be measured as *serial correlation* (Durbin and Watson, 1950; 1951), and any effects upon the statistical independence of sequential sets of data can be removed (using the approach of Theil and Nagar, 1961, as described by Johnston, 1963, and Elliott, 1973).

Analyses are directed toward explanation of differences in output over time for the group, as well as for individual workers. As a first step, zero-order correlations are examined for the first relay group—for the entire 23 periods, and separately for the seven periods prior to replacement of two unsatisfactory workers and for the 16 periods after this exercise of managerial discipline. In the second step, the best multiple regressions are determined for the group using all available periods for each of the three production measures, with correction for serial correlation where necessary. As a third and final step, this procedure is repeated for the production rates of each of the individual workers, first by forcing the group models upon the individual data and then by determining whether alternate models provide greater variance explanation.[8]

RESULTS

Zero-Order Relationships for the Group

Results from correlating all group data over the experimental periods are presented in Table 1, employing the maximum number of periods available for each pair of variables. The group dependent variables are net mea-

TABLE 1 Experimental Correlations—Group Outputs and Repair[a]

	Periods 1–23			Periods 1–7			Periods 8–23		
	Hourly Output	Weekly Output	Repair Time	Hourly Output	Weekly Output	Repair Time	Hourly Output	Weekly Output	Repair Time
Dependent Variables									
(1-G) Hourly Output, units/hr.									
(2-G) Weekly Output, units/wk.	.197			.973			−.356		
(3-G) Repair Time, min./day	.225	1.03		.693	.524		.187	.036	
Independent Variables Work Schedule									
(4) Hours per day	−.656	.378	.117	—[d]	—	—	−.549	.702	.199
(5) Days per week	−.629	.585	−.195	—	—	—	−.624	.891	−.174
(6) Net Hours per week[b]	−.758	.489	−.155	−.964	−.878	−.778	−.691	.920	−.077
(7) Weeks per period	.394	.480	.037	.349	.426	−.661	.040	.394	.028
Rest Pauses									
(8) Scheduled Rest Stops, no./ day	.261	.036	.374	.761	.626	.884	.425	−.229	.324
(9) Scheduled Rest Time, min./day	.693	.161	.427	.964	.877	.788	.425	−.229	.324
(10-G) Voluntary Rest Time, min./day	−.466	−.096	−.356	−.612	−.402	−.852	−.256	.129	−.189
Categoric Changes in Working Conditions[c]									
(11) Managerial Discipline	.887	.343	.118	—	—	—	—	—	—
(12) Economic Depression	.791	−.096	.256	—	—	—	.917	−.351	.245
(13) Defective Raw Materials	.101	.275	.806	—	—	—	−.198	.226	.863
(14) Temporary Replacement of Oper. 5	.244	.594	.651	—	—	—	.064	.567	.694
(15) Small Group Incentive	.552	.272	—	.771	.840	—	—	—	—

[a] All data employed are per-capita averages over all periods for which data were available (see Appendix 1); these Pearson product-moment correlations are for periods common to both variables indicated (in total 18, 21, or 23), and are uncorrected for serial correlation.

[b] Hours per day times days per week, minus scheduled rest time.

[c] Change indicated = 1, otherwise = 0.

[d] Dashes indicate no data or no variance in a variable.

sures of output quantity per worker per hour, and per week, as well as a negative measure of output quality which also is subsumed in the quantitative measure (repair time required per worker per day). These three performance variables were correlated over periods with each other and with the 12 independent experimental variables in work schedules, rest pauses, and categoric changes of working conditions that occurred during the five years analyzed for the first relay experiment. Results are presented separately for the entire 23 periods, for the first seven periods with the original five workers, and for the final 16 periods with the group containing three original and two replacement workers.

Because the variables are measured for sequential periods of time and their generalized historical dependence or serial correlation has not yet been measured, it would be premature to evaluate relationships in terms of statistical significance. However, there are in some cases very substantial simple relationships between group performance and experimental variables, yielding high levels of variance explanation (R^2). For example, period-by-period differences in rate of hourly output over 23 periods can be explained in large part (25 percent or more) by the categoric variables of managerial discipline and economic depression, with group hourly production apparently improved by management's replacement of two workers and by the depression. Also, fewer net hours per week, more scheduled rest time, and use of small group incentives appear to have improved hourly production rates.[9] Since most intercorrelations of these independent variables are smaller than their correlations with the dependent variable, prospects appear good for multivariate explanation of a large portion of variance in hourly output by known experimental variables. Separate correlations are presented in Table 1 for group hourly output with independent variables over periods 1-7 and 8-23—before and after the imposi-

tion of managerial discipline expressed by the replacement of operators 1A and 2A with operators 1 and 2. During the early periods, more rest time (leading to fewer net hours) and use of small group incentive payment seem to have been beneficial. In later periods, the economic depression and fewer net hours appear to have benefited hourly output. These shorter-term results are consistent with correlations over the entire 23 periods, where, in addition, the apparent effect of managerial discipline is shown.

Correlations for weekly output rates are also presented in Table 1, but show strong simple relationships over 23 periods only with the temporary replacement of operator 5 and with the days (and net hours) worked per week. A greater number of hours worked per week appears to have offset lower hourly rates when viewing weekly output. During periods 1-7 more rest time (reflected in slightly fewer net hours) and the introduction of small group incentives seem to have aided weekly output, while during periods 8-23 more net hours and the replacement of operator 5 seem to have been beneficial. In sum, the replacement of operator 5, more hours per week, more rest time, and use of small group incentives seem to have benefited group weekly output. Neither managerial discipline nor the economic depression shows the strong simple relationship to weekly output seen in Table 1 for hourly output. The replacement of operator 5 seems to have been important to weekly but not to hourly output, and more net hours seem to have benefited weekly output while detracting from hourly rate of output. On the zero-order surface, only rest time and small group incentive payment seem to have been useful to both rates of output.

Correlations for the third performance variable of repair time required per day (extent of poor quality output) also are presented in Table 1. Poor quality is strongly related to the use of defective raw materials and to the temporary replacement of operator 5, for periods 3-20 and for the later periods (8-20). During the early periods (3-7), lower quality is associated with more scheduled rest stops (and the attendant fewer net hours and less voluntary rest time taken) and with shorter experimental periods. Thus poorer quality output appears to result from a combination of factors which might affect quality more or less mechanically—from poor raw materials, an inexperienced worker, and from breaks in work routine by more frequent daily rest stops and more frequent changes in work schedule and conditions.

Multiple Analysis: Group Regression Equations

Each of the three dependent variables for the group has been regressed stepwise upon the 12 independent variables identified in Table 1 (data in Appendix 1). The results are presented in Table 2 as regression equations. Also presented are the multiple coefficients of determination (R^2 and cR^2, the latter "corrected" for the number of independent variables), the Durbin-Watson coefficients of serial correlation (DW), stepwise variance explanations, and the regression equations after correction for serial correlation, if necessary.

Differences in rates of hourly output by the first relay group are explained in model 1 through managerial discipline (79 percent), economic depression (an additional 14 percent), and through scheduled rest time (4 percent). Most of this 97 percent variance explanation appears to have resulted from the imposition of managerial discipline, which included better performing replacement workers as well as the disciplinary example, from the beginning of period 8.

However, the time-series data used to obtain model 1 are not statistically independent, as indicated by the Durbin-Watson coef-

ficient obtained (which is significantly distant from the neutral point of 2.00; cf. Durbin and Watson, 1951: Table 5). That is, the passage of time and unspecified historical factors appear to have influenced the regression residuals, making the use of critical values tables questionable in testing for significance of the regression equation. Correction for serial correlation using the Theil-Nagar (1961) approach is successful, as shown by the resulting nonsignificant Durbin-Watson coefficient of serial correlation. Variance explanation after correction is 94 percent, and the three independent variables show substantial and highly significant partial correlations with hourly output. Slope coefficients are altered little by correction: managerial discipline apparently resulted in a production increase of eight or nine units per worker per hour, the depression in an increase of six units, and scheduled rest time which ranged from zero to 30 minutes per day resulted in an increase of up to five units per worker per hour. As shown in Appendix 1, hourly output rose from some 50 units per worker per hour up to nearly 72 units by the end of the experiment, and most of this change is accounted for through the above slope coefficients.

Regression of weekly output of the first relay group upon experimental variables in model 2 yields as explanatory variables net hours per week,[10] then managerial discipline, economic depression, scheduled rest time, and finally the introduction of small group incentive payment. Although hours per week enters first as a regression variable, it provides only 24 percent variance explanation. Managerial discipline is again the major explanatory variable (56 percent), followed by the depression and rest time (8 percent each) and by small group incentive (1 percent), for total variance explanation of 97 percent. Since there is no serial correlation, the equation and each partial relationship can be tested for significance. All are substantial and highly signifi-

TABLE 2 Stepwise Regression Equations—Group[a]

Model 1:

$$X_{1-G} = 50.50 + 8.64\,X_{11} + 6.18\,X_{12} + 0.18\,X_9$$

	Intercept	Managerial Discipline	Economic Depression	Scheduled Rest Time
		$r_p = .928$	$r_p = .894$	$r_p = .758$

$R^2 = w\ 97.10\%$, $cR^2 = 96.64\%$, DW = 1.58 (p < .05)

Stepwise variance explan.:[b] 78.72% + 14.46% + 3.91%

Corrected for serial correlation (factor = 0.25):

$$X_{1-G} = 38.29 + 8.26\,X_{11} + 6.34\,X_{12} + 0.16\,X_9$$

		$r_p = .894$	$r_p = .859$	$r_p = .692$
		(p = .0000)	(p = .0000)	(p = .0007)

$R^2 = 94.48\%$, $cR^2 = 93.56\%$ (p = .0000), DW = 1.95 (NS)

Model 2:[c]

$$X_{2-G} = -716.33 + 66.52\,X_6 + 393.78\,X_{11} + 245.97\,X_{12} + 7.67\,X_9 + 105.32\,X_{15}$$

	Intercept	Net Hours Per Week	Managerial Discipline	Economic Depression	Scheduled Rest Time	Small Group Incentive
		$r_p = .977$	$r_p = .942$	$r_p = .845$	$r_p = .731$	$r_p = .423$
		(p = .0000)	(p = .0000)	(p = .0000)	(p = .0004)	(p = .0713)

$R^2 = 96.57\%$, $cR^2 = 95.56\%$ (p = .0000), DW = 1.98 (NS)

Stepwise variance explan.: 23.88% + 56.48% + 7.50% + 7.97% + 0.75%

Model 3:

$$X_{3-G} = 17.88 + 25.33\,X_{13} + 2.58\,X_8 + 7.50\,X_{12} + 0.35\,X_7$$

	Intercept	Defective Raw Mtls.	Scheduled Rest Stops	Economic Depression	Weeks per Period
		$r_p = .951$	$r_p = .763$	$r_p = .770$	$r_p = -.724$

$R^2 = 92.38\%$, $cR^2 = 90.03\%$, DW = 2.32 (p < .05)

Stepwise variance explan.: 64.98% + 14.01% + 5.00% + 8.38%

Corrected for serial correlation (factor = -0.40):

$$X_{3-G} = 22.36 + 25.46\,X_{13} + 3.08\,X_8 + 6.97\,X_{12} + 0.27\,X_7$$

		$r_p = .964$	$r_p = .808$	$r_p = .821$	$r_p = -.594$
		(p = .0000)	(p = .0005)	(p = .0003)	(p = .0251)

$R^2 = 94.90\%$, $cR^3 = 93.21\%$ (p = .0000), DW = 2.07 (NS)

---

[a] Independent variables are presented in order of appearance in stepwise multiple regression; n = 23 periods for output models and n = 18 periods for repair model.

[b] Stepwise variance explanation prior to correction for serial correlation.

[c] Stepwise model independent variables included net hours per week, excluding the highly correlated hours per day and days per week (cf. fn. 10).

cant, except for small group incentive (.05 < p < .10), which did not enter the stepwise regression for hourly output of the group. Slope coefficients in the weekly equation are comparable with those for hourly output (considering that the average work week contained 42 net hours), with additional factors of hours worked and the introduction of small group incentives. As shown in Appendix 1, weekly output ranged from about 2,100 to 3,200 units per worker, averaging some 2,600 units. Changes in net hours worked, with a range from 30.33 to 48 hours per week, could have accounted for a range of 1,175 units of weekly output per worker if not offset by changes in other variables. Managerial discipline and the economic depression could account for 394 and 246 units per week, and small group incentives for 105 units per week.

The third regression model presented in Table 2 seeks explanation of differences in quality of production as measured by repair time per worker per day. Stepwise regression for the first relay group shows explanation by the use of defective raw materials (65 percent), more frequent scheduled rest stops (14 percent), the economic depression (5 percent), and by fewer weeks per experimental period (8 percent). Total variance explanation is 92 percent. The acknowledged provision of defective raw materials in periods 14 and 15 appears to be the primary source of quality difficulty during the experiment, followed by increased disturbance of work routine by more rest stops and by shorter work periods containing unchanged working conditions, all apparently aggravated through stress induced by the depression. Correction of serial correlation, over the 18 periods for which repair data were available, did not substantially change slope coefficients. Interpretation of regression slopes shows the supply of defective raw materials accounting for 25 minutes of repair time per day, scheduled rest stops (zero

to six) for up to 18 minutes, the depression for seven minutes, and shorter experimental periods (two to 31 weeks) for a range of about eight minutes of repair time per day.

For each group dependent variable in Table 2, there are measured experimental variables which explain well over 90 percent of the variance observed in production characteristics. Most of the difference in quantitative production of the group is explained by the replacement of two mediocre workers by others who from the outset demonstrated better performance. Most of the difference in quality of production is explained by difference in quality of raw materials. However, for an understanding of the meaning of these statistical results, replications are required at the level of individual workers—to measure for workers 1A plus 1 and 2A plus 2 the effects of replacement, and to measure the effects of this disciplinary example upon workers 3, 4, and 5.

Replication:
Individual Multiple Regressions

In the remaining tables, multiple regression results are presented interpreting the individual performance data in Appendix 2.[11] The regressions include initially only the independent variables found useful in group models (Table 2). Wherever independent stepwise multiple regressions yield results different from the group equations, these results are presented in the table footnotes. All results presented have been corrected for serial correlation (except for two instances of incomplete correction), and the variance explanations presented have been adjusted to allow for number of independent variables.

Multiple regressions for individual rates of hourly output are presented in Table 3. For workers 1, 2, 3, and 4, all three independent variables of group model 1 are significantly related to hourly output. Independent stepwise

TABLE 3 Replication of Regression Equation 1—Individual Hourly Output (X_1) upon Independent Variables from Table 2

X_1 for Operator(s)	Intercept	Managerial Discipline	Economic Depression	Scheduled Rest Time	Variance Explanation	Durbin-Watson Coefficient
1A + 1[a]	29.67	+ 10.84 X_{11} r_p = .840 (p = .0000)	+ 7.59 X_{12} r_p = .758 (p = .0001)	+ 0.19 X_9 r_p = .583 (p = .0070)	87.15%	1.67
2A+2A[b]	49.60	+ 13.65 X_{11} r_p = .939 (p = .0000)	+ 8.07 X_{12} r_p = .874 (p = .0000)	+ 0.18 X_9 r_p = .641 (p = .0017)	96.42%	1.67
3[b]	51.63	+ 6.35 X_{11} r_p = .835 (p = .0000)	+ 2.74 X_{12} r_p = .591 (p = .0048)	+ 0.21 X_9 r_p = .749 (p = .0001)	91.12%	1.74
4[c]	21.78	+ 6.55 X_{11} r_p = .637	+ 5.78 X_{12} r_p = .595	+ 0.17 X_9 r_p = .570	65.79%	1.33
5[d]	20.83	+ 2.67 X_{11} r_p = .215 (p = .3621)	+ 7.52 X_{12} r_p = .532 (p = .0157)	+ 0.06 X_9 r_p = .164 (p = .4885)	28.33%	1.82

[a] After correction for serial correlation using factor of 0.40.

[b] Independent multiple regression yields:

X_{1-8} = 53.49 + 5.81 X_{11} + 0.14 X_9 + 2.96 X_{12} + 3.89 X_{15}, cR^2 = 93.53%
r_p = .853 r_p = .632 r_p = .688 r_p = .556 DW = 1.83 (NS)
(p = .0000) (p = .0028) (p = .0008) (p = .0109)

[c] After correction of serial correlation using factor of 0.60; not fully corrected.

[d] After correction for serial correlation using factor of 0.60; independent multiple regression yields after correction using factor of 0.40:

X_{1-5} = 41.45 − 7.95 X_{13} + 4.89 X_{12} − 0.35 X_6 + 3.27 X_{11}, cR^2 = 85.19%,
r_p = −.820 r_p = .661 r_p = −.670 r_p = .509   DW = 1.88 (NS)
(p = .0000) (p = .0021) (p = .0017) (p = .0261)

multiple regression shows no further variables to be important for workers 1, 2, and 4, but the additional variable of small group incentive payment benefiting worker 3. When model 1 is applied to worker 5, only the economic depression relates significantly to hourly output. Independent stepwise multiple regression for worker 5 does show managerial discipline as a positive factor, with the additional and negatively related variables of defective raw materials (X_{13}) and the number of hours worked per week (X_6). The best individual equations from Table 3 provide explanation of variance in hourly output which ranges from 96 percent for operators 2A and 2 down to 66 percent for operator 4. Managerial discipline appears to have had the greatest effect upon those most directly involved in the replacement (operators 1A plus 1 and 2A plus 2), but also is significant for operators 3, 4, and 5, with smaller slope coefficients. Depression slope coefficients are about the same for operators 1, 2, 4, and 5, and lower but still significant for operator 3. Scheduled rest time is about equally important to the hourly output of operators 1, 2, 3, and 4, but unimportant to operator 5 (for whom fewer working hours seem to have been useful). Defective raw materials appear to have had an adverse effect upon the hourly output of operator 5 only.

Model 2 results for individual weekly output rates, presented in Table 4, are similar to the regression results of model 1 for individual hourly output. In addition, net hours worked per week are positively associated with output for all five workers, but the model 2 variable of small group incentive payment has a significant effect only for worker 3 (see fns. to Table 4). The best individual equations show variance explanation of weekly output which ranges from 95 percent for operator 3 to 89 percent for operator 5.

Model 3 regressions of repair time (poor quality output) upon experimental variables are presented in Table 5 for individual workers. Although the group regression equation is not fully supported by any individual results, the main variable, the provision of defective raw materials, is significant and the most important variable for each individual. More frequent scheduled rest stops seem detrimental to production quality for three workers, while the economic depression and fewer weeks per experimental period seem to have contributed to poor quality for two workers. Independent stepwise multiple regression for individuals shows a negative influence of voluntary rest time upon work quality for operators 1A plus 1, negative influence of scheduled rest time for operator 3 (in place of number of scheduled rest stops), and a beneficial influence of managerial discipline upon work quality for operator 5. Best equations show variance explanations for repair time ranging from 98 percent for operator 5 down to 56 percent for operators 2A plus 2.

In general, the group output models (Table 2) are the best models also for individuals (Tables 3, 4, and 5), or are within a few percentage points of amended models in variance explanation. Median variance explanations for individuals using both the group and the best models are 87 percent for hourly output, 92 percent for weekly output, and 75 percent for repair time—somewhat lower than variance explanations for the group of 94 percent, 96 percent, and 93 percent. For quantity of output, the managerial intervention in replacing two workers and the advent of the economic depression were important to all individuals as well as to the group. Both factors may be viewed as exerting certain pressures upon the workers. For quality of output, quality of raw materials was of primary importance to all individuals and to the group.

These results differ starkly from most earlier descriptions of the findings of the Hawthorne experiments. The following section in-

TABLE 4 Replication of Regression Equation 2—Individual Weekly Output (X_2) Upon Independent Variables from Table 2

X_2 for Operator(s)	Intercept	Net Hours Per Week	Managerial Discipline	Economic Depression	Scheduled Rest Time	Small Group Incentive	Variance Explan.	Durbin-Wastson Coef.
1A + 1[a]	−661.18	+ 72.68 X_6 $r_p = .963$ ($p = .0000$)	+ 516.73 X_{11} $r_p = .884$ ($p = .0000$)	+ 320.25 X_{12} $r_p = .761$ ($p = .0002$)	+ 10.15 X_9 $r_p = .695$ ($p = .0014$)	103.24 X_{15} $r_p = .220$ ($p = .3814$)	91.59%	1.99
2A + 2[b]	−1173.33	+ 77.46 X_6 $r_p = .963$ ($p = .0000$)	+ 635.97 X_{11} $r_p = .942$ ($p = .0000$)	+ 361.84 X_{12} $r_p = .829$ ($p = .0000$)	+ 9.98 X_9 $r_p = .676$ ($p = .0021$)	120.08 X_{16} $r_p = .265$ ($p = .2880$)	93.40%	1.97
3	−641.62	+ 66.26 X_6 $r_p = .975$ ($p = .0000$)	+ 277.74 X_{11} $r_p = .891$ ($p = .0000$)	+ 128.22 X_{12} $r_p = .627$ ($p = .0053$)	+ 7.65 X_9 $r_p = .717$ ($p = .0008$)	192.76 X_{15} $r_p = .561$ ($p = .0154$)	95.44%	2.00
4[c]	−284.29	+ 69.22 X_6 $r_p = .962$	+ 310.10 X_{11} $r_p = .688$	+ 240.27 X_{12} $r_p = .598$	+ 9.10 X_9 $r_p = .654$	5.42 X_{15} $r_p = .012$	90.28%	1.44
5[d]	−19.70	+ 53.09 X_6 $r_p = .874$ ($p = .0000$)	+ 109.48 X_{11} $r_p = .218$ ($p = .3848$)	+ 257.13 X_{12} $r_p = .470$ ($p = .0490$)	+ 2.57 X_9 $r_p = .161$ ($p = .5239$)	51.99 X_{15} $r_p = .075$ ($p = .7686$)	70.57%	1.96

[a] After correction for serial correlation using factor of 0.40; independent multiple regression yields after correction using factor of 0.40:

$$X_{2-(1A+1)} = -667.78 + 72.72\ X_6 + 520.79\ X_{11} + 10.36\ X_9 + 320.45\ X_{12},\ cR^2 = 91.69\%,$$
$r_p = .962$ $r_p = .881$ $r_p = .695$ $r_p = .753$ DW = 1.91 (NS)
($p = .0000$) ($p = .0000$) ($p = .0010$) ($p = .0002$)

[b] After correction for serial correlation using factor of 0.10; independent multiple regression yields:

$$X_{2-(2A+2)} = -1380.15 + 78.36\ X_6 + 652.06\ X_{11} + 10.93\ X_9 + 365.12\ X_{12},\ cR^2 = 94.26\%$$
$r_p = .961$ $r_p = .951$ $r_p = .751$ $r_p = .833$ DW = 1.82 (NS)
($p = .0000$) ($p = .0000$) ($p = .0001$) ($p = .0000$)

[c] After correction for serial correlation using factor of 0.60; not fully corrected. Independent multiple regression yields after incomplete correction using factor of 0.60:

$$X_{2-4} = -284.06 + 69.22\ X_6 + 309.84\ X_{11} + 9.09\ X_9 + 240.20\ X_{12},\ cR^3 = 90.85\%,\ DW = 1.44$$
$r_p = .962$ $r_p = .688$ $r_p = .654$ $r_p = .598$

[d] After correction for serial correlation using factor of 0.60; independent multiple regression yields after correction using factor of 0.60:

$$X_{2-} = 124.38 + 48.30\ X_6 - 337.95\ X_{12} + 190.72\ X_{12} + 174.28\ X_{11},\ cR^2 = 89.13\%.$$
$r_p = .944$ $r_p = -.813$ $r_p = .620$ $r_p = .586$ DW = 1.86 (NS)
($p = .0000$) ($p = .0000$) ($p = .0046$) ($p = .0083$)

TABLE 5 Replication of Regression Equation 3—Individual Repair Time (X_3) upon Independent Variables from Table 2

X_3 for Operator(s)	Intercept	Defective Raw Mtls.	Scheduled Rest Stops	Economic Depression	Weeks per Period	Variance Explan.	Durbin-Watson Coef.
1A+1[a]	35.00	+ 28.85 X_{18} $r_p = .892$ $(p = .0000)$	+ 2.00 X_8 $r_p = .440$ $(p = .1563)$	+ 3.42 X_{12} $r_p = .316$ $(p = .2716)$	— 0.36 X_7 $r_p = -.452$ $(p = .1046)$	74.74%	2.06
2A+2A[b]	21.02	+ 17.46 X_{18} $r_p = .738$ $(p = .0017)$	+ 2.72 X_8 $r_p = .544$ $(p = .0359)$	+ 4.47 X_{12} $r_p = .370$ $(p = .1750)$	— 0.30 X_7 $r_p = -.424$ $(p = .1157)$	53.38%	2.05
3[c]	21.34	+ 19.98 X_{18} $r_p = .957$ $(p = .0000)$	+ 1.85 X_8 $r_p = .695$ $(p = .0058)$	+ 12.76 X_{12} $r_p = .953$ $(p = .0000)$	— 0.05 X_7 $r_p = -.137$ $(p = .6414)$	96.16%	2.09
4[d]	6.44	+ 14.02 X_{18} $r_p = .725$ $(p = .0034)$	+ 1.07 X_8 $r_p = .293$ $(p = .3096)$	+ 10.21 X_{12} $r_p = .664$ $(p = .0096)$	— 0.25 X_7 $r_p = -.481$ $(p = .0813)$	52.44%	1.92
5[e]	9.18	+ 46.57 X_{18} $r_p = .962$ $(p = .0000)$	+ 5.58 X_8 $r_p = .865$ $(p = .0001)$	+ 4.85 X_{12} $r_p = .348$ $(p = .2231)$	— 0.50 X_7 $r_p = -.774$ $(p = .0012)$	92.08%	1.92

[a] After correction for serial correlation using factor of -0.25; independent multiple regression yields:

$X_{8-(1A+1)} = 37.00 + 28.36\ X_{18} - 0.77\ X_{10-1} - 0.33\ X_7$, $cR^2 = 73.54\%$.

$r_p = .868$ $r_p = .579$ $r_p = -.503$ $DW = 1.99$ (NS)
$(p = .0000)$ $(p = .0187)$ $(p = .0469)$

[b] Independent multiple regression yields:

$X_{8-(2A+2)} = 22.41 + 15.28\ X_{18} + 3.32\ X_8$, $cR^2 = 56.20\%$, $DW = 2.23$ (NS)

$r_p = .732$ $r_p = .583$
$(p = .0013)$ $(p = .0177)$

[c] After correction for serial correlation using factor of $-.80$; independent multiple regression yields:

$X_{8-3} = 13.90 + 20.35\ X_{18} + 13.08\ X_{12} - 0.28\ X_7 + 0.21\ X_9$, $cR^2 = 91.67\%$,

$r_p = .937$ $r_p = .915$ $r_p = -.683$ $r_p = .596$ $DW = 2.04$ (NS)
$(p = .0000)$ $(p = .0000)$ $(p = .0050)$ $(p = .0191)$

[d] After correction for serial correlation using factor of 0.25; independent multiple regression yields:

$X_{3-4} = 8.51 + 12.68\ X_{13} + 8.14\ X_{12}$, $cR^2 = 58.89\%$, $DW = 2.34$ (NS)

$r_p = .689$ $r_p = .662$
$(p = .0022)$ $(p = .0038)$

[e] After correction for serial correlation using factor of 0.40; independent multiple regression yields after correction using factor of -0.40:

$X_{3-5} = 34.37 + 49.09\ X_{18} + 4.68\ X_8 - 11.74\ X_{11} = 0.48\ X_7 + 8.73\ X_{12}$, $cR_2 = 97.76\%$

$r_p = .990$ $r_p = .877$ $r_p = -.887$ $r_p = .772$ $r_p = .865$ $DW = 2.17$ (NS)
$(p = .0000)$ $(p = .0001)$ $(p = .0001)$ $(p = .0020)$ $(p = .0001)$

terprets the present results in juxtaposition to previous interpretations.

DISCUSSION

Multiple regression analyses over 23 periods of the first relay experiment at Hawthorne show that three variables—managerial discipline, the economic adversity of the depression, and time set aside for rest—explain most of the variance in quantity of output for the group and generally for individual workers. Two workers who exhibited undue independence from management (but, as shown in Appendix 2, did not have the lowest average production rates in the group) were replaced by two more agreeable workers. This exercise of managerial discipline seems to have been the major factor in increased rates of output for the now altered group, including increased production by the three individuals remaining. It may be speculated that improvement resulted from the positive example of the two new workers, as well as from the aversive effects of management's disposal of two of the original workers. Clear support is given to the suggestion by Carey (1967) that this intervention was a key part of the first relay experiment. As pointed out by Argyle (1953: 100), the Hawthorne researchers had provided "no quantitative evidence for the conclusion for which this experiment is famous—that the increase of output was due to a changed relation with supervision." Quantitative evaluation now does provide such evidence. However it is not "release from oppressive supervision," as suggested by Landsberger (1948:53), but its reassertion that explains higher rates of production.

Regarding the second independent variable resulting from the present analyses, the Hawthorne researchers as well as Argyle (1953) and Landsberger (1958) recognized that the economic depression beginning October 24, 1929, might have been a disturbing factor in the experiments. Yet they did not appear to suspect its positive influence on production. The increased importance of jobs and the real danger of losing them, because of the depression, may explain its positive contribution to output quantity for the group and for all individuals.

The third dimension resulting from these analyses is worker fatigue. In his review of the Hawthorne studies and of the first several decades of criticism and application, Landsberger (1958) agreed with the conclusion of the Hawthorne researchers that reduction of fatigue did not play much of a role in the first relay experiment. This seemed indicated to them by examination of individual work rates over time and by the findings from the mica splitting experiment. However, Argyle (1953) and Carey (1967) reviewed the same evidence and came to opposite conclusions. Their interpretations are supported by the present analyses, suggesting that physical or mental fatigue reduction through rest pauses also contributed to higher output rates for the group and for four of the five workers. In the case of worker 5, fatigue reduction by working fewer hours in the week appears to have increased the rate of hourly output. Crude analysis of data from the mica splitting experiment further suggests that reduction of fatigue is beneficial for production (Note. 9).

An additional variable found related to production is the use of an incentive pay system based upon the output of the small group rather than upon that of the department. Again, contrary to the views of the Hawthorne researchers and of most subsequent interpreters, some empirical evidence is provided here supporting the positive influence of small group incentives upon weekly output rates in the first relay experiment and upon hourly output rates in the second relay experiment (Note. 9). However, the effects of incentives in the first relay experiment are minor relative to the three factors discussed above, and thus will not be considered further.

In this statistical analysis of the first relay experiment, only the relatively small but consistent effect of rest pauses upon production quantity provides support for the contention that economic benefits result from humanitarian activity. The lack of substantial unexplained variance in any of the final models for output quantity indicates that the unmeasured supervisory and social interaction variables were not very important economically. As Carey (1967) suggested in his incisive but nonquantitative critique, reevaluation of the experiments does not support the conclusions of the Hawthorne investigators.[12] Still, there remains Carey's (1967:403) question of how it was possible for "conclusions so little supported by evidence to gain so influential and respected a place within scientific disciplines and to hold this place for so long." One explanation for this enthusiastic embrace of something scientifically unproved may lie in the particular emphasis of the Hawthorne conclusions, another in the nonsubstantive nature of most criticism of them. Conclusions of the Hawthorne studies seem to have been congenial to persons who were in agreement with the prevailing economic system, but were prepared to proceed from simple materialistic notions about work motivation on to more complex social theories, which could be seen as more useful, humane, and democratic. Authors who appear to have interpreted the Hawthorne studies in this way include those . . . edited by Cass and Zimmer (1975), and DeNood (1941), Friedman (1946), Homans (1941; 1949; 1950), Landsberger (1958), Miller and Form (1951), Nieder (1975), Sanford (1973), Shepard (1971), and Vroom (1964).

Most criticism in early years was ideological rather than substantive, in part directed, as noted by Landsberger (1958), against the ideology of Mayo (1919; 1933; 1945; 1947) and Whitehead (1936), and not particularly concerned with what the Hawthorne studies themselves had to say. This criticism did not treat seriously the main body of work by Roethlisberger and Dickson (1939), supplemented by Whitehead (1938). Examples of such rather misdirected interpretations include the writings of Bell (1947), Gilson (1940). Lynd (1937), Bendix and Fisher (1949), and Schneider (1950). But complaints by Sheppard (1949; 1950) and Hampden-Turner (1970) of reactionary tendencies at Hawthorne have been given some plausibility by Homans's (1941) and Wilensky and Wilensky's (1951) observations that union activities failed at Western Electric. Other social scientists have been diverted by the Hawthorne effect, described by Roethlisberger (1941:14): " . . . If a human being is being experimented upon, he is likely to know it. Therefore, his attitudes toward the experiment and toward the experimenters become very important factors in determining his responses to the situation" (cf. also Dickson and Roethlisberger, 1966, and Bishop and Hall, 1971). This concept of influence upon an experiment through the experiment itself was found either erroneous or misleading by Cook and Campbell (1976), Katz and Kahn (1966), Parsons (1974), and Rubeck (1975). Sommer's (1968) conclusion, that the "errors" called placebo or Hawthorne effect need themselves to be evaluated and understood, is most pertinent.

Perhaps discouraged by the inaccessibility of numerical data from the experiments (although outputs were graphed and most independent variables described by Whitehead, 1938), not one of the numerous commentators has attempted a quantitative interpretation of changes in output rates for nearly 50 years.[13] Indeed, except for Hare (1967) and Parsons (1974), most of the interpreters of the first relay experiment appear not to have recognized that there were more than 13 experimental periods, even though 15 periods had been described by Pennock (1930) and a total of 24 by Whitehead (1938; cf. Note 6).

In the social sciences—particularly where complex beliefs and processes are involved—there seems to be no substitute for quantitative analysis. Whether there are only few data available or, as in the present case, where there exists a massive body of data and description, quantitative analysis enables the scientist to separate fact from fiction. Much of the information from the Hawthorne experiments remains to be tapped and interpreted with this aim.[14]

CONCLUSION

This first statistical interpretation of the major Hawthorne experiment leads to conclusions different from those heretofore drawn. Most of the variance in production rates during the first relay experiment could be explained by measured variables. To assume that output changes resulted from unmeasured changes in the human relations of workers therefore seems injudicious, even though it was the assumption of the Hawthorne researchers and has been accepted and built upon by many social scientists over the past several decades.

The Hawthorne experiments, most of which involved small groups of workers, are exceptional in the accumulation of information over extensive periods of time under actual working conditions. The experiments drew attention to small group processes, and the studies' conclusions led to widespread acceptance of human relations as a primary factor in worker performance. Following dissemination of the findings, previously accepted and conceptually simpler mechanisms such as those of scientific management (Taylor, 1911) tended to be given less emphasis as determinants of work performance. These include

the possible benefits of fatigue reduction, use of economic incentives, the exercise of discipline, and other aspects of managerial control. But it is precisely such factors to which we are directed by empirical analyses of the Hawthorne data. In particular, the discharge and replacement of two somewhat insubordinate workers were followed by higher group and individual production rates in the first relay experiment. Fairly strong evidence has been provided in recent years showing that proclivity to exert close managerial control can benefit the economic performance of individual managers (Miner, 1965), of organizations (Kock, 1965), and of whole societies (Franke, 1973; 1974; 1977). If the empirical results from the Hawthorne experiments and from these more recent studies contain some general applicability to economic organizations, then more of our attention as social scientists might well be directed to managerial characteristics and processes and somewhat less to the human relations of workers. Quantitative analyses of the data from Hawthorne, as well as empirical studies of work groups in the decades subsequent (cf. Stogdill, 1974), unfortunately do not support a contention that improvements in human relations lead to improved economic performance. On the other hand, such activities as participative management, industrial democracy, and sensitivity or consideration training may have benefits transcending the criteria considered here.

The analytical procedures employed in the present study suggest feasibility of examining closely the building blocks of our disciplines, especially when quantitative information is available. This has long been done in the physical sciences, where development routinely includes the process of critical scientific review, secondary analysis, and replication of important studies. There appears great need as well as opportunity for such activities in the social sciences.

APPENDIX I Group Data from First Relay Experiment[a]

Period Number (Dates Included)	(1) Hourly Output	(2) Weekly Output	(3) Repair Time	(4) Hours Per Day	(5) Days Per Week	(6) Net Hours Per Week	(7) Weeks Per Period	(8) Scheduled Rest Stops	(9) Scheduled Rest Time	(10) Voluntary Rest Time
1 (4/25–5/10/27)	49.7	2385.60	—	8.75	5.5	48.00	2	0	0	—
2 (5/10–6/11/27)	49.1	2356.80	—	8.75	5.5	48.00	5	0	0	10.5
3 (6/13–8/6/27)	· 0	2448.00	14.9	8.75	5.5	48.00	8	0	0	13.7
4 (8/8–9/10/27)	1	2452.87	18.5	8.75	5.5	47.08	5	2	10	9.0
5 (9/12–10/8/27)	5.	2543.97	26.4	8.75	5.5	46.17	4	2	20	9.5
6 (10/10–11/5/27)	55.6	2515.90	31.7	8.75	5.5	45.25	4	6	30	0.5
7 (11/7/27–1/21/28)	55.9	2552.95	18.8	8.75	5.5	45.67	11	2	25	8.4
8 (1/23–3/10/28)	61.9	2692.22	23.2	8.25	5.5	43.17	7	2	25	2.8
9 (3/12–4/7/28)	63.9	2598.81	17.2	7.75	5.5	40.67	4	2	25	2.3
10 (4/9–6/30/28)	61.8	2822.41	15.8	8.75	5.5	45.67	12	2	25	5.5
11 (7/2–9/1/28)	62.8	2616.88	19.4	8.75	5.0	41.67	9	2	25	6.4
12 (9/3–11/24/28)	60.7	2913.60	13.4	8.75	5.5	48.00	12	0	0	14.3
13 (11/26/28–6/29/29)	66.5	3039.06	14.4	8.75	5.5	45.67	31	2	25	7.0
14 (7/1–8/31/29)	63.3	2637.71	48.5	8.75	5.0	41.67	9	2	25	6.9
15 (9/2/29–4/5/30)	66.2	3023.35	40.2	8.75	5.5	45.67	31	2	25	5.2
16 (4/7–5/3/30)	69.7	3183.20	30.5	8.75	5.5	45.67	4	2	25	4.6
17 (5/5–10/25/30)	69.2	2624.06	22.0	8.00	5.0	37.92	25	2	25	5.4
18 (10/29/30–2/7/31)	69.6	2406.79	22.0	8.00	4.5	34.58	15	2	25	7.1
19 (2/9–5/23/31)	69.3	2396.39	26.9	8.00	4.5	34.58	15	2	25	7.0
20 (5/25–11/14/31)	68.6	2601.31	24.2	8.00	5.0	37.92	25	2	25	6.0
21 (11/16–12/5/31)	69.6	2110.97	—	8.00	4.0	30.33	3	2	25	5.2
22 (12/7/31–2/6/32)	71.7	2718.86	—	8.00	5.0	37.92	9	2	25	4.6
23 (2/8–2/27/32)	71.5	2168.60	—	8.00	4.0	30.33	3	2	25	—

[a] For specific microfilm sources, contact first author (cf. note 14). Values of categoric variables: X_{11} over periods 1–7: 0; periods 8–23: 1; X_{12} over periods 1–14: 0, period 15: 0.74, periods 16–23: 1; X_{13} over periods 1–13 and 16–23: 0, periods 14–15: 1; X_{14} over periods 1–13 and 18–23: 0, period 14: 0.44, periods 5–16: 1, period 17: 0.04; X_{15} over periods 1–2: 0, periods 3–23: 1.

APPENDIX 2 Individual Data from First Relay Experiment[a]

Oper-ator:	(1) Hourly Output, units/hour					(3) Repair Time, min./day					(10) Voluntary Rest Time, min./day				
Period	1A + 1	2A + 2	3	4	5	1A + 1	2A + 2	3	4	5	1A + 1	2A + 2	3	4	5
1	50.5	49.7	49.7	49.7	48.3	—	—	—	—	—	—	—	—	—	—
2	47.8	48.0	49.5	51.1	48.9	—	—	—	—	—	—	—	—	—	—
3	48.4	50.4	53.6	52.2	50.5	19.0	13.5	12.3	10.6	19.0	10.0	12.6	12.0	12.7	5.3
4	51.5	50.7	53.6	53.6	50.8	19.7	16.3	13.4	9.4	32.8	13.7	17.0	13.0	16.5	8.3
5	54.1	55.4	56.9	56.1	52.9	34.6	37.4	17.4	11.4	31.5	8.8	4.8	11.0	13.9	6.5
6	55.2	54.7	56.8	56.8	54.6	38.0	36.3	21.2	12.5	50.3	9.8	9.3	9.3	12.8	6.5
7	54.0	53.9	58.9	58.2	54.2	23.5	23.0	14.2	6.2	27.0	0.3	1.1	0.2	0.5	0.6
8	62.8	64.5	62.2	63.1	56.8	39.0	25.2	19.0	6.3	26.4	11.4	6.1	10.3	9.0	5.1
9	65.5	68.0	63.0	63.5	59.5	30.5	16.8	16.3	6.0	16.3	0.5	5.3	1.3	4.5	2.2
10	63.9	64.9	62.1	62.8	55.2	24.1	20.0	12.5	3.5	18.7	—	4.6	0.5	5.0	1.6
11	65.6	66.4	63.9	62.9	55.0	33.6	27.6	13.1	9.6	13.2	0.2	7.6	3.6	11.2	4.9
12	62.5	63.9	59.7	61.3	56.1	23.7	22.9	11.0	3.8	5.6	—	8.9	4.3	13.8	4.8
13	67.4	71.9	64.3	69.1	59.7	22.3	19.0	13.8	7.8	8.9	15.0	20.6	11.2	15.8	8.9
14	64.5	70.6	62.0	69.4	50.0	59.9	42.7	40.7	30.0	69.0	5.0	10.0	5.4	9.2	5.6
15	68.8	73.9	64.0	71.3	52.7	48.8	36.7	36.8	18.4	60.2	6.1	8.4	7.1	8.0	5.1
16	72.7	76.8	67.5	73.0	59.6	39.5	31.7	31.7	19.2	30.5	5.1	6.0	5.1	5.2	4.5
17	69.6	75.9	65.6	73.7	61.5	28.0	20.3	26.1	14.6	21.1	3.9	4.4	6.1	4.8	4.2
18	69.1	76.4	64.9	72.8	64.9	21.0	25.0	26.0	13.7	24.5	4.6	5.0	6.3	4.9	6.4
19	72.9	74.8	64.1	69.6	65.3	32.8	30.0	30.6	19.6	21.3	6.3	5.7	9.2	6.2	8.0
20	72.5	76.3	63.4	66.5	64.0	28.7	25.0	26.0	22.7	18.6	6.1	5.9	8.3	6.9	7.6
21	70.2	72.5	67.0	68.9	67.7	—	—	—	—	—	5.0	5.4	6.8	6.6	6.4
22	75.0	76.4	68.6	73.1	65.8	—	—	—	—	—	3.7	4.6	6.2	5.5	5.8
23	77.1	78.0	66.9	73.1	67.1	—	—	—	—	—	3.6	3.6	5.0	5.1	5.6

[a]For specific microfilm sources, contact first author (cf. note 14). Individual weekly output rates can be calculated by multiplying individual values of variable (1), above, by variable (6) from Appendix 1.

NOTES

1. For a selection of studies testifying to the importance of the Hawthorne studies in the development of applied social science, cf. Homans (1941; 1950), Friedman (1946), Miller and Form (1951), Viteles (1953), Blum and Naylor (1968), Sanford (1973), Cass and Zimmer (1975), and Locke (1976).

2. Such interpretation has been taken to considerable lengths, as in the work of Roethlisberger and Dickson (1939), Homans (1950), and Whitehead (1938). The latter author did also employ statistical procedures but without application to the major dependent variables in the various experiments.

3. The primary sources describing and interpreting the Hawthorne experiments are the monumental *Management and the Worker* of Roethlisberger and Dickson (1939), two volumes of graphs and description by Whitehead (1938), and description and social application by Elton Mayo (1933; 1945; 1947).

4. The description and conclusion are extracted from Roethlisberger and Dickson (1939).

5. The experimental and analytical approaches of the Hawthorne experimenters have been criticized in these and other lights by numerous authors, including Carey (1967), Cook and Campbell (1976), and Farris (1969), and by those reviewed by Landsberger (1958).

6. There was also a 24th period, from March 1, 1932, to February 8, 1933, which is not considered in the present analyses. During this final period, all five operators were laid off and replaced by more senior workers who were inexperienced in the assembly of relays.

7. For a treatment of regression equations containing dummy variables, cf. Johnston (1963).

8. Zero-order correlation coefficients also have been calculated for individuals over the 23, 7, and 16 periods, and group and individual regression equations have been calculated for the first 7 and for the remaining 16 periods. No additional findings of note were obtained in these calculations, which thus are not included in the present report.

9. The effects of incentive system and rest pauses upon output also were shown in the data of the second relay and mica splitting experiments. (The data are presented but not analyzed by Roethlisberger and Dickson, 1939: 132, 148.) The incentive effect was tested in the second relay experiment, where a group of five operators worked in one period with the existing large group incentive arrangement, in a second period with the small group of five as basis for incentive pay, and in a final period after return to the large group incentive system. The mean rates of production per worker rose from 1,634 to 1,840 and then back to 1,531 unit components per hour. With the earlier periods serving as controls for the same workers in the next periods, t-test analysis shows a significant difference only between periods 1 and 2 ($t = 2.54$, $p < .05$). That is, there was a significant 12.6 percent improvement in rate of production that appeared to result from the use of a small group incentive system. Similarly for the five workers in the mica splitting test, analysis indicates a significant and even more substantial (15.5 percent) improvement in hourly production rate, apparently resulting from the reduction of fatigue by use of rest pauses and fewer working hours ($t = 3.34$, $p < .02$). Other positive effects of performance-contingent incentives and of fatigue reduction upon output rates have been reported in various settings (cf. Bass and Barrett, 1972; Cherrington et al., 1971; Taylor, 1911).

10. In this as in all other models presented, the variable net hours was included for potential regression equations, but the hours per day and days per week which are its constituents were excluded. However, models which included these variables also were examined. In no case did the resulting equation possess variance explanation superior to that of the corresponding model presented in this report.

11. These analyses at a lower level of aggregation may be viewed as testing to guard against the ecological fallacy in making inferences based upon group data (cf. Blalock, 1961; Dogan and Rokkan, 1969; Galtung, 1967; Robinson, 1950; Thorndike, 1939).

12. Acker and Van Houten (1974:156) similarly concluded that "the cumulative effect of coercion, paternalistic treatment, and special rewards resulted in a rise in productivity." Others that criticized the early evaluations of the first relay experiment are Argyle (1953), Blum and Naylor (1968), Farris (1969), Locke (1976), Moore (1947), Sykes (1965), and Viteles (1953). Acker and Van Houten further suggested that results for the female workers in the first relay experiment might not be applicable to male workers.

13. Parsons (1974) offered a behavioral theory to replace the social interaction theory of the Hawthorne investigators, but this theory also is rendered implausible by the present analyses. Still, quantitative testing of the feedback mechanism suggested by Parsons should be possible using the continuous production record available from the first relay experiment.

14. A "Guide to Hawthorne Records," which provides entry to the UWM and WPI microfilm files and to the comprehensive index of Mallach and Smith (1977), may be obtained from Franke. All data used in the present analysis are provided in Appendixes 1 and 2. We wish to encourage reappraisal of our calculations, as well as further investigation of these historically important experiments.

REFERENCES

Acker, Joan and Donald R. Van Houten (1974). "Differential recruitment and control: the sex structuring of organizations." Administrative Science Quarterly 19:152-63.

Argyle, Michael (1953). "The relay assembly test room in retrospect." Occupational Psychology 27:98-103.

Bass, Bernard M. (1960). Leadership, Psychology, and Organizational Behavior. New York: Harper.

Bass, Bernard M. and Gerald V. Barrett (1972). Man, Work, and Organizations. Boston: Allyn and Bacon.

Beer, Michael (1976). "The technology of organizational development." Pp. 937-93 in M. D. Dunnette (ed.), Handbook of Industrial and Organizational Psychology. Chicago: Rand McNally.

Bell, Daniel (1947). "Adjusting men to machines." Commentary 3:79-88.

Bendix, Reinhard and Lloyd H. Fisher (1949). "The perspectives of Elton Mayo." Review of Economics and Statistics 31:312-9.

Bishop, Ronald C. and James W. Hill (1971). "Effects of job enlargement and job change on contiguous but nonmanipulated jobs as a function of workers' status." Journal of Applied Psychology 55:175-81.

Blalock, Hubert M., Jr. (1961). Causal Inferences in Nonexperimental Research. Chapel Hill: University of North Carolina Press.

Blum, Milton L. and James C. Naylor (1968). Industrial Psychology: Its Theoretical and Social Foundations. New York: Harper & Row.

Bradford, L. P., J. Gibb and K. Benne (eds.) (1964). T-group Theory and Laboratory Method. New York: Wiley.

Campbell, Donald T. and Julian C. Stanley (1963). "Experimental and quasi-experimental designs for research on teaching." Pp. 171-246 in N. L. Gage (ed.), Handbook of Research on Teaching. Chicago: Rand McNally.

Carey, Alex (1967). "The Hawthorne studies: a radical criticism." American Sociological Review 32:403-16.

Cass, Eugene Louis and Frederick G. Zimmer (eds.) (1975). Man and Work in Society. New York: Van Nostrand Reinhold.

Cherrington, David J., H. Joseph Reitz, and William E. Scott, Jr. (1971). "Effects of contingent and non-contingent reward on the relationship between satisfaction and task performance." Journal of Applied Psychology 55:531-6.

Cook, Thomas D. and Donald T. Campbell (1976). "The design and conduct of quasi-experiments and true experiments in field settings." Pp. 223-326 in M. D. Dunnette (ed.), Handbook of Industrial and Organizational Psychology. Chicago: Rand McNally

DeNood, Neal B. (1941). "Book review: management and the worker." American Sociological Review 6:304-5.

Dickson, William J. and F. J. Roethlisberger (1966). Counseling in an Organization. Boston: Harvard University.

Dogan, M. and S. Rokkan (eds.) (1969). Quantitative Ecological Analysis in the Social Sciences. Cambridge, Ma.: MIT Press.

Durbin, J. and G. S. Watson (1950). "Testing for serial correlation in least squares regression, I." Biometrika 37:409-28.

Durbin, J. and G. S. Watson (1951). "Testing for serial correlation in least squares regression, II." Biometrika 38:159-78.

Elliott, J. Walter (1973). Economic Analysis for Management Decisions. Homewood: Irwin.

Farris, George F. (1969). "The drunkard's search in behavioral science." Personnel Administration 32:10-8.

Fleishman, E. A., E. F. Harris, and H. E. Burtt (1955). Leadership and Supervision in Industry. Columbus: Bureau of Educational Research, Ohio State University.

Franke, Richard Herbert (1973). "Critical factors in the post-war economic growth of nations: review of empirical studies and implications for participative organization." Pp. 107-19 in E. Pusić (ed.) Participation and Self Management, Vol. 5. Zagreb: University of Zagreb.

Franke, Richard Herbert (1974). An Empirical Appraisal of the Achievement Motivation Model Applied to Nations. Ph.D. dissertation, Graduate School of Management, University of Rochester.

Franke, Richard Herbert (1977). "Culture and industrial development." Paper presented at the International Conference on Social Change and Organizational Development, Inter-University Centre of Post-Graduate Studies. Dubrovnik.

Friedman, Georges [1946] (1955). Problèmes Humains du Machinisme Industriel. Paris: Librairie Gallimard. Trans. and ed. by Harold L. Sheppard as Industrial Society: the Emergence of the Human Problems of Automation. Glencoe: Free Press.

Galtung, Johan (1967) Theory and Methods of Social Research. New York: Columbia University Press.

Gilson, Mary B. (1940). "Book review: management and the worker." American Journal of Sociology 46:98-101.

Golembiewski, Robert T. and Arthur Blumberg

(1970). Sensitivity Training and the Laboratory Approach. Itasca: Peacock.

Hampden-Turner, Charles (1970). Radical Man. Cambridge. Ma.: Schenkman.

Hare, A. Paul (1967). "Small group development in the relay assembly testroom." Sociological Inquiry 37:169-82.

Homans, George Caspar (1941). "The Western Electric researches." Pp. 56-99 in National Research Council Committee on Work in Industry, Fatigue of Workers: Its Relation to Industrial Production. New York: Reinhold.

Homans, George Caspar (1949). "Some corrections." Review of Economics and Statistics 31:319-21.

Homans, George Caspar (1959). The Human Group. New York: Harcourt Brace.

Johnston, J. (1963). Econometric Methods. New York: McGraw-Hill.

Kahn, Robert L. (1975). "In search of the Hawthorne effect." Pp. 49-63 in Eugene Louis Cass and Frederick G. Zimmer (eds.), Man and Work in Society. New York: Van Nostrand Reinhold.

Katz, Daniel and Robert L. Kahn (1966). The Social Psychology of Organizations. New York: Wiley.

Kock, Sven E. (1965). Företagsledning och motivation. (Management and Motivation, with English summary.) Helsinki: Affärsekonomisk Förlagsförening.

Landsberger, Henry A. (1958). Hawthorne Revisited. Ithaca: Cornell University.

Likert, Rensis (1967). The Human Organization. New York: McGraw-Hill.

Locke, Edwin A. (1976). "The nature and causes of job satisfaction." Pp. 1297-349 in Marvin D. Dunnette (ed.), Handbook of Industrial and Organizational Psychology. Chicago: Rand McNally.

Lynd, Robert S. (1937). "Book review: leadership in a free society." Political Science Quarterly 52:590-2.

Mallach, Stanley and Steven Smith (1977). Records of the Industrial Relations Experiment Carried Out by the Western Electric Company at the Hawthorne Works, Hawthorne, Illinois. Index, University of Wisconsin-Milwaukee Library, Milwaukee.

Marrow, Alfred J. (1975). "Management by participation." Pp. 33-48 in Eugene Louis Cass and Frederick G. Zimmer (eds.), Man and Work in Society. New York: Van Nostrand Reinhold.

Mayo, Elton (1919). Democracy and Freedom. Melbourne: Macmillan.

Mayo, Elton (1933). The Human Problems of an Industrial Civilization. New York: Viking.

Mayo, Elton (1945). The Social Problems of an Industrial Civilization. Boston: Harvard University.

Mayo, Elton (1947). The Political Problems of an Industrial Civilization. Boston: Harvard University.

Miller, Delbert C. and William H. Form (1951). Industrial Society. New York: Harper.

Miner, John B. (1965). Studies in Management Education. New York: Springer.

Moore, Wilbert E. (1947). "Current issues in industrial sociology." American Sociological Review 12:651-7.

Nieder, Peter (1975). "Zum zusammenhang zwischen führungsverhalten, produktionsniveau und zufriedenheit." Gruppendynamik 2:127-39.

Parsons, H. M. (1974). "What happened at Hawthorne?" Science 183:922-32.

Pennock, G. A. (1930). "Industrial research at Hawthorne: an experimental investigation of rest periods, working conditions and other influences." Personnel Journal 8:296-313.

Price, James L. (1968). Organizational Effectiveness: An Inventory of Propositions. Homewood: Irwin.

Pusić, E. (ed.) (1973). Participation and Self Management. 6 Vols. Zagreb: University of Zagreb.

Robinson, W. S. (1959). Ecological correlations and the behavior of individuals. American Sociological Review 15:352-7.

Roethlisberger, F. J. (1941). Management and Morale. Cambridge, Ma.: Harvard University Press.

Roethlisberger, F. J. and William J. Dickson (1939). Management and the Worker. Cambridge, Ma.: Harvard University Press.

Rubeck, Patricia A. (1975). "Hawthorne concept—does it affect reading progress?" The Reading Teacher 28:375-9.

Sales, S. M. (1966). "Supervisory style and productivity: review and theory." Personnel Psychology 19:275-86.

Sanford, Aubrey C. (1973). Human Relations: Theory and Practice. Columbus: Merrill.

Schneider, Louis (1950). "An industrial sociology—for what ends?" Antioch Review 10:407-17.

Shepard, Jon M. (1971). "On Alex Carey's radical criticism of the Hawthorne studies." Academy of Management Journal 14:23-32.

Sheppard, Harold L. (1949). "The treatment of unionism in "managerial sociology'." American Sociological Review 14:310-3.

Sheppard, Harold L. (1950). "The social and historical philosophy of Elton Mayo." Antioch Review 10:396-405.

Sommer, Robert (1968). "Hawthorne dogma." Psychological Bulletin 70:592-5.

Stogdill, Ralph M. (1974). Handbook of Leadership. Glencoe: Free Press.

Sykes, A. J. M. (1965). "Economic interest and the Hawthorne researches." Human Relations 18:253-63.

Taylor, Frederick W. (1911). The Principles of Scientific Management. New York: Harper.

Theil, H. and A. L. Nager (1961). "Testing the independence of regression disturbances." American Statistical Association Journal 56:793-806.

Thorndike, E. L. (1939). "On the fallacy of imputing the correlations found for groups to the individuals or smaller groups composing them." American Journal of Psychology 52:122-4.

Viteles, Morris S. (1953). Motivation and Morale in Industry. New York: Norton.

Vroom, Victor H. (1960). Some Personality Determinants of the Effects of Participation. Englewood Cliffs: Prentice-Hall.

Vroom, Victor H. (1964). Work and Motivation. New York: Wiley.

Whitehead, T. N. (1936). Leadership in a Free Society. Cambridge, Ma.: Harvard University Press.

Whitehead, T. N. (1938). The Industrial Worker. 2 Vols. Cambridge, Ma.: Harvard University Press.

Whyte, William F. (1955). Money and Motivation: An Analysis of Incentives in Industry. New York: Harper & Row.

Wilensky, Jeanne L. and Harold L. Wilensky (1951). "Personnel counseling: the Hawthorne case." American Journal of Sociology 57:265-80.

Explanation and Critique

The Franke and Kaul article turned research in human relations management on its head. For years the "testing effect" had been the justification for a focus on increasing productivity through better personal relations between management and worker. As Franke and Kaul state:

> The researchers concluded from both the primary and the derivative experiments that *measured* experimental variables had little effect, but that the *unmeasured* quality of human relations of workers to management and peer group was responsible for most output improvements observed in the first four experiments (emphasis added).

The beginning of this part described how important it is to look for any and all other plausible explanations for the changes found in the postprogram characteristic of interest. The Hawthorne researchers concluded that a logical unmeasured effect, that of being tested, *caused* a productivity increase despite the varying of other measurable phenomena. In keeping with the tradition of researchers in the physical sciences, Franke and Kaul replicated the Hawthorne studies using the original Hawthorne data, more modern and sophisticated methodological techniques, and the urge to seek out all plausible explanations—the search for falsification.

In sifting through the original data, Franke and Kaul found no systematic way in which the original researchers dealt with the effects of the onset of the Great Depression (an effect of history, Chapter 15) and of the termination of two low-producing employees with new employees (an effect of both history and experimental mortality, Chapter 21). They took these and other unmeasurable effects, such as the onset of small-group incentives, and used a new methodology—pooled time-series analysis—to measure the effects of these two occurrences for the first time.

These "unmeasurable" effects were made measurable through the construction of so-called dummy variables. For each time period (unit of analysis) a score of "1" indicated the presence of the effect and "0" the absence of the effect. The estimated regression equations (even when corrected for serial correlation—other historical factors) indicate the effects of major independent variables (such as defective raw materials for repair time). These variables plus those measured by history and the effects of experimental mortality explain virtually all the variance in the dependent variables. The result is that there is not enough *unexplained* variance left over for the human relations (i.e., testing) for its explanation to be considered important. Hence, the findings of the Hawthorne studies have been overturned, or at least misinterpreted.

However, it would have been interesting to see how the findings might have changed had Franke and Kaul been able to *measure* the testing effect. For example, if the workers and/or management had been observed regarding the quality and quantity of their interpersonal relationships or had the workers been surveyed directly as to whether and how being singled out or given attention had altered their habits, these variables could be included in the regression equation. Then the impact of all three threats to internal validity (i.e., plausible explanations) could be partialed out and a more complete understanding of their impact and interaction assessed.

Did Franke and Kaul completely rule out the testing effect in the Hawthorne case? Did they do so for the testing effect altogether? Although they made a compelling empirical case for the dismissal of the testing effect in the current case, they failed to follow their own prescription for measuring all relevant variables and including them in the regression equations. Presumably they would have operationalized this effect had the original data allowed them to. However, they did reduce the primary importance given to the original finding and the change in management orientations practiced as a result.

Finding empirical fault with the original Hawthorne studies does not altogether end our concern with the effect of testing. A primary concern in studies that assess the effect of new prescription drugs is the placebo effect. The "true" effects of a drug are often assumed to be the difference between the effects found in those taking the real drug and those taking the placebo. In a much more refined, Solomon-like design, Sherman Ross and his associates partialed out not only the drug's effects (by way of using one group who took a pill and another for whom the pill was disguised) but also the placebo's effects (placebo versus control group).[2] They found evidence of a testing, or placebo, effect.

In evaluations in the social sciences, one must continue to be conscious of testing effects in a variety of designs. Care must be taken to establish a baseline of information without overly sensitizing the subject to patterns of behavior in which he or she would not naturally be inclined to engage. Take the example of political events at the beginning of the chapter as an example. Those who previously had not paid attention to political events were sensitized by the pretest to pay more attention to these events. This affected their posttest scores. With the prevalence of the media as instant information sources, one may wish to be concerned about their role in respondents' awareness of the events. In that way, the researchers can attempt to "measure" the Hawthorne effect in a way Franke and Kaul could not.

Knowledge of the impacts of testing raise questions regarding other articles. In Lana and King's article using the Solomon Four-Group Design (Chapter 3), how much "learning" on average, can be attributed to the viewing of the film as opposed to pretest? (*Hint:* Compute this from Table 2 of the article.) Was the Hawthorne effect a problem in the Seattle-Denver income maintenance experiment described by Skidmore in Chapter 5?

REFERENCES

1. Fred J. Roethlisberger and W. Dickson, *Management and the Worker* (Cambridge, MA.: Harvard University Press, 1939).
2. Sherman Ross, Arnold D. Krugman, Samuel B. Lyerly, and Dean J. Clyde, "Drugs and Placebos: A Model Design," *Psychological Reports* 10 (1962): 383–392.

18

Instrumentation

In instrumentation, internal validity is threatened by a change in the calibration of a measuring instrument or a change in the observers or scorers used in obtaining the measurements. The problem of instrumentation is sometimes referred to as *instrument decay*. For example, a battery-operated clock used to measure a phenomenon begins to lose time—a clear measure of instrument decay. But what about a psychologist's evaluating a program by making judgments about children before and after a program? Any change in the psychologist's standards of judgment biases the findings.

Sometimes the physical characteristics of cities are measured by teams of trained observers. For example, observers are trained to judge the cleanliness of streets as clean, lightly littered, moderately littered, and heavily littered. After the observers have been in the field for a while, they begin to see the streets and alleys as average, all the same. The solution to this problem of instrument decay is to retrain the observers.

An evaluation of the Responsive Public Services Program of Savannah, Georgia, by Rackham Fukuhara for the International City Management Association's (ICMA) Innovations Project follows. The Savannah program, begun in 1973, is considered a model program for the utilization of ongoing evaluation findings as inputs into the delivery of service and the process of budgeting. Initially, the street cleanliness program was highlighted. Following the Fukuhara description and evaluation, an excerpt from the 1986 Street Cleanliness Program is provided along with the procedure on which the Savannah program is based. While reading these items, try to determine where instrument decay could occur and what measures could be taken to deal with such decay.

Improving Effectiveness

Responsive Public Services

RACKHAM S. FUKUHARA

This report examines the Responsive Public Services Program (RPSP) implemented by the City of Savannah, Georgia. The purpose of this program is:

1. To measure the effectiveness of the services provided to each neighborhood against a city standard;
2. To identify specific geographic areas with deficient services;
3. To develop a plan for improving the delivery of city services in order to maintain an acceptable level of neighborhood quality;
4. To determine what resources are needed to achieve maximum and equitable service delivery.

The RPSP incorporates a citywide effort to systematically survey 11 conditions. These are: cleanliness; crime prevention; dog control; fire prevention; flood hazard; housing condition; land use compatibility; recreation use; street condition; street signs; and water and sewer adequacy.

Under the auspices of ICMA's Productivity Innovations Project, a management review team was sent to Savannah to assess the potential applicability of this program to other local governments. The findings of this review and a description of the Responsive Public Services Program are the subject of this report.

SAVANNAH'S APPROACH TO PROVIDING SERVICES

The public service perspective of the city manager, Arthur A. Mendonsa, is a key factor in understanding the Responsive Public Services Program. This perspective is exemplified in the following statements:

The general purpose of city government programs is to maintain acceptable standards of livability throughout all areas of the municipality. To accomplish this task, the city must identify those neighborhoods which fall below the desired level of livability and then design service programs which can correct problem conditions.

From our study of effectiveness measures, we have determined that the level of services being provided uniformly throughout the community is not adequate for some neighborhoods. This is a significant finding, for it means that we must discard the idea that it is enough to provide each neighborhood with the same service levels. Instead, we must plan our service programs to achieve a predefined quality within each neighborhood. This will mean that some neighborhoods will have to be supplied with a higher level of service than others if we are to achieve and maintain an acceptable quality of life in these neighborhoods.

It should also be noted that Mendonsa believes that a primary concern of public managers should be the determination of the

Source: *Innovations*, Report No. 10 (June 1976). From Fred S. Knight and Michael D. Rancer, eds. *Tried and Tested: Case Studies in Municipal Innovation.* International City Management Association, September 1978 (Management Information Service Special Report, No. 3).

impact of the services they provide. For example, the sanitation department is responsible for garbage collection. The end product is not the amount of garbage collected; rather, it is the resulting cleanliness of the neighborhood. To use another example, leisure services provides park facilities and recreational activities; however, the primary goal is to involve residents in the program by increasing their participation. The impact of services is an important element of the RPSP, and it is emphasized throughout the program.

BACKGROUND

In 1973 the joint City of Savannah and Chatham County Metropolitan Planning Commission prepared a Community Renewal Program (CRP). This study was an effort to determine the effectiveness of public service in meeting community needs. The CRP was followed by the city's Responsive Public Services Program initiated in the srping of 1974. The more comprehensive survey and research work undertaken in the RPSP: (1) updated the data collected previously; (2) was a source of information on additional service activities; and (3) developed further the methodology for measuring service effectiveness. The findings of the RPSP were published in August 1974, and since then they have been relied upon to make decisions on operations and to plan capital improvements. No further follow-up surveys have been conducted; however, the data base is being updated periodically through the use of departmental reports.

RESPONSIVE PUBLIC SERVICES

The RPSP is based upon the recognition that the city has certain responsibilities: (1) to maintain community livability standards; (2) to identify areas that are impacted by problem conditions; and (3) to respond to these neighborhood service deficiencies with programs targeted to the high need areas.

The Responsive Public Services Program employs an analytical approach combined with mapping and urban planning techniques. Savannah's 33 square miles were divided into 21 geographic areas called planning units. These areas incorporated census tracts and respected neighborhood and natural boundaries where possible. Land area, housing units, and the population of 118,000 were not equally distributed among the planning units.

Basically, four survey techniques were used to collect data:

1. *Field inspections using a trained observer.* The cleanliness survey used this technique. To evaluate effectiveness, sanitation workers were selected and trained to use the visual inspection method described in the Urban Institute manual *How Clean Is Our City?* This method measures a physical condition by simply counting each occurrence of a deficiency factor (for example, the amount of uncollected trash or the number of substandard garbage containers). The survey inspector also rates the observed condition by comparing it with a set of photographs illustrating the scoring system. Spot reinspections by supervisory personnel ensure quality control and consistency of ratings. Field inspection techniques were employed for the surveys of dog control, housing condition, street condition, and street signs. Except for the last, a random sample of blocks were surveyed in each planning unit.

2. *Citizen surveys.* To measure the effectiveness of the leisure services program and facilities, a recreation user survey was conducted, again using materials developed by the Urban Institute. This survey consisted of polling 5 percent of the households in each planning unit, using a standard interview questionnaire to obtain citizens' opinions of the services and their recommendations for improvement. Fifteen recreation leaders representing half of the planning units were also asked for their views.

3. *Special studies.* Geographic, geological, zoning, and public utility maps and studies were used to assess flood hazards, land use compatibility, and water and sewer adequacy for each neighborhood. These surveys consisted primarily of research and analysis with field work limited to verifying data or investigating problems. Also, flooding and sewer stoppages were monitored for deficiencies.

4. *Operational information.* For public safety, the number of crimes per capita and the number of fires per thousand structures were calculated for each planning unit, using departmental records. Every crime and fire incident was plotted by geographic location. This research and analysis was performed without field research.

Once the survey data were collected, the effectiveness measure for each livability condition was determined. Each of the 11 conditions was measured using quantified criteria. For example, a block might be given a numerical rating on the basis of the number of houses without access to municipal sewer lines. The individual ratings were combined with other rating factors into a composite score for the neighborhood.

Planning units were compared using a statistical method applying the concept of the normal curve. The citywide average was used as an indicator of the minimum acceptable service level. In other words, the average (i.e., the norm) became the established standard. Neighborhoods were rated by their relative deviation from the norm to identify problem conditions occurring in particular areas. The severity of the deficiency was ranked according to the magnitude of the score. With these rankings, the city was able to objectively distinguish the high need areas.

The survey findings have an impact on city operations and planning. Some examples of service improvements were: (1) sanitation workers were assigned to code enforcement to ensure that proper trash containers were being used; (2) special litter and trash pickups were provided to areas with severe deficiencies; (3) park and playground equipment was repaired or replaced; (4) leisure service activities were better matched with the neighborhood clientele; and (5) capital improvement programs were developed. (Several construction projects, for example, street paving, storm and sanitary sewers, fire hydrants, and water mains, were proposed and were funded with Community Development Act monies.) Although specific action plans will not be described here, it should be noted that planning units with significant problems were targeted for projects and programs to upgrade the services delivered by the city government to those particular neighborhoods. The 11 surveys are summarized in Table 1.

Resources and Organization

The city manager provided the leadership, executive commitment, and technical direction necessary for implementing the RPSP. A project team was organized to coordinate the program with the operating departments. This team was assembled for the four months' duration of the study. It was headed by a project director and three staff members transferred from the Model Cities program.

The RPSP operated in a decentralized manner. Personnel assigned to survey crews were obtained on a temporary basis from the agencies responsible for the service being evaluated. For example, recreation leaders were trained to conduct door-to-door interviews for the citizen survey. Securing direct departmental cooperation and involvement was essential to the reliability of the data gathering and the success of the entire program.

No additional permanent personnel were

TABLE I   Responsive Public Services Program Surveys

Service Product and Neighborhood Quality Goal	Effectiveness Measure and/or Level of Service Indicator	Survey Method	Action Plan
Cleanliness To provide a sanitation service that permits a healthy environment, removes unsightly trash and solid waste, frees streets, lanes, and yards from litter and debris, and enforces regulations concerning proper garbage and trash disposal.	Incidence of litter, debris, sand, leaves, and abandoned vehicles. Adequacy of trash containers.	Visual inspections of a random sample of block faces, using trained observers.	Concentrated code enforcement and trash cleanup. Additional street sweeping.
Crime Prevention To provide police protection which renders maximum security to persons and property, minimizes fear from crime and reduces preventable crime hazards.	To obtain a total crime rate for each neighborhood of no more than 100 crimes per 1,000 population.	Inventory incidence of crimes (burglary, larceny, automobile theft, robbery, murder, manslaughter, rape and aggravated assault). Using police records and plotting them on planning unit maps.	Monitor the performance of the Law Enforcement Assistance Administration funded Crime Prevention Unit, and the special traffic unit.
Dog Control Residents of every neighborhood should be freed from the fear to their persons and nuisance value to their property imposed by the threat of stray dogs.	Number of loose and/or unlicensed dogs and packs of dogs.	Visual inspection of a random sample of block faces during mid-day and the early morning hours.	A new program was adopted. However, the county assumed responsibility for animal control.
Fire Prevention To provide a fire protection system which has adequate means of defense against fire occurrences, efficient investigative methods which delineate fire hazards through a public information, education, and enforcement program.	To obtain an overall structure rating for each neighborhood of not more than 37 fires per 1,000 structures.	Inventory department records for a two-year period and delineate fires by class (dwelling, structure, vehicle, and trash, or open area), and by incidence and cause (preventable, unpreventable, and incendiary).	Pre-Fire Planning Program (inventory of building floor plans). Accelerated Code Enforcement. Arson Investigation Unit.

TABLE I (*Continued*)

Service Product and Neighborhood Quality Goal	Effectiveness Measure and/or Level of Service Indicator	Survey Method	Action Plan
Flood Hazard To provide a drainage system which prevents property damage flooding, permits convenient access to property, and allows convenient traffic flow during periods of heavy rainfall.	To obtain a flood threat deficiency score for all neighborhoods of not more than 20 vulnerable structures per 1,000. Structural damage by inconvenience and/or canal flooding. Incidence of inconvenienced transportation access, and street impasses.	Analyze flood plain studies and records of flood conditions. Field survey during heavy rains.	Capital projects were proposed and funded on a priority basis with Community Development (CD) monies.
Housing Condition Every neighborhood should be free from housing units which are in violation of the City Housing Code and are detrimental to neighborhood appearance and stability, or are otherwise inimical to the health, comfort, and well-being of the citizenry.	Number of dwellings with code violations. Cost to rehabilitate substandard housing.	Field inspection of a 5% sample of the housing stock using County Health Department Housing Inspectors.	A multi-million dollar housing program was implemented with CD block grant funds.
Land Use Compatibility To provide a compatible land use pattern that allows for developing and maintaining residential environs free from noise, odor, traffic and visual hazards imposed by adjacent industrial and heavy commercial use and permits proper access to, and adequate development space for commercial and industrial uses.	Incidence of environmental hazards.	Update land use maps and calculate mix of residential, commercial, industrial, open space, and institutional acreage. Identify causes of hazards.	Monitor neighborhoods in transition for future developments. Use zoning controls to maintain residential quality.

(*cont.*)

TABLE I (*Continued*)

Service Product and Neighborhood Quality Goal	Effectiveness Measure and/or Level of Service Indicator	Survey Method	Action Plan
Recreation Use Residents in all neighborhoods should be provided with year round public recreation opportunities which are accessible, varied, safe, physically attractive, free of crowdedness, and generally enjoyable.	To obtain public recreation usage by not less than 24% of the population for each neighborhood. (A recreation user is an individual who participates in a program or uses a facility at least ten times per year.)	Citizen survey of 5% sample of households. Recreation leader survey.	A multi-year capital facilities building plan and expanded personnel budget. Program goals and objectives and monitoring system. Equipment acquisition and replacement.
Street Condition To provide a system of streets that permits convenient traffic flow and convenient access to property and that is free of street surface conditions which create a nuisance to the adjoining properties or creates hazards or inconvenience to the neighborhood users of the streets.	Street paving, surface condition, and width. Presence of curbs and sidewalks.	Field inspection of all neighborhood street mileage to record observed conditions.	Specific street problems listed with a five-year capital plan, CD block grant, and public necessity property owner assessments. Annual maintenance and resurfacing program.
Street Signs To provide a street name sign system which properly identifies residential and arterial streets, and a traffic sign system which allows expedient travel, permits coordinated traffic flow, and is designed to lessen the probability of traffic accidents which result in the loss of lives and property damage.	Presence of street name signs and traffic (regulatory, warning, and special) signs. Condition of signs based on need for replacement.	Field inspections the length of all streets.	Contract for placement and replacement of signs. Maintenance and repair program.
Water and Sewer Adequacy To provide a water and sewer service which permits convenient access to sanitary sewer and water services to every residence, provides sufficient water supply for fire protection, and eliminates property damages due to sewer stoppages.	Access to water mains of adequate size and water pressure. Distance of structures to fire hydrants. Access to sewer lines.	Analyze water distribution maps. Map the location of all hydrants and apply hose reach standards. Analyze sewer system maps. Record sewer stoppages and lift station accidents (mechanical and solid stoppages) for a three month period.	Capital program for water main replacements. CD block grant. Installation of hydrants. Capital improvements programmed for CD block grant.

hired for the RPSP. This was consistent with the city manager's intention that evaluation become an integral part of Savannah's administration rather than an exceptional process. To supplement the normal city operating expenditures, a $35,000 U.S. Department of Housing and Urban Development "701" Comprehensive Planning Assistance grant helped support the RPSP activities.

The Steps to Implement the RPSP

- Determine which public service products contribute to neighborhood livability.
- Evaluate the quality of all neighborhoods in terms of the livability conditions affected by city services. This step provides for the measurement of the effectiveness of city services.
- Establish a numerical rating system for each condition and use this system to compare all neighborhoods with each other and with the community as a whole.
- Compute a city standard for all conditions so that a ranking system can be used to identify significant problem conditions for each neighborhood.
- Identify neighborhoods with substandard conditions by comparing the quality ratings of each planning unity with the city norm.
- Establish priorities for the improvements in city services, operations, and facilities that are needed to upgrade each neighborhood's conformance to the quality standard. Provide a cost analysis for the proposed improvement program.
- Obtain citizen and city council endorsement for the program. Implementing the specific projects targeted to fulfilling neighborhood needs.

Informational Uses

The Responsive Public Services Program was designed and implemented to measure the effectiveness of municipal services. This information was used in the following ways:

- The levels of service provided to neighborhoods were evaluated. Detailed compari-

sons of neighborhoods and of the degrees of differences among them provided a logical method for establishing city program priorities on the basis of objective (and subjective) criteria.
- Neighborhoods with severe public service deficiencies were clearly identified. The RPSP performed a valuable function by preparing a comprehensive needs assessment that was the basis for implementing program changes, re-allocating personnel and equipment, and in general improving operations.
- The comprehensive inventory of problem areas listed with priority ratings provided the city with a substantial plan for improving neighborhood conditions. Assistant City Manager Frank Wise states that with this information, it was possible to satisfactorily explain to citizens why storm sewers are being installed on Tenth Street, where residents experience flood hazards, rather than on Pine Street, where transporation is occasionally inconvenienced during heavy rains. Citizens can now understand the differences in priorities, and because of this they can accept the city's work program. In addition, the comprehensive information base demonstrates to citizens that the city is aware of the problem situations occurring throughout the community.
- Citizen communication was strengthened. The survey conducted for leisure services provided a vehicle for obtaining citizen feedback. (In a sense, citizen surveys are a market test of the demand for and satisfaction with the services being delivered.) The opinions represented an input that departmental personnel used to increase program effectiveness.

In the Community Development process public hearings were held to solicit citizen participation. The city administration is pleased with the outcome of these discussions, because the priorities established in the RPSP were validated by the results of the public meetings. The only lack of agreement occurred where interest groups advocated programs that did not match the city's interpretation of the intent of the federal legislation, for instance, in the priorities and funding of police and social services.

- The mayor and board of aldermen were presented with straightforward fiscal information on which goals, service level objectives, budgets, and multi-year planning could be based. The governing body was very receptive to the RPSP. They authorized the study and, upon its completion, they held a two-day working session to have the methods and findings explained. Policy alternatives were directed to them in a format that specified the need areas and the proposals for meeting the deficiencies.
- Capital improvement planning was made more effective. The RPSP report document was immediately put into use when the Community Development Act was adopted. The availability of these funds gave Savannah the revenue with which to implement a capital improvement program that would make a meaningful contribution to the community.

As a result of the attention devoted to data collection and analysis in the RPSP, the decision making process was rationalized. Service level deficiencies were identified and these problems were addressed.

ASSESSMENT

On June 9-10, 1976, a review team visited the City of Savannah to evaluate the general applicability of the Responsive Public Services Program for other local governments. The members of the review team were: John Dullea, city manager, Greenville, South Carolina; Curtis Branscome, city manager, Decatur, Georgia; Jerry Coffman, assistant city manager, Charlotte, North Carolina; and Fred Knight and Rack Fukuhara, ICMA staff. Differing views were expressed by the team on several aspects of the Savannah program. The findings are summarized below:

1. The RPSP concept is a useful tool for measuring effectiveness. Local governments need yardsticks in order to evaluate the service delivery function. Savannah has developed standards based on the citywide average, and it has used them to rate neighborhood conditions.

2. Dividing the community into geographic areas and ranking them according to deficiency levels are innovative methods for identifying programs. The surveys of neighborhood conditions provide a substantial needs assessment; however, they do not automatically analyze problems and develop alternative solutions. Problem analysis is a necessary second step in the process.

3. The RPSP is a decision making tool. Savannah has used the inventory of problems and has assigned priorities to specific projects and programs in order to plan service improvements for high needs areas. This is a significant move away from "squeaky wheel" decision making.

The review team recommended that the governing body should be involved early in the policy formulation process to include setting goals, establishing service level standards, determining action plans, and allocating resources.

4. Providing services deferentially and redistributing resources to areas of identified deficiencies are both progressive and responsive actions. Reallocation may be necessary, because the residents of problem areas may not be prepared to financially support the programs to improve the service level to even the minimum level.

The review team indicated that such a policy had the potential to become controversial, especially in a city in which the legislative body is elected by wards or districts. Individuals representing areas which are not targeted for improvement may feel their constituents are getting short-changed for their tax dollars.

The full impact of a program like the RPSP benefits the entire community by upgrading and maintaining the city's livability conditions. An explanation of the total benefits is a logical way of preventing opposition. And as a public choice, it is difficult to justify building tennis courts in one neighborhood while another has unpaved streets and lacks adequate storm drainage.

5. The technique used to calculate the citywide standard and deficiency ranking is too complex to be easily understood. The normal distribution curve and the standard deviation are statistically sound methods for developing city standards; however, even Savannah's staff suggests using a simpler index to measure service levels and to rank neighborhoods.

6. A wide range of cities can adapt the RPSP to fit their individual needs. Savannah has taken a basic approach using techniques developed in-house and by the Urban Institute. The city has been able to keep the system simple. To date, data collection has been a manual task. Savannah is currently investigating an automated system to track the needs assessment and the service improvements in a geographically based application. The review team pointed out that computer applications may exceed the capacity of some jurisdictions, and project monitoring can be accomplished with a manual record keeping system.

The transferability of the RPSP has been demonstrated, as Chatham County, Georgia, has recently (April 1976) completed similar surveys for the services it delivers. It is too early to evaluate the success of this application. And the review team has agreed that it is not possible to make a "final" assessment of the Savannah program, because the service improvements and all the other impacts cannot be evaluated after only two years.

The consensus of the review team was that the RPSP is a viable concept. The team was impressed by the fact that the program has had an impact that (1) has resulted in operational service improvements, and (2) has provided information that has strategically influenced decision making and priority setting. Local governments not currently involved in effectiveness measurement should consider the application carefully. It is a worthwhile approach that uses a basic methodology.

CONCLUSION

The City of Savannah has made a substantial contribution with the development of the Responsive Public Services Program. It is a comprehensive improvement process directed at the products of its government. The methodology has taken complex concepts and presented them in a format that can be replicated by other governments for specific services or across the board. The community information and ranking system has proved beneficial, because it has had an impact on policy making.

On the other hand, the methods for evaluating the effectiveness of public services still need further development, although significant advances have been made. Many functional areas require research and development in order to acquire both the indicators necessary to fully assess the adequacy of services as they contribute to the quality of community life and the techniques used to collect the data necessary for objective analysis and review.

REFERENCES

The following materials have been useful to cities involved in effectiveness measurement; and they have been used in the preparation of this report.

Blair, Louis H. and Schwartz, Alfred I. *How Clean Is Your City?* Washington, D.C.: Urban Institute, 1972.

Fisk, Donald M. and others. *How Effective Are Your Community Recreation Services?* Washington, D.C.: U.S. Department of the Interior, Bureau of Outdoor Recreation, April 1973.

Hatry, Harry P. and others. *Measuring the Effectiveness of Basic Municipal Services, Initial Report.* Washington, D.C., Urban Institute and International City Management Association, February 1974.

Webb, Kenneth and Hatry, Harry P., *Obtaining Citizen Feedback: The Application of Citizen Surveys to Local Governments.* Washington, D.C.: Urban Institute, 1973.

Yurman, Dan., "Focused Investments in the City. There is a Growing Trend to Target Community Development Funds into Select Neighborhoods. Memphis and Dayton Are Two Examples." *Practicing Planner.* (Washington, D.C.: American Institute of Planners) February 1976, pp. 16-23.

Appendix A
The 1986 Street Cleanliness Program

INTRODUCTION

For the first time in 1973, the City of Savannah attempted to examine the effectiveness of its service delivery programs within each neighborhood. The Community Renewal Program process included analyzing the city's planning units (clusters of neighborhoods); determining the present level of services being provided in them; setting an acceptable level of liveability; identifying the planning units which fell below the desired level of liveability by establishing a numerical rating system for each condition; comparing all planning units and devising a city-wide mean; and designing service programs to correct the conditions to bring them up to an acceptable level.

Conditions studied for each neighborhood included crime rates, fire rates, cleanliness levels, water and sewer service, quality of housing, and quality of streets. From this study, it was clear that the level of services being provided in some of the planning units was not effective. As a result, the City

planned programs to achieve an acceptable level of liveability for each planning unit. This meant that some areas had to be supplied with a higher level of services than others if the City were to secure and maintain liveability conditions in them at acceptable levels.

The CRP was renamed the Responsive Public Services Program document in 1974. This process and resulting document enabled the City to monitor the delivery of City services by physically measuring and tracking service delivery. The Responsive Public Services document is significant in its use as a tool by the City to equalize the delivery of city services to all residents and its use by various departments to:

- Project and plan for program improvements—the Department of Housing, Community and Economic Development
- Prepare five-year plans— the Engineering, Water, and Sewer Departments
- Allocate Capital Improvement Program funds—City-wide CIP Appropriations Committee

Source: City of Savannah, Georgia, *Responsive Public Services Program,* 1986.

- Estimate fixed assets totals—the Finance Departments
- Determine city-wide goals and objectives

The result of the establishment of this program is more effective overall planning by matching budget preparation activities with the need/conditions of the community and the City's general goals and objectives.

The 1985 RPSP was developed as an interim document to measure the City's service deliveries. However, with the development of the City's geo-data base information system, this document will be used as a basis for determining city-wide goals and objectives, thereby increasing the scope and significance of the document.

The purpose of the geo-data base is to provide an information resource that will support the operation and management of City government. A majority of City service delivery functions are dependent on knowledge of the physical elements that make up the City geographically. For example, land parcels, buildings, streets and utility networks are some of the elements needed for support. The location, composition and current status of these elements are critical factors to both management and operations within the City. Compiling information on these elements is in effect establishing a data base that eventually will be used by many departments of the City. This will reduce duplication of data collection updating procedures, improve data sharing between departments, and provide ready access to the data.

As a result of implementing the geo-data base information system, it will become possible to produce the RPSP on demand with graphic illustrations and more detailed information. The departments will be able to examine the effectiveness of projects and programs through the comparison of base data information to actual site conditions or problems.

Previously, the data have been collected, sorted, and manipulated manually. This year, all data were stored and manipulated through the City's central data management system known as the aMAPPER System. This resulted in greater flexibility in examining and analyzing the survey and departmental data.

Departments Included

Information from the following departments was used to examine service delivery goals and objectives:

- Fire
- Police
- Streets
- Water
- Sewer
- Drainage
- Housing
- Clean Environment
- Leisure Services
- Park and Tree
- Traffic Engineering

STREET CLEANLINESS CONDITIONS

The survey of street cleanliness conditions was conducted in conjunction with the street condition survey. Street segments were rated for cleanliness according to the following standards:

Street Cleanliness Standards

1. *Clean* - The street looks like it has recently been swept. No noticeable sand, dirt, leaves or litter.
2. *Lightly littered* - A few scattered leaves or small amount of sand or a little litter along at least a two-block area. The debris is not remaining as a result of having swept around cars.
3. *Moderately littered* - Leaves, sand, dirt, or litter have started to accumulate along at least a two-block area.
4. *Heavily littered* - There is a heavy accumulation of leaves, sand, dirt or litter along at least a two-block area.

The street and lane condition indices are designed to provide basic information about the cleanliness conditions and to permit comparison of these conditions among the planning units. The index scores for both streets and lanes are calculated by multiplying the number of segments in each condition category by a designated weight; the sums of these products are divided by the total number of segments surveyed. This computation and the standard condition weights are illustrated as follows:

Planning Unit 5	Condition Category	Weight
Street Cleanliness	Clean	39×0 n $= 0$
	Lightly Littered	$270 \times 3.33 = 899.10$
	Moderately Littered	$161 \times 6.67 = 1073.87$
	Heavily Littered	$6 \times 10 = 60$
	Total $= 2032.97$	
Index Score $= 2032.97 \div 476 = 4.27$		

Analysis

Of the 7,121 street segments rated for cleanliness conditions, 1,579 or 22 percent were rated clean (01), 4,084 or 57 percent were rated lightly littered (02), 1,332 or 19 percent were rated moderately littered (03), and 126 or 2 percent were rated heavily littered.

Six planning units fell in the Priority One category in street cleanliness conditions. They were planning units 9, 6, 1, 14, 18, and 5. In 1983, only 1 planning unit fell in the Priority One category, Planning Unit 23. However, in 1985, Planning Unit 23 is ranked as a Priority Two area.

In the Priority Two category, 12 planning units—17, 19, 27, 21, 22, 15, 2, 24, 20, 10, 23, 16—are found. This number compares to six Priority Two planning units in 1983.

Ten planning units—3, 13, 7, 12, 4, 8, 28, 11, 25, 26—fell in the Priority Three category of least severe cleanliness condition. In 1983, 21 planning units were found in this category.

Appendix B
Visual Inspection Procedure

DESCRIPTION OF THE PROCEDURE

The heart of the measurement system is a visual inspection procedure in which trained inspectors rate streets and alleys for cleanliness from accumulations of solid wastes, and other items when desired. The inspector gives a numerical rating to the litter condition on a street or alley.[1] The rating is the basis for measuring differences and changes over time and among neighborhoods. A set of photographs

Source: Louis H. Blair and Alfred I. Schwartz, *How Clean Is Our City?* Washington, D.C.: The Urban Institute, 1972.

Figure 1
Street Cleanliness

Clean — The street looks like it has recently been swept. No noticeable sand, dirt, leaves or litter.

Lightly littered — A few scattered leaves or small amount of sand or a little litter along at least a two-block area. The debris is not remaining as a result of having swept around cars.

Moderately littered — Leaves, sand, dirt, or litter have started to accumulate along at least a two-block area.

Heavily littered — There is a heavy accumulation of leaves, sand, dirt or litter along at least a two-block area.

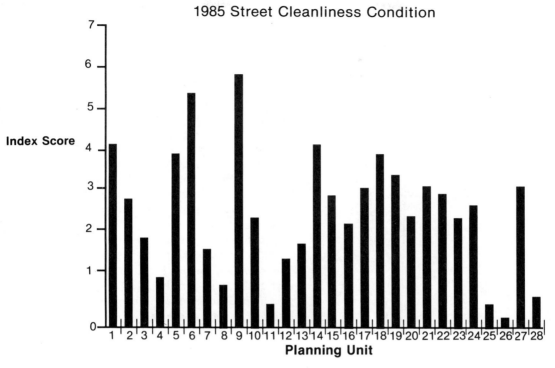

Figure 2
1985 Street Cleanliness Conditions

of scenes of streets and alleys, scaled to illustrate the range of litter conditions, is used as a standard for assuring consistent ratings of litter conditions by different inspectors, and in different parts of the community over different periods of time.[2]

Figures 1 and 2 show examples of the range of litter conditions for streets and for alleys in the District of Columbia and the applicable litter ratings. Cities with frequent occurrences of more severely littered conditions might provide photos for a condition "5". Cities with special types of litter—such as tumbleweed or palm fronds—might use different sets of photos.

The District of Columbia experience showed that the following inspection procedure is feasible and yields ratings that are reproducible. Inspectors rate the average litter

condition of streets and alleys on a scale of 1.0 to 4.0 using the photos as standards. Intermediate ratings of 1.5, 2.5, and 3.5 are used when the degree of litter falls between the conditions illustrated.

An inspector makes a rating by driving over a predetermined route past each block face or through each alley to be inspected. He observes the condition and notes the block or alley identification, the litter rating, and the presence of any other item of interest. The data from each inspection can be recorded on a form such as the one shown in Figure 3. For the type of data collected in the District of Columbia it was faster and less expensive to have the inspectors dictate their findings and location into a tape recorder for later transcription, rather than to complete the form by hand, which required the inspector to stop his

TABLE 1   Street Cleanliness Conditions

Planning Unit	Index Score
9	6.23
6	5.72
1	4.55
14	4.54
18	4.30
5	4.27
Priority One	
17	4.05
19	3.82
27	3.55
21	3.49
22	3.33
15	3.24
2	3.15
24	3.10
20	2.78
10	2.77
23	2.73
16	2.58
Priority Two	
3	2.17
13	2.03
7	1.93
12	1.69
4	1.26
8	1.0
28	0.75
11	0.57
25	0.54
26	0.34
Priority Three	

City-wide mean, 2.87.

vehicle. However, some jurisdictions may prefer to use a written report.

Tables would be prepared with figures showing the average litter ratings in each area (see Table 1 and the summaries of other data that are collected. When all the streets and the alleys are inspected in the high-intensity option, maps should be prepared showing the level of cleanliness on a block-by-block basis. Maps [can] illustrate how the data can be presented to show street litter conditions and locations of abandoned automobiles. The tabulated and mapped data should be compared

from one inspection period to the next to see what changes have taken place over time.

An inspector should be able to rate about 20 block-faces an hour or 7 to 10 alleys an hour for a low-intensity sampling inspection operation where he often has appreciable travel time between block-faces. He should be able to rate about 40 block-faces an hour or 15 alleys an hour when all streets and alleys are being inspected in the high-intensity option and there is no appreciable travel time between inspections.

We recommend that ratings of street cleanliness be restricted to the block face—the area between the center line of the street on one side and the property line on the other and bounded by the cross streets on either end of the block. In the D. C. experiment it was judged unsafe for the inspector to drive his vehicle and, at the same time, try to rate both sides of the street. An alley, however, can be safely inspected in its entirety.

We recommend that inspectors note the presence of health and fire hazards caused by accumulations of solid wastes. A health hazard may be defined as a substantial amount of unenclosed garbage that rats and other rodents could readily feed upon or be harbored in. A fire hazard may be defined as a pile of combustible solid waste within five feet of a building which, if ignited, could cause substantial damage to the building. We observed in alleys a strong correlation between high litter ratings and the presence of health and/or fire hazards.

INSPECTOR SELECTION, TRAINING, AND REPLICATION

The District of Columbia experience showed that certain persons with identifiable characteristics could perform the inspection function adequately after a three-day training period. The quality of the inspectors is critical to the success of the inspection system. After train-

Figure 1
Examples of Street Litter Conditions

Condition 1. Clean

Condition 2. Moderately Clean

Condition 3. Moderately Littered

Condition 4. Heavily Littered

Exhibit 6. FORMS FOR DATA COLLECTION

Figure 3
Form for Data Collection

321

TABLE 1   Illustrative Comparison of Street Litter Ratings

Service Area	Average Sample Litter Rating[a]		Percentage of Streets in Sample Rating 2.5 or Worse	
	June 1971	Dec. 1971	June 1971	Dec. 1971
1	2.43	2.11	15	7
2	1.80	1.79	0	0
3	3.13	2.53	61	22
4	2.10	2.32	10	25
5	1.58	1.44	0	0
6	2.71	2.76	31	38
Total[b]	2.38	2.27	29	25

[a] These average ratings would be obtained by inspecting a minimum of 30–50 block-faces in each service area for the low intensity option and an average of 1000–1500 block-faces in each service area for high intensity option. Statistical confidence limits for the averages should also be made available.

[b] Weighted averages based on number of blocks in the respective services areas.

ing, most persons are capable of making the visual judgments required. Less certain and thus requiring extra attention is whether an inspector will maintain the required performance quality over a long period of time.

Formal education requirements are not critical per se, other than the ability to read simple instructions. Candidates for inspectors should be conscientious individuals known to be able to perform with alertness repetitive and often tedious tasks over sustained periods (up to five hours a day, five days a week), to read maps well, and to be observant. Each inspector has to drive, read the road map, and report his judgments on litter conditions and other observations using a tape recorder.

The inspectors do not have to be sanitation department personnel. They may be volunteer citizens or persons from other departments. (Perhaps the ratings may have a higher degree of public credibility if they are not conducted by sanitation department personnel.)

An annual three-day training period should be satisfactory. Potential inspectors would be trained; previously trained inspectors would receive refresher training. The first day the trainees would be introduced to the purpose of the inspection operations, to the photo standards, and inspection reporting procedures. The second day field inspections would be conducted with all trainees and the instructor in one vehicle. The third day field inspections would be conducted with each trainee driving a vehicle accompanied by an instructor. After the three days of training the trainees would be considered inspectors and would perform on their own . . . .

Eighty to 100 ratings made by each inspector during the first two weeks of on-the-job inspection and about 10 percent of his ratings thereafter should be replicated by a judge, preferably the analyst in charge of the operation, to see that each inspector is consistently making accurate ratings. If the ratings are inaccurate, the inspector should be retrained, or if that fails, replaced.

ESTABLISHING BOUNDARIES

For comparison purposes, the city should be divided into inspection areas. These can be service areas or neighborhoods of particular interest. Inspections are then made to estimate conditions for each area. The boundaries can be ward lines, census tracts, or service district lines. The District of Columbia, containing approximately 6,000 blocks, had already been divided into nine service districts, each containing between 500 and 1,200 blocks. Many communities have already identified service areas for a variety of purposes.

The boundaries of the areas should be overlaid on a large-scale map of the city. Each block should be examined to determine if it is appropriate for inspection. Some blocks will be eliminated, perhaps because they are within a region in which the city does not provide refuse collection or street cleaning services. Each block-face and each alley remaining should be numbered consecutively. The number is a unique identifier which is used in the random selection of block-faces and alleys required for certain aspects of the measurement system operation.

TWO FIELD INSPECTION OPTIONS

A basic decision is whether to a) inspect a sample of streets and alleys, or b) inspect all streets and alleys in any given area.

To save time and reduce costs, only a sample of blocks and alleys needs to be inspected when the data are to be used solely for program and policy planning purposes. When the sample is selected in a statistically sound manner, considerable confidence in its being representative of the city can be obtained. The resulting inspection data will be useful for such purposes as determining which parts of the city are dirtier than others, for measuring the change in cleanliness over time, and for evaluating the broad effects of cleaning programs. They can be used to help determine and justify budget requests for additional forces as well as to help allocate forces among the various areas.

Inspection of all streets and alleys in an area requires substantially more time and expense. However, it has the advantage that maps can be produced showing litter conditions on a block-by-block basis allowing comparisons between areas and over time. Actual counts of items of concern . . . can be obtained. This information can be used to direct field forces and to evaluate individual work crew performances. We do not believe it is necessary to inspect all streets and alleys in the predominantly clean areas.

In the District of Columbia sample inspections were made in those service areas generally recognized as clean to establish base conditions for comparison with other areas and to detect any significant deterioration in conditions. In the moderately and heavily littered areas, all streets and alleys were inspected to provide location information for the direction of cleaning crews as well as to evaluate changes on a block-by-block basis.

The two options are described in more detail below.

Sample Inspection Option

The accuracy requirements and the resources available determine the size of the sample. We recommend generally that a sample of 30 to 50 block-faces and 30 to 50 alleys be inspected in each area. For that sample size, if the average litter ratings of the block-faces (or alleys) in two different samples[3] are compared and the absolute difference is 0.25 or more, one can conclude with 90 percent confidence that there is a statistically significant difference in litter conditions for the two areas and that the difference is not due to the chance selections of certain block-faces (or alleys). . . .[4]

The specific block-faces and alleys to be inspected in each neighborhood should be selected in a statistically random fashion. We have already recommended that each block-face and each alley should be uniquely numbered in each inspection area. Then 30 block-faces and 30 alleys should be selected using a set of random numbers. The block-faces and alleys selected should be marked on a map and given to the inspector. He should then plot a route between inspection points that minimizes total travel time. After the block-faces and the alleys have been inspected, the variances of the ratings (a statistical measure of the dispersion of the individual ratings about the average rating) should be calculated to determine if enough inspections were made. . . .

It may be desirable to know if statistically significant changes are occurring in the percentage of streets or alleys with ratings in excess of 2.5 or of any other percentages. Then the sample must be enlarged considerably to measure small changes in these percentages. Between 30 and 50 block-face inspections in an area will not provide a high degree of precision. For example, if the percentage of block-faces with ratings of 2.5 or worse is 10 percent for one sample, there is a tangible possibility (10 percent) that, had all block-faces been inspected, the value would have been lower than 3 percent or higher than 17 percent, rather than 10 percent. With about 120 to 200 block-face ratings—either from combining results from four inspection areas or by more intense sampling—the range decreases to about 7 percent and 14 percent respectively. . . .

Inspection of All Streets and Alleys

This option calls for the inspection of one side of all the streets and, if so determined, all the alleys, in moderately and heavily littered service areas and a light sampling as described above in the clean areas at least semi-annually. Depending upon what additional data are collected, high-intensity inspection can provide actual counts and locations of abandoned automobiles, . . . health and fire hazards on public/private property, broken pavements and clogged storm sewer basins, and even abandoned houses and exterior building violations.

Street inspection routes and alley inspection routes should be plotted on separate maps directing inspectors to make ratings of every public, traversable alley and of one side of essentially every street in the area. The routes should be simple and planned to minimize travel time; they will be used for all subsequent inspections. . . .

ALTERNATIVE INSPECTION PROCEDURES

Alternative inspection procedures can be developed. One obvious procedure would involve inspection of all streets and alleys once every year or two and sampling inspections for the other inspection periods. The sampling procedure would be based on an analysis of the data collected in the first inspection. A sampling inspection procedure could reduce inspection costs, based on the D. C. experience, by as much as 50 percent. There is a loss in data and it would not be possible to produce all of the maps that the full-inspection procedure allows.

A cluster sampling procedure can be developed where adjacent block-faces are selected, rather than random selection of each block-face. This reduces travel time and can reduce overall inspection costs. A city probably would need to engage a consultant with statistical test design experience to develop a proper cluster sampling procedure.

SCHEDULING OF INSPECTION

Statistical analysis of the D. C. inspection ratings showed that there was no substantial variation in litter ratings from one work day of the week to another or from one time of the day to another time in the same day. Inspections for street and alley cleanliness could be scheduled any day. We expect that the same stability in condition will be found in other communities and that this type of inspection can be conducted any or all days of the week. However, when the inspection system is used to evaluate the adequacy of collection frequency or whether or not collectors spill or scatter refuse, the timing of inspection must be related to cleaning operations.

NOTES

1. The litter rating scale is a rough measure of the area of ground covered by scattered litter. We used a scaled litter rating rather than the square feet of area covered for two reasons. First, it is far easier to assign a rating from 1 to 4 than to estimate the area covered with litter. Second, it is believed far easier for the decision-maker to visualize what, for example, a condition "3" looks like than to visualize what say 10 percent of the surface area covered resembles. Volume of litter was not used. It would be difficult to measure and we felt that the area covered by litter was a much more relevant measure than volume. Weight was not used because the density of solid wastes varies greatly depending on the type of waste.

2. A set of standard photographs was developed in the District of Columbia. Four hundred photographs were taken of scenes representative of the range of existing litter conditions on streets and alleys, and the variety of backgrounds, structures, and land uses in which the conditions occur in the District. These were then judged independently by 19 persons who separated the photos into four groups corresponding to four different levels of litter conditions, with "1" representing the cleanest condition and "4" the most littered condition. Photographs on which there was complete or nearly complete agreement concerning its condition rating among 19 persons were included in the set used as the visual inspection standard. A set of these photographs was provided to each inspector for a reference standard. A lithograph set is available from The Urban Institute. A procedure similar to the one just described could be used by any jurisdiction to develop its own inspection reference standard.

3. The samples may be taken from different service areas during one inspection operation to compare differences between areas or the samples may be taken from the same area at different periods of time to compare differences over time.

4. The accuracy of the ratings based on sample data is determined by the sample size selected and the ability of the inspectors to rate conditions precisely. The D. C. experience showed that, using a four-point scale with intermediate one-half point values, inspectors with acceptable performances could, on the average, rate conditions to well within one-quarter of a point of their actual value as determined by the judge.

Explanation and Critique

As can be seen from the ICMA evaluation by Fukuhara, Savannah's evaluation system is based on explicitly stated goals and measurable objectives. Without these, evaluation is difficult. In addition, the city officials and staff are committed to the goals of the evaluations and do use the findings as the basis for their decision making. Notice that Savannah does not rely on one data collection source or technique. In fact, they use multiple measures whenever feasible.

In his conclusion, Fukuhara suggests that effectiveness measures need to be updated and reassessed as necessary. Savannah, in constantly updating and evaluating their measures as well as their services, follows Fukuhara's prescriptions.

Appendix A is the summary of a recent Street Cleanliness Conditions Report as presented to the city. Notice that the results allow the city to give priority to areas according to need. Those neighborhoods needing greater than normal service to attain the city standard are given extra resources in terms of worker hours and other resources, according to City Manager Arthur (Don) Mendonsa. Mendonsa also notes that several changes have been made to the original RPSP reflecting the fact that Savannah is now physically larger, with a larger population, and with more planning and service delivery units. For example, dog control is no longer surveyed, whereas a number of new aspects—crime prevention, fire prevention, and housing conditions—have been added.

Notice that in Appendix B, "Visual Inspection Procedure," from *How Clean Is Our City?* a great deal of emphasis is placed on observer training and the periodic rechecking of trained inspectors.[1] This is done to allay instrument decay. Do training and auditing *assure* the reliability of the observations? Not necessarily. In Savannah the auditing arm of the city manager's office, the Resource Management and Control Program (REMAC), is housed in the productivity improvement and managerial analysis division whose auditors periodically reassess observers. When instrument decay is noted or inconsistency is found (and that does happen, even among fully trained employees), the audit officers, the appropriate subdivision of the city bureaucracy, and the manager's office get together to evaluate what went wrong and decide how to rectify the situation, which often includes a retraining of the observers. Mendonsa describes the relationship of REMAC with the RSP:

> The REMAC program uses industrial engineering techniques to assess the efficiency and effectiveness of City programs. The REMAC program is also used to determine the validity and accuracy of the condition standards used by departments. Essentially, every City department is reviewed under the REMAC program at least once every two or three years. Through the program we have imposed our measurement of condition standards and improved conditions in the community.[2]

The following example is from the Washington, DC, "Operation Clean Sweep" program, which was the model for Savannah's program. Here is a classic example where observers' ratings converged to require retraining of the raters:

> Most people perform the inspection operation after three days of training. It is essential that at least 10 percent of the streets and alleys rated by each inspector also be inspected by a judge to see if inspectors continue to make accurate ratings. We found that the ability of some inspectors deteriorated over time, requiring retraining or replacement of some persons.[3]

The Savannah case study is a good illustration of the use of ongoing evaluation studies. Having established baseline data by neighborhoods, the city can chart its progress using a time-series (i.e., reflexive) design. In this case, as the article indicates, Savannah has its own goals that act as generic controls—that is, the standard by which they can judge progress. Other cities may have other goals or priorities. Only if these goals are clearly articulated can such evaluations be successful.

REFERENCES

1. Louis H. Blair and Alfred I. Schwartz, *How Clean Is Our City?* (Washington, DC: Urban Institute, 1972), pp. 19-34.

2. Correspondence with Arthur A. Mendonsa, City Manager, City of Savannah, Georgia, dated October 7, 1987.

3. Louis H. Blair and Alfred I. Schwartz, *Measuring Effectiveness of Refuse Collection* (Washington, DC: Urban Institute, 1973), p. 22.

19

Regression Artifact

Variously called "statistical regression," "regression to the mean," or "endogenous change," a regression artifact is suspected when cases are chosen for inclusion in a treatment based on their extreme scores on a variable.[1] For example, the most malnourished children in a school are included in a child nutrition program. Students scoring highest in a test are provided a "gifted" program, whereas those with the lowest scores are sent to a remedial program. So what is the problem? Are not all three of these programs designed precisely for these classes of children?

The problem for the evaluation researcher is to determine whether the result of the program is genuinely caused by the program or by the propensity for a group over time to score more consistently with the group's average than with extreme scores. Donald Campbell and Julian Stanley view this as a measurement problem wherein deviant scores tend to have larger error terms:

> Thus, in a sense, the typical extremely high scorer has had unusually good "luck" (large positive error) and the extremely low scorer bad luck (large negative error). Luck is capricious, however, so on a posttest we expect the high scorer to decline somewhat on the average, the low scorers to improve their relative standing. (The same logic holds if one begins with the posttest scores and works back to the prettest.)[2]

In terms of our gifted and remedial programs, an evaluator would have to determine if declining test scores in the gifted program are due to the poor functioning of the program or to the natural tendency for extreme scorers to regress to the mean. Likewise, is any improvement in scores from the remedial program due to the program itself or to a regression artifact? Campbell and Stanley argue that researchers rarely *account for* regression artifacts when subjects are selected for their extremity although they may acknowledge such a factor may exist.

In the following article, Garrett Moran not only acknowledges a regression effect; he actually tests for this effect in an attempt to disentangle the effects of increased inspections and regression on workplace injuries.

Regulatory Strategies for Workplace Injury Reduction

A Program Evaluation

GARRETT E. MORAN

During the last few years great attention has been focused on the issue of safety in the workplace. Economists and policy analysts have vigorously debated the merits of government intervention in the "safety marketplace." This debate has focused both on whether such involvement is appropriate and, if so, what the optimal form for intervention should be. There seems to be widespread agreement that market imperfections exist, yet there is little confidence that a government remedy would improve the situation. As Wolf (1979) has so clearly shown, the character of the public sector often makes it unlikely that the legislature will succeed where the marketplace has failed.

Several economic theorists have argued that the social costs incurred as the result of the standards enforcement approach to safety enhancement, the approach almost universally employed in federal programs, far exceed the resulting benefits. A determination of this sort requires consideration of such issues as the valuation of human life and health, which are beyond the scope of this discussion (for example, see Viscusi, 1979, 1980). Other authors, notably Mendeloff (1980), argue that considerations other than that of economic efficiency must be brought to bear. This position admits a loss of efficiency is a genuine possibility,[1] but suggests that society as a whole may be willing to make such a trade-off in order to lessen the proba-

bility that identifiable subgroups may be unduly exposed to possible injury (Okun, 1975).

Regardless of which position one endorses on this question, an effective and inexpensive method for reducing injuries is called for. In the evaluation literature, much attention has been given to each aspect of this issue. Smith (1980) and Mendeloff (1980) both conclude that the regulation and inspection efforts of OSHA (Occupational Safety and Health Administration) probably, though not certainly, have a small, but statistically significant effect. Viscusi (1979, 1980) and others come to the opposite conclusion, claiming the injury rates are not changed by OSHA's programs. Differences in methodology and approach can certainly account for the seemingly contradictory results, but perhaps the most significant conclusion is that the determination of the effectiveness of such programs is a difficult and complex matter.

Mendeloff (1980: 103-105) cites data suggesting that workforce demographics alone account for a very substantial proportion of the variance in injury rates.[2] In developing a model of the possible impact of OSHA he points out that an inspection program of the typical sort can only be expected to reduce the probability of injuries that result from violation of an existing safety standard and are detectable in the context of periodic site visits. He concludes that this class of injur-

Source: Garrett E. Moran, "Regulatory Strategies for Workplace Injruy Reduction," EVALUATION REVIEW, Vol. 9, No. 1 (February 1985), pp. 21-33. Copyright © 1985 by EVALUATION REVIEW. Reprinted by permission of Sage Publications, Inc.

ies, which he labels injuries caused by detectable violations (ICDV's), represents a rather small proportion of the total. Because OSHA has historically targeted industry groups with high overall injury rates, he suggests that interindustry variation in the percentage of ICDV's may, in an aggregate analysis, obscure any effects the inspection program might have.

> It is rather easy to construct numerical examples that illustrate how such a situation could easily lead to underestimates of the OSHA inspection effect. For example, suppose that the ICDV category contains 10 percent of all injuries in the nontarget industries, but only 5 percent in the target industries. Suppose further that OSHA really has been effective, that ICDV injuries are going down by 5 percent in other industries and—because of the intense inspection effort—going down by 10 percent in the target industries. However, suppose that non-ICDV injuries are going up by 5 percent in all industries. Because of the injury mix, the calculations show that the overall target industry rate would go up by 4.25 percent, while the nontarget rate would go up by only 4.00 percent. Thus the lack of impact found by this study could be consistent with an actual program impact [Mendeloff, 1980: 94-95].

Economists, in particular, have suggested that a more effective approach than the combination of standards and inspections might be developed around the idea of an injury tax. Such a system would, they argue, completely avoid the issue of whether a cause of injury was detectable by inspection, might be less expensive to administer, and would more consistently provide economic incentives to proprietors to lessen the possible causes of injuries. The question of whether a tax system could perform in the intended manner will in all likelihood remain an academic one. Mendeloff (1980) cogently argues that the political environment is unlikely to permit passage of legislation that may be described as making it acceptable to harm workers as long as one could pay for the privilege.

In place of the taxation approach, Mendeloff (1980) calls for an approach that he labels THIRE, Targeting High Injury Rate Establishments. Such a program, by concentrating on the demonstrated "bad apples," would be politically appealing and because it would select firms with high injury rates compared to others in the same industry, it would avoid the problem of differential ICDV's that made it difficult to determine program effectiveness. He suggests that the time, penalty, and compliance costs associated with high inspection frequencies would serve as a form of injury tax on these dangerous establishments. The employer would thus have an incentive to reduce perils outside of the ICDV class, just so he could get the inspectors and the costs they impose "off his back."

> The crucial operating principle of the targeting program is that it imposes incremental costs on employers for each additional injury or injury loss. . . . Linking the frequency of inspection to relative safety performance may have an analytic rationale as well. Poorly performing establishments may plausibly carry out injury prevention more cheaply at the margin than high-rate establishments. Under a system based on changes in rates, a high-rate firm would not be inspected at all unless its rate worsened. Under a THIRE system, in contrast, it would be inspected frequently unless its rate improved [Mendeloff, 1980: 134].

Mendeloff admits that such a program might be less effective in practice than it would appear on paper. He acknowledges the possibility of worsened performance in industries with relatively low injury rates,[3] but he hypothesizes that the reductions obtained by what would effectively be a tax on any injury in the high-rate group would outweigh the increases in injuries caused by ICDV's in the lower-rate group. Also, postaccident investigations would continue in the entire population of firms, and the threat of future inclusion in the targeted population would theoretically provide motivation to prevent a deteriorating safety record. Given the possibility of such shifts in performance in the different groups of firms, Mendeloff suggests that THIRE be implemented on a regional basis so that control districts would be available for comparison. As an alternative or supplement, he suggests time-series data be collected on such a program so that it would be possible to separate, at least partially, the impact of the program from that of ongoing trends.

THE PAR PROGRAM

A program that demonstrates many of the features of THIRE has been in operation within the Mine Safety and Health Administration (MSHA) since 1975. This accident re-

duction program, identified by the acronym PAR, selects for special attention those metal/nonmetal mines which, on the basis of a weighted injury index, are shown to have significantly greater numbers of injuries than other comparable operations. The index numbers that serve as the selection criterion take into account the size of the operation, the rate of lost workday injuries and their seriousness, policy differences regarding the definition of lost workdays, the difference in rates compared to the national norm, and the upward or downward trend compared to the norm.

The analysis presented below focuses on mines from a single sector of the metal/nonmetal mining field—sand, gravel, and stone mines—and thus can be expected to have comparable proportions of ICDV's. As Table 1 illustrates, the targeting strategy of the PAR program clearly focuses intensive attention on the program mines. The mean numbers of in-

TABLE I Comparison of Quarterly Group Means

Variable	All Mines[a] N = 3855	PAR Mines N = 24	Non-PAR Hi N = 286
No. of miners	30.34	119.20	10.85
Hours worked/employee	495.87	536.42	439.84
No. of inspections	.80	1.61	.70
No. of orders	.08	.79	.05
No. of citations	2.53	8.92	1.45
No. of hours on site	6.51	22.09	4.12
Nonfatal day-lost injuries	.29	2.55	.25
No. of fatalities[b]	.003	.020	.004
Total number of injuries	.30	2.57	.26
Injury index	2.87	12.26	19.06
Fatality rate [c,d]	.22	.43	1.05
Injury rate[d]	14.55	61.23	95.40

NOTE:

All means differ significantly (Alpha = .05), except for those variables referenced in notes (a) and (b) below.

[a] The mines included in the PAR and Non-PAR Hi groups have been excluded from the All Mines group for purposes of the difference of means tests.

[b] PAR mines differ significantly from All Mines (Alpha = .01) and from Non-PAR Hi Mines (Alpha = .02), but there is no significant difference between All Mines and Non-PAR Hi Mines.

[c] There is a significant difference between All Mines and Non-Par Hi Mines (Alpha = .03), but there are no significant differences between either All Mines and PAR Mines or Non-PAR Hi Mines and PAR Mines.

[d] Fatality and injury rates are defined respectively as the number of fatalities or injuries per million hours worked.

spection, orders, citations, and inspector hours on site are all from two to ten times higher for the PAR mines than for the general population of sand, gravel, and stone mines (here labeled as "All Mines"). A comparison group of mines that also had recorded poor performance in the area of safety but had not been included in the PAR program (labeled Non-PAR Hi Mines) received even less attention than did the general population of mines.[4] The costs associated with such inspection-related activity should, according to Mendeloff's thesis, provide a substantial economic incentive to reduce dangerous conditions.

The mines in the program are larger than those excluded from PAR, having nearly four times as many miners as the general population. Examination of this table demonstrates that the program has certainly focused on the "bad apples," as defined in terms of absolute numbers of injuries. The mean number of total injuries (including fatalities and nonfatal, day-lost injuries) is more than eight times as high in the PAR mines, whereas the weighted injury index numbers, used as the selection criterion for the program, are more than three times as high. Thus, even when the injury data are weighted for the size of the operation and other relevant factors by the injury index numbers, the PAR mines are still substantially more hazardous places to work than the average.

Table 1 also shows clearly that there is another group of mines that may be even more dangerous workplaces than the PAR mines. The injury index numbers for the Non-PAR Hi group are, on average, 55 percent higher than those of the PAR mines and nearly seven times as high as the comparable figures for the general mine population. Although these mines were excluded from the PAR program due to their small size, they are of interest because they provide some basis for determining what patterns may emerge in the injury rate trends over time when no governmental intervention is involved other than the typical standards enforcement approach. This notion will be addressed at greater length below.

It appears that PAR does in fact meet the conditions for defining the THIRE program that Mendeloff has outlined. Let us turn our attention now to the issue of its effectiveness in reducing injuries.

METHODOLOGY

The overriding difficulty in evaluating a program of this sort is that of regression to the mean, a fact clearly recognized by Mendeloff (1980: 143-144) in his discussion of the THIRE approach. When mines are selected for participation based on their extreme scores, it is highly probable that regression artifacts will result in those scores decreasing, regardless of the presence of any intervention. The problem then becomes one of attempting to separate the effects, if any, resulting from the program from those that would have occurred due to statistical artifacts.

Campbell and Stanley (1963) recommend the use of the multiple time-series design as a means of addressing the problem. The difficulty persists, however, unless a sufficiently similar comparison group can be located. Although there is no wholly satisfactory way around this problem, it was determined that an approximate solution may be found by comparing PAR mines to others that had high-injury index numbers, yet were excluded from the program for other reasons. As was apparent in Table 1, the group of mines designated as Non-PAR Hi mines were significantly more injury prone than were the PAR mines. Unfortunately, they also differ on most other variables examined. Notably, these mines are quite small, averaging only about 10 miners compared to 30 in the general population and nearly 120 in the PAR group. The absence of a viable alternative dictates that this group serve as the comparison group. Regression techniques will be used to hold size differences between the PAR and Non-PAR mines constant.

A second difficulty is that mines were inducted into PAR at different points in time and were retained only until the index numbers suggested they were again in line with industry norms. This problem was dealt with by constructing a counter that had an initial value of zero, became one when the mine entered the program, and was incremented by one each quarter thereafter. This counter was intended to represent both the effect of the PAR program intervention and because mines would have been inducted into the program about the time of their peak injury index numbers, the regression artifact as well.[5] For the regression to the mean simulation comparison group (the Non-PAR Hi group) the counter assumed the value one when the mine had its peak injury index number and was incremented identically, thus representing the regression artifact alone.

In order to control for other influences on the mines that may be associated with the passage of time, a separate counter is included in the model. This variable had the initial value of one and was increased by one throughout the 22 quarters for which data were available.

Because reduction of the absolute number of injuries is the more important policy consideration, the dependent variable selected was the total number of injuries per mine per quarter.[6] This necessitated inclusion of an independent variable to measure exposure because, as was discussed above, the PAR mines tended to have more miners who worked longer hours than the Non-PAR Hi mines. The total number of hours worked per mine per quarter was consequently included in the model.

Quarterly data for all sand, gravel, and stone mines were obtained from MSHA for the period from the beginning of 1975 until the middle of 1980. The resulting pooled cross-sectional time-series data set was analyzed by means of weighted least squares (Kmenta, 1971; Berk et al., 1979: 385–410). This allowed for the appropriate corrections for the problems of heteroscedasticity and serial correlation that are likely to occur in data of this character.[7] From the full data set two subgroups were selected, consisting of the following: (1) all PAR mines; and (2) all mines not included in the PAR program that had, at one or more points during the time series, injury index numbers more than two standard deviations above the mean. The first group was of course the target of the analysis. The second group (the Non-PAR Hi mines) served as the regression to the mean simulation comparison group.

The first question is whether, controlling for the total exposure of miners to the workplace and any long-term trend factors, the number of injuries decreases as the result of exposure to the PAR program. Even if this occurs, it is necessary to determine whether a similar outcome is observed in the comparison group, that is, whether a regression to the mean effect produces a result similar to that found in the PAR mines. If PAR is effective, then any reduction in numbers of injuries seen in the PAR mines must be significantly greater than that found in the comparison mines.

This calls for a test of the research hypothesis that the PAR mines and the Non-PAR regression to the mean simulation comparison group constitute different populations. That is, any downward trend following the peak injury index quarter in the Non-PAR Hi mines must be significantly less steep than any downward trend resulting from the intervention of the PAR program. Inability to reject the null hypothesis that they are from the same population would suggest that any decline in numbers of injuries observed after their inclusion in the program could not confidently be attributed to the effects of the program but may instead be attributable to regression effects.

RESULTS

To test the above hypothesis, observations from the two groups of mines, those in the PAR program and those in the Non-PAR Hi comparison group, were pooled. The dependent variable was the absolute number of injuries per mine per quarter. The independent variables of primary interest were those counters indicative of the trend following induction into the PAR program or, in the case of the comparison group, the trend following the peak injury index number. While the two counters were treated as a single variable, the inclusion of a slope dummy variable that had the value of zero for comparison mines and the value of one if the mine had participated in the PAR program permitted distinctions to be made between the respective slopes. In recognition of the clear differences in the absolute numbers of injuries between the larger

PAR mines and the smaller mines of the comparison group, a dummy intercept was included in the model as well.

Two additional independent variables were included. The first was simply the time counter variable, which had the effect of controlling for any ongoing trends over the full time series. The final variable was the number of hours of exposure to the work setting. This last variable served the crucial role of controlling for the size of the mines, a function made particularly important by the clear disparity in size between PAR and comparison mines. The results of the estimated model are presented in Table 2.

The time trend counter indicates that, controlling for all other independent variables, there was an upward trend over the full time series such that the passage of one additional quarter was associated with an average increase of 0.0258 injuries. All else being equal, each additional ten thousand hours of exposure to the work setting was associated with a small (0.16) but statistically significant increase in the number of injuries. Finally we note that both the PAR/Post Peak counter

TABLE 2   Results of the Regression Model

Variable	Regression Coefficient	t Value	t Significance
Intercept	−0.0069	−0.147	0.8832
PAR/Post peak counter	−0.0281	−3.000	0.0027
Dummy intercept	1.1049	15.868	0.0001
Dummy PAR/Post peak	−0.1540	−9.261	0.0001
Time counter	0.0258	4.280	0.0001
Hours of exposure	0.000016	15.938	0.0001

F Value Full Equation (F Prob.)	F Value-Test of Equality of Two PAR/Post Counters (F Prob.)	N (310 mines × an average of 15.6 quarters)	R Square	Durbin Watson Statistic
294.94 (0.0001)	33.15 (0.0001)	4844	.2336	2.101

As noted above, this model includes weighted least squares corrections for the problems of autocorrelation and heteroscedasticity. These corrections make the R-Square statistic a misleading measure of goodness of fit.

and the slope dummy-PAR/Post Peak counter were, controlling for other variables, associated with decreases in the mean number of injuries per quarter. Inspection of the table reveals that the magnitude of decrease was more than six times as large in the PAR mines than in the comparison mines.

The associated Chow test of the null hypothesis that the two groups constitute a single population resulted in an F-statistic of 33.15 that is statistically significant (Alpha = 0.0001). We are thus able to conclude that the PAR program produced a substantially greater reduction in numbers of injuries than that resulting from the regression artifact alone.[8]

CONCLUSIONS

The above discussion pointed to the potential difficulty in drawing definitive conclusions regarding the effectiveness of programs designed to improve workplace safety. The current effort provides an additional illustration of the point. On the positive side, the (negative) partial slope coefficient associated with participation in the PAR program was six times as large as the comparable counter for the Non-PAR Hi group. Although regression artifact in the Non-PAR Hi mines led to a change when other variables are controlled, of −0.0281 injuries per quarter from the peak injury index number period, the comparable figure for PAR mines was −0.1540. If we assume that the PAR and comparison groups are otherwise comparable, we must conclude that the program was highly effective.

As examination of Table 1 indicated, the PAR and Non-PAR mines are quite different from each other. Reexamination of that table shows that PAR mines have twelve times as many miners as the Non-PAR Hi group, and that those miners work longer hours. Such differences between the two groups of mines

raise questions about what otherwise appears as clear evidence of the effectiveness of the PAR program. The inclusion of hours of exposure to the work setting should, however, provide an effective statistical control for the size differences between the PAR and Non-PAR Hi mines. Moreover, given the post hoc character of this evaluation and the limitations of the available data base, it is difficult to conceive of an alternate methodology that could more effectively control for the obvious threat to validity.

The importance of this study may ultimately lie less in its findings than in what it attempted. The literature is full of efforts to answer such questions as whether safety regulations taken generically have been effective or whether economic theory would suggest that an approach that could never be implemented given the political realities may be superior to what is currently in place. Although such issues may present academically interesting questions, they seem to offer little hope of making a genuine contribution to the improvement of safety enhancement methods.

By focusing instead on the evaluation of an approach that is both potentially effective and politically viable, one may hope to obtain knowledge that could be of greater practical value. It is unlikely that Congress will suddenly change its mind about an injury taxation scheme, but, should it be shown to be effective, an alternate approach to targeting of inspection effort could be readily adopted, perhaps without even the need for congressional approval. Conversely, a determination that such approaches, whatever their conceptual merit, are ineffective in application could result in theorists turning their attention to alternate and perhaps more fruitful methods.

The PAR program, with its targeting of high injury rate establishments, must be considered as an example of one such potentially promising approach. The results of this evaluation are indicative that the program may have been quite effective, although the lack of comparability between comparison and treatment groups on important dimensions calls for some caution in attempting to reach definitive conclusions. Given the promising yet indefinite findings of the current study, further research on this program is clearly warranted.

NOTES

1. It should be pointed out that the current work attempts only to examine the PAR program as an example of Mendeloff's (1980) targeting of a high injury rate establishment (THIRE) strategy. Attention is given only to whether the program is effective. No consideration is given to the relative effectiveness of such alternate approaches as workmen's compensation or conventional injury taxation proposals, nor are efficiency considerations brought to bear.

2. See Mendeloff (1980: 103-105). His model using only demographic factors and pay rate data explained 83 percent of the variation in annual injury rate changes.

3. Such a decline in performance in the previously better performing industries would be predicted both by standard deterrence theory and by such formal models as that developed by Langbein and Kerwin (1984). Langbein and Kerwin, paying particular attention to the effects of time delays and negotiated compliance, suggest that any simultaneous relaxation in agency policy on these factors may both exacerbate the problems of lessened compliance in the nontargeted firms and also serve to induce noncompliance in the targeted firms. For the sake of simplicity, it will be assumed here that no relaxation in these policies accompanied the development of the THIRE targeting strategy. It may also be noted that the evaluation strategy proposed by Mendeloff facilitates evaluation of such effects, though the current effort admittedly does not.

4. This comparison group, the Non-PAR Hi Mines, will be discussed in greater detail below. They were selected from the general population of sand, stone, and gravel mines exclusively on the basis of the injury index numbers. Mines were included in the group if they had,

at any point during the time series, an injury index number that was more than two standard deviations above the mean for all mines.

5. As a test of the assumption that induction into the PAR program would roughly coincide with the peak injury index number, a separate model was developed using the same counter assignment strategy for PAR and Non-PAR Hi groups. The results of this alternate model proved to be essentially identical to those obtained when the PAR mine counter was started upon entry into the program.

6. This included both fatal injuries and nonfatal, day-lost injuries. The same models were run using nonfatal day-lost injuries alone as the dependent variable, producing essentially identical results. Models were attempted using the number of fatalities alone as the dependent variable, but the results proved insignificant.

7. Autocorrelation was corrected by setting each variable equal to the value of that variable minus the product of rho and the one-period lag value of the variable. Heteroscedasticity was corrected by weighting the observations by the number of hours of exposure to the work setting through use of the SAS (1982) Proc Reg WEIGHT statement.

8. It should be mentioned that another model was developed that included an independent variable summing the various types of inspection and enforcement activities. The model was run for PAR Mines only with the same dependent variable. This produced a statistically significant partial slope coefficient, but the sign was positive, suggesting that inspection and enforcement activities were associated with increased numbers of injuries. The result is no doubt attributable to postaccident investigations occurring in the same quarter, yet experimentation with lagged enforcement activity failed to indicate any significant relationships, though the sign did become negative as was predicted.

REFERENCES

Ashford, N. (1976) Crisis in the Workplace: Occupational Disease and Injury. Cambridge, MA: MIT Press.

Berk, R. A., D. M. Hoffman, J. E. Maki, D. Rauma, and H. Wong (1979) "Estimation procedures for pooled cross-sectional and time series data." Evaluation Q. 3 (August): 385-410.

Campbell, D. T. and J. C. Stanley (1963) Experimental and Quasi-Experimental Designs for Research. Boston: Houghton Mifflin.

Cook, T. J. and F. P. Scioli, Jr. (1975) "Impact analysis in public policy research," pp. 95-117 in K. M. Dolbear (ed.) Public Policy Evaluation. Beverly Hills, CA: Sage.

Gordon, J. B., A. Akman, and M. Brooks (1971) Industrial Safety Statistics: A Re-examination. New York: Praeger.

Kmenta, J. (1971) Elements of Econometrics. New York: Macmillan.

LaGather, R. B. (1979) "The federal mine safety and health act." Labor Law J. 30 (December): 723-731.

Langbein, L. and C. M. Kerwin (1984) "Implementation, negotiation and compliance in environmental and safety regulation." Unpublished manuscript.

Lewis-Beck, M. S. and J. R. Alford (1980) "Can government regulate safety? The coal mine example." Amer. Pol. Sci. Rev. 74 (September): 745-756.

McDowall, D., R. McCleary, E. E. Meidinger, and R. A. Hay, Jr. (1980) Interrupted Time Series Analysis. Beverly Hills, CA: Sage.

Mendeloff, J. (1980) Regulating Safety: An Economic and Political Analysis of Occupational Safety and Health Policy. Cambridge, MA: MIT Press.

Nichols, A. L. and R. Zeckhauser (1977) "Government comes to the workplace: an assessment of OSHA." The Public Interest 49: 36-69.

Okun, A. M. (1975) Equality and Efficiency: The Big Tradeoff. Washington, DC: The Brookings Institution.

Sands, P. (1968) "How effective is safety legislation?" J. of Law and Economics 11 (April): 165-174.

SAS Institute Inc. (1982) SAS User's Guide: Statistics, 1982 Edition. Cary, NC: SAS Institute.

Smith, R. S. (1980) "The impact of OSHA inspections on manufacturing injury rates." Evaluation Studies R. Annual 5: 575-602.

Stokey, E. and R. Zeckhauser (1978) A Primer for Policy Analysis. New York: Norton.

Viscusi, W. K. (1980) "Labor market valuations of life and limb: empirical evidence and policy implications." Evaluation Studies R. Annual 5: 545-574.

Viscusi, W. K. (1979) "The impact of occupational safety and health regulation." Bell J. of Economics 10 (Spring): 117-140.

Wolf, C., Jr. (1979) "A theory of nonmarket failure: framework for implementation analysis." J. of Law and Economics 22 (April): 107-139.

Zeckhauser, R. (1975) "Procedures for valuing lives." Public Policy 23: 419-464.

Explanation and Critique

Garret Moran met his problem with regression artifact straightforwardly. In this analysis, his goal was to disentangle those effects from the efforts of the Mine Safety and Health Administration. As a clinical psychologist interested in workplace safety, Moran was concerned whether intensified investigations aimed at the worst offenders decreased injuries. Our concern in this chapter is more with the sensible way Moran tested for regression artifacts.

The accident reduction program, PAR, selected for special attention those mines with significantly greater numbers of injuries than comparable mines. The mines were chosen for treatment on the basis of their high injury rates, controlling for size and other relevant characteristics. Campbell and Stanley recommend the use of time-series designs with comparison groups to address the problem of regression artifact.[3] Moran therefore searched for a group of untreated mines to use as a comparison group. Because his evaluation was conducted after the fact, Moran did not have the luxury of randomly assigning mines to treated and untreated groups. He found a set of mines that also had high injury rates but that admittedly were different from the treated group on a number of important variables. This group Campbell and Stanley refer to as a nonequivalent group—one chosen for a match on extreme scores but lacking a match on other relevant variables. Moran used regression techniques to control for these differences, most notably size.

The most innovative aspect of this study was the modeling of the regression artifact. Mines were included in the PAR intervention when their injury and accident rates soared above comparable mines. Presumably, mines entered the program when they were at their worst. The program of inspection and intervention, if effectively operational, should have acted to reduce these rates at a pace above and beyond that anticipated by the regression effect. Therefore, Moran constructed a counter variable for each treated mine with an initial value of zero when it entered PAR. The counter was incremented by one for each additional quarter in the program. The comparable counter for the comparison group was initiated when each comparable mine reached its peak injury rate, with increments being added each subsequent quarter. For a treatment effect to have been present, the improvement for treated mines must have been statistically significantly better than that for the untreated mines, which would be improving by means of regression to the mean. Notice that Moran also controlled for history with a similar counter and a dummy variable to account for PAR participation.

Using a pooled time series design, Moran got the results in Table 2 of the article. He literally interpreted the regression coefficients (b's) as shown in Chapter 10, "Use of Statistical Controls" by associating the passage of time and hours of exposure in the work setting with increases in mean number of injuries per quarter while PAR participation and the regression artifact accounted for decreases in average injuries. By means of a significance test, he found that the PAR program had an impact above and beyond that attributed to the regression artifact.

The policy implications of these findings are obvious: PAR decreased injuries. With this information, policy makers can decide whether this impact justifies further funding or whether a cost-benefit or cost-effectiveness analysis (Chapters 13 and 14) should be conducted in tandem with the present analysis. However, this second step could not be taken without establishing independent impact. Moran provided the evaluator with a prescription for coping with regression artifacts when programs are targeted to extreme cases.

REFERENCES

1. *Endogenous change* is the term used by Peter H. Rossi and Howard Freman in *Evaluation: A Systematic Approach* (Beverly Hills, CA: Sage, 1986), p. 192.
2. Donald T. Campbell and Julian C. Stanley, *Experimental and Quasi-Experimental Designs for Research* (Boston: Houghton Mifflin, 1963), p. 11.
3. *Ibid.*, p. 49.

20

Selection Bias

The internal validity problem involving selection is that of uncontrolled selection. Uncontrolled selection means that some individuals (or cities or organizations) are more likely than others to participate in the program under evaluation. Uncontrolled selection means that the evaluator cannot control who will or will not participate in the program.

The most common problem of uncontrolled selection is target self-selection. The target volunteers for the program and other volunteers are likely to be different from those who do not volunteer. We have already seen how one investigator— Tim Newcomb (Chapter 6)—handled the problem of self-selection in one of the examples of the quasi-experimental designs. He compared volunteers for a weatherization program with a group of similar volunteers at a later time. In the article in Chapter 9, "The Effects of Early Education of Children's Competence in Elementary School" by Martha B. Bronson, Donald E. Pierson, and Terrence Tivnan, the investigators did not have this opportunity.

Reread the Bronson, Pierson, and Tivnan article, and keep in mind while you do so the problem of uncontrolled selection that the authors encountered.

Explanation and Critique

The article by Martha Bronson, Donald Pierson, and Terrence Tivnan is an example of a research project in which, in our opinion, the researchers were unable to rule out self-selection as an explanation for differences in the experimental and comparison groups. The researchers compared second-grade children who had participated in a preschool program—the Brookline Early Education Program (BEEP)—with other second graders who had not. The prechool program was voluntary and had as its main goal the reduction or elimination of school problems. The research project sought to assess the impact of the program after several years had passed since the children's participation in BEEP. The investigators matched each BEEP participant with a control by selecting a child at random from within the same classroom and sex group. The investigators found that the demographic characteristics of the two groups were quite similar.

BEEP children showed significant advantages over the comparison group in both mastery and social skills, with the largest differences being in the area of mastery skills. In addition, BEEP children with highly educated mothers showed significant advantages over comparison children regardless of the BEEP program level experienced by the participants (see Figure 2 in the article). The researchers concluded:

> The results of the study *suggest* [emphasis ours] the importance of a carefully planned program like the Brookline Early Education Project for all school systems. Education and support services to parents of young children coupled with early education programs for the children should be recognized as an essential part of a high quality elementary school curriculum.

In our view, the authors did not make their case. The selection of the control group (demographically similar children and families) did not control for all elements necessary to overcome the self-selection bias. Is it not possible that, on average, BEEP parents show more concern for their children and thus instill "better" behavior patterns in them through more training and care?

Let us look at the evidence in Figure 2 of the article. First, take the mothers who were college graduates. There is a difference between the BEEP children and comparison group for these mothers, *but there is no difference between BEEP children on the basis of the level of BEEP intervention*. This suggests to us that self-selection and all that it means in a child-rearing situation may be a relevant factor.

Second, examine the scores for children whose mothers were not college graduates. The relationship shown in Figure 2 of the article indicates some difference between the comparison group and all BEEP children, no difference between BEEP C and BEEP B treatments, and a significant difference between BEEP A and BEEPs B and C. Is it not plausible that self-selection differentiates BEEPs from non-BEEPs and that only the BEEP A treatment is really effective?

If these interpretation of Figure 2 are accurate, then one is forced to conclude that the only effective BEEP program is BEEP A for children of noncollege mothers. This is a far cry from the authors' conclusions quoted earlier. This is not to say that the conclusions we draw are more valid than those of Bronson, Pierson, and Tivnan, only that their comparison group does not overcome the self-selection problem. The difference between the BEEP children and the children in the comparison group is probably explained by differences in parenting *and* the BEEP program. There is not enough information, however, to allow us to weight the relative importance of either factor.

Questions of selection bias are prevalent in other articles as well. Consider the following questions. In reviewing the article by Skidmore *and* our "Explanation and Critique" in Chapter 5, do you buy our contention that a problem of selection bias actually validates the results? How are the problems of selection encountered by Newcomb (Chapter 6) similar to those in the Hirst and Goeltz article (Chapter 10)? Compare and contrast how each dealt with this threat to validity. Who, in your opinion, was more successful? Which selection factors nullify the use of the proposed control group in Chapter 11? Could selection bias have been overlooked by Houlden and Balkin in Chapter 14?

21

Experimental Mortality

The problem of experimental mortality is in many ways similar to the problem of self-selection, except in the opposite direction. In experimental mortality the concern is with the question of why subjects drop out of a program rather than why they participate in it. It is seldom the case that participation in a program is carried through to the end by all those who begin the program. Dropout rates vary from project to project, but unfortunately the number of dropouts is almost always significant. Subjects who leave a program may differ in important ways from those who complete the program. They may, for example, be those who are least benefiting from it. Thus, postprogram measurement may show an inflated result because it measures the progress of only the principal beneficiaries.

A good example of potential biases associated with experimental mortality is found in the article in Chapter 5, "Overview of the Seattle-Denver Income Maintenance Experiment Final Report." Review this article in terms of the way in which experimental mortality was handled.

Explanation and Critique

The researchers involved in the Seattle-Denver Income Maintenance Experiment should be recognized for the ways in which they attempted to overcome their problems of experimental mortality. The experiment involved almost 5,000 low-income families randomly assigned to three-year or five-year treatment. The experiment was launched in Seattle, Washington, in 1970 and was extended to Denver, Colorado, in 1972. Eligibility was restricted to families with total earnings of less than $9,000 per year if one head was employed or $11,000 a year if both husband and wife were employed. Although participants might lose their subsidies in the program if their annual incomes in a given year became too high, they retained their eligibility for the program and could move back in if their incomes fell below the prescribed levels.

In spite of strenuous efforts to keep track of families and to persuade them to continue in the experiment, some families dropped out. During the first 30 months of the experiment, 20 percent of the originally enrolled husbands, 15 percent of the originally enrolled wives, and 15 percent of single heads of families dropped out. The husband-wife differences are a result of different experimental mortality rates in the cases of couples that split up.

Although a 15 to 20 percent mortality rate is of concern, it is hardly unique. Other researchers have been satisfied with far higher rates.[1] What is unique, however, is that the research team attempted to estimate the impact of this loss on the study's outcome. Project researchers Philip Robins and Richard West used data from the Social Security Administration (on both attriters and nonattriters) to determine whether sample attrition generated serious biases in the estimates of labor supply response in the Seattle and Denver experiment. They found that estimates corrected for attrition were uniformly larger than estimates not corrected for attrition, contrary to their theoretical expectations. The biases were slightly larger for earnings than for employment status (never more than 2 percent). For example, the estimated earnings effect for husbands is 8 percent uncorrected for attrition and 10 percent corrected for attrition.[2]

Skidmore reports that, on the basis of this analysis of dropouts of both experimental and control families, for husbands any attrition bias is probably small. For wives, however, there is evidence of moderate attrition bias that goes in the opposite direction from that observed for wives who did not drop out. Thus the researchers warn: "When interpreting the results for female heads, therefore, it should be kept in mind that the observed responses might underestimate slightly the actual reduction." Virtually every experiment is plagued with the problem of dropouts. The researchers in the Seattle-Denver Income Maintenance Experiment attempted to deal with the problems of experimental mortality in two ways: (1) by doing everything possible to persuade families not to drop out, and (2) by estimating the impacts of mortality on the results. The efforts to counter the problem of attrition are documented in the appendix to Skidmore's article in Chapter 5.

As was the case with selection bias, questions of mortality are common to many of the articles in this book. Consider the following:

- How did McKay et al. (Chapter 2) deal with the fact that 18 percent of the treatment group were lost over the four years of the experiment? Do you find this to be satisfactory?
- In Ann Solberg's evaluation of community posthospital follow-up services (Chapter 4), 24 percent of the clients in the experimental group were "designated as dropouts because they refused services during the first few contacts or were resistive to the extent that the social workers stopped initiating contacts with them before the follow-up period ended." If individuals with similar attitudes could have somehow been subtracted from the control group, is it not probable that rehospitalization rates would have been about equal? Does this dropout rate invalidate the study?
- How much impact did experimental mortality have in the Hawthorne study (Chapter 17)?
- Were there experimental mortality problems associated with the evaluation done by Bronson, Pierson, and Tivnan in Chapter 9? Discuss your answer.
- Estimate the effects of mortality on the evaluation of the nutrition program in Chapter 11. Could anything have been done to improve the evaluation in this regard?

REFERENCES

1. Stephen P. Klein, Harry M. Bohannan, Robert M. Bell, Judith A. Disney, Craig B. Foch, and Richard C. Graves, "The Cost and Effectiveness of School-Based Preventative Dental Care," in *Evaluation Studies Review Annual*, ed. Linda H. Aiken and Barbara H. Kehrer (Beverly Hills, CA.: Sage, 1985), 10: 184. These authors report a loss of 52 percent of their baseline population in 48 months. Ronald D. Hedlund and Chava Nachmias report a 35 percent attrition rate between intake and termination interviews of Milwaukee County CETA-funded employees in "The Impact of CETA on Work Orientations," in *The Practice of Policy Evaluation*, ed. David Nachmias (New York: St. Martin's Press, 1980), pp. 80–114.

2. Phillip K. Robins and Richard W. West, "A Longitudinal Analysis of the Labor Supply Response to a Negative Income Tax Program: Evidence from the Seattle and Denver Income Maintenance Experiments," Research Memorandum 58, Center for the Study of Welfare Policy, SRI International, Menlo Park, CA., Dec. 1978. See also John H. Pencavel and Richard W. West, "Attrition and the Labor Supply: Effects of the Seattle and Denver Income Maintenance Experiments," Center for the Study of Welfare Policy, SRI International, Menlo Park, CA, Sept. 1978.

PART SEVEN

On Your Own

The previous chapter completes the presentation of new materials. Part VII attempts to aid you in making sense out of these materials. In Chapter 22, we take you through a fairly comprehensive critique of an evaluation to illustrate how one goes about the process of critiquing an evaluation.

The final chapter leaves you on your own. Chapter 23 presents the results of a typical and straightforward evaluation. We do not present an "Explanation and Critique," however. As the chapter title states, "Now It's Your Turn."

22

Putting It All Together: A Comprehensive Critique

In each of the preceding chapters, one specific evaluation design or potential cause of invalidity was examined discretely—that is, by itself. This was done to make learning about evaluations easier. It is obviously easier to learn about one technique or problem than it is to try to sort out several designs or threats to internal validity.

Now, however, this simplified form of learning is over, and it is time for a serious critique of an evaluation with more than one design and several threats to validity. The article, "Attitude Change and Mental Hospital Experience" provides an excellent opportunity to put it all together. The article features not one but two designs. Furthermore, the authors identify the first design as a "recurrent institutional cycles design" developed by Donald Campbell and Julian Stanley—a design not discussed in this book.[1] Furthermore, the second design does not perfectly fit the designs presented in Parts II, III, or IV. But this should pose no problem. Each real-world evaluation problem is unique, and you should not expect textbook designs to be completely appropriate for all problems. For each design described and illustrated, there are clearly numerous modifications. The recurrent institutional cycles design is a modification of a design already presented, as is the design adopted for the second experiment.

While reading the article, it might help you to view the two experiments as two cases (which they are). The authors were dissatisfied with the results of the first experiment and adopted a new design to overcome the weaknesses of the first evaluation.

Try to identify what the recurrent institutional cycles design actually is (based on your reading of the earlier chapters). Then focus on the threats to validity: What are these threats? Which threats could not be overcome, thus forcing the authors to adopt a new design and conduct a second experiment?

Then, what is the second design? Does it overcome the problems of the initial experiment? At the end, are you struck with serious reservations about the results? If so, there must be certain sources of invalidity that were not overcome successfully. Are there any "neat" aspects to the experiment? Have the authors been able to measure any external influences not attributable to the program?

We believe that if you can satisfactorily critique, not criticize, this case, then our objectives in writing and editing this book have been met.

Attitude Change
and Mental Hospital Experience

JACK M. HICKS
FRED E. SPANER

It is the thesis of this investigation that favorable attitudes toward the mentally ill may develop as a function of intimate exposure to the mental hospital environment. Specifically, attitudes of hospital employees will shift over time in a direction more favorable to the patient. Empirical support of this notion is suggested by Bovard (1951), who found that as frequency of interaction between persons increases, the degree of liking for one another increases. His study, however, involved college classes and may not be generalizable to the mental hospital.

Impressionistic evidence of the positive effects of mental hospital experience is provided by extensive work with student nurses (Perlman & Barrell, 1958). These observers report that at the beginning of psychiatric training student nurses see patients as "maniacal" and tend to emphasize the differences between patients and themselves. But, as their training progresses, "they begin to maximize the similarities between themselves and patients, and see the differences as predominantly differences in degree and not kind." Some experimental corroboration of these observations is offered by Altrocchi and Eisdorfer (1960).

Dissenting evidence of the positive effects of the hospital environment upon attitudes is suggested by Middleton (1953) who found greater prejudice toward mental patients among older, more experienced mental hospital employees than among younger, less experienced employees. However, this finding is difficult to interpret as evidence of attitude change due to the absence of pretest information.

In view of the paucity of systematic research and ambiguity of findings in this area, the present investigation was undertaken.

EXPERIMENT I

This study was an initial step toward further exploration of the effects of mental hospital experience upon attitudes toward the mentally ill. Attitude modification was measured among student nurses exposed to 12 weeks of psychiatric nursing training at the Veterans Administration Hospital, Downey, Illinois. Attitudes elicited immediately prior to training were compared to attitudes immediately following training.

The following hypothesis was tested:

There will be a favorable shift in attitude toward mental patients over a 12-week period of psychiatric nursing training.

Favorable attitude shift was defined as a change in response to attitude statements in the direction of judges' opinions of the most desirable attitudes for student nurses to have.

Psychiatric nursing training consisted of two main subdivisions: classroom instruction and ward experience. Classroom instruction involved 10 hours per week devoted to exploration of nursing care problems. Ward ex-

Source: "Attitude Change and Mental Hospital Experience," Jack M. Hicks and Fred E. Spaner. JOURNAL OF ABNORMAL AND SOCIAL PSYCHOLOGY, Vol. 65, No. 2 (August 1962 Copyright 1962 by THE AMERICAN PSYCHOLOGY ASSOCIATION. Reprinted by permission of publisher and author.

perience entailed 6 weeks on each of two clinical areas—the male section and the female section—of the Acute and Intensive Treatment Service.

Method

Subjects. Seventy-eight student nurses, sent to Downey from several schools of nursing in the Chicago area as part of their regular nursing training schedule, were used. They were there in groups of 48 and 30, 3 months apart. All had received an average of about 2 years' previous "nonpsychiatric" nursing training.

Materials. A five-point Likert questionnaire designed to elicit attitudes associated with mental patients was used. The scale contained 66 statements some of which were borrowed verbatim or modified from Gilbert and Levinson's (1956) CMI scale (Items 5, 7, 11, 15, 18, 19, 25, 31, and 38) and Middleton's (1953) "Prejudice Test" (Items 1, 2, 5, 10, 14, 17, 22, 23, 26, 34, 36, and 37). The remaining items were original with this study.

Design. The design for this study, presented in Table 1, was a "recurrent institutional cycles design" developed by Campbell and Stanley (1962). It is appropriate to those situations in which an institutional process (in this case, psychiatric nursing training) is presented continually to new groups of respondents. Group A was a posttest-only aggregate whose only exposure to the questionnaire was on the final day of their 12-week psychiatric training period. Group B was a pretest-posttest aggregate. These respondents received the questionnaire on the first morning of their arrival into the psychiatric setting, prior to any formal orientation or exposure to patients (Group B_1). They also received an identical form of the questionnaire on the final day of their training period (Group B_2).

Procedure. First exposure: For the pretest and posttest only conditions, the experimenter was introduced to the group by a nursing education instructor. The experimenter then asked their cooperation in participating in a survey of attitudes and opinions about mental illness. Confidentiality of results was assured. Group B_1 were asked to sign their names on the questionnaire. Group A were asked not to record names.

Second exposure: Group B_2 respondents, having already been exposed to the test situation, were not given the introduction and full instructions. The group was simply asked to participate in filling out another questionnaire concerning attitudes and opinions about mental illness. They were reminded to put their names on the questionnaires. The same test room and same experimenter were used for all conditions.

Composite scoring key: A total attitude score was derived for each respondent by the method of summated ratings. The directionality of each item was determined by asking five nursing education instructors to respond to each statement in accordance with their professional opinions as to the most desirable attitude for a student nurse to have. These ratings produced at least 80 percent interjudge agreement on 38 of the total 66 items. Item response categories were scored from zero

TABLE 1 Comparisons of Composite Score Means

Comparison	N	M	t
B_1 (Pretest)	48	103.1	11.55[a]
B_2 (Posttest)	48	118.3	
A (Posttest only)	30	107.6	1.96[c]
B_1	48	103.1	
A	30	107.6	4.67[c]
B_2	48	118.3	

[a] Significant at .0005 level, one-tailed.

[b] Significant at .05 level, one-tailed.

[c] Significant at .001 level.

through four, depending on the directionality of the statement.

Results and Discussion

The major statistical tests of the hypotheses shown in Table 1 were t tests of difference in mean composite scores between (a) Group B_1 (pretest) and Group B_2 (posttest), and (b) Group B_1 and Group A (posttest only).

The mean difference between B_1 and B_2 was 15.25. A direct-difference t test between these two means was highly significant and in the predicted direction ($p < .0005$). This finding strongly supported the hypothesis. The mean difference between B_1 and A was 4.5, reaching significance in the same direction as the B_1-B_2 difference ($p < .05$). Hence, support of the hypothesis was provided by both comparisons.

However, these results became less clear-cut in consideration of an unexpected divergence between the two posttest means. A t test between A and B_2 produced a convincingly significant difference ($p < .001$), with B_2 higher than A. This finding seemed noteworthy despite the fact that a t test did not show the unpredicted A-B_2 difference to be significantly greater than the predicted A-B_1 difference ($p > .05$). There appeared to be several plausible explanations. One possibility stemmed directly from the fact that B_2 received a pretest, whereas A did not. That is, the pretest may have influenced performance on the subsequent testing. According to Campbell (1957), a pretest may increase or decrease sensitivity to the experimental variable. Thus, there may have been an interaction between the attitude pretest and psychiatric experience.

Another possible cause of the A-B_2 discrepancy was a respondent selection bias. Group B may have had a higher mean attitude than Group A at the outset of psychiatric training. This consideration became particularly important since the nature of the field situation prevented random preselection by the experimenter. Although psychiatric nursing trainee assignments were made unsystematically, and were not expected to vary from group to group, this assumption could only be made on a priori grounds at this time.

A third source of confoundment pertained to names being asked of Group B_2 but not Group A. This fact may have "freed" Group A respondents to more readily express less favorable attitudes actually felt. Group B_2, on the other hand, because of the presence of their names, may have been more inclined to present themselves in a favorable light, giving answers which they knew the staff thought desirable.

A fourth possibility concerned the sheer fact of taking a pretest sufficing to produce systematic changes on the posttest. This phenomenon differs from test-treatment interaction in that it refers to the main effects of testing per se.

Finally, it is possible that "history" effects of a powerful extraneous influence unknown to the experimenter occurred prior to B_2, but not prior to A. An example would be a mental health publicity campaign occurring contemporaneously with the Group A training period. A related possibility is that psychiatric training itself differed in some important way for Groups A and B. It is certainly possible to imagine that some change in hospital personnel, goals, or other conditions may have affected the nursing education program.

EXPERIMENT II

This investigation was an attempt to (a) corroborate and refine the basic findings of Experiment I, and (b) clear up ambiguities in the results of Experiment I. It will be recalled that a small but significant difference in the predicted direction was found between a posttest-only and an independent pretest group, but that a highly significant difference between the two posttests created problems of interpretation. Basically, the same quasi-experimental design was used (institutional cycles design), but with additional controls and a modified measuring instrument. This design also resembles Campbell and Stanley's (1962) "nonequivalent control groups" design in that random preselection was not possible.

The primary advantage of Experiment II was in the introduction of control groups. This addition made two important contributions: First, it provided for the testing of a hypothesis more precisely related to the effects of psychiatric training. The hypothesis for Experiment I was limited to predicting "absolute" attitude shift over 12 weeks of psychiatric training. The study was not designed to differentiate between change as a function of psychiatric training and change produced by other variables. As much change may conceivably have occurred with no psychiatric training at all. Equipped with control groups, Experiment II may test the more meaningful hypothesis of whether or not attitude change will be relatively greater as a function of psychiatric training than some other treatment. Hypothesis I for this investigation is:

There will be greater favorable shift in attitudes toward mental patients over a 12-week period of psychiatric nursing training than over an equivalent period of nonpsychiatric nursing training. (Attitude change was defined as in Experiment I.)

A second advantage of control groups permitted light to be cast on factors related to the unpredicted mean difference between the posttests of Experiment I. In particular, it was possible to test for pretest "sensitization" to psychiatric experience. For Experiment I, there were pretested and unpretested groups for the experimental treatment only. For Experiment II, there were pretested and unpretested groups for both experimental and control conditions. Due to the suggestive finding of Experiment I, the following hypothesis may be stated:

There will be a significant interaction between pretest attitude and psychiatric experience. This interaction should have a favorable rather than a dampening effect upon posttest attitudes.

An alternative possibility which can be tested as part of the analysis of the above hypothesis concerns the main effects of testing. In this consideration, pretested respondents would have significantly more favorable attitudes than unpretested respondents to a comparable degree on both experimental and control conditions.

Experiment II was also designed to test for recruitment differences among groups of respondents, another of the suggested confounders of Experiment I. This analysis was made by testing for nonlinearity among mean attitudes of all pretest conditions, both Experimental and Control.

It was also conjectured that the unpredicted difference between the posttests of Experiment I was due to instructions to record names on the questionnaires for one group but not the other. In order to check out this possibility, an additional experimental group was tested with "no name" instructions.

One further test designed to clarify Experiment I was considered. The reader will recall the suggestion that the two posttest means differed due to "history" effects of extraneous influences occurring concomitantly with psychiatric training, or subtle changes in psychiatric training itself. Such confounders were controlled for in Experiment II by the inclusion of two pretest-posttest psychiatric groups differing in terms of a 3-month separation in experimental treatment. If either or both of these effects are manifest, differential attitude change between the two groups would be expected.

Method

Subjects. A total of 354 student nurses were used. Two hundred twenty-four were members of the experimental groups receiving 3 months of intensive psychiatric nursing training. The remaining 130 were control respondents who, not yet having reached the psychiatric phase of nursing training, were encountered somewhat earlier in their overall programs. There was considerable overlap in this respect, however, since entrance of students into psychiatric training was distributed fairly evenly over the second half of the 3-year registered nurses training program. The only prerequisite for psychiatric training was at least 18 months of previous general hospital training.

All Experimental subjects took their psychiatric training at the Veterans Administration Hospital, Downey, Illinois, as part of their normal nursing training schedule. They came in aggregates of approximately 50 at 3-month intervals from seven schools of nursing in the Chicago area. Control respondents were tested while undergoing pediatric, surgical, obstetrical, or other phases of nursing training at two of the seven home hospitals of the nursing schools mentioned above. Respondents were not randomly assigned by the experimenter.

Materials. The Experiment I questionnaire was used except for slight modifications in format and content. In terms of format, the six-point forced-choice Likert adaptation, employed by Cohen and Struening (1959) was adopted. This represented an elimination of the ? category used too liberally by Experiment I respondents, being replaced by two categories: not sure but probably agree, and not sure but probably disagree.

The content of the questionnaire was modified to the extent of eliminating 5 items and adding 26 new ones, making a total of 87 for the Experiment II questionnaire. The 5 eliminated items were unsatisfactory because of highly skewed response distributions. One of these items was Number 22 from Middleton's (1953) Prejudice Test. The addition of

26 items was an attempt for better representation of the attitude universe of interest. Of these items, 4 were borrowed from Middleton's Prejudice Test (Items 4, 18, 29, and 30) and 8 were taken from Cohen and Struening's (1959) Opinions about Mental Illness questionnaire (Items 8, 14, 34, 35, 39, 41, 42, and 48). The remaining 14 items were original with this study. A special feature of the revised questionnaire was the retention of 21 nonshifting items from Experiment I. These items were included as an indicator of the degree to which Experimental respondents discriminate among items in the process of demonstrating attitude change. Fourteen items which showed significant change in the same direction on both B_1–A and B_1–B_2 comparisons in Experiment I were also retained.

Design. The 354 respondents made up eight conditions, five treatment conditions and three control conditions. Experimental groups are referred to in Table 2 as Groups A, B, F, G, and H. Groups C, D, and E are Control groups. The lettering, A through H, is related to the chronological order in which the different groups were encountered over a 9-month period. The Experimental groups were of two types: pretest-posttest and posttest-only. Groups A and H (comparable to Group A of Experiment I) were posttest-only (or unpretested) whose only exposure to the questionnaire was on the final day of their respective 12-week psychiatric training periods. Groups A and H differed in that A was tested 9 months prior to H; and Group A respondents were asked to record their names on the questionnaires, while H respondents remained anonymous. Groups B and G were Experimental pretest-posttest aggregates, comparable to Group B of Experiment I. These subjects were pretested immediately upon arrival at Downey and prior to any of the scheduled activities (Conditions B_1 and G_1). They were posttested on an identical form of the questionnaire after completion of

TABLE 2
Experimental Design

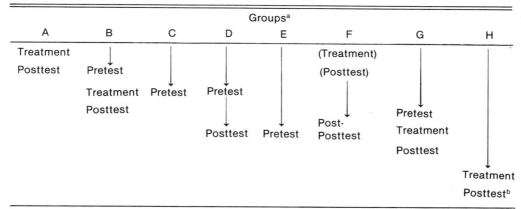

				Groups[a]			
A	B	C	D	E	F	G	H
Treatment					(Treatment)		
Posttest	Pretest				(Posttest)		
	Treatment	Pretest	Pretest				
	Posttest					Pretest	
			Posttest	Pretest	Post- Posttest	Treatment	
						Posttest	
							Treatment
							Posttest[b]

[a]In chronoligical order.
[b]Respondents asked not to record names.

all scheduled psychiatric activities 12 weeks later (Conditions B_2 and G_2). A 3-month separation in the span of time (12 weeks) during which training was received denotes the principal difference between these two groups.

In order to determine the longer-range effects of psychiatric experience upon attitude changes, an additional Experimental group (Group F) was tested. Of the 24 individuals in this group, 14 had participated previously in Experiment I and 10 in Group B of Experiment II, discussed above. These subjects ranged from 1 to 10 months of "postpsychiatric" general hospital training, with a mean of 5.25 months.

Control groups were also of two types: pretest-posttest and pretest-only. There were two pretest-only groups (C and E), so-called as a convenient label for "one-shot" testing administered at times prior to psychiatric training. Minor differences between Groups C and E were in terms of time and hospital at which testing took place. The final condition to be discussed pertains to Group D, a non-psychiatric pretest-posttest aggregate. This group, representing the basic control for testing of Hypothesis I, received 12 weeks of general hospital training between pretest and posttest.

Procedure. The identical procedure was used as described in Experiment I. The same experimenter presided over all sessions, with one exception. A substitute examiner was used for Condition G_2. Instructions were the same. All groups were requested (on both pre- and posttest) to record their names in the upper right-hand corner of the questionnaire except Group H. Group H was asked not to record names.

As in Experiment I, the method of summated ratings were used. Directionality of the new attitude statements was established by the same five nursing education instructors used in Experiment I. Items retained from Experiment I were not "rekeyed." Eighty percent interjudge agreement was achieved on 59 of the 87 items. Items were scored from one through six for analysis purposes.

Results

A post hoc measure of test-retest stability of the 59 keyed items was obtained by matching pretest-posttest scores for Control Group D. The Pearson coefficient was .82. Similar Pearson r's were obtained between pretests and posttests of Experimental Groups B and G of .55 and .57, respectively.

Internal consistency of the keyed items was estimated as a by-product of average item-total correlations (Guilford, 1950, p. 494). Two independent matrices of item-total correlations were computed. Groups A, B, and G were combined, as well as Groups C, D, and E, yielding average item-total correlations of .34 and .30, respectively. Resulting internal consistency reliabilities were .88 and .86. The average item-total r's were also squared to provide estimates of .11 and .09 mean item intercorrelations.

An overall picture of mean attitudes and attitude shifts is presented in Figure 1. A cursory inspection reveals both markedly higher attitude scores for psychiatric groups than Control groups overall, and sharp increments in attitude favorability over the 12-week psychiatric training period. Mean attitude increments for Experimental Groups B and G were 21.57 and 21.43, respectively, both of which are highly significant ($p < .0005$, one-tailed), thus, strongly supporting the hypothesis of Experiment I.

The Tukey test for multiple comparisons, reviewed by Ryan (1959), was employed for the assessment of Hypothesis I. A three-way comparison was made between Experimental Groups B and G, and Control Group D in terms of degree of favorable attitude shift.

Groups B and G exceeded D in magnitude of favorable attitude shift by mean differences of 16.71 and 16.57, respectively. Both of these increments exceeded their respective "wholly significant difference" ($\overline{\text{WSD}}$) set at the .01 level of confidence indicated in Table 3. The third comparison between Groups B and G produced no significant difference, as expected. These comparisons unequivocally supported Hypothesis I as shown graphically in Figure 2.

Pretest-treatment interaction was tested by a fourfold analysis of variance for unequal and disproportionate cell frequencies. Experimental versus Control groups made up the row main effects, whereas pretested versus unpretested groups were represented in the columns. As noted in Table 4, and also graphically in Figure 3, there was no significant interaction between pretesting and psychiatric nursing experience ($F < 1$). Therefore, Hypothesis II was rejected in that there was no evidence of pretest sensitization to the experimental variable.

Table 4 does present, however, strong evidence of the main effects of testing. Mean posttest attitudes of pretested respondents were found to be significantly higher than corresponding mean attitudes of posttest-only subjects ($p < .001$).

The significant main effects of the experimental variable are also shown in Table 4. Overall mean posttest attitudes of psychiatric nurses are shown to be significantly more favorable than posttest attitude scores of the nonpsychiatric groups. This analysis does not reflect attitude *shift*, however, and does not bear directly on Hypothesis I.

Results of a one-way analysis of variance are presented in Table 5, testing for nonlinearity among group mean pretest attitudes. The between-groups variance was less than the within-groups variance, hence rejecting the nonlinearity hypothesis ($F < 1$) regarding recruitment nonequivalence.

The hypothesized difference between "names" and "no names" was tested by comparing the attitude means of posttest-only Experimental Groups A and H. The means for the two groups were 263.65 and 265, respectively. An uncorrelated t was < 1, failing to support the hypothesis.

The effects of "history" and/or undetected changes in the experimental variable were tested by comparing the mean shifts of two psychiatric groups, B and G. A test for this hypothesis was conveniently provided by

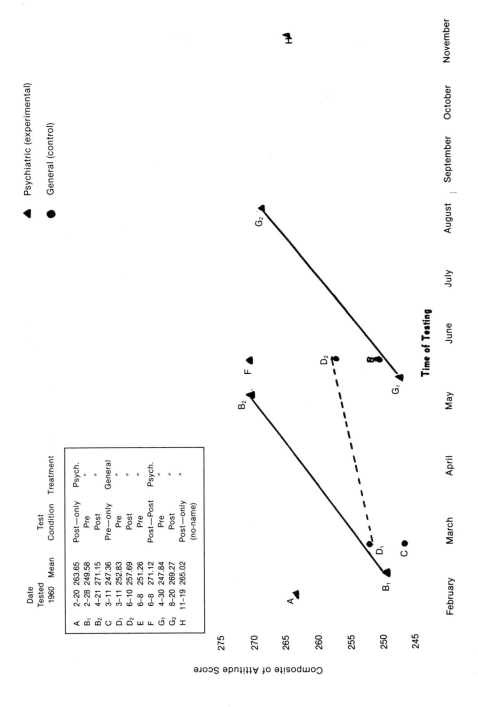

Figure I

Mean Attitudes and Attitude Shifts for All Groups

TABLE 3   Multiple Comparisons Test of Differential Attitude Shift

Comparison	Difference	$\overline{WSD}$
$(\overline{X}_{B_1}-\overline{X}_{B_2}) - (\overline{X}_{D_1}-\overline{X}_{D_2})$	16.71	9.37[a]
$(\overline{X}_{G_1}-\overline{X}_{G_2}) - (\overline{X}_{D_2}-\overline{X}_{D})$	16.57	8.81[a]
$(\overline{X}_{B_1}-\overline{X}_{B_2} - (\overline{X}_{G_1}-\overline{X}_{G_2})$	.14	8.81

[a] Significant at .01 level.

TABLE 4   Analysis of Variance of Mean Attitude Differences as a Function of Testing and Treatment

Source	df	MS	F
Pretest	1	3932.5	11.00[a]
Treatment	1	14,543.3	40.68[a]
Interaction	1	140.2	.39
Error (w)	326	357.5	

[a] Significant at .001 level.

Table 3. As previously mentioned, the mean difference (.14) in shifts between Groups B and G is far below the $\overline{WSD}$ of 8.81. Thus, no history effects or changes in psychiatric training appear evident.

The testing of 24 "post-posttest" respondents (Group F) made it possible to estimate the stability of attitude change. Since most of these respondents were previous members of psychiatric pretest-posttest conditions, they were compared accordingly with pretest-posttest Groups B and G. The postposttest mean attitude of Group H was

271.12, a level remarkably comparable to a posttest mean of 271.15 for Group B and 269.27 for Group G. The durability of attitude change, at least for a period of several months, seems clearly demonstrated.

A comparison of degree of shifts was also made between shifting and nonshifting items of Experiment I. The criterion of item shift on Experiment II was a significant mean difference on the B_1-B_2 comparison. A Yatescorrected χ^2 was a nonsignificant 1.73 ($p >$ .05). Hence, items which shifted on Experi-

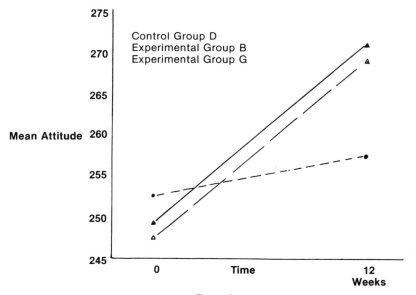

Figure 2
Mean Attitude Shift over 12-Week Period

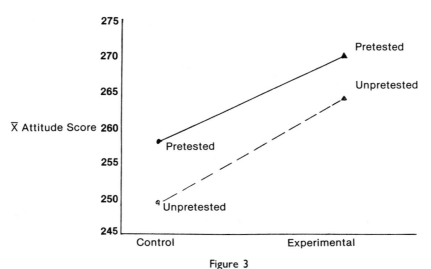

Figure 3

Conjunctive Effects of Testing and Treatment on posttest Scores

ment I did not shift to a significantly greater extent on Experiment II than items which did not shift on Experiment I.

DISCUSSION

Of the several additional subsidiary hypotheses concerning the unpredicted difference between the posttests of Experiment I, only that which concerned pretest main effects was supported. It appears, therefore, that the significantly higher mean attitude of Condition B as compared to Condition A of Experiment I may be traced to transfer effects from Pretest Condition B with Group A not being so benefited by a pretest "booster." This interpretation

does not follow from two investigations of attitude change by Lana (1959a, 1959b), who found neither pretest sensitization nor testing effects. A third study by Lana and King (1960), however, did show testing main effects without test-treatment interaction when a learning task was used. These results are directly in line with those of this investigation, suggesting the presence of a learning factor in the attitude questionnaire used.

In conclusion, then, it may be stated with confidence that 12 weeks of psychiatric training was demonstrated to be unequivocally effective in producing attitude change toward mental illness over and above the noise level of pretest transfer effects. Furthermore, the absence of troublesome interactions strengthens the generalizability of these findings beyond this particular experimental arrangement.

TABLE 5   Analysis of Variance of Recruitment Differences

Source	df	MS	F
Between groups	4	252.5	< 1
Error	234	338.9	

SUMMARY

Two quasi-experiments were performed as part of an ongoing project to investigate the effects of overall mental hospital experience upon modification of attitudes toward the mentally ill. Four hundred thirty-two student nurses served as respondents overall. Attitudes were measured by the Likert technique before and after 12 weeks of psychiatric nursing training. In Experiment I, attitudes on both posttests were observed to be significantly higher in a favorable direction than a pretest. A complication arose, however, with respect to an unpredicted significant difference between the posttests. Experiment II was basically a refinement of Experiment I. Control groups were added to the design, the questionnaire was revised, and a larger N used. Control respondents were student nurses in general hospitals not as yet having reached the psychiatric phase of their training. The basic hypothesis that psychiatric subjects would make a significantly greater favorable shift in attitudes over a 12-week period than nonpsychiatric subjects was strongly supported. The evidence suggests that the posttest discrepancy in Experiment I was probably due to pretest main effects, with the "pretested" posttest condition manifesting a higher mean attitude than the unpretested group.

REFERENCES

Altrocchi, J., & Eisdorfer, C. Changes in attitudes toward mental illness. Unpublished manuscript, 1960.

Bovard, E. W. Group structure and perception. *J. abnorm. soc. Psychol.*, 1951, 46, 398-405.

Campbell, D. T. Factors relevant to the validity of experiments in social settings. *Psychol. Bull.*, 1957, 54, 297-312.

Campbell, D. T., & Stanley, J. C. Experimental designs for research in teaching. In N. L. Gage (Ed.), *Handbook of research on teaching.* Chicago: Rand McNally, 1962.

Cohen, J., & Struening, E. L. Factors underlying opinions about mental illness in the personnel of a large mental hospital. Paper read at American Psychological Association, Cincinnati, 1959.

Gilbert, Doris, & Levinson, D. J. Ideology, personality, and institutional policy in the mental hospital. *J. abnorm. soc. Psychol.*, 1956, 53, 263-271.

Guilford, J. P. *Fundamental statistics in psychology and education.* (2nd ed.) New York: McGraw-Hill, 1950.

Lana, R. E. A further investigation of the pretest-treatment interaction effect. *J. appl. Psychol.*, 1959, 43, 421-422. (a)

Lana, R. E. Pretest-treatment interaction effects in attitudinal studies. *Psychol. Bull.*, 1959, 56, 293-300. (b)

Lana, R. E., & King, D. J. Learning factors and determiners of pretest sensitization. *J. appl. Psychol.*, 1960, 44, 189-191.

Middleton, J. Prejudices and opinions of mental hospital employees regarding mental illness. *Amer. J. Psychiat.*, 1953, 10, 133-138.

Perlman, M., & Barrell, L. M. Teaching and developing nurse-patient relationships in a psychiatric setting. *Psychiat. quart. Suppl.*, 1958, 31, 1-13.

Ryan, T. A. Multiple comparisons in psychological research. *Psychol. Bull.*, 1959, 56, 26-47.

Explanation and Critique

In the face of conflicting research results concerning the effect of student nurses' hospital experience on attitudes toward psychiatric patients, Jack Hicks and Fred Spaner sought to systematically assess changes in the attitudes of nurses that occurred between their entering the psychiatric training program and their leaving it. Hicks and Spaner used the *institutional cycles design,* which is appropriate when an institutional process (in this instance, psychiatric nursing training) is presented continuously to new groups. There are a number of instances when this design would be appropriate. For instance, any training process—student teaching, geriatric nursing training, apprenticeship programs—would be a candidate.

But what actually is this design? It is merely a label attached to a design that patches together aspects of the Solomon Four-Group Design and the pretest-posttest comparison group designs. The label is instructive to point out instances when the use of this patchwork makes sense. In such a design, a number of comparisons can be made—as Hicks and Spaner do. Gathering data in this manner allows a researcher to make comparisons between pretest and posttest scores (B1-B2), between pretest and posttest only scores (B1-A), and between posttested scores (B2-A).

Hicks and Spaner used 66 Likert items scored ordinally, (e.g., a five-point scale in which 1 was unfavorable and 5 was favorable) that were drawn from existing indexes or were modifications of them. (This is a common practice. There is a whole body of testing literature that deals specifically with measuring the validity and reliability of measures and scales. You should use a tried-and-true measure rather than reinventing the wheel with each new research endeavor. In addition, it adds to the cumulative nature of this research.) "Favorable" attitudes were determined by a panel of judges who examined possible attitude items and ranked answers as "favorable" to "not favorable" toward patients. Use of expert opinions was reasonable in this instance or in any instance in which there are no existing measures that perfectly match the study's needs. The attitude index was a summation of the responses to these items after all items were recoded to reflect the same scale.

The subjects were nurses on two psychiatric training rotations. They were judged to be similar on a number of characteristics; for example, all had two years' nursing training. Random assignment was impossible because of the nature of the timing of the rotation. Nurses were not systematically or randomly assigned to class cohorts. They entered the nursing school when they wished. Thus, the investigators had no reason to believe there were systematic differences between the cohorts.

Using a difference of means test (t-test), Hicks and Spaner compared the pre- and posttest results. If training were to have a positive effect on favorable attitudes, the B2 and A mean scores would have to be significantly higher than the B1 mean score. That, in fact, was what they found. To rule out any effects of the pretest on the posttest results, the A and B2 mean scores would have to be the same (not significantly different from each other). The latter result did occur. Not only were the A and B2 scores different, but the B2 score was higher. The substantive meaning of this result is that the pretested nurses had favorable scores that were even higher than those without the pretest but with the same treatment (i.e., training).

These results troubled Hicks and Spaner. Rather than being satisfied that the training appeared to have a positive impact, they sought to explain the differences between A and B2 scores. The plausible explanations revolved around threats to internal validity, mostly the effect of testing. The various threats resulting from testing that they suggest are interesting. First, what were the effects of the pretest on the posttest response? This is what one typically asks when doubtful about testing effects. Second, did the pretest experience in any way interact with the psychiatric training experience to, in this case, enhance the favorable result? This interaction effect is above and beyond the main effects postulated in the first example. So, was it the pretest that affected the result, or did the pretest do something to enhance the training effects? Did the pretest sensitize the Group B nurses during the training to make them react more favorably to the patients? This question was compounded by the fact that the responses by the Group B nurses were not confidential. This situation cannot be helped when one needs to link the responses at B1 to those at B2 without using a numbered coding scheme (which might have helped). Did this lack of confidentiality result in nurses' answering questions in line with what they believed their evaluators would regard as favorable? Even though Hicks and Spaner postulated no systematic differences between the two groups, could any selection bias have been explored? Finally, did anything (i.e., history) occur before B2 that did not occur before A?

Typically, there is no easy way to evaluate these other effects after the fact; they are often estimated if addressed at all. However, the beauty of an institutional cycles design is that there will be new entrants into the cycle and the effects can be measured. The nursing rotation allowed Hicks and Spaner to redesign the initial experiment with the result being Experiment II.

Hicks and Spaner physically controlled for other explanatory variables by adding nonequivalent control groups (Section III). The members of the basic control groups were nurses who were in a nonpsychiatric rotation who had not completed a psychiatric rotation. These nurses had slightly less hospital experience than those in the treatment groups. Within the treatment groups, there were also control groups to control for confidentiality and time.

The attitude instrument was also modified slightly on the basis of the results in Experiment I. By forcing respondents to make a favorable versus unfavorable decision (i.e., by removing the "don't know/no opinion" category), Hicks and Spaner increased the variation in the attitudinal score. In other words, they reduced the propensity to give a neutral response, which really is not unique. Apparently Hicks and Spaner believed that nurses would have some feeling rather than no feeling regarding these attitudes. This belief is similar to the idea among some political scientists that there are fewer pure Independent voters than Republican and Democratic leaners. The leaners are not allowed to hide their leanings under the cloak of fashionable independence.

Systematically, Hicks and Spaner constructed control groups to test each of the possible threats suggested in Experiment I. Their Table 2 displays the groups in terms of their experimental status and the timing of the test. Although the experiment was designed to verify the findings in Experiment I, Hicks and Spaner also did a good job of showing how to test the validity threats.

The findings are clearly presented and straightforward. (Unfortunately, most evaluation results are not so clear-cut!) First, did the treatment favorably affect attitudes? The result in both Table 3 and Figure 2 indicate that attitudes improved with the training program. The pretest scores are similar, and the change in the scores between the pre- and posttest indicates that the treatment versus control change is significant. In addition, the effects across the two treated groups appear to be similar, and their respective differences from the control group are similar. The pattern of the attitude change does not change over time (the three months between Groups B and G).

The fourfold analysis of variance in Table 4 of the article was used to determine whether and which testing effects were operative. Hicks and Spaner found no significant interaction between the pretest and the treatment. However, there were consistent and significant effects of the pretest results as compared with the posttest results. There was an effect of taking the pretest and more favorable posttest scores for both the experimental and control groups.

Was there a recruitment effect? If there were a difference, it would show up on the pretest scores. Hicks and Spaner performed an analysis of variance to see if the scores on the pretests were different among the groups. The idea was that if the difference between groups was more different than the difference within the groups, then there were systematic differences between the groups (i.e., the groups were not equivalent or similar to begin with). Hicks and Spaner found more variation within the groups than between them. Thus, they conclude that there is no systematic variation—that is, no selection bias. This does not mean that there were no differences between the groups in Experiment I. Because of the results from Experiment II, Hicks and Spaner assumed that there were no selection effects in Experiment I.

Did lack of confidentiality enhance posttest scores? To determine the answer, Hicks and Spaner compared groups that received the treatment and posttest-only attitude test. The groups differed only regarding whether they were asked to identify themselves on the instrument. Thus, the testing effect was controlled for; no pretest was given. Again, they found no difference in the posttest scores, which indicated that there was no enhancement based on pleasing the examiner. The inference is that it did not make a difference in Experiment I either. Rather, the difference that emerged in Experiment I was due to the main testing effects.

One of the reasons Hicks and Spaner had two pretest-posttest groups was to determine whether history played a part in the differences between A and B2. Apparently all the posttested A's were in one class cohort and the B's were in another. In Experiment II, the two pretest-posttest groups (B and G) were from different cohorts that began their training three months apart. By looking at the mean shifts in both groups, Hicks and Spaner concluded that history was not a factor because there were no significant differences between the shifts. History was not a contributing factor across that three-month period.

This finding is bolstered by the fact that the post-posttest results from Group F were similar to those of B and G. Not only did there appear to be no history effect across those three periods, but the results indicated that the effect was fairly durable. The authors did not indicate how they chose the nurses from Group F. Perhaps they tried to follow up on all, used participants from one participating school or hospital, or chose convenient subjects. The threat to validity they did not address in this aspect of the study was experimental mortality.

One of the neat and orderly aspects of this design was that with each new nursing cohort, the researchers were able to have a clean slate with which to work (i.e., untreated nurses with similar pretraining), so the experiments could be done over and over again. This luxury is not normally afforded evaluators. However, when the opportunity is presented, it allows one to take a second shot at the research and improve on the initial design. From these results, Hicks and Spaner were able to question the results of Lana and King discussed in Chapter 3. Now that you are an accomplished "critique-er" of evaluations, how would you reconcile these disparate findings?

REFERENCE

1. Donald T. Campbell and Julian C. Stanley, "Experimental Design for Research in Teaching," in *Handbook of Research in Teaching,* ed. N. L. Gage (Chicago: Rand McNally, 1962), pp. 171-246.

23

Now It's Your Turn

Now it is your turn to produce a thorough critique of an article, of a practical program evaluation. The following article by Leonard A. Jason, Kathleen McCoy, David Blanco, and Edwin Zolik evaluates two attempts within a community to decrease dog litter.

In selecting the article for this chapter, we were not trying to be cute. Dog litter is a nagging problem for public administrators in many communities. Thus, this is a good example of how a simple evaluation can be applied to solutions to mundane, everyday problems. This is hardly a "pure" evaluation, nor is it very sophisticated. But can one quarrel with the findings?

The article is clear and concise and the methodology is not difficult to understand (it has no statistics). It provides a nice opportunity for a student of evaluation to provide both (1) a "scientific" critique of the evaluation, and (2) a "practical" critique of the evaluation. In other words, what are the evaluation's technical problems, if any? And, given the nature of the problem, would you have done it any other way?

Decreasing Dog Litter

Behavioral Consultation to Help a Community Group

LEONARD A. JASON
KATHLEEN MCCOY
DAVID BLANCO
EDWIN S. ZOLIK

A primary mission for behavioral community psychologists is the strengthening, through consultation, of both formal and informal support systems within communities (Jason, 1977). Support systems represent an intertwined matrix of networks, including political groups, self-help organizations, block clubs, natural helpers, conservation groups, volun-

---

Source: Leonard A. Jason, Kathleen McCoy, David Blanco, and Edwin S. Zolik, "Decreasing Dog Litter: Behavioral Consultation to Help a Community Group," Vol. 4., No. 3 (June 1980), pp. 355–369. Copyright © 1980 by EVALUATION REVIEW. Reprinted by permission of Sage Publications, Inc.

tary associations, and the like. Their stability and viability have an important impact upon the health, well-being, and sense of identity and meaning of community residents (Caplan, 1974). Harnessing and working with the talent and resources already existing within communities represent high-priority needs (Sarason, 1976).

An endemic problem plaguing urban areas and rousing the wrath of community dwellers concerns accumulations of dog waste. Because of this problem, children and adults must exercise inordinate care to sidestep ubiquitous dog messes on lawns and sidewalks. In addition, this litter seriously detracts from the visual attractiveness of a community. Academically based psychologists might find neighborhood groups eager to collaborate on the amelioration of this quantifiable community sore-spot.

Uncollected dog feces in urban areas also represent an often neglected but nevertheless insidious health hazard (Cruickshank et al., 1976). Dogs are the chief hosts of roundworms (*Toxocara canis*), a disease which is a threat to barefooted children, since the worms can pass directly through a child's skin (Moffet, 1975). Echinococcosis is another disease which can be acquired when wind or flies transport parasite eggs from dog feces to homes, where they are deposited on human food (Van der Hoeden, 1964). Dog waste is responsible for transmitting these diseases as well as others (e.g., fish tapeworms, *brucellosis canis*, and *leptosprosis*). Given these potential health hazards, efforts to identify effective strategies to motivate dog owners to pick up dog droppings are strongly warranted.

The impetus for a series of studies on dog litter was provided during an invited presentation at a graduate-level seminar in community psychology at DePaul University. During this talk, a representative from a Chicago alderman's office indicated that dog droppings had generated the most resident complaints in his geographic area. Following this meeting, a research group at DePaul University was formed to study this dog litter problem.

In the first study, a class of DePaul undergraduates was asked to rank ten types of litter (e.g., broken glass, dog defecations, food, paper, and so forth) on a ten-point scale, with anchor points ranging from "not offensive" (1) to "extremely offensive" (10). Dog defecations were ranked as the most offensive type of litter (mean $X = 9.4$). These findings are congruent with resident complaints and confirm the seriousness of the dog litter problem.

As the next step in the research project, all fresh defecations in an eight- by five-block area in a residential section on the north side of Chicago were counted. In this target area, 1,147 droppings were observed, suggesting enough was regularly deposited to warrant an attempt at monitoring daily droppings on a specific block. An area was selected which met the following criteria: (a) dogs and owners could be unobtrusively observed from a building, and (b) a moderate amount of droppings had been found in the area. Throughout the study, the target area was observed for five hours each day, and all defecations were removed from the area daily. During the baseline week, only 5 percent of dog owners picked up after their dogs, and over 19 pounds of dog defecations were accumulated on the target block. Posting signs aimed at prompting pick-up behaviors was ineffective in modifying dog owner behaviors. When dog owners were instructed on how to pick up dog droppings, over 80 percent picked up after their dogs had defecated. Pick-up rates decreased modestly during a reversal period and increased with reimplementation of treatment. At a three-month follow-up, there was a 68 percent reduction in dog litter in the intervention area, and at a five-month follow-up, there was an 82 percent reduction in dog feces in streets surrounding the target area (Jason et al., 1979).

A Chicago alderman asked the first author to present the above study at a hearing in City Hall, as support for an ordinance he was introducing which would require dog owners to carry a "pooper scooper." The proposed ordinance passed, and the author's testimony was later presented on television and radio stations, as well as in several newspapers. (The follow-up data reported above were probably affected by the passage of this ordinance.) Subsequently, several citizen groups in Chicago contacted the investigators for help in setting up their own intervention programs. The present study describes a nine-month collaborative relationship between an academically based research team and one of the community groups which expressed interest in ameliorating the dog litter problem in its neighborhood. The experiment investigated the process whereby behavioral techniques, validated through methodologically rigorous designs, could be adopted and utilized by community residents in combatting an inveterate litter problem. Advantages and potential barriers in collaborating with neighborhood-based groups on the amelioration of environmental problems are delineated.

STUDY 1

Method. Two members of Southeast Lakeview Neighbors, a community group on the north side of Chicago, contacted the first author in order to obtain more information about his "bag intervention" with dog owners. An ad hoc committee of about twenty members of Southeast Lakeview Neighbors wanted to mount an intervention aimed at alleviating the dog nuisance problem in their community. During the following six weeks,

the first author attended four planning meetings where strategies and plans for the intervention were discussed. Throughout these meetings, expertise was provided the members in order to help them devise an intervention and build in an evaluation component.

Dependent Variables. During the first meeting, the committee members decided to identify the streets in their community with the greatest accumulations of fresh dog litter (defined as having color and form). Each member surveyed designated streets, and two connected streets (each was about 198 meters) with the highest density were selected for the intervention. A DePaul research assistant also surveyed all streets (a second observer recorded data on two streets to obtain a reliability estimate). Defecations were collected and weighed on nine mornings prior to the intervention and six mornings after the intervention. (On two occasions, interrater reliability was obtained.)

Procedure. The committee members picked a Saturday in early October to implement the intervention. From 8:00 A.M. to 5:30 P.M., three to four members, in two-hour shifts, patrolled the streets. During the intervention, two Chicago aldermen helped distribute bags during one shift. Committee members approached dog owners and said, "Hi. We're from Southeast Lakeview Neighbors. Are you aware of the new ordinance about carrying a receptacle to clean up after your dog?" Following an answer, the worker replied, "Here is a copy of the new ordinance. Would you like some newspaper or a plastic bag in case you don't have anything with you?" If the bag was taken or the owner had a bag, the worker said, "Thanks for keeping the streets clean." If the bag was refused, the worker said, "We just want everyone to be aware of the new ordinance so we can keep our neighborhood clean." All workers were asked to use the script above in their interactions with dog owners. Role-playing was used to teach the workers the script. Interveners recorded whether the dogs were on a leash, whether the owners knew of the new ordinance, and whether the owners took a bag, had their own, or refused. During the intervention, a research assistant followed teams of dog interveners on thirty-eight occasions in order to collect reliability data.

In addition to the intervention, a Girl Scout troop agreed to have a group of eight Girl Scouts patrol the streets for several hours, giving out flyers urging owners to pick up after their dogs.

Results

Reliability. Two DePaul University observers independently monitored droppings on two streets, and they reached an average agreement of 93 percent. On 24 sides of streets, dog dropping estimates were obtained from both community residents and a DePaul research assistant. The correlation coefficient for these estimates was .90 $(p < .01)$. On two occasions, two DePaul observers counted dog defecations and weighed the droppings. Both observers reached a 100 percent agreement on these two dependent measures. On the day of the intervention, the DePaul observer and the Lakeview residents reached an average interrater reliability of 90 percent on the following variables: whether the dog defecated, whether the owner picked up the droppings, whether the dog was on a leash, whether the owner had knowledge of the ordinance, whether the owners took a bag, had their own, or refused, and whether the owners were missed.

Dependent Variables. Prior to the intervention, 1,377 fresh droppings were counted by the DePaul observer in a four- by two-block area.

Figure 1 presents data on the number of droppings and their weight, before and after the intervention. Before the intervention, an average of 36 droppings weighing 6.8 pounds was deposited on the streets daily. Following the intervention, there was an average of 33 droppings weighing 6.3 pounds. The most prominent effects were observed during the first few days after the intervention. During the day-long intervention, 71 dog owners were approached. The majority of dogs (59 percent) were on a leash, 68 percent of owners knew about the dog ordinance, 45 percent took a bag, 27 percent had their own, 18 percent refused to take a bag, and 10 percent were missed. Of 12 owners whose dogs defecated in the target area, 8 (67 percent) picked up the feces. Of the 4 who did not pick up, 2 refused to take a bag and 2 took bags but did not pick up the droppings.

Discussion

This study demonstrated that an academically based research team could profitably work with a neighborhood action group in designing and evaluating an intervention aimed at reducing dog litter. The community residents had identified a serious aesthetic and health problem: approximately six pounds of dog droppings deposited daily, or about a ton of feces left in the target areas each year. Different members of the community, including two Chicago aldermen, over twenty residents, and a Girl Scout troop, joined together in working harmoniously toward the resolution of this problem.

The intervention was relatively successful on the day bags were given out: Only 18 percent refused to accept a bag and 67 percent picked up after their dogs. Many of the owners offered comments indicating they were concerned and angry about the dog litter problem. For example, one owner stated, "I can't stand the shit anymore. And if you get it on the shoes, you have to throw the shoes

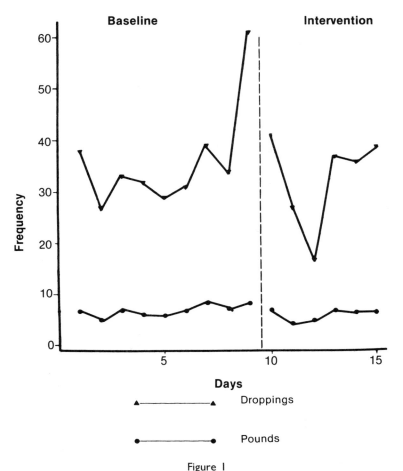

Figure I
Daily Rates of Droppings and Pounds Before and after the Intervention

away." A minority of owners refused bags and seemed rather indignant about the intervention. One owner who refused the bag said, "This is my property and I keep it clean." When another owner refused the bag and stated, "Dog haters are stupid people," a person walking on the street who heard the exchange said to the owner, "Hey, meathead, get the mutt off the street." We quickly intervened to prevent any further altercation. These episodes suggest that the issue of picking up droppings is highly controversial: Some community residents feel strongly that

owners should be more responsible, while some owners feel that they are not responsible for picking up their dogs' droppings.

For the first few days after the intervention, rates of dog litter declined by about two pounds daily; however, rates subsequently increased. There are several reasons that might account for this lack of maintenance of gains. It is conceivable that some owners were away for the weekend and consequently were not approached by the interveners. Also, some individuals might initially have complied with the requests to pick up dog feces but, when prompts were withdrawn, returned to their old behavior patterns. Both explanations suggest that longer-term interventions might reach more owners and more potently instill pick-up behaviors.

The ad hoc community group remained motivated and encouraged by the generally positive responses of owners. While the group temporarily recessed during the winter months, they were interested in launching a more extended intervention when better weather returned. Study 2 describes the intervention implemented in the spring of 1978.

STUDY 2

Method. Three and one-half months following the first intervention, the second author met with the community group to plan a more extended intervention. At that meeting, the intervention, script, and design of the study were agreed upon. The DePaul research team agreed to evaluate the intervention, whereas the community residents supplied the labor to implement the second project.

The ground surrounding a nursing home was selected for the intervention because unobtrusive observations could be made from the home's third floor. Since the nursing home was situated on a corner of a block, the observed target area consisted of two half-blocks, each perpendicular to the other. Part of the target area was on the site of the first intervention.

Dependent Variables. Prior to the baseline phase of study 2, and one month following the end of study 2, fresh dog defecations in the target and the four- by two-block surrounding area were counted. During the baseline phase, one of three DePaul University observers counted the number of dogs walked in the target area on Sundays between 8:30 A.M. and 5:30 P.M. (stray dogs

were eliminated from all analyses). In addition, observers recorded whether the dog was on a leash, whether the dog defecated, whether the droppings were picked up, and whether the dog owner had a visible receptacle to pick up droppings. During intervention phases, the observer also recorded whether the bag was accepted or refused and whether the owner had a bag which was not overtly visible (e.g., in the pocket) or the owner was missed.

Experimental Design. The study employed an ABAB design. Observations always occurred on Sundays.

Baseline. During this four-day period, which lasted one month, owners and dogs were observed. On the day before observations started, a metal sign was posted in the target area, which said: "Remove animal litter. You must always remove your pet's excrement and carry means to do so. Subject to $200 fine." Posting of the sign was not part of the planned intervention; however, the sign remained posted throughout the experiment.

Intervention. The program was implemented on four of the subsequent six Sundays (rain prevented the intervention from occurring on two Sundays). Ten different members of Lakeview Neighbors took two-hour shifts during various Sundays. Approached owners were greeted with the following: "Hi. I'm from Southeast Lakeview Neighbors. Do you know it is illegal not to pick up after your dog?" If the owner did not have a visible receptacle, the following was asked: "Would you like a bag and paper to pick up your dog's droppings?" If the bag was accepted or a receptacle was visible, the Lakeview Neighbors member said: "Thank you for helping keep your neighborhood clean." Each dog owner was then given an information sheet, composed by a neighborhood veterinarian, identifying the role of fecal matter in spreading worms to dogs and humans. If a dog defecation was picked up, the owner was given a circular token with the words "Scoop Poop" and a sketch of pooper scooper on it.

Baseline. During this period, data were collected on only two consecutive Sundays (weather and missing data due to observer absence eliminated two possible days of observations). The first observation during this phase occurred three weeks after the previous intervention. In this phase, dogs were unobtrusively observed from the third floor of the nursing home.

Intervention. The intervention described above was reimplemented during the two Sundays following the second baseline phase.

Reliability. The DePaul observers independently counted dog defecations in the target area prior to the baseline period. One reliability session, lasting from 45 to 90 minutes, was conducted during each of the four phases of the experiment.

Results

Reliability. Two observers reached 94 percent agreement in counting the number of defecations in the target area. During the baseline phase, two observers reached 100 percent agreement on the number of dogs,

defecations, pick-ups, and whether a pooper scooper was visible and the dog was on a leash. During the intervention phases, observers agreed 100 percent of the time on the number of dogs and pick-ups. Agreement was 90 percent for whether a pooper scooper was visible, accepted, refused, in the pocket, or the owner was missed.

Dependent Variables. Table 1 and Figure 2 present data describing the four phases of the second project. During the baseline phase, no dog defecations were picked up. With implementation of the intervention, pick-up behavior increased to 87 percent. In addition, 80 percent of the owners either had a visible pooper scooper, accepted the bag, or had bags in their pockets. During the intervention, the number of dogs on leashes also increased. Three and four weeks following the end of the intervention, over 50 percent of the owners continued to pick up. With reimplementation of the intervention, pick-up rates increased to 89 percent. While rejection rates increased during the last phase, many who refused a bag gave plausible reasons for their refusals (e.g., the dog only defecated in the backyard, the bag had already been used and deposited).

One month following the intervention, rates of defecations in the target area had been decreased by 88 percent (216 droppings were counted before the first baseline phase and 27 during the follow-up). In addition,

TABLE I   Dog Owner Behavior During the Four Experimental Phases of the Second Intervention (in percentages)

	Baseline	Intervention	Baseline	Intervention
Picked up	0	87	53	89
On leash	40	66	66	68
Pooper scooper visible	0	50	50	44
Accept bag		10		11
Reject bag		8		16
Bag in pocket		20		20
Missed		12		9

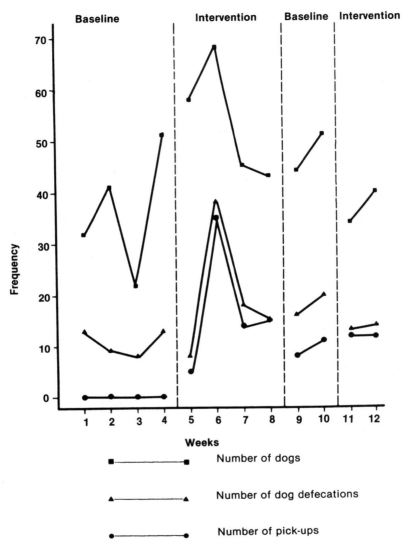

Figure 2
Daily Dogs, Defecations, and Pick-Ups Over Time

there was an 80 percent decrease in the overall community rates (i.e., when the number of defecations in a four- by two-block area before the first study, 1,377, was compared to the count one month following the end of the second study, 281). The number of droppings per side of street significantly decreased from 44.4 to 9.1 (t[30] =4.53, p < .01).

DISCUSSION

The study's principal contribution was to demonstrate the superiority of a more extended intervention, as illustrated by the second project, in bringing about at least short-term decreases in neighborhood dog litter. Mounting an intervention for one day brought about changes which lasted only temporarily. In contrast, when the dog intervention occurred for four Sundays, positive carry-over effects were noted for up to four weeks later. Whereas no community residents picked up during the first baseline, over 50 percent did so following the four-week intervention. In addition, positive generalization effects were noted in a four- by two-block area one month following the end of the intervention.

In the second project, a sign was posted in the target area before the baseline phase, and this did not result in any defecations being picked up. This finding supports a previous study (Jason et al., 1979) which found signs to be ineffective in increasing pick-up behavior. It is possible that signs would be more effective if compliance was enforced by police officials. However, during the course of the entire study no dog owner was observed being fined for either not having a pooper scooper or not picking up dog feces. Even though a dog ordinance was in effect during the course of each project, the present study suggests it was not being enforced by city police.

The community intervention elicited both positive and negative responses from the owners. Comments accompanying bag refusals included: "You must not like dogs"; "Look lady, go somewhere and flake off"; "I don't want to be hassled"; "If you're so concerned why don't you pick it up"; and "Give me your address and I'll mail you the defecation." Many others commended the interveners, saying: "I think it is a great idea, especially if you can get it to generalize"; "Some of these areas are regular shit factories. We need to do something about it." Several owners suggested that containers should be placed on the streets so droppings and bags could be placed in them. Many community residents began recognizing the interveners. One driver passing through the area said, "Make sure those dogs don't go on the lawns." These comments, along with those from the first project, indicate that many residents endorse responsible pick-up behavior and a vocal minority of owners resent any efforts to modify their behavior.

At the intervention end, community interveners and some personnel in the nursing home were asked if they had seen changes in the amount of dog litter in the target area. All indicated they saw decreases. Several of their comments included: "Yes, I notice people picking up. I think in this neighborhood, the intervention is needed"; "I think it was very helpful. At least it started people thinking"; and "I think the intervention is good, but we can't let up; it's not complete but it helps. If people are intimidated, they'll pick up." In general, nursing home personnel and community interveners felt quite positive about the attempt to alter dog owner pick-up behaviors in their neighborhood.

In introducing evaluation into community collaborative projects, several issues need to be addressed. For example, community members need to be appraised of the benefits stemming from the evaluation process, the importance of standardized procedures, the need for comprehensive training sessions, and the importance of supervision to ensure adequate implementation of intervention procedures. Members of the Lakeview community group were remarkably receptive to all evaluation procedures utilized. In part, this positive set might have been facilitated by the relevancy and usefulness of data collected in the previous study (Jason et al., 1979), which received considerable media exposure, highlighting the seriousness of the dog litter problem in Chicago. In addition, the community members believed that quantification of procedures and benefits accrued through the present interventions could provide necessary feedback concerning the project's efficacy, and could be used by other community groups confronted with similar difficulties.

Potential advantages in consulting with community groups include: (a) engendering among people a more positive public image of resources accessible within universities and of the beneficial capabilities of behavior modification techniques, (b) utilizing community input for identification of urgent issues needing amelioration, and (c) precipitating the mobilization of forces which might exert long-term positive influences on the rectification of community problems. Difficulties in mounting such programs include: (a) miscommunications due to failures in adequately understanding the culture and traditions of the members of particular communities, and (b) resistance on the part of community residents who might feel dominated by scientists demanding excessive quantification and rigor. The latter difficulties were avoided by devoting several sessions to becoming familiar with the traditions and values of the community and the university, and utilizing input from community members in devising intervention procedures and evaluation methodologies.

There are several methodological flaws in the studies presented above. For example, intervention phases were often too short, behaviors were unstable, several intervention components were employed simultaneously, and different criterion variables were employed in the different interventions. We hope that future studies will better control for these methodological difficulties.

The present study describes a successful collaborative effort between an ad hoc community group and a university-based research team. The planned interventions succeeded in ameliorating a serious community health and aesthetic problem. While the community group contributed resources for the mounted interventions, the community psychologists provided requisite training in behavioral technologies and evaluated the interventions' efficacy. Strengthening informal networks of support systems within a community represents a high priority for community psychologists (Leutz, 1976; Sale, 1973).

REFERENCES

Cruickshank, R., K. L. Standard, and H. B. L. Russell (1976) Epidemiology and Community Health in Warm Climate Countries. New York: Churchill Livingstone.

Caplan, G. (1974) Support Systems and Community Mental Health. New York: Behavioral Publications.

Jason, L. A. (1977) "Behavioral community psychology: conceptualizations and applications." J. of Community Psychology 5:303-312.

Jason, L. A., E. S. Zolik, and F. Matese (1979) "Prompting dog owners to pick up dog droppings." Amer. J. of Community Psychology 7: 339-351.

Leutz, W. N. (1976) "The informal community caregiver." Amer. J. of Orthopsychiatry 46: 678-688.

Moffet, H. L. (1975) Pediatric Infectious Diseases. Philadelphia: J. B. Lippincott.

Sale, J. S. (1973) "Family day care: one alternative in the delivery of developmental services in early childhood." Amer. J. of Orthopsychiatry 43: 37-45.

Sarason, S. B. (1976) "Community psychology, networks, and Mr. Everyman." Amer. Psychologist 31: 317-328.

Van Der Hoeden, J. (1964) Zoonosis. Amsterdam: Elsevier.

Reflections

We decided to title these concluding remarks "Reflections" rather than "After-word," "Epilogue," "Postmortem," or some similar term because we want to reflect on what we hope we have accomplished. We also use these pages to correct for the "oops" factor—as in, oops, we forgot to cover thus and so.

The lessons presented in the preceding chapters are sometimes difficult but always necessary if evaluation is to become what it really is, that is, fun. Evaluation is the artistic use of scientific principles. It is an opportunity not just to do something well but to be creative in doing it. Every evaluation problem has some unique quality about it. Thus, every evaluation is different. Evaluators have an opportunity to do things in life that are denied to many others: to be creative in their jobs and to use their minds to solve problems. It is our hope that you will see the challenges posed by evaluation problems and will rise to those challenges.

There are several ways for you to tell how valuable the lessons contained in this book have been to you. If your thought process has changed in the ways we have intended it to change, you will know it. First, if the lessons have come through loud and clear, you will never again consider using the simple before-and-after design except for the very simplest of evaluations—and then you will think twice about it. You will know, without thinking about validity problems or anything else, that the design is so fundamentally flawed as to be unusable under most circumstances. One of the articles in this book illustrates one of the few situations in which we consider the design to be appropriate. In evaluating the Red Cross nutritional program, Edwards, Acook, and Johnson essentially used the simple before-and-after design effectively.

The second important lesson we hope the book has made clear is that in evaluation it is always important to keep an eye out for confounding factors. It is not so important in day-to-day-evaluation work to keep your eyes open for the seven sources of invalidity—history, maturation, testing, instrumentation, regression artifact, selection, and experimental mortality. (There are in fact more than seven if interactive and reactive effects are included.) It *is* important to be constantly alert for any confounding factors. This applies to evaluative work in general, not only to formal evaluations. Take the case in which we were involved recently.

We were conducting a massive survey (500,000 people) for the Catholic Church in a major metropolitan area. We were assisting the church in identifying issues of most concern to Catholics. The one issue the survey showed to be most important to Catholics was the church's inability to attract priests and sisters to its work. This issue was shown to be more important than issues such as birth control, abortion, Catholic schools, and the role of women in the church. These results caught everyone, including church officials and our research team, by surprise. That is, until we looked for confounding factors. On Wednesday of our survey week (the surveys went out on Monday), one of the major newspapers in the area featured a front page story on the problems the church was having attracting men and women to the clergy and sisterhood. We know that this story biased the responses, but we have no idea how much bias was introduced. A small item but a confounding effect—and a lesson. History as a source of invalidity need not cover a long period. The impact of a historical event can occur in one day, and undoubtedly also in a shorter time if it is an event of great importance.

While we are on the subject of validity, we should be aware that there are other validity problems often associated with evaluation. These problems are associated with measurement. A program may be designed to change attitudes, or behavior, or skill, or any number of things. If the evaluator is unable to measure accurately the change in attitudes, or behavior, or skill, then it will be impossible to evaluate the program. This book is not about measurement, and we will not dwell on measurement here beyond introducing a few measurement concepts. There are a number of excellent texts that cover instrument design and measurement in detail.[1]

Whatever one is measuring, there is always the question as to what extent the measure is reliable and valid. A test is reliable to the extent that, under constant conditions, it will give the same results (e.g., measure the same attitude at the same strength). The problem is in determining reliability. Ideally, one would wish to determine the reliability of an instrument by repeating the test on the same people who have already taken it, but this poses practical difficulties. Some people will remember certain answers and will give them again just to be consistent (thus the test will appear more reliable than it may be), others will think about the subject between the test and retest and may change their positions. In any event, instrument reliability poses some problems for the evaluator, and there are ways to measure the reliability of instruments (e.g., alternative forms method, split-half method). Most good methods books describe such techniques.[2]

Reasonable reliability is one necessary attribute of a measurement instrument; the other is validity. By validity is meant the success the instrument has in measuring what it is designed to measure. Can difference between individuals' scores on the test or instrument be taken as true differences in the characteristic under study? An unreliable scale thus also lacks validity. But a reliable scale is not also necessarily valid.

There are several types of measurement validity. The first and simplest is *face validity*. Does the instrument "look like" the concept it is supposed to measure? If an instrument is supposed to measure management attitudes, do attitudes about management run through the instrument items? If so, the instrument has face validity.

A related concept, but one that is more rigorous and systematic, is known as *content validity*. Does the instrument cover the full range of the attitude (all of its components), and does it cover it in a balanced way? If so, the instrument has content validity. Content validity is essentially a matter of expert judgment.

Criterion validity subsumes predictive validity and concurrent validity, which are essentially the same thing except that predictive validity refers to some time in the future. *Concurrent validity* is thus concerned with how well the instrument can describe the present criterion, whereas *predictive validity* is concerned with how well the instrument can forecast the future criterion. The Law School Admission Test (LSAT), for example, is designed to predict how individuals will do in law school.

One more test of validity in instrumentation is *construct validity*. The essence of construct validity is its dependence on theory. Is the instrument constructed in such a way that it measures a theoretical construct—for example, religiosity or IQ?

We bring these concepts of measurement validity up not to create confusion but to make things clearer. When you hear the terms face validity, content validity, criterion validity, predictive validity, concurrent validity, or construct validity, remember that these all refer to the measurement instrument. The other validity problems—history, maturation, testing, instrumentation, regression artifact, selection, and experimental mortality—all refer to the evaluation design.

We have spent a significant portion of this book on problems of internal validity and, except for a brief mention in Chapter 1, have tended to ignore external validity—that is, the generalizability of findings. It deserves a brief mention here if only because to some degree there is a trade-off between internal and external validity. The stronger the internal validity of the evaluation design, the less likely the results are to be generalizable (in practice, not in theory).

There are ways, however, that generalizability, or external validity, can be increased.[3] The most obvious is through random sampling from a designated universe which allows the evaluator to generalize to that universe. The major polling organizations, for example, randomly sample telephone numbers from the nation so that they can generalize the results to the entire United States. Unfortunately, with most real-world problems random sampling is not possible. Imagine the problems one would have conducting the Seattle-Denver income maintenance experiment on a random basis throughout the United States.

A more practical approach is to choose heterogeneous groups to extend external validity. This is exactly what happened in Seattle and Denver. The experiment included married couples, female-headed households, childless couples, blacks, whites, Hispanics, and so on. Generalization to specific groups and to the entire population becomes plausible, if not scientific.

Generalization to modal instances is another practical way of increasing external validity. Cook, Cook, and Mark explain:

> If a widespread program of group counseling sessions for poor students with bad academic records in inner-city schools was under consideration, we would want to know about the effectiveness of group counseling for such students, and not for middle-class suburban children. Thus the model requires one to specify targets of generalizability in advance, and then to plan the selection of persons, settings,

and times so that there is a common sense correspondence between the planned targets and the achieved sample.[4]

We would like to conclude "Reflections" with one of our favorite evaluation stories by Michael Patton.[5]

It concerned an evaluation of a program established by a state legislature as a demonstration program to teach welfare recipients the basic rudiments of parenting and household management. The state welfare department was charged with the responsibility for conducting workshops, distributing brochures, showing films, and training case workers on how low-income people could better manage their meager resources and how they could become better parents. A single major city was selected for pilot testing the program, and a highly respected independent research institute was contracted to evaluate the program. Both the state legislature and the state welfare department were publicly committed to using the evaluation findings for decisionmaking.

The evaluators selected a sample of welfare recipients to interview before the program began. They collected considerable data about parenting, household management, and budgetary practices. Eighteen months later, the same welfare recipients were interviewed a second time. The results showed no measureable change in parenting or household management behavior. In brief, the program was found to be ineffective. These results were reported to the state legislators, some of whom found it appropriate to make sure the public learned about their accountability efforts through the newspapers. As a result of this adverse publicity, the legislature terminated funding for the program—a clear instance of utilization of evaluation fundings for decisionmaking.

Now, suppose we wanted to know why the program was ineffective. That question could not be answered by the evaluation as conducted because it focused entirely upon measuring the attainment of intended program outcomes, i.e., the extent to which the program was effective in changing the parenting and household management behaviors of welfare recipients. As it turned out, there is a very good reason why the program was ineffective. When the funds were initially allocated from the state to the city, the program became immediately embroiled in the politics of urban welfare. Welfare rights organizations questioned the right of government to tell poor people how to spend their money or rear their children: "You have no right to tell us to manage our households according to white, middle-class values. And who is this Frenchman named Piaget who's going to tell us how to raise our American kids?"

As a result of these and other political battles the program was delayed and further delayed. Procrastination being the better part of valor, the first parenting brochure was never printed, no household management films were ever shown, no workshops were held, and no case workers were ever trained. In short, *the program was never implemented—but it was evaluated!* It was then found to be ineffective and was killed.

The Lesson: Be sure the program exists before you evaluate it.

REFERENCES

1. For example, see Delbert C. Miller, *Handbook of Research Design and Social Measurement* (White Plains, NY: Longman, 1983), Don A. Dillman, *Mail and Telephone Surveys: The Total Design Method* (New York: Wiley Interscience, 1978) and Earl R. Babbie, *Survey Research Methods* (Belmont, CA: Wadsworth, 1973).

2. For example, see David Nachmias and Chava Nachmias, *Research Methods in the Social Sciences* 3rd ed. (New York: St. Martins Press, 1987); Julian J. Simon and Paul Burstein, *Basic Research Methods in the Social Sciences* 3rd ed. (New York: Random House, 1985); and Earl R. Babbie, *The Practice of Social Research* 3rd ed. (Belmont, CA: Wadsworth, 1983).

3. Thomas D. Cook, Fay Lomax Cook, and Melvin M. Mark, "Randomized and Quasi-Experimental Designs in Evaluation Research," in *Evaluation Research Methods: A Basic Guide,* ed. Leonard Rutman (Beverly Hills, CA: Sage, 1977), pp. 108–109.

4. *Ibid.*

5. Michael Q. Patton, *Utilization-Focused Evaluation* (Beverly Hills, CA: Sage, 1978), pp. 149–150.

Index

Page numbers in *italics* indicate illustrations. Page numbers followed by *t* indicate tables.

F*ck it. Let's do this!

THIS F*CKING BUCKET LIST IS THE
CREATION OF

AND

IF FOUND, PLEASE CONTACT US URGENTLY:

MASTER LIST

BUCKET LIST ITEM	☑	BUCKET LIST ITEM	☑
1		26	
2		27	
3		28	
4		29	
5		30	
6		31	
7		32	
8		33	
9		34	
10		35	
11		36	
12		37	
13		38	
14		39	
15		40	
16		41	
17		42	
18		43	
19		44	
20		45	
21		46	
22		47	
23		48	
24		49	
25		50	

MASTER LIST

BUCKET LIST ITEM	✓	BUCKET LIST ITEM	✓
51		76	
52		77	
53		78	
54		79	
55		80	
56		81	
57		82	
58		83	
59		84	
60		85	
61		86	
62		87	
63		88	
64		89	
65		90	
66		91	
67		92	
68		93	
69		94	
70		95	
71		96	
72		97	
73		98	
74		99	
75		100	

EXPLORING GOAL SETTING

Name: _____   Name: _____

What personal characteristics or
traits are you most proud of?

What are some ways you could put
these personal characteristics into
action to achieve your goals?

Who inspires you? What of their
qualities and achievements do
you most admire? How could you
emulate these in planning your own
goals?

EXPLORING GOAL SETTING

Name: _____

Name: _____

Which works of art (books, music, art, poetry, movies or even TV shows) inspire you most? What parts of them do you admire most? How could they inspire your own personal goals?

It's never too late! What forgotten goals or dreams have you previously had that might be worth a revisit for 2020?

If a genie granted your dream goal today, what would your life look like? Describe in vivid detail!

EXPLORING GOAL SETTING

Name: _____

Name: _____

Define success for yourself when it comes to your goal. What tangible specifics (locations, dates, emotions, possessions, money, job status etc.) will exist when the goal has been achieved?

Focus on the journey! How will you feel after you've taken small steps towards your goal? How will you feel once you've achieved your quarter-way and half-way milestones?

Challenges and setbacks: How will you be gentle and forgiving if you should steer off-course? How would you redirect your focus to get back on track with your goals?

EXPLORING GOAL SETTING

Name: _____   Name: _____

What are some of your happiest
memories? How could these
moments inspire goals that inspire
similar joy and gratitude?

What kinds of things may have
prevented you achieving your
goals previously? What will you do
differently, or what resources will
you need to ensure your new goals
are achieved?

What impact will working toward,
and achieving your goals have on
loved ones? How will your success
improve their lives?

GOAL SETTING WORD PROMPTS

1	ACCOLADE	57	CARING	113	DELIVER	169	FAR OUT	224	GRATITUDE
2	ACCOMPLISH	58	CAROUSE	114	DELVE INTO	170	FASCINATING	225	GROUND
3	ACCOMPLISHMENT	59	CAUSE	115	DESIGN	171	FASHION	226	GROUP
4	ACCUMULATE	60	CELEBRATION	116	DESIROUS	172	FATHER	227	HALLOWEEN
5	ACQUIRE	61	CEREMONY	117	DEVELOP	173	FEARLESS	228	HANG AROUND
6	ACT	62	CHALLENGING	118	DEVISE	174	FEAST	229	HANG OUT
7	ACTION	63	CHANCE	119	DIFFERENT	175	FEAT	230	HAPPENING
8	ACTUALIZE	64	CHARMING	120	DIG INTO	176	FEATHER IN CAP	231	HAPPINESS
9	AD-LIB	65	CHILDREN	121	DISCIPLINED	177	FESTIVITY	232	HARDY
10	ADVANCE	66	CHOOSE	122	DISCOVER	178	FETCHING	233	HATCH
11	ADVENTURE	67	CHRISTMAS	123	DISHY	179	FIND	234	HAVE A BALL
12	AFFECT CHANGE	68	CIRCUMSTANCE	124	DISPORT	180	FINISH	235	HAVE A LOOK
13	AGGREGATE	69	CLEANSE	125	DISPOSED	181	FIRE UP	236	HEAP
14	ALLURING	70	CLUSTER	126	DISTINCTION	182	FIX	237	HEARTEN
15	AMASS	71	COINCIDENCE	127	DISTRACTION	183	FLING	238	HEAVENLY
16	AMBITIOUS	72	COLLECT	128	DIVERSION	184	FLIRTATIOUS	239	HELP
17	AMBROSIAL	73	COLLEGE	129	DO	185	FLOCK	240	HEROIC
18	AMEND	74	COLORFUL	130	DONATION	186	FLYING	241	HOLIDAY
19	AMUSEMENT	75	COME UP WITH	131	DREAM	187	FOLLOW	242	HOME
20	ANNIVERSARY	76	COMPLETE	132	DREAM UP		THROUGH	243	HONESTY
21	APPEALING	77	COMPOSE	133	DRINK TO	188	FOOD	244	HONOR
22	APPEARANCE	78	COMPUTER	134	DRIVE	189	FOOLERY	245	HOP
23	AROUSE	79	CONCEIVE	135	EAGER	190	FOREIGN	246	HOT
24	ART AND DESIGN	80	CONCENTRATE	136	EARN WINGS	191	FOREST	247	HOTEL
25	ASSOCIATE	81	CONCLUDE	137	EDUCATION	192	FORGE	248	HUDDLE
26	ATHLETICS	82	CONCOCT	138	EFFECT	193	FORGIVENESS	249	HUMOR
27	ATTAIN	83	CONFIDENT	139	ELATE	194	FORM	250	HUNT
28	ATTAINMENT	84	CONGREGATE	140	ELEVATE	195	FORMULATE	251	IMAGINE
29	AVANT GARDE	85	CONSECRATE	141	EMBOLDEN	196	FRAME	252	IMPRESS
30	BABY	86	CONSTRUCT	142	EMPLOYMENT	197	FREEDOM	253	IMPROVE
31	BEACH	87	CONTINGENCY	143	EMPOWERMENT	198	FRIENDS	254	IMPROVEMENT
32	BEAUTIFUL	88	CONVERGE	144	ENACT	199	FRISK	255	IMPROVISE
33	BETTER	89	CONVERSATIONAL	145	ENDOWMENT	200	FROLIC	256	INCIDENT
34	BIKE	90	COOK UP	146	ENERGIZE	201	FULFILL	257	INCLINED
35	BIKING	91	COOKING	147	ENHANCE	202	FUN	258	INCREASE
36	BIRTHDAY	92	COURAGEOUS	148	ENKINDLE	203	FUTURE	259	INDIVIDUAL
37	BIZARRE	93	COURSE	149	ENLIVEN	204	GAIN GROUND	260	INFLUENCE
38	BLESS	94	CREATE	150	ENTERPRISE	205	GALLANT	261	INFORM
39	BOLD	95	CREATIVITY	151	ENTICING	206	GALVANIZE	262	INFUSE
40	BOOK	96	CROWD	152	ENVIABLE	207	GAME	263	INITIATE
41	BOOST	97	CRUISING	153	ENVIRONMENT	208	GAMING	264	INQUIRING
42	BRAZEN	98	CUISINE	154	ENVISION	209	GARDEN	265	INSPECT
43	BREAKTHROUGH	99	CULTIVATE	155	ESTABLISH	210	GENERATE	266	INSPIRIT
44	BRING ABOUT	100	CURIOUS	156	EVENING	211	GENEROUS	267	INSTALL
45	BROTHER	101	CUTE	157	EVENT	212	GET DONE	268	INSTILL
46	BUCKET LIST	102	DALLIANCE	158	EXALT	213	GET TOGETHER	269	INSTITUTE
47	BUILD	103	DATING	159	EXAMINE	214	GIFT	270	INTERESTED
48	BURROW	104	DAUGHTER	160	EXCITE	215	GIVE LIFE TO	271	INTOXICATING
49	BUSINESS	105	DAUNTLESS	161	EXCLUSIVE	216	GIVE RISE TO	272	INTREPID
50	CABIN	106	DECISION	162	EXCURSION	217	GLAMOROUS	273	INTRODUCED
51	CALL UP	107	DECORATION	163	EXHILARATE	218	GLOBAL	274	INVENT
52	CAPER	108	DEDICATE	164	EXPEDITION	219	GLOBE-TROTTING	275	INVEST
53	CAPTIVATING	109	DEED	165	EXPERIENCE	220	GLORIFY	276	INVIGORATE
54	CAPTURE	110	DELECTABLE	166	EXTERNAL	221	GO INTO	277	INVITE
55	CAR	111	DELICIOUS	167	EXTRAORDINARY	222	GOLD STAR	278	JEST
56	CAREER	112	DELIGHT	168	FALL/AUTUMN	223	GRANT	279	JOB TITLE

280	JOIN
281	JOKE
282	JOKING
283	JOYFUL
284	JUBILATE
285	JUNKET
286	KEEP
287	KICK UP HEELS
288	LAND
289	LANDMARK
290	LARK
291	LAUD
292	LAY FOUNDATION
293	LEAP
294	LET LOOSE
295	LIBIDINOUS
296	LINE
297	LIVE
298	LIVE IT UP
299	LODGE
300	LONG SHOT
301	LOOK INTO
302	LOOK UP
303	LOTTERY
304	LOVE
305	LUSCIOUS
306	LUXURY
307	MAGNIFICENT
308	MAKE
309	MAKE MERRY
310	MAKE OVER
311	MAKE STRIDES
312	MAKE THE SCENE
313	MAKE UP
314	MANAGE
315	MARRIAGE
316	MARVEL
317	MASS
318	MATCH
319	MATTER
320	MEET
321	MEET AGAIN
322	MEMORIALIZE
323	MEMORIES
324	MEND
325	MERRIMENT
326	MILESTONE
327	MIRACLE
328	MOBILIZE
329	MONEY
330	MOOR
331	MOTHER
332	MOTIVATE
333	MOVE
334	MOVEMENT
335	MOVIE

336 MUSIC	392 POKE	448 REFORM	493 SCHOLARSHIP	537 SPRING	581 TRAVERSE
337 MUSTER	393 POLISH	449 REFRESH	494 SCOPE	538 SPRUCE	582 TREKKING
338 NAVIGATION	394 POUR IN	450 REFURBISH	495 SCORE	539 SPRUCE UP	583 TRIP
339 NEGOTIATE	395 PRACTICE	451 REJOICE	496 SCOUT	540 SPUNKY	584 TRIUMPH
340 NEPHEW	396 PRAISE	452 REJOIN	497 SCRIPT	541 SPUR	585 TROPHY
341 NERVY	397 PRANK	453 REKINDLE	498 SEAFARING	542 STABILIZE	586 TROPICAL
342 NIECE	398 PRECIOUS	454 RELATIONSHIP	499 SEAL	543 STACK UP	587 TRY
343 NOVEL	399 PREPARATION	455 RELAXATION	500 SEARCH	544 START	588 TURNING POINT
344 OBSERVE	400 PREPARED	456 RELIABLE	501 SECURE	545 START BALL ROLLING	589 UNAFRAID
345 OBTAIN	401 PROBE	457 REMAKE	502 SEDUCTIVE	546 START OFF	590 UNCOMMON
346 OCCASION	402 PROCLAIM	458 REMODEL	503 SEEK	547 STATION	591 UNDERTAKING
347 OCCUPATION	403 PRODUCE	459 RENEW	504 SELF-CONFIDENCE	548 STAY	592 UNFAMILIAR
348 OCCURRENCE	404 PROFIT	460 RENOVATION	505 SELF-DRIVEN	549 STEAMY	593 UNFLINCHING
349 OFF-THE-CUFF	405 PROGRESS	461 REPAIR	506 SENSUAL	550 STIMULATE	594 UNITE
350 ONE AND ONLY	406 PROJECT	462 RESEARCH	507 SET DOWN	551 STIR	595 UNIVERSITY
351 OPPORTUNITY	407 PROMOTE	463 RESOLUTE	508 SET IN MOTION	552 STOCKPILE	596 UNUSUAL
352 ORDER	408 PROMOTION	464 RESOLVE	509 SET RIGHT	553 STOPOVER	597 UP FOR
353 ORGANIZE	409 PROMPT	465 REST	510 SET UP	554 STORY	598 UPGRADE
354 ORIGINATE	410 PROPEL	466 RESTORE	511 SETTLE	555 STRAIGHTEN OUT	599 UPLIFTING
355 OUTLANDISH	411 PROSPECT	467 RESURRECT	512 SEXY	556 STRANGE	600 VACATION
356 OUTRAGEOUS	412 PROUD				
357 OUTSIDE CHANCE	413 PROVIDE				
358 OVERHAUL	414 PROVOCATIVE				
359 OVERNIGHT	415 PUBLICIZE				
360 PAINT TOWN RED	416 PUNCH				
361 PAINTING	417 PURIFY				
362 PARENT	418 PURSUIT				
363 PARTY	419 PUT				
364 PASS	420 PUZZLED				
365 PASSAGE	421 QUESTIONING				
366 PASTIME	422 QUICKEN				

 BUCKET LIST BRAINSTORMING: CLOSE YOUR EYES AND DROP YOUR PEN AT RANDOM (OR CHOOSE A NUMBER BETWEEN 1 AND 625). BRAINSTORM IDEAS BASED ON ONE OR MORE OF YOUR RANDOMLY CHOSEN WORD PROMPTS.

367 PATCH UP	423 QUIET	468 RETIREMENT	513 SHAPE UP	557 STRIKE	601 VALIANT
368 PATIENCE	424 RACK UP	469 RETRIEVE	514 SHARPEN	558 STRIKING	602 VALOROUS
369 PAUSE	425 RACY	470 REUNITE	515 SHIFT	559 STUDY	603 VENTURE
370 PEACEFUL	426 RAFFLE	471 REVAMP	516 SHOT IN THE	560 SUAVE	604 VIDEO
371 PECULIAR	427 RAISE	472 REVEL	DARK	561 SUGGESTIVE	605 VISIT
372 PEREGRINE	428 RAISE HELL	473 REVERE	517 SIGHTSEEING	562 SUMMER	606 VOYAGE
373 PERFECT	429 RALLY	474 REVISE	518 SIGN	563 SWARM	607 WAGER
374 PERFORM	430 RAMBLE	475 REVITALIZE	519 SIRE	564 SWING	608 WALK
375 PERFORMANCE	431 RARE	476 REVIVE	520 SISTER	565 TAKE OFF	609 WANDER
376 PERK UP	432 REACH	477 RICHES	521 SITUATION	566 TALENTED	610 WANDERLUST
377 PERSEVERING	433 REACTIVATE	478 RIDE	522 SKILLS	567 TEASING	611 WARMTH
378 PERSISTENT	434 READY	479 RIDING	523 SKYROCKET	568 TECHNOLOGY	612 WAY OUT
379 PHASE	435 REALIZE	480 RING IN	524 SOJOURN	569 TEST	613 WAYFARING
380 PHENOMENON	436 REASSEMBLE	481 RISK	525 SOLVE	570 THING	614 WEALTH
381 PHOTOS	437 REASSURE	482 RISQUÉ	526 SON	571 THRONG	615 WEDDING
382 PICK UP	438 RECESS	483 ROMANCE	527 SONG	572 THROW DICE	616 WEEKEND
383 PILE UP	439 RECONCILE	484 ROMANTIC	528 SPARE MOMENTS	573 TIME	617 WEIRD
384 PLACE	440 RECONDITION	485 ROMP	529 SPARE TIME	MANAGEMENT	618 WELCOMING
385 PLAN	441 RECONVENE	486 ROUND UP	530 SPARK	574 TIME OFF	619 WIN
386 PLAY	442 RECOVER	487 ROUSE	531 SPAWN	575 TITILLATING	620 WING
387 PLEASING	443 RECREATE	488 SABBATICAL	532 SPEC	576 TOUCH	621 WINTER
388 PLEASURE	444 RECREATION	489 SAILING	533 SPECULATION	577 TOUCH UP	622 WONDER
389 PLUCK	445 RECTIFY	490 SCARE	534 SPICY	578 TOUR	623 WORK UP
390 PLUCKY	446 RECUPERATE	491 SCENE	535 SPIRITED	579 TRANSIT	624 WRITE
391 POETRY	447 REFINE	492 SCHEME	536 SPORT	580 TRAVEL	625 WRITING

MIND MAP

Start with a central idea or keyword (see "goal setting word prompts" on page viii) and work your way out, adding to the idea with variations (think: who? what? when? where?) or combine with other keywords to discover new possibilities.

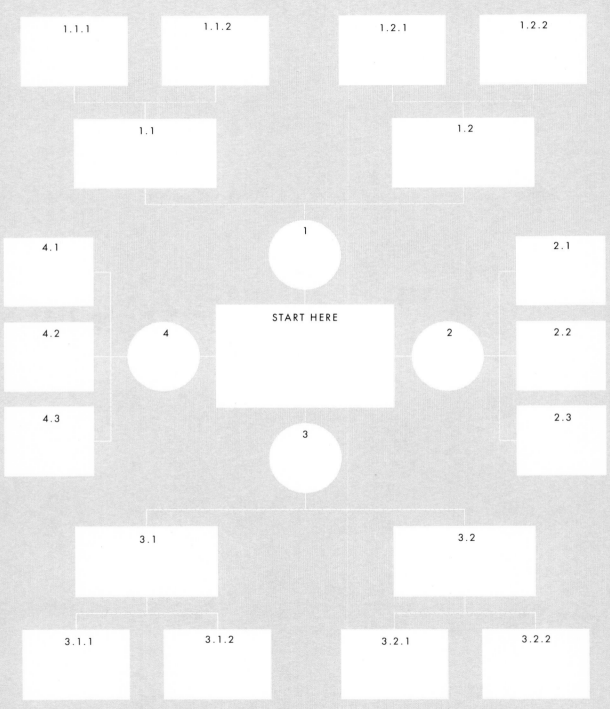

1.1.1

1.1.2

1.2.1

1.2.2

1.1

1.2

4.1

1

2.1

4.2

START HERE

4

2

2.2

4.3

2.3

3

3.1

3.2

3.1.1

3.1.2

3.2.1

3.2.2

TIP: Think about switching things up by combining your key idea with an unusual or unexpected time (classic example: Christmas in July). Time can include seasons, time of day, particular days of the week, months, anniversaries, birthdays and holidays.

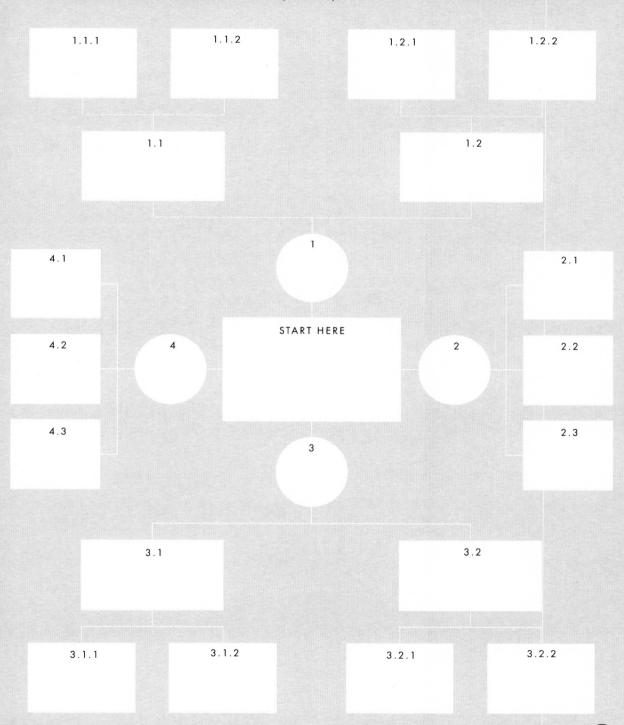

1.1.1

1.1.2

1.2.1

1.2.2

1.1

1.2

1

4.1

2.1

START HERE

4.2

4

2

2.2

4.3

2.3

3

3.1

3.2

3.1.1

3.1.2

3.2.1

3.2.2

MIND MAP

TIP: Think about desired outcomes such as emotions, or improvements to finances, skills or relationships. How would you both like to feel after completing a challenge? Revived, refreshed, and refocused? Motivated and energized? Confident and skillful?

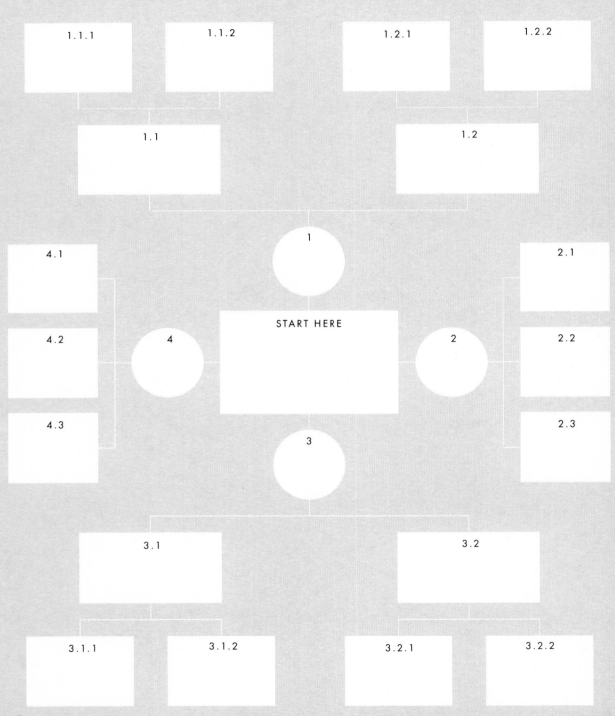

1.1.1

1.1.2

1.2.1

1.2.2

1.1

1.2

1

4.1

2.1

START HERE

4.2

4

2

2.2

4.3

3

2.3

3.1

3.2

3.1.1

3.1.2

3.2.1

3.2.2

TIP: Consider how adding different people to your bucket list idea would add interest to a simple activity. People you might consider might include family, friends, relatives, co-workers, long-lost friends, and even exes and enemies!

MIND MAP

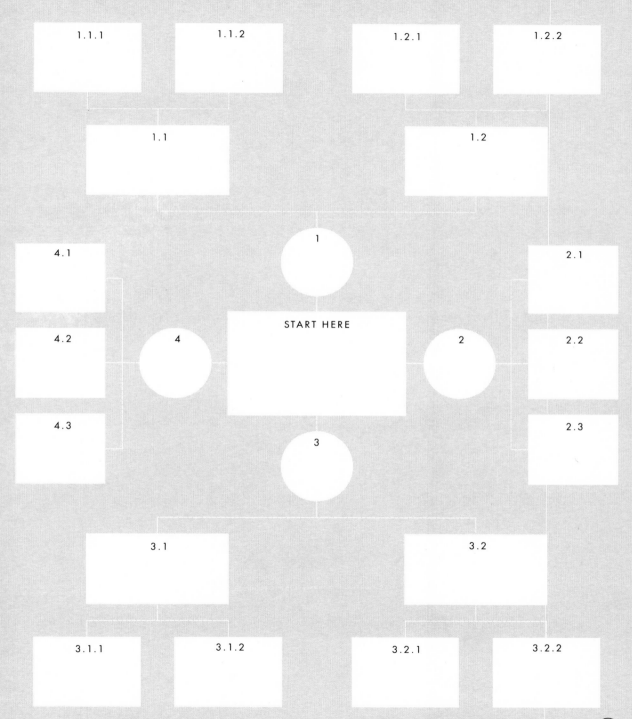

1.1.1

1.1.2

1.2.1

1.2.2

1.1

1.2

4.1

1

2.1

4.2

4

START HERE

2

2.2

4.3

2.3

3

3.1

3.2

3.1.1

3.1.2

3.2.1

3.2.2

MIND MAP

TIP: Don't get too caught up in technicalities or details when mind-mapping. Keep an open mind and allow spontaneity and intuition take over. Often it's the random or nonsense ideas that will lead you to something unexpected and amazing!

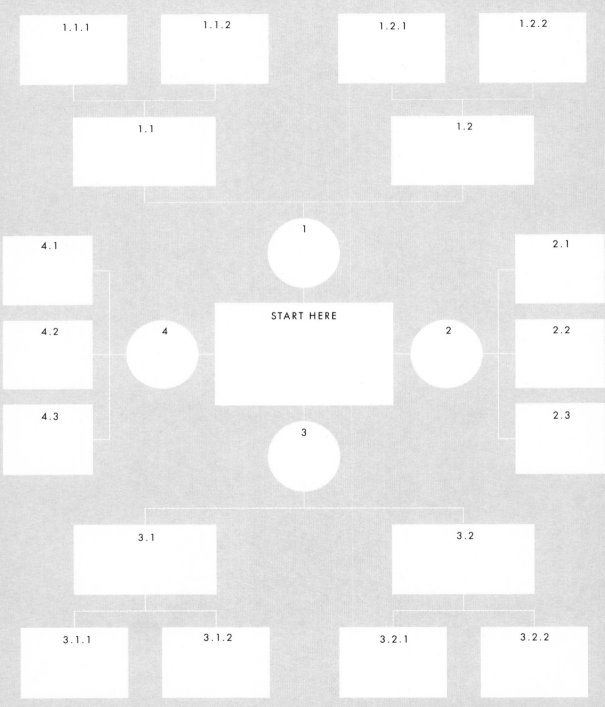

1.1.1

1.1.2

1.2.1

1.2.2

1.1

1.2

4.1

1

2.1

4.2

4

START HERE

2

2.2

4.3

2.3

3

3.1

3.2

3.1.1

3.1.2

3.2.1

3.2.2

TIP: Location, location! How might different locations make your initial idea more interesting. Think about some unexpected or unusual locations to switch up even simple ideas (e.g. candlelit dinner but in a rainforest, or a picnic lunch but in your partner's office).

MIND MAP

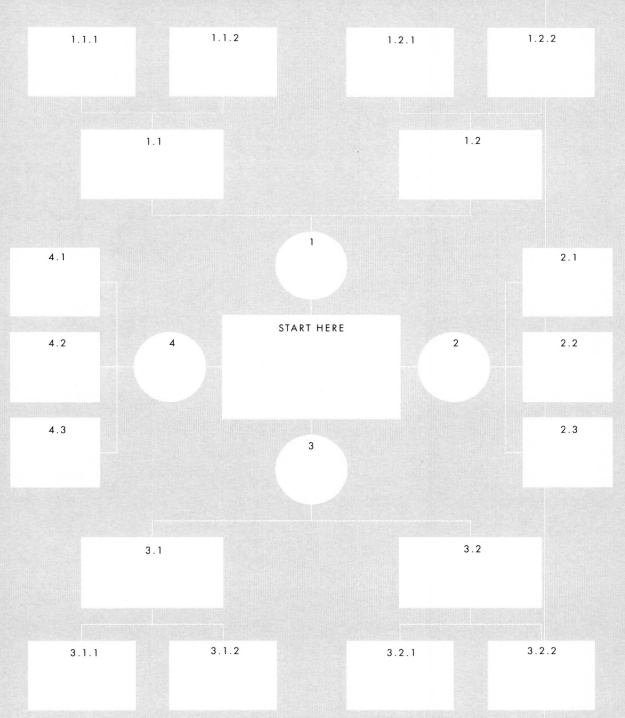

1.1.1

1.1.2

1.2.1

1.2.2

1.1

1.2

1

4.1

2.1

START HERE

4.2

4

2

2.2

4.3

2.3

3

3.1

3.2

3.1.1

3.1.2

3.2.1

3.2.2

MIND MAP

TIP: Highlight the best ideas for further exploration. If you strike a golden bucket list idea, transfer it to a bucket list item planning page. From there work on fleshing out the challenge idea in terms of schedule, budget, and planning details to make it a reality.

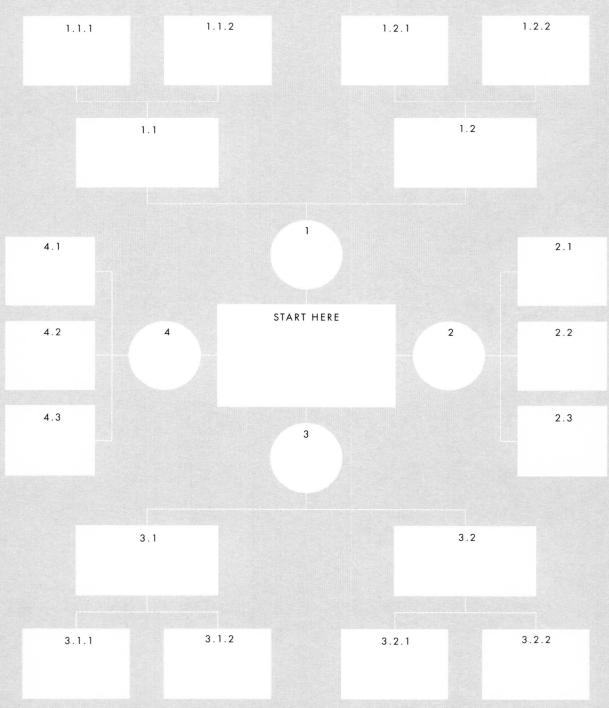

MIND MAP

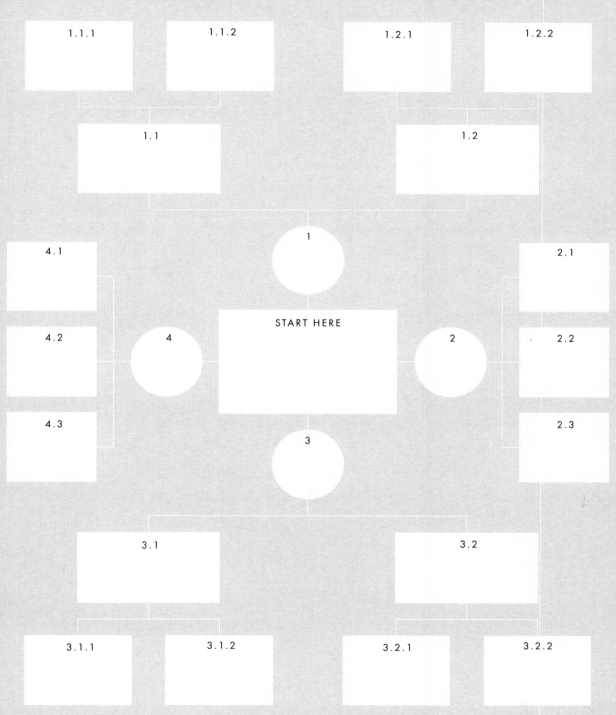

1.1.1

1.1.2

1.2.1

1.2.2

1.1

1.2

4.1

1

2.1

4.2

4

START HERE

2

2.2

4.3

2.3

3

3.1

3.2

3.1.1

3.1.2

3.2.1

3.2.2

MAJOR GOAL SUMMARY

This major goal is:

_____

_____

It will be accomplished by this date:

_____

This goal is important to us because...

_____

_____

_____

We will need to prepare the following resources to achieve this goal:

_____

_____

_____

_____

✐ **Goal Totem**

Insert a visual reminder (drawing, text, clipping)
that powerfully symbolizes this major goal.

MAJOR GOAL PROGRESS CHART

	JAN	FEB	MAR	APR	MAY	JUN	JULY	AUG	SEPT	OCT	NOV	DEC
100%												
90%												
80%												
70%												
60%												
50%												
40%												
30%												
20%												
10%												
0%												

MAJOR GOAL SUMMARY

This major goal is:

....
....
....

It will be accomplished by this date:

....

This goal is important to us because...

....
....
....
....

We will need to prepare the following resources to achieve this goal:

....
....
....
....

Goal Totem

Insert a visual reminder (drawing, text, clipping)
that powerfully symbolizes this major goal.

MAJOR GOAL PROGRESS CHART

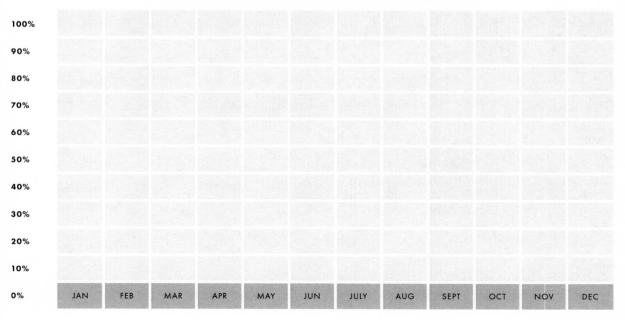

	JAN	FEB	MAR	APR	MAY	JUN	JULY	AUG	SEPT	OCT	NOV	DEC
100%												
90%												
80%												
70%												
60%												
50%												
40%												
30%												
20%												
10%												
0%												

MAJOR GOAL SUMMARY

This major goal is:

_____

_____

It will be accomplished by this date:

_____

This goal is important to us because...

_____

_____

_____

We will need to prepare the following resources to achieve this goal:

_____

_____

_____

_____

✎ Goal Totem

Insert a visual reminder (drawing, text, clipping)
that powerfully symbolizes this major goal.

MAJOR GOAL PROGRESS CHART

	JAN	FEB	MAR	APR	MAY	JUN	JULY	AUG	SEPT	OCT	NOV	DEC
100%												
90%												
80%												
70%												
60%												
50%												
40%												
30%												
20%												
10%												
0%												

MAJOR GOAL SUMMARY

This major goal is:

....
....
....
....

It will be accomplished by this date:

....

This goal is important to us because...

....
....
....
....

We will need to prepare the following resources to achieve this goal:

....
....
....
....

✤ Goal Totem

Insert a visual reminder (drawing, text, clipping)
that powerfully symbolizes this major goal.

MAJOR GOAL PROGRESS CHART

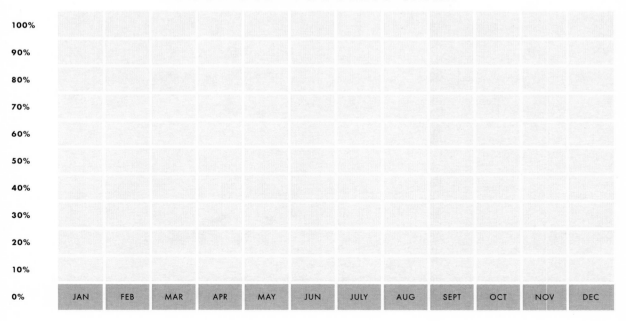

	JAN	FEB	MAR	APR	MAY	JUN	JULY	AUG	SEPT	OCT	NOV	DEC
100%												
90%												
80%												
70%												
60%												
50%												
40%												
30%												
20%												
10%												
0%												

MAJOR GOAL SUMMARY

This major goal is:

_____

_____

_____

It will be accomplished by this date:

_____

This goal is important to us because...

_____

_____

_____

_____

We will need to prepare the following resources to achieve this goal:

_____

_____

_____

_____

✒ Goal Totem

Insert a visual reminder (drawing, text, clipping)
that powerfully symbolizes this major goal.

MAJOR GOAL PROGRESS CHART

	JAN	FEB	MAR	APR	MAY	JUN	JULY	AUG	SEPT	OCT	NOV	DEC
100%												
90%												
80%												
70%												
60%												
50%												
40%												
30%												
20%												
10%												
0%												

The List

ITEM #1:

PRIORITY ★ ★ ★ ★ ★

SUMMARY: THIS WOULD BE F*CKING PERFECT FOR US BECAUSE...

_____
_____
_____
_____
_____
_____
_____

MAKE IT F*CKING HAPPEN: HOW? WHEN?

_____
_____
_____
_____
_____
_____
_____
_____

BUDGET

$

ANTICIPATED DATE

/ /   TO   / /

ACTION LIST

⊘ _____
⊘ _____
⊘ _____
⊘ _____
⊘ _____
⊘ _____
⊘ _____
⊘ _____
⊘ _____
⊘ _____
⊘ _____

REVIEW

DATE COMPLETED: / /

WHAT HAPPENED? (PEOPLE MET, HIGH POINTS, EXPECTATIONS VS REALITY)

_____
_____
_____
_____
_____
_____
_____
_____
_____

Success!

ONCE COMPLETE, PLACE A CHECK HERE
TO TAKE IT OFF YOUR BUCKET LIST

RATE THIS ACTIVITY

★ ★ ★ ★ ★

ITEM #2:

PRIORITY ★ ★ ★ ★ ★

SUMMARY: THIS WOULD BE F*CKING PERFECT FOR US BECAUSE...

_____

_____

_____

_____

_____

_____

MAKE IT F*CKING HAPPEN: HOW? WHEN?

_____

_____

_____

_____

_____

_____

REVIEW

DATE COMPLETED: / /

WHAT HAPPENED? (PEOPLE MET, HIGH POINTS, EXPECTATIONS VS REALITY)

_____

_____

_____

_____

_____

_____

_____

_____

_____

BUDGET

$

ANTICIPATED DATE

/ /   TO   / /

ACTION LIST

- ⊘
- ⊘
- ⊘
- ⊘
- ⊘
- ⊘
- ⊘
- ⊘
- ⊘
- ⊘
- ⊘

Success!

✓

ONCE COMPLETE, PLACE A CHECK HERE
TO TAKE IT OFF YOUR BUCKET LIST

RATE THIS ACTIVITY

★ ★ ★ ★ ★

ITEM #3:

PRIORITY ★ ★ ★ ★ ★

SUMMARY: THIS WOULD BE F*CKING PERFECT FOR US BECAUSE...

_____

_____

_____

_____

_____

_____

_____

MAKE IT F*CKING HAPPEN: HOW? WHEN?

_____

_____

_____

_____

_____

_____

_____

REVIEW

DATE COMPLETED: / /

WHAT HAPPENED? (PEOPLE MET, HIGH POINTS, EXPECTATIONS VS REALITY)

_____

_____

_____

_____

_____

_____

_____

_____

_____

BUDGET

$

ANTICIPATED DATE

/ / TO / /

ACTION LIST

⊘ _____
⊘ _____
⊘ _____
⊘ _____
⊘ _____
⊘ _____
⊘ _____
⊘ _____
⊘ _____
⊘ _____
⊘ _____

Success!

ONCE COMPLETE, PLACE A CHECK HERE
TO TAKE IT OFF YOUR BUCKET LIST

RATE THIS ACTIVITY

★ ★ ★ ★ ★

ITEM #4:

SUMMARY: THIS WOULD BE F*CKING PERFECT FOR US BECAUSE...

_____

_____

_____

_____

_____

_____

MAKE IT F*CKING HAPPEN: HOW? WHEN?

_____

_____

_____

_____

_____

_____

REVIEW

DATE COMPLETED: / /

WHAT HAPPENED? (PEOPLE MET, HIGH POINTS, EXPECTATIONS VS REALITY)

_____

_____

_____

_____

_____

_____

_____

_____

_____

BUDGET

$

ANTICIPATED DATE

/ /   TO   / /

ACTION LIST

⊘
⊘
⊘
⊘
⊘
⊘
⊘
⊘
⊘
⊘
⊘

Success!

ONCE COMPLETE, PLACE A CHECK HERE
TO TAKE IT OFF YOUR BUCKET LIST

RATE THIS ACTIVITY

★ ★ ★ ★ ★

ITEM #5:

PRIORITY ★ ★ ★ ★ ★

SUMMARY: THIS WOULD BE F*CKING PERFECT FOR US BECAUSE...

_____

_____

_____

_____

_____

_____

_____

MAKE IT F*CKING HAPPEN: HOW? WHEN?

_____

_____

_____

_____

_____

_____

_____

BUDGET

$

ANTICIPATED DATE

/ /   TO   / /

ACTION LIST

⊘ _____
⊘ _____
⊘ _____
⊘ _____
⊘ _____
⊘ _____
⊘ _____
⊘ _____
⊘ _____
⊘ _____
⊘ _____

REVIEW

DATE COMPLETED: / /

WHAT HAPPENED? (PEOPLE MET, HIGH POINTS, EXPECTATIONS VS REALITY)

_____

_____

_____

_____

_____

_____

_____

_____

_____

Success!

ONCE COMPLETE, PLACE A CHECK HERE
TO TAKE IT OFF YOUR BUCKET LIST

RATE THIS ACTIVITY

★ ★ ★ ★ ★

ITEM #6:

SUMMARY: THIS WOULD BE F*CKING PERFECT FOR US BECAUSE...

_____

_____

_____

_____

_____

_____

_____

MAKE IT F*CKING HAPPEN: HOW? WHEN?

_____

_____

_____

_____

_____

_____

_____

REVIEW

DATE COMPLETED: / /

WHAT HAPPENED? (PEOPLE MET, HIGH POINTS, EXPECTATIONS VS REALITY)

_____

_____

_____

_____

_____

_____

_____

_____

_____

BUDGET

$

ANTICIPATED DATE

/ / TO / /

ACTION LIST

- ⊘
- ⊘
- ⊘
- ⊘
- ⊘
- ⊘
- ⊘
- ⊘
- ⊘
- ⊘
- ⊘

Success!

ONCE COMPLETE, PLACE A CHECK HERE
TO TAKE IT OFF YOUR BUCKET LIST

RATE THIS ACTIVITY

★ ★ ★ ★ ★

ITEM #7:

SUMMARY: THIS WOULD BE F*CKING PERFECT FOR US BECAUSE...

_____
_____
_____
_____
_____
_____
_____

MAKE IT F*CKING HAPPEN: HOW? WHEN?

_____
_____
_____
_____
_____
_____
_____

REVIEW

DATE COMPLETED: / /

WHAT HAPPENED? (PEOPLE MET, HIGH POINTS, EXPECTATIONS VS REALITY)

_____
_____
_____
_____
_____
_____
_____
_____
_____

BUDGET
$

ANTICIPATED DATE
/ /   TO   / /

ACTION LIST
- ⊘
- ⊘
- ⊘
- ⊘
- ⊘
- ⊘
- ⊘
- ⊘
- ⊘
- ⊘
- ⊘

Success!

ONCE COMPLETE, PLACE A CHECK HERE
TO TAKE IT OFF YOUR BUCKET LIST

RATE THIS ACTIVITY
★ ★ ★ ★ ★

ITEM #8:

SUMMARY: THIS WOULD BE F*CKING PERFECT FOR US BECAUSE...

_____
_____
_____
_____
_____
_____
_____

MAKE IT F*CKING HAPPEN: HOW? WHEN?

_____
_____
_____
_____
_____
_____

BUDGET

$

ANTICIPATED DATE

/ /   TO   / /

ACTION LIST

⊘ _____
⊘ _____
⊘ _____
⊘ _____
⊘ _____
⊘ _____
⊘ _____
⊘ _____
⊘ _____
⊘ _____
⊘ _____

REVIEW

DATE COMPLETED: / /

WHAT HAPPENED? (PEOPLE MET, HIGH POINTS, EXPECTATIONS VS REALITY)

_____
_____
_____
_____
_____
_____
_____
_____
_____

Success!

ONCE COMPLETE, PLACE A CHECK HERE
TO TAKE IT OFF YOUR BUCKET LIST

RATE THIS ACTIVITY

★ ★ ★ ★ ★

ITEM #9:

PRIORITY ★ ★ ★ ★ ★

SUMMARY: THIS WOULD BE F*CKING PERFECT FOR US BECAUSE...

_____

_____

_____

_____

_____

_____

_____

MAKE IT F*CKING HAPPEN: HOW? WHEN?

_____

_____

_____

_____

_____

_____

_____

REVIEW

DATE COMPLETED: / /

WHAT HAPPENED? (PEOPLE MET, HIGH POINTS, EXPECTATIONS VS REALITY)

_____

_____

_____

_____

_____

_____

_____

_____

_____

_____

BUDGET

$

ANTICIPATED DATE

/ /   TO   / /

ACTION LIST

⊘

⊘

⊘

⊘

⊘

⊘

⊘

⊘

⊘

⊘

⊘

Success!

ONCE COMPLETE, PLACE A CHECK HERE
TO TAKE IT OFF YOUR BUCKET LIST

RATE THIS ACTIVITY

★ ★ ★ ★ ★

ITEM #10: ⬚

SUMMARY: THIS WOULD BE F*CKING PERFECT FOR US BECAUSE...

_____
_____
_____
_____
_____
_____
_____

MAKE IT F*CKING HAPPEN: HOW? WHEN?

_____
_____
_____
_____
_____
_____
_____

BUDGET

$

ANTICIPATED DATE

/ /   TO   / /

ACTION LIST

⊘ _____
⊘ _____
⊘ _____
⊘ _____
⊘ _____
⊘ _____
⊘ _____
⊘ _____
⊘ _____
⊘ _____
⊘ _____

REVIEW

DATE COMPLETED: / /

WHAT HAPPENED? (PEOPLE MET, HIGH POINTS, EXPECTATIONS VS REALITY)

_____
_____
_____
_____
_____
_____
_____
_____
_____
_____
_____

Success!

✓

ONCE COMPLETE, PLACE A CHECK HERE
TO TAKE IT OFF YOUR BUCKET LIST

RATE THIS ACTIVITY

★ ★ ★ ★ ★

ITEM #11:

PRIORITY ★ ★ ★ ★ ★

SUMMARY: THIS WOULD BE F*CKING PERFECT FOR US BECAUSE...

_____

_____

_____

_____

_____

_____

_____

MAKE IT F*CKING HAPPEN: HOW? WHEN?

_____

_____

_____

_____

_____

_____

_____

REVIEW

DATE COMPLETED: / /

WHAT HAPPENED? (PEOPLE MET, HIGH POINTS, EXPECTATIONS VS REALITY)

_____

_____

_____

_____

_____

_____

_____

_____

_____

BUDGET

$

ANTICIPATED DATE

 / /   TO   / /

ACTION LIST

⊘
⊘
⊘
⊘
⊘
⊘
⊘
⊘
⊘
⊘
⊘

Success!

ONCE COMPLETE, PLACE A CHECK HERE
TO TAKE IT OFF YOUR BUCKET LIST

RATE THIS ACTIVITY

★ ★ ★ ★ ★

ITEM #12:

SUMMARY: THIS WOULD BE F*CKING PERFECT FOR US BECAUSE...

_____

_____

_____

_____

_____

_____

MAKE IT F*CKING HAPPEN: HOW? WHEN?

_____

_____

_____

_____

_____

_____

REVIEW   DATE COMPLETED: / /

WHAT HAPPENED? (PEOPLE MET, HIGH POINTS, EXPECTATIONS VS REALITY)

_____

_____

_____

_____

_____

_____

_____

_____

BUDGET

$

ANTICIPATED DATE

/ /   TO   / /

ACTION LIST

⊘

⊘

⊘

⊘

⊘

⊘

⊘

⊘

⊘

⊘

⊘

Success!

ONCE COMPLETE, PLACE A CHECK HERE
TO TAKE IT OFF YOUR BUCKET LIST

RATE THIS ACTIVITY

★ ★ ★ ★ ★

ITEM #13:

SUMMARY: THIS WOULD BE F*CKING PERFECT FOR US BECAUSE...

_____

_____

_____

_____

_____

_____

_____

BUDGET

$

ANTICIPATED DATE

/ /   TO   / /

ACTION LIST

⊘

⊘

⊘

⊘

⊘

⊘

⊘

⊘

⊘

⊘

⊘

MAKE IT F*CKING HAPPEN: HOW? WHEN?

_____

_____

_____

_____

_____

_____

_____

REVIEW

DATE COMPLETED: / /

WHAT HAPPENED? (PEOPLE MET, HIGH POINTS, EXPECTATIONS VS REALITY)

_____

_____

_____

_____

_____

_____

_____

_____

_____

Success!

✓

ONCE COMPLETE, PLACE A CHECK HERE
TO TAKE IT OFF YOUR BUCKET LIST

RATE THIS ACTIVITY

☆ ☆ ☆ ☆ ☆

ITEM #14:

SUMMARY: THIS WOULD BE F*CKING PERFECT FOR US BECAUSE...

_____

_____

_____

_____

_____

_____

_____

MAKE IT F*CKING HAPPEN: HOW? WHEN?

_____

_____

_____

_____

_____

_____

BUDGET

$

ANTICIPATED DATE

/ /   TO   / /

ACTION LIST

- ⊘
- ⊘
- ⊘
- ⊘
- ⊘
- ⊘
- ⊘
- ⊘
- ⊘
- ⊘
- ⊘

REVIEW   DATE COMPLETED: / /

WHAT HAPPENED? (PEOPLE MET, HIGH POINTS, EXPECTATIONS VS REALITY)

_____

_____

_____

_____

_____

_____

_____

_____

_____

_____

Success!

✓

ONCE COMPLETE, PLACE A CHECK HERE
TO TAKE IT OFF YOUR BUCKET LIST

RATE THIS ACTIVITY

★ ★ ★ ★ ★

ITEM #15:

PRIORITY ★ ★ ★ ★ ★

SUMMARY: THIS WOULD BE F*CKING PERFECT FOR US BECAUSE...

_____

_____

_____

_____

_____

_____

_____

MAKE IT F*CKING HAPPEN: HOW? WHEN?

_____

_____

_____

_____

_____

_____

REVIEW

DATE COMPLETED: / /

WHAT HAPPENED? (PEOPLE MET, HIGH POINTS, EXPECTATIONS VS REALITY)

_____

_____

_____

_____

_____

_____

_____

_____

_____

_____

BUDGET

$

ANTICIPATED DATE

/ / TO / /

ACTION LIST

⊘
⊘
⊘
⊘
⊘
⊘
⊘
⊘
⊘
⊘
⊘

Success!

✓

ONCE COMPLETE, PLACE A CHECK HERE
TO TAKE IT OFF YOUR BUCKET LIST

RATE THIS ACTIVITY

★ ★ ★ ★ ★

(15)

ITEM #16:

PRIORITY ★★★★★

SUMMARY: THIS WOULD BE F*CKING PERFECT FOR US BECAUSE...

_____
_____
_____
_____
_____
_____
_____

MAKE IT F*CKING HAPPEN: HOW? WHEN?

_____
_____
_____
_____
_____
_____

BUDGET

$

ANTICIPATED DATE

/ /   TO   / /

ACTION LIST

- ⊘
- ⊘
- ⊘
- ⊘
- ⊘
- ⊘
- ⊘
- ⊘
- ⊘
- ⊘
- ⊘

REVIEW   DATE COMPLETED: / /

WHAT HAPPENED? (PEOPLE MET, HIGH POINTS, EXPECTATIONS VS REALITY)

_____
_____
_____
_____
_____
_____
_____
_____
_____
_____

Success!

ONCE COMPLETE, PLACE A CHECK HERE
TO TAKE IT OFF YOUR BUCKET LIST

RATE THIS ACTIVITY

★★★★★

ITEM #17:

SUMMARY: THIS WOULD BE F*CKING PERFECT FOR US BECAUSE...

_____

_____

_____

_____

_____

_____

_____

MAKE IT F*CKING HAPPEN: HOW? WHEN?

_____

_____

_____

_____

_____

_____

REVIEW
DATE COMPLETED: / /

WHAT HAPPENED? (PEOPLE MET, HIGH POINTS, EXPECTATIONS VS REALITY)

_____

_____

_____

_____

_____

_____

_____

_____

_____

BUDGET

$

ANTICIPATED DATE

/ /   TO   / /

ACTION LIST

⊘
⊘
⊘
⊘
⊘
⊘
⊘
⊘
⊘
⊘
⊘

Success!

ONCE COMPLETE, PLACE A CHECK HERE
TO TAKE IT OFF YOUR BUCKET LIST

RATE THIS ACTIVITY

★ ★ ★ ★ ★

17

ITEM #18:

SUMMARY: THIS WOULD BE F*CKING PERFECT FOR US BECAUSE...

_____
_____
_____
_____
_____
_____
_____

MAKE IT F*CKING HAPPEN: HOW? WHEN?

_____
_____
_____
_____
_____
_____

REVIEW

DATE COMPLETED: /   /

WHAT HAPPENED? (PEOPLE MET, HIGH POINTS, EXPECTATIONS VS REALITY)

_____
_____
_____
_____
_____
_____
_____
_____
_____
_____

BUDGET

$

ANTICIPATED DATE

/   /   TO   /   /

ACTION LIST

- ⊘
- ⊘
- ⊘
- ⊘
- ⊘
- ⊘
- ⊘
- ⊘
- ⊘
- ⊘
- ⊘

Success!

ONCE COMPLETE, PLACE A CHECK HERE
TO TAKE IT OFF YOUR BUCKET LIST

RATE THIS ACTIVITY

★★★★★

18

ITEM #19:

PRIORITY ★ ★ ★ ★ ★

SUMMARY: THIS WOULD BE F*CKING PERFECT FOR US BECAUSE...

_____

_____

_____

_____

_____

_____

_____

_____

MAKE IT F*CKING HAPPEN: HOW? WHEN?

_____

_____

_____

_____

_____

_____

_____

BUDGET

$

ANTICIPATED DATE

/ /   TO   / /

ACTION LIST

⊘
⊘
⊘
⊘
⊘
⊘
⊘
⊘
⊘
⊘
⊘

REVIEW

DATE COMPLETED: / /

WHAT HAPPENED? (PEOPLE MET, HIGH POINTS, EXPECTATIONS VS REALITY)

_____

_____

_____

_____

_____

_____

_____

_____

_____

_____

_____

Success! ✓

ONCE COMPLETE, PLACE A CHECK HERE
TO TAKE IT OFF YOUR BUCKET LIST

RATE THIS ACTIVITY
★ ★ ★ ★ ★

ITEM #20:

SUMMARY: THIS WOULD BE F*CKING PERFECT FOR US BECAUSE...

_____

_____

_____

_____

_____

_____

MAKE IT F*CKING HAPPEN: HOW? WHEN?

_____

_____

_____

_____

_____

_____

REVIEW

DATE COMPLETED: / /

WHAT HAPPENED? (PEOPLE MET, HIGH POINTS, EXPECTATIONS VS REALITY)

_____

_____

_____

_____

_____

_____

_____

_____

_____

BUDGET

$

ANTICIPATED DATE

/ /   TO   / /

ACTION LIST

⊘
⊘
⊘
⊘
⊘
⊘
⊘
⊘
⊘
⊘
⊘

Success!

ONCE COMPLETE, PLACE A CHECK HERE
TO TAKE IT OFF YOUR BUCKET LIST

RATE THIS ACTIVITY

★ ★ ★ ★ ★

ITEM #21:

SUMMARY: THIS WOULD BE F*CKING PERFECT FOR US BECAUSE...

_____

_____

_____

_____

_____

_____

MAKE IT F*CKING HAPPEN: HOW? WHEN?

_____

_____

_____

_____

_____

_____

REVIEW

DATE COMPLETED: / /

WHAT HAPPENED? (PEOPLE MET, HIGH POINTS, EXPECTATIONS VS REALITY)

_____

_____

_____

_____

_____

_____

_____

_____

_____

BUDGET

$

ANTICIPATED DATE

/ /   TO   / /

ACTION LIST

⊘ _____
⊘ _____
⊘ _____
⊘ _____
⊘ _____
⊘ _____
⊘ _____
⊘ _____
⊘ _____
⊘ _____
⊘

Success!

ONCE COMPLETE, PLACE A CHECK HERE
TO TAKE IT OFF YOUR BUCKET LIST

RATE THIS ACTIVITY

★ ★ ★ ★ ★

ITEM #22:

SUMMARY: THIS WOULD BE F*CKING PERFECT FOR US BECAUSE...

_____

_____

_____

_____

_____

_____

MAKE IT F*CKING HAPPEN: HOW? WHEN?

_____

_____

_____

_____

_____

_____

REVIEW

DATE COMPLETED: / /

WHAT HAPPENED? (PEOPLE MET, HIGH POINTS, EXPECTATIONS VS REALITY)

_____

_____

_____

_____

_____

_____

_____

_____

_____

BUDGET

$

ANTICIPATED DATE

/ /   TO   / /

ACTION LIST

⊘ _____

⊘ _____

⊘ _____

⊘ _____

⊘ _____

⊘ _____

⊘ _____

⊘ _____

⊘ _____

⊘ _____

⊘ _____

Success!

✓

ONCE COMPLETE, PLACE A CHECK HERE
TO TAKE IT OFF YOUR BUCKET LIST

RATE THIS ACTIVITY

★ ★ ★ ★ ★

ITEM #23:

SUMMARY: THIS WOULD BE F*CKING PERFECT FOR US BECAUSE...

_____

_____

_____

_____

_____

_____

_____

MAKE IT F*CKING HAPPEN: HOW? WHEN?

_____

_____

_____

_____

_____

_____

_____

REVIEW

DATE COMPLETED: / /

WHAT HAPPENED? (PEOPLE MET, HIGH POINTS, EXPECTATIONS VS REALITY)

_____

_____

_____

_____

_____

_____

_____

_____

_____

BUDGET

$

ANTICIPATED DATE

/ /   TO   / /

ACTION LIST

⊘
⊘
⊘
⊘
⊘
⊘
⊘
⊘
⊘
⊘
⊘

Success!
✓

ONCE COMPLETE, PLACE A CHECK HERE
TO TAKE IT OFF YOUR BUCKET LIST

RATE THIS ACTIVITY

★ ★ ★ ★ ★

23

ITEM #24:

SUMMARY: THIS WOULD BE F*CKING PERFECT FOR US BECAUSE...

_____

_____

_____

_____

_____

_____

_____

MAKE IT F*CKING HAPPEN: HOW? WHEN?

_____

_____

_____

_____

_____

_____

REVIEW

DATE COMPLETED: / /

WHAT HAPPENED? (PEOPLE MET, HIGH POINTS, EXPECTATIONS VS REALITY)

_____

_____

_____

_____

_____

_____

_____

_____

_____

_____

BUDGET

$

ANTICIPATED DATE

 / /   TO   / /

ACTION LIST

⊘
⊘
⊘
⊘
⊘
⊘
⊘
⊘
⊘
⊘
⊘

Success!

ONCE COMPLETE, PLACE A CHECK HERE
TO TAKE IT OFF YOUR BUCKET LIST

RATE THIS ACTIVITY

★★★★★

24

ITEM #25:

PRIORITY ☆ ☆ ☆ ☆ ☆

SUMMARY: THIS WOULD BE F*CKING PERFECT FOR US BECAUSE...

_____

_____

_____

_____

_____

_____

MAKE IT F*CKING HAPPEN: HOW? WHEN?

_____

_____

_____

_____

_____

_____

_____

REVIEW

DATE COMPLETED: / /

WHAT HAPPENED? (PEOPLE MET, HIGH POINTS, EXPECTATIONS VS REALITY)

_____

_____

_____

_____

_____

_____

_____

_____

_____

BUDGET

$

ANTICIPATED DATE

/ /   TO   / /

ACTION LIST

⊘
⊘
⊘
⊘
⊘
⊘
⊘
⊘
⊘
⊘
⊘

Success!

✓

ONCE COMPLETE, PLACE A CHECK HERE
TO TAKE IT OFF YOUR BUCKET LIST

RATE THIS ACTIVITY

☆ ☆ ☆ ☆ ☆

ITEM #26:

PRIORITY ★ ★ ★ ★ ★

SUMMARY: THIS WOULD BE F*CKING PERFECT FOR US BECAUSE...

_____

_____

_____

_____

_____

_____

MAKE IT F*CKING HAPPEN: HOW? WHEN?

_____

_____

_____

_____

_____

BUDGET

$

ANTICIPATED DATE

/ /   TO   / /

ACTION LIST

⊘ _____
⊘ _____
⊘ _____
⊘ _____
⊘ _____
⊘ _____
⊘ _____
⊘ _____
⊘ _____
⊘ _____
⊘ _____

REVIEW

DATE COMPLETED: / /

WHAT HAPPENED? (PEOPLE MET, HIGH POINTS, EXPECTATIONS VS REALITY)

_____

_____

_____

_____

_____

_____

_____

_____

_____

_____

Success!

ONCE COMPLETE, PLACE A CHECK HERE
TO TAKE IT OFF YOUR BUCKET LIST

RATE THIS ACTIVITY

★ ★ ★ ★ ★

ITEM #27:

PRIORITY ★ ★ ★ ★ ★

SUMMARY: THIS WOULD BE F*CKING PERFECT FOR US BECAUSE...

_____

_____

_____

_____

_____

_____

_____

MAKE IT F*CKING HAPPEN: HOW? WHEN?

_____

_____

_____

_____

_____

_____

REVIEW

DATE COMPLETED: / /

WHAT HAPPENED? (PEOPLE MET, HIGH POINTS, EXPECTATIONS VS REALITY)

_____

_____

_____

_____

_____

_____

_____

_____

_____

BUDGET

$

ANTICIPATED DATE

/ /   TO   / /

ACTION LIST

⊘
⊘
⊘
⊘
⊘
⊘
⊘
⊘
⊘
⊘
⊘

Success!

ONCE COMPLETE, PLACE A CHECK HERE
TO TAKE IT OFF YOUR BUCKET LIST

RATE THIS ACTIVITY

★ ★ ★ ★ ★

ITEM #28:

PRIORITY ★ ★ ★ ★ ★

SUMMARY: THIS WOULD BE F*CKING PERFECT FOR US BECAUSE...

_____

_____

_____

_____

_____

_____

_____

MAKE IT F*CKING HAPPEN: HOW? WHEN?

_____

_____

_____

_____

_____

_____

REVIEW

DATE COMPLETED: / /

WHAT HAPPENED? (PEOPLE MET, HIGH POINTS, EXPECTATIONS VS REALITY)

_____

_____

_____

_____

_____

_____

_____

_____

_____

BUDGET

$

ANTICIPATED DATE

/ /   TO   / /

ACTION LIST

⊘
⊘
⊘
⊘
⊘
⊘
⊘
⊘
⊘
⊘
⊘

Success!

ONCE COMPLETE, PLACE A CHECK HERE
TO TAKE IT OFF YOUR BUCKET LIST

RATE THIS ACTIVITY

★ ★ ★ ★ ★

28

ITEM #29:

SUMMARY: THIS WOULD BE F*CKING PERFECT FOR US BECAUSE...

_____

_____

_____

_____

_____

_____

_____

MAKE IT F*CKING HAPPEN: HOW? WHEN?

_____

_____

_____

_____

_____

_____

REVIEW   DATE COMPLETED: / /

WHAT HAPPENED? (PEOPLE MET, HIGH POINTS, EXPECTATIONS VS REALITY)

_____

_____

_____

_____

_____

_____

_____

_____

_____

_____

BUDGET

$

ANTICIPATED DATE

/ /   TO   / /

ACTION LIST

⊘
⊘
⊘
⊘
⊘
⊘
⊘
⊘
⊘
⊘
⊘

Success!

ONCE COMPLETE, PLACE A CHECK HERE
TO TAKE IT OFF YOUR BUCKET LIST

RATE THIS ACTIVITY

★ ★ ★ ★ ★

29

ITEM #30:

PRIORITY ★ ★ ★ ★ ★

SUMMARY: THIS WOULD BE F*CKING PERFECT FOR US BECAUSE...

_____

_____

_____

_____

_____

_____

MAKE IT F*CKING HAPPEN: HOW? WHEN?

_____

_____

_____

_____

_____

_____

BUDGET

$

ANTICIPATED DATE

/ /   TO   / /

ACTION LIST

⊘ _____
⊘ _____
⊘ _____
⊘ _____
⊘ _____
⊘ _____
⊘ _____
⊘ _____
⊘ _____
⊘ _____
⊘ _____

REVIEW

DATE COMPLETED: / /

WHAT HAPPENED? (PEOPLE MET, HIGH POINTS, EXPECTATIONS VS REALITY)

_____

_____

_____

_____

_____

_____

_____

_____

_____

Success!

✓

ONCE COMPLETE, PLACE A CHECK HERE
TO TAKE IT OFF YOUR BUCKET LIST

RATE THIS ACTIVITY

★ ★ ★ ★ ★

ITEM #31:

PRIORITY ★ ★ ★ ★ ★

SUMMARY: THIS WOULD BE F*CKING PERFECT FOR US BECAUSE...

_____

_____

_____

_____

_____

_____

_____

MAKE IT F*CKING HAPPEN: HOW? WHEN?

_____

_____

_____

_____

_____

_____

_____

REVIEW   DATE COMPLETED: / /

WHAT HAPPENED? (PEOPLE MET, HIGH POINTS, EXPECTATIONS VS REALITY)

_____

_____

_____

_____

_____

_____

_____

_____

_____

_____

BUDGET

$

ANTICIPATED DATE

/ /   TO   / /

ACTION LIST

⊘
⊘
⊘
⊘
⊘
⊘
⊘
⊘
⊘
⊘
⊘

Success!

ONCE COMPLETE, PLACE A CHECK HERE
TO TAKE IT OFF YOUR BUCKET LIST

RATE THIS ACTIVITY

★ ★ ★ ★ ★

31

ITEM #32:

PRIORITY ★ ★ ★ ★ ★

SUMMARY: THIS WOULD BE F*CKING PERFECT FOR US BECAUSE...

_____

_____

_____

_____

_____

_____

MAKE IT F*CKING HAPPEN: HOW? WHEN?

_____

_____

_____

_____

_____

_____

BUDGET

$

ANTICIPATED DATE

/ /   TO   / /

ACTION LIST

⊘ _____

⊘ _____

⊘ _____

⊘ _____

⊘ _____

⊘ _____

⊘ _____

⊘ _____

⊘ _____

⊘ _____

⊘ _____

REVIEW   DATE COMPLETED: / /

WHAT HAPPENED? (PEOPLE MET, HIGH POINTS, EXPECTATIONS VS REALITY)

_____

_____

_____

_____

_____

_____

_____

_____

_____

Success!

✓

ONCE COMPLETE, PLACE A CHECK HERE
TO TAKE IT OFF YOUR BUCKET LIST

RATE THIS ACTIVITY

★ ★ ★ ★ ★

ITEM #33:

PRIORITY ⭐ ⭐ ⭐ ⭐ ⭐

SUMMARY: THIS WOULD BE F*CKING PERFECT FOR US BECAUSE...

_____

_____

_____

_____

_____

_____

_____

MAKE IT F*CKING HAPPEN: HOW? WHEN?

_____

_____

_____

_____

_____

_____

REVIEW
DATE COMPLETED: / /

WHAT HAPPENED? (PEOPLE MET, HIGH POINTS, EXPECTATIONS VS REALITY)

_____

_____

_____

_____

_____

_____

_____

_____

_____

BUDGET
$

ANTICIPATED DATE
/ /   TO   / /

ACTION LIST

⊘
⊘
⊘
⊘
⊘
⊘
⊘
⊘
⊘
⊘
⊘

Success!

ONCE COMPLETE, PLACE A CHECK HERE
TO TAKE IT OFF YOUR BUCKET LIST

RATE THIS ACTIVITY

⭐ ⭐ ⭐ ⭐ ⭐

ITEM #34:

SUMMARY: THIS WOULD BE F*CKING PERFECT FOR US BECAUSE...

_____

_____

_____

_____

_____

_____

_____

MAKE IT F*CKING HAPPEN: HOW? WHEN?

_____

_____

_____

_____

_____

_____

BUDGET

$

ANTICIPATED DATE

/ /   TO   / /

ACTION LIST

⊘ _____
⊘ _____
⊘ _____
⊘ _____
⊘ _____
⊘ _____
⊘ _____
⊘ _____
⊘ _____
⊘ _____
⊘ _____

REVIEW

DATE COMPLETED: / /

WHAT HAPPENED? (PEOPLE MET, HIGH POINTS, EXPECTATIONS VS REALITY)

_____

_____

_____

_____

_____

_____

_____

_____

_____

Success!

✓

ONCE COMPLETE, PLACE A CHECK HERE
TO TAKE IT OFF YOUR BUCKET LIST

RATE THIS ACTIVITY

★ ★ ★ ★ ★

ITEM #35:

SUMMARY: THIS WOULD BE F*CKING PERFECT FOR US BECAUSE...

_____

_____

_____

_____

_____

_____

_____

MAKE IT F*CKING HAPPEN: HOW? WHEN?

_____

_____

_____

_____

_____

_____

_____

REVIEW

DATE COMPLETED: / /

WHAT HAPPENED? (PEOPLE MET, HIGH POINTS, EXPECTATIONS VS REALITY)

_____

_____

_____

_____

_____

_____

_____

_____

_____

BUDGET

$

ANTICIPATED DATE

/ /   TO   / /

ACTION LIST

⊘
⊘
⊘
⊘
⊘
⊘
⊘
⊘
⊘
⊘
⊘

Success!

ONCE COMPLETE, PLACE A CHECK HERE
TO TAKE IT OFF YOUR BUCKET LIST

RATE THIS ACTIVITY

★ ★ ★ ★ ★

ITEM #36:

PRIORITY ★ ★ ★ ★ ★

SUMMARY: THIS WOULD BE F*CKING PERFECT FOR US BECAUSE...

_____

_____

_____

_____

_____

_____

MAKE IT F*CKING HAPPEN: HOW? WHEN?

_____

_____

_____

_____

_____

_____

REVIEW

DATE COMPLETED: / /

WHAT HAPPENED? (PEOPLE MET, HIGH POINTS, EXPECTATIONS VS REALITY)

_____

_____

_____

_____

_____

_____

_____

_____

_____

_____

_____

BUDGET

$

ANTICIPATED DATE

/ /   TO   / /

ACTION LIST

- ⊘
- ⊘
- ⊘
- ⊘
- ⊘
- ⊘
- ⊘
- ⊘
- ⊘
- ⊘
- ⊘

Success!

✓

ONCE COMPLETE, PLACE A CHECK HERE
TO TAKE IT OFF YOUR BUCKET LIST

RATE THIS ACTIVITY

★ ★ ★ ★ ★

ITEM #37:

PRIORITY ★ ★ ★ ★ ★

SUMMARY: THIS WOULD BE F*CKING PERFECT FOR US BECAUSE...

_____

_____

_____

_____

_____

_____

MAKE IT F*CKING HAPPEN: HOW? WHEN?

_____

_____

_____

_____

_____

_____

REVIEW   DATE COMPLETED: / /

WHAT HAPPENED? (PEOPLE MET, HIGH POINTS, EXPECTATIONS VS REALITY)

_____

_____

_____

_____

_____

_____

_____

_____

_____

BUDGET
$

ANTICIPATED DATE
/ /   TO   / /

ACTION LIST

⊘
⊘
⊘
⊘
⊘
⊘
⊘
⊘
⊘
⊘
⊘

Success!

ONCE COMPLETE, PLACE A CHECK HERE
TO TAKE IT OFF YOUR BUCKET LIST

RATE THIS ACTIVITY

★ ★ ★ ★ ★

ITEM #38:

SUMMARY: THIS WOULD BE F*CKING PERFECT FOR US BECAUSE...

_____
_____
_____
_____
_____
_____
_____

BUDGET

$

ANTICIPATED DATE

/ /   TO   / /

ACTION LIST

⊘ _____
⊘ _____
⊘ _____
⊘ _____
⊘ _____
⊘ _____
⊘ _____
⊘ _____
⊘ _____
⊘ _____
⊘

MAKE IT F*CKING HAPPEN: HOW? WHEN?

_____
_____
_____
_____
_____
_____

REVIEW   DATE COMPLETED: / /

WHAT HAPPENED? (PEOPLE MET, HIGH POINTS, EXPECTATIONS VS REALITY)

_____
_____
_____
_____
_____
_____
_____
_____
_____
_____

Success!

✓

ONCE COMPLETE, PLACE A CHECK HERE
TO TAKE IT OFF YOUR BUCKET LIST

RATE THIS ACTIVITY

★ ★ ★ ★ ★

ITEM #39:

PRIORITY ★ ★ ★ ★ ★

SUMMARY: THIS WOULD BE F*CKING PERFECT FOR US BECAUSE...

_____

_____

_____

_____

_____

_____

_____

MAKE IT F*CKING HAPPEN: HOW? WHEN?

_____

_____

_____

_____

_____

_____

_____

REVIEW

DATE COMPLETED: / /

WHAT HAPPENED? (PEOPLE MET, HIGH POINTS, EXPECTATIONS VS REALITY)

_____

_____

_____

_____

_____

_____

_____

_____

_____

BUDGET

$

ANTICIPATED DATE

/ /   TO   / /

ACTION LIST

⊘
⊘
⊘
⊘
⊘
⊘
⊘
⊘
⊘
⊘
⊘

Success!

ONCE COMPLETE, PLACE A CHECK HERE
TO TAKE IT OFF YOUR BUCKET LIST

RATE THIS ACTIVITY

★ ★ ★ ★ ★

ITEM #40:

SUMMARY: THIS WOULD BE F*CKING PERFECT FOR US BECAUSE...

_____
_____
_____
_____
_____
_____
_____

MAKE IT F*CKING HAPPEN: HOW? WHEN?

_____
_____
_____
_____
_____
_____
_____

REVIEW   DATE COMPLETED: / /

WHAT HAPPENED? (PEOPLE MET, HIGH POINTS, EXPECTATIONS VS REALITY)

_____
_____
_____
_____
_____
_____
_____
_____
_____

BUDGET

$

ANTICIPATED DATE

/ /   TO   / /

ACTION LIST

⊘ _____
⊘ _____
⊘ _____
⊘ _____
⊘ _____
⊘ _____
⊘ _____
⊘ _____
⊘ _____
⊘ _____
⊘ _____

Success!

ONCE COMPLETE, PLACE A CHECK HERE
TO TAKE IT OFF YOUR BUCKET LIST

RATE THIS ACTIVITY

★ ★ ★ ★ ★

ITEM #41:

SUMMARY: THIS WOULD BE F*CKING PERFECT FOR US BECAUSE...

_____

_____

_____

_____

_____

_____

_____

MAKE IT F*CKING HAPPEN: HOW? WHEN?

_____

_____

_____

_____

_____

_____

_____

REVIEW

DATE COMPLETED: / /

WHAT HAPPENED? (PEOPLE MET, HIGH POINTS, EXPECTATIONS VS REALITY)

_____

_____

_____

_____

_____

_____

_____

_____

BUDGET

$

ANTICIPATED DATE

/ / TO / /

ACTION LIST

⊘

⊘

⊘

⊘

⊘

⊘

⊘

⊘

⊘

⊘

⊘

Success!

✓

ONCE COMPLETE, PLACE A CHECK HERE
TO TAKE IT OFF YOUR BUCKET LIST

RATE THIS ACTIVITY

★ ★ ★ ★ ★

ITEM #42:

SUMMARY: THIS WOULD BE F*CKING PERFECT FOR US BECAUSE...

_____

_____

_____

_____

_____

_____

_____

MAKE IT F*CKING HAPPEN: HOW? WHEN?

_____

_____

_____

_____

_____

_____

_____

REVIEW

DATE COMPLETED: / /

WHAT HAPPENED? (PEOPLE MET, HIGH POINTS, EXPECTATIONS VS REALITY)

_____

_____

_____

_____

_____

_____

_____

_____

_____

_____

BUDGET

$

ANTICIPATED DATE

/ /   TO   / /

ACTION LIST

- ⊘
- ⊘
- ⊘
- ⊘
- ⊘
- ⊘
- ⊘
- ⊘
- ⊘
- ⊘
- ⊘

Success!

✓

ONCE COMPLETE, PLACE A CHECK HERE
TO TAKE IT OFF YOUR BUCKET LIST

RATE THIS ACTIVITY

☆☆☆☆☆

ITEM #43:

SUMMARY: THIS WOULD BE F*CKING PERFECT FOR US BECAUSE...

_____
_____
_____
_____
_____
_____

BUDGET

$

ANTICIPATED DATE

/ /   TO   / /

ACTION LIST

- ⊘
- ⊘
- ⊘
- ⊘
- ⊘
- ⊘
- ⊘
- ⊘
- ⊘
- ⊘
- ⊘

MAKE IT F*CKING HAPPEN: HOW? WHEN?

_____
_____
_____
_____
_____
_____
_____

REVIEW

DATE COMPLETED: / /

WHAT HAPPENED? (PEOPLE MET, HIGH POINTS, EXPECTATIONS VS REALITY)

_____
_____
_____
_____
_____
_____
_____
_____

Success!

✓

ONCE COMPLETE, PLACE A CHECK HERE
TO TAKE IT OFF YOUR BUCKET LIST

RATE THIS ACTIVITY

★ ★ ★ ★ ★

ITEM #44:

PRIORITY ⭐⭐⭐⭐⭐

SUMMARY: THIS WOULD BE F*CKING PERFECT FOR US BECAUSE...

_____

_____

_____

_____

_____

_____

MAKE IT F*CKING HAPPEN: HOW? WHEN?

_____

_____

_____

_____

_____

_____

_____

REVIEW   DATE COMPLETED: / /

WHAT HAPPENED? (PEOPLE MET, HIGH POINTS, EXPECTATIONS VS REALITY)

_____

_____

_____

_____

_____

_____

_____

_____

_____

BUDGET

$

ANTICIPATED DATE

/ /   TO   / /

ACTION LIST

⊘
⊘
⊘
⊘
⊘
⊘
⊘
⊘
⊘
⊘
⊘

Success!

ONCE COMPLETE, PLACE A CHECK HERE
TO TAKE IT OFF YOUR BUCKET LIST

RATE THIS ACTIVITY

⭐⭐⭐⭐⭐

44

ITEM #45:

SUMMARY: THIS WOULD BE F*CKING PERFECT FOR US BECAUSE...

_____

_____

_____

_____

_____

_____

_____

MAKE IT F*CKING HAPPEN: HOW? WHEN?

_____

_____

_____

_____

_____

_____

_____

REVIEW
DATE COMPLETED: / /

WHAT HAPPENED? (PEOPLE MET, HIGH POINTS, EXPECTATIONS VS REALITY)

_____

_____

_____

_____

_____

_____

_____

_____

_____

_____

BUDGET

$

ANTICIPATED DATE

/ /   TO   / /

ACTION LIST

- ⊘
- ⊘
- ⊘
- ⊘
- ⊘
- ⊘
- ⊘
- ⊘
- ⊘
- ⊘
- ⊘

Success!

✓

ONCE COMPLETE, PLACE A CHECK HERE
TO TAKE IT OFF YOUR BUCKET LIST

RATE THIS ACTIVITY

★ ★ ★ ★ ★

ITEM #46:

SUMMARY: THIS WOULD BE F*CKING PERFECT FOR US BECAUSE...

_____
_____
_____
_____
_____
_____

MAKE IT F*CKING HAPPEN: HOW? WHEN?

_____
_____
_____
_____
_____
_____

REVIEW

DATE COMPLETED: /   /

WHAT HAPPENED? (PEOPLE MET, HIGH POINTS, EXPECTATIONS VS REALITY)

_____
_____
_____
_____
_____
_____
_____
_____
_____
_____

BUDGET

$

ANTICIPATED DATE

/   /   TO   /   /

ACTION LIST

- ⊘
- ⊘
- ⊘
- ⊘
- ⊘
- ⊘
- ⊘
- ⊘
- ⊘
- ⊘
- ⊘

Success!

✓

ONCE COMPLETE, PLACE A CHECK HERE
TO TAKE IT OFF YOUR BUCKET LIST

RATE THIS ACTIVITY

★ ★ ★ ★ ★

ITEM #47:

PRIORITY ⭐ ⭐ ⭐ ⭐ ⭐

SUMMARY: THIS WOULD BE F*CKING PERFECT FOR US BECAUSE...

_____

_____

_____

_____

_____

_____

MAKE IT F*CKING HAPPEN: HOW? WHEN?

_____

_____

_____

_____

_____

_____

REVIEW

DATE COMPLETED: / /

WHAT HAPPENED? (PEOPLE MET, HIGH POINTS, EXPECTATIONS VS REALITY)

_____

_____

_____

_____

_____

_____

_____

_____

_____

BUDGET

$

ANTICIPATED DATE

/ /   TO   / /

ACTION LIST

- ⊘
- ⊘
- ⊘
- ⊘
- ⊘
- ⊘
- ⊘
- ⊘
- ⊘
- ⊘
- ⊘

Success!

ONCE COMPLETE, PLACE A CHECK HERE
TO TAKE IT OFF YOUR BUCKET LIST

RATE THIS ACTIVITY

⭐ ⭐ ⭐ ⭐ ⭐

ITEM #48:

SUMMARY: THIS WOULD BE F*CKING PERFECT FOR US BECAUSE...

_____

_____

_____

_____

_____

_____

_____

MAKE IT F*CKING HAPPEN: HOW? WHEN?

_____

_____

_____

_____

_____

_____

_____

REVIEW

DATE COMPLETED: / /

WHAT HAPPENED? (PEOPLE MET, HIGH POINTS, EXPECTATIONS VS REALITY)

_____

_____

_____

_____

_____

_____

_____

_____

_____

_____

BUDGET

$

ANTICIPATED DATE

/ / TO / /

ACTION LIST

⊘
⊘
⊘
⊘
⊘
⊘
⊘
⊘
⊘
⊘
⊘

Success!

✓

ONCE COMPLETE, PLACE A CHECK HERE
TO TAKE IT OFF YOUR BUCKET LIST

RATE THIS ACTIVITY

★ ★ ★ ★ ★

48

ITEM #49:

SUMMARY: THIS WOULD BE F*CKING PERFECT FOR US BECAUSE...

_____

_____

_____

_____

_____

_____

MAKE IT F*CKING HAPPEN: HOW? WHEN?

_____

_____

_____

_____

_____

_____

REVIEW

DATE COMPLETED: / /

WHAT HAPPENED? (PEOPLE MET, HIGH POINTS, EXPECTATIONS VS REALITY)

_____

_____

_____

_____

_____

_____

_____

_____

BUDGET

$

ANTICIPATED DATE

/ /   TO   / /

ACTION LIST

⊘
⊘
⊘
⊘
⊘
⊘
⊘
⊘
⊘
⊘
⊘

Success!

ONCE COMPLETE, PLACE A CHECK HERE
TO TAKE IT OFF YOUR BUCKET LIST

RATE THIS ACTIVITY

★ ★ ★ ★ ★

ITEM #50:

SUMMARY: THIS WOULD BE F*CKING PERFECT FOR US BECAUSE...

_____

_____

_____

_____

_____

_____

MAKE IT F*CKING HAPPEN: HOW? WHEN?

_____

_____

_____

_____

_____

_____

REVIEW
DATE COMPLETED: / /

WHAT HAPPENED? (PEOPLE MET, HIGH POINTS, EXPECTATIONS VS REALITY)

_____

_____

_____

_____

_____

_____

_____

_____

BUDGET

$

ANTICIPATED DATE

/ /   TO   / /

ACTION LIST

- ⊘
- ⊘
- ⊘
- ⊘
- ⊘
- ⊘
- ⊘
- ⊘
- ⊘
- ⊘
- ⊘

Success!

ONCE COMPLETE, PLACE A CHECK HERE
TO TAKE IT OFF YOUR BUCKET LIST

RATE THIS ACTIVITY

★ ★ ★ ★ ★

ITEM #51:

SUMMARY: THIS WOULD BE F*CKING PERFECT FOR US BECAUSE...

_____

_____

_____

_____

_____

_____

_____

MAKE IT F*CKING HAPPEN: HOW? WHEN?

_____

_____

_____

_____

_____

_____

_____

REVIEW

DATE COMPLETED: / /

WHAT HAPPENED? (PEOPLE MET, HIGH POINTS, EXPECTATIONS VS REALITY)

_____

_____

_____

_____

_____

_____

_____

_____

_____

BUDGET

$

ANTICIPATED DATE

/ /   TO   / /

ACTION LIST

⊘
⊘
⊘
⊘
⊘
⊘
⊘
⊘
⊘
⊘
⊘

Success!

✓

ONCE COMPLETE, PLACE A CHECK HERE
TO TAKE IT OFF YOUR BUCKET LIST

RATE THIS ACTIVITY

⭐ ⭐ ⭐ ⭐ ⭐

ITEM #52:

SUMMARY: THIS WOULD BE F*CKING PERFECT FOR US BECAUSE...

_____

_____

_____

_____

_____

_____

_____

MAKE IT F*CKING HAPPEN: HOW? WHEN?

_____

_____

_____

_____

_____

_____

_____

REVIEW

DATE COMPLETED: /   /

WHAT HAPPENED? (PEOPLE MET, HIGH POINTS, EXPECTATIONS VS REALITY)

_____

_____

_____

_____

_____

_____

_____

_____

_____

_____

_____

BUDGET

$

ANTICIPATED DATE

/   /   TO   /   /

ACTION LIST

- ⊘
- ⊘
- ⊘
- ⊘
- ⊘
- ⊘
- ⊘
- ⊘
- ⊘
- ⊘
- ⊘

Success!

ONCE COMPLETE, PLACE A CHECK HERE
TO TAKE IT OFF YOUR BUCKET LIST

RATE THIS ACTIVITY

★ ★ ★ ★ ★

ITEM #53:

SUMMARY: THIS WOULD BE F*CKING PERFECT FOR US BECAUSE...

_____

_____

_____

_____

_____

_____

MAKE IT F*CKING HAPPEN: HOW? WHEN?

_____

_____

_____

_____

_____

_____

REVIEW

DATE COMPLETED: / /

WHAT HAPPENED? (PEOPLE MET, HIGH POINTS, EXPECTATIONS VS REALITY)

_____

_____

_____

_____

_____

_____

_____

_____

_____

_____

_____

BUDGET

$

ANTICIPATED DATE

/ / TO / /

ACTION LIST

- ⊘
- ⊘
- ⊘
- ⊘
- ⊘
- ⊘
- ⊘
- ⊘
- ⊘
- ⊘
- ⊘

Success!

ONCE COMPLETE, PLACE A CHECK HERE
TO TAKE IT OFF YOUR BUCKET LIST

RATE THIS ACTIVITY

★ ★ ★ ★ ★

ITEM #54:

SUMMARY: THIS WOULD BE F*CKING PERFECT FOR US BECAUSE...

_____

_____

_____

_____

_____

_____

MAKE IT F*CKING HAPPEN: HOW? WHEN?

_____

_____

_____

_____

_____

_____

REVIEW

DATE COMPLETED: /   /

WHAT HAPPENED? (PEOPLE MET, HIGH POINTS, EXPECTATIONS VS REALITY)

_____

_____

_____

_____

_____

_____

_____

_____

BUDGET

$

ANTICIPATED DATE

/   /   TO   /   /

ACTION LIST

- ⊘
- ⊘
- ⊘
- ⊘
- ⊘
- ⊘
- ⊘
- ⊘
- ⊘
- ⊘
- ⊘

Success!

✓

ONCE COMPLETE, PLACE A CHECK HERE
TO TAKE IT OFF YOUR BUCKET LIST

RATE THIS ACTIVITY

★ ★ ★ ★ ★

ITEM #55:

SUMMARY: THIS WOULD BE F*CKING PERFECT FOR US BECAUSE...

_____
_____
_____
_____
_____
_____

MAKE IT F*CKING HAPPEN: HOW? WHEN?

_____
_____
_____
_____
_____
_____

REVIEW

DATE COMPLETED: / /

WHAT HAPPENED? (PEOPLE MET, HIGH POINTS, EXPECTATIONS VS REALITY)

_____
_____
_____
_____
_____
_____
_____
_____

BUDGET

$

ANTICIPATED DATE

/ /   TO   / /

ACTION LIST

⊘
⊘
⊘
⊘
⊘
⊘
⊘
⊘
⊘
⊘
⊘

Success!

✓

ONCE COMPLETE, PLACE A CHECK HERE
TO TAKE IT OFF YOUR BUCKET LIST

RATE THIS ACTIVITY

★ ★ ★ ★ ★

ITEM #56: _____

SUMMARY: THIS WOULD BE F*CKING PERFECT FOR US BECAUSE...

_____
_____
_____
_____
_____
_____
_____

MAKE IT F*CKING HAPPEN: HOW? WHEN?

_____
_____
_____
_____
_____
_____
_____

REVIEW

DATE COMPLETED: / /

WHAT HAPPENED? (PEOPLE MET, HIGH POINTS, EXPECTATIONS VS REALITY)

_____
_____
_____
_____
_____
_____
_____
_____
_____
_____

BUDGET
$

ANTICIPATED DATE
/ /   TO   / /

ACTION LIST

⊘
⊘
⊘
⊘
⊘
⊘
⊘
⊘
⊘
⊘
⊘

Success!

ONCE COMPLETE, PLACE A CHECK HERE
TO TAKE IT OFF YOUR BUCKET LIST

RATE THIS ACTIVITY

★ ★ ★ ★ ★

ITEM #57:

SUMMARY: THIS WOULD BE F*CKING PERFECT FOR US BECAUSE...

_____

_____

_____

_____

_____

_____

MAKE IT F*CKING HAPPEN: HOW? WHEN?

_____

_____

_____

_____

_____

_____

REVIEW
DATE COMPLETED: /   /

WHAT HAPPENED? (PEOPLE MET, HIGH POINTS, EXPECTATIONS VS REALITY)

_____

_____

_____

_____

_____

_____

_____

_____

BUDGET

$

ANTICIPATED DATE

/   /   TO   /   /

ACTION LIST

- ⊘
- ⊘
- ⊘
- ⊘
- ⊘
- ⊘
- ⊘
- ⊘
- ⊘
- ⊘
- ⊘

Success!

✓

ONCE COMPLETE, PLACE A CHECK HERE
TO TAKE IT OFF YOUR BUCKET LIST

RATE THIS ACTIVITY

★★★★★

ITEM #58:

SUMMARY: THIS WOULD BE F*CKING PERFECT FOR US BECAUSE...

_____

_____

_____

_____

_____

_____

_____

MAKE IT F*CKING HAPPEN: HOW? WHEN?

_____

_____

_____

_____

_____

_____

BUDGET

$

ANTICIPATED DATE

/ /   TO   / /

ACTION LIST

⊘ _____

⊘ _____

⊘ _____

⊘ _____

⊘ _____

⊘ _____

⊘ _____

⊘ _____

⊘ _____

⊘ _____

⊘ _____

REVIEW

DATE COMPLETED: / /

WHAT HAPPENED? (PEOPLE MET, HIGH POINTS, EXPECTATIONS VS REALITY)

_____

_____

_____

_____

_____

_____

_____

_____

_____

_____

_____

Success!

✓

ONCE COMPLETE, PLACE A CHECK HERE
TO TAKE IT OFF YOUR BUCKET LIST

RATE THIS ACTIVITY

★ ★ ★ ★ ★

ITEM #59:

SUMMARY: THIS WOULD BE F*CKING PERFECT FOR US BECAUSE...

_____

_____

_____

_____

_____

_____

_____

MAKE IT F*CKING HAPPEN: HOW? WHEN?

_____

_____

_____

_____

_____

_____

_____

BUDGET

$

ANTICIPATED DATE

/ /   TO   / /

ACTION LIST

⊘ _____
⊘ _____
⊘ _____
⊘ _____
⊘ _____
⊘ _____
⊘ _____
⊘ _____
⊘ _____
⊘ _____
⊘ _____

REVIEW

DATE COMPLETED: / /

WHAT HAPPENED? (PEOPLE MET, HIGH POINTS, EXPECTATIONS VS REALITY)

_____

_____

_____

_____

_____

_____

_____

_____

_____

_____

Success!

ONCE COMPLETE, PLACE A CHECK HERE
TO TAKE IT OFF YOUR BUCKET LIST

RATE THIS ACTIVITY

★ ★ ★ ★ ★

ITEM #60:

SUMMARY: THIS WOULD BE F*CKING PERFECT FOR US BECAUSE...

_____
_____
_____
_____
_____
_____
_____

MAKE IT F*CKING HAPPEN: HOW? WHEN?

_____
_____
_____
_____
_____
_____
_____

REVIEW

DATE COMPLETED: / /

WHAT HAPPENED? (PEOPLE MET, HIGH POINTS, EXPECTATIONS VS REALITY)

_____
_____
_____
_____
_____
_____
_____
_____
_____
_____
_____

BUDGET
$

ANTICIPATED DATE
/ / TO / /

ACTION LIST

- ⊘
- ⊘
- ⊘
- ⊘
- ⊘
- ⊘
- ⊘
- ⊘
- ⊘
- ⊘
- ⊘

Success!

ONCE COMPLETE, PLACE A CHECK HERE
TO TAKE IT OFF YOUR BUCKET LIST

RATE THIS ACTIVITY

★ ★ ★ ★ ★

60

ITEM #61:

SUMMARY: THIS WOULD BE F*CKING PERFECT FOR US BECAUSE...

_____

_____

_____

_____

_____

_____

_____

MAKE IT F*CKING HAPPEN: HOW? WHEN?

_____

_____

_____

_____

_____

_____

_____

BUDGET

$

ANTICIPATED DATE

/ /   TO   / /

ACTION LIST

⊘ _____
⊘ _____
⊘ _____
⊘ _____
⊘ _____
⊘ _____
⊘ _____
⊘ _____
⊘ _____
⊘ _____
⊘ _____

REVIEW

DATE COMPLETED: / /

WHAT HAPPENED? (PEOPLE MET, HIGH POINTS, EXPECTATIONS VS REALITY)

_____

_____

_____

_____

_____

_____

_____

_____

_____

_____

_____

Success!

✓

ONCE COMPLETE, PLACE A CHECK HERE
TO TAKE IT OFF YOUR BUCKET LIST

RATE THIS ACTIVITY

★ ★ ★ ★ ★

ITEM #62:

SUMMARY: THIS WOULD BE F*CKING PERFECT FOR US BECAUSE...

_____
_____
_____
_____
_____
_____

MAKE IT F*CKING HAPPEN: HOW? WHEN?

_____
_____
_____
_____
_____
_____

REVIEW

DATE COMPLETED: / /

WHAT HAPPENED? (PEOPLE MET, HIGH POINTS, EXPECTATIONS VS REALITY)

_____
_____
_____
_____
_____
_____
_____
_____
_____
_____

BUDGET

$

ANTICIPATED DATE

/ /   TO   / /

ACTION LIST

- ⊘
- ⊘
- ⊘
- ⊘
- ⊘
- ⊘
- ⊘
- ⊘
- ⊘
- ⊘
- ⊘

Success!

ONCE COMPLETE, PLACE A CHECK HERE
TO TAKE IT OFF YOUR BUCKET LIST

RATE THIS ACTIVITY

★ ★ ★ ★ ★

ITEM #63:

PRIORITY ★ ★ ★ ★ ★

SUMMARY: THIS WOULD BE F*CKING PERFECT FOR US BECAUSE...

_____
_____
_____
_____
_____
_____
_____

MAKE IT F*CKING HAPPEN: HOW? WHEN?

_____
_____
_____
_____
_____
_____

REVIEW   DATE COMPLETED: / /

WHAT HAPPENED? (PEOPLE MET, HIGH POINTS, EXPECTATIONS VS REALITY)

_____
_____
_____
_____
_____
_____
_____
_____
_____

BUDGET

$

ANTICIPATED DATE

/ /   TO   / /

ACTION LIST

⊘
⊘
⊘
⊘
⊘
⊘
⊘
⊘
⊘
⊘
⊘

Success!

ONCE COMPLETE, PLACE A CHECK HERE
TO TAKE IT OFF YOUR BUCKET LIST

RATE THIS ACTIVITY

★ ★ ★ ★ ★

ITEM #64:

PRIORITY ★★★★★

SUMMARY: THIS WOULD BE F*CKING PERFECT FOR US BECAUSE...

_____

_____

_____

_____

_____

_____

MAKE IT F*CKING HAPPEN: HOW? WHEN?

_____

_____

_____

_____

_____

_____

BUDGET

$

ANTICIPATED DATE

/ /   TO   / /

ACTION LIST

⊘ _____

⊘ _____

⊘ _____

⊘ _____

⊘ _____

⊘ _____

⊘ _____

⊘ _____

⊘ _____

⊘ _____

⊘ _____

REVIEW   DATE COMPLETED: / /

WHAT HAPPENED? (PEOPLE MET, HIGH POINTS, EXPECTATIONS VS REALITY)

_____

_____

_____

_____

_____

_____

_____

_____

_____

_____

Success! ✓

ONCE COMPLETE, PLACE A CHECK HERE
TO TAKE IT OFF YOUR BUCKET LIST

RATE THIS ACTIVITY

★★★★★

ITEM #65:

SUMMARY: THIS WOULD BE F*CKING PERFECT FOR US BECAUSE...

_____

_____

_____

_____

_____

_____

_____

MAKE IT F*CKING HAPPEN: HOW? WHEN?

_____

_____

_____

_____

_____

_____

REVIEW

DATE COMPLETED: / /

WHAT HAPPENED? (PEOPLE MET, HIGH POINTS, EXPECTATIONS VS REALITY)

_____

_____

_____

_____

_____

_____

_____

_____

_____

BUDGET

$

ANTICIPATED DATE

/ /   TO   / /

ACTION LIST

⊘

⊘

⊘

⊘

⊘

⊘

⊘

⊘

⊘

⊘

⊘

Success!

ONCE COMPLETE, PLACE A CHECK HERE
TO TAKE IT OFF YOUR BUCKET LIST

RATE THIS ACTIVITY

★ ★ ★ ★ ★

ITEM #66:

SUMMARY: THIS WOULD BE F*CKING PERFECT FOR US BECAUSE...

_____

_____

_____

_____

_____

_____

_____

MAKE IT F*CKING HAPPEN: HOW? WHEN?

_____

_____

_____

_____

_____

_____

_____

REVIEW

DATE COMPLETED: / /

WHAT HAPPENED? (PEOPLE MET, HIGH POINTS, EXPECTATIONS VS REALITY)

_____

_____

_____

_____

_____

_____

_____

_____

_____

_____

BUDGET

$

ANTICIPATED DATE

/ /   TO   / /

ACTION LIST

- ⊘
- ⊘
- ⊘
- ⊘
- ⊘
- ⊘
- ⊘
- ⊘
- ⊘
- ⊘
- ⊘

Success!

ONCE COMPLETE, PLACE A CHECK HERE
TO TAKE IT OFF YOUR BUCKET LIST

RATE THIS ACTIVITY

★ ★ ★ ★ ★

ITEM #67:

PRIORITY ★ ★ ★ ★ ★ ★

SUMMARY: THIS WOULD BE F*CKING PERFECT FOR US BECAUSE...

_____

_____

_____

_____

_____

_____

_____

MAKE IT F*CKING HAPPEN: HOW? WHEN?

_____

_____

_____

_____

_____

_____

_____

BUDGET
$

ANTICIPATED DATE
/ /   TO   / /

ACTION LIST

⊘ _____
⊘ _____
⊘ _____
⊘ _____
⊘ _____
⊘ _____
⊘ _____
⊘ _____
⊘ _____
⊘ _____
⊘ _____

REVIEW

DATE COMPLETED: / /

WHAT HAPPENED? (PEOPLE MET, HIGH POINTS, EXPECTATIONS VS REALITY)

_____

_____

_____

_____

_____

_____

_____

_____

_____

Success!

ONCE COMPLETE, PLACE A CHECK HERE
TO TAKE IT OFF YOUR BUCKET LIST

RATE THIS ACTIVITY

★ ★ ★ ★ ★

ITEM #68:

SUMMARY: THIS WOULD BE F*CKING PERFECT FOR US BECAUSE...

_____
_____
_____
_____
_____
_____
_____

BUDGET

$

ANTICIPATED DATE

/ /   TO   / /

ACTION LIST

⊘
⊘
⊘
⊘
⊘
⊘
⊘
⊘
⊘
⊘
⊘

MAKE IT F*CKING HAPPEN: HOW? WHEN?

_____
_____
_____
_____
_____
_____
_____

REVIEW

DATE COMPLETED: / /

WHAT HAPPENED? (PEOPLE MET, HIGH POINTS, EXPECTATIONS VS REALITY)

_____
_____
_____
_____
_____
_____
_____
_____
_____
_____

Success!

ONCE COMPLETE, PLACE A CHECK HERE
TO TAKE IT OFF YOUR BUCKET LIST

RATE THIS ACTIVITY

★ ★ ★ ★ ★

ITEM #69:

SUMMARY: THIS WOULD BE F*CKING PERFECT FOR US BECAUSE...

_____

_____

_____

_____

_____

_____

BUDGET

$

ANTICIPATED DATE

/ /   TO   / /

ACTION LIST

- ⊘
- ⊘
- ⊘
- ⊘
- ⊘
- ⊘
- ⊘
- ⊘
- ⊘
- ⊘
- ⊘

MAKE IT F*CKING HAPPEN: HOW? WHEN?

_____

_____

_____

_____

_____

_____

REVIEW

DATE COMPLETED: / /

WHAT HAPPENED? (PEOPLE MET, HIGH POINTS, EXPECTATIONS VS REALITY)

_____

_____

_____

_____

_____

_____

_____

_____

Success!

ONCE COMPLETE, PLACE A CHECK HERE
TO TAKE IT OFF YOUR BUCKET LIST

RATE THIS ACTIVITY

★ ★ ★ ★ ★

ITEM #70: _____

SUMMARY: THIS WOULD BE F*CKING PERFECT FOR US BECAUSE...

_____
_____
_____
_____
_____
_____
_____

MAKE IT F*CKING HAPPEN: HOW? WHEN?

_____
_____
_____
_____
_____
_____
_____

REVIEW

DATE COMPLETED: / /

WHAT HAPPENED? (PEOPLE MET, HIGH POINTS, EXPECTATIONS VS REALITY)

_____
_____
_____
_____
_____
_____
_____
_____
_____

BUDGET

$

ANTICIPATED DATE

/ / TO / /

ACTION LIST

- ⊘
- ⊘
- ⊘
- ⊘
- ⊘
- ⊘
- ⊘
- ⊘
- ⊘
- ⊘
- ⊘

Success!

✓

ONCE COMPLETE, PLACE A CHECK HERE
TO TAKE IT OFF YOUR BUCKET LIST

RATE THIS ACTIVITY

★ ★ ★ ★ ★

ITEM #71:

SUMMARY: THIS WOULD BE F*CKING PERFECT FOR US BECAUSE...

_____

_____

_____

_____

_____

_____

MAKE IT F*CKING HAPPEN: HOW? WHEN?

_____

_____

_____

_____

_____

_____

REVIEW
DATE COMPLETED: / /

WHAT HAPPENED? (PEOPLE MET, HIGH POINTS, EXPECTATIONS VS REALITY)

_____

_____

_____

_____

_____

_____

_____

_____

BUDGET

$

ANTICIPATED DATE

/ /   TO   / /

ACTION LIST

- ⊘
- ⊘
- ⊘
- ⊘
- ⊘
- ⊘
- ⊘
- ⊘
- ⊘
- ⊘
- ⊘

Success!

ONCE COMPLETE, PLACE A CHECK HERE
TO TAKE IT OFF YOUR BUCKET LIST

RATE THIS ACTIVITY

★ ★ ★ ★ ★ ★

ITEM #72:

SUMMARY: THIS WOULD BE F*CKING PERFECT FOR US BECAUSE...

_____
_____
_____
_____
_____
_____
_____

MAKE IT F*CKING HAPPEN: HOW? WHEN?

_____
_____
_____
_____
_____
_____
_____

REVIEW

DATE COMPLETED: / /

WHAT HAPPENED? (PEOPLE MET, HIGH POINTS, EXPECTATIONS VS REALITY)

_____
_____
_____
_____
_____
_____
_____
_____
_____
_____

BUDGET

$

ANTICIPATED DATE

/ /   TO   / /

ACTION LIST

- ⊘
- ⊘
- ⊘
- ⊘
- ⊘
- ⊘
- ⊘
- ⊘
- ⊘
- ⊘
- ⊘

Success!

ONCE COMPLETE, PLACE A CHECK HERE
TO TAKE IT OFF YOUR BUCKET LIST

RATE THIS ACTIVITY

★ ★ ★ ★ ★

ITEM #73:

SUMMARY: THIS WOULD BE F*CKING PERFECT FOR US BECAUSE...

_____

_____

_____

_____

_____

_____

MAKE IT F*CKING HAPPEN: HOW? WHEN?

_____

_____

_____

_____

_____

_____

REVIEW

DATE COMPLETED: / /

WHAT HAPPENED? (PEOPLE MET, HIGH POINTS, EXPECTATIONS VS REALITY)

_____

_____

_____

_____

_____

_____

_____

_____

BUDGET

$

ANTICIPATED DATE

/ /   TO   / /

ACTION LIST

- ⊘
- ⊘
- ⊘
- ⊘
- ⊘
- ⊘
- ⊘
- ⊘
- ⊘
- ⊘
- ⊘

Success!

✓

ONCE COMPLETE, PLACE A CHECK HERE
TO TAKE IT OFF YOUR BUCKET LIST

RATE THIS ACTIVITY

☆ ☆ ☆ ☆ ☆

ITEM #74:

SUMMARY: THIS WOULD BE F*CKING PERFECT FOR US BECAUSE...

_____

_____

_____

_____

_____

_____

MAKE IT F*CKING HAPPEN: HOW? WHEN?

_____

_____

_____

_____

_____

REVIEW   DATE COMPLETED: / /

WHAT HAPPENED? (PEOPLE MET, HIGH POINTS, EXPECTATIONS VS REALITY)

_____

_____

_____

_____

_____

_____

_____

_____

_____

BUDGET

$

ANTICIPATED DATE

/ /   TO   / /

ACTION LIST

- ⊘
- ⊘
- ⊘
- ⊘
- ⊘
- ⊘
- ⊘
- ⊘
- ⊘
- ⊘
- ⊘

Success!

ONCE COMPLETE, PLACE A CHECK HERE
TO TAKE IT OFF YOUR BUCKET LIST

RATE THIS ACTIVITY

☆☆☆☆☆

ITEM #75:

SUMMARY: THIS WOULD BE F*CKING PERFECT FOR US BECAUSE...

_____
_____
_____
_____
_____
_____

MAKE IT F*CKING HAPPEN: HOW? WHEN?

_____
_____
_____
_____
_____
_____

REVIEW

DATE COMPLETED: / /

WHAT HAPPENED? (PEOPLE MET, HIGH POINTS, EXPECTATIONS VS REALITY)

_____
_____
_____
_____
_____
_____
_____
_____
_____

BUDGET

$

ANTICIPATED DATE

/ /   TO   / /

ACTION LIST

- ⊘
- ⊘
- ⊘
- ⊘
- ⊘
- ⊘
- ⊘
- ⊘
- ⊘
- ⊘
- ⊘

Success!

ONCE COMPLETE, PLACE A CHECK HERE
TO TAKE IT OFF YOUR BUCKET LIST

RATE THIS ACTIVITY

★ ★ ★ ★ ★

ITEM #76:

SUMMARY: THIS WOULD BE F*CKING PERFECT FOR US BECAUSE...

_____
_____
_____
_____
_____
_____
_____

MAKE IT F*CKING HAPPEN: HOW? WHEN?

_____
_____
_____
_____
_____
_____

REVIEW   DATE COMPLETED: / /

WHAT HAPPENED? (PEOPLE MET, HIGH POINTS, EXPECTATIONS VS REALITY)

_____
_____
_____
_____
_____
_____
_____
_____
_____
_____

BUDGET

$

ANTICIPATED DATE

/ /   TO   / /

ACTION LIST

- ⊘
- ⊘
- ⊘
- ⊘
- ⊘
- ⊘
- ⊘
- ⊘
- ⊘
- ⊘
- ⊘

Success!

✓

ONCE COMPLETE, PLACE A CHECK HERE
TO TAKE IT OFF YOUR BUCKET LIST

RATE THIS ACTIVITY

★ ★ ★ ★ ★

ITEM #77:

SUMMARY: THIS WOULD BE F*CKING PERFECT FOR US BECAUSE...

_____

_____

_____

_____

_____

_____

_____

MAKE IT F*CKING HAPPEN: HOW? WHEN?

_____

_____

_____

_____

_____

_____

_____

REVIEW   DATE COMPLETED: / /

WHAT HAPPENED? (PEOPLE MET, HIGH POINTS, EXPECTATIONS VS REALITY)

_____

_____

_____

_____

_____

_____

_____

_____

_____

BUDGET

$

ANTICIPATED DATE

/ /   TO   / /

ACTION LIST

⊘

⊘

⊘

⊘

⊘

⊘

⊘

⊘

⊘

⊘

⊘

Success!

✓

ONCE COMPLETE, PLACE A CHECK HERE
TO TAKE IT OFF YOUR BUCKET LIST

RATE THIS ACTIVITY

★ ★ ★ ★ ★

ITEM #78:

SUMMARY: THIS WOULD BE F*CKING PERFECT FOR US BECAUSE...

_____

_____

_____

_____

_____

_____

MAKE IT F*CKING HAPPEN: HOW? WHEN?

_____

_____

_____

_____

_____

_____

REVIEW

DATE COMPLETED: / /

WHAT HAPPENED? (PEOPLE MET, HIGH POINTS, EXPECTATIONS VS REALITY)

_____

_____

_____

_____

_____

_____

_____

_____

_____

BUDGET

$

ANTICIPATED DATE

/ / TO / /

ACTION LIST

⊘
⊘
⊘
⊘
⊘
⊘
⊘
⊘
⊘
⊘
⊘

Success!

ONCE COMPLETE, PLACE A CHECK HERE
TO TAKE IT OFF YOUR BUCKET LIST

RATE THIS ACTIVITY

★ ★ ★ ★ ★

ITEM #79:

SUMMARY: THIS WOULD BE F*CKING PERFECT FOR US BECAUSE...

_____

_____

_____

_____

_____

_____

MAKE IT F*CKING HAPPEN: HOW? WHEN?

_____

_____

_____

_____

_____

_____

REVIEW   DATE COMPLETED: / /

WHAT HAPPENED? (PEOPLE MET, HIGH POINTS, EXPECTATIONS VS REALITY)

_____

_____

_____

_____

_____

_____

_____

_____

BUDGET
$

ANTICIPATED DATE
/ /   TO   / /

ACTION LIST

⊘
⊘
⊘
⊘
⊘
⊘
⊘
⊘
⊘
⊘
⊘

Success!

✓

ONCE COMPLETE, PLACE A CHECK HERE
TO TAKE IT OFF YOUR BUCKET LIST

RATE THIS ACTIVITY

★ ★ ★ ★ ★

ITEM #80:

PRIORITY ⭐⭐⭐⭐⭐⭐

SUMMARY: THIS WOULD BE F*CKING PERFECT FOR US BECAUSE...

_____
_____
_____
_____
_____
_____
_____

MAKE IT F*CKING HAPPEN: HOW? WHEN?

_____
_____
_____
_____
_____
_____
_____

REVIEW

DATE COMPLETED: / /

WHAT HAPPENED? (PEOPLE MET, HIGH POINTS, EXPECTATIONS VS REALITY)

_____
_____
_____
_____
_____
_____
_____
_____
_____

BUDGET

$

ANTICIPATED DATE

/ / TO / /

ACTION LIST

- ⊘
- ⊘
- ⊘
- ⊘
- ⊘
- ⊘
- ⊘
- ⊘
- ⊘
- ⊘
- ⊘

Success!

✓

ONCE COMPLETE, PLACE A CHECK HERE
TO TAKE IT OFF YOUR BUCKET LIST

RATE THIS ACTIVITY

⭐⭐⭐⭐⭐

ITEM #81:

SUMMARY: THIS WOULD BE F*CKING PERFECT FOR US BECAUSE...

_____
_____
_____
_____
_____
_____
_____

MAKE IT F*CKING HAPPEN: HOW? WHEN?

_____
_____
_____
_____
_____
_____
_____

REVIEW   DATE COMPLETED: / /

WHAT HAPPENED? (PEOPLE MET, HIGH POINTS, EXPECTATIONS VS REALITY)

_____
_____
_____
_____
_____
_____
_____
_____

BUDGET

$

ANTICIPATED DATE

/ /   TO   / /

ACTION LIST

⊘
⊘
⊘
⊘
⊘
⊘
⊘
⊘
⊘
⊘
⊘

Success!

ONCE COMPLETE, PLACE A CHECK HERE
TO TAKE IT OFF YOUR BUCKET LIST

RATE THIS ACTIVITY

★ ★ ★ ★ ★

ITEM #82:

PRIORITY ★ ★ ★ ★ ★

SUMMARY: THIS WOULD BE F*CKING PERFECT FOR US BECAUSE...

_____
_____
_____
_____
_____
_____
_____

MAKE IT F*CKING HAPPEN: HOW? WHEN?

_____
_____
_____
_____
_____
_____
_____

REVIEW

DATE COMPLETED: / /

WHAT HAPPENED? (PEOPLE MET, HIGH POINTS, EXPECTATIONS VS REALITY)

_____
_____
_____
_____
_____
_____
_____
_____
_____

BUDGET

$

ANTICIPATED DATE

/ / TO / /

ACTION LIST

- ⊘
- ⊘
- ⊘
- ⊘
- ⊘
- ⊘
- ⊘
- ⊘
- ⊘
- ⊘
- ⊘

Success!

✓

ONCE COMPLETE, PLACE A CHECK HERE
TO TAKE IT OFF YOUR BUCKET LIST

RATE THIS ACTIVITY

★ ★ ★ ★ ★

ITEM #83:

SUMMARY: THIS WOULD BE F*CKING PERFECT FOR US BECAUSE...

_____

_____

_____

_____

_____

MAKE IT F*CKING HAPPEN: HOW? WHEN?

_____

_____

_____

_____

_____

BUDGET

$

ANTICIPATED DATE

/ /　TO　/ /

ACTION LIST

⊘ _____

⊘ _____

⊘ _____

⊘ _____

⊘ _____

⊘ _____

⊘ _____

⊘ _____

⊘ _____

⊘ _____

⊘ _____

REVIEW

DATE COMPLETED:　/ /

WHAT HAPPENED? (PEOPLE MET, HIGH POINTS, EXPECTATIONS VS REALITY)

_____

_____

_____

_____

_____

_____

Success!

ONCE COMPLETE, PLACE A CHECK HERE
TO TAKE IT OFF YOUR BUCKET LIST

RATE THIS ACTIVITY

★ ★ ★ ★ ★

ITEM #84:

SUMMARY: THIS WOULD BE F*CKING PERFECT FOR US BECAUSE...

_____
_____
_____
_____
_____
_____

MAKE IT F*CKING HAPPEN: HOW? WHEN?

_____
_____
_____
_____
_____
_____

REVIEW

DATE COMPLETED: / /

WHAT HAPPENED? (PEOPLE MET, HIGH POINTS, EXPECTATIONS VS REALITY)

_____
_____
_____
_____
_____
_____
_____
_____

BUDGET

$

ANTICIPATED DATE

/ /   TO   / /

ACTION LIST

- ⊘
- ⊘
- ⊘
- ⊘
- ⊘
- ⊘
- ⊘
- ⊘
- ⊘
- ⊘
- ⊘

Success!

ONCE COMPLETE, PLACE A CHECK HERE
TO TAKE IT OFF YOUR BUCKET LIST

RATE THIS ACTIVITY

★ ★ ★ ★ ★

ITEM #85:

SUMMARY: THIS WOULD BE F*CKING PERFECT FOR US BECAUSE...

_____

_____

_____

_____

_____

_____

MAKE IT F*CKING HAPPEN: HOW? WHEN?

_____

_____

_____

_____

_____

_____

_____

REVIEW
DATE COMPLETED: / /

WHAT HAPPENED? (PEOPLE MET, HIGH POINTS, EXPECTATIONS VS REALITY)

_____

_____

_____

_____

_____

_____

_____

_____

_____

BUDGET
$

ANTICIPATED DATE
/ /   TO   / /

ACTION LIST

- ⊘
- ⊘
- ⊘
- ⊘
- ⊘
- ⊘
- ⊘
- ⊘
- ⊘
- ⊘
- ⊘

Success!

ONCE COMPLETE, PLACE A CHECK HERE
TO TAKE IT OFF YOUR BUCKET LIST

RATE THIS ACTIVITY
★ ★ ★ ★ ★

ITEM #86:

SUMMARY: THIS WOULD BE F*CKING PERFECT FOR US BECAUSE...

_____

_____

_____

_____

_____

_____

MAKE IT F*CKING HAPPEN: HOW? WHEN?

_____

_____

_____

_____

_____

_____

_____

REVIEW

DATE COMPLETED: /   /

WHAT HAPPENED? (PEOPLE MET, HIGH POINTS, EXPECTATIONS VS REALITY)

_____

_____

_____

_____

_____

_____

_____

_____

BUDGET

$

ANTICIPATED DATE

/   /   TO   /   /

ACTION LIST

⊘
⊘
⊘
⊘
⊘
⊘
⊘
⊘
⊘
⊘
⊘

Success!

ONCE COMPLETE, PLACE A CHECK HERE
TO TAKE IT OFF YOUR BUCKET LIST

RATE THIS ACTIVITY

★ ★ ★ ★ ★

ITEM #87:

SUMMARY: THIS WOULD BE F*CKING PERFECT FOR US BECAUSE...

_____

_____

_____

_____

_____

_____

MAKE IT F*CKING HAPPEN: HOW? WHEN?

_____

_____

_____

_____

_____

_____

REVIEW

DATE COMPLETED: / /

WHAT HAPPENED? (PEOPLE MET, HIGH POINTS, EXPECTATIONS VS REALITY)

_____

_____

_____

_____

_____

_____

_____

_____

BUDGET

$

ANTICIPATED DATE

/ /   TO   / /

ACTION LIST

- ⊘
- ⊘
- ⊘
- ⊘
- ⊘
- ⊘
- ⊘
- ⊘
- ⊘
- ⊘
- ⊘

Success!

ONCE COMPLETE, PLACE A CHECK HERE
TO TAKE IT OFF YOUR BUCKET LIST

RATE THIS ACTIVITY

★ ★ ★ ★ ★

ITEM #88:

SUMMARY: THIS WOULD BE F*CKING PERFECT FOR US BECAUSE...

_____

_____

_____

_____

_____

_____

_____

MAKE IT F*CKING HAPPEN: HOW? WHEN?

_____

_____

_____

_____

_____

_____

_____

REVIEW

DATE COMPLETED: /   /

WHAT HAPPENED? (PEOPLE MET, HIGH POINTS, EXPECTATIONS VS REALITY)

_____

_____

_____

_____

_____

_____

_____

_____

_____

BUDGET

$

ANTICIPATED DATE

/   /   TO   /   /

ACTION LIST

⊘ _____
⊘ _____
⊘ _____
⊘ _____
⊘ _____
⊘ _____
⊘ _____
⊘ _____
⊘ _____
⊘ _____
⊘ _____

Success!

ONCE COMPLETE, PLACE A CHECK HERE
TO TAKE IT OFF YOUR BUCKET LIST

RATE THIS ACTIVITY

★ ★ ★ ★ ★

ITEM #89:

SUMMARY: THIS WOULD BE F*CKING PERFECT FOR US BECAUSE...

_____

_____

_____

_____

_____

_____

_____

MAKE IT F*CKING HAPPEN: HOW? WHEN?

_____

_____

_____

_____

_____

_____

REVIEW

DATE COMPLETED: / /

WHAT HAPPENED? (PEOPLE MET, HIGH POINTS, EXPECTATIONS VS REALITY)

_____

_____

_____

_____

_____

_____

_____

_____

_____

BUDGET

$

ANTICIPATED DATE

/ /   TO   / /

ACTION LIST

- ⊘
- ⊘
- ⊘
- ⊘
- ⊘
- ⊘
- ⊘
- ⊘
- ⊘
- ⊘
- ⊘

Success!

ONCE COMPLETE, PLACE A CHECK HERE
TO TAKE IT OFF YOUR BUCKET LIST

RATE THIS ACTIVITY

★ ★ ★ ★ ★ ★

ITEM #90:

SUMMARY: THIS WOULD BE F*CKING PERFECT FOR US BECAUSE...

_____
_____
_____
_____
_____
_____

MAKE IT F*CKING HAPPEN: HOW? WHEN?

_____
_____
_____
_____
_____
_____

REVIEW

DATE COMPLETED: / /

WHAT HAPPENED? (PEOPLE MET, HIGH POINTS, EXPECTATIONS VS REALITY)

_____
_____
_____
_____
_____
_____
_____
_____

BUDGET

$

ANTICIPATED DATE

/ /   TO   / /

ACTION LIST

- ⊘
- ⊘
- ⊘
- ⊘
- ⊘
- ⊘
- ⊘
- ⊘
- ⊘
- ⊘
- ⊘

Success!

✓

ONCE COMPLETE, PLACE A CHECK HERE
TO TAKE IT OFF YOUR BUCKET LIST

RATE THIS ACTIVITY

☆ ☆ ☆ ☆ ☆

ITEM #91:

PRIORITY ★ ★ ★ ★ ★

SUMMARY: THIS WOULD BE F*CKING PERFECT FOR US BECAUSE...

_____

_____

_____

_____

_____

_____

_____

MAKE IT F*CKING HAPPEN: HOW? WHEN?

_____

_____

_____

_____

_____

_____

_____

REVIEW

DATE COMPLETED: / /

WHAT HAPPENED? (PEOPLE MET, HIGH POINTS, EXPECTATIONS VS REALITY)

_____

_____

_____

_____

_____

_____

_____

_____

_____

BUDGET

$

ANTICIPATED DATE

/ / TO / /

ACTION LIST

⊘
⊘
⊘
⊘
⊘
⊘
⊘
⊘
⊘
⊘
⊘

Success!

✓

ONCE COMPLETE, PLACE A CHECK HERE
TO TAKE IT OFF YOUR BUCKET LIST

RATE THIS ACTIVITY

★ ★ ★ ★ ★

(91)

ITEM #92:

PRIORITY ★ ★ ★ ★ ★

SUMMARY: THIS WOULD BE F*CKING PERFECT FOR US BECAUSE...

_____
_____
_____
_____
_____
_____
_____

BUDGET

$

ANTICIPATED DATE

/ /   TO   / /

ACTION LIST

⊘
⊘
⊘
⊘
⊘
⊘
⊘
⊘
⊘
⊘
⊘

MAKE IT F*CKING HAPPEN: HOW? WHEN?

_____
_____
_____
_____
_____
_____
_____
_____

REVIEW   DATE COMPLETED: / /

WHAT HAPPENED? (PEOPLE MET, HIGH POINTS, EXPECTATIONS VS REALITY)

_____
_____
_____
_____
_____
_____
_____
_____
_____

Success!

ONCE COMPLETE, PLACE A CHECK HERE
TO TAKE IT OFF YOUR BUCKET LIST

RATE THIS ACTIVITY

★ ★ ★ ★ ★

ITEM #93:

PRIORITY ★★★★★

SUMMARY: THIS WOULD BE F*CKING PERFECT FOR US BECAUSE...

_____
_____
_____
_____
_____
_____
_____

MAKE IT F*CKING HAPPEN: HOW? WHEN?

_____
_____
_____
_____
_____
_____
_____

BUDGET
$

ANTICIPATED DATE
/ /   TO   / /

ACTION LIST
⊘
⊘
⊘
⊘
⊘
⊘
⊘
⊘
⊘
⊘
⊘

REVIEW

DATE COMPLETED: / /

WHAT HAPPENED? (PEOPLE MET, HIGH POINTS, EXPECTATIONS VS REALITY)

_____
_____
_____
_____
_____
_____
_____
_____

Success!

ONCE COMPLETE, PLACE A CHECK HERE
TO TAKE IT OFF YOUR BUCKET LIST

RATE THIS ACTIVITY
★★★★★

ITEM #94:

SUMMARY: THIS WOULD BE F*CKING PERFECT FOR US BECAUSE...

_____
_____
_____
_____
_____
_____

MAKE IT F*CKING HAPPEN: HOW? WHEN?

_____
_____
_____
_____
_____
_____

BUDGET

$

ANTICIPATED DATE

/ /   TO   / /

ACTION LIST

- ⊘
- ⊘
- ⊘
- ⊘
- ⊘
- ⊘
- ⊘
- ⊘
- ⊘
- ⊘
- ⊘

REVIEW

DATE COMPLETED: / /

WHAT HAPPENED? (PEOPLE MET, HIGH POINTS, EXPECTATIONS VS REALITY)

_____
_____
_____
_____
_____
_____
_____
_____

Success!
✓

ONCE COMPLETE, PLACE A CHECK HERE
TO TAKE IT OFF YOUR BUCKET LIST

RATE THIS ACTIVITY

★ ★ ★ ★ ★

ITEM #95:

SUMMARY: THIS WOULD BE F*CKING PERFECT FOR US BECAUSE...

_____

_____

_____

_____

_____

_____

_____

MAKE IT F*CKING HAPPEN: HOW? WHEN?

_____

_____

_____

_____

_____

_____

REVIEW
DATE COMPLETED: / /

WHAT HAPPENED? (PEOPLE MET, HIGH POINTS, EXPECTATIONS VS REALITY)

_____

_____

_____

_____

_____

_____

_____

_____

BUDGET
$

ANTICIPATED DATE
/ /   TO   / /

ACTION LIST

⊘
⊘
⊘
⊘
⊘
⊘
⊘
⊘
⊘
⊘
⊘

Success!

✓

ONCE COMPLETE, PLACE A CHECK HERE
TO TAKE IT OFF YOUR BUCKET LIST

RATE THIS ACTIVITY

★ ★ ★ ★ ★

ITEM #96:

SUMMARY: THIS WOULD BE F*CKING PERFECT FOR US BECAUSE...

_____

_____

_____

_____

_____

_____

MAKE IT F*CKING HAPPEN: HOW? WHEN?

_____

_____

_____

_____

_____

_____

REVIEW   DATE COMPLETED: / /

WHAT HAPPENED? (PEOPLE MET, HIGH POINTS, EXPECTATIONS VS REALITY)

_____

_____

_____

_____

_____

_____

_____

_____

BUDGET

$

ANTICIPATED DATE

/ /   TO   / /

ACTION LIST

⊘
⊘
⊘
⊘
⊘
⊘
⊘
⊘
⊘
⊘
⊘

Success!

ONCE COMPLETE, PLACE A CHECK HERE
TO TAKE IT OFF YOUR BUCKET LIST

RATE THIS ACTIVITY

★ ★ ★ ★ ★

ITEM #97:

SUMMARY: THIS WOULD BE F*CKING PERFECT FOR US BECAUSE...

_____
_____
_____
_____
_____
_____

MAKE IT F*CKING HAPPEN: HOW? WHEN?

_____
_____
_____
_____
_____

REVIEW

DATE COMPLETED: / /

WHAT HAPPENED? (PEOPLE MET, HIGH POINTS, EXPECTATIONS VS REALITY)

_____
_____
_____
_____
_____
_____
_____
_____

BUDGET

$

ANTICIPATED DATE

/ /   TO   / /

ACTION LIST

- ⊘
- ⊘
- ⊘
- ⊘
- ⊘
- ⊘
- ⊘
- ⊘
- ⊘
- ⊘
- ⊘

Success!

ONCE COMPLETE, PLACE A CHECK HERE
TO TAKE IT OFF YOUR BUCKET LIST

RATE THIS ACTIVITY

★ ★ ★ ★ ★

ITEM #98:

SUMMARY: THIS WOULD BE F*CKING PERFECT FOR US BECAUSE...

_____
_____
_____
_____
_____
_____

MAKE IT F*CKING HAPPEN: HOW? WHEN?

_____
_____
_____
_____
_____
_____

REVIEW

DATE COMPLETED: /   /

WHAT HAPPENED? (PEOPLE MET, HIGH POINTS, EXPECTATIONS VS REALITY)

_____
_____
_____
_____
_____
_____
_____
_____
_____
_____

BUDGET

$

ANTICIPATED DATE

/   /   TO   /   /

ACTION LIST

⊘
⊘
⊘
⊘
⊘
⊘
⊘
⊘
⊘
⊘
⊘

Success!

✓

ONCE COMPLETE, PLACE A CHECK HERE
TO TAKE IT OFF YOUR BUCKET LIST

RATE THIS ACTIVITY

★ ★ ★ ★ ★

ITEM #99:

PRIORITY ☆ ☆ ☆ ☆ ☆

SUMMARY: THIS WOULD BE F*CKING PERFECT FOR US BECAUSE...

_____

_____

_____

_____

_____

_____

_____

MAKE IT F*CKING HAPPEN: HOW? WHEN?

_____

_____

_____

_____

_____

_____

REVIEW

DATE COMPLETED: / /

WHAT HAPPENED? (PEOPLE MET, HIGH POINTS, EXPECTATIONS VS REALITY)

_____

_____

_____

_____

_____

_____

_____

_____

_____

_____

BUDGET

$

ANTICIPATED DATE

/ /   TO   / /

ACTION LIST

⊘
⊘
⊘
⊘
⊘
⊘
⊘
⊘
⊘
⊘
⊘

Success!

ONCE COMPLETE, PLACE A CHECK HERE
TO TAKE IT OFF YOUR BUCKET LIST

RATE THIS ACTIVITY

☆ ☆ ☆ ☆ ☆

ITEM #100:

SUMMARY: THIS WOULD BE F*CKING PERFECT FOR US BECAUSE...

_____

_____

_____

_____

_____

_____

MAKE IT F*CKING HAPPEN: HOW? WHEN?

_____

_____

_____

_____

_____

_____

REVIEW   DATE COMPLETED: / /

WHAT HAPPENED? (PEOPLE MET, HIGH POINTS, EXPECTATIONS VS REALITY)

_____

_____

_____

_____

_____

_____

_____

_____

BUDGET

$

ANTICIPATED DATE

/ /   TO   / /

ACTION LIST

- ⊘
- ⊘
- ⊘
- ⊘
- ⊘
- ⊘
- ⊘
- ⊘
- ⊘
- ⊘
- ⊘

Success!

ONCE COMPLETE, PLACE A CHECK HERE
TO TAKE IT OFF YOUR BUCKET LIST

RATE THIS ACTIVITY

★ ★ ★ ★ ★

ITEM #101:

SUMMARY: THIS WOULD BE F*CKING PERFECT FOR US BECAUSE...

_____

_____

_____

_____

_____

_____

_____

MAKE IT F*CKING HAPPEN: HOW? WHEN?

_____

_____

_____

_____

_____

_____

_____

REVIEW

DATE COMPLETED: /   /

WHAT HAPPENED? (PEOPLE MET, HIGH POINTS, EXPECTATIONS VS REALITY)

_____

_____

_____

_____

_____

_____

_____

_____

_____

BUDGET

$

ANTICIPATED DATE

/ /   TO   / /

ACTION LIST

⊘

⊘

⊘

⊘

⊘

⊘

⊘

⊘

⊘

⊘

⊘

Success!

ONCE COMPLETE, PLACE A CHECK HERE
TO TAKE IT OFF YOUR BUCKET LIST

RATE THIS ACTIVITY

★ ★ ★ ★ ★

THE PERFECT COMPANION
THE F*CK IT! MONTHLY CALENDAR PLANNER

- ✓ **Goal Planning**: Establish a series of long-term goals for the year, with prompts to summarize goal outcomes, reasons and required resources. Include a drawing, picture or text to visualize your goal.

- ✓ **Goal Progress Chart**: At at-a-glance view of each major goal's progress. Monitor your journey to goal accomplishment with this simple bar chart.

- ✓ **Exploring Goal Setting**: These pages are an opportunity to pause and reflect on opportunities for self-improvement through goal achievement. Explore ways that others have inspired you; identify personal characteristics and qualities that will help you accomplish goals; and develop a tangible vision of what goal accomplishment will look like for you.

- ✓ **Goal Check-In**: At the end of each month, you'll be guided to reflect on your goals' progress on the Goal Check-In page. This page includes three important questions to help stay accountable to your plan, and reinforces the importance of the goals you've set. These questions are designed to prompt internal dialog and self-reflection about your goal's progress, and reinvigorate commitment over the coming month.

- ✓ **Monitor progress using your Monthly Goal Progress chart**: Shade in the completion scale for particular goals to give yourself a visual reinforcement of progress and success.

- ✓ **Goal Setting Word Prompts**: A fun activity to help inspire new goals or flesh out ideas for self-improvement. This list contains 600+ seed words to prompt development of goal statements and/or contemplate themes not previously considered.

- ✓ **Monthly Dream Board**: Compiling your monthly vision board helps visualize what can be accomplished in the short term. Collage together photos, clippings, drawings, and quotes to envision goals and inspire commitment.

IN STOCK NOW AT AMAZON.COM

bit.ly/goalweekly

Made in United States
North Haven, CT
11 December 2021

12366519R00076

<u>NO</u>
FOOD
OR
DRINKS
ALLOWED
IN THE
STUDIO

THANK YOU

RicTV Inc.
Presents
We Want Clean Food
13 Episodes From the Public Television Series
Ric Orlando's TV Kitchen

By Ric Orlando

Cover Photography: Chris Fitzpatriick

Graphic Design: Michael Corsentino

Photograhy: Michael Corsentino
(except where otherwise noted)

Editing: Kelly Ward, Laura Corrado
Margo Orlando

Editorial Consultant: Liz Corrado

Clean Food Press
1411 Rt. 212
Saugteries, NY 12477
www.rictv.com

Printed in USA

This book, like everything else I do, is dedicated to
Lizzie, Margo, Willie and Terry.

Table of contents

We want clean food!

The First Rant

Taped July 29, 2002

Welcome! My name is Ric Orlando, and this is My TV Kitchen.

My motivation in this TV kitchen is mostly to share my opinions with you. I am a deliciously opinionated chef. I have cooked a million meals, and after the first 500,000 I realized there was more to making food than just technique and skill: there must also be a sensibility and a conscience. I want to share that part with you. My mission is to get you to love to cook—to get you to use your hands and to connect—to get you to think about the connection between your mind and your soul, and your body, and your food, and the world around you.

We have developed a pretty hectic lifestyle these days, and the comments I get most often when I speak publicly are: "I'm in too much of a hurry to cook," and "What do you have that's quick that even *I* can make?" and "Can you show me some professional shortcuts?" Frankly, what I'm going to tell you is more like therapy than cooking secrets.

Cooking is not where you should be cutting corners. I figured this out all by myself because running a restaurant and cheffing with three school-aged kids and a loving wife in law school is pretty complex, too.

When I ask people what the rush is (why do you need to have a meal started, cooked, eaten, over and done with in an hour?) I'm told the same story: "I get home from work and I'm too tired to cook, so we have something quick, then I veg out and watch TV until I crash."

Let me tell you a story that most of you probably already know, though sometimes it's good to hear it from somebody on TV (we have authority!). I too have a TV, and I turn it on occasionally, usually late at night. I have something like 400 channels, and of these 400 channels, 390 of them are showing incredibly stressful material.

When I lie in bed and flip through the electronic guide, I find murder, mayhem, revenge, more murder, rape, controversy, horrible news, bad-mannered pundits interrupting each other, misinformation, lies, deceit, conceit, propaganda, general violence or what my wife's family in Queens calls the "Rape-Slain Show." The amount of stress-inducing programming on television is completely out of whack with reality. The idea of rushing through an unhealthy, chemical-laden supper, just to "veg out" to the content of 21st Century television is so far from relaxing, it is inconceivable!

As a health-oriented chef I am often asked questions like "What can I do about my blood pressure? What am I doing wrong, what should I be eating?" Well, there is a simple answer: if you are choking down processed food just so you can get stressed out by a triple homicide adventure show—I needn't go any further. You know the answer already, don't you?

Cooking is like therapy— it's like taking a long, hot bath...

Reprioritize, baby!

Let's start again. Let's say you got home at 6:00 and you were done with dinner by 6:45 because you microwaved some processed—but *low-fat*—counterfeit food, then you plunked down in front of the television until you became comatose. You are never winding down. You've had no chance to let the day go. You are never connecting with your physical and sensual world. You need to *play with your food* sometime during the day! If you are not giving yourself the opportunity to use your senses of touch, taste and smell, you are missing a major ingredient of life. Reestablishing that part of your life, by creating simple but wholesome food, will help you relax. Doing it as a hobby—a little gardening a few weekends a year, a dozen dinner parties a year—is nice, but a daily escape is better. My prescription for peace of mind is to spend some time in the kitchen every day.

Try to make dinner four or five days a week (actually prepare a meal and then sit, relax and enjoy it with someone with whom you can speak...). When you prepare a meal by touching—cutting the vegetables, washing the fish, trimming the meat, feeling the grains in your hands—you are getting *in* touch. The more you use your hands, the more whole you become, and the more whole the feeling you have for cooking and eating becomes. Then, instead of always feeling too rushed to cook because you want to watch TV and chill, your evenings will melt away into relaxing pleasure.

When you get home, put on some music. No news—once a day is enough news for anyone. (And now with these news update tickers on the bottom of the screen, we are hypnotized! Give it a rest.) And skip the ads, please. They're just there to make you feel inadequate anyway, so give 'em a break.

So where were we? Oh yes, you've put on some music and you have laid out some ingredients. Now spend half an hour making a fresh meal. Maybe your kids or partner can help. Take your time—be European—and don't plan on eating until 7:30 or 8:00 pm. Now, when you eat, linger for an hour and digest. Talk about things, not just the bad things, but the amusing things too. Then by 9:00 or 9:30, if you are ready to turn on the tube, you've already unwound. Wait 'til you see how absurd that channel guide looks once you've let some of the sap out of your spine. This really is the ultimate therapy. Using your hands, your soul and your mind to create sustenance takes such an edge off life!

The nutritional advantage of making your own food is also crucial. When you combine fresher and Cleaner meals, made from scratch, with patience and meditation during the preparation *and* the eating of the meal, your whole life improves. Now try it: a little wine, a little dinner—it's not unreasonable, that is the healthy choice—it is a worthy lifestyle change.

About the Recipes

Oh, brave New World that has such cookable stuff in it...

My culinary style is an amalgamation of some of the world's best-known food ideas and my own personal bent for art, culture and good health. It is also a way of thinking about what to expect from eating food and drinking spirits. I turn over rocks, chit-chat with a myriad of grandmothers and taste whatever the world has to offer, smiling all the time.

My simple mantra of "Clean is Best" drives all the recipes in this book. These recipes are extremely healthful according to me, but I won't venture to label them "health food." What our society calls health food is well-intentioned, but it seems to have been designed to be a primal fuel first, and a flavorful experience second (or third...). Many Americans have backlashed against health food, finding it boring, almost depressing. Boring food is not healthy food. Food is much more than fuel for our bodies; it propels our personalities. Why did our earliest ancestors delve into using seasonings in the first place? After all, if we were just bipeds looking for food, where did all the artistry come from? So my philosophy is to cook with the Cleanest stuff because it is good body fuel and cook with aggressive flavors because that makes excellent soul food.

I utilize marinades, quick broil-and-baste dishes and simple bases for stews and sauces to make my cooking easier. I will show you how to create big, homey meals, full of textural and flavorful "surprise" day in and day out, without starting over from scratch. Surprise appears in things like the unexpected volume of a particular herb, the startling crunch of fennel seeds, or the tart explosion of a whole, grilled, fresh-from-the-garden tomatillo. Tonight's vinaigrette, with some fresh cherry tomatoes and some garam masala, becomes the sauce for tomorrow's salmon on the grill. You can go there! No amount of plate decoration can compare with the sensual stimulation of Clean and assertive cooking. With good, Clean ingredients, my food is very cookable for everyone.

As you will see as you use this book, I always recommend organic foods over commercial foods. Grass-fed meats and free-range birds are the only way to go. I avoid hydrogenated, refined and altered fats like the plague! Margarine is not allowed in my house. I use naturally saturated fats in moderation. Even organic duck and goose fat, pork lard and schmaltz still have a place in a healthful diet. I use sea salts but do not recommend using iodized salt. I use only limited amounts of refined sugar and white flour.

That is the whole idea. Please come along on this Clean Food ride!

If you are unsure of sourcing Clean Food in your area, I have included a rough sourcing page at the end of this book.

My simple mantra of "Clean is Best" drives all the recipes in this book.

To Be or Not to Be Organic?

This question has become much easier to answer! First rule: as often as you can, buy organic. Make one of the most important statements in your life and keep yourself and your family healthy by buying organic food. The more we use our consumer dollars to buy organic, the louder the message is to big business: WE WANT CLEAN FOOD! Remember that businesses do respond to our demands. In the 1950s and '60s, when we decided that we wanted year-round access and simplicity in the kitchen, the huge commercial food producers responded by forcing food production, limiting the variety available in the marketplace, and lowering the standard of flavor in our food.

Our food supply has become so driven by chemicals that it isn't even as nutritious as it once was. Vegetables and fruits raised in depleted, "propped-up" soil don't deliver anything to the table. It is the minerals from well-composted soils that make food healthy. Though there is conflicting wisdom in the lobbyist-polluted American information system, the Organic Retailers and Growers Association of Australia has recently completed an extensive study comparing organically cultivated vegetables from well-composted soils with commercially grown "supermarket" tomatoes. Their study concluded that the organic tomatoes were 20% higher in vitamin C, higher in beta carotene, ten times higher in potassium, seven times higher in calcium and six times higher in zinc. Higher levels of vitamins and minerals were also found in beans, silver beet and capsaicin.

It is reasonable to believe that naturally composted soil and rotated crops will provide better nutrients than will dirt pumped full of weed killers and steroids. Organic farming brings healthy food back to the table. In order to grow organically, composting and crop rotation are essential. When the soil is made healthy, the plants are actually stronger themselves and are more resistant to pests and disease. On the other hand, the more synthetic the growing procedure, the more the producers rely on pesticides and chemical growth stimulants to keep bringing food to market. Remember that when we discuss pesticides, that includes sprays for insects, weeds and other vermin. Many of these are WWII-era neurotoxins and are notoriously destructive and carcinogenic, regardless of what the FDA has to say.

WE WANT CLEAN FOOD!

Lots of organic vegetables are now available most of the year. In the winter, lettuces come from Southern California, Arizona and now Mexico. Root vegetables and some stalk vegetables are also in the market year-round. However, a commitment to buying organic produce also means making a pledge to common sense. One of the ways in which we have allowed the corporate agri-culture to produce less than desirable food is by demanding that absolutely every vegetable under the sun be available all year round. As I said before, big business will do what it can to respond to our demands. If we want red tomatoes in February, some laboratory will figure out a way to make them happen, even if that means genetically engineering them to grow in ice cubes! Remember that food is alive and responsive to its environment. Anyone who has ever had a vegetable garden knows that normal produce has variations in size and color. When all of the tomatoes on a shelf look exactly the same, don't you get a little suspicious? Are these the Stepford tomatoes? And is that really what you want rushing through your bloodstream en route to your heart and brain?

Do you want CLEAN WATER?

Clean Food helps keep our water clean, too.

The EPA has found 98 different pesticides in the groundwater of 40 states, contaminating the drinking water of over 100 million people. The agency has identified agriculture as one of the largest ground water polluters nationwide.

Organic Farming helps to protect our water supply in two ways. First, there are no polluting chemicals added to the soil in organic farming. This protects and conserves water resources from nitrogen contamination and toxic sediments.

And second, Organic agriculture actually requires less water because the process of building good soil through composting, cover cropping and crop rotating builds a living soil that retains moisture so it uses less water!

source: www.living-foods.com

To help keep our produce marketplace Clean and sane, try to think seasonally when buying stuff for cooking. Insisting on white asparagus, yellow tomatoes or fresh peas in winter will just bring us more of the same chemically-assisted suicide we have commissioned all along. Shop for produce in your local co-op or health food store, which is committed to carrying organics all year. When you see organics in the larger supermarkets, support that idea with your dollars and watch the effect it has on inventory and price over the long haul.

What about the price of organic food? That's easy. Organic food is more costly than commercial food. In most cases it is about double the price. But does that mean that it is "expensive"? I believe that is a relative question; we do have the cheapest food *in the world!* That is one of the great, yet strange, American truths. Our insistence on cheap food has created this monster of genetically engineered, chemically fed foodstuff. Let's do some

I can make dinner for four with an organic roasted chicken, organic brown rice, organic carrots and organic salad for about $5 per person.

math: a regular head of romaine lettuce is $0.89 in Walmart, an organic head is $1.59 in the health food store, while a Macdonald's hamburger is $0.89. Two people can have a beautiful organic Romaine salad for the same price as they can each have a Macdonald's hamburger. Notice the value? These absurd comparisons are fun. Is a loaf of organic bread the same price as a pack of cigarettes? Is an organic apple cheaper than Blue Gatorade? Are you having fun yet? I can make dinner for four with an organic roasted chicken, organic brown rice, organic carrots and organic salad for about $5 per person. That's the same as a trip to the pizza shop. So, the price of organic food is really a matter of perspective. If you cook for your family at home with fresh stuff, using organic food, it will cost you about the same as buying frozen prepared dinners or eating out in a chemical-rich "budget" restaurant.

There is a cynical saying that goes: "You'll never go broke under-estimating the intelligence of the American public." I believe exactly the opposite: we as a culture are craving knowledge. But since knowledge is power, we are being denied access to it in mainstream sources. Don't give up. Look outside the mainstream. Get on the internet, enter those chat rooms and do your own research. The information we seek is out there. It all starts with Clean Food. Clean Food is one of the greatest secrets to health and happiness.

A New World Pantry

There is a world of cool stuff out there to cook with. If you like to cook, you'd better like to shop. Tap into your hunter-gatherer instincts! Stocking up on interesting pantry items should be your idea of a fun day of leisure. Some people cycle, some hike—I explore the markets! Making a trip to the health food store, a gourmet shop, an Asian or ethnic market and to the specialty aisle of the supermarket is like venturing down a new road filled with intrigue and inspiration. This is a great chance to get kids—even teenagers—interested in cooking. Having a good stash of old world and new world basics will make recipe completion quick and easy and make experimentation more fun. Organize your shelves so that you can see what you have on hand. Maybe you should try removing your cabinet doors like my wife did. (I have since furnished our kitchen with a huge open-shelved pantry unit, circa 1940!)

You can learn a lot about people by glancing into their refrigerators. Those college habits of Chinese leftovers, ketchup packets, grated cheese, bottles of soda and some old chive creme cheese just don't cut it anymore. In this world of corporate food, one of the best ways to fight back is to keep a well stocked fridge. Many cooler items last a long time (sometimes too long...) so you can develop a culinary arsenal in a matter of weeks. Every time you go to the grocer, add a good mustard, some olives or a nice bottle of hot sauce to your pantry. You'll get more satisfaction from these than you will from that glamour magazine and they cost about the same. There will never again be a time when you say there's nothing to cook. If all you have to eat in the house is a bag of macaroni, but you have a nice collection of condiments on hand, we can make dinner rock!

Condiments and Cool Goodies

I love cooking with condiments. When I began cooking professionally I was somehow persuaded that using some of the newer ethnic condiments like pre-made curry paste and Asian seasoning sauce was, in a sense, cheating—though it was perfectly acceptable to use Tabasco, mustard, soy sauce and other "traditional" condiments. Silly, isn't it? That bias has been injected into the psyches of a whole legion of chefs trained in old school kitchens. (I can still see the smirk on that pink, juicy face of a particular chef when he was given a tour of my kitchen. He picked up a bottle of Indonesian ketchup and commented that I was "still cooking with ketchup." Ah, so now I am here having fun and he is busy salting prime rib number 11,234!)

Condiments will continue to be developed because they add zest to food and make our cooking easier. I have no problem with that. Just be cautious when buying your condiments, read the labels and make smart decisions. Many Asian items are full of MSG. Many Indian items contain artificial colors. Try to avoid these items in a Clean cooking kitchen. There are many great choices that are not packed with chemicals. There are more ethnic condiment choices available in health food stores and even in green grocers and ethnic markets. The whole world is catching on to the European, Canadian and American demand for pure food. Your choices will continue to grow. Try some new items in your cooking and collect your own favorite condiments.

When I gaze into my fridge or at my pantry, these are the items that I can always rely on to be there, waiting for my love. This is romance by the refrigerator light!

French Dijon mustard
Pommerey or grainy mustard
Chinese mustard
German mustard
English mustard
Okay, Ketchup (Organic is good!)
Anchovies three ways: salted, in vinegar and in oil
Prepared horseradish
Safflower mayonnaise (no canola or hydrogenated oils)
Assorted flavors of all-fruit preserves
Chunks of real Romano and Parmigiano-Reggiano cheese
Feta cheese
Soy sauce
Tahini paste
Wheat-free tamari
White and red miso
Firm tofu
Japanese Plum (Ume) Sauce
Organic Worcestershire sauce
Tamarind paste
Wasabi, powder or paste (without food coloring)
All-natural Hoisin sauce
Mirin (sweet rice wine)
A fine assortment of fish sauces
Fermented black beans
Dried shrimp
Chili-garlic paste (Sri Rachi)
Sweet chile sauce

Chile oil

Curry oil

Fermented bean paste

Thai curry pastes (red, green, panang, masaman, sour yellow)

Pickapeppa Sauce

Sambal Olek

Hot sauces (American style—Tabasco or Louisiana, Caribe mustard-fruit
habanero style—Matouk's, Trinidad or Lottie's, to name a few)

Note on hot sauces: I recommend avoiding any capsaicin oleo resin-extract sauces. These are novelty sauces that are made with chemical simulations of the hot pepper and can be hazardous to your health. Ask at any hot sauce shop and they will tell you which ones to avoid.

Ah, so now I am here having fun...

Dairy

My kids love milk and drink it by the quart. This has motivated me to make milk-buying a serious thing. In this modern age of chemically invigorated foods, cows are pushed too hard to produce milk. The use of Bovine Growth Hormones is a major scandal, in my opinion. The milk from non-organically raised cows is tainted with hormones, pesticides and antibiotics, which are stored in the milk-fat. There are scary new studies correlating the early onset of puberty in girls with drinking milk containing those hormones fed to cows. Ouch! I absolutely recommend buying milk that is BGH-free, organic and preferably grass-fed. If you can find traditional milk that has been pasteurized but not homogenized (that's the "cream-on-the-top" milk, making a comeback in artisan dairy farms), go for it! The process of homogenizing milk shatters the fat molecules into tiny fragments, enabling your body to absorb far too much fat. Even if you buy low-fat milk, if it is homogenized, you will absorb more fat from it than from whole milk in its natural state. *That's a fact.* If you want a richer taste, simply add a splash of cream and gently stir, as it was done in the old days.

If you haven't tried goat's milk and sheep's milk, why haven't you? Been under a cow lately? Goat, sheep, cow, what's the big deal? They are all farm animals with their own wonderful perfume!

Goat's milk is bright and tangy, almost like yogurt. It has excellent enzymes that help to stabilize and balance your digestion. It is awesome on oatmeal or drizzled on fresh berries.

Fermented dairy products are magnificent additions to your diet. Think about the last time you took antibiotics. Antibiotics indiscriminately destroy bad AND good bacteria. We need good bacteria to keep our intestines working properly. That doesn't just mean feeling good, that means working properly. Many allergies develop when our bodies' natural bacteria become out of balance. Consuming fermented dairy products on a reasonably regular basis helps to ensure that your body keeps its good bacteria thriving. Interestingly, in areas of the world whose diet does not contain much dairy, vegetables are fermented and eaten to achieve the same positive effects. Cool, huh? So if you think Kim Chee or Fish sauce stinks, ask a Korean what he thinks of the aroma of sour cream!

Open your fridge to these goodies:

*Organic full fat milk, raw or pasturized,
  not homogenized if possible*

Organic lactose-free milk

BGH-free heavy cream

Pasteurized, NOT homogenized milk

Organic yogurt, organic buttermilk

*Creme fraiche, Clabber, English Double Devon Cream
  and sour cream*

Unsalted organic butter

Goat's and sheep's milk

Flavored and plain Kefir or Quark

Pastured and/or Organic Eggs

For years now, we've harbored suspicion against one of our most basic foods, the egg. The egg got a bad rap for being one of the causes of high cholesterol. Wrong!

The secret is in seeking out and eating eggs from hens that are allowed to roam freely and eat the foods that nature has intended them to eat. The grasses, insects and flowers that free-range chickens get to eat deliver super trace minerals into our systems when we consume the eggs. It's all about assimilating the earth from a food source that consumes it.

Eggs from chickens that have been tube-fed genetically modified, high-fat grains are not very good for you, because the chickens' own systems are out of balance. The Omega 6 and Omega 3 fatty acids in eggs from a naturally pastured hen are in perfect balance for our bodies. Research shows that eating pasture-raised eggs raises HDL (or good cholesterol) levels, reduces triglycerides and decreases insulin requirements. This is basic science. When the fatty acids are balanced in food, your body doesn't need to produce cholesterol to defend itself from the free radicals associated with "bad fats."

A study by Michigan State University's Food Science and Human Nutrition Department reported that people who ate up to three eggs daily had better cholesterol counts than those who ate fewer than one egg per day. A fun fact to know and share!

What about "Omega 3" Eggs? These come from chickens that are fed an inordinate amout of flax seed. Eat a piece of fish every couple of days or take a fish oil supplement and stop worrying! I can't imagine chickens being happy when they are force-fed too much of anything.

Olives, Capers & Pickles

I can't get enough olives, capers and pickles. We have so many in our refrigerator that we sometimes can't close the door...that's when it's time to liquidate some into a killer sauce for lentils or pasta.

In a good Mediterranean deli, you can buy loose olives. Buy three to four ounces at a time to keep them fresh. Most quality olives do not come pitted, except for Calamatas from Greece. I do not think it's necessary to buy pre-seasoned olives. Seasoning them yourself with some olive oil, crushed pepper, garlic and herbs is fun and cheap. A nice olive-pitter is a kitchen tool that helps, although I like smacking them with the side of a knife and picking the meat off with my fingers. It keeps my hands softer, younger-looking...

Minimal Supply for Security:

Green Olives: Manzanilla, Spanish queens, Cerignolas Green, Arbequina, Catalan, Picholine, Sicilian Style

Black and/or Red Olives: Morrocan or Nyon oil-cured and/or sun-dried olives, Calamata, Tunisian, Nicoise, Spanish Empeltes, Cerignolas Black, Colossal Ripe Olives

Capers: Nonpareile capers, salt-packed capers, capotes, caperberries

Pickles: Kosher dills, half sours, cornichons, bread-and-butters

Peppers: Pickled cherry peppers, pepperoncini, pickled jalapeños, chipotles en adobo, serrano peppers en adobo

I can't get enough...

Oils: A Few Good Ones are Enough

If you are really concerned about your health, don't be penny-wise and pound-foolish. Refined oils, along with hydrogenated fats, are the real nemesis in the American diet!

What is a Refined Oil and Why is it UGLY?

When commercial oil is processed for human consumption, it is combined with caustic acids. The introduction of these caustic acids removes the beneficial free fatty acids. The oil is then filtered, degummed, bleached, deodorized, rescented, stabilized and colored. Often, synthetic anti-oxidants are added to replace what was lost in the refining process. Lastly, a defoamer is added before it gets to market. The oil is often sold in clear containers even though sunlight and flourescent light destroys most of the remaining advantageous fatty acids. The process of hydrogenation is intended to create a solid fat with smooth, rich mouthfeel. The hazard lies in the process of shattering fat molecules into smaller parts, which are much more easily absorbed into our intestines than are fat molecules in their natural state. Additionally, all of the essential fatty acids are destroyed in the processing, leaving a basically indigestible product.

A quick walk through a modern American supermarket will reveal to you that the staggering majority of the foods we are sold contain processed fats. And just about any commercial deep-fried food is fried in processed fat. So, if the FDA recommends that we should consume less of these foods, I agree. But without essential real fats, we become out of balance and our vital organs and blood cells begin to break down.

Real stuff won't kill you.

Spend the extra few bucks and buy unrefined and expeller-pressed oils. They are essentially virgin oils and retain their excellent nutrient value. I use unrefined or semi-refined oils as a rule. For hotter pan-frying and wokking, I use natural peanut oil, cold-pressed palm oil or organic pork lard and duck fat, as they are highly saturated and retain their fatty acid composition under high heat better than light oils.

For light sautéing I use olive, grapeseed, safflower, sesame and peanut oils or organic butter. For salad dressings I rely on olive, safflower, sunflower and grapeseed oil, except on Asian dishes where sesame and peanut oils come into play. See the list that follows for some of the other special occasion oils I use for drizzling and seasoning.

I also keep clarified duck fat in my refrigerator for special occasions. I really don't fear duck fat. Anything that makes you feel that good can't be all bad. Besides, haven't you heard of the French Paradox? In the regions of France where duck fat is consumed regularly, cholesterol problems are minimal. Some American medical spokespersons are crediting the Euro-diet paradox on wine consumption. My theory has more to do with a diet that is rich in locally raised fruits, vegetables, meats, fish and grains. Real stuff won't kill you. (More on this throughout the book!) Whenever I buy a chunk of organic pork, I render the fat to make the most spectacular pork lard on the planet. You want good cornbread? Try organic pork lard!

Please take care of your oil to keep it fresh. I recommend buying reasonably small packages of oil, enough for about a month or two. Store your oil in a cool dark place, preferably in the refrigerator. It may appear cloudy, but that will diminish as the oil returns to room temperature. Also, avoid oils in clear glass and, especially, plastic containers. Sunlight and fluorescent light damage the Omega 3 fatty acids present, diminishing the oil's nutritional value and plastic will leach chemicals into the oil. Yuck!

Oils allowed in a Clean Food kitchen:

Extra virgin olive oil (Greek, Italian, American and Spanish!)

Expeller-pressed high oleic safflower oil

Expeller-pressed sunflower oil

Cold-pressed peanut oil

Red or golden palm oil

Toasted and cold-pressed sesame oils

Unrefined coconut oil

Organic butter

Clarified duck, goose and chicken fat from organic birds

Walnut oil

Grapeseed oil

Hazelnut oil

Avocado oil

Almond oil

Vinegars

Vinegar is one of the original seasonings. The Romans loved vinegar and the most exciting antique recipes from Europe and China utilized vinegars in the Agri-Dolce or sweet-and-sour method of seasoning. The acidity really picks up the palate and can bring a simple dish to a high level of sophistication. Real vinegar is also a natural disinfectant and detoxifier. The acids in vinegar help us maintain a proper pH balance in our intestines. Choose your vinegar carefully. For instance, white vinegar and now "red" vinegar are not made from wine—they are made from neutral spirits (whatever?) and shouldn't be used for anything other than cleaning and egg coloring!

A true vinegar is made from "the mother." If you've ever seen a small layer of filmy or cloudy, solid veil-like substance floating in the bottom of your vinegar, you have encountered traces of the mother in good quality vinegar. The mother is a natural culture that not only converts the fruit juice or wine to vinegar, it is also widely believed to be one of the great gifts to humankind. There are volumes of documents in libraries and on the web, some very real, some truly false and some just unabashed lore, available to all curious investigators.

A true vinegar is made from "the mother."

I love vinegar and I use many kinds in my cooking on a daily basis. You'll find a growing array of vinegars made with organically produced fruit appearing on health food store shelves, and it's all pretty inexpensive. As for flavored or infused vinegar like tarragon, roasted garlic or hot pepper—well, that's your call. Some are pretty good, but they are so easy to make yourself that buying them seems like a misguided way to invest in a Clean pantry. Buy some organic white wine vinegar and stick a sprig of tarragon from your garden in it. Seal it up and leave it alone. Within a few days you will taste the essence of the herb.

Vinegars I cannot do without are:

Balsamic

Red wine

Brown rice and/or rice wine

Sherry

Cider

Umeboshi (plum)

White wine and/or champagne

Raspberry

There are other nice vinegars to be found in quirky markets. I particularly like Muscatel vinegar.

Try making your own vinegars!

Buy a bottle of real (not distilled) red or white wine organic vinegar. Look for the veil-like substance in the vinegar. That is the mother. Now get a very clean cask or a jar and fill it almost to the top with good quality red or white wine of your choice. Add some of the mother from the vinegar you bought to the wine and seal it with wax paper and a rubber band (to allow breathing). In about a month, you will have your own vinegar. Now you can add herbs, peppercorns, garlic, shallots or chiles to this vinegar. Though you don't really save money doing this, it is fun. You can also use the mother from this vinegar over and over again.

Dried Chiles

The home cook's interest in exotic ingredients is at an all-time high, and the dried chile, whether hot or mild, is as tantalizing as it is mysterious. Chile peppers are high in vitamins C and A and iron. They help reduce stress by increasing circulation. They are also proven to help with bronchial, asthmatic and respiratory problems. There is no real documentation linking chiles to digestive maladies. On the contrary, the most recent studies have shown that capsaicin, the enzyme in chile peppers that makes them taste hot assists in the body's processing of food, making the digestive system's acid delivery more balanced and efficient. There is also evidence that because of the trickery capsaicin plays on the brain, chiles may very well be addictive!

Store chiles in an airtight container or steep them in a vinegary dressing with lime, lemon or pineapple and let them soften. I often freeze-dry chiles for a few days when I first buy them. I am amazed by how many times I have had grain moths hatch in a bag of chiles. Freezing them will destroy any microscopic larvae that may possibly be present. (I'd rather deal with this problem myself than encourage chile producers to take the drastic step of applying post-harvest pesticides like citrus fruit growers do or, worse yet, irradiation!)

Here are the chiles I keep in my pantry:

New Mexican reds
These are your basic red chiles found on decorative ristras. Sometimes called Chimayos or Colorados, they have a pure chile flavor and moderate heat level. They can be used to make beautiful red chile purees, real chili and dry rubs for barbecue. Toasted and ground, they are the quintessential chiles for chile powder.

Guajillos

Guajillos are a dried form of the Mirasol chile. They are moderately hot with a hint of plum or currant flavor. Pastes or pestos made with guajillos will keep for two weeks in the refrigerator. They add fun and frolic to a variety of dishes. "Paint" or stripe creamy soups with guajillo pesto. Mix 50-50 with basil pesto and spoon some on top of each clam, add a slice of bacon and bake for the most intense clams casino ever. Mix with Dijon mustard and herbs and baste roasts or serve them with cold beef or pork. It's great!

Cascabels

Cascabels are dried Mexican cherry peppers. They are named for their percussive rattle. They are mildly pungent with a subtle cocoa flavor. They are used pureed in soup or toasted and crumbled in salsas, on pizza or in stews. They are also great marinated in cider vinegar with garlic and herbs.

Chipotles

Chipotles are ripe, red jalapeño peppers that have been slowly smoked over the burning branches of jalapeño plants mixed with mesquite, alder, apple or peach wood. They have a very intense flavor and a fairly strong heat. They add a dimension to gourmet cooking that I can only describe as INVALUABLE. Add just one chipotle to beef, veal or turkey stock and let simmer to add a whole new dimension to demiglace and gravy. Grind one up into a cup or two of cocktail sauce. Soak them in vinegar, salt and oil until they soften and mix with mayonnaise for the best turkey club ever. I keep both dried and canned chipotles en adobo on my shelf.

Ancho chiles

Ancho chiles are a dried form of Poblano peppers. They are bittersweet, mildly pungent and complex. Used in a wide range of dishes, they have prune and cocoa nuances. This puts them on the same plate with beef, venison and other hearty game dishes. Anchos are also a perfect match with chocolate, making them the Mole Poblano chile.

Habaneros a.k.a. Scotch bonnets a.k.a. Jamaican hots
Hottest of the hot, this "King of the Yucatan" chile is commonly used in tropical hot sauces, jerks and salsas. Habaneros have a misleading fruity flavor at first, followed by an incendiary finish. I describe their flavor as "Cantaloupe from Hell!" In the Caribbean, one or two seeded bonnets are sautéed with onions, garlic, red beans, allspice berries, thyme and scallions as a base for peas and rice. Add two or three crushed habaneros to a pot of marinara sauce and explore a true fra diavolo! Wow! They match well with sweet things like mango, banana, papaya, peach and pineapple and "dirty" seasoning like allspice, thyme, marjoram, sage, cinnamon, and nutmeg.

Dried cayenne, Szechuan chiles or chile de arbol
These basic hotskis are perfect for making chile oil, picking up a stirfry or crushing into a pot of pasta.

There is also evidence that because of the trickery capsaicin plays on the brain, chiles may very well be addictive!

Dried Spices

To set the record straight, I classify dried seeds, roots and berries as spices, and leaves and flowers as herbs. There are a few exceptions like saffron, dried star anise and onion powder, but for the most part we can live with this categorization, right?

The best flavors come from freshly ground spices. They are actually mellower that way. When the spices have been ground too far in advance (like the stuff in the supermarket), the juices and water contained in the seeds have evaporated, leaving the pungent oils all alone and creating an unbalanced flavor. Try to buy your spices in small quantities and grind them as you need them. If you grind more than you need, just store the leftovers in a twist of plastic wrap. Always buy non-irradiated organic spices. The preservative treatment that commercial spices receive will make you sick— really. Besides, the good stuff is actually cheaper than the tasteless dust sold in the supermarket.

Remember, this is the minimum allowed by my law. More spices are always welcome.

Here is a list of dried spices I need to know I have, to sleep well:

Allspice berries

Annato seeds

Arrowroot

Coriander seeds

Cumin seeds

Caraway seeds

Cardamom pods

Cloves

Cinnamon (whole and ground— I did say there are always exceptions)

Dry ginger

Crystallized ginger

Fennel seeds

Fenugreek

Gumbo filé

Garlic powder

Galanga root

Yellow mustard seeds

Black mustard seeds

Madras curry powder

Peppercorns, black or tellicherry, white, green and pink

Whole nutmeg

Onion powder

Szechuan pepper

Sea salt, as many kinds as you can afford!

Sesame seeds, natural unhulled, hulled white and black

Turmeric

Herbs

I love herbs! If you get anything from this book it should be how important herbs are to your cooking. I use mostly fresh herbs but there is a place for dried herbs, too. Many Cajun recipes use dried herbs. Dried herbs are also great for making stock and in long-cooking dishes, as their flavor gets more pronounced as they reconstitute in the pot.

One of the best ways to have great dried herbs in your kitchen is to dry them yourself. Whenever I buy a bunch of fresh herbs from the market, I use what I need and then wrap the bases of the stems with a rubber band and tack it to the wall near the stove. In a few weeks, when the bunch is dried out completely, I put it in a clean and dry jar with a tight-fitting lid and store it in a cabinet. This works great for most herbs that I would use dry. Cilantro, basil and parsley are the only herbs that I don't have an application for in their dried form. Other herbs, like the many basils I love, can be frozen. I have freezer bags full of all kinds of herbs from last year's garden in my freezer. In the middle of January, crumbling that frozen globe basil into fish stew is a beautiful thing.

These are the herbs that I buy in dried form (organic only) to keep in my pantry:

Greek and Mexican oregano

Methi leaves

Savory

Thyme

Rosemary

Tarragon

Herbs that I buy or grow fresh, include all of the above, and...:

Lemongrass

Red sage

Purple sage

Garden sage

Yellow sage

Pineapple sage

Cantaloupe sage

Chervil

Lemon thyme

Orange thyme

Lavender

Lemon balm

Lemon verbena

Marjoram

Anise hyssop

Epazote

Mexican marigold mint
  (also known as Texas tarragon)

French tarragon

Russian tarragon

Grow as many as you can...

The following herbs must be used in their fresh state or frozen. Grow as many as you can and snip the tops just before they develop flowers. I snip all summer and by September my plants are nice and bushy, ready to process into pestos, oils and coulis. In small doses, any of these herbs is also an excellent addition to salad greens:

Any form of basil (regular garden basil, Thai basil, globe basil, African black basil, piccolo basil, cinnamon basil, lemon basil, salad leaf basil...)

Parsley, curly and Italian flat leaf

Spearmint, peppermint, chocolate mint, orange mint

Summer savory

Sorrel

Lovage

Burnet

Chives

Garlic chives

Recao (saw-leaf cilantro)

Cilantro

I have freezer bags full of all kinds of herbs...

I must admit that basil is my favorite food. The slightest hint of the aroma of basil intoxicates me. I'm sure it has to do with my Amalfi coast DNA.

At New World we grow up to seven varieties of basil every year. I have a lot of fun adding basil to desserts and salads. The look of inquisitive surprise I see on the face of the customer who has encountered a sprinkling of lemon basil tops in their Double Dark chocolate cake with lemon curd filling is priceless.

Allowing your palate to dictate where and when you use herbs is crucial. We tend to intellectualize when cooking—which is fine, as long as we don't forget to add in the sensual part. Taste some combinations of herbs and other base foods and see what your DNA tells you. You will be surprised at the results and maybe you will add a few new twists to your own cooking repertoire!

Beth Bliss

Sweeteners

Let's get down to it. White stuff is the killer—sugar, flour, cocaine, heroin—they're insidiously addictive and they destroy your health. It may seem nuts to compare sugar with heroin, but in laboratory tests, rats became addicted to both and their health gradually deteriorated. Getting white sugar out of your diet is a challenge if you dine out a lot, but in your own kitchen it's pretty easy. Brown sugar is not the answer. (Remember that commercial brown sugar is actually processed white sugar with some of the molasses added back in.) I have tried numerous substitutes, but for a combination of flavor, cookability and health sense visit your local health food store or shop on-line and stock up any of the following raw sugars:

Succanat (naturally milled cane juice)

Turbinado sugar ("Sugar in the Raw")

Evaporated cane juice ("Florida Crystals")

Barley malt

Other traditional sweeteners in my pantry include:

Honey

Blackstrap molasses

Pure maple syrup

These are all more complex than processed white sugar. Your body processes them a little more slowly and evenly. Succanat, turbinado and evaporated cane juice work in most recipes that call for white sugar and they all taste just like sugar.

For those of you who need to avoid any sugar because of diabetes or other health restrictions, try stevia. Stevia is an amazing herb from Paraguay that sweetens like aspartame. Get this—it is a leaf, not a chemical. There is absolutely no glucose reaction from stevia and it has actually been proven to *reduce* blood glucose levels while sweetening food! Stevia is truly a miracle sweetener and our American chemical sweetener lobby does not want Americans knowing about it. Thanks to expensive lobbying, the FDA has classified stevia as a dietary supplement, not a food.

The Japanese have adopted stevia into their mainstream diet and use it to sweeten about 33% of the confections made in that country, while we have once again allowed our markets to be purchased by the group that can afford to lobby the hardest. Well, in this case it is certainly mainstream America's loss. But you can find stevia in your local health food store and there is an abundance of unbiased information about stevia on-line.

White stuff is the killer—sugar, flour, cocaine, heroin—they're insidiously addictive and they destroy your health.

Flours, Grains & Breads

The tandem of bromated, bleached, processed white flour and refined white sugar creates the one-two punch that has delivered Americans that dreaded disease, Type II Diabetes. If you eat processed foods (candy bars, cereal, cookies, cakes, sandwiches, fried foods, snack bars, pasta, canned soups, gravies—have I left anything out?) you are likely eating highly processed white flour. This stuff, combined with refined sugar, is a silent killer, forcing your metabolism into high-speed mode and then allowing it to crash within an hour or so. So, you hit the flour or sugar again to get back up into high gear and then you crash again. Sound familiar? Let me help you beat the cycle by turning you on to some superior selections.

First of all, watch the quality of the breads you buy and think about the quantity of the bread you eat. One sandwich is two slices—that's plenty for an average day's consumption. If the inside is really snowy white and the air bubbles are uniform, it's probably fake—by fake I mean that the flour is bromated and contains various dough conditioners—SUPER unhealthy. If your area has an artesan baker, that's usually a good place to get bread made with milled flour, natural starter and little else. There are now many sources on the web for artesan breads.

Enjoy whole grain bread or spelt bread for sandwiches. It won't be as chewy as we have become accustomed to. That's okay. That chewiness is a pretty synthetic experience anyway. Lightly toasted spelt bread makes an excellent sandwich. Also, try doing bread with dinner the way many Europeans do—as dessert! The bread, cheese and fruit dessert course is common and lets you get filled up on food first, so that you don't eat a loaf of bread before dinner!

Buy organic, unbleached and unbromated all-purpose flour for general cooking and breading use. Use less as a rule by blending it with some of the following alternatives:

For everyday use, get stone-ground whole wheat flour. Not all whole wheat is the same. The stuff they use to make cheap whole wheat bread is barely better than white flour. Like brown sugar, it is often highly processed white flour with some of the bran added back in. Useless. Stone-ground wheat is like extra virgin olive oil. All the good stuff is still in there.

Another great general-use flour is brown rice flour. It is used in Asian cooking for light frying and baking. Rice flour is also an excellent binder for thickening stews and sauces.

For baking options, try spelt and kamut flour. Both of these grains are ancient relatives of wheat and are very Clean and healthy. Many breads and pizza recipes can be made using these flours exclusively or in combination with wheat flour. For muffins, cookies, and pancakes I have fun with wild rice flour, organic cornmeal (yellow or blue), amaranth flour and oat flour. They all have an affinity for sweetness and your kids won't know the difference. (See Episode Nine for information on brown rice.)

About Gluten Intolerance

There is a growing awareness of a condition named Celiac's disease which effects 1 in every 133 Americans. It is charactorized by a toxic reation to gluten. It is a very serious disorder that goes undiagnosed in millions of people, mostly of Euorpean descent. Wheat, rye, barley and oats are the grains that celiacs should not consume. Both spelt and kamut are versions of wheat. Bulgur is wheat that's been specially processed. Triticale, a grain crossbred from wheat and rye, is definitely on the toxic list. Gluten intolerance symptons include digestive disorders, weight loss and nutritional deficiencies and may contribute to arthritis, skin diseases and acne, asthma, autism and schizophrenia. Often, the symptoms are mistakenly treated with topical medications that ease the symptoms without addressing the true source. Ceiliac's disease may have a cumulative effect on your immune system and your general heath. Sound intense? It is intense. To find out more about Celiac's disease ask your doctor or visit http://celiac.com/.

Flours:

Stone-ground whole wheat flour

Unrefined white flour

American corn meal

Almond flour

Chick pea flour

Hominy grits

Polenta

Corn flour (Red, White, Yellow and Blue)

Masa

Cassava flour

Lentil flour

Potato flour or starch

Matzoh meal

Split pea flour

Spelt flour

Rye flour

Kamut flour

Amaranth flour

Brown rice flour

White rice flour

Grains (all organic):

Brown rice (use long grain for every day consumption, side dishes and stir fries, brown basmati for pilafs, sweet brown rice for puddings and risotto, short grain brown for paellas and pilaus)

Unhulled barley

Quinoa

Amaranth

Millet

Teff

Bulgur

Buckwheat groats

Whole oats

Cross cut oats

Hominy or posole

Wheat berries

Pasta and Noodles

Okay, this was a tough one for me. I grew up in a Southern Italian household and pasta was a daily event for me. I know now that pasta made with refined flour *shouldn't* be a daily experience. The "pasta crash" is that wonderful feeling about 45 minutes after eating that either puts you to sleep or beckons you to dessert! Look, I didn't quit pasta, I just put it in perspective. I eat semolina pasta once or twice a month at most. I eat brown rice pasta twice a week. It is a smart road to get on and it will lead us to a healthier place.

On the way there, there are some pasta variations that you should consider. I have tried many whole grain pastas and they do take a little getting used to. Good pasta is all about mouthfeel. That silky, glutenous Durum wheat texture is almost inimitable. However, these satisfying versions of pasta are also very delicious. One of the secrets I have found when using alternative pastas is to cook them all the way, strain and put them into the sauce to soak up some of the flavor.

Brown rice pasta is probably the closest to semolina in mouthfeel. Brown rice pasta is a complex carbohydrate that is digested slowly and efficiently. It has a slightly nutty flavor and a smooth texture and I really like it. We serve excellent brown rice pasta at my café. It doesn't take much getting used to. After one or two tries, it quickly becomes part of your culinary repertoire because it makes you feel great!

Quinoa, whole wheat and kamut pasta are slightly grainier but are acceptable in baked pasta casseroles. Artichoke and Jerusalem artichoke pastas are combined with wheat and are also fantastic.

As for traditional pasta, the real thing is the real thing! If you can afford this book, you can afford to pay two or three dollars for a pound of pasta that will feed four people. The budget pasta on the market today is usually flimsy and made with inferior wheat. We serve Bionature, an Italian pasta made from organic semolina, in my kitchens. It is delicious. If you can't find the organic stuff, eat what the Italians eat—Dececco, DelVerde, Tama or Rummo are good brands. Fresh specialty pastas are all fun and delicious, too.

For Asian cookery there are numerous noodles made with buckwheat and semolina. Try using soba noodles in a stir-fry. Or how about using brown rice spaghetti in your next lo mein? Of course there are times when there is no substitute, as in making pad Thai—only rice vermicelli will do and that's cool. After all, you aren't going to make it every day, are you?

I didn't quit pasta, I just put it in perspective...

Rice TV

The "Ric-ter" Scale

In the following recipes, as on our house menu at New World Home Cooking Co., the heat and spiciness of each dish is rated numerically via my "Ric-ter" scale.

Here is how my dishes are rated:

*0-3: Mild. Seasonings may include garlic, herbs, citrus.

*4-6: Assertive, but not hot, as in sauce au poivre, a bowl of chili or ginger sauce.

*7-8: Authentically spicy Caribe, Thai or Central American-style hot...balanced, delicious, the real thing.

*9-10: Over the top, for aficionados only. At New World, we warn our customers that dishes ordered at *9 or hotter cannot be returned.

Occasionally when someone orders a dish rated as a *7 or more, they go into a panic after the first bite. If this is you, file this advice: eating hot food is like diving into a cold pool naked. Deal with the initial shock and you will adjust quickly; jump right out and you will end up sitting on the deck shivering by yourself! Choose according to your own preference, but if you dive in...KEEP SWIMMING! The bright, strong flavorings and spices in good clean cooking are easier on your digestive system than bland food with additives. That is a physiological fact, Jack!

Episode One: Seafood for Keeps

Taped July 29, 2002

‘The industry is trying to convince the public that the environmentalists are leading an orchestrated effort to put small, family-owned fishing companies out of business. The truth is exactly the opposite...’

Recipes:

Portuguese Fisherman's Stew

Pale Ale-Lemongrass Mussels

Wild Salmon Wrapped in Corn Husks on the Grill

In this show I am preparing eco-friendly dishes using some of our favorite seafood—shrimp, cod, mussels, squid and wild salmon. The great thing is that we will use sustainable alternatives—seafood that is both environmentally safe and also bountiful. I was on a panel at a Sustainable Seafood Conference at the Culinary Institute of America in the spring of 2002. What was most striking to me was how technology has changed fishing and the way the seafood industry markets its products. Sustainability and species survival are serious issues because the American seafood industry, like our produce, grain, and meat industries, has consolidated its offerings to increase profitability.

Just compare the seafood on display at an American supermarket's seafood section to an Asian or traditional Mediterranean fish market. The American supermarket may have six to ten choices at the most. An Asian fish market has at least twice, sometimes four to five times as many choices. This American consolidation of market choices creates a stressful situation for many seafood species. On the one hand we are being told that we should be eating more seafood and, on the other hand, we are being offered a small percentage of what is out there to eat. Salmon, sword, haddock, halibut, flounder, sea bass, sole, trout, catfish and a few old standby shellfish items are the whole of our selection. Lemme see, how many edible species are there in the sea...hundreds? Thousands? If our demand for fish is increasing, so should our number of choices. Diversifying our tastes will lessen the stress on the oceans' livestock, which will diminish the tension between the environmental and industrial camps.

The seafood industry lobby is trying to convince the public that the environmentalists are leading an orchestrated effort to put small, family-owned fishing companies out of business. The truth is exactly the opposite: if all of our fish came from independent family companies out there bringing us their catch, we wouldn't be in the pickle we are in today. Just as in all other segments of farming, the family-owned company segment of the fishing industry is shrinking. It is the corporate industrial fishing interests that have created this imbalance: since the mid-1980s the impact of the computer revolution has been felt everywhere, including the fishing industry. The major corporate players, with their ability to send out fleets for weeks at a time, harvesting megatons of seafood with advanced technological devices, have changed the entire concept of commercial fishing. Don't be misled by misinformation. There is a monumental difference between the romantic idea of a small fishing boat and its quirky crew chasing down a school of cod and a multinational corporation's massive fleets and lobbying strength. This ain't about Hemingway! It's about exploitation and future vision—or lack of it.

So, when I refer to a seafood choice as "sustainable," I am referring to two things: the state of the species and the environmental impact of how that species is harvested.

The state of the species is measurable in many cases. The average size of a swordfish brought to market in the 1960s was over 200 pounds. In 2000 it was under 80 pounds. Keep in mind that the average swordfish doesn't procreate until it reaches about 150 pounds. That is bad math, baby! If we are catching fish before they spawn, we will eventually be out of fish. That is not an alarmist statement, it is an obvious conclusion.

Here's how I learned about sustainability practices first hand: I grew up on the Connecticut coast. When I was very young I recall fishing with my uncles in Long Island Sound, catching striped bass that were bigger than I was. What majestic fish they were! Strong and shiny with noble heads and dense striped bodies, they were the very image of a great catch. We ate big filets out of foil packs at barbecues and out of my grandmother's casserole pot smothered in tomato sauce on rainy Fridays. I loved fishing stripers from Long Island Sound when I was in my early teens.

Then they started disappearing. We could fish for hours without seeing one striped bass. Plenty of blue and skate, but no stripers. Eventually a size limit was introduced. It was illegal to take in a fish under 36 inches long. Then 40 inches. Then there was a complete ban on catching them. An effort to protect an overfished species was underway, but at that time in my life I perceived it as an inconvenience and an injustice. I, like the rest of the fisherman on Long Island Sound moved on to other fish—tautog, blue, fluke and rockfish.

This is where nature in all of her wisdom outdoes us. In 2002, twenty years after I caught my last striper, the great fish is back. Striped bass is now on restaurant menus and in fish markets all over the East Coast. Given a respite from being fished, a species will return to full strength in a relatively short span of time. Lesson learned? We can't just consume massive catches of a particular fish from the same place year in and year out without eventually diminishing the species.

This is where making sustainable choices plays an incisive role. Commercial fishing is an industry with a product line and financial goals. Like the rest of American industry, it has experienced rapid technological advances. Tracking and catching fish is no longer a sport, it is a science. Large vessels use radar and sonar to observe the fish before harvesting them. This has led to many species' being fished to the brink of extinction. The best way to choose is to check the reports of public interest nonprofit groups like the Audubon Society. Unlike many government agencies, which are subjected to intense lobbying by those who can afford the most, these groups have no financial interest in fish. That's where I put my faith.

Now we return to my basic theme of keeping the food industry honest: use your $$$$! Diversify your seafood choices. Try new things. Learn how to cook mackerel and wolf fish and sea trout. The Alaskan black sable fish used in today's recipe is hardy because it is not one of the major fish marketed in America. It is a great alternative to Chilean sea bass and Atlantic cod with its buttery, white, flaky flesh.

Remember: industry is listening to one thing—your money. If we all want to eat swordfish every night, the industry is eager to make it happen by any means possible, including genetic modification and decimation of an ancient member of the food chain. Not exactly the best thing, is it? Be wise and taste new things! I won't steer you wrong in this. There are more delectable items in the sea than we could taste in a lifetime. Let's mix it up!

The second aspect of sustainability we should become aware of is the environmental impact of repeated harvesting. This is especially crucial along our coasts, although it is important on the open seas as well.

The ocean is crowded with millions of species depending on each other for survival. We can't just damage or diminish one area without affecting another one drastically. For instance: harvesting clams and mussels is currently a dredging process. The ocean floor is overturned and sifted to harvest most shellfish. Imagine the destructive effect on plant life and small species at the bottom of the food chain. When these guys are eliminated, the bigger guys who dine on them stop coming around, and then the even bigger guys stop coming around and the circle is broken. I know it sounds simplistic, but that's the way it is. We don't know enough about nature to mess with it! After all, because we are just a part of the process, we are limited in how much we can understand it. Hell, we don't even know what 90% of our own brain does yet! What makes us think we could tweak the ecosystem in the ocean without it coming back to bite us—hard?

On the subject of shellfish—or as the Italians have named it "frutta di mare," the fruit of the sea—there are some illuminating developments. Rope-grown mussels are a great example of sustainable seafood. The mussels are grown on ropes submerged in the sea. To harvest these mussels, workers simply retrieve the ropes. Nice, Clean and smart. Raised beds are also being used for oyster, clam and scallop farming. That keeps the harvester from destroying virgin ocean floor with every scoop. There is more information about these methods on-line. Look it up and inform yourself. The more we learn, the smarter we are.

Shrimp are another major element in the sustainable seafood discussion. There are two major negatives to shrimp harvesting that must be addressed sooner rather than later. (There is good news so keep reading!) Traditional shrimp farmers used small nets and simply scooped up all of the shrimp they could carry in their nets and small boats. There could be a harbor full of fishermen with their hand-held nets out there and they couldn't impact the ecosystem if they wanted to.

But modern technology has had a disastrous impact. Shrimp are now caught by huge trolling-nets dragged along the bottom of the ocean. And guess what? This method is more than nature can handle. You see, not only humans love shrimp—so do young grouper, red snapper and a myriad of the oceans' finest. So when these shrimp trollers are harvesting tons of shrimp at a time, their nets are filled with these other species—including many of the undersized young fish. This is known as "bycatch." The bycatch of shrimp is more than 50%! That means that more than half of what is pulled up in these shrimp nets is something other than shrimp.

Unfortunately, the stress of being retrieved in a net full of tons of struggling cohabitants usually kills many of the smaller fish caught. This is considered part of the cost of doing business.

The second pitfall of our demand for shrimp is shrimp farming. The process of farming shrimp is very polluting. Ancient Mangrove swamps in Southeast Asia are used to farm shrimp—good habitat, cheap land, great deal for the shrimp farmers, right? Wrong! After a few years of ingesting the waste produced by digestive tracts of tons of shrimp, these swamps become devastated toxic sites, unusable for generations. The shrimp farmers move on and the local native peoples are left with a sick harbor and far fewer fish to harvest for themselves. Bad deal all around.

The good news about shrimp, which I promised earlier, is that there are some harvesting alternatives finally becoming available. The spot shrimp that we are going to use in the following recipes are harvested in a sustainable manner. Instead of being netted, they are trapped in cages, which prevents the massive bycatch of current shrimp harvesting. These are cold water shrimp from Alaska, sweet and good!

On the one hand we are being told that we should be eating more seafood, and on the other hand, we are being offered a small percentage of what is out there to eat.

Portuguese Fisherman's Stew

Serves 4. Ricter Scale *4

This fish stew, called a caldierada, provides a great example of the Mediterranean and North African influences in Portuguese cooking. The Portuguese were the backbone of the development of the great North-eastern fishing industry. Their hearty nature and robust palate have made their cuisine one of the best-kept culinary secrets in Europe. The seafood items in this dish are all similar to those used on Cape Cod 100 years ago, but they are alternative, sustainable choices. Once all fish were bountiful. Now we have to make the commitment to diversify our fish choices.

One 12-ounce Alaskan black sable (a.k.a. Black Cod) or Alaskan halibut filet
32 rope-grown mussels
1 pound fresh Maine shrimp or Alaskan spot shrimp
12 ounces Nantucket Bay scallops
8 ounces Monterey Bay calamari
1/3 cup red bell pepper, diced medium
2/3 cup white onion, diced medium
3 tablespoons extra virgin olive oil
2 teaspoons garlic, finely minced
3 tablespoons tomato paste
1 cup Vinho Verde or other tart white wine
1/2 teaspoon curry powder
1/2 teaspoon black pepper
1/3 teaspoon ginger, grated
1 teaspoon fresh cilantro, minced
1/2 teaspoon fresh thyme leaves
1/2 teaspoon dry oregano
1 fresh bay leaf or three dry ones, whole
1/3 cup fresh parsley, chopped
1 teaspoon crushed red pepper
4 cups organic canned tomatoes, roughly diced
16 ounces canned clam juice

First prepare your seafood: cut the filet into eight relatively equal chunks and rinse with cold water. Cut the squid into 1/4-inch thick rings, not too thin or it will curl up on itself. Rinse with cold water. Check the mussels for beards or debris and scrub well. Rinse with cold water. Use scissors to cut the shell on the back of the shrimp. *Leaving the shell on,* remove the digestive vein and rinse with cold water. Rinse the scallops with cold water. Set the seafood aside until your stew is ready for it. Keep it away from the stove—and the cat—but not in the fridge.

Now make the stew. Use a heavy stainless or porcelain-lined pot or Dutch oven with a lid. Over medium-high heat, wilt the onions and peppers in the olive oil. Turn up the heat and add the garlic. Let it sizzle until it releases its aroma but does not change color. Add the tomato paste and stir it in well with a wooden spoon. Now add the wine and all of the herbs and spices except the parsley—that goes in at the end. Bring it to a boil and cook over high heat for three to four minutes to evaporate most of the alcohol from the wine. Now add the canned tomatoes and their juice and the fish stock or clam juice. Simmer for 15 minutes to let all the flavors settle in together. Turn the heat to medium-low and let the sauce reduce at a delicate simmer. Add the fish filet first and let it cook about three minutes. Gently—gently—don't let the sauce boil hard. Now stir in the shrimp and scallops.

Cook for two or three more minutes and add the mussels. Cover and cook for two more minutes. Remove the lid, add the squid and stir gently. Put the cover on the pot and turn off the heat. Leave it covered for five minutes. The seafood will gently finish cooking in the steaming sauce. Fish out the bay leaves. Serve in big bowls with a fork, a spoon, bread and hot sauce on the side. Garnish with plenty of parsley.

Ric's tip: *it is important to keep the internal temperature of seafood below boiling (212°F). Once it has reached 160°F it is fully cooked. There is no need to cook it any further unless you prefer tough, rubbery food. When it is boiled its essential liquids begin to evaporate and it will become dry. By lowering the heat and covering the pot you create a delicate steaming situation.*

Pale Ale-Lemon Grass Mussels

Serves 4. Ricter Scale *7

We're just getting started here and I am sure it's already pretty clear to you that a bowl of braised seafood is my idea of a good time. Maybe it's my Sicilian and Amalfi roots. I just can't resist anything in a shell in a broth.

I used to be a devotee of big, wild mussels until I learned how they were harvested: huge machines dredge the ocean floor, wreaking havoc on the ecosystem. Any other life forms, both plant and animal, that are existing there are uprooted and destroyed. Sorry, for my money this can't be good. Rope-grown mussels are grown on ropes (duh) suspended from docking structures. There is minimal impact on the other living creatures.

There is another positive to rope-grown shellfish: they are not embedded in the ocean silt. Most hazardous materials, such as sewage residue and heavy metals, that are dumped in the ocean sink to the bottom and remain in the upper layers of sediment where the mollusks live. Eating rope-grown seafood is an excellent way to minimize your consumption of stuff you'd rather not consume!

This concoction has been refined over the years. My old friend, Johnny Levins, the electrifying chef of the Green Street Grill in Cambridge, Massachusetts, turned me on to beer and lemongrass cookery. Your whole house will smell bewitched.

Ric Orlando

2 tablespoons garlic, pureed

3 medium shallots, minced

1 tablespoon roasted peanut oil

32 ounces quality bottled clam juice

1 stalk lemongrass, cut into 2-inch segments

4 chipotles en adobo, minced

*2 tablespoons Texas tarragon a.k.a. Mexican marigold mint
(a combination of 1 tablespoon fresh tarragon, 1 teaspoon
basil and 1 teaspoon minced mint leaves can be used to
substitute for Texas tarragon)*

1 teaspoon basil

1 teaspoon cilantro

6 ounces Bass or other delicious pale ale

5 pounds rope-grown mussels, scrubbed and debearded

2 tablespoons organic butter (optional)

1 medium tomato, diced small

1 cup sliced scallions

In a large wok or pot with a tight-fitting lid, sizzle garlic and shallots in oil for one minute and then add all the clam juice and lemongrass. Simmer briskly for five minutes, then add the chipotles and herbs. Cook for two more minutes then add the ale. Cook for one more minute, add all of the mussels and cover. Cook over medium heat, covered, for three minutes. Turn off the heat, add the organic butter and re-cover the pan, allowing the mussels to steam without boiling.

Ladle into big bowls, with plenty of broth. Sprinkle each bowl with diced tomatoes and scallions.

Wild Salmon Grilled in Corn Husks

Serves two as a dinner, four as a lunch or appetizer. Ricter Scale *0

Grilling fish wrapped in corn husks is a cooking method dating back to pre-Columbian times. The husk protects the delicate flesh of the fish and imparts a sweet, nutty aroma to the dish. The corn husks I use are the large and sturdy New Mexican variety. (They are available in most gourmet stores, Mexican stores, or see my page on sourcing at the end of this book.) You can use our native Northeast husks, just double them up to prevent burning.

The salmon used in this dish have been harvested in an environmentally clean manner. If you cannot obtain the salmon, try any full-flavored filet. Wild striped bass, Connecticut blackfish, Alaskan sable or halibut, or West Coast corvina filet are great alternatives.

Four 4-ounce Alaskan king or sockeye salmon filets

6-8 large corn husks, soaked in warm water until soft

2 large lemons, washed and sliced into thin rounds

2 large oranges, washed and sliced into thin rounds

2 large leeks, split, dark greens discarded, washed well

2 large firm apples, cored and sliced into thin half moons

2 bunches fresh dill, cilantro, basil, chervil or tarragon
 (or a mix of any of these)

4 tablespoons organic fromage blanc or other mild goat cheese

2 tablespoons olive oil

pinch of salt and black pepper

Preheat your grill to medium hot. Soak the corn husks until pliable. Use one sheet to tear strips for tying your bundles; tear eight 1/4-inch-thick strips lengthwise and reserve. Lay out four large husks to fill. Layer equal amounts of each ingredient onto each husk in the following order:

lemon slices

orange slices

leeks

apples

a few pinches of your fresh herb(s)

1 fish filet

1 tablespoon goat cheese

splash olive oil

salt and pepper to taste and a few more pinches of herb(s)

Grill fish right side up—with the fish and the goat cheese up and the fruit on the bottom—for four to five minutes, or until the husk begins to get darkened and a little black around the edges. As the heat penetrates the fruits on the bottom, they will begin to caramelize and release steam that will gently cook the fish. Now move the fish to a cooler part of the grill and allow it to gently finish steaming for two to three more minutes. Carefully peel open and serve right in the husks!

Ric TV Seafood Buying Recommendations

BEST CHOICES
Anchovies
Bluefish
Catfish
Clams
Crab: Blue, Stone, Dungeness
Crawfish
Atlantic Herring
Hake
Hoki (New Zealand Cod)
Mackerel: Atlantic, Spanish
  Mahi Mahi or Dorado
Mussels (rope grown)
Oysters (farmed)
Rainbow Trout (farmed)
Sable (Black Cod)
Salmon (Wild Alaskan)
Sardines
Scallops, (farmed)
Shrimp/Prawns:
Northern Maine and
  trap-caught spot prawns
Squid (Calamari)
Striped Bass (farmed)
Sturgeon (farmed)
Tilapia (farmed)
Tuna: Pacific Albacore

MODERATE RISK
Blackfish a.k.a. Tautog
Bluefish
Flounder: "Summer Flounder", Fluke
Halibut (Pacific)
Lobsters
Pollack
Salmon (wild from WA, OR, BC
  Canada)
Scallops (Bay)

Striped Bass
Snapper
Snow Crab
Sole
Tilefish
Tuna: Yellowfin
Weakfish a.ka. Seatrout
Yellowtail Snapper

**GIVE THESE A CHANCE
TO REBUILD**
Alaska King Crab
Atlantic Cod
Grouper
Haddock
Halibut (Atlantic)
Lingcod
Monkfish
Orange Roughy
Pacific Rockfish (Rock Cod)
Salmon (farmed)
Scallops (Sea)
Scrod
Seabass: Chilean
Shark: all species
Red Snapper
Shrimp/Prawns: farmed and wild
  trawler-caught
Skate
Swordfish, especially fish caught
  under 180 lbs
Toothfish: Patagonian a.k.a. Chilean
  Seabass
Tuna: Bluefin
Yellowtail Flounder

Episode Two:
Sexy Snacks
Taped July 29, 2002

"My mission is to convince you that there are definite health benefits to seeking out and eating what I like to call Clean Food."

Recipes:

Poké of Cured Salmon and Tuna

Wasabikko Deviled Eggs

Strawberry and Goat Cheese Bruschette

As a chef I am in constant contact with food. And the food with which I am in contact has been changing at an alarming rate over the last decade. Finding food that is not made with genetically modified ingredients, and hasn't been injected with chemicals and sprayed with stabilizers, is becoming quite challenging. My mission is to convince you that there are definite health benefits to seeking out and eating what I like to call Clean Food. Clean Food means food that has been grown, harvested and prepared in a traditional manner. Clean Food is sexy food. Clean Food makes you feel sexy after you eat it!

As we venture forth into the jungle of health information, there is one recurring truth that continues to surface through the marketing muck: that the traditional diets of regional peoples are the healthiest diets of all. Are they low-fat, low-calorie, high-carbohydrate diets like the one the FDA recommends for us? Not exactly. The healthy, ancestral diets of the world are based on fresh, local ingredients, in balance and harmony with the seasons. Clean fats combined with fresh fruits, vegetables and legumes constitute the optimum diet. Thinking about food in this way is the healthiest approach possible. It's Clean, sexy food!

The three recipes I offer today all contain a fair amount of fat, but it's all unprocessed, "good" fat. Most traditional diets contain considerably higher amounts of fat than our own FDA recommends. They also contain more calories. Our bodies *need* fat and a fair amount of it to operate properly. Fats carry vitamins A, D, E and K. Fats are found in every single cell of the body. Why do you think they are called Essential Fatty Acids? The challenging task is learning the difference between good and bad fats and then learning where to get good, Clean fats. Consuming a reasonable amount of Clean fat not only increases your HDL or "good" cholesterol, it actually lowers your LDL or "bad" cholesterol.

That is sexy!

New World Poké of Cured Alaskan Salmon and Tuna Serves eight. Ricter Scale *5

Poké is a popular and spicy seafood tartar from Hawaii. There are as many recipes for poké as there are for, say, potato salad. That's good, because once you have a feel for making poké, you can design your own according to your own tastes. For me, this is the perfect kind of cocktail dish—beautiful, assertive and settling. The intense protein fix and the excellent fats from the fish will keep you and your guests sated while mingling. This is very important when you are pouring delicious sparkling wines!

About the good fats—the acids in the tuna and salmon are never exposed to heat, so they are in perfect condition! The seaweed also contains the important trace minerals naturally found in the sea—selenium, zinc and iodine. Seaweed is Clean Food at its best.

1/4 cup wakame (dried green seaweed), hijiki (black seaweed), or arame (brown "twig" seaweed), reconstituted

6 ounces sushi-grade tuna

6 ounces sushi-grade raw Alaskan salmon or gravlax (see recipe below), or you may substitute any fine quality cured salmon

2 tablespoons finely chopped scallions

1 tablespoon grated ginger

1 small Thai chile, sliced into thin rings or
  1 teaspoon crushed red pepper flakes

2 tablespoons sesame seeds

2 tablespoons dark soy sauce

1 tablespoon toasted sesame oil

1 tablespoon sweet vinegar or Mirin

1 package of brown rice-tamari crackers, endive petals or Romaine hearts

Put the seaweed in a work bowl. Cover with three cups warm water and allow it to reconstitute (about five minutes). It will bloom to two to three times its size, so make sure your bowl is big enough! When it has bloomed, strain and squeeze out any excess water.

Dice the fish into small pieces—slightly bigger than minced. In a glass bowl, toss gently with the seaweed and all of the other remaining ingredients except the crackers. Refrigerate for 15 minutes to allow the flavors to mingle, like your guests. Serve cold, spooned onto rice-seaweed crackers, endive petals or Romaine hearts.

Gravlax Salt and Sugar Cured Salmon
Serves four with leftovers. Richter Scale *0

One 2-pound filet of wild sockeye or king salmon, skin still on

1/4 cup strong Dijon mustard

1/2 cup sea salt

1/4 cup turbinado sugar or organic sugar ("Florida's Crystals")

1 tablespoon coarsely ground coriander seeds

Place the salmon on a plate with the skin side down. Use your hands to rub the mustard into the flesh of the fish. Mix all the dry ingredients and sprinkle the mixture onto the filet like a thin coating of snow. Carefully wrap the whole thing in plastic wrap or waxed paper.

Set another plate on top of the fish, creating a gentle press and refrigerate. Let the fish cure for two to three days. Rinse under cold water to remove most of the curing salt before serving. Store the leftovers in the refrigerator!

Finding food that is not made with genetically modified ingredients and hasn't been injected with chemicals and sprayed with stabilizers is becoming quite challenging.

Wasabikko Deviled Eggs

Serves six to eight. Richter Scale #5

Wasabikko is fish roe flavored with wasabi. If you have eaten sushi, you have probably had tobikko or Japanese-style caviar. Made from the roe of smaller fish like smelt or flying fish, it is quite affordable. The wasabi flavor in wasabikko is unusually delicious. The combination of eggs and mayonnaise with the pop and crunch of the fish roe and the pungency of the wasabi is WILD! Serve these at your next cocktail party and video-tape the expressions on your guests' faces as they let the texture of these eggs develop in their mouths. You will be creating culinary erotica!

1 tablespoon frozen wasabi or wasabi powder

1/2 cup or more of prepared safflower mayonnaise

1 dozen large free-range chicken eggs

2 – 3 tablespoons wasabikko, plus more for garnish

Whisk the wasabi into the mayo and set aside. Hard-boil the eggs, then cool and carefully peel them. Rinse the eggs gently under cold water to remove any residual shell pieces. Cut the eggs in half lengthwise and remove the yolks to a medium-sized mixing bowl. Put the cooked whites on a serving platter. Whisk the wasabi-infused mayonnaise into the yolks to blend. Whisk thoroughly until the mixture is smooth. (An electric hand mixer is perfect for this job.) Fold two to three tablespoons of wasabikko into the prepared mayonnaise. Fill a piping bag, fitted with a large star tip, with the yolk mixture and pipe into each white half. Garnish with a sprinkling of wasabikko. Serve cold.

Strawberry, Tomato and Basil Salad on Goat Cheese Bruschette

Serves four. Ric-ter Scale *3

Local strawberry season is one of those agricultural events that starts with a trickle, proceeds to a flood and then dries up almost overnight. When Fourth-of-July berries are plentiful at farm stands, this is the dish to use them in to knock your friends' socks off. The complex textures and tart accents of pepper and vinegar are sensational. This recipe provides a good opportunity to use up those delicious berries that may be slightly bruised or imperfect. I served this dish at the 1999 Taste of the Nation event in Fishkill, New York and my 10-year-old son, Willie, helped me serve. So many people were puzzled by the combination of strawberries and basil that he began barking in his deep raspy voice, "Just taste it!" to the guests. He was as big a hit as the food was!

For the Dressing:

1 cup balsamic vinegar

1/4 cup dry red wine

1 tablespoon Worcestershire sauce

3 tablespoons evaporated cane juice or organic sugar

For the Salad:

3 cups ripe strawberries, hulled and cut in half lengthwise

2 cups ripe tomatoes, diced

20-25 fresh basil leaves

coarsely ground black pepper

fruity extra-virgin olive oil

For the Toast:

Twelve 1/2-inch-thick slices Italian or French bread

8 ounces fromage blanc or other mild, soft goat cheese

Put all of the dressing ingredients in a non-reactive pot, bring to a boil and reduce by half. Let the mixture cool. Tear or gently chop the basil into bite-size pieces. Add the strawberries, tomatoes and chopped basil to the cool dressing and fold gently together. Gently toast the bread slices in a toaster oven or broiler. Spread each with a schmear of goat cheese. With a slotted spoon, put a spoonful of berries and basil onto the goat cheese toasts. Drizzle with some of the remaining dressing and grind a little more black pepper on the top, if you like.

That's my "co-star" Kevin on the right.

Episode Three:
We Do Chicken, Right?

Taped July 30, 2002

'The flavor of organic and real free-range chicken is richer, and the texture more substantial, because the chicken develops muscle from actually walking around in the barn and in the pasture.'

Recipes:

Punjabi Style Chicken

Simple Vietnamese Chicken Soup

Chicken Stuffed with Chevre, Sage and Prosciutto

The Chef's Treat

Today we're going to talk about one if my real pet peeves—the "I don't wanna know" syndrome! We all say we want Clean Food, but when we try to discuss some of the real issues, we get all squeamed-out! If you want real food, you have to deal with the facts. The fact is that happy farm animals are excellent food for many of us. In Europe and Asia the majority of birds are sold with their heads still attached, so the buyer can better inspect the animal. That always grosses Americans out, but it should do just the opposite. Don't you want to know where your food comes from?

If we can connect with that concept and buy intelligently, we'll have Clean Food—if not we'll just get more "mystery nuggets!" Look, I'm here to entertain you and at the same time I want to turn you on to Clean Food.

The mantra is "We want Clean Food," and we'll go out of our way to get it!

Let's get to work! Today's show is called "We Do Chicken, Right?" Everybody loves chicken, especially kids. And why not? It is inexpensive, neutral tasting and easy to cook. It's also a Clean protein source that makes us feel good. We humans have been cooking and eating domesticated chicken since about 4000 BC. Chicken breeding in America was in full swing during the mid-1800s, but it was between the World Wars that commercial chicken farming became a multi-million dollar industry. To continue to meet the demand for America's chicken love, chicken producers have added many questionable practices to their processes. They use artificial growth hormones and stimulants, antibiotics and synthetic feed to get those girls up to weight and into the market more quickly. And why wouldn't they fatten them up and get them to market in half the time? When it gets to that level, it's not farming—it's food manufacturing! As long as we accept it, it will be done!

The health benefits of chicken are best realized from eating the best chickens. Let me give you a little RicTV guide to help you out—sort of a RicTV seal of approval.

There are various grades and names of chicken on the market. The most popular is "Fresh Grade A Chicken." Our culture's favorite food term is "fresh." It conjures up cozy, farmy homestead images of security. Sadly, fresh is probably the least meaningful term there is on a food label. It only means the food is not canned or frozen. So-called fresh or "regular" chicken is commonly pumped with growth hormones for rapid development. These birds are indiscriminately fed antibiotics to counteract the squalid conditions they live in—like living in high rise coops with no central plumbing, for instance—Man, I'd hate to live on the ground floor! Okay, don't moan—the more we acknowledge, the better off we are! Wanna hear more?After it's slaughtered, the bird is infused with artificial and/or so called "natural flavors" to enhance the flavor of the meat. Hmmm—why would a chicken need "chicken flavor" added to it, anyway? And that's the "Grade A" stuff! The lower grades are really scary— they're used for processed nuggets, cutlets and other manufactured chicken meals. Calling these items chicken is like calling Kool-Aid juice. The chemicals used in this kind of chicken production are harmful to our bodies and our environment.

What About Free-Range or Pastured Chicken?

This is what we should all be eating, period. Where can you find it? It's around. You just may have to change a few shopping habits to get it. It's readily available at many butcher shops, larger health food stores and better supermarkets and you can also find local sources on the internet.

The flavor of organic and real free-range chicken is richer and the texture more substantial because the chicken develops muscle from actually walking around in the barn and in the pasture. It's also able to graze freely on grains, grasses and insects, which makes the meat more flavorful and higher in natural minerals.

This is absolutely the best option for feeding chicken to your family. The relativey high price is still really cheap in the grand scheme of things. Think about it. A home-cooked meal with fresh veggies, spuds, salad and a four-pound organic bird will easily feed a family of four for under 20 bucks, or at around the same price as a trip to Fast Food Chain A, B or C.

The other type of chicken you'll encounter in the market is "Minimally Processed" or "Natural" Chicken. Minimally processed chicken means just that—it has been minimally processed. Its head, feet, entrails and feathers were removed, it was washed and packaged to ship. This term also indicates that there have been no preservatives, artificial flavors or stabilizers added to the chicken after it has been slaughtered. That seems fine, except, what about before it was slaughtered? "Minimally processed" on a label has nothing to do with the way a chicken has been raised. The hormones and antibiotics are still in there...

The more I have cooked chicken, the more I'm convinced there is no free lunch—the money we save buying bargain chicken is the money we spend on medicines and drugs later in life! Don't encourage the big producers. The more you buy, the more they produce. Remember: they are food manufacturers responding to your demand! These scary techniques, developed over the last 30 years to produce these pseudo-chickens, are a direct response to our consumer demand. We have the absolute power of the dollar on our side. If we begin to insist on Clean poultry and we spend our money on it, not only do we and our families eat better, we also create a healthier environment. What's the mantra? WE WANT CLEAN FOOD!

Punjabi Style Chicken Serves four. Ricter Scale *4

Watch out, Punjabi style cooking is coming your way! Tandoori recipes are hitting the mainstream at a break-neck pace. Indian fast food has reached the food courts and I am not convinced that's a good thing. Sure, it's cool to have high school kids chowing down aloo paratha after school, but does that mean Indian versions of Olive Garden or Taco Bell are going to redefine America's perspective of another one of the world's most complex and majestic cuisines? Let's hope not.

The succulence and salinity of tandoori cooking are so accessible to the American palate that we all should be making it at home in a Clean and fresh way with free-range birds, no food coloring and no MSG.

It is low in fat because the chicken's skin is removed before cooking, and it is a relatively cheap dish to prepare. The marinated meat can stay fresh stored safely under refrigeration for a week. It is also extremely easy to make. In this rendition, we are going to eliminate any need for a tandoor, those legendary clay pots used in the Punjab for rapid searing and sealing of meats and breads. All you need is a heavy skillet or "sizzle platter" and an oven that cranks.

For the Marinade:

4 chicken thighs

4 chicken legs

1–1/2 tablespoons ginger

1/4 medium Spanish onion, coarsely chopped

1 tablespoon salt

1 cup yogurt

1/2 cup lemon juice

2 teaspoons garam masala

2 tablespoons paprika

For the Finish:

1 each red, yellow and green peppers, julienne

1 small red onion, thinly sliced

2 lemons, 1 sliced in thin rings and one juiced

1 teaspoon of safflower oil or clarified butter

cilantro sprigs for garnish

Remove the skin from the chicken; reserve for stock or broth.

Peel the ginger , then drop it down the shoot of your rapidly running food processor. Turn off the machine, add the onion, lemon juice and spices. Blend and grind fine until the mixture is very smooth. Then, using a rubber spatula, remove all the mixture into a mixing bowl and fold in the yogurt until there are no streaks. Add the chicken pieces to this mixture and toss to coat completely. Store in the refrigerator in a non-reactive vessel covered with plastic wrap. Let it all marinate for at least 24 hours, or up to three days, turning daily.

For the meal: preheat oven to 550°F. Remove chicken from the fridge and shake off most of the marinade. Put it on a plate and allow to stand for twenty minutes to remove the chill. Put sizzle platter or heavy oven-proof skillet on high heat. While pan is heating, toss the sliced peppers, onions and lemon rings with the oil in a mixing bowl. Drop about half of the pepper-onion-lemon mix into the raging hot skillet. Be careful of flare-ups: always have a snug-fitting lid at the ready just in case.

Add the chicken to the pan and shake. Let cook for one minute and then, using tongs, turn the chicken. Pour the rest of the pepper mix over the chicken and quickly add the juice from the squeezed lemon, then put the entire skillet in the oven. Allow it to cook for 15-20 minutes, then remove the pan from the oven to the stovetop. Poke the thickest part of a thigh with a sharp, pointy knife. If the juices run clear, the chicken is done. If not, give it another minute or two in the hot oven. Cover loosely with foil and let it stand for a few minutes to allow the molecules to stop shakin'.

Simple Vietnamese Chicken Soup

Serves four. Ric-ter Scale *3

This is a beautiful broth and noodle soup, light on the actual meat. Notice that we are making broth here, not stock. The idea is to create seasoned water that captures all of the essence of cooked chicken. This is similar to Italian brodo, except with ginger. The ginger-roasting technique is very cool. It will make your house smell like a wicca ceremony has been taking place—good for you! (The burning ginger skin may make a bit of smoke, so check your smoke alarm. If you disarm it, please remember to rearm it before retiring.) The side dish of hot pepper and lime is the perfect pick-me-up for chicken broth. If you have an excellent Southeast Asian hot sauce in your arsenal, by all means, use that too!

wings, backs, gizzards, necks and skin of two chickens

one 1x2-inch piece of ginger

1 teaspoon white peppercorns

1 carrot, julienne

1 scallion, julienne

1 seranno pepper, julienne

1 cup mung bean spouts

1 lime, quartered

4 nice spearmint sprigs

4 medium cilantro sprigs

sea salt

one 10-ounce package of bean thread noodles

Put 10 cups of water in a heavy pot. Add just enough salt to make the water taste a little less salty than finished soup. Get it? Good. Add the chicken and bring to a boil. Skim the froth off the top and reduce to a gentle simmer.

Now prep the ginger. With the skin on, put the whole piece of ginger right on the direct heat of the burner of your stove and blacken the entire outside—sort of like roasting a pepper. Make sure it is thoroughly black. Remove the ginger from the heat and let it get cool enough to handle. Bring it to the sink and scrub the black skin off under running water. Use a washcloth or a brush. Now dry it off and chop it into three or four pieces and put it in the simmering broth. Add the peppercorns. Cook very gently for 15-20 more minutes. While cooking, skim as much fat from the surface as you can. Meanwhile, soak the noodles in plenty of hot tap water, enough to cover by at least three inches.

Remove from heat and let cool a few minutes, then strain out the solids, reserving both the broth and the solids. Pick off any chicken meat from the backs and wings and add them to the broth. Discard the peppercorns, bones, necks and ginger pieces (or eat them—chicken necks and roasted ginger with hot sauce make a nice snack!) Bring the broth back to a simmer to serve. Add the carrot julienne to the soup just before serving. Adjust the salt to your liking.

To serve, set up four deep bowls. Put a sprig of mint and cilantro in the bottom of each bowl, topped with a handful of soaked noodles.

Ladle the hot broth into each bowl, covering the noodles. Give each guest a small plate with a lime wedge, some hot pepper pieces, scallions and mung sprouts on the side to add to the soup.

Chicken Breasts Stuffed with Sage, Chevre and Prosciutto

Serves four. Ric-ter Scale *0

Let's start out with this premise: chicken on the bone is superior to chicken off the bone. Raise your hackles? Well, in my humble opinion, chicken on the bone has better flavor, aroma, texture and more subtleties than any cutlet ever could have. Don't let me be misunderstood, there is plenty of room for both me and boneless chicken on this planet. It simply comes in second!

This recipe is a beautiful variation on the well-conceived—but almost always dry—chicken saltimbocca. Saltimbocca means "jump in the mouth," and that is exactly what this dish will do! Note the technique for cooking breasts on the bone. It works for this cut regardless of the preparation. If you are using a broiler, start bone-side-up; if you choose to use a grill, start bone-side-down, making sure the rib cage is facing the heat.

4 chicken breast halves on the bone

1 cup mild fromage blanc or other soft goat cheese

1 scallion

3 large sprigs of fresh sage

2 thin slices prosciutto

sea salt

fresh black pepper

extra virgin olive oil

2 lemons, one juiced, one sliced into thin rings

Use a thin-bladed boning knife to make a cut in the wing-end of the breast (the thick end) through the skin, just wide enough to fit the blade. Push the blade down into it, along the meat, parallel with the surface. Move the blade back and forth just a bit, making a long, narrow pocket.

Hand-mince the scallion and the prosciutto very fine. Pull the leaves off the sage, reserving the stems. Mince the sage very well, also. Fold together the minced scallion, sage, prosciutto and goat cheese. Add a generous cracking of fresh pepper but no salt. Put into a pastry bag with a narrow tip. Pipe the filling into the slit in each breast until the filling is well compacted into the meat. Rub each breast with olive oil and the juice of the lemon. Salt and pepper the entire outside of the chicken to taste.

Preheat your broiler and get out your broiling pan. Put the lemon rings and sage sprigs down on the pan with a few drops of olive oil. Place the breasts skin-side down on the lemon, sage and oil.

In the broiler, put the pan as close as possible to the heat source without having the chicken come in contact with it. Cook with the bone side up for 10-15 minutes or until the bones are well browned and slightly blackened at their high points. Remove the pan and carefully turn the chicken over, return it to the broiler, but a bit further away from the heat. Cook for an additional 10 minutes, or until the skin is golden brown. Turn off the broiler and let the chicken stand in there for about five minutes so that the juices run down—that's your sauce!

The Chef's Treat
(Chicken Livers and Hearts on a Skewer)
Serves one. Ricter Scale #2

This simple and savory recipe is a variation on one of my favorites— chicharones. The liver and heart are marinated with a quintessentially Latin-style dry adobo powder, and grilled in a skillet using the chicken fat for browning.

From the chicken we butchered:
the livers
the heart
the fat we removed from the cavity
1 tablespoon or more of RicTV adobo seasoning
sea salt
bamboo skewer

Trim the livers of any fat and sinew and cut into three or four small pieces. Trim the fat from the heart and cut the heart in half. Thread heart and liver on to a bamboo skewer. Sprinkle generously with adobo and marinate until you are done rendering the fat.

To render the fat, put the reserved fat from processing the chicken and the trim from the heart and livers in a small pot and cover with water. Cook over medium heat until the water has evaporated, about 15 minutes. When the water is evaporated, the pot will begin to sizzle. Remove the pot from the heat and discard the remaining solids. Pour the fat into a skillet and place over medium-high heat. Add the heart-on-a-skewer and cook on one side until it's golden and caramelized. Turn it over and cook the other side until it is cooked through, but still pink in the middle, about four to five minutes.

Enjoy right away, it's the chef's treat!

What's so awful about Offal?

Organ meats, also known as Offal or Variety meats, have fallen out of favor with the modern American. That is a shame. Common concerns are high cholesterol and toxicity. Here is my call on this. Organ meats from organic animals are unbelievably healthy. They are full of vitamin A, minerals, monosaturates and antioxidants. They are so high in antioxidants that they actaully help to detoxify your own organs! Not only that, they add exciting texture to your meal. Smooth chicken liver mousseline, gently sauteed sweetbreads, antichuchos (Peruvian style beef heart) or the excellent Uruguayan ravioli with spinach and brains are some of the most sensual foods on earth! When something is so good for you and so sexy to eat, how could you pass it up?

'The money we save buying bargain chicken is the money we spend on medicines and drugs later in life!'

Episode Four:
It's My Party and
I'll Fry If I Want To

Taped July 30, 2002

Now let's guiltlessly make some good, traditional and delicious fried foods the way they were meant to be!

Recipes:

Paper Bag Fried Chicken

Fritto Misto Tempura Style

Smooth Tomato Sauce

Chocolate and Black-Raz-Gooseberry Wontons

Welcome to my TV Kitchen. I am Ric Orlando and today anything goes.

We live in a big crazy world and at any given time there must be at least half a billion people cooking something. They are all living their lives and loving some kind of regional dish they eat—even if it is gruel, it's someone's gruel that they come to have a connection with and affection for.

And there is infinite wisdom in humanity. The more we study our traditions and ourselves, the more we will learn about where we are and where we shouldn't be heading. We have to keep our traditions of cooking alive. There is a corporate culture trying to morph our culinary habits into some super-market miracle, but real food is the real thing that we all need and want.

Today's show is wittily named "It's My Party and I'll Fry If I want To," and the phrase of the day is Saturated Fat!

That's a phrase that scares the BEJESUS out of us—saturated fat is the killer in the kitchen, the murderer on the menu, the devil in the diet. Help me please! Saturated fat has been unjustly demonized! Has anyone here ever researched the importance of saturated fats in our diets? Let's see, some facts about saturated fats...

1. 50% of our cell membranes are made from saturated fats;

2. They are vital to our bones because saturated fat helps us to assimilate calcium (look at the constitution of milk and cheese!);

3. They enhance the immune system by protecting the liver;

4. They reduce stress! The heart draws on saturated fat reserves in times of stress;

5. Analysis of the fat in arterial clogs shows that only one quarter of it is saturated; the majority is polyunsaturated, from refined vegetable oils!

There are two types of fat that are used in my kitchen—raw, cold-pressed monosaturated seed fats like olive, sunflower, safflower and grapeseed oils and rich saturated fats like duck fat, lard, coconut, palm and peanut oils. Why? Because they are stable! What does stable mean? It means they are not *rancid*. Does anyone out there know where most of the cholesterol in our bloodstream comes from? It comes from US! We produce it in our livers. It's our bodies' natural defense against free radicals.

Saturated fat is the killer in the kitchen, the murderer on the menu, the devil in the diet...

Why are free radicals bad? Because they damage our blood vessels, and make us prone to tumors and plaque build-up. And where do free radicals come from? Mostly from oxidized or rancid VEGETABLE oils. And when does vegetable oil become rancid? When it is exposed to heat. And what kinds of oils are not suited for high heat exposure? Polyunsaturated vegetable oils—the kinds that are in almost everything on the shelf in most markets! But how could it be exposed to high heat before I've even opened it? It happens in the extensive refining and detoxifying process. The oil is heated to over 400ºF.

Had enough?

I'm not saying you should fry every day. What I am saying is that frying is a traditional cooking method of most of the people of the world. It wasn't an issue until we introduced highly processed oils and hydrogenated oils into our cooking. All hydrogenated oils are chemically altered versions of vegetable fat made to resemble saturated fats. Duh—as if your body doesn't know the difference...

Frying in the correct fat makes all the difference in the world. If the fat remains stable when heated, you will not have increased cholesterol. Don't forget, your best bet is to fry at home—most restaurants have stopped using saturated fats and have switched to hydrogenated vegetable oils— and we're paying the price with our health.

Now let's guiltlessly make some good, traditional and delicious fried foods the way they were meant to be!

Frying safety tips: these recipes require a safe frying vessel. I recommend a cast iron kettle, a Dutch oven, or a wok with a stove ring to stabilize it. For safety's sake, you should always have a suitable, snug-fitting lid when frying, just in case of emergency. A large skillet, inverted, could be a lid for a wok, for example. Always check this out before you start heating the oil. If, for some unforeseen reason, there is a flare up, don't panic, and NEVER, EVER use water to put out a grease fire. Cover the frying vessel tightly and turn off the heat source. Don't lift the lid off for at least five minutes. This will allow any gasses to burn themselves out.

Paper Bag Fried Chicken Serves four. Ricter Scale *0

Fried chicken is a classic American meal that really satisfies. Get the kids in on this one. Shakin' in the bag is really funny when a little kid tries it. When we filmed this show, I had my eight-year-old-son, Terry, come up and shake the chicken. It was pointed-out by many enamored audience members that the little guy shook everything BUT the bag of chicken!

Get a fry thermometer.

one 3-pound free-range frying chicken

2 cups fine corn flour (or substitute masa harina)

1/2 cup corn meal

2 tablespoons sea salt

a generous cracking of black pepper

a pinch of dry thyme

2 quarts rendered duck or goose fat, or pork lard, or you may substitute peanut oil or safflower oil

Cut the chicken into the following portions:

2 legs

2 thighs

2 full wings

one back

one neck

4 breast pieces (done by splitting the whole breast into two single breast pieces and then cleaving each of those pieces in half)

Put all the dry ingredients in a large, clean paper grocery bag. Add the chicken pieces and roll up the bag. Shake well. Let the chicken stay in the bag while you heat the oil.

Using a heavy cast iron kettle with a lid (a Dutch oven or an electric fry pan wok will work also), heat the fat to 325°F (use that fry thermometer). Remove the chicken from the bag to a cookie sheet. Make sure the chicken is fully coated with the corn flour seasoning. Carefully put as many chicken pieces into the oil as you can without crowding. If you cannot fit all of the chicken, it's okay, do two batches. Fry the chicken for 15 minutes, tending to it and gently turning any pieces that poke out above the oil. If you are cooking two batches, remove the first batch to a pan and hold in a 200-degree oven while the second batch finishes. Don't cover it with foil, however. Covering it will contain the escaping steam and that will soften its crispy crust.

Note the genetic foot posture of me and my son Terry.

Fritto Misto Tempura Style

Serves four or more. Ric·ter Scale *0

A classic fritto misto—or mixed fry—is a perfect example of peasant cooking from central and Southern Italy. Fresh veggies lightly fried in excellent oil is a very healthy treat for adults and kids, too. It is a perfect summer snack that utilizes the sweetest vegetables of the season in yet another way and it supplies us with the vital fatty acids that we need!

Remember, this is very different from those hydrogenated, MSG-laden, processed fried veggies served in most diners. The real deal is the real deal—and well worth the effort!

My Sicilian grandmother was a mad veggie fryer. When I was a kid, it was one of the ways that I really enjoyed eating my veggies. Squash blossoms, small slices of eggplant, small zucchini, Spring onions, celery hearts, string beans—nothing escaped the boiling-in-oil treatment! She served them with a dish of smooth tomato sauce and a generous grating of sharp Romano cheese. The cheese would lightly melt on contact with the hot veggies. It produced a smell that I will always remember.

The secret here is to fry in very hot oil, somewhere around 400° F, sealing the crust around the veggie. Then as the veggie rests and drains—and becomes cool enough to eat—it gently steams within its crust to a perfect al dente texture.

Doing a recipe like this at home from scratch is fun for the entire family. Have the kids get their hands dirty dipping and dredging the veggies. Be careful when frying, though—I let the kids watch from stools a few feet away from the stove—we don't want any slipping or splishing going on around here!

A note on the oils recommended: sunflower and grapeseed oils are among the healthiest and most traditional choices available. The virgin olive oil is used for flavor. That's your choice, as it will add a few bucks to the cost of this dish. Either way, the oil should not be used again. Once it is cool, simply pour it into a plastic bag, tie it off tightly and throw it away.

4 ounces virgin olive oil

12 ounces grapeseed or sunflower oil, or pomace olive oil

ice water

eggs

unbleached organic flour or white rice flour

sea salt

lemon wedges

fresh Parmigiano-Reggiano, Romano, Sardo or Sonoma Dry Jack cheese

smooth tomato sauce (recipe follows)

Use any combination of the suggested veggies below.
  Use what is freshest for you at the time:

small zucchini

small yellow squash

squash blossoms

small button mushrooms

oyster mushrooms

mixed cherry tomatoes

small string beans

snap peas

regular or baby carrots

small eggplant, any variety

scallions, spring onions or rings of small onions

baby beets, stemmed and cut in quarters

celery hearts

baby bok choy

baby artichokes, split or quartered

Anything else? Use your imagination!

Wash your vegetables well, and cut them into moderate pieces. Some items like tomatoes, blossoms, snap peas and small mushrooms can be left whole. When cutting items like carrots or squash, make sure that they are thick enough to have some texture when they are cooked, and thin enough to cook through in the center. One quarter inch is usually a good thickness. Always remove the stem on the bottom end of vine veggies like squash. Those ends are bitter.

Heat oil to 350°F. In a large bowl, quickly whisk an egg into two cups lightly salted ice water. Sprinkle in a cup of rice flour or organic white flour and stir until incorporated, but not completely smooth. Dredge a few pieces of veggies into the batter and fry right away. Don't over-crowd the wok—that will bring the temperature down and your veggies won't cook evenly. Cook until evenly golden, about three minutes. Remove with a slotted skimmer to a pan lined with a brown paper bag (paper towels) to drain, and cover loosely with foil to keep warm. If you are frying for a crowd, you can hold the fried veggies in a 185-degree oven while you work.

Continue frying in batches until done. (If you need to make more batter, it's easy, so go for it!) Put the finished veggies on a plate and grate a snowy layer of cheese on them. Serve with lemons and smooth tomato sauce.

Smooth Tomato Sauce

one 20-ounce can of excellent organic tomatoes

1 pinch of crushed red pepper

1 clove garlic, peeled and thinly sliced

3 tablespoons extra virgin olive oil

3-4 basil leaves, coarsely chopped

1 small spring parsley, coarsely chopped

Use a heavy skillet for this one. Open the can of tomatoes to have it ready. Add the oil to the pan and heat to medium. Add the garlic and crushed pepper, and turn the heat to high. Shake the pan. As soon as the edges of the garlic become a nut brown color, remove the pan from the heat, add the tomatoes all at once and return the pan to the heat. Bring to a rolling boil, add the herbs and cook for two minutes. Remove from the heat and when the mixture is slightly cooled, puree it in a blender until it is very smooth. Reheat gently to serve.

Why the heck is tomato sauce called Marinara Sauce anyway?

Marinara simply means "sailor's style". Tomatoes are indigenous to the New World. The Spanish brought them back to Europe and they were introduced into the Spanish kingdom of Naples around 1550. Tomatoes became very popular in Naples and tomato sauce originated in the Naples area. Because the tomatoes first arrived on boats, the sauce was named for the sailors who delivered them. The name Marinara is not very appropriate anymore, if you use organic California tomatoes like I do. I prefer Filetto di Pomodori or Tomato sauce. If you are from the east coast, you may even prefer "Gravy!"

Chocolate-Black-Raz-Goose-Berry Wontons Serves four. Ricter Scale *0

twelve 2-1/2 inch square wonton wrappers

2 cups peanut oil for frying

1 lemon

1 cup each of blackberries, raspberries, and gooseberries

1 additional cup of raspberries for the sauce

1 cup and 3 tablespoons evaporated cane juice

2 tablespoons confectioner's sugar, plus 2 tablespoons for garnish

1 cup organic chocolate chips

1 cup organic heavy cream

juice of one lemon

zest of one lemon

Whip heavy cream with two tablespoons of confectioner's sugar and the zest of the lemon until stiff. Refrigerate until ready to use.

Put half a cup each of the blackberries, raspberries, and gooseberries in a bowl with three tablespoons of evaporated cane juice. Stir well with a wooden spoon. Strain, reserving any accumulated juices for the sauce. Puree one cup of the raspberries with the reserved mixed-berry juice, the juice of the lemon and the remaining cane juice. Strain through a sieve to remove any seeds.

Lay out a wonton wrapper. Put a scant tablespoon of the sugared berries in the center. Add about four or five chocolate chips. Fold the wrapper over into a triangle. Spread a bit of water on the edges and press tightly to seal. Repeat until you have used up the wonton wrappers.

Heat the oil to 400ºF. Fry the wontons until golden brown. Remove from the oil onto paper towels and quickly blot dry. Put on a decorative plate and use reserved berries, berry sauce and whipped cream to dress up the plate. Sprinkle with the remaining confectioner's sugar.

Gooseberries and Tomatillos?

Goosberries are native to Europe. Gooseberry preserve was favored when serving a goose, hence the name. Through the middle ages in some regions, gooseberries were called "feverberry." The fruit had a reputation for its cooling property; an ability to control fevers.

Tomatillos are native to Mexico and Central America and are the gooseberry's savory cousin. Both plants grow on a bush and the fruit itself is individually encased in a papery, Chinese lantern-like pouch. Tomatillos are the primary ingredient in the Mexican staple Salsa Verde.

I'm not saying you should fry every day. What I am saying is that frying is a traditional cooking method of most of the people of the world. It wasn't an issue until we introduced highly processed oils and hydrogenated oils into our cooking.

Episode Five: Something's Fishy

Taped July 31, 2002

"Eskimos, the Japanese, and Mediterranean peoples have been eating oily fish for generations."

Recipes:

Grilled Escolar with Guava Sauce

 and Raw Mushrooms

Bloody Mary Bluefish

Boston Mackerel Puttanesca Fresca

Before we get to today's rant, I have to tell you a story about this show. We had to produce a creative tag to end this episode because I screwed up the first ending royally. We were in such a groove by this stage of shooting that we didn't worry about anything not coming off right—and we got nailed. I put a fully prepared batch of bluefish into the convection oven to cook on stage right before the taping began. Then about 15 minutes into the show, I assembled another one. I was working on the premise that the first dish of blue would be perfectly bubbling and ready to present as I popped the raw one into the oven. But no-o-o-o! The oven thermostat had failed and instead of having a 400-degree oven on the stage, I had a 140-degree oven! So the early blue was dead raw! Well, I couldn't present it like that and we were committed to live cooking with no major edits—so here's what we did: I simply ignored the fish, finished the show and had a nice day, thank you very much. We finished up the evening and the audience went home. I don't even know if they were wondering about the blue, we were all so happy.

After the audience left I finished the bluefish in the repaired oven. We then recorded a 60-second tag for the very end of the show. The setting is the same cooking studio, but dark and empty. There is a shadowy stage hand sweeping the floor in the background. A single dim light shines on my director, Steven Honeybill, and myself as we sit at a small table eating this beautiful dish of steaming bluefish. I look into the camera, smile and then address Steve. "I'll bet they thought we forgot this Bluefish by mistake!" We both laugh diabolically and continue eating as the light fades to black. Now that is television...

What is Clean Food? Is it low-fat, synthetic food made in laboratory? No! Is it refined and processed food with added nutrients? No! Clean Food is real food—organic vegetables; real, pasture-grazed meats and eggs; and excellent, wild fish. The more we try to "fix" our food, the weirder it gets. Let's pun, shall we? GET BACK TO THE EGG—WE WANT CLEAN FOOD!

That brings us to today's episode, "Something's Fishy!" We're going to cook some oily, fishy fish—and we're going to make it taste great—trust me!

During my career as a chef, I can't even count how many times I've been told that people don't like fishy fish. And yet in my café, it sells like... like...FISHCAKES! So, what is the big secret to making fishy fish delish? Acid, dude! Any oily fish should be paired with bright and acidic complements. Butter sauces exaggerate the oils in fish, while fruits, olives, tomatoes and vinegar balance the oils—just like salad dressing—Got oils? Add acid! Which brings us to the phrase of the day: Omega 3 Fatty Acids.

Why do we want to eat these oily fish anyway? That's what our grandparents ate! Yes, and that's exactly why! If you've been alive during the last decade you have learned that oily fish are the most abundant source of Omega 3 fatty acids in the world. The Omega 3 fatty acids in oily fish lower your triglycerides. And triglycerides are like a poisonous vine—as your triglycerides climb, so do your chances of developing diabetes and heart disease. Eskimos, the Japanese, and Mediterranean peoples have been eating oily fish for generations. The fact is oily fish are an amazing food source and most of them are cheap! Only the well-marketed varieties like fresh tuna and wild salmon are pricey.

Before we cook I want to address some other misinformation about oily fish. We have heard negative news about traces of heavy metals being in oily fish. Well, this is where nature is very cool. Wild, oily fish do contain small traces of metals, but they're also rich in antioxidants and ORGANIC minerals like zinc, magnesium, and selenium, which protect your blood cells from poisonous metals and help your body eliminate any harmful materials. Don't mess with Mother Nature—She knows best!

Now, let me show you how to convert oily, throw-away fish into Clean, succulent suppers...

What is Clean Food? Is it low-fat, synthetic food made in laboratory? No! Is it refined and processed food with added nutrients? No! Clean Food is real food—organic vegetables; real, pasture-grazed meats and eggs; and excellent, wild fish. The more we try to "fix" our food, the weirder it gets. Let's pun, shall we? GET BACK TO THE EGG—WE WANT CLEAN FOOD!

Grilled Escolar with Guava Sauce and Raw Mushroom Salad

Serves four. Ric-ter Scale *0

Escolar is an unusual fish from the South Pacific that is renowned for its oil content. The American markets have given it the nickname "white tuna," which has it jumping onto upscale menus up and down our coasts. That's ironic, because it is actually called "oilfish" by natives of Australia and New Zealand. Imagine a surly waiter describing the Pacific oilfish special! It is essentially a "junk fish" that has made good in America. It has a very soft and rich flavor and a super sexy texture, somewhat like a buttery swordfish. I recommend it as an appetizer because it is so rich. Its fat molecules are very large like those in castor and like cod liver oil, so eating too much can have a laxative effect. Eating just enough, however, is an ethereal experience. The combination of this luxurious fish teamed with tangy, musky guava and the mineral flavors of the raw mushrooms and truffle oil make for a truly memorable first course or tasting course. I love guava on upscale dishes. It's like inviting a gorilla-in-a-gown to a cocktail party; it has a soft pink color and a tangy-sweet flavor, yet I can truly say that it smells like an animal. There is a muskiness to its flesh that brings out the beast in me...

For the Fish:

*one 12-ounce escolar filet cut into four 3-ounce pieces,
about 1/2 to 3/4-inch thick*

2 tablespoons olive oil

juice of one lemon

a generous pinch of saffron

a generous pinch of sea salt

a generous grinding of black pepper

For the Guava Glaze:

2 ounces fresh orange juice

2 ounces dry sherry

1/4 cup evaporated cane juice

2 ounces rice vinegar

1 teaspoon shallots, pureed super fine

1/2 teaspoon garlic, pureed super fine

*1/2 cup guava puree, or seeded guava flesh pureed
with 1 tablespoon of water*

1 teaspoon cumin seeds, toasted and coarsely ground

2 teaspoons dry mustard

1/2 cup organic canned tomatoes with juice

1 teaspoon hot chile powder

1 teaspoon black pepper

1 tablespoon organic butter

In a non-reactive pot, boil the orange juice, sherry, vinegar, shallots and garlic for 10 minutes at medium-high heat. Add all remaining ingredients except the butter and cook at a gentle heat for 10-15 more minutes. Remove from heat and allow to cool. Puree until very smooth in blender. When ready to serve, add the butter and reheat in a skillet, swirling to incorporate the butter. Do not boil hard.

For the Raw Salad:

3 ounces oyster mushrooms, stemmed and thinly shaved,
* or 3 ounces enoki mushrooms, trimmed*

1/2 cup garlic chives or regular chives, cut thinly on
* a bias into 1-inch pieces*

1/2 pound thin asparagus, broken off at the perfect place
* and sliced very thinly on a bias*

a pinch of sea salt

cracking of black pepper

a few drops of truffle oil

1 squeeze of lemon

Put the escolar on a plate and coat evenly with the marinade. Preheat grill or ribbed grillpan until hot. Grill the escolar carefully on one side, scarring it nicely. Turn it over and move it to a cooler side of the grill (if using a grillpan, just turn off the heat) and let the fish finish very gently until it is just cooked.

Heat the sauce. Line each of four plates with the sauce. Add a small stack of the mushroom salad on each plate, and put the fish piece next to it on the plate. Taste all of the components together to get the full effect.

Bloody Mary Bluefish Roast

Serves four. Richter Scale *0

Having grown up on the Connecticut coast, I know that bluefish is the fish of choice in summer. When fresh, it is sublime. For the locals, blues come in many forms. There are the big blues, which are most common in fish markets. They run from four to twenty pounds or more and are strikingly beautiful. The middle-sized blues, known as harbor blues, run from twelve ounces to three pounds. They are often served in shoreline restaurants. A single two-pound fish makes a nice dinner for one. They are not as oily as the big blues and are more popular with the locals. They give a great fight when caught, too. The most legendary in the kitchen, however, are the little guys. They are five to nine inches long, weigh less than a pound, and are called snapper blues. They are extremely easy to catch—when they are running. In late summer you can see the water sparkling as they gorge themselves on whitebait. They pour into the harbors, inlets and river mouths in schools. Just cast an eighth-ounce shiny lure in and reel up. You will catch as many snappers as you can carry until the tide changes and they dart off to another feeding ground. When I was a young boy (long, long ago) my uncle Vinny and his friends taught us how to snapper-fish. We would bring home big pickle buckets of them and my grandmother (who was in her 70s at the time) would behead, gut and split the hundred or so snappers that we would bring home. She would then lightly bread them and wrap them in wax paper. Into the freezer they went. Later that year, as we gathered to watch the football games on TV, she would heat up the olive oil. She would fry up 50 or 60 snappers, and set them out on a big platter lined with newspaper. We guys would drizzle hot sauce on them and consume every last one. There was always a gnarly pile of bones and tails that went out for the cats at the end of the game! We loved those cats.

four 6-ounce fresh, skinless bluefish filets

2 cups fresh organic tomato en concassee (peeled, seeded and diced)

2 ounces hot pepper vodka

1 cup tomato juice

3 tablespoons freshly grated horseradish

a few drops of Tabasco

a few drops of Worcestershire

1 tablespoon lemon juice

1 teaspoon celery seeds

2 cups matchstick-julienne celery

4-5 lemons, washed well and sliced into thin wheels

Preheat oven to 400°F. Arrange the lemons and celery on a baking pan. Arrange the bluefish on the lemons and celery. In a martini shaker, mix the tomato juice, vodka, lemon, horseradish, celery seeds, lemon juice, Tabasco and Worcestershire and shake well. Take a sip for good measure and then pour the rest over the fish. Sprinkle the tomato concasee on top and bake for 15 minutes or until it's done. Serve hot, or room-temperature at an outdoors event. Garnish with celery leaves.

Blue-Fishin'!

Bluefish comprise less than 1% of the U.S. Atlantic coast commercial fishery landings, in terms of both weight and dollar value. In contrast, the recreational value of this species is enormous. Bluefish comprise about 15% by numbers and nearly twice as much by weight of Atlantic coast sport fish landings. About 90% of the average 55 million kg of bluefish taken annually over the past 7 years (about 8 times more than the commercial catch) were hooked by anglers in the mid-Atlantic region. We eastcoasters love to fish for Blues. Bluefish are finally beginning to be regulated, so that their survival as a species will never be in doubt and I will be able to watch my grandchildren fish for blues.

Boston Mackerel Puttanesca

Serves four. Ricter Scale *0

Boston mackerel is a glorious fish. It has a very supple texture and its flavor is much milder than its reputation.

24 ounces Boston mackerel filet, skinned and
  portioned into 4 equally-sized pieces

4 cups coarsely diced ripe tomatoes

2 tablespoons garlic, finely minced

4 anchovies, minced

1/2 cup capers with some juice

1/2 cup pitted oil cured black olives, coarsely chopped

a generous grinding of black pepper

2 tablespoons extra virgin olive oil, plus one extra tablespoon for the pan

1 cup chopped parsley

Toss well all of the ingredients (except the mackerel) in a glass bowl. Let stand at room temperature (not in a warm place) for at least 20 minutes, but not more than one hour before serving.

Crack some pepper on each of the mackerel filets but don't salt them. Use a non-stick skillet. Bring to medium-high heat and add the extra tablespoon of olive oil. Put the filets in with the top side down (not the side the skin was removed from) and cook until lightly caramelized, about three to four minutes. Carefully turn each filet over and cook for about a minute. Now pour the entire contents of the sauce from the bowl into the skillet. Swirl it around for a few seconds, turn off the heat and cover with a lid or a heavy plate. Let stand for a few minutes so that the fish gently steams through. Serve each plate with plenty of sauce and accumulated juices.

Episode Six:
That's Spicy, Baby
Taped July 31, 2002

One of the best ways to fight food irradiation is to use your $$$$. Get on the internet or to your health food store and track down clean spices. There are many independent spice companies that sell excellent organic and non-irradiated herbs and spices...

Recipes:

New World's Pan-Blackened Stringbeans

Ric's Mustard Remoulade

Seafood Creole

Rabbit "con Tutti gli Odori"

We all know that the cool rule of the neo-cool chef is Fresh Herbs All the Time. If you've ever watched me cook, you know that I am a huge proponent of using fresh herbs in the kitchen—and lots of 'em! But there are some times when dried herbs are not just suitable, but maybe even better than fresh for particular effects and cooking methods. Other times a balance of the two is needed to achieve a harmony of flavors. Slow cooking and high amounts of acid will dissipate the flavor of a fresh herb while the dried herb will have a chance to reconstitute or develop over time in a sauce with, say, tomatoes or wine.

First let's separate the herbs from the spices. For the most part, herbs are leaves and flowers, spices are seeds and bark. Are there exceptions? Sure, there are a few like saffron, which is considered a spice even though it is a flower tendril...But, essentially, herb–leaf, spice–seed.

Most importantly, all dried herbs and spices are not the same! This fact is essential to Clean cooking.

Most commercial dried herbs and spices are dried using sulfur and other chemicals, then are treated with preservatives and are finally, mostly—here's where we get to the word of the day—irradiated. I certainly don't want anything to do with irradiated food. It is bad business all around. Keep your radiation off my food! Besides all the obvious environmental problems and potential long term health effects of irradiation, it also destroys up to half the nutrients in the food. No thanks!

Write somebody—like your senator or congressperson—stop that madness now!

One of the best ways to fight food irradiation is to use your $$$$. Get on the internet or to your health food store and track down clean spices. There are many independent spice companies that sell excellent organic and non-irradiated herbs and spices that are better—and cheaper—than the scary stuff. That's what I use in my café. The stuff is perfect for cooking and has no salty aftertaste that sulfured spices have.

The best bet is to dry some of your own herbs. (The only herbs I don't recommend drying are cilantro and parsley.) Clip 'em, tie 'em up and hang 'em someplace safe, crumble what you need and bingo! Dried herbs for you, year-round! This works well when you buy a pack of herbs and can't use it all up.

Nancy Bundt

New World's Pan-Blackened Stringbeans Serves four to six. Ricter Scale *6

New World's pan-blackened stringbean appetizer is the single most ordered dish at the café. I receive requests for the recipe via e-mail, snail mail, by telephone and in person. I love when a diner walks right up to our open kitchen on a busy night with his plate of blackened beans and exclaims that he absolutely must find out how to make them. Happily, with proper ventilation, this dish is a breeze to prepare. Essentially rooted in a classic Szechuan recipe, these just-cooked, still-crunchy, nice-and-spicy string-beans with an American twist are a hit at any party.

Note: okay folks, here's the real story of those stringbeans...When I was the chef at Justin's in Albany, we did not have a grill. All of our meats and fish were either broiled in a salamander or seared on cast iron. On a heavy-volume night, I would have as many as four cast-iron skillets raging on the back burners of the stove. I tried cooking everything on hot cast iron in those days. Having limited options sometimes forces creativity.

One hectic night I came up three orders short of vegetables while plating up a large table. In a moment of panic, I tossed a handful of stringbeans in the boiling pasta water to cook them lightly. Well, I re-moved them from the water a little too soon. In my rush to get them cooked and finish plating those last three dinners, I dumped the beans into the hottest skillet on hand...a white-hot blackening pan laden with residual blackening seasoning. I moved them around to finish them and put them on the plate with the rest of the entrees. Nine people eating dinner...nine different dishes and one topic of conversation...those string-beans! The table ordered three side orders so everyone could taste them. The server exclaimed that if I didn't put these on the menu, I was nuts!

2 pounds fresh stringbeans, stems picked off

1 batch New World Cajun seasoning

2 tablespoons safflower, sunflower or corn oil

1-1/2 teaspoons cayenne

4 teaspoons ancho chile powder

3 teaspoons cornmeal

1 teaspoon dry oregano

1 teaspoon dry thyme

3 teaspoons Kosher salt

3 teaspoons finely ground black pepper

1-1/2 teaspoons paprika

1 teaspoon onion powder (not flakes)

1-1/2 teaspoons garlic powder (not granules)

Be sure that your kitchen is properly ventilated before you attempt to blacken any food indoors. Open the windows and doors and disable the smoke detectors. (Don't forget to hook them back up again afterwards!) If you don't want to smoke up the house, you can always prepare this dish outside. Heat the skillet to white-hot indoors, then, when you are ready to put the beans into the pan, bring everything outside. Scoot, though; the skillet should be kept hot enough to blacken the beans for full a minute or two.

Fold all the seasonings together thoroughly. Fill a medium-sized pot three-quarters full of water. Bring to a rolling boil while you preheat a cast-iron skillet or heavy wok until very hot, about ten minutes, over high heat. Plunge the stringbeans into the boiling water and cook them for 30 seconds, until they are bright green, forkable but still a bit crisp. Drain the beans but do not rinse them, and put them in a work bowl big enough to toss them around in. Add the oil and toss to coat them evenly. Sprinkle the seasonings over the beans and toss to coat evenly. When you are ready to blacken them, dump the beans into the hot skillet. If your skillet is small, this may need to be done in batches. Don't overload the skillet. Using tongs, move the beans around to blacken them evenly in the seasoning. The idea here is to char the spices, not the beans themselves.

Serve the beans mounded on fresh greens, garnished with lemon wedges, with 1/2 cup of Mustard Remoulade Sauce for dipping.

Ric's Mustard Remoulade Sauce

This is a killer sauce that we also serve with chilled shrimp or oysters.

2 tablespoons paprika

3/4 tablespoons Tabasco sauce

1 teaspoon Worcestershire sauce

1/4 teaspoon celery salt

1/4 cup pommerey mustard

1/3 cup Dijon mustard

1/2 teaspoon gumbo filé powder

1/4 teaspoon dried tarragon

1 teaspoon grated or finely minced onion

1 teaspoon grated or finely minced scallion

1 teaspoon grated or finely minced celery

1 cup safflower, sunflower or other neutral-flavored oil

In a food processor, combine all the ingredients except the oil and process well. Then, with the machine running, add the oil in a steady stream to emulsify.

Down Home Seafood Creole

Serves four. Ricter Scale #5

There is no one recipe for Creole sauce. From household to household, from county to county and from state to state, the Creole cooking style incorporates as many influences as there are on the planet! French, Spanish, Italian, African, Asian—all make their way into a Creole kitchen. This recipe, then, is a stripped down representation of bare bones, pre-supermarket style Creole sauce. All of the fresh veggies and dried spices combine to let the ingredients speak for themselves. Note that aside from the parsley, all of the spices in this dish are dry. This allows the spices to intensify as the sauce cooks, bringing all of the earthy flavors into the complexity of the sauce. These earthy flavors really harmonize with the naturally musky essence of catfish.

6 cups cooked rice, preferably long grain brown

1 pound catfish or trout filet, cut into four pieces

8 ounces Narragansett Bay scallops

1 pound medium-sized Maine or Alaskan spot shrimp

12 fresh or frozen crawfish

2 tablespoons safflower or sunflower oil

6 scallions, roots removed, chopped end to end (use the white parts for cooking and the green part for garnish)

1 cup yellow onion, diced

1 red bell pepper, diced medium

1 green bell pepper, diced medium

2 celery ribs, chopped medium-small

3 large, ripe, fresh tomatoes, peeled, seeded, stemmed and coarsely chopped, or 10 ounces chopped canned organic tomatoes with juice

2 teaspoons minced garlic

1 cup sliced okra

2/3 cup dry red wine

1/2 cup canned clam juice or fish stock

1 bay leaf

1 teaspoon dry thyme

1/2 teaspoon dry rosemary, crumbled

1/2 teaspoon dry marjoram

1/4 cup chopped fresh flat leaf parsley (reserve half for garnish)

1/2 teaspoon black pepper

1/2 teaspoon cayenne

1/2 teaspoon dry mustard powder

1 teaspoon gumbo filé or sassafras powder

2 teaspoons Worcestershire sauce

2 teaspoons Louisiana-style hot sauce

2 teaspoons lemon juice

small pinch sea salt

Preheat oven to 400°F. Use a large, heavy, ovenproof skillet with a tight-fitting lid. Add the oil and the onions to the pan and cook over medium heat until the onion is softened but not brown. Add the scallion whites, garlic, celery and bell peppers. Cook for four to five minutes until the vegetables are wilted. Add all of the other ingredients except the seafood and bring to a boil. Cook vigorously for three to four minutes, then cover and reduce heat to medium-low. Cook covered for 15 minutes or until the okra and aromatics are cooked.

Remove the pan from the heat and arrange the seafood in the skillet with the sauce, spooning some of the sauce on top of the seafood. Put the entire pan in the oven and cook for 15 minutes. Serve over rice with plenty of sauce. Garnish with chopped scallion greens and parsley.

Rabbit con Tutti gli Odori

Serves four. Richter Scale #2

Rabbit is a Clean, healthy meat choice that we Americans should eat more of. It is white, lean, inexpensive to produce and yes, it tastes like chicken! Have you ever wondered why we phased rabbit out of our culinary repertoire? After all, it is still very popular in Europe.

Maybe it has to do with the cartoons we grew up watching. The rabbit was always cute and was always the good guy. Chickens are not very memorable characters, aside from Foghorn Leghorn, and he doesn't come off as foodstuff. Maybe the fledgling chicken industry did a better job of lobbying the animation industry than the rabbit farmers did. More paranoid ranting, I know...

1 large frying rabbit sectioned into:

2 hind legs

2 forelegs

1 loin split and cut in half, giving you four pieces

2 tablespoons olive oil

tutti gli odori—all of the herbs and aromatics:

1 tablespoon fresh basil

1 tablespoon dry thyme

6 juniper berries

1 tablespoon black peppercorns

1 tablespoon fennel seeds

1 tablespoon fresh sage

1 tablespoon fresh rosemary

2 teaspoons dry marjoram

1 teaspoon dry oregano

2 tablespoons fresh parsley

2 teaspoons sea salt

1/4 teaspoon freshly grated nutmeg

1 medium yellow onion, diced

4 cloves of garlic, smashed

1/4 cup water

1 cup red wine

1 cup organic canned tomatoes with juice

flour and water for sealing the lid

Use a spice mill to grind the juniper, fennel and peppercorns to a coarse grind. Put that into a food processor with the remaining herbs and spices, the onion and the garlic. Add the water and puree to a medium paste. Use your hands to rub this paste all over the rabbit pieces. In a heavy pot with a proper fitting lid, heat the oil to medium and add the rabbit. Cook for three minutes, turn, and add the wine and tomatoes. Remove from the heat and hermetically seal. (To do this, make a paste of 1/4 cup flour and 1/4 cup water. Rub the paste around the rim of the pot. Put a piece of waxed paper or foil over the top of the pot and cover with the lid.)

Return to the heat. Cook at the lowest heat possible for three to four hours. The steam from the rabbit will create a sublime juice. Remove from the pot gently and serve in small bowls. The only accompaniment should be a slice of sourdough bread.

Episode Seven:
El Super Latina Cocina

Taped August 1, 2002

"The word of the day is GRASS! (Uh oh, the chef is from Woodstock, I knew this would happen sooner or later...) No, no, I am talking about the stuff that grows in a pasture..."

Recipes:

Ric's Ropa Vieja

Cuban Black Beans

Simple Brown Rice

Island Yams

Tostones

Good Greens

RicTV has a Mantra: We Want Clean Food!

You may be wondering, What's the difference? Just give me the cheapest stuff you have! You wouldn't do that to your car, would you? You wouldn't do that to your house—why would you do it to your family?

And what about you and your body and your essence? Would you really say, just give me the diluted, chemically processed, artificially flavored, synthetically textured meal? No! Deep down, no matter what your politics are, you want Clean Food. This is a simple fact—food has CHANGED recently—meat is raised in boxes instead of grasslands, vegetables are cloned and synthetic—have you ever seen a display of tomatoes which all look exactly alike? What are those?

Let me get to today's show, "El Super Latino Cocino!" What's that? And the word of the day is GRASS! (Uh oh, the chef is from Woodstock, I knew this would happen sooner or later...) No, no, I am talking about the stuff that grows in a pasture—the stuff that cows are supposed to eat.

You know that the Latin culture eats a lot of meat—boiled, fried, fried in lard? Yet, in their native countries, this is an extremely trim and vital culture. My stepfather is from Ponce, Puerto Rico and he grew up on a farm—he won't touch commercial meat. Guess what he wants—he wants Clean Food. His cows always lived on the farm and grazed on the lush green hillsides, they ate grass and wild stuff, and then they were dinner. Grass-fed beef is Clean Food! The magic of the earth is in the meat—not the hormones and steroids that are in feed-lot beef.

Most Latinos in their native lands enjoy grass–fed meat. These are trim and beautiful real meat eaters, because that meat is not pumped-up red meat! It is Clean Food!

Would you really say, Just give me the diluted, chemically processed, artificially flavored, synthetically textured meal? No! Deep down, no matter what your politics are, you want Clean Food.

Ric TV

Ric's Ropa Vieja

Serves six to eight. Ricter Scale *1

Ropa vieja, which translates as "old rags" or "dirty laundry," is one of the world's great peasant meat dishes. The long cooking with acidic components, tomatoes, wine, soy sauce and beer, leaves the beef in tender shreds—hence the nickname. Essentially Cuban, ropa vieja transcends all cultures and is one of the most popular dishes at New World. This recipe has been requested by some of my customers to be served at Bar Mitzvahs, Catholic weddings, tropical theme parties and even Christmas dinners.

The quintessentially Latin flavor comes from the fresh green sofrito.

salt and freshly ground black pepper to taste

3 tablespoons safflower or peanut oil

5 pounds fresh grass-fed beef brisket or chuck shoulder,
  trimmed of excess fat and cut into fist-sized chunks

1 batch green sofrito (see recipe)

12 ounces lager beer, like Red Stripe, Budweiser or Corona

2 cups dry red wine

1/2 cup soy sauce

1/2 cup minced Spanish onion

1/4 cup minced garlic

1/2 cup stuffed Manzanilla green olives

1/4 cup capers (capotes, the large ones, are best for this recipe)

4 cups organic plum tomatoes with juice, squished
  through your fingers

3 ounces organic canned tomato paste

1/2 cup bell pepper cut into 1-inch strips

Fresh Green Sofrito:

1/2 cup coarsely chopped green pepper

8 medium peeled garlic cloves

1/2 cup coarsely chopped Spanish onion

1/2 cup chopped cilantro, packed, (stems and leaves both)
  or Recao if available

1 tablespoon Kosher salt

a generous cracking of freshly ground black pepper

1/8 cup olive oil

1/8 cup water

To make the sofrito, mince the cilantro stems and leaves from end to end into very short pieces. (The stems are full of flavor and if you can mince them finely, they won't be stringy.) Puree the cilantro with the bell pepper, onion, garlic, salt and pepper and olive oil in a food processor, adding a few tablespoons of water to make a soft pesto.

In a heavy pot, lightly sauté the sofrito in the oil. Don't let it brown.
Salt and pepper the meat and, when the sofrito is lightly cooked and begins to smell good, add the meat to the sofrito in the pot. Using a large spoon, turn the meat in the sofrito, coating it well. Add all of the rest of the ingredients except the bell pepper and tomato paste. Add enough water to cover the meat. Bring to a boil, skim off the froth that forms, then reduce to a slow simmer to braise for two to three hours. Add more water if necessary to keep the meat covered. (Cooking the meat at a very low simmer will create a very tender dish. If you boil it too hard too long, the proteins in the meat with tighten, leaving it chewy and dry.) After two to three hours of cooking, break the meat up into shreds with the back of a spoon. Add the tomato paste and bell pepper strips and cook slowly for an additional 20-30 minutes. Make sure the meat is covered with liquid at all times while cooking.

Tostones (tose-TONE-aze)

Serves four. Ricter Scale *0

Tostones is the Latino nickname for fried green plantains (pronounced plan-tins). I have never heard anyone refer to a single tostone—it's always tostones!

3 or 4 medium green to light yellow plantains, peeled

peanut or safflower oil or organic lard for frying

Peel and slice plantains on a slight bias about 1/3-inch thick. Heat oil to 325°F. Fry plantain pieces until they're golden around the edges. Remove from the oil and, while they're still hot, tap them down with the back of a skillet or a meat mallet until they're flattened by about half their thickness and the warm center squishes out around the edges a bit. Fry again until golden. Drain and serve topped with a squeeze of lime and hot sauce if you like.

Tia Sulma's Vegetarian Black Beans
Serves four. Richter Scale *1

Beans rule! They're like little soldiers lined up ready to fight for your life. Maybe that's why a Spanish teacher I once knew called his students "little gandules," Spanish for pigeon peas. Beans are high in soluble fiber, B vitamins and iron. They help lower cholesterol. What a concept! Is that why all over the world (Asia, Europe, South America, the American South) pork is paired with beans? Beans are also a great blood sugar balancer and are great for your colon. I was once told by a nutritionalist for a large supermarket chain that I made "Colon-Friendly" cuisine. That would be quite a slogan, wouldn't it? "Visit New World, Home of Colon-Friendly Cuisine!"

Remember also to think about the soil that these little guys have thrived on. Is it nutritious or synthetic? Buy organic beans, dude. They are so cheap that there is no excuse not to. This recipe is meatless, and is intended as a side dish. It is more aromatic and lighter than many of the robust Latin-style bean dishes that are meant to be complete meals.

1 pound dried organic black beans

1 tablespoon coriander, ground

2 teaspoons ground cumin

1 teaspoon black pepper

1 teaspoon Kosher salt

1/2 teaspoon ground cloves

1 teaspoon crumbled bay leaf

1/2 cup sherry

I was once told by a nutritionalist for a large supermarket chain that I made "Colon-Friendly" cuisine.

Pick over the dried beans for stones, put them in a heavy pot and cover by at least two inches with cold water. Bring the beans to a rolling boil. Turn off the heat, skim off any coagulation on the surface and let soak for half an hour or so. Strain, rinse and return to the pot with a new batch of water. Add all remaining ingredients. Return to a boil, skim the surface, then reduce heat to very low. Cook slowly for another half to one hour until beans are soft but still round, firm but not chalky—we'll call them perfect.

The real fiber of the issue

The word on fiber is that we should get all that we can. It can reduce cholesterol and stabilize blood sugar. Millions of Americans actually take fiber pills to make sure they get enough. But recent research published in Britain's *Lancet* and *The New England Journal of Medicine* states that too much fiber (the kind found in most supplements and cereals) does not prevent the development of polyps that may lead to colon cancer as many of the fiber pill manufacturers claim.

Now what? Forget the quick fixes and stick with the RicTV mantra of eating a Clean food diet with plenty of whole foods, nuts, legumes and fresh vegetables and you will get enough fiber. Eat an apple a day. Lay off the processed fruit juices which have all of the sugar and none of the fiber and eat the whole fruit. Whole fruits and vegetables are loaded with the best fiber and are easy on the system. Remember, Clean, organic whole foods give you what you need.

Brown Rice to Go with those Black Beans Serves four. Ricter Scale #1

I'm guessing that 99% of the Cubans in the world eat white rice with their black beans. I won't slander the flavor of white rice, but please, consider this: white rice is a simple carbohydrate that converts to sugar in your system extremely quickly. If you are planning on dancing or playing ball after dinner, enjoy your white rice. It will burn hot and fast and then you'll be ready for another meal in two hours. But if you are realistically going to spend an evening sitting, talking, maybe watching a little tube, then by all means, cook the brown rice. It is a slow-burning carbohydrate that won't leave you hanging! And you thought it was the MSG in Chinese food that made you crash and crave within two hours of eating it! It's the white rice! Let's put it behind us. Switching from white to brown rice has very measurable long-term health benefits.

In this recipe, I keep the rice fairly straightforward so it won't fight with the beans. Fancy, highly seasoned rice is appropriate on many tables, but here simple rice is a vehicle for the ropa vieja and the beans.

2 cups long grain organic brown rice

2 tablespoons safflower oil

1 thin slice of lime

2 teaspoons salt

3 cups cold water

In a heavy pot with a lid, heat the oil. Add the lime, salt and rice. Use a wooden spoon to stir and coat the rice with the oil. Let it cook for 15-30 seconds to release its aroma. Stir again, then add the water AND DON'T STIR ANY MORE. Bring to a boil uncovered, then cover snugly and reduce the heat to very low. Allow it to cook UNDISTURBED for 30-40 minutes. Let it stand covered but off the heat for a few minutes to settle in. DON'T STIR. Flake the rice with a cook's fork or chopsticks into a serving bowl.

Island Yams Serves four. Richter Scale *0

Yams, or sweet potatoes, are another one of those super foods that somehow have fallen out of favor in the commercial American diet. They are full of fiber, vitamins A, C, and E and selenium. They are amazing for your eyes, your heart and your immune system. Why don't we eat more of them? Is it because of those sickeningly sweet canned yams in our collective memory? Simply prepared, they have mass appeal. Just cook these guys like regular spuds and the kids will love 'em.

6 medium organic sweet potatoes or yams

boiling water, lightly salted

1/2 stick of butter

one ripe orange

one lime

Kosher salt

a generous cracking of black pepper

Peel the yams and cut into 1-inch thick rounds. Boil the yams until they soften up (about 25-30 minutes). Turn off the heat and cover. Let them sit for a few more minutes until they are tender. Strain and transfer them to a heavy bowl. Add the butter in small pieces and mash well. Zest the orange and lime and add it to the sweeties. Cut the orange and lime in half and squeeze out the juice into the bowl, watching out for any orange seeds. Add the salt and pepper and mash again.

A note about using citrus zests: when you are using oranges and limes, wash them well with soap and water before using the zests. Even organic citrus fruits may have organic waxes or oils on them to protect them during shipping and storage. Most commercial citrus has tons of post-harvest pesticides and fungicides sprayed onto the skins. Any word that ends in "-cide" is usually not Clean Food!

Good Braised Greens, Peasant Style

Serves four. Ric-ter Scale *0

This simple technique for cooking greens has Caribe and Asian touches. It really allows the greens to be themselves. I have omitted garlic from this particular version for two reasons. First, because in the grand scheme of this meal, there is already enough garlic to depopulate all of Transylvania! Secondly, kale is notorious for its gas-producing effect. Adding garlic only enhances that feature. If you are making these greens as a stand-alone side dish, if you live alone, or if your partner is eating with you, feel free to add a little garlic.

Another great food fact is that kale is absolutely one of the best cancer-fighting foods on the planet. It is rich in A and C vitamins as well as cartenoids, those powerful cancer-fighting agents. It is vital to remember that organically grown kale will have higher amounts of nutrients than chemically grown kale, because the soil in which it was grown has been nurtured and fortified with organic fertilizer and compost. Have you ever read the recurring stories of folks from the deep south who have lived to be over 100 years old even though they smoked for 90 of those years? Could it be that the great amount of greens in their diet was continually repairing them? Food for thought.

The nutrient value of raw versus cooked greens

So, you don't want to cook your greens because you have read that they lose their nutritional value when cooked. Simmer this. We are not cows and do not have the digestive chemistry to assimilate all that we need from most raw foods. So, it is true that cooking greens destroys some of the cancer fighting cartenoids in greens. However, you body is able to absorb almost all of the remaining nutrients from greens that have been cooked. Not overcooked, just cooked enough to release their bright green hue and make them tender. When you eat raw greens, you pass most of it through your system as fiber. The best way to get the nutritional benefits of raw greens is to juice them (or chew them for about an hour!)

*1 pound red Russian or green kale, stripped
of stems and washed*

*1 pound calalloo, dandelion greens or
Lacinata kale*

one handful of cilantro stems (optional)

1 tablespoon peanut oil

1 cup Spanish onions, thinly sliced

salt and pepper

water for steaming

Use a large wok or high-sided sauté pan with a snug-fitting lid. Turn the heat to high and add the oil, and heat until moderately hot. Add the onions. Let them sizzle, but don't let them brown. Sprinkle generously with salt and pepper (the salt will temper the bitterness of the greens.) Add the greens and cilantro stems. DON'T STIR!* Add about half a cup of water or just enough to create steam. Cover snugly and cook for three to five minutes or until tender but still brightly colored. Remove from heat, but leave covered until ready to serve. Now you may toss thoroughly before serving.

***I suggest you try my technique** of steaming the greens **on** the salted onions. The onions, salt and pepper will flavor the steam for even cooking. When the greens are done cooking, stir the onions into the greens.*

Food has CHANGED recently—meat is raised in boxes instead of grasslands, vegetables are cloned and synthetic...

Episode Eight: Deer Me

Taped August 5, 2002

'Did you ever wonder how boring it must be to be a fish in a tank?'

Recipes:

Venison Bolognese Sauce with

 Brown Rice Fettucine

Texas Style Venison Fajitas

Slang Jang Relish

Hong Kong BBQ Venison Chops

Last week we had a wonderful dinner here at the studio. The mixed crowd was of all ages. We really got into some good, healthy politics, and it was so great to be at the same table with smart people who have been through some amazing times. They have so much knowledge, and they have "fight" inside. They continue to fight for what they think is right. (I wonder if our generation will have that "fight" as we grow older?) And you know, they really liked the RicTV mantra, We Want Clean Food.

If you really want Clean Food, you're going to have to fight, too! There are many who would let our food supply homogenize into pseudo-nutritious processed space bars—and why not? They'd be easier to produce, sanitary, and certainly more profitable. But is that food? No! WE WANT CLEAN FOOD! We've got the fight in us tonight!

Which brings us to tonight's episode, "Deer Me," an episode about venison. And the word of the day is WILD! Venison is essentially a wild food. One of the ways we keep the fight in our spirit is to eat wild foods. When I say "wild" I don't necessarily mean *completely* wild. I mean that the food has had to fight, in the way Nature intended it to, to survive. We keep our spirit alive by eating this stuff!

Let's check this out. We are talking about food as energy. If you want to be well and feel well, you need to consume nutrients that are well, as well! Great, healthy, Clean foods have had to fight to survive. It is Darwinism at its best. Have you ever seen a hen in the barnyard? She pokes, she scratches, she turns over stones...all in that genetically programmed search for food. That is the chicken's nature. A chicken raised in a box with a feed tube shoved down its throat has no survival skills. It has no vital energy. There is no vitality passed on to you when you eat it.

It's exactly the same for farm-raised fish; wild fish migrate, forage and have to have the instincts and drive to survive. Farm-raised fish are like fish in a fish tank. Did you ever wonder how boring it must be to be a fish in a tank? Imagine what the spirit of fish raised in a tank is like. Do you want that essence passed on to you when you have dinner?

My theory applies to fruits and vegetables, too. Veggies that are raised in real soil with organic nutrients reach their roots deep into the ground to survive and thrive, while vegetables produced in what is essentially dead soil will just kinda grow without having to probe the soil for the nutrients they need. Their environment is pumped with synthetic feed and growth stimulants so the plants develop no will to live.

That brings us to the star of tonight's episode: venison. Venison is the ultimate Clean Food! This is food with spirit! Corny as it seems, that spirit is what comes with eating forest animals.

A few summers ago I was cooking at the New York Garlic Festival. Our booth was positioned next to a local volunteer rescue squad's booth. We were making blackened stringbeans, fajitas, and garlic-mashed potatoes. We had a very popular booth. When there was a lull, a strawberry flat-topped fellow in the rescue squad's booth, his T-shirt blotched with sweat and his face brick-red from the sun, asked me about my café. He wanted to know what kind of food we served and whether we served "deer meat." I responded that yes, not only did we sell deer meat, but we sold pig meat and cow meat too. He smiled and smacked his lips. Told me he liked cow meat, too.

The point here is that there is a fantastic word for deer meat. That word is "venison." Venison comes from the Latin "Venatio," or the hunt or chase, and is related to the word "venerate," which means to desire, as in to desire meat for dinner. Cool, huh? There are three types of venison available for consumption. First, there is truly wild venison. This is the stuff you or your friends kill during deer season. There is very little risk in eating this meat. If you are an experienced hunter yourself and are confident in the manner that the meat was processed and handled, you should have no concerns about eating this venison rare. If you hunt but are uncertain about your own skills at properly handling a fresh carcass, bring it to a licensed butcher or USDA station for butchering. On the other hand, if you are worried about whether or not you should eat the meat your auto mechanic or paperboy has given you, please be safe and use a recipe, like the following Bolognese recipe, that involves cooking the meat completely.

The second type of venison, readily available in gourmet stores and by mail order, is "essentially" wild venison. This is venison that has been raised on a large nature preserve. These deer basically have the same lifestyle as completely wild deer, except there is some inspection and regulation of the herd as it grows. *This is the best choice for venison.* It is still very lean, richly mineral-flavored and full of all the essential nutrients that make venison a superior red meat choice. This meat may also be served dead rare, even raw in a carpaccio or tartare presentation. Go for it!

The third type of venison is truly farm-raised. These deer are raised in captivity, on medium-sized farms, are fed a combination of hays and grains and are allowed to graze. I don't think this is a good idea. What makes any meat a healthy, healing food, is our ability to assimilate its wild diet through eating its flesh. I'm back to that again: real food is Clean Food. Stick with it!

There is a fantastic word for deer meat. That word is "venison."

Meat Comparison

Here is a comparison of the content of Venison and other popular meats. All figures are based on grams per 4 oz. portion.

SPECIES	FAT	PROTEIN	CALORIES	CHOLESTEROL
Axis Venison	1.9	26	120	59
Fallow Deer	2.4	26	127	75
Whitetail Deer	2.2	27	128	70
Beef, Top Loin, Grazed	23	21	300	75
Beef - Top loin, Standard	26.1	21	323	79
Lamb	4.9	24	142	75
Pork, center loin chop	24.8	31	355	108

Venison Bolognese Sauce

Serves four. Richter Scale *0

This is a simply perfect Bolognese sauce. It is true to its Northern Italian roots. As opposed to many of those overly spiced and greasy meat sauces served in family-style Italian restaurants, this recipe uses just a touch of garlic and a touch of cream. The fresh nutmeg really brings the flavor of the forest to life. It was traditionally served in a small portion as one of many courses. If you are doing the American thing and having a big bowl for dinner, serve some braised greens, steamed string or Roma beans or a crisp salad on the side.

1 pound ground venison
1 tablespoon organic butter
1 tablespoon extra virgin olive oil
3 tablespoons minced shallots
1 teaspoon minced garlic
sea salt and fresh black pepper to taste
a generous pinch of fresh sage
a generous pinch of fresh Italian parsley
one 20-ounce can organic tomatoes, squished through your fingers
1/2 cup organic heavy cream
a nice grating of fresh nutmeg
freshly grated Parmigiano-Reggiano or Sardo cheese
1 pound brown rice fettucine, cooked

Gently heat oil and butter. Add the venison to the pan and very lightly salt and pepper it. Cook the venison until brown, but not cooked hard. Remove most of the venison with a slotted spoon. Add the shallots to the pan and cook until soft but not brown, then turn up the heat and add the garlic. Cook for an additional minute then add the parsley and sage, stir and add the venison back in. Stir well and add the tomatoes. Bring to a boil and reduce heat. Cook gently for five minutes, stirring often. Add the cream, stir it in well and grate a bit of nutmeg over the top. Cook for an additional three minutes and serve over cooked pasta. Top with chopped parsley and grated nutmeg. Serve with excellent Parmigiano-Reggiano on the side.

Texas Style Venison Fajitas with Slang Jang Relish Serves four. Ricter Scale #6-7

For the Marinade:

1 1/2 pounds "Denver leg" or sirloin of venison

2 cloves garlic crushed

1/2 teaspoon ancho chile powder

1/4 teaspoon ground cloves

2 teaspoons cumin powder

2 teaspoons dried Mexican oregano

2 teaspoons soy sauce

2 teaspoons molasses

3 tablespoons chopped cilantro

2 teaspoons balsamic vinegar

4 tablespoons safflower oil

For Wrapping:

8 flour tortillas

8 sprigs of cilantro

Venison is essentially a wild food. One of the ways we keep the fight in our spirit is to eat wild foods.

Cut the meat into 3/4 to 1-inch-thick pieces so it will grill evenly. It doesn't matter how big they are since you will be slicing it all for the fajitas.

Combine the chile powder, cloves, cumin and oregano. Using a dry skillet, lightly toast this mix on medium heat until a hint of smoke appears. Stir and remove from heat. Combine with the wet ingredients to make the marinade. Put the marinade in a bowl and dip each piece of meat into it. Turn to cover every inch of meat generously, making sure there are no parts of the meat that are untouched by the marinade. Wrap the venison in plastic wrap and refrigerate for no less than six hours and no more than four days.

Preheat your grill to medium-high heat. Remove the meat from the refrigerator and allow it to lose its chill for a few minutes before grilling. Put meat over the hottest coals and let it stand on the high heat for three to four minutes or until the outside is just charred. Turn the meat over and cook for one minute on high heat and then move to the cooler part of the grill and allow it to finish cooking very slowly. In three to four minutes you should have perfectly medium-rare venison sirloin ready to slice.

Remove the meat to a plate and let stand for a few minutes, so that when you cut it you don't lose all of the juices. Slice the meat against the grain (pretend it's wood) into thin strips. Take each tortilla and warm it over the grill or an open stove flame to soften it up. Layer a sprig of cilantro, a few slices of venison and a generous tong-ful of slang jang relish (recipe below) onto the warm tortilla. Roll it up and consume with joy.

Slang Jang Relish

Serves four to six. Richter Scale *7

When I was first starting out in this business I cooked in some great kitchens in the Boston-Cambridge area. I had one of my most penetrating experiences at a strange fine-dining room called the Wild Goose, in the famed tourist destination, Quincy Market. Architect Ben Thompson owned three restaurants; Ben's Chowder House and the Landmark Café were perpetually full, and the Wild Goose was notoriously slow. The menu consisted of game and some exotic seafood and was priced two or three notches above what the upper tier of Quincy Market tourists would even consider shelling out for a meal. The Wild Goose was Mr. Thompson's fully staffed downtown playground for himself, his partners and his clients. When Ben needed to "wow" a city planner or politician, it was lunch at the Goose. Any incidental business was a bonus. Must be nice.

Chef Emmett Fox had a profound influence on me. He was from Texas and I was from Connecticut. I showed him how to fry belly clams and he showed me how to use ancho chiles and more. I worked in all three of the restaurants but eventually became its main lunch guy up at the Goose. I was not nearly qualified for that level of dining yet, but sometimes the pressure of learning on the job is the best way to go!

Slang Jang was something Emmett introduced in the casual café. It was the kind of relish Emmett and his sister E-Jo (for lack of a better spelling...) would stack up on burgers or chicken sandwiches. It was my idea to incorporate it into a venison presentation. To Emmett's surprise, it outsold the venison prep with the tarragon buerre rouge! I have come across a few other variations since those days at the Goose, but this version is over the top. I made this on the Today Show on July 4, 1996. I am still penpals with people based on their experience with this slang jang!

1 medium yellow pepper, julienne

1 medium red pepper, julienne

1 medium poblano pepper, julienne

2 jalapeños, julienne (not seeded—unless you care to miss out on the fun!)

1/2 Spanish onion, peeled and thinly sliced

1/2 red onion, peeled and thinly sliced

3 large ripe tomatoes, quartered, all seeds and guts scraped out and cut into thin strips

1 tablespoon cumin, ground

1/4 cup gold tequila

1/8 cup spicy mustard

1 tablespoon fresh black pepper

1/4 cup of your favorite BBQ sauce

2 tablespoons sunflower oil

Toss all ingredients together in a large bowl and let stand for 20 minutes. Meanwhile, preheat a wok, sauté pan, or skillet large enough to hold the entire contents of the bowl, to high. Dump the mixture all at once into the pan and let it sit for 30 seconds. Use a spoon to turn the contents over as best as you can. Let it cook another 30 seconds. Turn off the heat. Leave the pan on the stove. Let the slang jang continue to wilt in the hot pan until it is cool enough to handle.

Real food is Clean Food. Stick with it!

Hong Kong BBQ Venison Chops

Serves four. Ric-ter Scale *5

Boston, Manhattan, Queens, Philly, Frisco— these are some of the best places in America to get good Hong Kong BBQ. There is nothing like the aroma of simply marinated meats hanging under bright heat lamps waiting to be hacked up just for you! Using the basics of Chinese cooking (ginger, hot bean paste, soy, garlic, Hoisin sauce), this is some of the most savory BBQ going! In this recipe we keep it all exceptionally Clean by avoiding the basic condiments and using many root ingredients like coriander, orange juice, molasses and anise stars.

In this presentation we are really going over the top by using venison loin chops. They are the most expensive cut of venison and for good reason. The loin chops are mild, richly textured and absolutely luxurious to eat. Consider this a special occasion dish. Does the marinade work with anything else, you ask? Dude—it works with anything! From trout to tofu, this dark and intense sauce is fabulous!

eight 4-ounce venison loin chops (at least 1 inch thick)
6 anise stars
3 tablespoons ginger, minced
3 cloves garlic, crushed
2 tablespoons coriander seeds
2 tablespoons orange juice
1/2 cup tamari sauce
4 tablespoons rice vinegar
1 tablespoon Worcestershire sauce
1 cup water
1/2 cup molasses
1/2 cup fermented bean paste
1/2 cup evaporated cane juice
1/4 cup sesame oil
8 whole scallions, washed
1 small head of savoy cabbage cored and cut into eighths
4 heads baby bok choy, cored and split in half lengthwise

This recipe will make both marinade and sauce for the venison. In a non-reactive bowl, mix together all of the ingredients except the sesame oil, venison, scallions and cabbage. Divide the mixture in half, putting one half in a small pot and leaving the other half in a bowl.

To make the marinade, whisk the sesame oil into the ingredients in the bowl. Dip each chop in this mix to thoroughly coat and then arrange in a glass or plastic container. Cover with the remaining marinade. Marinate for at least four hours or up to three days. Remember to turn the chops daily for even marinating. To make the sauce, cook the ingredients in the small pot over medium-low. Simmer gently for 45 minutes or until reduced by about one-third and slightly thickened. Strain through a fine strainer. This is your finishing sauce.

When you are ready to cook the venison, start a nice BBQ fire. Make sure there is a hot, concentrated heat spot on one part of your grill and a low and slow spot on the other. While the fire is heating up, remove the chops from the marinade to a plate. Let them sit out to remove the chill. Add the cabbage, bok choy and scallion wedges to the marinade. Turn to coat and remove to the same plate as the venison. When the fire is nice and hot, put the chops down to cook. Let them cook in one hot place for two to three minutes to sear. Baste once with the finishing sauce, turn the chops over and let them cook an additional minute over the hottest part of the fire. Baste again. Now move them to a cooler part of the grill and stand them up on their t-bones. This helps let the radiant heat warm the chops without drying out the surface of the meat.

While the meat is finishing (about three more minutes) put the marinated veggies on the hot grill and cook for a few minutes, turning regularly. Cook those chops to a nice medium-rare. This is a very lean cut of meat and over-cooking the chops will make them tough. Serve with the grilled veggies, steamed brown rice and more of the finishing sauce on the side.

Episode Nine:
Zillions Served, Why Brown Rice is Good

Taped August 5, 2002

White flour and white rice and white sugar and foods stripped of their natural nutrients and goodness are NOT clean. And we want Clean Food!

Recipes:

Lobster Fra Diavolo with Brown Rice Spaghetti

No Crash Risotto

Risi e Pisi

So, here is my riddle for today: when is WHITE not CLEAN? When we are talking about food! White flour and white rice and white sugar and foods stripped of their natural nutrients and goodness are NOT clean. And we want Clean Food!

"Evil white stuff" has taken on a new meaning in this new millennium: the White Carb Menace! We are up to our necks in it, and it's messing with everything. Most ingredients served in "family" restaurants are laced with white carbohydrates. Modified food starch, stripped-down flours and all forms of processed grains are everywhere.

At one point my wife decided to try avoiding wheat consumption to see if she had Celiac's disease, a "gluten intolerance." It was impossible for us to dine out! Every sauce base, every breading, every filling and almost all the basic sauté dishes had some amount of white flour. Combine this with the white sugars that were in our beverages—yes, high fructose corn syrup is a simple carb sugar, too.

This is not natural. This is not normal. I don't care if bread is the staff of life, there shouldn't be this much modified, processed, stripped down carbohydrate in our bodies. And the ones who have it worst are our kids. Kids are hammered with empty carbs at every turn. I have not found one child-oriented snack in the supermarket that did not have simple carbs in it. NOT ONE! That is scary. Sure, kids are attracted to sweet stuff, but white starches and sugars are not the only answer. By the way, have you been in a school lately? There are simple, stripped-down sugar foods everywhere. Soda machines, candy machines, processed foods in the café, even candy in the classroom. This is not Clean Food! I say, put kids who are struggling with their concentration on a CLEAN DIET. Ditch the white flour, blue drinks and processed snacks in school. Kids need Clean Food! I anxiously await the results—I predict that kids' concentration and behavior will improve if they are on a clean diet.

What about you—are you one of the "Trillions Served?" Do you want Clean Food? Then you need to get out of the simple carb trap and begin to eat complex carbohydrates. One of the greatest things you can add to your diet is brown rice. Brown rice is a complex carbohydrate and one of the healthiest foods there is. It can really be seen as a life-saver. It gives you a constant, slow burning energy and keeps you from being hungry every 20 minutes or so.

One of my many food theories has to do with what is known as "Chinese Restaurant Syndrome." Many people who experience a "crash" after eating Chinese restaurant food blame their reaction on MSG. There is also a widely held opinion that two hours after eating Chinese food, you'll be hungry again. Maybe it's actually because of all the white rice that comes with it! Do you *normally* consume two or even three cups of white rice for dinner?

Here is one more illustration of the virtues of brown rice: my wife's father, Angelo, lives with us. He has been diabetic for over 30 years. He still craves pasta, though he knows it is one of the worst foods he can possibly eat. Whenever he eats regular white or semolina pasta, his blood sugar count jumps to over 300, then crashes down again, leaving him depressed and drowsy. Is this you? Actually, eating is supposed to provide your body with fuel; you are not supposed to fall asleep after eating.

So my wife, Liz, and I used Angelo as our Guinea pig. We began to serve him small portions of brown rice pasta, combined with free-range meats and fish, for dinner and we monitored his blood sugar levels. Result: when he eats brown rice pasta his blood sugar levels barely rise at all and he stays awake and happy. You should see how thrilled he is! He can eat pasta again without the sugar jolt and post-pasta crash. The complex carbohydrates in brown rice seem truly miraculous.

In one of today's recipes we will make risotto using brown rice. On the menu at New World we actually call it "No Crash" risotto. This is big for me. Getting away from the white stuff is a matter of survival!

Getting Ahead on Brown Rice

It is a good habit to make a few cups of brown rice every week and keep it in the fridge. It is so simple. The ratio for making brown rice is one part rice to one and one half parts water. Add a pinch of salt and a drop of oil or butter and bring to a boil. Once it boils, cover it snugly, reduce the heat to very low and allow it to steam gently for about 45 minutes. Use a fork to flake the rice out onto a cookie sheet to cool, then store it in an airtight container in the fridge for up to one week. I like to count on about 3/4 cup raw rice per person, per meal.

Brown Rice and Mushroom Risotto

Serves four. Ric-ter Scale *1

For the Risotto:
6 cups cooked short grain sweet brown rice
olive oil
1 tablespoon organic butter
1/2 Spanish onion, minced
1 cup leeks, sliced in rings (1 medium leek should do)
1/4 cup carrot, diced small
1 clove of garlic, minced
4 ounces brandy
4 large portabello mushrooms, sliced
1 cup oyster mushrooms, string-roots trimmed and reserved
1 cup crimini mushrooms, quartered lengthwise
2 tablespoons fresh sage, coarsely chopped

For the Garnish:
grated Parmigiano-Reggiano, Sardo or Asiago (Romano is too sharp)
truffle oil

For the Stock:
olive oil
chopped leek tops
any garlic peels
stems from sage
stems from the portabellos
trimmings from the oyster mushrooms
1/8 cup dried forest mushrooms or porcini (a few pieces)
1/4 cup brandy
1 tablespoon sea salt
a few whole peppercorns
4 cups water
2 cups cream

If you have your rice pre-cooked, the making of this dish is about timing. Put the mushrooms in to roast while you make the stock. Getting everything ready in advance is not a bad idea. You can roast the mushrooms, cook the rice and make the stock up to three days in advance. Just be sure to store them in the refrigerator, covered well.

To roast the mushrooms, preheat the oven to 500ºF. Put the sliced portabello, crimini and oyster mushrooms in a bowl. Toss them with olive oil, salt and pepper them well and put them on a sheetpan. Roast for 10 minutes or until they are sizzling and golden around the edges. Remove from the oven and let them cool down while you finish the dish.

To make the stock, in a heavy pot, sauté the mushroom stems and leek tops with the olive oil until golden. Put in the dried mushrooms and brandy. Turn up the heat and let it all cook until the brandy flames up. Add water, garlic peelings, cream and sage stems and bring to a rolling boil. Reduce the heat to a low simmer, add the salt and peppercorns and continue to simmer for 20 minutes to infuse the flavor. Press on the solids to extract all of the flavor, strain out and reserve the liquids. Discard the solids.To make the risotto, use a heavy-bottomed pan large enough to hold everything with room for stirring and cooking and use a wooden spoon for stirring. In that heavy pan use some olive oil to sauté the onion, leek and carrot. When wilted and lightly golden around the edges, add the garlic. Now add the brandy and flame. When the flame has died down, stir well. Add the cooked rice and stir well. Add about half of the reserved stock and stir again with a wooden spoon.

Cook the risotto, gently adding the rest of the stock a little at a time until it is all gone. Add the sage and a handful of the cheese. Stir. Fold in the roasted mushrooms and add any accumulated oil and juices from the mushroom roasting pan. Cook for one more minute to warm the mushrooms. Plate it up and top with the grated cheese and a drizzle of truffle oil.

Lobster Fra Diavolo with Brown Rice Spaghetti

Serves four. Ricter Scale #6

This dish was made using lobster (and the risotto was made with truffle oil) because I wanted to show my audience that brown rice is not proletariat-hippie food. It is awesome and it works well with luxurious items like lobster and expensive mushrooms. The fra diavolo sauce recipe is perfect as it is. It needs no seafood, actually! It also works well with squid, scallops, shrimp, mussels, clams, octopus, scungilli or whatever seafood fra diavolo dish you care to make—just remember, think sustainable!

two 12 ounce packages of brown rice spaghetti

two 1-1/4 pound lobsters, cooked, meat removed and coarsely chunked

extra virgin olive oil

3 large cloves garlic, peeled and thinly sliced

2 tablespoon diced onion

2 fresh hot peppers, Italian style or a serrano or jalapeño, stemmed and cut into a few big pieces with the seeds intact

one 20-ounce can of organic tomatoes, whole or diced

a few sprigs fresh parsley

a few sprigs fresh oregano

(**Note:** I urge you to leave the hot peppers in big pieces so that they are visually evident. The flavor will be imparted beautifully but the extreme heat of biting down on a pepper will be a matter of choice. If you can see the peppers, you can avoid them if you choose to.)

Brown rice pasta cooks pretty much the same as regular wheat pasta, but is not as forgiving. If it is overcooked, it gets gloppy. ("Gloppy" is a technical term used by renowned chefs and six-year-old kids.) If the pasta is too al dente it will break up when stirred, so keep an eye on it. It's not rocket science, but it did take me a few tries to get brown rice pasta cooking right. I keep trying to remember my first attempts at cooking regular pasta, but my memory seems to get stuck on some Humble Pie concert. Anyway...put on a large pot of water to cook the pasta. Lightly salt it. When the water is boiling, add the pasta and stir. While the pasta cooks, make the sauce.

Use a big skillet for the sauce. Have the canned tomatoes opened. If they are diced, leave them as they are. If they are whole, put them in a bowl and squish them through your fingers. Turn the heat to high. Add the olive oil and let it heat for a minute. Add the onion and cook for one minute, or until it is wilted but not brown. Now add the garlic and about half of the hot pepper. Cook until the garlic begins to get just a little golden color around the edges. (Now, go and gently stir the pasta.)

Add the tomatoes to the garlic pan all at once. Stir and add the lobster chunks and any accumulated juices. Stir again (check your pasta) and add a generous handful of chopped parsley and fresh oregano. Stir gently and turn the heat down to very low. When the pasta is done, strain it and add it to the sauce. Stir gently to coat. Pour the whole thing into a big serving bowl or serve right out of the skillet and top with more chopped herbs. Serve with a side of olio santo (recipe below). Do not add cheese or I will track you down and abstract it from you.

Olio Santo (Oil of the Saints)

1 cup extra virgin olive oil

1 nice, fresh hot pepper, stemmed and cut into a few pieces

In a small, heavy pot, heat the oil and the pepper together very slowly until the pepper is fully wilted but not brown. Let it cool in the pot. Use this oil to drizzle on pasta, fish, steaks, eggplant or your lover's toes. It can be stored, *loosely covered*, in a cool dark place. Use a square of wax paper and a rubber band to cover it. If you create an airtight seal on cooked vegetables, you can create botulism. You don't want to do that. Let it breathe.

Risi e Pisi

Serves four. Richter Scale *0

This is truly peasant food. When I was a schoolboy, this was my favorite dish. Either rice or macaroni and peas. If a friend invited me over for a nice American roast meat dinner I always wished it was rice and peas. It didn't occur to me that we were poor—I assumed we were rich because we had rice and peas and plenty of cheese!

6 cups cooked brown rice

1 pound organic frozen or fresh peas

1 cup Prosciutto di Parma sliced into thin strips (or substitute the following dry cured specialties: real Westphalian, Sarrano or Smithfield ham. Use dry cured ham. Avoid using processed cold cuts.)

1 tablespoon organic butter

1 tablespoon olive oil

1 small yellow onion, minced

2 tablespoons minced celery

2 cups homemade chicken stock or health food store-bought free-range chicken stock

fresh thyme

fresh parsley

fresh Parmigiano-Reggiano or Romano cheese

sea salt

fresh black pepper

Heat the butter and olive oil together until the butter begins to foam. Add the celery and onions and cook slowly until the onions begin to develop a golden color. This should take about ten minutes. Now add the ham and cook for another two to three minutes. Turn the heat up all the way and add the peas. Stir to coat the ham well with the onions and oil. Cook for a minute or so and then add the stock and a generous handful of fresh thyme leaves and chopped parsley. Season the broth to taste with salt and pepper. Don't forget that you will be garnishing with lots of salty cheese, so don't over-salt the broth. Stir and add the rice. Cook over medium-high heat until the rice is warm through. This will be a little soupier than risotto. Serve in bowls topped with fresh pepper, parsley and a generous grating of Romano or Parmigiano-Reggiano cheese.

Note for more flavor: if you have the time, you can infuse the thyme— and the cheese. Simply chop the thyme you will need for this dish and save the thyme stems. Then grate the cheese you need and save the cheese rind. Now, put your broth or stock in a small pot and add the cheese rind and/or thyme sprigs. Cook that for a few minutes to infuse even more flavor into your broth!

Note on a great vegetarian rendition: if you'd like to prepare a vegetarian rendition of this dish, try substituting mesquite-smoked tofu pieces for the ham and use a light vegetable stock instead of chicken broth. If you are vegan and are avoiding butter, go with straight olive oil. If you have to avoid the finishing touch of grated cheese, you have my sympathies.

'Actually, eating is supposed to provide your body with fuel; you are not supposed to fall asleep after eating.'

Episode Ten: In Watermelon Sugar

Taped August 6, 2002

Dive back in for another cooling spoonful...

Recipes:

Tropical Chicken Thighs with Watermelon Salsa

Grilled Squid and Watermelon Sambal over Rice

New World's Watermelon Gazpacho

How did we get here? How did we get to a place where we have to chant for Clean Food? What does "Clean Food" mean, anyway? And how much free-range and organic is enough and how do we get it onto our plates at a price that makes sense? This is the culinary challenge of our time. Becoming a Clean Food cook is like becoming a defender of sanity.

The DeMedicis, Escoffier and Brillat-Savarin had it made; they didn't have to cope with American ingenuity! To be Clean Food cooks, let's go back to post-World War II America to understand why it matters so much. Through the boom years of the 1950s and early 1960s, women at home—housewives—were targeted by the new breed of television marketers and the product that was being sold was Convenience. So, quicker and more easily prepared foods appeared on the newly innovated Supermarket shelves. Frozen veggies, cake mixes and precooked meats in exciting packages were quickly accepted into our homes. And why not? They were less expensive and advertisements claimed that they tasted as good as homemade. In a matter of a few years, the American palate was converted shall we say, subverted to one that enjoyed, perhaps even preferred, pre-fabricated Salisbury steak over fresh cooking. In addition, the American housewife was freed from the drudgery of making food from scratch. (If you are ever in a suburban house built in the early 1960s, you may notice that the kitchen is the smallest room in the house.)

Through the late '60s and into the '70s the economic structure changed and housewives were no longer the primary target of marketing. Those same women became busy working moms without the time to cook fresh meals every night. Additionally, more Americans remained single longer and lived alone or with roommates in apartments. It was the Mary Tyler Moore era. Single people who worked all day really didn't need to cook anything complicated. After all, they were just cooking for themselves. Things had to be made even easier. Faster and faster food was introduced. As the microwave entered the kitchen, the sci-fi future of two-minute hot meals in styrofoam became a reality.

On a parallel time line, a backlash was beginning. As mainstream cuisine became synthetic, many better-informed and more progressive Americans searched for alternatives. The health food industry was setting its roots. It began a counter-culture movement and many of its supporters were not exactly your cookie-cutter Americans. Shopping at the co-op was an anti-establishment statement. But as many younger Americans were becoming enlightened to the virtues of whole grains, yogurt and the vegetarian lifestyle, the health food industry built a solid foundation.

During the 1980s and through the 1990s, those '60s housewives became the "empty nesters," and the early health food generation evolved into the New-Age culture. Both were continuing parallel paths and both became more aware of their bodies and the effects that food has on them. That consciousness started a renaissance of good cooking in America. Gourmet, classic and ethnic foods permeated our markets. Vegetarian items like tofu and tempeh became mainstream. World culture became pop culture. The waves of celebrity chefs and food media kept growing. The layers of information about styles of cooking, nutrition and the cleanliness of food were rushing like a river that had burst its banks, ultimately overwhelming the cook at home. Suddenly, making dinner for a group of guests was like being in a competition with the world's greatest chefs and nutritionists at the same time. That's no fun and you can't win!

So, as we enter the 21st Century we are searching for clarity and sanity in our food choices. We want to know more about the effects of food on our health and personal well-being. We want to understand the environmental impact of the production of food. We want to safely buy and cook food and we want it to taste amazing. WE WANT CLEAN FOOD!

Let's get into tonight's show: "In Watermelon Sugar!" And the word of the day is Lypocene.

Lypocene is found in certain red foods—watermelon, tomatoes, red grapefruit and tropical fruits like guava—but not berries. Lypocene is a powerful cartenoid. A cartenoid is an antioxidant. Antioxidants protect us from bad free radicals (not that free, *radical people—like me—*are bad!) in our blood. Free radicals are a real nemesis to our health. One of the main sources of free radicals in our American diet comes from rancid oils like the commercial vegetable oil compounds used in fast foods and low-end restaurants. Remember, they are not just used for deep frying anymore. These super-hydrogenated oils are used in most frostings, cookies, desserts, many soups and on the griddle for making eggs. (It ain't the eggs that are bad, baby!) If you have been reading this book, you must be hip to my stance on that stuff by now!

Free radicals are marauders in the body. They attack cell membranes and red blood cells. They are a factor in diseases like arthritis, Parkinson's, Alzheimer's and cataracts. There is an absolute correlation between high amounts of free radicals in the blood and cancer, heart disease, build-up of plaque and premature aging. So there you have it. Free radicals suck! We need to do what we can to keep them out of our bloodstream. Eating the right foods will help.

Watermelon is loaded with lypocene, vitamin C and potassium. These are all excellent free radical fighters. So, watermelon is a good Clean Food! Here are some recipes that give you options for getting watermelon into your diet some place other than cookouts! (Note that in the following recipes, leftover watermelon is a perfectly adequate choice. Use it up!)

Curry-Mustard Chicken Thighs with Ric's Way-Cool Watermelon Salsa

Serves four. Ric-ter Scale *6

For the Watermelon Salsa:

4 cups watermelon, diced in to 1/2-inch cubes

2 cups mixed tomatoes, diced the same as the watermelon

1 cup scallions, sliced into thin rings

1 teaspoon fresh ginger, minced

a generous splash of good Caribe hot sauce like Matouk's, Martin's Island or Inner Beauty

2 tablespoons cider vinegar

1 tablespoon dark rum

pinch of Madras or Blue Mountain curry powder

1 teaspoon fresh thyme, minced

1/2 teaspoon sea salt

Toss everything together in a non-reactive bowl. Keep it cool until the chicken is ready. Delicious!

For the Curry Mustard Chicken:

8 free-range chicken thighs

1/4 cup strong French Dijon or English mustard

3 tablespoons safflower or sunflower oil

1 tablespoon turmeric

1 small shallot, minced

1/4 cup white wine

1 tablespoon Madras or Blue Mountain curry powder

2 tablespoons lemon juice

pinch of dry thyme

Use a non-reactive bowl large enough to hold the marinade and the chicken. Whisk together everything except the chicken. Using tongs, add the chicken and turn to coat all areas thoroughly. Leave it in the bowl and cover with plastic wrap. Refrigerate for at least 20 minutes or overnight before cooking.

To cook the chicken in a broiler, remove from the marinade letting any residual marinade remain on the thighs. Put the chicken on a cookie sheet with the skin side down. Broil close to the heat for about 8 to twelve minutes, or until the flesh on the bone-side is golden brown and the chicken is beginning to sizzle. Turn the chicken over and place the rack one rung lower so that it is about three inches from the heat source. Cook until the skin looks perfectly brown and is blistering and bubbling. Turn the temperature from broiler to 300°F and bake for an additional five to ten minutes. Serve hot with an accompaniment of watermelon salsa and more Caribbean hot sauce on the side.

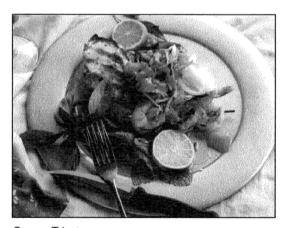

Gregor Trieste

Ric's Way-Cool Watermelon and Grilled Squid Sambal Serves four. Ricter Scale #7

This sambal, or marinated condiment, is a really special recipe. The rollercoaster of sensations experienced while eating this dish will keep it ensconced in your vault of summer secrets. If you cannot grill the squid, try scorching it in a raging-hot but dry cast iron skillet.

4 cups seeded watermelon cut into bite-sized pieces

1/2 cup red or yellow bell pepper, julienne

1/4 cup carrots peeled, split lengthwise and sliced paper thin

1 cup cucumber split lengthwise and sliced paper thin

1 cup red or Vidalia onions, sliced into thin rings

1 medium poblano chile, julienne

1 (or more!) hot Thai chile, sliced into thin rings

1 teaspoon garlic, finely minced

2 tablespoons rice vinegar

1 tablespoon lime juice

2 tablespoons Thai fish sauce

1 tablespoon peanut oil

1 cup chopped unsalted peanuts

1/2 cup coarsely chopped cilantro, leaves and smaller stems

2 tablespoons chopped fresh spearmint

2 tablespoons chopped fresh basil

4 cups cooked brown rice

1 cup mung bean sprouts

8 sprigs cilantro for garnish

Toss everything except the brown rice, cilantro sprigs and mung bean sprouts together in a non-reactive bowl. Fill each of four deep bowls with a cup of brown rice, a handful of mung bean sprouts and a few cilantro sprigs. Spoon on a generous amount of watermelon sambal. Top with coarsely chopped, grilled squid (recipe below) and serve with chopsticks and cold beer.

Grilling the Squid

Serves four. Richter Scale *2

2 pounds cleaned squid, tubes and tentacles

2 tablespoons sesame oil

1 tablespoon cold-pressed peanut oil

2 tablespoons tamari

1 scallion, minced

2 tablespoons orange juice

1 tablespoon Chinese sweet vinegar

2 tablespoons ginger, minced

2 tablespoons molasses

1 teaspoon Chinese five-spice powder

Gregor Trieste

Whisk together all ingredients except squid until smooth. Toss in the squid and stir to coat. Marinate the squid for five or ten minutes before cooking. Remove the squid and grill rapidly on high heat. It's done as soon as it is opaque. As the pieces of squid come off the grill, place them on a cutting board and coarsely chop them, then place them on top of the bowls of rice and sambal.

Watermelon Gazpacho

Serves eight. Ricter Scale *6

This is a cool and refreshing soup you will come back to all summer. Not only does it cool you off and heat you up at the same time, it also makes you popular! You will be asked for this recipe, so be prepared! It's a great way to use up leftover watermelon. The chiles add important flavor, so don't wimp out. If you encounter a spicy bite, dive back in for another cooling spoonful of watermelon juice. It will cool you right off!

2 pounds red watermelon, seeded and pureed in a blender, rendering about 6 cups watermelon puree (see the note on watermelon)

1/2 cup cider vinegar

1/4 cup water

1 medium cucumber, peeled, seeded and diced, plus one cucumber peeled and coarsely chopped

1/2 medium red onion, diced, plus the other half coarsely chopped

4 tablespoons each coarsely chopped basil, spearmint and cilantro

4 tablespoons red bell pepper, finely diced

1/2 cup diced jicama

1 teaspoon fresh garlic, minced

1 teaspoon cumin

3 serranos or 1 jalapeño chile, sliced into very thin rings with seeds

2 teaspoons salt

3 tablespoons lime juice

1/2 teaspoon ground pepper

To puree the watermelon, follow these guidelines. This will simplify an otherwise annoying job. Fill your blender about one-third of the way with chunks of watermelon. Add half the vinegar and all of the water. Pulse the blender on low until the watermelon gets caught up and begins to puree. Turn the machine to "liquify" and run until the watermelon is smooth. Now here's the trick: pour about half of this puree into a large, non-reactive bowl. Use the remaining half of the watermelon puree as the medium to puree more watermelon. Continue until you have pureed enough watermelon to yield 6 cups, plus the cucumber and red onion noted above. If you need to add more liquid, add the remaining vinegar and the lime juice. Do not add more water. In a pinch you can add back some of the pureed watermelon to create enough of a liquid base to finish pureeing the cucumbers and onions.

Mix in all of the other ingredients and stir gently. Chill well.

Serve ice-cold, garnished with chopped cilantro and a lime wheel.

> Frozen veggies, cake mixes, and precooked meats in exciting packages were quickly accepted into our homes. And why not? They were less expensive and advertisements claimed that they tasted as good as homemade.

Episode Eleven: Chocolate and Chiles

Taped August 7, 2002

If that's not happiness then what is?

Recipes:

White Chocolate-Dipped Serrano Chiles

Coquilles St. Louis

Bittersweet Chocolate and

 Goat Cheese Truffles

Mole Poblano Turkey Tenderloins

Well, here we are at another episode of RicTV. And today we are going to push the envelope...Today's show is about taking Clean Food to a new place. We are going to use Clean Food to find the word for today: Happiness!

There are some great foods that are strictly New World foods. Let's list some of the foods that we love that are indigenous to the New World: corn, tomatoes, potatoes, turkey, pumpkins, and, oh yeah, chocolate and chiles! Do you want to stimulate your tastebuds to the extreme? Let's get some euphoria cooking!

In the kitchen, there are two proven euphoria inducers: chocolate and chiles. And, yes, chocolate and chiles can both be Clean Food!

Let's talk about chocolate first. To the Mayans, cocoa pods symbolized life and fertility. Talk about happiness! I second that, life, fertility and Clean Food! Chocolate has two true qualities that earn it the RicTV stamp of approval:

1. Chocolate contains phenolics. Those are the same antioxidants found in red wine! If that's not happiness then what is? Plus, chocolate can help you fight cancer and balance cholesterol.

2. Chocolate contains phenylethylamine, or PEA, a chemical found in the brain. For example, when you fall in love your PEA level rises and you feel happy. When you are reprimanded by the boss, your PEA level plunges and you feel lousy. We can raise our PEA levels when we are feeling low by eating chocolate. And, uh, that's good.

Just one tip: *keep your chocolate Clean. Don't muddy the waters. Avoid chocolates and candy that contain hydrogenated fats and refined starches! Stick with the pure stuff and you'll feel good in the short and the long run.*

Now onto chiles: we could do an entire series on chiles. They give me so much happiness! Chiles are perfect Clean Food. They taste great and are really good for you. Try every chile you can. If you use a variety of chiles, you help to sustain the agricultural heritage of many indigenous people. That is also a Clean Food thing! As corporations are pressuring regional Mexican peoples to produce just two peppers—jalapeños and red cayenne or "Tabasco" peppers—for hot sauce, there are many heirloom peppers that will become more and more rare. Not only does this threaten the agricultural and gastronomic heritage of many people, it also increases the chance for pestilence and poor harvest. If the crop diversity is lost and the fields are planted with only one or two varieties of pepper, all it takes is one blight to destroy the whole crop and threaten the livelihood of the workers. This is the danger of mono-agriculture. When the crops are diverse, a natural defense against losing an entire harvest is put into place.

The three main aspects that make chiles a RicTV Clean Food are:

1. Chiles are loaded with trace minerals and vitamins A and C.

2. Chiles actually enhance digestion. The capsaicin in chiles helps your system produce a perfect balance of digestive fluids. The myth that chiles give you heartburn has to do with something else: because chiles help you to digest more efficiently, you'd better be careful to eat Clean Food with chiles, or watch out! If you eat processed, spiced up foods with lots of hydrogenated fats like budget Mexican food or less-than-honest pizza shop cuisine for instance, those chiles will enhance your absorption of stuff that maybe you would rather not absorb quite so well.

3. Chiles play a cool trick on your brain: when you eat hot stuff, your brain is fooled into thinking that your mouth has been burned by heat. Heat heat, not chile heat! So it rushes endorphins into your system. Yes, endorphins are your body's natural pain killer. This is where you get that chile BUZZ, as it is known in my hometown of Woodstock, New York.

In summation: chocolate makes you blissful and chiles make you euphoric. They both contribute to good health and they both taste remarkable. Sounds like a recipe for happiness to me!

To the Mayans, cocoa pods symbolized life and fertility. Talk about happiness!

White Chocolate Dipped Chiles— Crazy Candy! Serves four. Ricter Scale *7

This is a wild little surprise that we serve on Valentine's Day on our Safe Sex platter. Did I say Safe Sex Platter? What is that?

Every Valentine's Day at my café we serve an appetizer for two called Safe Sex. It consists of 10 pairs of simple but surprisingly sexy tastes. In addition to these crazy, candy-dipped chiles, the plate includes items such as: mango, wrapped in basil leaves; huge Cerignola olives; aged Valdeon bleu cheese from Spain; wasabi deviled eggs; baby octopus kim chee; a spoon of caviar on a cold potato; chilled asparagus spears with grainy mustard; slices of avocado splashed with homemade lime and chile sauce; strawberries soaked in aged balsamic vinegar; grilled skewers of beef heart...you get the idea.

All of these items, and the rest of the plate, seem simple by themselves, and yet they create a stunning symphony of one-bite affairs. Oh, and did I forget the kicker here? You have to be fed these bites by your lover. Is that enough? Of course not. You are fed these delights one at a time—BLINDFOLDED! That is why we call it Safe Sex—there is daring, trust and pure sensual stimulation going on here. When you taste something as simple as that Cerignola olive blindfolded, it is beyond sexy! Everything is amplified when you eliminate one of your senses.
In this case, eating is beyond exotic, it's erotic!

12 fresh serrano peppers, washed and blotted dry
1/2 cup fennel seeds
1 cup white chocolate, chopped

Using a dry skillet over medium heat, gently toast the fennel seeds until they lightly smoke, then pour them onto a plate. Melt the white chocolate slowly over a double boiler. *Make sure that the bowl is not touching the water.* Carefully dip each chile in chocolate to coat, then sprinkle with the seeds and lay on a sheet of waxed paper to set. When you bite into the chile, smile!

Coquilles St. Louis

Serves four as an appetizer, two as a dinner. Richter Scale *4

This dish is a sublime variation on the old school coquilles St. Jacques, which is scallops baked in their shells, topped with a rich béchamel-based cheese sauce. The harmony of the salty-sweet scallops, the rich blue, the smoky chipotle powder and the silky white chocolate is unimaginably good. The sneaky heat of the chipotle powder and the whisper of white chocolate carry this creation far beyond the expected. So have you figured out why I call them coquilles St. Louis? C'mon. Because of the bleus used!

4 large sea scallop shells

20-30 Taylor Bay or Narragansett Bay scallops

4 slices baguette, toasted

2 tablespoons butter plus enough for lightly buttering the bread

1/2 cup organic, unrefined white flour

1 1/4 cup organic milk

1/4 cup crumbled Stilton bleu cheese

1/4 cup Gorgonzola cheese

1/4 pound white chocolate

1 tablespoon chipotle chile powder

Use a small, heavy-bottomed sauce pot. Make a basic béchamel by melting the butter over low heat and adding the flour. Stir well to make a roux. Add the milk and whisk to incorporate completely. When it is warm, add the cheese and stir well, still over low heat, to make a nice creamy sauce.

In each scallop shell place a thin slice of toasted and buttered baguette. Put five to seven scallops on the baguette. Top generously with cheese sauce. Using a cheese grater, grate a light snowy coating of white chocolate over each one and sprinkle lightly with smoked chile powder. Bake at 450°F for about five to seven minutes or until bubbling. Serve immediately.

Bittersweet Chocolate and Fromage Blanc Truffles

Serves four to six. Ricter Scale *4

I love chocolate, chile and lemon. A beautiful flavor of minerals and earth comes to life in your mouth when these flavors are combined. It is essential that you use pure ancho chile powder in this recipe. Regular commercial chile powder usually contains salt, garlic, cumin and other ingredients which, although they may work with chocolate (see the Mole recipe), don't work with this dish. The final rolling in the spices brings a wonderful, bitter element to these truffles. That makes it for me. I really don't like my chocolate to be too sweet. These are the optimum for me.

About "Fromage Blanc"—As mountains go, the Adirondacks, Berkshires, and Catskills are extremely old. There is a lot of old spirit permeating the hills and meadows here. Maybe that helps make the earth give such great flavor to the foods produced here. This area is home to the producers of some of the finest goat cheeses made in America. Coach Farms, Capri and Nettle Meadows all produce outstanding organic goat's-milk products. We buy an Adirondack "Fromage Blanc" from Nettle Meadows in Warrensburg, New York, that is unsalted and extremely mild. There, farmer Laurie Goodhart feeds her goats a selection of aromatic herbs and flowers that gives the cheese a uniquely sensual bouquet. If you can acquire such a soft and unsalted chevre, try it in this recipe. If not, try some of the soft goat cheeses that are available in your area. Some are brighter and more tangy than others; for this particular recipe, I recommend the mildest cheese you can get.

8 ounces best quality bittersweet chocolate, chopped

6 ounces fresh Fromage Blanc (unsalted goat's cheese)

2 tablespoons confectioner's sugar

1/2 teaspoon vanilla extract

1/8 teaspoon lemon extract

2 tablespoons pure ancho chile powder

2 tablespoons cocoa powder

2 tablespoons cinnamon

In a stainless steel bowl set over a pan of barely simmering water, melt the chocolate, stirring until it is smooth. Remove the bowl from the pan and let the chocolate cool slightly. In another bowl, whisk together the goat cheese, the confectioner's sugar, the vanilla and the lemon extract until the mixture is light and fluffy. Whisk in the chocolate until the mixture is combined well. Chill the mixture covered with waxed paper for one hour, or until it is firm. Roll the mixture into balls about 3/4 inch in diameter.

Put the chile powder, cocoa powder and cinnamon in a bowl. Roll each truffle in this spice mix. Chill the truffles on a baking sheet lined with waxed paper for 30 minutes or until they are firm. The truffles keep in an airtight container, chilled, for three days. This recipe makes about 24 truffles.

Variation: put the chile, cocoa, and cinnamon in separate bowls. Roll a few truffles in just one of each spice separately, so that you end up with a trio of cinnamon, chile, and cocoa flavored truffles. The straight-chile truffles will be pretty hot at first, but the sugar and fat in the chocolate will cool off the chile heat in a short time.

Turkey Mole de Ric Serves four to six. Richter Scale #5

When someone tells you that the French invented *cuisine*, kindly remind them that the early dynasties of this hemisphere were developing a complex and disciplined "cuisine" back when the French were still living in caves. In my opinion, though the French have mastered the art of cooking for sure, they still haven't topped the sophistication of the original mole sauce prepared in Puebla, Mexico, 500 years ago. A mole sauce (pronounced MO–lay) is true testament to the artistry and the sensory appreciation of these great people. The chocolate gives mole its mystique as well as its balance. The negro chiles have a resonance similar to that of bitter cocoa, especially if you allow them to slightly toast when they are roasted.

Mole Negro de Ric

1 cinnamon stick

6 negro or Pasilla chiles

*4 ancho chiles (If you don't have negro or Pasilla chiles
  use about a dozen anchos instead).*

1/4 cup sunflower or safflower oil

1/4 cup whole shelled almonds

1 tablespoon sesame seeds plus a few more for garnish

2 teaspoons dried Mexican oregano

1/2 teaspoon allspice powder

1/2 teaspoon cloves

1 teaspoon cinnamon

1 teaspoon garlic, minced

1 small onion, thinly sliced

2 tablespoons dark raisins or 5 dried black mission figs, stemmed

4 large ripe tomatoes, coarsely chopped

3 tablespoons evaporated cane juice or turbinado sugar

1/2 cup chopped unsweetened chocolate

two raw 6-inch corn tortillas, torn into strips

Preheat oven to 400ºF. Put the chiles on a cookie sheet and lightly toast them in the oven for about three minutes. The chiles should plump up and release a rich aroma. Remove from the oven and take off the hard stems. (Save the cookie sheet and leave the oven on for the second part of this recipe.) In a small saucepot, bring four cups of water, chicken or turkey stock to a boil. Add the cinnamon stick and toasted chiles, stir and reduce heat to very low. Let cook for ten minutes and then cover tightly. Turn off the heat and let the chiles soak until softened and plump. This stock will be used later in the recipe.

Put all of the remaining ingredients except the chocolate and tortilla strips into a mixing bowl and coat well with the oil. Pour it all out on the cookie sheet and roast in the 400-degree oven for about eight to twelve minutes, or until the mixture begins to brown around the edges and smells really good. Remove from the oven and, using a rubber spatula or wooden spoon, scrape it back into the mixing bowl.

Now remove the cinnamon stick from the soaked chiles. Use a slotted spoon to remove the chiles from the soaking liquid. Add them to the bowl of roasted ingredients and reserve the liquid. Add the strips of tortilla and the chocolate to the roasted ingredients. Stir well, then puree in batches in a food processor, adding some of the warm stock slowly until you achieve a nice smooth consistency, like ketchup. Strain through a sieve for the smoothest texture possible. Serve warm over the turkey, chicken, or eggplant. Garnish with sesame seeds.

Turkey Tenders to Serve with Mole Sauce Serves four. Ricter Scale #1

8 turkey tenderloins

pinch of sea salt

pinch of ancho chile powder

4 tablespoons duck fat, lard or sunflower oil

1/2 cup of water

Heat the duck fat in a heavy skillet that has a lid. Season the turkey lightly on all sides with salt and chile powder. Sear the turkey on all sides, obtaining a golden color. Add the water. Cover and reduce heat to very low and let poach for five to seven minutes or until perfectly moist and succulent. Dress it up with plenty of mole sauce.

"Try every chile you can. If you use a variety of chiles, you help to sustain the agricultural heritage of many indigenous people."

White Chocolate Dipped Chiles Pg.156

Episode Twelve: We Hate Tofu!
Taped August 7, 2002

I mentioned "food trends" earlier. How many of you think that eating soy and tofu is a trend? WRONG! Going back to 1,000 BC, soy has been known in China as one of the five sacred grains—the others are millet, barley, wheat and rice.

Recipes:

Sublime Mango, Tofu and Tomato Salad

　with Basil Coulis

Spiced Chocolate-Tofu Pudding

East-West Pesto-Stuffed Tofu in Miso Broth

Grilled Alaskan Salmon with Miso Vinaigrette

Tempeh, Potato and Smoked Mozzarella

　Napoleons with Agri-Dolce Tomato Sauce

You know, I've been cooking for a few hundred years now and, as the food trends come and go, I still love my job! I love working with my hands and my mind! I use my mind to choose Clean Food and use my hands to get in touch with it. When your food is prepared using fresh, straight-from-the-earth ingredients, I know that you too will come to love Clean Food.

Anyone can use flavor bases loaded with chemicals like MSG, refined starches and hydrogenated fats to create a pleasing mouthfeel. But there is more to enjoying food than pleasing your mouth! And when you cook with organic, free-range and natural foods as nature intended, you feel good; you not only get good mouthfeel, you get good body-feel and mind-feel, too.

So, for tonight's episode we are going to do something fun. The show is called, "We Hate Tofu!" because that is what I have been told by you! I can't count how many times folks have vowed to me that they hate tofu. Now, I can see being indifferent about tofu. But how can you hate it? It is relatively innocuous, it's not like gin or anchovies or something. It is really mild, polite and pretty much a wallflower. There should be no hate here! Hopefully I can persuade you to have a fresh perspective. Don't forget: I am a chef—I can do anything!

Make sure the label says non-GMO and organic!

I mentioned "food trends" earlier. How many of you think that eating soy and tofu is a trend? No! Going back to 1,000 BC, soy has been known in China as one of the five sacred grains—the others are millet, barley, wheat and rice.

Word of the day: Isoflavones. So we hate tofu and the word of the day is Isoflavones. Soy foods such as miso, tempeh, tofu, and edamame—pronounced eh-deh-mah-may, that's Japanese for fresh soybeans—contain cholesterol-lowering phytochemicals called isoflavones. Soy iso-flavones may help prevent LDL, or bad cholesterol, from oxidizing and sticking to artery walls. Fermented soy like in soy sauce, tempeh and miso also contains blood-thinning enzymes that help prevent strokes. There is research showing that isoflavones may even help lessen the symptoms of menopause.

But there have also been recent studies establishing that while soy has many excellent properties, it should not be our sole source of protein. Just like everything else in America, huge conscienceless multinationals have gotten hold of soy and are forcing it down our collective throats. This may not be to our healthiest advantage. Soybeans are high in phytates. This is an organic acid, present in the bran or hulls of all seeds. In balance, they aren't harmful. But when they are consumed in an unnatural proportion, they can have negative effects on many aspects of our health. Over-con-sumption of phytates blocks the uptake of essential minerals in the intestinal tract.

Nature has figured us humans and our food out quite well, so trust her. Keep it all in perspective and in balance. Soy is processed by our bodies best when we have some other forms of protein in our diet. The original soy-eaters have understood this for generations; the Japanese traditionally eat tofu in a mineral-rich fish broth, and the Chinese and Vietnamese often pair tofu and pork. Edamame are commonly eaten as part of a sushi meal.

So try to avoid the intense marketing and misinformation of the multi-national food/chemical companies and keep soy in its place as a delicious addition to a diverse diet. You shouldn't eat cheeseburgers every day and you shouldn't eat tofu every day. Keep it all in balance and make it delicious.

Now, please make sure you buy Clean soy! Make sure the label says non-GMO and organic! Genetically modified soybeans are not Clean Food!

Soybeans

Soybeans account for over 50% of the world's oil seed production. You guessed it, America is the leading producer of soybeans in the world.

World soybean production in 1999

United States	46%
Brazil	20%
Argentina	14%
China	9%
India	3%
Paraguay	2%
EU	1%
All others	5%

Source: American Soybean Association

Sublime Mango, Tofu and Ripe Tomato Salad with Basil Coulis

Serves four. Ricter Scale *1

In the Hudson Valley and nearby northern New Jersey and Connecticut, ripe tomatoes in season are as spectacular a sensual experience as any I know. Really! For two or three weeks, from late August through mid-September, we harvest a slew of varieties: Big Boys, Patios, Sungold, Lemon, Zebra, Red and Yellow Roma, Baby Pear and of course, Beefsteaks. Often we serve them fresh from the vine, still warm from the late afternoon sun. These are truly love-apples, oozing with juices, tart, sweet and fleshy.

One day, on a visit to New World, Olivier Mouton of the Rothschild wine family tasted our organically grown Sungold tomatoes and was absolutely dazzled by them. (He actually went to our garden and took a soil sample back to France!)

As we sat and sipped some of his nice flinty Bordeaux, he contemplated making wine with those little golden gems. I insisted that the fruitiness was more like a peach or a mango than a grape, and sliced some mango for him to taste what I was thinking. Now, the combination of tomatoes and mango with basil is constantly on our menu until the season, alas, ends. If you can get Thai basil, or grow some, it is undoubtedly the best kind for this dish. This dish can easily be made using fresh Mozzarella instead of tofu, but it is a great way to illustrate the neutral quality of tofu. Like fresh Mozzarella, it is a simple curd that marries well with bright acids and herbs.

Nature has figured us humans and our food out quite well, so trust her. Keep it all in perspective and in balance.

Ric TV
Ortapde's Kitchen

For the Basil Coulis:

1 cup extra-virgin olive oil

*1 packed cup fresh basil leaves, regular,
opal or Thai*

1 teaspoon sea salt

1 teaspoon fresh black pepper

Puree in a blender until smooth and green.

For the Salad:

1-2 pounds ripe tomatoes, your choice of variety

2 blocks of firm tofu, rinsed

2 large medium-ripe mangoes

torn basil leaves for garnish

To assemble the salad, slice the tomatoes, mangoes and tofu and arrange them on plates in a manner that pleases you. Drizzle with the coulis and scatter some chopped basil leaves on the plate. That's all! Simple and sublime.

Spiced Chocolate-Tofu Pudding

Serves four. Ric-ter Scale *0

This is almost too easy. It is a perfect dessert for someone with a dairy allergy and can be made in advance, spooned into wine glasses and chilled for up to two days. Just make sure it is covered and refrigerated. It's perfect with fresh berries.

7 ounces medium-firm tofu

6 ounces bittersweet chocolate

1 tablespoon barley malt

pinch of allspice

Carefully melt the chocolate over a double boiler. Using a rubber spatula, scrape it all into the bowl of your food processor, add the tofu, barley malt and allspice. Turn on the machine and let it run for three to four minutes, until the mixture is as smooth as silk. Pour into Martini glasses, coffee cups or whatever tickles your fancy. Cover with plastic wrap to keep the refrigerator aromas away and chill for at least 30 minutes or even up to three days before eating. As we stated before, tofu has a meek personality so it will pick up other flavors quickly. Make sure these little moussies are covered well and also make sure that your utensils, processor bowl and blade are well cleaned.

Ric's Tip: Plastic food processor bowls can and will absorb strong food odors, especialy garlic and onions, and as we all know, food processors are used for chopping garlic and onions a lot. Clean your processor parts in hot water and use a combination of baking soda and white vinegar to power out the aromas. It will foam up like a big volcano, but when the fizz subsides, just use a clean sponge to thoroughly wipe the enitre surface of all of the parts and rinse well with warm water. That should do the trick.

East-West Pesto-Stuffed Tofu in Miso Broth
Serves four to six. Ricter Scale *1

So you ask me, what's pesto? "Pesto" comes form the word "pestle." The pesto that we are so familiar with is the ubiquitous Genovese pesto featuring pignoli, garlic, basil and sharp cheese. Let's take liberties. Use that pestle—or in this case a food processor—to make herbal pastes to flavor your cooking beautifully. Call it pesto. Go ahead, there is no Culinary Terminology cop listening!

This preparation combines Asian and Italian in a synchronistic way. Nuts, ginger, sesame, greens—yum! We presented this dish at the Culinary Institute of America's Winter Dining Series in 1998 and we wooed the tofu haters into love. It was paired with a Cal-Italian red, Barbera, from Monte Volpe. What a knockout course! The soft red wine picked up on the nuts and sun-dried tomatoes, while the red miso was reminiscent of red meat juices. Perfecto!

3 blocks extra firm Tofu

1 cup walnut halves

1/2 cup sun-dried tomatoes

1–1/2 tablespoons grated ginger

2 packed cups cleaned arugula, coarsely chopped

1 large garlic clove

1/2 cup scallion greens, chopped

1/2 cup basil, coarsely chopped (reserve the stems for miso broth)

1 tablespoon barley malt

2 tablespoon olive oil

1 cup black sesame seeds and sesame oil for searing

1/8 cup dark sesame oil for sautéeing the tofu

(Look Ma, no added salt!) Preheat oven to 375°F. Put the walnuts on a cookie sheet and roast in a 375-degree oven for six to eight minutes or until golden and their sweet aroma is released.

If your sun-dried tomatoes are soft and moist, simply pour hot tap water over them and let them soak for 10 minutes to soften a bit more. If they are very dry and firm, bring a small pot of water to a boil, put in the tomatoes and cover. Turn off the heat and let them soak for 10 to 15 minutes to soften.

Put the tomatoes, walnuts, arugula, ginger, garlic, scallion greens, basil, barley malt and olive oil in your food processor and pulse until it begins to break down a bit. Now run the machine for 20-30 seconds. Scrape down the sides and run it again until you have the semi-smooth consistency of a classic pesto. Set aside while you prepare the tofu and the broth.

To stuff the tofu, split the tofu in half like a layer cake. Now take each half and "x" cut it—that is, quarter it into four equal triangles. Cut a 1-inch slit into the long side of each triangle. Using something very small, like a demitasse spoon, stuff as much pesto into each triangle as you can without cracking it. Be careful and work with delicate hands. Pour the sesame seeds onto a plate and gently stamp one side of each triangle into the sesame seeds. Set them aside until the miso broth is ready.

There have also been recent studies establishing that while soy has many excellent properties, it should not be our sole source of protein..

Ric TV

Miso Broth

This also works as a deliciously simple soup with brown rice and tofu cubes.

5 cups water

1/2 cup medium carrot, matchstick–julienne

1/2 teaspoon garlic, minced

1/2 cup dried hijiki or arame seaweed

1 medium leek, white part only, julienne

1/2 cup shittake mushrooms, stemmed
  and thinly sliced

3 tablespoons dry sherry

reserved basil stems tied up with string

1 quarter-sized slice of ginger

1 teaspoon ground star anise

3 tablespoons tamari

a generous cracking of black pepper

1/4 cup red miso paste

Put all ingredients except the miso in a non-reactive pot. Bring to a boil and then simmer 15 minutes. Remove the basil stem bundle and stir in the miso. Now prepare the triangles.

Heat a large skillet, preferably non-stick, and add the sesame oil. When the oil gets nice and hot and begins to smoke, carefully put in the tofu triangles, sesame seed side down. Cook for two to three minutes or until nicely caramelized. Use tongs and gently turn over each triangle. Ladle miso broth into the skillet, being careful not to pour the broth on the triangles. You don't want to wash the sesame seeds off the tofu. Add enough broth to come about three-quarters of the way up the side of the triangles. Bring to a boil then turn off the heat. This will warm the tofu through.

For the Finish:

4 cups cooked brown rice

1 cup of sun-dried tomatoes, julienne

1 cup sunflower sprouts (optional)

1 cup basil leaves, coarsely chopped

1 cup scallions, cut on a long bias

To plate four servings, use large bowls with a low profile. Put a generous serving of rice into the center of each bowl. Sprinkle with equal amounts of the remaining garnish ingredients. Arrange four triangles per person around the rice, on top of the garnish. (Ah—garnish on the bottom, now there's something new!) Ladle in enough miso broth to cover the tofu by about half. Serve with a fork and a spoon.

Grilled Alaskan Salmon with White Miso BBQ Sauce Serves four. Ric-ter Scale *4

This glaze works on just about anything grilled from steaks to mushrooms. Keep this recipe handy, you'll want to use it all BBQ season!

four 6-ounce Alaskan salmon paillards or cutlets

3 tablespoons white miso paste

2 tablespoons wasabi powder

1–1/3 tablespoons barley malt

1/2 teaspoon garlic, minced finely

2 teaspoons hot water

2 tablespoons scallions, finely minced

1 teaspoon crushed red pepper or a small Szechuan chile, crumbled

1/2 cup dark sesame oil, plus one tablespoonful for the wok

2 cups carrots, long matchstick-julienne

2 cups daikon, long matchstick-julienne

2 cups leeks, long matchstick-julienne

1 cup ginger, long matchstick-julienne

Preheat your grill or a ribbed cast iron skillet to medium hot. Whisk together the miso and hot water. Add the wasabi, crushed pepper, garlic, scallions and barley malt. That's your miso BBQ sauce. Easy, right? Brush the salmon with sauce on one side and cook that side down on the grill for about three minutes. While it is cooking, baste with more sauce. Carefully turn the salmon over and cook for one to two more minutes, depending on the thickness of the paillards. Continue basting while it cooks.

Meanwhile, use a wok or deep skillet to sear the veggies. This is where the burner on your gas grill comes in handy. Get the wok very hot and then add the tablespoon of sesame oil. Now add the ginger and the vegetables julienne, and let them cook undisturbed for 15 seconds. Now, stir vigorously, turn off the heat and allow the veggies to wilt in the wok while you finish the salmon. Place a pile of veggies on the plate and top with the grilled salmon however it pleases your aesthetics. Drizzle with some more BBQ sauce. Eat. Yum.

Tempeh, Potato and Smoked Mozzarella Napoleons with Agri-Dolce Tomato Sauce Serves four. Ricter Scale *1

This dish is cool. There are lots of flavors and textures to work through as you enjoy tempeh in a unique way. Tempeh is a fermented soybean cake, bound by rice. There are variations that use barley, wild rice or even millet as a binder, but brown rice and soybeans constitute the standard-issue tempeh rectangle. Tempeh is a near perfect way to eat soybeans. The beans have been fermented first, which makes them easy to digest. Caramelizing the outside of the tempeh accentuates its nuttiness—I'm sure it would do the same to you, too.

Since the tempeh, potatoes and smoked Mozzarella are all richly flavored and richly textured, I have added two bright components to contrast from that depth of flavor. The layering of cilantro sprigs between the layers really adds some green and earthy notes and the "agri-dolce," or sweet-and-sour tomato sauce, makes you salivate and cleanses your palate.

Try to make all the slices of similar circumference. You will be stacking them up like cold cuts. You can cook any tempeh and potato scraps in a wok.

twelve 1/4-inch thick slices tempeh

12 thin slices of potato

12 slices smoked Mozzarella

1 bunch of cilantro

a 50/50 combination of safflower
    and extra virgin olive oil

Cut the tempeh in half, sideways, like cake layers. Cut in half from above making rectangles in the 2"x3" range. Slice the potato into slices the long way so they are in the same size range as the tofu. The potatoes should be about 1/16-inch thick, or at least double the size of a potato chip. If the potatoes are too thin you miss the texture, but if they are too thick, they won't cook through.

Use a nonstick skillet. Sauté the tempeh in the oil blend on each side until golden. Reserve. Now sauté the potato slices until browned around the edges. Make the sauce, then assemble the towers.

For the Sauce:

2 tablespoons olive oil

1/4 cup minced shallots

3 ounces aged balsamic vinegar

1 tablespoon molasses

1 cup Thai basil, chopped

1 teaspoon fresh black pepper

16 ounces organic tomatoes with juice

So try to avoid the intense marketing and misinformation of the multi-national food/chemical companies and keep soy in its place as a delicious addition to a diverse diet.

Use a deep skillet. Slowly cook the shallots in the oil until they are a deep amber color, but not black. Add the balsamic vinegar and the molasses and reduce until it is sticky and caramel-like. Add the tomatoes and basil and increase the heat to high. Cook vigorously for five minutes. Remove from the heat and let cook down a bit. Puree in a blender.

Assembly:

Preheat oven to 400°F. Use a nice casserole dish or sizzle platter. Use a paper towel to smear a thin layer of olive oil on the bottom of the casserole pan. Assemble your napoleons: place a piece of tempeh down first. Add a small smear of sauce. Now layer a potato slice. Pinch off a small sprig of cilantro and layer it on the potato. Add another smear of sauce and a slice of Mozzarella. Repeat. Put a piece of tempeh on top to finish. Use the palm of your hand to gently press it together. Make the other three towers the same way. Ladle some sauce over each stack and bake for 10 minutes or until the cheese is melted. Serve hot, with the remaining sauce on the side.

Episode Thirteen: Garlic Show #1

Taped August 7, 2002

"I want you to think about where your food comes from: how meat and fish are raised, and what goes into the soil your vegetables and grains come from..."

Recipes:

Roasted Garlic Bread Pudding

Sopa de Ajo

Chimmichurri Steaks on the Grill

Simple Filetto di Pomodori with Sun-Dried Olives

Well folks, if you've just tuned in, this is RicTV. It's me, Ric Orlando, "deliciously opinionated" chef and father of three and devoted husband. And this TV kitchen is a place where we cook (yes, it is a cooking show) but it is also a place where—I hope—I get you to think. I want you to think about where your food comes from: how meat and fish are raised; what goes into the soil your vegetables and grains come from; and about what genetically modifying food means today—and what it might mean a few hundred years from now. Clean Food means a lot of things. If you want to be a great cook, you have to buy great stuff and Clean stuff is a no-brainer!

Yes, today's show is called "Garlic Show #1." I know how much you all love garlic. There is no way I can get all of the garlic lore and garlic myth and garlic facts and garlic dishes into one half-hour show! So let me promise you now, just as sure as I am standing here, that if you support this show and get your friends to email in their testimonies of love and somehow we produce subsequent seasons of RicTV, there will always be a garlic show included. By the time I am 95 years old, I may have exhausted the subject of garlic—but I doubt it!

We love garlic because garlic is the ultimate Clean Food! Garlic cleans *us!* In the first *American Cookbook*, Amelia Simmon wrote that "Garlicks, 'tho used by the French, are better adapted to the uses of medicine than cookery!" Well, she has a point, though I wouldn't say *better* used as medicine. Garlic is both food and medicine! It is one of the most potent healers on the planet. Yes, garlic really does ward off evil. When in doubt, trust the old peasant legends. They had the trial and error thing on their side! They didn't care about poll-takers and bureaus of vital statistics. There were those who cut their finger and died of gangrene and those who cut their finger, applied garlic paste, healed and lived to the ripe old age of 45. Those legends rippled through the forest back then the way the exaggerated animation of digital data transfer appears to travel on ".com" commercials.

Okay, back to earth. We are talking about garlic and the word of the day is ANTI! Garlic is a powerful ANTI...! This isn't a New-Age theory, this is proven stuff. Garlic is an antioxidant, anti-allergen, anti-asthmatic, anti-histamine, antibacterial, anti-stress and anti-tumor food! These are facts! Physicians around the world who think outside the box have known this for centuries. There is more medicinal garlic information on the web than just about anything except—you know what! (No, unfortunately it's not anti-porn.)

Why it works

Garlic contains very high amounts of the minerals germanium and selenium. Both are extremely supportive of our immune systems. There is also an unusual form of sulfur in garlic called sulfhydryl amino acids. These are powerful antioxidants that work against cell-damaging free radicals. Garlic does not cure or kill but it activates our healthy cells to defend the body against invaders and bad bacteria.

Believe it or not, aged garlic extract has actually received a patent and has patents pending for use as an anti-oxidant, anti-tumor agent, immune enhancer, liver protective agent, anti-stress agent, acidophilus (good digestive bacteria) growth stimulant and an anti-fungal agent. Wow!

Source: Prescription for Dietary Wellness

Garlicky Grilled Sirloins with New World Chimmichurri Sauce

Serves four. Ricter Scale #3

Chimmichurri sauce is classic fusion food. The Italians in Argentina helped to develop this ubiquitous Gaucho marinade. The bright flavors and high levels of acidity help to tenderize the intensely rich and chewy grass-fed beef from the Pampas. If you are eating Clean Food, grass-fed beef is sure to be on your menu and chimmichurri will become a staple marinade for your beef. It is also perfect as a basting and finishing sauce on all grilled fish, poultry and meats. And it makes a great dressing for any type of bean salad.

Check out my tip in this recipe. I'll give you a tip on how to use less marinade so you can have plenty of chimmi left for sauce.

1/2 teaspoon seeded jalapeños

6 cloves of garlic

2 tablespoons minced onion

1/2 cup parsley, coarsely chopped

3/4 teaspoon sea salt

a twist of your black pepper mill

1 tablespoon cilantro

2 ounces sherry vinegar

2 ounces lemon juice

1 bay leaf, finely crumbled

1/4 teaspoon cumin seeds

1/4 cup safflower or grapeseed oil

1/4 cup extra virgin olive oil

four 12-ounce grass-fed sirloin or shell steaks

1 ripe tomato, cored and diced small

Grind everything except the oil, the steaks and the tomato in a food processor until medium-fine. Add the oil in a steady stream to emulsify. Your marinade is done. **Now here is my tip for using less marinade:** put about half of this stuff in a mixing bowl. Using tongs, dip and coat each steak in the chimmi, then wrap them in waxed paper or plastic bags to marinate for at least six hours or, preferably, overnight.

Fire up your grill or grill pan. Remove the steaks from the bags. Discard the bags or wraps including the marinade that was left in them. Put the steak on the hottest place on the grill and leave it alone for three minutes. Now you can turn it to a different angle to achieve those desired hashmarks. I had a cook from Texas who referred to that diagonal black grid on all properly food-styled steaks as "the ol' 10 o'clock-two o'clock method." Whatever makes you crow, I guess. Just try to let the steak stay in one place for a few minutes so that it actually caramelizes. Many grill-people have this annoying habit of banging the steak around the grill like a dog does with a menacing chew toy. Try not to hurt it. Treat it nicely and it will retain all of its juices for you!

If your meat is one inch thick, cook it for four to five minutes on one side and turn it over. Baste it with chimmi when you turn it over. Move the steak to less direct heat and finish cooking gently for three to four minutes for medium-rare, five minutes for medium. After that, you're on your own. Please don't overcook grass-fed beef (or any, for that matter). If you are uncomfortable about eating meat medium-rare, buy a different cut that lends itself to braising. A great pot roast out-performs a lousy steak in my opinion! To serve, put a small pool of chimmichurri on a plate. Set the steak on the chimmi and garnish with diced ripe tomato pieces. It may be the best steak you've ever eaten.

Note: you can store chimmichurri covered at room temperature for two to three days or refrigerated for two weeks. Stir or shake to re-emulsify before use.

Ric TV

Roasted Garlic Bread Pudding

Serves six to twelve. Ricter Scale #1

This recipe uses a lot of mellow, roasted garlic, it's easy and affordable to make and is a great alternative to potatoes, rice or pasta. Serve it as a side dish with hearty meat, game or poultry dishes.

24 cloves unpeeled garlic

2 cups organic milk

2 cups organic heavy cream

5 free-range eggs

1 ounce bourbon or brandy (optional)

1/2 teaspoon sea salt

a generous cracking of black pepper

1 teaspoon fresh thyme leaves (or a small pinch of dry)

1 teaspoon fresh rosemary, minced (or a small pinch of dry)

1/3 cup grated Romano, Sonoma Dry Jack or Asiago cheese

2-3 cups Italian or French bread roughly torn into pieces, crust removed

1 cup sliced, blanched almonds

To roast garlic, preheat your oven to 425°F. Snip the very top of each clove and toss the cloves with a touch of olive oil, salt and pepper. Bake on a sheet for 20-30 minutes or until softened. Let sit until cool to the touch, then gently peel each clove. If the garlic is roasted just right, you can squeeze it out of the peel like butter. Mash the cloves with the back of a fork. Mix the garlic and all other ingredients except the bread and almonds. Use an electric mixer or wire whisk (and a resilient arm) to bring the custard together. Get it nice and fluffy.

Arrange the bread in the baking pan evenly. There should be some space for the custard mix to fill in. Pour the mix over the bread, shaking it gently to settle and top with the almonds. Bake in a 425-degree oven for 40 minutes or until the top gets golden brown but the custard is still a bit loose—after all, it is pudding! Serve hot, with a spoon.

To reheat: Cover with a sheet of parchment and then a layer of aluminum foil. Heat in a 300-degree oven 15 minutes or until warmed through.

Why parchment? The parchment provides protection from the microscopic bit of aluminum that may cling to your food when heating it.

"Garlic is both food and medicine! It is one of the most potent healers on the planet. Yes, garlic really does ward off evil. When in doubt, trust the old peasant legends."

Sopa de Ajo Serves six. Ricter Scale *0

This is my absolute favorite garlic soup recipe. I developed it from a collection of different recipes. Add the cream for a New England thing—turn all soups into chowdah!—or, you may omit the cream, with outstanding results. A bowl of piping-hot sopa de ajo is at home on the same table with seared bitter greens, fresh figs and a bottle of Alberiño. A mug of chilled sopa garnished with white grape halves is a great, quick, Barcelona-style lunch. Garnishing with plenty of chopped parsley, which contains chlorophyll, will help to dissipate that lovely garlic breath some people fear.

2 cups pinenuts

16 cloves of garlic, peeled and sliced thin

4 tablespoons extra virgin olive oil

4 teaspoons salt

generous grinding of black pepper

2 tablespoons fresh thyme leaves or 1 tablespoon dried thyme

1 cup white wine

8 cups chicken or vegetable stock or packaged low-salt free-range chicken broth (available at most health food stores)

3 cups French or Italian peasant bread (not whole grain or sourdough), trimmed of crust, torn into small, thumbnail-size pieces

1 cup organic heavy cream at room temperature

1/2 cup chopped parsley and/or halved white grapes for garnish

Place the pinenuts, garlic and olive oil in a large heavy-bottomed pot and set it over medium-low heat. Cook slowly until the garlic and nuts are sandy-brown and smell rich and nutty, about 10 minutes.

Sprinkle in the salt, pepper and thyme and stir well to coat the almonds and garlic. Add the wine and turn up the heat all the way. Bring to a boil and let the wine reduce by half. Puree in batches until very smooth, in a blender or food processor, adding some of the stock if necessary to make a smooth puree. Return the puree to the pot, add the remaining stock and bring it all to a boil. Reduce the heat just a bit and let the soup boil moderately for 10-15 minutes.

Reduce the heat a bit more and let the soup come down to a strong simmer. Add the bread and stir well. Use the back of a wooden spoon to break up the bread against the side of the pot until it disintegrates. Reduce the heat to a gentle simmer until ready to serve.

Stir in the cream and garnish with the chopped parsley and/or white grapes cut in half. Wait until you taste the warm tangy grape enrobed in rich, creamy garlic soup!

Ric's Filetto di Pomodori with Sun-Dried Olives Serves four. Ricter Scale *1

I made this dish on the show because I knew my daughter, Margo, was going to be in the audience, and at this period of her life, this was about all she ate. There is something fear-inspiring about having a famished 15-year-old girl in a television studio. One never knows what could happen. There's a lot of power there!

The technique for this recipe is very Barese, very Pugliese, very Basilicata—we're talking hot-weather Italians here. Use excellent olive oil. Get some color on that garlic. Add some nice tomatoes, maybe a handful of your herb of the day. Bring it to a boil. It's done. Don't mess around. Add macaroni and enjoy. This is very different from the Calabrese or Neapolitan style of cooking. No onions. No paste. No wine. True peasant cooking is so honest it's hard to believe sometimes!

1 pound brown rice pasta—spirals or penne are best for this recipe

2 teaspoons sea salt

one 20-ounce can organic tomatoes

4 large cloves garlic

3 tablespoons extra virgin olive oil

1 cup sun-dried or oil-cured black olives

1/4 chopped basil or Italian parsley, your choice

Bring six quarts of water and the sea salt to a boil. Add the pasta to the boiling water, stir and cook just like regular pasta. While the pasta is cooking put a heavy skillet over medium heat. Open the can of tomatoes. Peel the garlic cloves and slice into pieces about the same thickness as a dime. Add extra virgin olive oil to the pan and turn the heat to high. When the oil begins to shimmer and is quite hot, add the garlic. Carefully shake the pan and then let the garlic cook until it is nicely bronzed around the edges. Add the olives and swirl to coat with the hot oil. Remove the pan from the direct heat, add the tomatoes and return the pan to the heat. Cook the sauce until the pasta is ready. Strain the pasta. Use a potato masher or a heavy spoon to break up the tomatoes just a bit. Add the strained pasta to the sauce. Add the herbs and stir the pasta and sauce together. Cook for one minute and remove from heat. Eat.

'Garlic is an antioxidant, anti-allergen, anti-asthmatic, antihistamine, antibacterial, anti-stress and anti-tumor food! These are facts!'

Hi ---I'm Ric Orlando and this is My TV KITCHEN! Whew, are we going to have some fun

RIC ORLANDO'S TV KITCHEN
Taped July 29-August 7, 2002

Director: Stephen Honeybill

Co-Producer: Ric Orlando

Assistant Producer: Courtney Haydock

Videotape Editor: Paul Minni

Theme Music Composed and Performed by: Ric Orlando

Additional Music: Margot Corrado-Orlando
Published by RicTV Music (BMI)

Production Assistant: Barbara Lawton

Audio: Dan Scheivert

Floor Manager: Melissa Bigge

Studio Cameras:
Kevin Keithly
Jesse Keithly
Eric Browne

Production Engineer: Tim Stah

Maintenance Engineer: David Lastarza

Lighting: Kevin Keithly

Set Construction:
Ron McGowty
Ken Girard

Broadcast Graphic Design: Adrienne Cochrane

Publicity: Marcy Stryker

Still Photography:
Michael Corsentino
Chris Fitzpatrick

Director of Finance and Accounting: Julie Raskin

Kitchen Assistants:
Carlos Arroyo
Heather Ludwig
Justin Sedlak
Heather Stadler
Janet vanRijsewijk

Audience Coordinators:
Mary Hunt
Jackie Pierce
Joyce Stah

Production Interns:
Erin Huth
Jamie Cheung

Production Assistance provided by:
Adventure in Food Trading Company
Aunt Debbie's Gourmet Mushrooms
Catskill Mountain Moccasins
Cavoli's Knife Grinding Service
Chef Works
Amy Kenyon
Morgan Linen Services Inc.
Nettle Meadow Goat Cheese
New World Home Cooking Co.
Price Chopper

Skate Creek Farm
Stone Ledge Farm
Sunflower Natural Foods of Woodstock, NY
Tartan Textile Services
The Cousins Fish Markets, Inc.
Liz Corrado
Margot Corrado-Orlando
Willie Orlando
Terrence Rex Orlando
Laurie Goodheart
Sham Morris

Senior Producer: Stephen Honeybill

Executive Producer: Marianne Potter

Sourcing Clean Food

I have made one thing abundantly clear throughout this book: to cook and eat Clean Food, you have to change some of your basic shopping habits. If you think that you can source Clean Food by shopping exclusively at your major supermarkets, you are mistaken. The whole mission of supermarkets is to provide convenience. But in consolidating sources, a supermarket must compromise. Only the major distributors and cartels have adequate inroads for getting their products on supermarket shelves. It is comparable to getting all of your news from one TV channel. There are powerful machines and mountains of money at work here! In fact, many large chain supermakets are beholden to massive suppliers. To depend upon reliable deliveries of commodities on a 24-7-365 basis, many strange marriages must be established.

Here is one bizarre example. In the Northeast there are a handful of market bases for providers of perishable food items. These perishables are then distributed to markets, stores and other establishments. The products have traditionally come from both regional and non-regional sources. Californian, Mexican and Southeastern produce that used to be trucked in during the off-season to keep a steady flow to market is now shipped year-round. So now the smaller Northeastern farms are competing with huge plantations and corporate farms from warmer climates.

How did this happen? Read on. The markets needed a year-round commitment and of course, Northeast growers can't do that. For local family farmers, access to their own regional market became almost impossible. So if you lived the Albany area, for instance, which is surrounded by farmland, the only way to get local produce was to travel to the farms themselves. National chain supermakets don't carry a represenative amount of local produce anymore because they are contracted to buy from the powerful

To cook and eat Clean Food, you have to change some of your basic shopping habits.

corporate suppliers in exchange for guaranteed year–round supply. This has systematically put the medium–sized vegetable farm out of business in the Northeast. This damage will never be undone.

And a major reason all of this happened is that our own eating habits changed. As we demanded tomatoes in February, the corporate distributors managed to provide them (though I would hardly venture to call those things tomatoes.) This gave disproportionate power to the corporate food providers and squeezed out the local food in the local markets.

Public opinion is clear. The majority of us will pay a little more to buy food from our own area when given a choice. You have the choice. You just need to understand it and act on it.

The sources listed below are guidlelines. These are suppliers that I use myself. Use the internet and your own local farmers markets to create your own list of reliable food sources. Local is better. Visit you area's health food stores, co-ops, specialty stores, butchers, fish markets and ethnic markets. Establish a connection by introducing yourself and shopping regularly. Build trust.

Eat well. Have fun.

Chefs and farmers began to organize...

The following are excellent resources for general information on sustainable food production and organic farming:

http://www.baumforum.org

http://www.nofaic.org

http://www.organicandnaturalnews.com

http://www.slowfood.com

http://www.localharvest.org

Organic General Stores

http://www.organickitchen.com

http://www.ecomall.com/biz/food.htm

http://www.orgfood.com

http://www.organictrading.com/

Organic Produce Delivered to your door

http://www.calliehill.com

Wild and Sustainable Seafood
http://www.ecofish.com

Grass-fed Meats and Wild Game

http://www.harmonyvalleyfarm.com (Beef)

http://www.brokenarrowranch.com (Game Meats)

Specialty World Adventures in Food, Albany NY, 518-436-7603

Northwind Farm, Tivoli, NY, 845-757-5591

Coffee
http://www.catskillmtcoffee.com

Teas
http://www.divinitea.com

Cheese
Olde Chatham Sheepherding Co. http://blacksheepcheese.com
Nettle Meadows Goat Cheese http://thefoodstores.com/gc/home.htm

http://www.fromages.com (All French Cheese)

Chemical Free Herbs and Spices
http://www.frontierherb.com
http://www.atlanticspice.com
http://www.sanfranciscoherb.com

If you think that you can source Clean Food
by shopping exclusively at your major supermarkets, you are mistaken. The whole mission
of supermarkets is to provide convenience.
But in consolidating sources, a supermarket
must compromise.

Rie TV

'Thanks to the entire New World crew for tolerating ...er... I mean supporting me and my eccentricities for the last 10 years. Thanks to Michael for the understanding and beauty he brought to this project and thanks to Kiwi for not shutting me up. Thanks to Marianne for sticking her neck out and sticking with me like glue for all these years and thanks to Steve for taking the dive. Last but not least, thanks to Melissa for running a tight stage.'